A HISTORY

OF THE

CONFEDERATE

NAVY

A HISTORY OF THE

CONFEDERATE

NAVY

RAIMONDO LURAGHI

TRANSLATED BY PAOLO E. COLETTA

Naval Institute Press ▪ Annapolis, Maryland

First published in Italian as *Marinai del Sud: Storia della Marina confederata
nella Guerra Civile Americana, 1861–1865* by Rizzoli in 1993.

LIBRARY OF CONGRESS CATALOGING-IN-PUBLICATION DATA

Luraghi, Raimondo.
[Marinai del Sud.   English]
A history of the Confederate Navy / Raimondo Luraghi.
p.   cm.
Includes bibliographical references and index.
ISBN 1-55750-527-6 (alk. paper)
1. Confederate States of America.   Navy—History.   2. Confederate
States of America—History, Naval.   3. United States—History—Civil
War, 1861–1865—Naval operations, Confederate.   I. Title.
E596.L8713   1996
973.7′57—dc20   95-49315

Printed in the United States of America on acid-free paper ∞

03 02 01 00 99 98 97 96   9 8 7 6 5 4 3 2

First printing

To the beloved memory of my mother

Contents

Illustrations

Another picture of the CSS *Stonewall*
The CSS *Shenandoah*

Maps

Preface

All historical research starts with a problem. Soon after I finished writing my history of the American Civil War, I began to worry about a twofold problem. First, how did an agricultural country with a limited industrial plant and almost no merchant marine succeed in building a navy that successfully confronted the formidable navy of the Northern states through four years of merciless fighting? Second, why, despite a staggering number of books on the American Civil War, has almost no historian tried to answer that question? J. Thomas Scharf's book is not a satisfactory history; it is instead a true mixture of facts and news, put together in a disorderly fashion with little critical sense. It is, of course, a mine of invaluable factual information, indispensable to any naval historian, but it certainly is not a *history.*

Such thoughts came to me some twenty-eight years ago; I was then much younger and had more élan, more daring (and more rashness) than I do now, so, I boldly started a research program that would keep me busy for almost twenty-seven years of careful work, carry me sometimes to the edge of despair, yet give me immeasurable satisfaction. I soon discovered why some historians had overlooked the Confederate States Navy.

During the evacuation of Richmond, the Navy Department had burned its archival records. This led to the belief that writing an organic history of the Southern naval organization and effort would be almost impossible, which frightened many a researcher away from what looked like a dreary, unrewarding, and hopeless enterprise. Such disregard, in turn, engendered another legend, resulting from the lack of careful and painstaking in-depth research on the issue, namely, that the only strategic aim of the Confederate navy was to break the blockade. Because the blockade was never broken, the Confederate navy was considered a failure. And who wants to study the story of a failure?

Plunging full-time into this research, visiting archives and repositories in the United States and abroad, looking carefully for any scrap of paper about the Confederate States Navy, I began to suspect that both legends were just that, baseless, and I began to develop a theory in direct opposition to such legends.

Meanwhile, I ran across the scholarly and perceptive works of a fellow historian (who, I am delighted to say, has become a warm friend of mine), William N. Still, Jr. By his painstaking, intelligent, and sharp research on single problems regarding several aspects of the Confederate navy, Still reached conclusions that provided the foundation for my job. Still's writings also showed that serious archival research could produce results. Still's outstanding studies emboldened me, and I went to work.

And work it was! I had to dig in depth in almost fifty archives and repositories, situated in four different countries, including the United States. I had to cross the ocean from Europe to the United States more than forty times, spending in this country, all in all, more than six years. I had to build up in my home in Italy a complete library of my own on the naval side of the Civil War which amounts now to some two thousand books, hundreds of pamphlets, and thousands of photocopies and microfilms.

It was, in a sense, an appalling job. No single big and complete collection of records existed to make research easy. It was like putting together the splinters of a beautiful china pot and doing it without showing that it had to be glued together; it was like toiling along meandering paths. How many times I felt discouraged is useless to say; yet, in the end, I achieved it.

Now that the book is done, I feel almost like a father, who is looking at his son, born late in life and ready to take the perilous way into the mighty world, and who, as in the old Roman republic, invokes protection on the path to life for his child: *"quod faustum, felix fortunatumque sit!"*

I closed my research in 1988. The Italian edition had to be produced and appeared first. The book then had to be translated and the translation carefully read, corrected, and double-checked. At last, it had to be submitted to publishers in the United States, which was far more time-consuming than foreseen. Luckily, I met with the staff of the Naval Institute Press, who acted swiftly as soon as they got the manuscript. I shall be forever grateful to them.

From the moment I ended the research in 1988, I decided not to change the book any more. Twenty years of research work were, indeed, more than enough. Since that time several books on the Civil War at sea have been published, and many of them are very good. Of course, I read all that was published on the subject after I had finished researching and writing. I found several of those books to be excellent, scholarly, and well conceived. They agree in the main with my conclusions so I had nothing substantial to change in this book. For the present American edition, I tried to add to the bibliography at least some of the most valuable books published recently.

I believe that somebody, in the near or distant future, will rise to challenge some of my conclusions and theses. Any challenge is welcome: a scientific book is written to be challenged; historical theses are by no means eternal truths; and every generation writes its own history. Yet I beg the would-be challenger to be fair and equitable enough to check *all* the records and sources—both manuscript and printed—on which I founded my conclusions to be sure he can honestly draw from them a different interpretation, or if he can, find sources that escaped me and would tell the contrary of what this book says.

A last question remains. Why did I get interested in the American Civil War? There is no clear-cut answer. Among Italian people interested in history I am by no means isolated; suffice it to say that two Italian editions of this book sold out in a couple of years. The United States is a great and fascinating country, and no event was considered more important than the Civil War in shaping it as it is today. That war was so momentous and awesome that its impact on America was believed to have been as great as the Renaissance, the Protestant Reformation, or the French Revolution was on Europe and the world. It was the first great war of the industrial age, the forerunner of the two world wars. Hence the desire to understand, to know more. This is a partial answer.

Acknowledgments

The reader will kindly understand that when a historian had been working on a book for more than twenty years, he has received the cordial and friendly help of so many people that listing every one of them is all but impossible. Human memory is imperfect and likely to become more flawed with the passing of years. Should I attempt a complete listing of all the persons and institutions that helped me in this venture, I would certainly fall into omissions and mistakes. The list I offer here is certainly not complete; still, all those who helped me are in my heart and my thankfulness toward them—all of them—shall last forever.

Therefore, I shall limit myself to a tentative, incomplete list, arranged (more or less) in alphabetical order. Writing this list, I realized sorrowfully how many of them are no longer with us, starting with my beloved mother, who encouraged me in many ways, discussed problems and topics with me, was always helpful with her healthy common sense, but did not live to see this book realized. To her beloved memory the book is inscribed, and this is my first acknowledgment.

Edwin C. Bearss and Margie Riddle Bearss, both prominent military historians, supplied books, maps, information, and suggestions and organized several convivial meetings for me with historians (always around a bottle of good bourbon!). Xavier de Boisrouvray, Director, Archives de la Loire-Atlantique, supplied valuable information on Confederate shipbuilding in France. The late Eleanor Brockenbrough offered invaluable help in wading through the "high sea" of manuscripts and papers at the Confederate Museum, made acute and thoughtful suggestions, and supplied several out-of-print books; she shall live forever in my heart and that of my (then) little son Nino, who developed for her a moving and ever-lasting affection. E. Milby Burton, late Director of the Charleston Museum, not only supplied suggestions together with a very rare book, but, very kindly, agreed to take several pictures of the artillery pieces of the Charleston Battery and graciously donated them. The late Fred Coker and the staff of the Library of Congress Manuscripts Division were helpful. Kenneth Coleman, University of Georgia, supplied some important books and valuable suggestions. Paolo E. Coletta, U.S. Naval Academy, Emeritus, translated this book into English and offered generous hospitality (and valuable suggestions) during several of my stays in Annapolis, Maryland. M. L. Courville, Conservateur de la Bibliothèque de Nantes, France, supplied information and invaluable data as well as rare essays on the first submarines in France. Charles H. Dufour, New Orleans, Louisiana, supplied some of his very valuable books. A. W. Furse, Cammel Laird Company, Liverpool, England, not only opened the archives of the firm to me but kindly supplied copies of important papers, invaluable for the story of Confederate shipbuilding on the Mersey. Eugene D. Genovese, in long, friendly conversations, offered valuable suggestions on the economic and social sides of the story and supplied many an important book. The late William E. Geoghegan of the Smithsonian Institution supplied first-rate opinions and information on the structure of Confederate ironclads and called my attention to the important Willink Papers. Lilla Hawes and the staff at the Georgia Historical Society Library, Savannah, Georgia, provided kind assistance. James Heslin and the staff of the New-York Historical Society, beyond helping to locate several important letters in the Gustavus V. Fox and John Ericsson papers, supplied a rare copy of the long out-of-print *Confidential Correspondence of Gustavus Vasa Fox.* Robert W. Hill and Paul R. Rugen, New York Public Library, were helpful. Robert Holcombe and the staff of the Confederate Naval Museum, Columbus, Georgia, supplied information, suggestions, and invaluable data. Ari Hoogenboom's suggestions and information were very useful in handling the Fox and Ericsson papers. Valuable assistance was provided by Richard M. Hurst, Buffalo and Erie County Historical Society, and E. L. Inabinett and the staff of the South Caroliniana Library, Columbia, South Carolina. The late Mary Johnson, as well as Sarah D. Jackson, together with Henry P. Beers, Lee Saegesser, and everybody on the National Archives staff during my years of research helped, suggested, accepted cheerfully the most extravagant requests for documents and papers, and told me about some overlooked collections such as that containing several harebrained projects to sink the *Virginia.* The late J. Ambler Johnston, Richmond, Virginia, made invaluable suggestions deriving from years of study of the American Civil War, as did several members of the

Commonwealth Club of Richmond. The late William Kennon Kay, Historian at the Richmond Military Park, during years of close friendship, supplied information, suggestions, and exchange of ideas, always—or frequently—*in convivium* (he was also a first-rate cook of Southern food) in his two hospitable houses, the first one on the Seven Days' battlefield, the second on Confederate Avenue, Richmond, where he organized for my benefit long meetings with several Civil War specialists and who helped to track down many a hard-to-find volume of the *Official Records*. I also thank Bettie King, Richmond Public Library, Richmond, Virginia, and H. R. Lacroix, Chambre de Commerce de Bordeaux. Alexander Lawrence of Savannah, Georgia, with extreme kindness, supplied a copy of his outstanding—and very difficult to obtain—book on Savannah in the Civil War. Philip K. Lundeberg, Smithsonian Institution, supplied valuable technical information about U.S. submarines. Louis H. Manarin and the staff of the Virginia State Archives were helpful. Dean James A. Moncure, formerly at the University of Richmond, and Professor Horace Montgomery, University of Georgia (together with Professors Vincent P. De Santis, Notre Dame, Vincent Carosso, New York University, and the academic authorities at all these institutions) secured for me long periods of visiting professorships at their institutions enabling me to spend months, indeed, years in the United States, which were invaluable for this research. Cynthia Moseley, Spartanburg, South Carolina, with extreme kindness, freely put her collection of J. K. Stevens's letters and her dissertation at my disposal. Harriet C. Owsley and the staff at the Tennessee State Archives, the late James W. Patton, J. Isaac Copland, Carolyn A. Wallace, and the staff at the Southern Historical Collection were always courteous, always helpful, always ready to extend a friendly hand. William H. Pease and Jane Pease, both prominent historians of the Old South and warm friends of mine, supplied books, suggestions, and hospitality in their friendly homes in Orono, Maine, and Charleston, South Carolina. Elena Pinto Surdi and the staff of the Library of the Centro di Studi Americani, Rome, Italy, including Elena Potsios and Umberto Fongoli, supplied books almost impossible to find in Europe. I thank Mrs. T. Granville Prior and the staff at the South Carolina Historical Society, Charleston, South Carolina. The late William M. E. Rachal (together with the staff of the Virginia Historical Society) not only worked painstakingly to help me locate the most important papers among the collections of the society but became in time a warm friend. Alas, he, too, as indeed too many in this list, was carried away by an illness that never forgives. The late Mattie Russell and the staff at Duke University Library gave good assistance. George G. and Gracie Shackelford, Blacksburg, Virginia, supplied books, conversation, and generous hospitality. Richard J. Sommers and the staff at the

U.S. Army History Institute Archives were the source of unending exchanges of ideas, and Sommers also helped to locate papers useful for the history of Confederate raiders. Warren F. Spencer, University of Georgia, kindly lent a copy of his manuscript on the C. S. Navy in Europe. William N. Still, Jr., a warm friend, contributed to the genesis and birth of this book in ways that cannot be overstated. He not only read the entire manuscript, offering thoughtful observations, but provided countless suggestions, discussions, information, articles, and books, an authentic treasure trove. It was he who led me to the extremely important Shelby Iron Works Papers. Meriwether Stuart from Richmond, Virginia, freely put at my disposal first-rate information from his research about Union spies inside the C. S. Navy Department. Patricia Sweet, Mark A. Palmer (and the entire staff) at the Alabama Department of Archives and History, over and above their kind and friendly help, told me about the hitherto almost ignored papers of Admiral Semmes. Andrea Testa, Casale Monferrato, Italy, one of my finest graduates, carefully perused the papers of Count Sclopis at the Accademia delle Scienze, Turin. Emory M. Thomas, University of Georgia, a longtime friend, offered important suggestions and even gave up a project of his on the C. S. Navy to grant me a free hand in the field. Frank E. Vandiver, also a friend, supplied valuable suggestions and very kindly lent his copies of blockade runners' papers. Saul Viener, Richmond, Virginia, together with his brother, kindly helped in many ways and supplied valuable information about the relic of the ironclad *Tecumseh* at Mobile Bay. Richard Von Doenhoff, Chief, Naval History Division Archives, was helpful. Lee A. Wallace, Jr., prominent military historian, beyond giving invaluable information and suggestions, called attention to the importance of the Van Benthuysen Papers (even supplying the microfilm of them) and helped locate the hitherto almost unexploited Rains Papers. The late Bell I. Wiley, a friend, was always prodigal in suggestions, information, and books. Stephen R. Wise (author of an outstanding book on blockade running) read the manuscript, offering a treasure of thoughtful observations. Mary E. Wood, Athens, Georgia, kindly authorized me to consult the Joel S. Kennard Papers at the University of Georgia Special Collections.

Two persons who deserve special mention are the late E. Merton Coulter, one of the most prominent historians of the Confederacy, who authorized me to roam freely in his fabulous private library, and Albert Krebs, Conservateur de la Bibliothèque Nationale, Paris, who lent out his precious copies of Admiral Lepotier's works and was even willing to have them mailed between Paris and Turin.

Other friends and colleagues who freely offered their help and suggestions in many ways, including some kind hospitality, are Genevieve

Barksdale, William L. Barney, Richard E. Beringer, Nash Boney, Charles J. Brockman, Jr., Steve A. Channing, John and Rose Cunningham, Marie Delaney, Don Doyle, Eric Foner, William Gresham, Herman Hattaway, Ludwell H. Johnson, Archer Jones, Lawrence Kaplan, Lee Kennett, John C. Leland, William H. Parks, Mary Clark Roane, James J. Robertson, Jr., Charles P. Roland, James M. Russell, William Salomone, Joan Scarpaci, Martin Shotzberger, Phinizy Spalding, George B. Tindall, Willie Lee Rose, and C. Vann Woodward.

I also send my most hearty thanks to staff and personnel of the following institutions, whose help was of the utmost importance and who liberally authorized me to make use of their invaluable collections and to quote them: Alabama State Department of Archives and History, Montgomery, Alabama; Buffalo and Erie Historical Society Library, Buffalo, New York; Charleston Library Society, Charleston, South Carolina; Confederate Museum Library, Richmond, Virginia; Confederate Naval Museum, Columbus, Georgia; Duke University Library, Durham, North Carolina; East Carolina University Library, Greenville, North Carolina; Emory University Library, Atlanta, Georgia; Florida Historical Society, Tampa, Florida; Georgia Historical Society Library, Savannah, Georgia; Georgia State Archives, Atlanta, Georgia; Library of Congress, Washington, D.C.; Louisiana State University Archives, Baton Rouge, Louisiana; Mariners Museum, Newport News, Virginia; Maryland Historical Society Library, Baltimore, Maryland; Miami University Library, Oxford, Ohio; Mississippi Department of Archives and History, Jackson, Mississippi; National Archives, Washington, D.C.; Naval Historical Foundation, Washington, D.C.; Naval History Division, Washington, D.C.; New-York Historical Society Library, New York, New York; New York Public Library, New York, New York; Norfolk Public Library, Norfolk, Virginia; North Carolina Department of Archives and History, Raleigh, North Carolina; Richmond Public Library, Richmond, Virginia; Rice University Library, Houston, Texas; South Carolina Department of Archives and History, Columbia, South Carolina; South Carolina Historical Society, Charleston, South Carolina; South Caroliniana Library, Columbia, South Carolina; Southern Historical Collection, Chapel Hill, North Carolina; Tulane University Library, New Orleans, Louisiana; U.S. Naval Academy, Chester W. Nimitz Library, Annapolis, Maryland; University of Alabama Library, Tuscaloosa, Alabama; University of Florida Library, Gainesville, Florida; University of Georgia Library, Athens, Georgia; University of Virginia Library, Charlottesville, Virginia; Valentine Museum, Richmond, Virginia; Virginia Historical Society Library, Richmond, Virginia; Virginia State Archives, Richmond, Virginia; William and Mary College Library, Williamsburg, Virginia.

European institutions are Accademia delle Scienze, Turin, Italy; Archives de la Marine, Chateau de Vincennes, France; Cammel Laird Company, Liverpool, England; Centro di Studi Americani, Rome, Italy; Public Record Office, London.

Also acknowledged is the courtesy of the Vicksburg Centennial Commission, Vicksburg, Mississippi; the North Carolina Department of Archives and History, Raleigh, North Carolina; the Louisiana State University Press, Baton Rouge, Louisiana; and the South Carolina University Press, Columbia, South Carolina.

The maps printed in this book come through the courtesy of the publishing house Rizzoli Libri Grandi Opere S.p.A., Milan, Italy.

The research for this book was also made possible by several travel grants supplied by the Italian Commission for Cultural Exchanges with the United States. I send my most hearty thanks to the then president, Cipriana Scelba, to the present-day president, Professor Chiarenza, to its secretary, Dr. Filadoro, and to the whole staff. I also thank the USIS offices in Italy for multifarious help.

Particular thanks are extended to the painstaking and perceptive editor of this book, Trudie Calvert, and to the staff of the Naval Institute Press, whose efficiency, professionalism, and above all exquisite kindness were invaluable: no praise would indeed suffice for them.

Last but by no means the least, is my wife, Germana. During years of work, she added to the burden of our ménage and our two children that of helping me in many ways, reading the manuscript, locating errors in typing, suggesting changes, additions, and modifications, always helpful, always unobtrusive, always present. Suffice it to say that she cheerfully supported the condition of being the wife of the last prisoner of the American Civil War.

All these people and institutions added tremendously to this book and made it far better. Yet they bear no responsibility for any mistake or flaw; I am the only one responsible.

Raimondo Luraghi

A HISTORY
OF THE
CONFEDERATE
NAVY

O N E

Birth of a Navy

At sunset on 18 February 1861, in a train crossing the eastern part of Alabama, headed toward Montgomery, a man in his fifties studied the passing landscape. Though he wore civilian dress, the features of a sailor were evident in his slender and strong body, in his face burned and tanned by the sun and ocean winds, and in his sharp, piercing eyes accustomed to gazing at far horizons.[1]

Commander Raphael Semmes, formerly of the U.S. Navy, had just made the most momentous decision of his life.[2] After thirty-five years of honorable service, he had, three days earlier, addressed to the secretary of the navy a letter of resignation in which he renounced his position, his rank, and his career.[3] Several Southern states had just seceded from the Union to organize a new independent Confederacy. Semmes and other naval officers had been invited to leave the U.S. Navy to serve their native land. True, he was from Maryland, which remained in the Union, yet Maryland had always been considered a Southern state, and Raphael Semmes had dedicated himself to the new Southern nation.[4]

As the train moved south the air became warmer and balmy; two days earlier, Semmes had left a cold and snowy Washington, D.C. All around, pine forests were ablaze, casting a fantastic glare over the train. The man looking wearily from the window felt that he was coming back to the bosom of his own people and that his heavy heart was relaxing. Semmes later wrote:

> Under the happy influence I sank, as the night advanced and the train thundered on, into the first sound sleep which had visited my weary

eyelids since I had resigned my commission and read at the foot of the letter accepting my resignation, my name inscribed as plain "Esq." This night-ride through the burning pine woods of Alabama afterward stood as a great gulf in my memory, forming an impassable barrier, as it were, between my past and my future life. It had cost me pain to cross the gulf, but once crossed, I never turned to look back. When I washed and dressed for breakfast, in Montgomery, the next morning, I had put off the old man, and put on the new. The labours and associations of a lifetime had been inscribed in a volume which had been closed, and a new book, whose pages were as yet all blank, had been opened.[5]

The new book was, in truth, opening for a whole people, and in that very hour millions of persons saw, as did Commander Semmes, their individual destiny coincide with the collective drama of the South.

During a long period whose roots were grounded in the colonial era (and even directly back to the European heritage),[6] the English colonies (after 1776, the United States of America) had been developing in several different directions and orientations that generated different social structures and economic institutions, distinct cultures, even different civilizations that, toward the middle of the nineteenth century, were culminating (at least in the South) in a distinct national consciousness.[7] In the end, following a period of relative equilibrium between North and South, the latter had begun to persuade itself that a series of events (the strongest being, perhaps, the industrial revolution emerging in the North) was reducing it to an inferior condition, a substantially semicolonial status.[8]

The election as president of the United States of Abraham Lincoln, who symbolized a strong centralized national power and had won almost no votes in the South, had pushed angry and frustrated Southerners to play the momentous card of independence.[9] They feared an attack on slavery that would subvert the very foundations of the Southern social structure. Lincoln, however, although stating that he would take no action against slavery in the Southern states, confirmed his unequivocal determination to prevent the "peculiar institution" from penetrating the western territories, which were the common domain of the whole Union, and which (as he had said many years earlier) he intended to reserve for the "home of free white people."[10] This intent seemed discriminatory to Southerners, a blatant expression of what they considered their inferior, quasi-colonial status within the Union.[11]

The independence movement soon swept the South, except for the so-called border states,[12] immediately involving the states of the Deep South. On 20 December 1860 a convention elected by the people of South Carolina met in Charleston and unanimously approved an ordinance affirming that "the union now subsisting between South Carolina and other states, under the name of the 'United States' is hereby dissolved."[13] On 9 January 1861 another convention voted Mississippi out of the Union; on the tenth it was Florida's turn, followed on the eleventh by Alabama, on the twelfth by Georgia, on the twenty-fifth by Louisiana, and on 1 February by Texas.

On 4 February 1861 a convention of representatives from the seven seceded states met in Montgomery, Alabama, to launch the new Confederacy. On 8 February a provisional Constitution of the Confederate States of America was unanimously approved.[14]

After the provisional framing of the constitutional bases of the Confederacy, the constituents deemed it both opportune and necessary to design the basic institutional structures without waiting for the special committee, elected on 9 February 1861 to draft a definitive Constitution, to end its work.[15] Although some nurtured illusions, to wiser heads it appeared improbable that the North would peacefully agree to recognize Southern independence. The Northern threat was real: indeed, the South needed to organize a defense in the shortest time possible.

Among the most immediate needs were defensive armaments. The provisional Constitution gave the pro-tempore Congress (a transformation of the Constitutional Convention) the power to raise armies and (Art. 1, Section 5, paragraph 13) "To provide and maintain a Navy."[16] To undertake these tasks Congress on 12 February created a series of standing committees, among them one on naval affairs headed by Charles M. Conrad, a wealthy planter and lawyer from New Orleans, the major maritime city of the new Confederacy.[17]

A constitutional provision introduced by Representative Colin J. McRae, merchant and businessman from Mobile, Alabama, who would later have prominent if indirect ties with the Confederate navy, authorized Congress to wield executive power until a president-elect could be seated. Therefore, the Committee on Naval Affairs set immediately to work. On 13 February it requested and obtained the mandate to include in any plan relative to naval organization "suitable provisions" for officers of the U.S. Navy who would resign to serve the Confederacy. On the fourteenth, the committee won authority to call south naval experts deemed necessary for consultation.[18] On the same day telegrams were sent to native Southern naval officers instructing them to resign and proceed to Montgomery.

It was in answer to such a message that Semmes had tendered his resignation from the U.S. Navy and come to the capital of the new Confederacy. The situation he found there on 19 February 1861 was hardly encouraging: there were only four captains (Duncan N. Ingraham, Josiah Tattnall, Victor M. Randolph, and Lawrence Rousseau) and four commanders (Ebenezer Farrand, Thomas W. Brent, Harry J. Hartstene, and

Semmes himself).[19] Not all of these were in Montgomery. A meeting with the Committee on Naval Affairs was attended by only Rousseau, Ingraham, Randolph, and Semmes, together with a military engineer, Major William H. Chase, commanding the land forces of the state of Florida at Pensacola.[20]

The position of the men who were meeting with the Committee on Naval Affairs was strange and offered little hope. They were civilians and former naval officers; indeed, they had not yet entered the service of a nonexistent Confederate navy that lacked even a secretary. At the time of the meeting the South had not a single warship of any importance;[21] the only navy yard available was that at Pensacola, and it was of very modest size, more of a repair and coaling station than anything else. Still worse, it was blockaded by a Federal garrison stationed at Fort Pickens on Santa Rosa Island, which, with a supporting naval squadron, effectively closed the bay.[22] It was certainly not yet war; still, it was not peace either.

Taking this poor situation into account, the experts examined what documents were available. Notable among these was a letter addressed on 13 February to the Military Council of the state of Louisiana by Major Pierre Gustave Toutant Beauregard, who had resigned from the U.S. Army. He would publish the letter two days later in the *Daily Delta* of New Orleans. In it Beauregard stressed the enormous importance of the Mississippi River and the vulnerability of the great port of New Orleans, which could be easily reached by enemy vessels coming from the Gulf of Mexico. Beauregard (who, in 1852, as an army engineer, had served on a special commission to study the conditions of navigation on the unpredictable Mississippi delta and was himself a Louisiana Creole) had a deep knowledge of the area. To forestall enemy vessels from entering the delta he proposed rehabilitating and reinforcing the defenses of Forts Jackson and St. Philip, located on the lower course of the river, and building underwater obstructions; also, he offered futuristic and revolutionary solutions such as the use of the great theater lights of the Drummond system to illuminate the waters during the night, as well as electrically controlled explosive underwater devices that would blow up enemy ships.[23]

Thus for the first time there appeared in a typical sector of naval war a land officer who in the future would be closely tied with naval operations. The attention paid by the experts to his ideas (very interesting, sensible, destined for great development) already placed in bold relief how 90 percent of the naval war in the South would be fought: a desperate and unequal battle to protect the land against the sea, to repel an enemy known from the beginning to have uncontestable control of the waters.

Painfully aware of this truth, the committee recommended accepting Beauregard's proposals for New Orleans and extending them to four more seaports—Mobile, Pensacola, Savannah, and Charleston—and suggested acquiring in each state some small ship to be armed as a patrol boat or gunboat. As for the immense problem of developing coastal defenses in the South, the committee had no suggestions, stating that this meant dealing with items that required "much deliberation and the command of considerable means."[24] But there were as yet no means, and no time to acquire them. At that moment, the only naval forces the Confederacy could deploy were the very modest ones hurriedly gathered by the states at the time of their secession.

South Carolina had been the first to take the fateful path to separation. Its governor, Francis Pickens, early concerned with naval problems, had provided on 18 December 1860 (before the people's convention of the state, assembled the day before, declared secession, which, however, appeared certain and impending) for fitting out two small vessels as patrol boats, their main mission to keep an eye on the Federal troops at Fort Moultrie in Charleston Harbor.[25]

When on 30 December the state left the Union, the South Carolina legislature had to acknowledge that the shore communities were concerned about the potential threat from the sea and considered themselves in serious danger, a conclusion with which the state authorities agreed. It was indeed ominous that, from the very moment of secession, when other states had not yet acted and the Confederacy had not yet been born, Southerners felt the sea to be hostile and dangerous, expecting the greatest threat to come from that direction.[26]

The legislature therefore created a Coast Police, and the governor responded on 11 January 1861 in his annual message by announcing a project to outfit three propeller-driven patrol ships, to be based at Charleston, Beaufort, and Georgetown, using for that purpose $150,000 appropriated by the legislature.[27] But he underscored the extreme difficulty of procuring even those modest vessels and stressed the need to protect the coasts with fortifications, for which he had already provided (and was still providing) careful inspections by officers of land troops.[28] Thus began to appear that peculiar orientation (which prevailed even inside the Committee for Naval Affairs) by which land forces would have to fight against sea power, a struggle in which, it was supposed, Southern naval forces would play at best an auxiliary function.

Governor Pickens had to content himself with little sea power. True, officers were not lacking: after the state seceded, officers who had resigned from the U.S. Navy began to arrive: Lieutenant Commander James H. North, designated to command the Coast Police;[29] then, in early February, the old and eminent Captain Duncan N. Ingraham, soon nominated the senior captain of the service.[30]

Means, however, were lacking. The destruction of the South Carolina State Archives in the great conflagration that during the 1865 campaign reduced the capital, Columbia, to ashes, prevents a complete listing of the vessels, which were very modest: the former revenue cutter *Aiken,* with one gun; the tug *James Gray* (rechristened the *Lady Davis* after the birth of the Confederacy); two or three small sailers, formerly in the Lighthouse Service; several other small steamers *(Catawba, Gordon, Seabrook)* each armed with one piece of small caliber and hastily fitted out.[31]

Mississippi announced its secession on 8 January 1861, Florida on the tenth, Alabama on the eleventh. Mississippians had not—nor hoped to have—anything resembling a navy; on 13 January they limited themselves to occupying Ship Island, off Biloxi, in the Gulf of Mexico.[32]

Pierre le Moyne d'Iberville, the founder of the French Empire in the Gulf, had been the first, in 1699, to identify the strategic importance of the île du Mouillage (Ship Island) for controlling the mouths of the Mississippi;[33] yet the Mississippians (and, later, the Confederate government) did not appear to have so considered it. Although the Confederates occupied the island and built very good fieldworks,[34] they later evacuated Ship Island, which was then taken over by the Federals on 16 September 1861, without firing a shot. Obviously, to defend the island (and the internal waters that separate it from the coast), an adequate naval force with guns would have been needed; but nothing would or could be done to create one.[35]

The state of Mississippi, however, was concerned with another front. Its entire western border was bounded by its great namesake river. Therefore, the governor soon had heavy artillery in place that commanded the stream from the heights of Vicksburg. This step provoked frantic alarms and lively protests from the northwestern states.[36] The Confederate Congress, sitting in Montgomery, therefore, declared on 26 February 1861 that peaceful navigation of the Mississippi was open to any state riverine to both the great river and its tributaries; yet this move did not appease the Northwest.[37]

Florida succeeded, following its ordinance of secession, in taking over the Pensacola Navy Yard together with its forts except one—Fort Pickens—that still blockaded the bay. The only ship it could seize was a schooner in the service of the Coast Survey.[38] In addition to Fort Pickens, there remained in Federal hands Forts Taylor and Jefferson, built on the islands at the apex of the Florida peninsula.

Alabama militia succeeded, without firing a shot, in seizing the vital forts that protected the roadstead and port of Mobile. A revenue cutter

A History of the Confederate Navy

and a tug of the Lighthouse Service also fell into their hands, but these ships were of very little value.[39]

More substantial in organizing a naval force was the action of the state of Georgia following its secession on 19 January. On the twenty-second, the secession convention voted to enlist any available officer of Georgian citizenship, either from the army or navy of the United States. On the twenty-fifth it was decided to buy or build three steamers, two of which would eventually form the modest nucleus of the Georgia navy.[40] The first officer to tender his service was the former U.S. lieutenant commander John McIntosh Kell,[41] who, during four years of naval warfare, would demonstrate his outstanding qualities as a sailor. Kell was nominated to command the Georgia navy, until it went to the old Captain Josiah Tattnall, with the rank of flag officer.[42] Kell then went on to command the gunboat *Savannah,* a side-wheeler of 406 tons displacement, armed with only a 32-pounder and most unseaworthy.[43] From New York, Georgia acquired the steamer *Huntress,* of five hundred tons. She was a side-wheeler too, but faster and more seaworthy.[44]

Even though Louisiana (which seceded on 28 January 1861) faced both the Gulf of Mexico and the Mississippi, at first it did not outfit a remarkable naval force: only two revenue cutters of a few tons each.[45] Yet it succeeded in seizing the forts that closed the river below New Orleans.

After seceding on 1 February 1861, Texas took possession of the revenue cutter *Dodge.*

According to J. Thomas Scharf (whose data are, however, not fully reliable),[46] the new Confederacy inherited from the U.S. Navy many outstanding officers but no more than some ten auxiliary vessels of little displacement and armed with a dozen cannon of small caliber and low class. All together, they could not muster the battery of even a single Federal sloop.

Still, the Confederate Congress proceeded without delay and with remarkable optimism to build the structures of the new state. On 9 February it had unanimously elected the president of the Confederacy (who, according to the provisional Constitution, would be the supreme commander of the armed forces), former senator Jefferson Davis from Mississippi. The vice-president-elect was Alexander Stephens of Georgia.[47] Proceeding at once to Montgomery, Davis took his oath and was inaugurated. The as yet nonexistent Confederate navy thus had at hand its supreme commander.

What kind of commander was he to be? What conceptions did he have about the tasks and the importance of a navy? And how capable was he of commanding it? There is no need here to reconsider the complex personality of the man and statesman Jefferson Davis. He had had a long and comprehensive military career: in addition to serving as secretary of war of the United States, he fought in Mexico as the colonel of a volunteer Mississippi regiment and distinguished himself for gallantry at the battle of Buena Vista, where he was severely wounded. Upon Mississippi's secession, he was appointed general of state troops. He would have preferred to serve the new Confederacy in military uniform rather than as its president.

Davis had some knowledge of naval affairs, having for a short time served as interim secretary of the navy.[48] The man upon whose shoulders would fall the full responsibility of creating and directing the Confederate navy during four long years of war, Secretary Stephen Russell Mallory, never charged Davis with incompetence, lacking concern, or arbitrary intrusion into naval problems.[49] The only criticisms Mallory made of Davis were aimed solely at faults he thought he discovered in the president's personal character,[50] and such criticisms appeared on a single occasion, surrounded by praise. Later, Mallory mentioned the president's reluctance to agree that men suitable for naval service be transferred to it from the army.[51] In fact, Davis conveyed Mallory's concern to Congress, though, it appears, somewhat mildly.[52]

Thus, if it is correct that the army was always first in Davis's thoughts, enjoying substantial priority over the navy (which he considered more or less an auxiliary force), it is also true that the South, lacking both human and material resources, had to face the ever-worsening depletion of the ranks of line regiments. Besides, if one might trust as witness a man who would become a most dangerous enemy of the Southern navy (Rear Admiral David Dixon Porter), Jefferson Davis, even before secession, had expressed the firm assurance that the South would have "a Navy to be proud of."[53]

Before the Navy Department was formally organized, President Davis made a decision that was not consonant with the need to create a Southern naval force: he sent Commander Raphael Semmes to the North to acquire arms and ammunition. The letter of instructions given Semmes spoke only of arms and material for the army,[54] and it seems strange that the president did not hesitate to deprive the future navy of one of its best men, putting him (even temporarily) in service to the land forces.[55]

At the same time, however, Congress and the president were taking a step of the highest importance. The day after Davis spoke to Semmes, on 20 February 1861, Congress by law instituted the Department of the Navy.[56] On the twenty-fifth the president, by special message, informed the Congress that he had appointed former senator Stephen Russell Mallory from Florida as secretary of the navy. There was some opposition, but Congress finally approved the appointment on 4 March.[57]

Mallory went to work immediately. Indeed, he would be one of the only two cabinet members in Davis's administration to remain in office during the entire conflict between North and South and the entire life of the Confederate States of America, the other being the postmaster general, John H. Reagan. Mallory's retention was undoubtedly owing to the deep confidence that Jefferson Davis always maintained for the head of the Southern navy, but perhaps also the "terrestrial" frame of mind of the president caused him to grant naval affairs only secondary attention, contenting himself with knowing that the secretary was a trustworthy person to whom he could substantially give carte blanche.[58]

Mallory was able to collaborate with Davis rather than antagonize him, and the president discerned what very few among his contemporaries or those who came later were able to recognize: the outstanding ability, alertness, and understanding of situations that (despite his limits and his mistakes, and these were neither few nor of trifling importance) helped Mallory to assess the needs of the moment and to determine the naval strategy that, with the limited means at his disposal, was the best the Confederacy might follow and constituted a substantial and in many ways a surprising success.[59]

Yet it is not by chance that both contemporaries and historians have so ill-treated Mallory, hitting him more with silence than with criticism. In his personality and his life there apparently was no exceptional charisma. He was not, like Jefferson Davis, full of human pathos, endowed by an extreme, almost excruciating sensitivity, sharp, capable of elevating himself to become a symbol of the desperate will and the heroic tragedy of the South, object of "inextinguishable hatred and of unconquered love." Nor was he, like General Robert E. Lee, gifted with an Olympian and serene austerity, blessed by the gods of war with the sparkle of military genius, as gigantic in victory as in defeat. Neither did he, like Thomas J. "Stonewall" Jackson, embody the unyielding Puritan hero of a dead age. He was not a Hector, a Hannibal, or a Cromwell and certainly not a Churchill or a Fisher. His personality lacked that tragic prominence that made the other protagonists of the Civil War so terribly grand, making of each of them a symbol, an embodiment of the drama of an era and a people.

Nonetheless, the dramatic component was not wholly absent from Mallory's war vicissitudes; it remained concealed, and he never became a symbol of the tragedy of the South. The stirring story the world saw was that of the Confederate navy, conjured up from nothing to fight against the heaviest odds; facing in an unequal and awesome struggle an overpowering opponent; capable of defying it by performing heroic deeds that commanded respect even from the enemy; and overwhelmed in the end

man of the Committee on Naval Affairs, of which he was already a member. In this way he became one of the major spokesmen of United States naval policy. As usual, he committed himself totally to his duty. In the Library of Congress he painstakingly studied problems of naval history and technology, never forgetting to get practical information from seamen.

During his tenure, he gave a vigorous impulse to the navy of the United States. One of the problems he had to face was the navy's abundance of superfluous personnel. Moreover, slow promotion compelled officers to vegetate for a long time in lower ranks, where many lost any inclination to improve their professional expertise. A few reached the higher ranks when they were too advanced in age, sometimes ill, narrow-minded, conservative, lacking any impulse. There was no lack of skilled officers, but they risked being forestalled by those prone to routine and red tape, who were often incompetent.

Solving the problem was the task of the Naval Retiring Board, which, after checking the records of all officers, mercilessly pruned the "dry branches." Its work was extremely positive, even if, in some cases, it risked hitting people who did not deserve it. The outcome was a storm of protest over Mallory's head and an obstinate hatred for him that would make itself felt in the future.[63]

At the same time Mallory was also working to modernize naval vessels. Thanks essentially to his enterprise, six screw-propeller steam frigates and six first-class and six second-class sloops, also screw-propeller steamers, were built, the most up-to-date warships in the world, envied by Great Britain herself.[64]

Yet Mallory was looking toward a grander future. Indeed, he tried (albeit fruitlessly) to push a project, already checked by Congress, for the construction of an armored ship, designed by Robert L. Stevens, for the defense of New York Harbor.[65] Mallory failed, yet his effort provides a glimpse into his future naval strategy.

The advanced naval reforms solicited and championed by Mallory persisted. He thus contributed perhaps more than anybody else to building the big navy against which he must, years later, fight almost empty-handed.

Indeed, when Mallory was appointed secretary of the Confederate navy, he had nothing effective to count on. Only on 8 March did the Confederate Congress approve a law to grant him some civil servants:[66] a chief clerk who handled only administrative matters, four clerks, and a messenger.[67] It was a very small staff.

On 11 March Congress passed another law to complete the structure of the Navy Department. It would be composed of four chiefs of bureaus and the commander of the Marine Corps.

The Office of Ordnance and Hydrography dealt initially with the entire vital sector of arms and ammunitions of every kind: research, projecting, production, acquisition, testing, and allocation as well as all nautical instruments and charts and everything pertaining to navigation (lighthouses, buoys, and the thorny problem of pilots). The Office of Orders and Details was to direct naval operations, but with very limited powers because they included only executive duties, and act—with greater power—as an office of personnel. This bureau attended first to the drafting and delivering, according to directives from the secretary, of all orders and dispositions, to the assignment and destination of personnel, and also to the administration of military justice and discipline. Later, this office would be charged with other tasks, not all consistent with its functions: supply and storage of fuel (coal and wood); fitting out and replenishing ships (except for weapons and ammunitions, which fell to the Office of Ordnance and Hydrography); and management of the Naval Rope Walk.[68] The Office of Medicine and Surgery was not only to organize and direct naval hospitals but also to produce and acquire medicinal drugs as well as medical and surgical stores, direct medical personnel, and, over and above any other duty, provide surgeons and infirmaries on board ships.[69] Finally, the Office of Provisions and Clothing was to secure (by means of direct production, acquisition, or requisition) all the food supplies for the personnel, either afloat or ashore, also small stores for the use of crewmen, and the management of the naval treasury, including pay for officers and enlisted men.[70] At first, even the supplying of fuel and fitting out of ships belonged to this office; later, that task went to the Office of Orders and Details. Last, there was the Marine Corps Command.

Thus, at least on paper, the framework of the Confederate naval command had been supplied. Yet the naval secretary and four bureau chiefs did not form a board of admiralty such as that implemented by the British, at least during serious wartime circumstances. No decision was taken jointly, and the ultimate responsibility for every determination rested with the secretary alone. His decisions were made under orders from the president, who, however, always granted him ample discretion. Undoubtedly, the chief of the Office of Orders and Details acted as the first adviser to the secretary, but in a very informal way. Mallory always lent an attentive ear to his suggestions but made decisions by himself. A limited power of decision fell to the Office of Orders and Details when the secretary was absent or ill.

The creation of such an office, rising apparently from a suggestion offered by Mallory himself to the president of the congressional Committee on Naval Affairs, undoubtedly represented a useful innovation compared to the U.S. Navy, which had none. There the secretary had to deal personally with the drafting of all the orders and the assignment of personnel, which caused a tremendous waste of time and risked his becoming busy with trifles. In the Confederate navy the responsibility lay with the head of the office, under the secretary's supervision.

A negative aspect of the naval establishment was giving the Office of Orders and Details responsibility for providing coal and fitting out ships. Even worse was the lack of an office of yards and docks and of an office of construction, equipment, and repair, both of which existed in the U.S. Navy. Such duties were divided between the Office of Ordnance and Hydrography and that of Orders and Details, with consequent overlapping of responsibilities, confusion, and slowing of work. Naval construction was later provided for by organizing, alongside the offices already existing, two new billets of chief constructor and engineer in chief. The first was charged with planning and constructing ships (directly or by supervising private shipyards with which the navy could contract to execute or complete its projects). The second was charged with planning, producing, and distributing steam engines.

Yet the most feeble point in the Confederate naval command was the absence of a chief of staff, or of what in the U.S. Navy would in 1915 be the chief of naval operations. Mallory was all and everything: administrator and head of the navy, author and executor of naval strategy, and the man responsible for the conduct of maritime and coastal operations.

Through almost five grim years of war, burdened by such almost inhuman responsibility, he did indeed do his duty well (if not without unavoidable blunders), yet he was able to learn from his mistakes and produced the best naval strategy possible in such a grievous situation. Still, the presence of a skillful chief of staff might have accelerated and made the work of the command machinery more resilient and avoided many blind alleys before reaching the proper road.

Mallory's counterpart, Gideon Welles, secretary of the U.S. Navy, was handicapped by a lack of expertise. Nicknamed "Father Neptune" because of his flowing beard, Welles was blessed with a keen and bright mind. Yet he had been a political journalist and had no naval experience except four years as head of the Office of Provisions and Clothing, where he had shone mainly as a careful administrator. Soon, however, thanks to a series of happy chances, not least of which was the outstanding ability of President Lincoln to select individuals to carry out his policy, Welles would have at his side (with the rank of assistant secretary of the navy) a resourceful, competent, and talented man, Gustavus Vasa Fox. Usually called "captain" because of the rank he had acquired in the merchant marine, he had also served for more than ten years in the navy. Fox soon became, in all but name, chief of staff of the U.S. Navy.[71]

At the end of June 1861 the U.S. Navy also had what amounted to a true operations office in the Blockade Strategy Board, headed by a prominent seaman, Captain Samuel Francis Du Pont.[72] Mallory would never have near him a personality or organization of this sort. The Chief Clerk, a Virginian, E. M. Tidball, who had served in the same position in the U.S. Navy for a decade, would never be more than an energetic and competent bureaucrat.[73] Such were the greatest flaws in the organization of the Confederate navy.

The law that became effective on 16 March 1861 with the signature of President Davis, other than providing for the Navy Department, gave a provisional table of personnel as follows: four captains, four commanders, thirty lieutenants, five naval surgeons and five assistant surgeons, six paymasters, and two chief engineers. The president could enroll as many masters, midshipmen, engineers, naval constructors, boatswains, gunners, carpenters, sailmakers, petty officers, junior ratings, and enlisted men as he needed, up to a total of three thousand.[74]

On 16 March Davis designated as the four captains Lawrence Rousseau, Josiah Tattnall, Victor M. Randolph, and Duncan N. Ingraham. The four commanders were Ebenezer Farrand, Thomas W. Brent, Raphael Semmes, and Henry J. Hartstene. Among the medical officers, W.A.W. Spotswood became surgeon general and thus was in charge of naval medicine. Notable among the lieutenants were James H. North and John M. Kell.[75]

All else was lacking: the sailors, the vessels, the weapons. There was not much time to conjure up all this. Exactly twenty-seven days later, the Confederate batteries, as a retort to what Southerners considered an unendurable challenge to the very existence of the Confederacy, opened fire on Fort Sumter in Charleston Harbor. On 13 April the fort surrendered; on the fifteenth, the president of the United States, Abraham Lincoln, by a proclamation, declared the existence of a rebellion and called for seventy-five thousand militia volunteers to subdue it; between 17 and 20 April, Virginia, Arkansas, Tennessee, and North Carolina left the Union to enter the Confederacy.

Mallory now faced a wholly unheard-of task: to build a navy from almost nothing while at war and in a war in which the enemy had from the first cannon shot complete mastery of the sea.

T W O

Financial Means, Personnel, and Organization

Virginia's secession resulted in the transfer of the Confederate capital from Montgomery to Richmond in the Old Dominion, seat of the oldest British colonial settlement in the New World, "mother of Presidents," and home of George Washington and Thomas Jefferson. Why should the center of the new Confederacy not be located there?

It might be asserted that the move was a major strategic blunder. Montgomery was located far from the enemy's most probable invasion routes, relatively well protected, inaccessible from the sea. Richmond, by contrast, was very close to what would soon become the front line; it was a railway focal point and the location of the only relatively large war industry (the Tredegar Iron Works), and it was easily threatened from the sea. Montgomery would have been a better choice, Atlanta even superior.[1]

Yet it was not easy to avoid the lure of Virginia. After long and anxious debate, on 31 May 1861 President Davis sent a special message to Congress communicating that he had signed an act relocating the capital of the Confederate States of America to Richmond.[2] Davis was the first to move there; his cabinet members followed in early June.

Leaving Montgomery on 31 May, Mallory reached Richmond on 3 June. On the fourth, having settled himself as best he could, he was already at work, even if harassed by violent attacks of gout, which gave him almost unbearable pain in one hip.[3]

Mallory and his partners met in Richmond a climate quite different from that which had greeted the birth of the Confederacy in Montgomery. There, the prevailing mood had been elation and hope, together with happiness for the event, seen as an auspicious one. Here, instead, was the somber and ominous prospect of imminent war. In short, in Montgomery (notwithstanding frenzied activity and some dark foreboding) one got the impression of living through a great *kermesse,* hardly bothered by fierce attacks from bloodthirsty mosquitoes.[4] In Richmond, instead, one felt in the immediate rear-front, in a city bustling to make itself ready for the war at its door.[5]

Virginia had contributed to the navy a few small ships, a substantial number of good officers who joined those already enlisted, and, most important, the Gosport Navy Yard at Norfolk.

In Richmond, at the corner of Franklin and Ninth streets, in front of the leafy trees of Capitol Square, there was at the time (between Franklin and Main streets, with its front on Ninth) a great brick building. Formerly the Mechanic Institute, it now became the headquarters of the War and Navy Departments. From his office on the second floor, Mallory would direct Confederate naval strategy throughout four years of war. Not far away, on Bank Street (which, perpendicular to Ninth, bordered the southern side of Capitol Square), in a fine, recently built palace of gray stone (formerly the local Custom House and today Richmond's main post office) were located the offices of President Davis and the secretaries of state and the treasury.[6]

Mallory had had no more than twenty-seven days of uncertain peace to organize a navy; and even then he had been distressed by the increasingly strained situation in Charleston Harbor. After the first acts by Congress and the president, he needed to move on to more complicated problems that required much greater effort.

The first urgent problem Mallory had to face after 12 March 1861 was to obtain the funds necessary to organize the navy, to put it to work, and to finance the naval war. Two centuries earlier, the great warlord Raimondo Montecuccoli had straightforwardly said that three things were indispensable for the conduct of war: "Money, money, and still more money."[7] Mallory was perfectly aware of this truth.

The mechanism available to the naval secretary to get the necessary funds was apparently very simple. He had to submit to Congress, via the Joint Committee on Naval Affairs (then, following the adoption of the permanent Constitution, the similar committees of both chambers), an estimate of expenses for successive ordinary and extraordinary appropriations required to fund them. Congress would then deliberate such appropriations.

At this point, however, the matter began to get complicated. The Confederacy never had anything like a navy portfolio that would grant it a proper independent budget. Funds were appropriated by Congress from time to time, in reply to specific requests, via the Treasury Department, to which Mallory had to send proper requirements on each occasion, practically through draft letters.[8]

The outcome was a series of setbacks and delays and haggling that complicated the already intricate conduct of naval war to the point that naval strategy was at the mercy of the Confederacy's financial policy. Such a situation was by no means due to the ill-will of the secretary of the treasury, Christopher G. Memminger (who, indeed, always tried to do his best) but to the strictness of the Confederate finance and economy, which influenced, at least in part, the events of naval war, sometimes catastrophically.[9] The Southern navy thus had to keep closer and more complicated relations with the secretary of the treasury than with any other department, including the secretary of war or the secretary of state. There were many elements of reciprocal interplay.

I do not intend to deal too deeply here with the problem of Confederate financial policies, yet some introductory remarks must be made to elucidate the subsequent ups and downs of the navy.

The navy's ties with the Treasury Department involved three primary sets of problems. First there was the policy by which the Confederacy sought to finance its war effort and thus the life of its land and naval forces. When the war began, the secretary of the treasury, Christopher G. Memminger,[10] after settling into an empty office that had not even been swept, gave thought to the foundation of the financial policy of his government: a specie reserve of bullion and foreign exchange. It did not take him long to acknowledge the lamentable truth that the North remained in possession of 67.5 percent of the specie reserves while the South had only 32.5 percent.[11]

Yet Memminger did not even consider seizing the specie reserves held in the banks, contenting himself with what could be found in the offices of the mint in Louisiana, amounting to no more than $600,000,[12] a truly small beginning! At this point, to meet the costs of the approaching war (just as the naval secretary, as of 12 March 1861, when hostilities had not yet begun, had produced an estimate of requirements for the period until 4 February 1862 of $2,065,110),[13] the Treasury Department could take only one road, the royal road followed in any similar emergency: recourse to taxation.

A prominent American economist, Albert Gallatin, in his day underscored that the organization for levying an extraordinary war tax must be prepared in time of peace, something obviously impossible for the new Southern nation.[14] While the financial machinery was being put into gear, it was therefore necessary to issue treasury notes and to borrow. This, however, needed to be only a temporary measure if the Confederacy were to escape falling into a disastrous inflation.

A loan must mobilize all the resources of the nation and, if possible, the reserves of specie and foreign exchange kept by the banks. This, for a number of reasons (not least, the inadequacy of monetary reserves in Southern banks, which feared being driven into bankruptcy), was more difficult than anticipated. The attempt to float a specie loan almost failed; throughout the war, the South was never able to put together more than $8 to $9 million in specie or foreign exchange.[15]

The substantial wealth of the South lay in its agricultural staples, primarily its cotton crop, which, alone, provided 33.83 percent of the gross national product of the United States.[16] Cotton was a gigantic asset: its average annual production amounted to 4,500,000 bales (about 2,225,000,000 pounds)[17] and represented, until the Civil War, the main export commodity of the old Union. At an average price of 11.5 cents per pound, cotton for the astonishing amount of $184,500,000 had been exported in 1860,[18] enough to adjust the trade balance of the United States, a fact that lay at the base of much of the grievance that drove the South out of the Union.

Could the Confederate Treasury Department float loans by exploiting such immense wealth? The answer was obviously no. Cotton could not be immediately converted into cash unless put up for sale on the world market,[19] something which the Confederate Treasury did not seem to have considered when it launched a produce loan finally formalized on 6 May 1861.[20] Such a loan should have been subscribed to by planters who would contribute cotton, tobacco, rice, and sugar (the most important crops of the South), which the government would then sell on foreign markets after paying the subscribers in Confederate bonds, good for paying taxes.

The loan was a failure. The fact was that the planters, before helping the government, needed to be helped themselves. Following the break with the North, they found themselves with their cotton unsold and their debts falling due. What they needed was either immediate payment for their entire harvest by the government (which would then dispose of it on overseas markets)[21] or immediate granting of credit. If either was unavailable and they had to give up their crops in exchange for bonds usable only to pay future taxes, they would go bankrupt.[22] Yet nothing was done for them, at least for the time being, and the planters were left to cope with their problems.

The produce loan gave the Confederate government in all 417,000 bales of cotton (about one-eleventh of the total crop) plus near-insignificant amounts of rice, sugar, grains, tobacco, and molasses.[23] So the Confederacy had to face the unpalatable truth: the only way to mobilize its potential wealth in cotton was to sell it immediately on foreign markets for ready cash. And because this had to be done through maritime trade (only a negligible amount could be exported across the Mexican border, in part because of the inadequacy of rail transportation), Treasury Department policy intersected with naval policy.

A basic naval task is to protect national maritime trade; however, this requires the existence of a navy, which, in turn, depends on possessing ships. The lamentable situation of the Confederate fleet and shipbuilding suggested therefore the wise policy of acquiring ships overseas, a matter to which Mallory had already given thought.

In which markets could Confederate vessels be bought? Semmes's mission to the North evidently having failed (as should have been expected), there remained only Canada and the industrial maritime countries of Europe, Great Britain first, then France. The difficulty was that such markets required cash payment in gold or in foreign exchange (which was the same), and it was up to the Treasury Department to provide the needed funds. This was the third point at which treasury and navy policies intersected. Indeed, the last two problems were tied closely together (and both with the first one) because the only effective wealth the Confederacy had by which theoretically to open any door on European markets was, once again, cotton. We thus are back to the starting point: no cotton exports, no money; no money, no ships; and no ships, no cotton export.

Given this situation, the solution might have been as follows: send to Europe, or to the West Indies, or to any neutral market, the largest possible amount of cotton before the outbreak of hostilities closed ocean routes to Southern trade. This step—if taken jointly with another one solicited by many sides, that is, the government's quick seizure, in whole or in part, of the planters' cotton crop—meant virtually the nationalization of foreign trade, a step from which the free-trade-minded South refrained. In the end, the Confederacy would be compelled to adopt such a resolution—but too late.

Nevertheless, for the time being, there was one who had not only thought of an analogous action but also immediately offered a plan. This was George Alfred Trenholm, a wealthy merchant, shipping agent, and banker of Charleston, South Carolina, a man who would have in the future deeper and deeper ties with the Southern navy.[24]

Skillful, able, competent in trade and finance as few others were, deeply committed to the Southern cause, Trenholm had for some time hoped to institute a transatlantic steamship line between Charleston and Liverpool (where a unit of his firm was located) and another one with the West Indies. Now, he understood that the famed East India Company was putting up for sale ten of its best steamers, four of larger displacement and six smaller ones, all with iron hulls and capable of being fitted with guns.[25] The cost of such ships ready for sea (for which Charles K. Prioleau, Trenholm's Liverpool agent, had already advanced a preemptive right) was two million pounds. This could be covered by forty thousand bales (about nine thousand tons) of cotton, priced (on the Southern market) at $2 million. The ships might then enter Confederate ports, possibly loaded with useful goods, and go back with more cotton to be placed in storage in Bermuda or Havana.[26]

It is uncertain when Trenholm brought his proposal before the Confederate government; in any case, it occurred before the Northern blockade of the South was effective.[27] Even though the secretary of the treasury, Memminger, favored the plan, the government rejected it.[28] Mallory provided the most serious objection by observing that the ships, having a draft of more than ten feet, would not be able to enter most Southern seaports.[29] Nevertheless, this was the only concrete possibility for establishing a considerable stock of cotton overseas before the blockade net was made very tight. Yet for many reasons it did not happen.

To make matters worse, several elements hindered the export of cotton. First was the decision by Congress—desperately seeking funds—to place upon cotton an export duty of one-eighth of a cent per pound, or about $2.50 per ton.[30] In itself, it was not a heavy tax, but, unfortunately, it coincided with repeated attempts by well-meaning "people's committees" to put an embargo on cotton exports, under the illusion that a cotton famine might force the big maritime powers to pressure the North into lifting its blockade. In truth, the Confederate authorities never consented to any such embargo; their opposition was lukewarm and clumsy, but to say that the Southern government favored the embargo idea would be utterly false. Still, there was no strong decision to control foreign trade and use cotton as a means for financing the war, in part because of the predominant free-trade philosophy held by most Southerners.[31]

The Confederate Treasury Department policy (at least until 1864) remained oriented toward financing the war with loans and, mainly, the ever-increasing issue of treasury forced-tender notes. The consequence was exactly what should have been avoided: a fearful and uncontrollable increase in inflation. The resort to taxation basically failed. It could not have been otherwise: without a market in which to sell their crops and without means of paying their debts, planters would be unresponsive to taxes.[32]

Inflation compelled secretaries (among them, Mallory) constantly to modify their estimates, in part because of the difficulty of facing expenses with a currency that was endlessly being depreciated.[33] The situation of the navy was the worst. The inability of the Treasury Department to regulate trade and the need of the navy to spend much money on foreign markets raised to extreme levels the rates of exchange that had to be accepted and later compelled the South to export cotton with enormous risks and at ruinous prices.

All this would have dreadful consequences for any financial operations the navy might have to conduct overseas. Already, on 11 May 1861, when inflation was not yet felt, Mallory, who had just proposed immediately putting $2 million on the English market "for the probable cost of ten steam gunboats for coast defense of the Confederate States, to be built or purchased as may be more convenient," had to content himself, at Memminger's request, with sending only $600,000, of which $400,000 was in letters of exchange on London and $200,000 through a letter of credit on the Fraser and Trenholm Bank of Liverpool. (And this did not take into account Trenholm's personal loss, to which he was exposed by making the operation possible.) [34] The situation would only darken in the future.

The answer would be found in 1864 through a radical revolution of the entire Confederate economic policy, mainly in the field of foreign trade. One cannot but admire the open-mindedness, courage, and determination with which such steps were taken. But this occurred too late.

Among recipients of funding in the Confederacy, only the President's house received less than the navy. During the entire conflict, the Confederacy spent a total of $107,000,000 for the navy, compared with $2,180,700,000 for the army, or more than twenty times less.[35] As a partial remedy the navy (whose administrative management seems to have been outstanding) finally found a way of self-financing. Indeed, during the last eighteen months of the war, it would be able to lend money to other bureaus of the Southern government.[36]

In the estimate of expenses written by Secretary Mallory on 12 March 1861, out of $2,065,110, $522,217 was for personnel stipends and pay.[37] This was a small sum, yet the Confederacy had planned a relatively small navy, of not more than 3,000 officers and enlisted men. This number was substantially maintained, rarely growing to above 4,000. The top was reached in the spring of 1864, with 753 officers of all ranks and 4,450 enlisted men.[38] In the same year, the Marine Corps included 749 officers, noncommissioned officers, and rank and file.[39]

By comparison, the great Union navy began with 11,422 officers, sailors, and marines and grew in 1865 to 6,759 officers, 51,357 sailors, and 3,850 marines, enlisting during the entire war more than 84,000 men.[40] It is thus easy to understand the limits of the Confederate navy and the extremely difficult situation of inferiority it endured.

Mallory at the beginning of the conflict had no problems deriving from scarcity of officers. Although not all Southerners had resigned from the U.S. Navy, they arrived in adequate numbers. On 22 May 1861 the U.S. secretary of the navy, Gideon Welles, noted that he had accepted the resignations of four captains, seven commanders, twenty lieutenants, six surgeons, six of other ranks and categories, and forty-one midshipmen.[41] According to Scharf, out of a total of 2,234 officers of the navy and Marine Corps, 671 were Southerners. Of these, 321 resigned to cast their lot with the Confederacy while 350 remained on the Union list.[42]

Mallory thus ran the risk of having too many officers when Virginia (which, after secession, had organized its own navy) entered the Confederacy.[43] He resolved the problem temporarily by accepting in the Confederate navy only those Virginia officers who had resigned from the U.S. Navy following the state's secession.[44] The others (who had resigned earlier for private reasons) were assigned to the coast artillery.[45] Some of these were perhaps too hurriedly assigned so that later it was necessary to recall them despite opposition from land commanders.[46]

Owing to this situation, the law of 16 March 1861 was substantially amended to make room for newcomers (some of them first-rate). It was clear that the old law was neither suitable nor adequate to take care of those officers. New provisions were therefore prepared and approved. During the reworking of the law, the ranks of officers were reorganized and equivalency was achieved with those of the army. The Confederate navy—and Mallory as well—displayed a creative and innovative spirit in relation to the old U.S. Navy, creating a more cogent and better-structured articulation of ranks and their assignments (even if many of them remained on paper and were never covered).

After shelving a first pharaonic project that included nine admirals, the ranks were definitively settled with two laws, of 24 December 1861 and 21 April 1862. According to these laws, the officers were divided into two groups: line officers, who formed the elite of the navy and who alone could be given responsibility for command, and limited-duty officers such as engineers, paymasters, and surgeons. Both groups included commissioned officers, who had a commission signed by the president of the Confederacy and approved by Congress, and warrant officers, who had a warrant signed by the naval secretary. Commissions were revocable only as a punitive measure, but warrants were revocable at any time.[47]

The following table shows the ranks of naval officers of the Confederacy and the corresponding grade in the Confederate army. The lieutenant commanding was more a function than a rank. Normally, the lieutenant commanding was a first lieutenant serving as a ship commander but at his regular pay. There was also the charge of flag officer, but this was not

Corresponding Ranks of the Confederate Navy and Army

NAVY	ARMY
Commissioned officers	
Admiral	General
Vice-admiral	Lieutenant general
Rear admiral	Major general
Commodore	Brigadier general
Captain	Colonel
Commander	Lieutenant colonel
Lieutenant commanding	Major
First lieutenant	Captain
Second lieutenant	Lieutenant
Warrant officers	
Passed midshipman	Lieutenant (j.g.)
Midshipman	

an effective rank: it was simply a temporary role given to a commodore or captain who commanded a naval squadron. Under the rank of midshipman was that of master, for which the Confederate army had no parallel.[48]

Some of the ranks listed in the table were never used. The law of 21 April 1862 (which was never amplified) provided for four admirals, ten captains, thirty-one commanders, one hundred first lieutenants, twenty-five second lieutenants, and twenty masters "in line of promotion" (i.e., waiting to be promoted to a higher rank).

By a specific law the Confederacy provided for granting naval officers serving with army detachments a military rank in addition to the naval one, an element of great future significance because it granted greater interdependence in the South between sea and land operations. Last, "provisional" ranks, limited to "the duration of war," were provided. They were somewhat similar to those held by reserve officers, yet they would end with the termination of hostilities if those affected could not obtain permanent rank.[49]

Limited-duty officers and their numbers included engineers, that is, engineer in chief (1); chief engineers (12); first (50), second (50), and third (150) assistant engineers; paymasters, including paymaster (12), assistant paymaster (40); surgeons, including surgeon general (1); surgeon (10); passed assistant surgeon (15), and assistant surgeon (30). The number of midshipmen was set at 106.[50]

Obviously, so that the officer corps could recruit young men, it was necessary to establish a naval academy, a primary concern to Mallory. An auxiliary cruiser, the *Patrick Henry*, part of the James River Squadron, was in time assigned as a school-ship. Because it could accommodate only some of the midshipmen, it was decided that the rest would be trained by the old practice of learning on warships already in service. Yet Mallory thought that the building of a few barracks near Drewry's Bluff (where the school-ship *Patrick Henry* was stationed) would enable all midshipmen to gather in one place. He firmly held—and from the beginning underscored—the inadequacy of professional and scientific training available to midshipmen aboard various units.[51]

The academy's superintendent was the learned and esteemed Lieutenant William H. Parker.[52] The cadets had to pass examinations in navigation, naval science, naval tactics, gunnery, various weapons, engineering, English, foreign languages (French and German), design, topography, mathematics, physics, history, and moral conduct.[53]

With great hesitancy, because he had lost his notes and was pressed by the needs of service, Lieutenant Parker wrote a special handbook of naval science for the academy's use,[54] as well as a compilation of rules of discipline and moral conduct to be followed while on board the school-ship.[55]

The corps of Confederate cadets was capable and earnest. At the end of the war, after the fall of Richmond, they had to fulfill the extremely difficult mission of preserving and delivering to President Davis what wealth remained of the treasury of the Confederacy. The well-trained cadets, armed as an infantry unit, after an exhausting march joined the president near Abbeville, South Carolina, and handed over to him and his cabinet the treasury intact, observing stern discipline to the end.[56]

The Confederate navy was plagued throughout the war with the inadequacy of pilots. Because the nautical charts of the time were, at best, uncertain, naval officers could not operate in coastal waters without experienced pilots. Following the method in use by the U.S. Navy, arrangements were made to employ civilian pilots who received regular pay.[57] In many cases, pilots would desert their duty; others were careful and efficient. The Confederacy gave particular care to those pilots who served in the area around Wilmington, North Carolina, the favorite docking place for blockade runners. Many pilots there were granted a military rank. The system of managing pilots and lighthouses, marking navigable canals, and locating wrecks was placed under the control of naval officers.[58]

The uniforms of the corps of officers consisted of a cap, frock coat, and trousers, all in gray (the famed Confederate gray), already adopted by the army. That color, unusual for a navy, was certainly not liked by the officers, yet, keeping discipline, they normally wore it.[59]

To promote the best and bravest officers to higher ranks, promotion by seniority was for the most part abandoned. Instead, a law stated that all the admirals and a substantial number of officers of lower ranks might be nominated or promoted only for acts of gallantry in war.

After the officer corps was organized, there arose the problem of non-commissioned officers and enlisted men. The South lacked such skilled personnel. In the old U.S. Navy most were of Northern birth. Further, out of the 5,539,812 tons of merchant shipping belonging to the old Union, the South had possessed only about 500,000, whereas New York State alone had 1,740,940 and New England 1,839,158.[60] The number of sailors was distributed in the same proportion. Worse yet, before Mallory was able to proceed with his duties, almost any man capable of naval service had been enrolled in the army, which showed little desire to release them.[61] Therefore, Mallory had to engage in a long and wearisome quarrel to reclaim them, facing the ill-will of army officers who, themselves hard-pressed by lack of men, declined to give them back. The same was true with the marines: recruiting officers in Montgomery and New Orleans had to strive endlessly to raise the required number of men.[62]

When the government was persuaded by Mallory that the navy lacked sufficient enlisted men, it promoted a series of laws to solve the problem. The law of 2 October 1862 authorized draftees to select the navy or the Marine Corps; that of 1 May 1863 ordered the transfer of all sailors from the army to the navy. Because that law was widely disregarded, another law of 22 March 1864 transferred to naval service twelve hundred men from the army, of whom nine hundred were to come from departments east of the Mississippi River.[63]

Yet, notwithstanding the government's pressure, such laws were not obeyed by army commanders, who were overwhelmed by the scarcity of men fit for service to fill up the depleted ranks of their regiments. Thus the already small navy struggled almost fruitlessly to complete its muster rolls.[64]

In the last months of the conflict desertion threatened a further weakening of the ranks. Mallory had to fight this problem with drastic orders: that all sailors who had already deserted from the Union navy could not set foot on land or take part in patrols. In addition, for any event that might offer the opportunity to desert, two officers must be detailed, together with the most trustworthy men.[65] Ultimately, desertion did not significantly increase; the great majority of Confederate sailors kept their combat stations to the very end.

The Marine Corps should originally have been composed of a battalion of six companies commanded by a major. Here, too, Mallory's action was innovative. He introduced the battalion/company system, unfamiliar in the Marine Corps of the United States and followed at the time only by

British Royal Marines. This system cost more, yet it \
than the old one and—most important—it allowed t,
employed, if need be, in autonomous separate units.[66]

The law of 20 May 1861, in addition to increasing the nu
ions, provided that the Marine Corps would include 46 ot,
men and be commanded by a colonel. The latter, named on
Lloyd J. Beall, an experienced officer from Maryland who
thirty years in the U.S. Army (but not with the marines). Beall
of great skill.[67] Later it was decided that, because their tasks
participating in many detached minor operations, the marines co,
more noncommissioned officers than normally provided.[68]

The Confederate Marine Corps, which would perform its difficul
honorably, never had more than 753 men, including officers, noncom,
sioned officers, and rank and file, whereas the Marine Corps of the Un,
States grew during the war to 3,881 effectives, of which 90 were officers
Mallory, as early as March 1861, had personally taken care of the creatio
and regulation of the corps.[70] As an organization, it was small yet adequate for the small navy of the Confederate States, and it did well, when
compared with that of the North, which was at least six times larger.
Mallory always gave it his particular attention, seeing that it was speedily
and well trained so as to become militarily efficient in the shortest time.[71]

Well commanded and well drilled by expert and capable officers, the
Confederate Marine Corps was, conceptually, far more advanced than that
of the United States because its organic battalion structure facilitated a
kind of training, well ahead of its time, that prepared it as a mobile striking force to be used as elite troops in amphibious operations. Misfortune
dictated that it was never possible for the Confederacy to use its Marine
Corps in such a manner even if operations of a major scale had been
planned and then abandoned because of other needs.[72] At any rate, it was
Mallory's desire that the marines enter action at the earliest moment.[73]

Despite their small number, the Confederate marines were present on
the lines of battle everywhere: aboard warships in either the coastal waters
or on the high seas, as naval police at sea and at naval bases, with coast
defense batteries, and on the firing line in land battles. Organized according to farsighted and innovative rules, they were a worthy part of a
proud, little navy that would show a brighter mind and a stronger heart
than destiny could afford it.[74]

In addition to the problem of military personnel, Mallory soon had to
face a perhaps more serious issue. The scarcity of military industries in
the South and consequently the militarization of nearly all productive
gear posed the problem of finding skilled workmen, which assumed enormous and troublesome dimensions in the history of the Southern navy.

uickly, the shortage of workers for naval needs became even more seri-
us than the shortage of sailors. The appeals of the naval secretary for
killed workmen became more and more frantic.

The primary problem was the dearth of skilled labor in the South. This
was so serious, Mallory complained, that at the beginning of 1862 only
half of the workers needed had been found so that the naval construction
program was in danger of being scuttled.[75] Several months later the engineer in chief lamented that he lacked mechanics, smelters, and blacksmiths, that most of these were in the army, and that their pay was excessively high.[76]

The situation was so serious that the president had to intervene personally. Many skilled workmen, he noted, were foreigners who had been
brought to the Confederacy from Europe at great cost and with the pledge
that they would never be drafted into military service; yet some states
were drafting them in violation of that agreement. It was a grave difficulty,
which put the central and state governments in conflict.[77]

Still, opposition and obstacles were endless. The president had to insist
that personnel of the naval works at Columbus, Georgia, who had been
drafted into the army, be sent back to their jobs.[78] Nevertheless, as late as
1865 Mallory still complained that skilled workmen of his department had
been enlisted into an infantry battalion and sent to the front because of
the dearth of soldiers and had been absent from their jobs for 107 days,
more than 50 percent of the workdays of the year. Still worse, several of
them had reacted by deserting. The curse of desertion eventually impover-
ished the field regiments.[79]

When the problem of putting together the indispensable enlisted personnel had been solved, there remained the need to feed and clothe them
and provide them with medical and surgical care. Supplying food and
clothing was the task of the Office of Provisions and Clothing. Originally
directed by Paymaster John De Bree, who had served as such for forty-
four years in the U.S. Navy, the job passed in April 1864 to James A.
Semple, who had been De Bree's deputy, a man with the same expertise
but more energetic, active, and vigorous, because younger.[80] The civilian
agent for food procurement, requisition, production, and storage was
William F. Howell, a man of greater ability and skill than most, wise,
farsighted, and resourceful.[81]

Under the vigorous direction of Mallory and these men, first among
them Howell and his co-workers, the provisions service was speedily and
well organized. The able and clever Howell established a central supply
agency in Augusta, Georgia, with an auxiliary agency at Montgomery,
Alabama.[82] In both places he put up warehouses for grains, flour, vegetables, dried fruits, meat, ham, and lard. For bread baking, by private con-

tractors, he succeeded in turning ten barrels of flour a day into bread in Augusta and a similar amount in Montgomery, at the reasonable price of fifteen cents per pound. Up to the fall of 1863 he obtained between a thousand and twelve hundred barrels of flour.[83] A mill and a bakery for the navy were built at Albany, Georgia, where there was also created, at Mallory's initiative,[84] a navy packing plant to pack meat, both canned and in barrels.[85]

The navy did not lack coffee and tea, which were hard to secure because of the blockade. As late as the fall of 1864, Paymaster Semple could state that in the warehouses at the Rocketts Navy Yard, near Richmond, there were, in addition to hardtack and flour for eight months, meat for six months, rice and beans for six months, sugar and molasses for five months, and tea and coffee for eight months.[86] In the navy's central warehouse at Charlotte, North Carolina, there were one hundred thousand pounds of coffee, thirty thousand pounds of sugar, and a thousand pounds of tea. At that time the naval mill and bakery at Albany, Georgia, turned out between five and six thousand pounds of hardtack daily that would be soon increased to eight thousand, more than enough to satisfy the navy's needs.[87]

This was an almost incredible achievement by the leaders of the Southern navy: in a country that was heavily blockaded, close to starvation (if not because of the blockade itself, surely from the near failure of the transportation network), and in which the army did not eat each day, the navy, thanks to the ability of its organizers and to Mallory's farsightedness in choosing his staff, never lacked anything and, indeed, occasionally supplied the army.[88] Indeed, Paymaster De Bree once suggested that the food allowance of the navy be reduced to avoid unpleasant comments by the army.[89]

Such accomplishment is even more remarkable if one keeps in mind the multifarious, ever-growing adversities the navy had to face to get the necessary supply of food. First and foremost, it had to struggle against inflation and ever-increasing prices, for which the funds at hand never sufficed. Mallory, however, took personal care that, at whatever cost, the sailors would never lack fresh vegetables to prevent scurvy.[90]

It was also necessary to ensure that naval supply agents not collide with army ones.[91] The navy had to accept the role of the "poorer relative," and barrels of salted meat destined for its use sometimes failed to arrive because they were shipped as private merchandise.[92] The army, either because of military requirements or its need for supplies, frequently claimed precedence over, hampered, or interrupted rail transport of the navy without requesting leave to do so.[93] Somehow the able William F. Howell succeeded in being almost everywhere, disentangling garbled situations, overcoming difficulties, securing food in some magical way, and delivering it on time.[94]

The hardships regarding uniforms, clothes, details of barracks furniture and fittings, and small stores increased. Again, the army needs were so great that those of the small fleet were given second consideration. Yet Mallory saw to it that marines as well as sailors were properly provided for.[95] He put his agents overseas to work ordering clothes, mainly from Great Britain[96] but also from France.[97] The hardest problem to solve was that of shoes, because, although cloth ones could be produced at home, those made of leather had to be imported or, at least, it was necessary to import all material for making them.

Happily, Howell succeeded in finding a local supply of leather for manufacturing sea boots, keeping their price between $15 and $20 a pair at a time when inflation was overwhelming the Confederacy.[98] In Augusta, Georgia, a naval factory was put up to produce uniforms, barrack stores, and footwear, and another warehouse was erected for food storage, all owing to Howell's energy.[99] Thus even if some complaints arose about the regularity of the uniforms,[100] to the very end of the conflict, Confederate sailors were "dressed in a comfortable manner."[101]

Care of the ill and wounded was entrusted to the Office of Medicine and Surgery, under the direction of Surgeon General W.A.W. Spotswood, who had served for thirty years as a naval medical officer. With great energy the navy organized its own hospitals, which in 1863 (after the excellent one at Norfolk had been lost), numbered four—in Richmond, Virginia; Charleston, South Carolina; Savannah, Georgia; and Mobile, Alabama—all well furnished with clean and comfortable beds, blankets, and bedsheets.[102] In addition, there were several infirmaries.[103]

Naval ships were always provided with medical personnel and male nurses; the Office of Medicine and Surgery printed a handbook for these personnel.[104] The hardest problem was providing medical drugs, most of which were imported through the blockade. A naval pharmaceutical laboratory was put up in Richmond so that the navy (unlike the army) never suffered a lack of medicines.[105]

The Confederate navy had its own flag and insignia. Initially, it adopted the national flag of the Confederacy, the "stars and bars" (three great horizontal stripes alternating red-white-red and, high to the left, a blue field with the eleven stars of the Confederacy in a circle). Then, on 26 May 1863, the navy adopted as its standard the one Congress had approved on the first of the month. High on the left of a white field was a great square reproducing the army war flag. The streamers were red-blue-red with white intervals; the stars were on the blue field; the jack was the same as the square of the standard.[106]

A History of the Confederate Navy

The main problem, however, was that of the ships upon which these flags were to wave. Through tremendous exertions, the vessels would be built and ride the waves of oceans, seas, and treacherous rivers. Over them, fighting against the heaviest odds, the flag of the Confederacy would float through the smoke of the guns and the stormy winds of hurricanes, earning the respect, even the admiration, of its enemies.

THREE

Building and Outfitting Warships

To create a navy from nothing, the Confederacy faced, in addition to the critical problems of money, personnel, and supplies, a far more momentous one: the need for warships.

The few auxiliary ships that composed the state navies were almost farcical: they were useful only for limited operations as coast police, and it would have been foolish to expect them to oppose an attack or a strong amphibious landing by the enemy. The conclusion was obvious: if a Confederate navy were to exist, warships must be acquired either in America or in Europe or be built from the bottom up. Because construction time was necessarily long and fraught with obstacles, Mallory at first chose to get what he needed through acquisition.[1]

Fortunately, the enemy, even if potentially formidable, had its own difficulties, which could give the Confederacy some valuable breathing space. On paper, the U.S. Navy looked extremely powerful: of its ninety ships, forty were steamers, some of them the most modern in the world. The fifty sailing ships, however, were obsolete, although they could be used as floating batteries or auxiliary blockaders. Of the forty steamers, only twenty-four were ready for action (the others being in various stages of construction or under repair) and, of them, nineteen were scattered around the world: in the Mediterranean (three), Equatorial Africa (four), off Brazil (two), in the East Indies and Japan (four), in the Pacific (four), and off Mexico (two). Only six were ready for action, although all the others, except two, had received orders to return home immediately. Of these, two were in New York, one in Washington, and two off Pensacola,

Florida.[2] This situation gave the South a small respite, and Mallory intended to take advantage of it.

The opportunities for acquiring ships within the Confederacy appeared insignificant or almost so. Virginia's secession brought another five small ships, the most notable of them being the paddle wheeler *Patrick Henry*, of thirteen hundred tons. She was quickly commissioned as an auxiliary and singled out to become the future school-ship.[3] The rest, such as North Carolina's four small vessels, each armed with a single gun,[4] counted for little. On 17 March 1861 Mallory had sent a team of officers headed by Captain Lawrence Rousseau to New Orleans to acquire any good ship that was available.[5]

The results of his mission were disappointing. Purchased were two small vessels named the *Habana* and *Marquis de la Habana,* which would later be converted into auxiliary cruisers. The first, rechristened the *Sumter* (the second was renamed *McRae*), was earmarked by destiny for a career that would earn her an everlasting place both in history and in legend.[6] To these were added another that would become the gunboat *Jackson* and two small ones to serve on the lakes near New Orleans.[7]

It was very little, and making the situation worse was the failure of secret agents sent to buy ships in the North and in Canada. Indeed, the Federal authorities, closer, with more money, and, perhaps, quicker to act, had bought all serviceable vessels on the Northern and Canadian markets.[8]

At this point Mallory was left with only two choices: turn toward the European markets or adopt a determined shipbuilding policy. In the second case, he must act quickly because the ominous fact that the North, although possessing formidable shipyards, had hurried to buy on the Northern and Canadian markets all available ships capable of being converted into war vessels revealed the magnitude of the coming threat.

The problems to be solved were as follows: Was the South capable of building warships in the available time and in the required number? And what kind of ships should be built?

The second question would be answered by the naval strategy the South would adopt. The first one required that the South have industrial plants and raw materials, as well as a supply of skilled workmen and an adequate transportation system.

As is well known, the South was, compared with the North, a primarily agricultural region, founded on an underdeveloped and basically backward economy. Nor could the then-existing Southern industries change the situation. While in the North only 40 percent of the population was engaged in agriculture, in the South it was 84 percent. Even in New Orleans, the major city of the South and one of the biggest in the Union as a whole, only 3 percent of its dwellers were employed in industry.[9] The South's urban population amounted to 9.6 percent while that of the North was 36 percent.[10]

Those who assert that the backward agricultural status of the South meant that it was wholly lacking in industrial enterprise are wrong because various industries prospered there. Still, two facts must be kept in mind: first, although the South in 1860 had only 159 plants with a capital investment of $9,596,000, in the North New England alone had as many as 570 plants with a capital investment of $69,260,000, or almost eight times as much; second, the capital invested per plant in the South averaged $60,325 whereas in the Northeast it averaged $121,508. The North was therefore a land of big, modern shops while the Southern ones (with few exceptions) remained relatively small.[11]

Harold D. Woodman, among the most authoritative and insightful scholars of the Southern economy, has proved that the South depended economically on the North in a form of semicolonial status.[12] Eugene D. Genovese and others have stressed that Southern industry was subordinate to agriculture and had the fundamental function of supplying its needs and not vice versa, as in the North.[13]

At the time of secession, the U.S. Navy had ten naval shipyards.[14] Of these, eight were in the North, leaving only two in Confederate hands. Of the two, that at Pensacola was very small. In the 1850s it had built two warships, yet it remained a second-rate yard.[15] Moreover, its roadstead was sealed up by U.S. naval forces, which, from 3 May on, blockaded it,[16] and a Federal land force was stationed at Fort Pickens on Santa Rosa Island, effectively closing up any passage.

Certainly better was the other navy yard that fell into Confederate hands, the one at Norfolk, Virginia, among the largest and most modern in the United States.[17] Even though, at the time of its evacuation on 19 April 1861, sailors of the Federal navy had torched all the buildings as well as ships in the roadstead and in the drydock, the captured plants were of inestimable value, as were also the more than a thousand heavy guns found there.[18] Norfolk would certainly be helpful, but its location exposed it to enemy attack; therefore its possible loss should be foreseen.

In such a situation, nothing remained but to exploit the South's limited industry and eventually to create new plants from scratch. And indeed, the Confederate navy performed miracles. First, the South had private shipyards, most of them small, suitable only for building barges or fishing boats.[19] According to the census of 1860, there were 36 shipyards, both large and small, a number that seems too small. The census fails to mention any shipyard in Mississippi[20] although it had three.[21] The same was true for Tennessee, which at least had the vestiges of the Memphis Navy

Yard, begun but never completed.[22] If the number 36 shipyards of any dimension seems wrong, that of 145 given by the businessman and newspaperman Thomas P. Kettell appears to be greatly overstated.[23] The truth, as correctly observes William N. Still, Jr., must lie somewhere between the two extremes.

During the war, in addition to exploiting the shipyards large and small (except those that immediately fell into enemy hands) the Southern navy built or requisitioned about twenty more.[24] Among these were those at Richmond, Virginia; Charlotte, North Carolina; Yazoo City, Mississippi; Selma, Alabama; and Columbus, Georgia.[25]

For domestic naval construction, the Confederate navy oriented itself according to three guidelines: direct institution of new navy yards; control of private shipyards over which naval agents, either lawfully or not, took direct management; and contracts with private shipyards to which the navy would provide specific ship designs, closely controlling their work.[26]

As a whole, the story would be one of unprecedented exertions, an unending and strenuous battle against the Rock of Sisyphus, which always seemed to fall back, crushing the small band of brave men at war against one of the most powerful navies in the world. The first disaster would be the fall into enemy hands of the only two navy yards remaining in the South, those at Norfolk and Pensacola, then the loss of the most important private shipyards, those at Memphis and New Orleans. There would follow an unending struggle to shift the naval construction sites hundreds of miles inland, along rivers, in areas unreachable by the enemy navy. Last, there would be the desperate defense of the lines of communication, without which every attempt to obtain indispensable war supplies for the shipyards would have been futile.

In such a destitute setting, during the four years of the war, according to Still, "the Southern Confederacy converted, contracted for, or laid down within its borders at least 150 warships."[27] Of them, about 50 percent were completed and commissioned into service. These were certainly very few compared with the almost 600 warships successfully commissioned by the North,[28] yet much for a country that had to start from nothing and to face heavy odds that would dishearten anyone less stubborn.

The man entrusted with the frightening responsibility of directing Confederate shipbuilding was John Luke Porter of Virginia. Designated a naval constructor on 1 October 1859 at the request of Florida for the Pensacola Navy Yard, Porter had then served at the Norfolk and Washington, D.C., navy yards and transferred back to Pensacola on 17 April 1861. He had thus acquired considerable experience in his field.[29] On 1 May 1861 he resigned his commission from the U.S. Navy and tendered his service to the Confederacy. As soon as Norfolk fell into Southern hands Mallory sent him there.[30]

The Confederacy did not establish a Bureau of Construction and Repair, perhaps because it first sought to exhaust all the possibilities of acquiring warships already built. This helps to explain why it was not until the fall of 1862 that the Confederacy created the office of chief constructor and entrusted it to Porter.[31] The assignment did not become effective until 30 April 1863, yet Porter had already long been exercising its functions.

Many historians have been harsh with John Luke Porter,[32] yet he performed his duties commendably.[33] The original plans for the construction of Confederate naval vessels, to be found in many archives and repositories, show that he drafted most of them, including several for ships built in Europe.[34] With help from his deputies, Joseph Pierce and William H. Greaves, Porter directed the construction of many of them. On balance, one is amazed by how much one man, amid dreadful adversity, was able to accomplish.[35]

Because it was necessary to build warships from the keel up (or radically convert merchant ships into auxiliaries), the problem of acquiring raw materials immediately assumed major dimensions. First among these materials were lumber and iron. At the time, the most important raw material for building warships was timber. The Confederacy had immense, almost boundless forest reserves.[36] Indeed, the South amply supplied the timber requirements of Northern shipyards, which still were able to get a good deal of lumber before the South completely closed all trade with the enemy in this priceless commodity.[37] Yet the most prominent historian of Southern naval construction, William N. Still, Jr., maintains that the true problem for the South was the absence of seasoned timber and that Confederate warships captured by the Federal navy were condemned because the raw timber used for their hulls caused them to leak badly.[38]

Still is such an authority on the subject that his opinions warrant the highest respect. Yet different conclusions seem warranted. Naval constructors and master carpenters always considered the seasoning of timber as extremely important; but of even greater importance for them was the time of tree cutting, the best times being during the full moons of January and August[39] to avoid the seasons when the vital activity of the tree was at its peak and the wood was richer in sap and therefore less workable.[40] Although seasoning was very important for the longevity of the ship, this was a secondary consideration if one had to build in a hurry. Canadians, for instance, had a good market for cheap ships built of raw wood.[41] Moreover, in the seventeenth century the Dutch had used raw timber to build the glorious ships of Tromp and de Ruyter, which assured them command of the sea for quite a while.[42]

The use of raw wood meant that a ship would last no more than six years rather than twenty.[43] The English were compelled to use largely unseasoned timber, as in the ships that fought at the battle of Trafalgar, the victorious fleet of Nelson and Collingwood.[44] Therefore, the situation for the Confederates was not serious, especially if one considers that along with white oak, cypress, poplar, and black walnut the South had two of the best woods in the world for naval construction: live oak and pitch pine.

The live oak *(Quercus virginiana)* is among the notable features of the Southern landscape. Their age-old tree trunks, of imposing dimensions, with the large, shadowy crown rich with leaves of a dark green sheen, generally covered with festoons of Spanish moss, dominate their environment, usually alone, making themselves known by their huge size. They provide a very strong and durable wood, compact, hard as steel, resistant to rot, lacking acids that might corrode metal nails. It was a widely held opinion of shipbuilders that ships built from live oak could last for a century. Because live oak has essential oil rather than sap, it does not require much seasoning even if such would make it even more durable.[45]

The government of the United States had early taken a census of this valuable tree, which grows generally in a band situated totally in the South that stretches from the ocean shore to about sixty miles inland.[46] In 1832 Secretary of the Navy Levi Woodbury had made it the subject of a special report to Congress in which he estimated that the nation had about 150,000 live oak trees, which could provide almost three million cubic feet of lumber.[47]

Yet this formidable wood was extremely heavy, seventy-six pounds per cubic foot,[48] a specific weight greater than that of water, which made ships very heavy and therefore required strong motive power.[49] Although it was ideal for building the framework, planking was better made from another first-rate Southern wood: pitch pine *(Pinus palustris)*, firm, resinous, and durable. It also did not require seasoning because a resin impervious to water replaced the sap in its fibers.[50]

The Confederacy therefore had abundant lumber of outstanding quality. The problem, however, was that, except for a small supply on hand, trees had to be felled, cut, planed, and transported. Live oak, in addition to being very heavy, tended to grow in inaccessible and difficult areas, usually far from rivers. This created a serious transportation problem, which would frequently force the Confederates to make do with inferior lumber.

Next (and equal in importance to lumber) was iron, which had just obtained prominence in naval technology. As William N. Still, Jr., put it, "It is nearly impossible to exaggerate the effect of iron production on the entire Confederate war effort."[51]

The iron problem of the Confederate navy must be considered from three perspectives: extraction, production, and manufacturing. Iron ore was found in every Southern state except Louisiana, Mississippi, and Florida. In 1860 the South produced about one-sixth of the iron ore extracted in the United States (such a small percentage that it was not even mentioned in the official census).[52] A problem, however, was that the areas of greatest production—Kentucky, Tennessee, and West Virginia—almost immediately fell into enemy hands. The mines of Virginia, Georgia, and Alabama therefore had to be depended upon.[53]

There were even more problems: the inadequacy of transportation, lack of skilled workmen, small size and distance of ore deposits, and the fact that, in addition to naval demands, the army, too, was an insatiable consumer of iron products. The result was that never during the war was the problem of supplying iron for the navy resolved in a satisfactory way. Therefore, many railroad trunk lines had to be torn up to use their rails.[54] Two other sources were the careful gathering of scrap iron and the importation of iron through the blockade that the Federals soon enforced.[55]

The naval bureau charged with the responsibility for securing iron was the Office of Ordnance and Hydrography until the end of June 1863, when by a single-handed decision the secretary of war stated that the Nitre and Mining Bureau (a section of the army's Bureau of Ordnance) would assume complete control over the extraction of iron, copper, lead, zinc, coal, and every other mineral product useful for war purposes.[56] Therefore, for mineral supplies the navy became subordinated to the army, with predictable results, even though Secretary Mallory never failed to send agents to prospect and develop new mines.[57]

If, as Still put it, the fate of the Confederacy depended on "iron and time," the situation was one of extreme concern, for there was little iron and far less time. In the Civil War era, production depended upon cast iron furnaces. Cast iron bars could be used without change for secondary casting or, after being reheated in a blast furnace, mixing (puddling), and hammering, could be transformed into wrought iron or steel of different grades of carbon, cemented or nitrated. The iron bars could then be rolled in a rolling mill.

In 1860 the South had thirty-nine furnaces, which produced 36,790 tons of cast iron bars. Yet it is unclear where the 91,498 tons of ore needed to feed the furnaces came from, that is, entirely from Southern mines (most improbable) or by purchases from the North. The North's overwhelming superiority is clear, however, for in the same year it produced 868,798 tons of cast iron bars, and to these should be added the 81,971 tons produced in Maryland, Missouri, and Kentucky, which either remained in the Union or soon fell into enemy hands. The total at Northern disposition thus amounted to almost one million tons, more than twenty times that of the South.

The small Southern production was largely concentrated in Tennessee (seventeen furnaces producing 22,302 tons) and Virginia (sixteen furnaces turning out 11,646 tons); both states, located on the front line, were soon threatened by invasion. One of them, Tennessee, was quickly almost completely lost.[58]

Total Southern production of wrought iron and steel in 1860 was 26,252 tons from eighty-four ironworks and rolling mills, mostly of insignificant size, little more than blacksmith shops, since the total number of workmen in such business was only 2,009, or 23.92 per firm. In contrast, the North produced 451,369 tons, which, added to the production of Maryland, Missouri, and Kentucky (31,463 tons), came to nearly half a million tons (482,832 tons, to be precise), or 18.32 times the Southern production. Tennessee had thirty-five plants that produced 5,144 tons. Fortunately for the South, its major producer was Virginia: 17,889 tons from twenty plants.[59]

Clearly, the South was inferior to the North in iron production. Yet with an astonishing show of energy and doggedness, the South made "hay from straw." After much soul-searching, the Confederate government decided upon a policy of intervention to increase and direct production. First, every private citizen wishing to create a new industry that would support the war effort received a loan equal to 50 percent of the capital invested and an advance of 30 percent of the value of the estimated production. The Confederacy thus obtained a quasi-property right in these firms, which, obviously, could produce only for the government. Profits from this production were at first limited by law to 75 percent, then reduced to 33.5 percent, and finally to 25 percent to keep the purchase prices low. A logical decision that followed froze prices: no change could be made without the authorization of a proper committee, the object being to keep pace with inflation.

Extremely strict controls were placed upon exempting workers from compulsory military service. Exemptions were denied to those who did not work efficiently for the government, thus forcing the undisciplined out of business. Then, an iron-handed control was established on railway transportation.[60] In addition, in more than one case, as in that of the Bibbs Iron Company of Alabama, the government expropriated several firms through forced acquisition.[61]

This policy was soon rewarded. Between 1862 and 1865, in the two main iron-producing states, Alabama and Virginia, there were created, respectively, thirteen and fifteen new furnaces. Unfortunately, in the meantime many extant ones were captured by the enemy;[62] consequently, ironworks, rolling mills, and cannon foundries lacked enough raw material to supply the urgent demand of the armed forces. It was worse for the navy, which had to compete with the army.[63]

The third and most important point was the manufacturing of iron products. The navy needed essentially five different kinds of products: plate, anchors, chains, nuts and bolts, nails, and the like; heavy guns (all of iron, whereas army fieldpieces were most often made of bronze); shell and shot for artillery; small arms; and ship engines.

The full responsibility for acquiring these items belonged to the Bureau of Ordnance and Hydrography, which was headed by Captain Duncan N. Ingraham, an old, experienced officer who had held the same responsibility in the U.S. Navy from 1850 to 1860 and proved an outstanding choice. He was well supported by his chief clerk, Joseph P. McCorkle, who also had performed the same task in Washington before secession. Able and competent, he would serve successively under three chiefs of ordnance. Ingraham quickly had his office working at full speed.

In November 1861 he was transferred to command the Charleston Squadron. His successor was his deputy, the hardworking and competent Commander George Minor from Virginia.[64] In March 1863, Minor left his office to his former collaborator, Commander John Mercer Brooke, who kept the responsibility until the war's end.

Brooke deserves detailed observation because, as Tom Wells correctly noted, he was more than merely a first-rate officer: he had the glint of genius.[65] Brooke was thirty-seven years old, having been born on 18 December 1825 in Tampa, Florida. In the U.S. Navy he was outstanding for his speculative mind, talent and intelligence, and the depth of his scientific knowledge. From 1851 onward he served in the Naval Observatory. There, he drafted the first nautical map of the route from California to China, inventing for use in those seas a bathometer that won him a gold medal from the Berlin Academy. When secession occurred, he went South.[66]

Directed by men of such high caliber, the Office of Ordnance and Hydrography was among the most efficient agencies not only in the navy but in the entire Confederacy. And the problems to be solved were pressing indeed. First, the South lacked even a single rolling mill capable of rolling two-inch plate. Thanks to the exertions of the leaders of the Ordnance Bureau, in a short time one firm, J. R. Anderson and Company, of Richmond, Virginia (which would go down in history under the old

A History of the Confederate Navy

name of Tredegar Iron Works), whose directors were skilled and patriotic, succeeded in converting its rolling mill as required.[67]

Founded in 1839, Tredegar had quickly grown until it was one of the better metallurgical firms of America, even though it was far from being a giant like those in Pennsylvania and New York. Today, the wayfarer in Richmond who walks down Fourth Street toward the James River banks will quickly reach a peaceful area where the past still makes itself felt in the old-fashioned appearance of the houses. There, on Gamble's Hill, a little, quiet park faces the bank of the river a few dozen yards away. Between it and the canal, high sheds, chimneys, and red brick walls of nineteenth-century industrial buildings can still be seen among the shrubbery: the Tredegar.[68] (The canal, which reached beyond Lynchburg, was the artery that connected the foundries of the Shenandoah with the coal basin of Richmond and the metallurgical plants of the city.)

Today all is silent there, and bushes surround the decrepit buildings; yet during the Civil War the Tredegar employed as many as a thousand workers, some free, some slave. From it came not only armor plates but guns, among them many heavy pieces for the navy; boilers and engines for ships; land and sea torpedoes; gun carriages; and railroad cars, rails, and locomotives.

Tredegar's owner, Joseph Reid Anderson, had turned to industry after serving for some time in the Engineer Corps of the United States.[69] Energetic, farsighted, able, gifted with rare organizational capability, he was the right man to solve extremely difficult tasks. Already, on 1 April 1861, he had met Secretary Mallory in Montgomery and discussed with him the costs of manufacturing heavy naval ordnance, announcing that he intended to equip Tredegar as soon as possible to produce gun carriages.[70] In short order the navy developed close ties with Tredegar.

The second firm that in 1861 succeeded in equipping itself for rolling plate of the size required by the navy was that of Schofield & Markham, of Atlanta, Georgia, soon known as the Atlanta Rolling Mill and taken under complete control by the navy.[71] The Atlanta Rolling Mill soon began to produce in high gear. For example, it rolled the armor plates for the big ironclad *Mississippi*.[72] On 7 August 1862 Commander George Minor stated that the mill had produced ten thousand tons of plate.[73]

The third and last rolling mill that so equipped itself was not put into operation until 1863. It was the Shelby Iron Company of Columbiana, Alabama. Created by an association between foundrymen and iron mine owners, the Shelby soon became one of the most promising enterprises of the South.[74] The Confederate government made a contract with it which would guarantee a good quantity of wrought iron.[75] The contract was closed for a total output of twelve thousand tons annually for three years, an amount Shelby never reached.[76] Indeed, at the end of 1862 deliveries had fallen to four thousand tons, yet, the company pledged to begin soon rolling plates of the thickness requested.[77]

A bulky exchange of correspondence began between the director of the company, A. T. Jones, and the secretary of the navy, who required eighteen hundred tons of plate immediately. Jones replied to Mallory that he was willing to place the entire output of the rolling mill at his disposal.[78]

Relations between the Shelby Company and the Confederate authorities were uneasy. The firm faced demands from many sources—armor for warships being built in Alabama and for those on the Mississippi and orders from the army.[79] But workmen were unavailable.[80] Shelby kept up at least with the needs of the navy; from it came armor plates for many an ironclad, among them the famed *Tennessee II*.[81]

Unfortunately, the Tredegar, the Atlanta Rolling Mill, and the Shelby were the South's only rolling mills. No others were capable of producing armor plate. Even these three firms, which worked as hard as possible for the navy, did so only within their means. First, they lacked workmen, many of whom were daily swallowed up by the army. Jones at the Shelby lamented that, had he had an adequate labor supply, he could have guaranteed an output of forty tons of plate per day.[82]

The production of anchors, chains, nuts and bolts, and the like came from several sources, some small, some large, such as Winship's Foundry and Machine Shop in Atlanta, which furnished the hardware for the ironclad *Mississippi*.[83] Yet the Tredegar held first place in this field.[84]

The most critical problem was that of heavy guns. Because the enemy already commanded the sea, it was a question of life or death. Even before the vessels of the future Southern fleet were ready, provision had to be made for the urgent needs of coast defense, which were complicated by the presence of many rivers and waterways, navigable highways for an invader.

Luckily for the South, the capture on 20 April 1861 of the Norfolk Navy Yard left in Confederate hands, in addition to a great deal of materials including several ships whose hulls, even if partly burned, were well worth salvaging, 450 naval gun carriages;[85] 2,800 barrels of powder (some 333,000 pounds);[86] and more than a thousand heavy or coastal guns.[87]

Such a large plunder of ordnance was true manna for the Confederacy, particularly for coastal defense, because its ships were few and small. The delivery of big guns to several places began immediately.[88] Unfortunately, however, many of the Norfolk cannons were of relatively small caliber, 24-, 32-, and 64-pounder smoothbores, and many were obsolete.[89] Also the pieces (about a thousand) already placed in many coastal zones were

A History of the Confederate Navy

of the same kind, except for a few recently acquired,[90] which portended poorly for the future.

Commander A. B. Fairfax, ordnance chief at Norfolk, was a resourceful and energetic man. He went to work without delay to convert as many of the 32-pounder smoothbores as he could by rifling them and reinforcing their breeches with a strong iron band, greatly improving their efficiency.[91] It was nevertheless a stopgap solution.[92]

Obviously, if the Confederacy intended to arm its future warships with guns as powerful as those of the enemy and properly defend its coastline, it must pursue the two usual ways of obtaining up-to-date and powerful weapons. First, it could purchase them abroad and import them through the blockade (yet here the navy was in competition with the army, which sought the lion's share, so that only a few score heavy naval guns were imported, though they were first-rate).[93] Second, and more important, the Confederacy could itself produce naval ordnance. Yet what industrial resources did it have for such a purpose?

Within the Confederacy's boundaries in 1861 there were only two cannon foundries. These, which had earlier worked for the armed forces of the old Union, were the Tredegar and the Bellona Foundry. Almost half of the 2,300 pieces of artillery produced in the Confederate States during the entire conflict were cast at Tredegar.[94] Of them, 173 were heavy guns and thus useful to the navy for both ships and coast defense.

The other plant, the Bellona Foundry, was located along the right bank of the James River about fifteen miles from Richmond. Today bucolic peace reigns there: just a few ruined walls, a molding box for cannons, and a rough cast of an artillery piece speak of the era of one of the most formidable wars in history. During the conflict, however, the foundry was full of frenzied life. It succeeded in making 135 heavy guns and was thus second to the Tredegar among firms providing ordnance.[95]

This exhausts the list of existing private plants that could be depended upon to provide naval guns. Still, there were some minor firms that might start producing them. The authoritative Larry J. Daniel and Riley W. Gunter list forty-seven (other than those already mentioned and Confederate-owned plants).[96]

Among the most notable ones were the Phoenix Furnace of New Orleans, which began working on 30 January 1862 and provided its first heavy gun by 10 March, and Bennett & Lurghs, also of New Orleans, which had sixty tons of the best cast iron on hand and pledged to deliver its first guns by 15 March 1862 and then produce four guns a month. Last, again in New Orleans, was the Patterson Iron Works, which would deliver its first consignment on 10 March 1862 and then produce eight cannons a month.[97] Yet these New Orleans firms were destined to fall into enemy hands on 25 April 1862. There were others, but they normally produced for the army.

The navy thus depended upon the foundries of Richmond, Tredegar and Bellona. Yet, through its own initiative it finally succeeded in creating the most efficient of all firms: the Naval Gun Foundry at Selma, Alabama.[98] The origin of this plant was owing to the initiative of Colin J. McRae, who was a member of the Committee on Naval Affairs at the Montgomery Convention. A successful businessman, able and active, McRae was charged by the Confederate government with superintending the production and acquisition of iron ore in Alabama. There he was struck by the characteristics of Selma, located on the river that is the namesake of the state, about two hundred miles from the sea, near (no farther than fifty miles from) Alabama's iron and coal mines, and near the Shelby Iron Works. In addition to the navigable river, Selma had excellent railroad connections both with the coast and with several inland centers.[99]

In Selma there was an old plant, the Alabama Manufacturing Company, which could be used to house a naval iron factory. McRae recommended that his government acquire it.[100] Richmond's authorities (perhaps shortsightedly) showed no interest in undertaking the venture themselves. McRae therefore sought private financing and bought the plant in his own name. He had received substantial encouragement, mainly from the navy's chief of ordnance, George Minor, who had already written to urge that the new factory be put into shape to produce heavy guns, adding that he would send McRae the necessary drafts and plans.[101]

In June 1862 McRae received an official position that added to his job: the appointment as government agent to pursue his unofficial task of securing iron in Alabama.[102] He faced numerous difficulties. None of these had been overcome when, in January and February 1863, he was asked to go to Europe as general financial agent of the Confederate government. He agreed on condition that the Southern military authorities acquire the Selma Foundry at the price he had paid for it.[103]

For a while, the Selma Foundry was jointly managed by the army and navy, but the latter ultimately assumed full responsibility for it.[104] The new chief of ordnance, John Mercer Brooke, appointed his most valued collaborator, Captain Catesby ap R. Jones, as commander of the foundry.[105] Brooke's choice could not have been better. Beyond such gifts of character as energy, steadiness, carefulness, and courage, Jones had an exceptional mind and was a scientist and a mechanical engineer. Even after the war, corresponding with his former enemies, he continued to contribute to the technical development of artillery. The U.S. Navy admiral David Dixon Porter said that he and Brooke were the two naval officers whose loss had been a disaster for the Union.[106]

At Selma, Jones had to begin from scratch. He found a small, pleasant city of the Deep South which, located on the navigable Alabama River, had been a good port for shipping cotton in peacetime. The site of civil rights marches in the 1960s, today Selma lives a peaceful and somewhat sleepy life. Nothing is left but a marker to indicate the place of the Naval Gun Foundry that cast some of the best and most powerful heavy cannons in the world. Gone also is every vestige of the nearby navy yard where at least four floating batteries and ironclads were launched: the *Huntsville, Tuscaloosa,* the famed *Tennessee,* and one whose launching went badly.[107] Yet there are still, along the riverbanks, the colorful buildings that at one time served as cotton warehouses as well as quarters for Confederate commanders. It is a corner of an old-fashioned, somewhat forgotten South, left intact as a witness to the past.

Upon assuming management of the foundry in June 1863, Jones found it in deplorable condition. Yet during the entire war the Selma Foundry turned out at least 143 guns, of which more than 100 were heavy naval cannons (the rest being light mortars, howitzers, and some experimental pieces).[108] At least eighteen 12- and 24-pounder bronze boat howitzers were cast at Selma; many others came from Tredegar[109] and from the Columbus, Georgia, Naval Iron Works which, by the beginning of 1865, had delivered more than 80 to the navy.[110]

The Selma Naval Gun Foundry also produced artillery projectiles. By 31 July 1863 it had delivered 2,858 shots and shells; then its production escalated to 30 a day so that in the end it produced several thousand, of which many were destined for the army.[111] At the beginning of 1865 Secretary Mallory could proudly claim that the Selma Naval Gun Foundry was fully capable of producing all the shot and shells for naval guns and for the entire navy.[112]

Other than at Selma, the production of shot and shells and gun carriages for the navy was the special duty of three ordnance works established by the navy itself. These were originally located at the Norfolk Navy Yard, where a big Nasmyth steam hammer was installed,[113] at New Orleans, and at Charleston. When Norfolk and New Orleans had to be evacuated, the two ordnance works were transferred respectively to Charlotte, North Carolina (together with the entire Norfolk Navy Yard), and to Atlanta, Georgia.

After moving to Charlotte, the Norfolk Navy Yard (whose machinery had been saved)[114] rapidly resumed operations, as did the Naval Ordnance Work, under the energetic command of Captain Richard L. Page. It was given a new, gigantic steam hammer, the greatest in the entire

South. It soon acquired another that had been salvaged before the fall of the Pensacola Navy Yard[115] and then a third, even larger.[116] Thanks to their power, armor-piercing projectiles of steel with a high carbon standard were provided for naval artillery,[117] as well as propeller shafts for such ironclads as the *Virginia II.*[118]

The considerable production of the New Orleans Ordnance Works[119] was still further increased after it was moved to Atlanta under the direction of Lieutenant David P. McCorkle (brother of the chief clerk of the Ordnance Bureau). Here, too, in addition to gun carriages, both shells and armor-piercing projectiles were produced.[120] When Atlanta, too, was lost, the ordnance works were moved again, to Augusta, Georgia.[121]

Shell could also be produced in the Naval Ordnance Laboratory at Richmond (devoted, however, mainly to chemical and specialized production under the direction of Lieutenant Robert D. Minor, brother of the chief of the bureau)[122] and at Tredegar.

Small arms were bought mostly in Europe. With his first shipment, agent James D. Bulloch sent five hundred revolvers with ammunition and a thousand short Enfield rifles with bayonets, enough to distribute to almost all personnel.[123] The Confederate navy adopted a revolver produced by the firm of A. Le Mat of Paris. In 1862 Mallory ordered three thousand items through Bulloch.[124] The Le Mat revolver, fitted with a second barrel capable of firing large shotgun bullets, was particularly suitable for hand-to-hand fighting during boarding. The first model, however, had several problems.[125]

Local contributions of small arms were not lacking. In April 1863 the Haimans firm of Columbus, Georgia, already manufacturing cutlasses, began large-scale production of the naval version of the Colt revolver.[126]

A problem closely connected with artillery and also belonging to the Ordnance Bureau was that of explosives. For this purpose, throughout the Civil War, almost exclusive use was made of black powder, generally composed of four parts of nitrate, one of carbon, and one of sulfur. Slow and dangerous to produce, hygroscopic, and unstable, black powder was a poor explosive because of the damaging crusting it produced inside weapons, the dense smoke it generated, and its tendency to break shells into a few large fragments rather than many splinters. Black powder nevertheless remained the basic explosive. Guncotton (nitrocellulose) had been invented in 1846, contemporarily with nitroglycerin, which the Italian Ascanio Sobrero produced for the first time in a laboratory. Even though the innovative Mallory thought of using guncotton as a charge for torpedoes,[127] it remained the explosive of the future. No satisfactory way had been found to stabilize it and to make it tractable.[128] Instead, of fundamental importance was fulminate of mercury, used for all primers and percussion caps in both cannons and small arms.

A good quantity of powder had been found in Norfolk, but it had to be shared with the army, which used enormous amounts. The prospects of production appeared negligible: in 1860 the South had only two powder mills of dwarfish size, one in Tennessee with ten workers, the other in South Carolina with only three.[129] Initially, as a stopgap remedy, the navy bought what powder was held in private hands[130] or raked up what could be found scattered in barracks and local arsenals.[131] Sometimes a few crumbs were obtained. On 17 September 1861, 126 pounds of gunpowder were acquired by the navy in New Orleans at a cost of $1,425; on 18 November another 5,974 pounds for $11,984; and on 22 December 550 pounds for $756.50.[132]

Requests for powder were pressing. As early as 6 September 1861 enemy naval forces were threatening to enter the outlet of the Apalachicola in Florida. From there came frantic requests to hurry down powder and primers. All Mallory could do was to send a distressed appeal to the secretary of war for at least two thousand pounds of explosives.[133]

It was impossible to continue thus. True, now and then some powder was imported by running the blockade. In November 1861, for example, the steamer *Fingal* moored at Savannah carrying, among other items, forty-eight tons of powder for the navy,[134] a little less than the fifty-five tons Mallory had requested from his European agent.[135] This was but a drop in the ocean, and the Bureau of Ordnance began to study a definitive solution—to imitate the army, which, under the urging of that outstanding organizer, General Josiah Gorgas, had created in Augusta, Georgia, the greatest powder works in the world.[136]

The first choice for locating a powder mill was Petersburg, Virginia, but the plant was transferred to Columbia, South Carolina, in the summer of 1862.[137] The appointed superintendent, T. Baudery Garesche, rose to the occasion. So experienced and well chosen was Garesche that Mallory soon announced that there was now more than enough powder.[138]

It was possible to obtain fair quantities of the most critical component of this explosive, nitrate, together with charcoal from the Nitre and Mining Bureau of the army, but the navy prospected for new mines, and not only for nitrates.[139]

The navy had no problem in getting fulminate of mercury primers. They were produced in adequate quantity by the Naval Ordnance Laboratory situated first in New Orleans and then transferred to Richmond under the direction of R. D. Minor.[140]

Engines and boilers were among the gravest problems. As Mallory wrote: "No marine engines such as are required for the ordinary class of sloops of war or frigates have ever been made in any of the Confederate States, nor have workshops capable of producing them existed in either of them. Parts of three such engines only have been made in Virginia, but the heavier portions of them were constructed in Pennsylvania and Maryland."[141]

In charge of this very important section was the engineer in chief, William P. Williamson, appointed on 21 April 1862.[142] Unfortunately, despite the importance of his task, he lacked, as the chief constructor, a specific branch of the navy under his own orders and instead had to depend directly upon the naval secretary. Williamson, from North Carolina, a veteran of the U.S. Navy, appears to have been competent and fitted for his duty. Yet Tom H. Wells, with authority deriving from his former position as a naval officer, was very severe with him.[143] True, Williamson never reached the standard of a Brooke, and several of his subordinates seem to have been more efficient and capable than he was. Still, one must consider the numerous adversities he had to face.

Mallory was not planning to power his prospective ships with engines built only inside the Confederacy. Frequent use would be made of obsolescent engines rescued from other ships, even riverboats. Some engines were obtained from Europe, but there were not enough of them.[144] The Confederacy was paying the bitter price of lacking its own adequate and efficient war industry and being compelled to depend upon foreign sources. It was forced to turn to local production. Some domestic firms, fitted out in great haste, succeeded in producing some engines and their boilers. Among these were the Patterson Iron Works of New Orleans[145] and the firm of James M. Eason, of Charleston, South Carolina.[146] Even putting aside the early loss of New Orleans, this was certainly not enough. More energetic action was needed.

At the beginning, Tredegar again came to the rescue. In addition to repairing the engines of some gunboats, it produced those for the ironclad *Richmond* and for three other craft.[147] Other than Tredegar, the navy contracted with the Shockoe Manufacturing Company of Richmond, owned by the Talbott brothers. Shockoe was a thriving and sound firm that specialized in producing small steam engines and, after 1854, locomotives.[148] By contract, the firm started, in September 1862, to build engines and boilers exclusively for the navy, first for small gunboats,[149] later for ironclad vessels.[150]

Finally, in March 1862 the Ordnance Bureau sent an officer to Columbus, Georgia, to investigate the possibility of opening "extensive government works."[151] A fine river port on the Chattahoochee (which flows into the Apalachicola, then to the Gulf of Mexico), well connected by railroad to the strategic areas of the Confederacy, Columbus is still a pretty city, not excessively defaced by modernization, with ample tree-lined avenues at its center, nice buildings, and tied to Alabama by several bridges. When the Civil War began, it had about ten thousand citizens and several industrial plants.[152]

The most important industry was the Columbus Iron Works, which produced bronze and pig iron castings and small steam engines. In the spring of 1862 it passed into the hands of Confederate naval authorities by a contract of unlimited rental. Used first for producing boat howitzers, it then engaged in the extensive production of engines and boilers under the name of Columbus Naval Iron Works.[153]

To assume direction of such an organization the navy appointed a man of outstanding ability and experience—Chief Engineer James H. Warner, who assumed command in September 1862.[154] Under his energetic lead (among other things, he invented a steam pump that was adopted after the war by the U.S. Navy), the firm went into full production. The first addition Warner made to the plant was a great boiler shop.[155] By October 1862 it was building engines and boilers for several ironclads and minor vessels.[156]

In a short while the Columbus Naval Iron Works became the most important manufacturer of naval engines in the Confederacy and even produced some for merchant ships.[157] The engines and boilers made here were of the best quality and universally praised. On 1 November 1864 the power plants of six out of the ten armored ships under construction in the South came from Columbus.[158] Next to this firm, in the same area but separated from it, was the navy yard commanded by Lieutenant Andrew McLaughlin, who started shipbuilding as soon as possible.

In addition to iron, other metals needed for fitting out naval ships were copper, tin, zinc, and lead. Copper was used to produce percussion caps. It also accounted for 87 to 92 percent of the metal to make bronze for guns.[159] Further, either in pure form or as bronze (an alloy with tin) or as brass (an alloy with zinc), it served to make many important parts of naval engines (faucets, valves, bushings, and so on). In its pure state it provided the sheathing for hulls to prevent corrosion and rotting. As an alternate to lead, it could be used to make "sabots" for the large shells used by big rifled guns.

The only copper mines in the South were near Ducktown, in southeastern Tennessee. Two others, located in Virginia, were of little significance.[160] Other sources, located in Arkansas or Arizona, were too far away to be of much use to the Confederacy, except perhaps locally.[161] Ducktown mine, the property of the Union Consolidated Mining Company, an enemy firm, had been seized by the Confederate government. It was then entrusted to William H. Peet, who worked it throughout the war. Nearby, in the small town of Cleveland, Tennessee, Peet also directed the Tennessee Copper Rolling Works.[162]

On 29 August 1861 Peet proposed to Mallory that he could supply the navy with all the copper it needed.[163] The contract pledged to consign to the navy a thousand tons of copper in ingots, bars, and sheets: fifty tons within the first six months, the rest according to need. Yet the navy received much less because the Ducktown mine and nearby rolling mill never provided more than a total of five hundred tons.[164] At the end of 1863, moreover, the Ducktown mine was taken by the enemy,[165] thus leaving the South without copper save what it could obtain from small mines hurriedly put into operation or recover by melting alembics or scraps.

The only solution was to try to import copper through the blockade, as had already been done for tin and zinc, of which the Confederacy had absolutely none,[166] and to stop sheathing its warships' hulls.[167] In the end these exertions brought some results,[168] for at the beginning of 1865 John Mercer Brooke could tell Secretary Mallory that the amounts obtained from overseas would suffice for many months.[169]

As for lead, other than being used to manufacture bullets (and here the army's need was far greater than the navy's), it served to make "sabots" for large shells as well as piping and parts of engines and other shipbuilding installations. The Confederacy had a priceless and abundant source in the mines of Wytheville in southwestern Virginia. The Southern government quickly took over these mines "for the duration" of the war.[170] Their total output during the period had been calculated at 1,591 tons.[171] Yet an almost equal amount was imported. Between 1 November 1863 and 1 March 1864, 685 tons of lead were brought through the blockade into the ports of Wilmington and Charleston.[172]

Among the most indispensable requirements for building and operating a navy, either for propulsion or for manufacturing and working iron, was coal. Even if Maryland, Kentucky, Missouri, and Tennessee, the bigger coal producers in the South, were all, sooner or later, in large part lost to the Confederacy, Virginia and Alabama had enough deposits. In 1860, 895,000 tons of coal were extracted in Virginia and only 20,000 in Alabama,[173] yet the latter, with its extensive reserves, soon took first place.

In Virginia, the basin of Clover Hill, near Richmond, produced ample first-rate coal for Tredegar. As Kathleen Bruce writes, "It is doubtful whether the Confederacy could have persisted without the Richmond coal."[174] In Alabama, the most important mines were those of Montevallo. In addition, coal came from a small mining area near Egypt, North Carolina.[175]

A History of the Confederate Navy

Responsibility for procuring coal at first fell upon the Office of Provisions and Clothing; it was then transferred to the Office of Orders and Details, which assigned the duty to Commander John K. Mitchell as superintendent of coal contracts.[176] Finally, in June 1863, the invaluable fuel passed under the control of the army's Nitre and Mining Bureau, which assumed the duty for the navy also.[177] The last arrangement was unsatisfactory to the navy, however, which in 1864 had to assign one of its own officers to assume responsibility for procuring coal.[178] The Naval Ordnance Bureau dealt on its own account for coal for its industrial plants,[179] and the commanders of the several naval squadrons tried to buy on the open market the small amounts needed to fill their bunkers.[180]

Coal available in the South was bituminous. The Confederacy had no anthracite except what it could acquire through capture. Its use was contested by the army.[181] The main problems arose from contracting with suppliers and transporters. In mid-1862 accords had been signed for the supply of twenty-five thousand tons.[182] Another contract signed with the Tredegar stipulated that all the coal extracted from its mines that exceeded its needs be consigned to the navy.[183] Yet some contracts (such as that for eight thousand tons signed with Robert Jemison, Jr., of Tuscaloosa, Alabama) went bad: Jemison provided nothing.[184] The Naval Station at Mobile, Alabama, had to turn to the "open" (i.e., black) market, which was quickly exhausted.[185]

A very important producer, Phineas Browne, of Montevallo, Alabama, whose papers provide the most valuable documentation on this thorny problem, complained of many difficulties while seeking to keep faith with his contract. First was the usual shortage of workers, which affected all industries in the Confederacy throughout the war, then the lack of professional miners, who had always been in short supply in the South, even before the war. The great evil that became a true nightmare for the South's civil and military leaders and in the end caused the collapse and breakdown of the Confederate supply system was the appalling inefficiency of transportation.[186]

Railroad problems increased as the war went on. For supplying coal either to the Atlanta Rolling Mill or the Columbus Navy Yard, as well as to the extremely important Savannah and Charleston naval squadrons, the navy had in all only forty-five railroad freight cars. These were worn out from incessant use. One can easily imagine the consequences of their wear and tear. No wonder, for example, that Flag Officer Ingraham, in Charleston, lamented that he was unable to get the minimum of fifteen tons a day needed by his squadron.[187]

Naval officers sought all possible means, even building a special trunk line to link the existing Alabama-Mississippi railroad with a place on the

Alabama River where coal could be delivered by barges, which soon became the main means of transportation.[188] Of simple construction, each barge could carry between twenty and twenty-five tons.[189]

The problem was far from solved, however, either because of the intrinsic difficulties of water transportation (rocks and shoals) or because transportation could not take place until river waters began to rise, which usually occurred after about 20 December and could last until June. Consequently, for about six months water transportation was barred except to rafts, which had little loading capability and were slower and hard to steer.[190]

Coal soon became still another difficult problem for the navy, even if the South had more than it needed. The Office of Orders and Details made an accurate inventory of available supplies;[191] yet, given the amount needed (the Charleston Squadron alone burned two hundred tons a month), the fires of warships had to be stoked with wood, saving coal for active operations.[192]

The Confederate navy never lacked resinous materials (pitch, turpentine) because the forests of North Carolina gave an ample supply.[193] The secretary of the navy had to provide rope by creating its own agency for doing so, the Naval Rope Walk at Petersburg, Virginia, which began production in January 1863.[194] This plant not only satisfied naval needs but also requests from the army, coal mines, railroads, and firms that ran navigable canals.[195] By April 1863 it was in full and regular production under the leadership of its commander, Lieutenant S. W. Corbin.[196]

On 30 September 1864 Captain Sidney Smith Lee, then head of the Bureau of Orders and Details, claimed proudly that the plant had produced 163,665 pounds (or 74,304 kilograms) of rope, 38,800 kilograms for the navy, 22,819 for the army, 10,000 for other customers, with an additional 3,185 in storage. In addition to supplying the navy with all the rope it needed at no cost to itself, the Rope Walk had netted a profit of $5,650.[197] Nor was ingenuity lacking. Given the scarcity and poor quality of Southern hemp and with its production concentrated almost wholly in Kentucky and Missouri, soon taken over by Federal forces,[198] Mallory, after failing to get hemp by an appropriation of $40,000,[199] resorted to the main national commodity, cotton. At Petersburg, thanks to the ingenuity and resourcefulness of local directors, excellent braided and tarred cotton rope was produced.[200]

At the end of 1864 the Naval Rope Walk was threatened by the advance of the armies of General Ulysses Grant. Mallory therefore had to move it before it fell into enemy hands.[201] From this moment on, records fail to address the subject, so it appears probable that Secretary Mallory, beset by even more serious problems, was never able to put the Rope Walk in motion again before the fall of the Confederacy.

If we can here draw some conclusion, it is that Mallory's concern about the extreme difficulty of building warships within the boundaries of the Southern Confederacy was well founded. The naval secretary justly perceived that the South would need from twelve to eighteen months to build a warship worth the name.[202] As had been amply demonstrated, the South had the potential, and, in general, all the raw materials needed, but it lacked to an almost disastrous degree modern and efficient industrial plants and a transportation system. To clinch this point, two references must suffice, one from the first historian of the Southern navy, J. Thomas Scharf, a former officer of that organization, the other by James Russell Soley, the "official" historian of the enemy.

Scharf writes that, on the eve of war, the South "possessed within its limits resources only in the rude, crude, and unmanufactured state. The timber for his ships stood in the forest, and when cut and laid was green and soft; the iron required was in the mines, and there were neither furnaces nor workshops; the hemp for the ropes had to be sown, grown, reaped, and then there were no rope walks. The Southern States had never produced a sufficiency of iron for the use of their people in time of peace. . . . Without a rolling mill capable of turning out a 2.5 iron plate, nor a workshop able to complete a marine engine, and with a pressing need to build, equip and maintain ships-of-war, the embarrassments and difficulties which Mr. Mallory encountered may be estimated."[203]

Soley writes: "The South entered upon the war without any naval preparation, and with very limited resources by which its deficiencies could be promptly supplied. Indeed, it would hardly be possible to imagine a great maritime country more destitute of the means for carrying on a naval war than the Confederate States in 1861."[204]

Thus, even if Mallory went to work building ships rather quickly and with astounding energy (the first contracts, however, were not signed until June 1861),[205] his first thought was to acquire warships in Europe. As early as 8 May 1861, while still in Montgomery, he had sent his first and most trusted agent, Commander James Dunwoody Bulloch, across the ocean.[206]

In spite of the enormous importance of the missions to Europe and the prominent part they played in the naval war and in the building up of the Southern navy, the Confederacy would soon find itself facing dire reality: if it did not want to succumb, it must build the most important core of its naval power within its own borders.

The energy which Mallory and his valiant collaborators displayed in handling the matter as well as the amazing results they realized still leave us astounded. During its short life the Confederacy built or laid down 150 warships. Even if less than half of them were completed and took part in operations, the number itself is remarkable. But what is still more astounding is how much industry the Southern navy successfully created to achieve its results: some twenty shipyards, including at least four naval ones; a rolling mill for producing armor plate; two plants for engines and boilers, of which the one in Columbus became the most important in the South; a foundry for heavy and very heavy guns; a powderworks; three artillery plants; a laboratory for caps, primers, and booby traps; and a rope walk.

There were in addition a bakery; two plants for packing foods; at least one distillery; two factories for the production of clothing and shoes; a laboratory for medical and sanitary supplies; several hospitals; and, finally, four warehouses for foods and barrack equipment. To these should be added several firms controlled by naval authorities even though (theoretically) still in private ownership. We thus see at a glance the dimensions of the organization Mallory managed to create.

All this in 1861 still required time, and war would not wait. Therefore, before anything else, Mallory concentrated upon large-scale acquisition of warships in Europe. His thinking about choices was precise and knowledgeable; it depended upon the naval strategy that he was devising.

Before dealing with the missions in Europe and their success (or failure, as the case may be) it is therefore indispensable to discuss at length from its roots the first phase of Confederate naval strategy. This was, in turn, decisively influenced by the technological revolution that was radically changing the essence of naval problems which, more than that, hinged upon it. It will therefore be necessary above all to deal with the dimensions and effects of such a revolution.

F O U R

The Technological Revolution
and the First Phase of
Confederate Naval Strategy

It is impossible to understand the substance of Confederate naval strategy as Secretary Mallory elaborated it unless one keeps in mind the revolutionary transformation in maritime technology that occurred toward the middle of the nineteenth century.

On this subject Alfred Thayer Mahan wrote: "A naval captain who fought the Invincibile Armada would have been more at home in the typical warship of 1840 than the average captain of 1840 would have been in the advanced types of the American Civil War."[1]

The extraordinary events that changed naval warfare were spawned by the industrial revolution. These can be reduced basically to four: invention of the steam engine and screw propeller, new and extremely powerful naval ordnance, and, as a result of the last, armored ships. Soon to appear and terrorize the seas of the Civil War was the last and most revolutionary innovation: underwater warfare.

In Admiral Horatio Nelson's day the ship of the line—the major warship of the great navies, called the capital ship—had reached its perfection. Imposing, stately under its towering forty sails,[2] with heavy armament that could include up to one hundred guns, the ship of the line was the apparently invincible tool of sea power.

And yet, toward the mid-1800s, it "dissolved into history and legend."[3] Its death knell was rung by a small ship displacing but a few tons, the *Savannah,* which in 1819 was the first to cross the Atlantic under the motive power of a steam engine. True, the *Savannah* was small and used steam power only as an auxiliary to her sails, but the die had been cast.

In a short while the steamer would render obsolete the sailing ship, which for centuries had dominated the seas, and make it a museum piece. Independent of the winds, able to breast the strongest currents, and capable of navigating both coastal and internal waters in practically any weather (bad weather, at least rough seas, was greatly feared and in general avoided by sailers), and laughing at dead calms, the steamer would soon become the queen of the seas.

True, the steamer depended on coal supplies. Therefore, at first steamers still made part-time use of sails to save valuable fuel while cruising. Yet in battle the steamer could be completely self-governing, able to move without concern for winds and currents, to attack, retreat, and undertake any operation it desired.

One is thus amazed by the reluctance with which naval men initially regarded substituting steamers for sailers. This was in part because the first steamers were propelled by paddle wheels. Their engine, therefore, had a small power-to-weight ratio (one horsepower per ton), which caused an enormous waste of fuel and, consequently, kept their range very short. In addition, because the engines were located well above the waterline, they were dangerously exposed to enemy fire. Paddle wheels also offered conspicuous targets along the sides.[4]

In 1836 a Swedish engineer, John Ericsson, patented a screw propeller in England. This son of a mining inspector was born on 31 July 1803 in central Sweden and early displayed a genius for mechanical inventions. Self-taught, then an officer in the Swedish Army Corps of Engineers, he moved to Great Britain, where he started a promising career as a civilian engineer. He first invented a locomotive that almost took the prize of priority from George Stephenson, then designed, tested, and patented a naval screw propeller.[5]

Even if Ericsson had competitors (great inventions often mature in the minds of many persons unknown to one another),[6] the screw propeller had relatively quick success mainly owing to his efforts. He aroused the enthusiasm of Captain Robert F. Stockton, U.S.N., who had conspicuous wealth and enjoyed a prominent social position. Stockton persuaded Ericsson to emigrate to the United States and financed the building of the first screw-driven ship.[7]

The advent of the screw stimulated a further revolution in naval technology. It made possible a great increase in the weight-to-power ratio over that of the paddle wheeler and thus enormously reduced fuel consumption. Thus the competition between sailers and steamers was won by the latter only with the advent of the screw propeller. Further, the screw in warships made it possible to place engines and boilers well below the waterline, in the hold, safe from enemy gunfire. The screw itself, being under water, was also protected. Thus, by removing an element of weakness and vulnerability, it also freed the sides for emplacement of artillery.

The screw did not arrive a moment too soon because at the same time naval ordnance had progressed to the point of changing warfare at sea. In Nelson's day the big sailing ships that were the backbone of a fleet had become so strong as to be nearly unsinkable. Not a single ship of the line was sunk by gunfire in the battle of Trafalgar. They could withstand terrific pounding from the solid shot used at the time. Their frames and planking were built with great skill and the intrinsic elasticity and porosity of wood tended to reduce damage to a minimum. The only tactic available for artillery fire was to seek to dismast enemy ships and capture them by boarding.[8]

To render artillery fire more effective had long been the concern of many men. Why not fire exploding shells instead of solid shot? For centuries this had been impossible except for very short pieces (mortars and howitzers) with a small powder charge, which had only a short range and little piercing power. Experiments to fire shell with guns, begun in France in 1761, failed. The heavy charges required often caused the shell to explode inside the barrel, primarily because of the low standard of cast iron metallurgy, as well as the defective and hygroscopic nature of both fuses and shells.[9]

The man who finally solved the problem was not a naval officer but an artillerist. Born at Metz in 1783, a graduate of the famed Ecole Polytechnique, Henri-Joseph Paixhans started to study the problem in 1809. Not until 1821 did he publish the first edition of his work, which was destined to revolutionize naval warfare. It was entitled *Nouvelle force maritime.*[10]

Paixhans denied being an inventor. Truly, it was the progress already made in casting iron as well as in fuses and shells that enabled him to experiment in ways unavailable to his predecessors. If not an inventor, he was certainly a man with ingenious ideas. He thought not only of firing shells from guns but also of building a piece able to fire horizontally big eight-inch mortar shells by using heavy charges, giving them the same dynamic power as solid shot. The problem, which he succeeded in solving, was to create a gun and a carriage steady enough to withstand the punishment from the report generated by the great charges needed both to fire large projectiles and to give them enough initial speed so that they would succeed, at the end of their trajectory, in piercing the side of a big ship, exploding inside.[11]

Experiments with Paixhans's gun were carried out at Brest by the French navy in January 1824. The target, the old eighty-gun ship of the line *Le Pacificateur,* was practically destroyed by only sixteen shells.[12]

Paixhans's gun truly closed an era. One could say that in 1824 by the firing of his shells he had at one stroke sunk all the world's navies. Yet many years passed before his doctrines were fully proved. This occurred on 30 November 1853, during the Crimean War, when the Turkish fleet in the Black Sea, anchored at Sinope, was surprised by a Russian squadron commanded by Admiral Pavel Stefanovic Nakimov. The fire from Russian shell guns made short work of the Turkish ships, sinking all of them except for one that managed to escape.

Paixhans now served in the Conseil des Travaux, an agency composed of naval officers, naval constructors, and artillerists, created in 1831 to supervise new naval technology. He strongly underscored the confirmation Sinope had provided for his theories. Now, he correctly held, there was only one solution for warships: to protect themselves with armor at least eight inches thick.[13]

Thus began the dramatic contest between armor and gun, for as armor improved, artillery was preparing its reply through the invention of rifled guns and armor-piercing projectiles. How to rifle guns was a problem that had tormented technicians for centuries. Obviously, if a projectile could be made to spin about its axis, it would enjoy greater stability. It would then be possible to fire shells with a cylindrical-conical nose that would explode on contact, thus eliminating the dangerous fuse except for a special kind (shrapnel). In addition, the reduced dispersion of gas would grant greater kinetic energy, hence providing more penetrating strength than that of smoothbore guns.[14]

The first to build an effective rifled gun was the Sardinian general Giovanni Cavalli, in 1833. After useless experiments with round shots, in 1845 Cavalli introduced cylindrical-conical shells.[15]

Test results proved them to be exceptional. Cavalli had at the same time obtained longer range and immensely greater penetrating power. Rotation stabilized the shell, while its elongated form, reducing air resistance by half, enabled it to be fired at higher speed and with high piercing force even by guns much smaller than smoothbores. This in turn permitted the concentration of maximum kinetic energy upon the minimum space of a target. From such a beginning would be developed the armor-piercing projectiles used during the Civil War.

The Americans, however, had followed a different road. This was, possibly, because they (as Louis Napoléon held in his work on artillery)[16] were unable to devote much time to theoretical study about the resistance of iron and steel, or, maybe, because of their tendency to prefer practical experience over pure theory.

The true explanation might be found elsewhere. From the time of the War of 1812 with Great Britain, when the Royal Navy had sailed up the

Potomac and landed at Washington, D.C., and the Royal Marines set the White House on fire, the United States lived under the nightmare of an attack from the sea by overwhelming British naval power. Undoubtedly this fear resulted in the strengthening of the U.S. Navy. Unable to match the Royal Navy, however, the Americans had moved mainly along two lines: an elaborate and formidable system of coast defense and heavy artillery pieces along the coast that would keep ships far from shore (vessels still were made of wood at the beginning of the nineteenth century).

For coast defense a gun was invented that was unknown in Europe—the Columbiad. The exact origin of the name remains unknown, yet its random use has left us "an inheritance of confusion."[17] What is known is that its inventor was Major George Bomford, of the Engineer Corps, later chief of the Ordnance Department of the United States, and that it began to be drafted about 1811, on the eve of the war with the immensely powerful United Kingdom.[18]

According to the most generally accepted account, Bomford named his piece "Columbiad" under the inspiration of the epic poem by Joel Barlow, which he read in its magnificent 1807 edition.[19] The inventor clearly wanted to underscore the "Americanness" of the new weapon designed to defend the independence of the New World. Perhaps also he had in mind the name of the Federal District of Columbia, seat of the capital of the United States, always threatened and soon to be violated by the enemy and which, more than any other place, symbolized the New World which must be defended against all possible aggression by the Old World.

From a technical viewpoint, the Columbiad was truly remarkable. Antedating Paixhans's experiments by twelve years, it for the first time solved the problem of firing huge shells (of eight to ten inches) by means of a cannon, or more exactly, by a quasi-cannon. Paixhans may have known of Bomford's invention.

Yet the Columbiad was a purely coastal gun, not adaptable (at least at the time) for shipboard use.[20] It combined the distinctive characteristics of cannon, mortar, and howitzer. Like the howitzer, it had a chamber that permitted firing with reduced charges,[21] yet it had a long barrel like that of a cannon (of more than ten calibers length). Finally, because it used a reduced charge, it normally fired with an elevation of up to forty degrees, similar to a mortar. For this reason, in its original version it was too unstable for shipboard use. It therefore was a coastal gun, as its inventor intended.

In its long history, however, the Columbiad evolved. Used first on a large scale as a seacoast defense gun, it was later almost abandoned, but in 1844 it was modified and made longer and heavier.

A later and more revolutionary transformation came at the hands of Captain Thomas J. Rodman, a U.S. Army artillery officer. A scientist and inventor, Rodman had observed that the current system of casting cannons involved a series of flaws. Normally the gun, cast solid, was then bored cold. For small pieces, all went well, but in the case of big guns, the cooling of a large mass, proceeding from the outside to the interior, caused the largest diameter of the gun to contract first, producing invisible cracks that more often than not caused the gun to burst when fired. Rodman developed a process by which the gun was cast hollow, with cooling then proceeding from the interior to the exterior by a continuous flux of water.[22]

The new system permitted casting of huge Columbiads of ten, fifteen, even up to twenty inches. The last was a monster more than nineteen feet long, weighing 115,000 pounds without carriage, able to fire shells weighing more than 1,600 pounds. Obviously, being smoothbores, such pieces fired projectiles at a slow or moderate speed. Yet the loss of kinetic energy caused by slow speed was made up for by the tremendous mass of the projectile. The effect that they might have on a ship was terrifying, like gigantic blows from a monster bludgeon.[23]

The U.S. Navy followed a similar line with some differences. The navy was fortunate to have another man of genius, Commander John A. Dahlgren, later chief of naval ordnance and a future admiral. A smart scientist, Dahlgren realized that the possibilities opened up by the advent of new and heavy naval cannons and the screw propeller indicated the adoption by warships of few but very powerful guns (unlike the old sailing ships, which had many guns of limited power) and that these should be all of the same caliber. Thus Dahlgren, with astounding foresight, posed the problem of the monocaliber ship, one destined to be solved only half a century later, by Vittorio Cuniberti.[24]

Consequently, Dahlgren set out to design, among others, a smoothbore gun of the Paixhans type for the U.S. Navy. His cannon, cast in several calibers but principally of eleven inches, turned out to be among the best artillery pieces in the world. Cast solid, it was, however, shaped on the basis of accurate studies of the pressures that firing exerted upon metal at various points. Its chamber's shape (also derived from scientific studies) permitted the greatest possible exploitation of the propelling force. The standard Dahlgren gun could fire a shell weighing 170 pounds.[25]

Even if in Europe nobody dared think of such monster pieces as Rodman's Columbiad (no wonder that Jules Verne, in his *From the Earth to the Moon,* would ascribe to the minds of former Northern artillerists of the Civil War the idea of building a tremendous gun able to fire a projectile as far as the moon), with Rodman's and Dahlgren's innovations, both the coast and the naval artillery of the United States were turning away from rifled guns. They sought to obtain the most from a solution that, even though it had a few years earlier revolutionized the world of naval warfare, already appeared obsolescent.

On the eve of secession, although the United States Ordnance Department had designed and built an excellent three-inch rifled fieldpiece, only private firms had experimented with heavy rifled guns. First among these was the firm of Robert Parker Parrott, a former artillery officer and, after 1836, superintendent of the big gun foundry at West Point, near Cold Springs, New York. From 1849 on, he had devoted himself wholly to the invention and construction of great rifled guns. In 1861 he patented a model of rifled cannon strengthened at the breech by a band of wrought iron. More followed: a first-rate field gun and pieces of thirty pounds (4.5 inches), one hundred pounds (6.4 inches), two hundred pounds (8 inches), and even a three-hundred-pounder (10 inches). Still, being muzzle-loaders and made of cast iron, these guns were subject to a dangerous tendency to burst at the muzzle after numerous firings.[26]

Such was the evolution of maritime technology, both civil and military, when Mallory began to draft his strategy for the Confederate navy. To hold that this evolution influenced his strategy understates the case. In reality, technology affected Confederate naval strategy in its very bases and ground rules, in the cardinal point upon which the talented secretary built it: technology would be the tool that appeared to offer a breath of hope in facing a war that otherwise would be hopeless or lost before it began.

Confederate naval strategy developed from four elements: the environment and the conditions it imposed; the overwhelming, indeed total naval preponderance of the enemy, which appeared to grant him the initiative; the naval strategy that the enemy himself planned and executed (i.e., the nature of the threat, which helped to determine the ways and directions of possible reply); and, most important, because it seemed to offer to the Confederates their only hope of seizing the initiative from the enemy, the new technological framework.

The French admiral A. Lepotier, in what still remains the most brilliant study of the strategic framework of the American Civil War at sea,[27] correctly stated that this was probably the only occasion in the course of history when, at the beginning of a conflict between two nations facing the ocean, one of the two had incontestable and total dominion over the waters.

The Southern seashore, indeed, consisted of thirty-five hundred nautical miles of coastline, as long as the whole European coastal perimeter from Hamburg to Genoa, with more than 189 harbors or navigable river mouths to be defended, and was, Lepotier stated, "so indented, as to be difficult to fix the boundaries between land and sea, because both elements join via banks, islands, estuaries, branches of the sea, watercourses and channels, which make all these coasts prize zones for amphibious operations."[28] In addition to the maritime frontier, the South had to defend its inland waterways, for the entire country is crossed by deep rivers that are navigable to a great distance from the sea.

First there was the Mississippi, the immense "Father of Waters," navigable even by large seagoing ships along its entire course and of such importance that the American Union had placed it under maritime law. It was therefore a true internal sea, 1,097 nautical miles long within Confederate territory, starting from Cairo, on the extreme southern point of Illinois and a Union outpost, to the sea, even if the distance as the bird flies is only 480 miles.[29] Second, there were so-called minor rivers, high at the end of spring, very low in the fall, which would have extremely important effects on military operations.

No war ever revealed a greater interdependence between land and maritime events. "To deal with them separately," writes Lepotier, "without underscoring this uninterrupted interdependence, would be to completely distort the facts and reach wrong conclusions."[30]

Let us now ask two questions: Did the Union leaders fully understand how naturally vulnerable the Confederacy was? And how did they plan to exploit such vulnerability by means of a naval strategy?

Following the bombardment of Fort Sumter, the war at sea opened with two measures resurrected from the dead world of sailing ships. Both governments seem to have ignored the age in which they were living and fighting.

First, the Confederate president, Jefferson Davis, had decided immediately to answer President Lincoln's proclamation of 15 April 1861[31] in which he had called upon the governors of the states for seventy-five thousand militia to quell the "rebellion" of the South. That proclamation clearly signified the beginning of warlike actions against the new Confederacy. Davis therefore retorted on the nineteenth with his own proclamation urging resistance against a threatened invasion. Yet the Confederate president, who was able to appraise the overwhelming naval strength of the enemy which had enabled the Union to keep several forts (even if the attempt to succor Fort Sumter had failed) and who was also aware of the riches the North was gaining through its flourishing maritime trade, invited by his proclamation "all those who may desire, by service in private armed vessels on the high seas, to aid this Government in resisting . . . to make application for commissions or letters of marque and reprisal to be issued under the seal of these Confederate States."[32] This was nothing but *guerre de course* by means of privateers, as in the seventeenth century. Lincoln gave him tit for tat by issuing on the same day another proclamation in which he announced the intention of the U.S. government "to set on foot a blockade" of the states in rebellion.[33]

Certainly, the Union government hesitated before proclaiming its blockade. According to Northern political doctrine, the Confederate States of America did not exist as a separate power, the problem being only a domestic rebellion. Now the question was, Could a nation blockade a supposedly nonexistent one? The U.S. naval secretary, Gideon Welles, doubted that it could. He therefore recommended proclaiming the closing of "rebel" ports rather than a blockade. This was the normal course to follow in case of insurrection, and it would have transferred the question into a purely domestic one and avoided a feared internationalization of the conflict.

Unfortunately for the Union, Welles's thesis was untenable. How could hundreds of ports along thousands of miles of coasts be declared closed? From London, the British secretary of state, Lord John Russell, discreetly let it be known that such a thesis was clearly absurd.[34] Lincoln, therefore, taking the Southern government's offer of letters of marque and reprisal as a pretext, resolved to proclaim a blockade.

These were two backward actions. As during the age of sail, the weaker power threatened to launch swarms of privateers against the enemy's maritime trade; in its turn, the stronger declared a "paper" blockade, reserving the right to apply it when and where it appeared to be possible and opportune.

In keeping with seventeenth-century practice, the two naval secretaries had no voice in these discussions because they had no competence in a subject that traditionally was of pertinence to the heads of state and the two respective secretaries of state. Indeed, after the presidents, the secretaries of state were the second to sign all proclamations. Although the Southern attempt to launch privateers upon the seas failed, the initial Northern blockade proclamation generated developments of enormous importance, far beyond the expectations of their initiators.

Mallory, who had not been consulted on privateering (and, according to custom, should not have been),[35] had clearly seen that the blockade proclamation contained the essence of the enemy's naval strategy, and it was this that he had to answer, albeit certainly not by means of the blunt and obsolete weapon of privateering.

What strategic problem did Mallory face? The naval power of the Union was such that he could not find any example in history of a similar situation being reversed during the course of a conflict. Successful improvising in naval warfare is almost impossible; the creation of a fleet with a

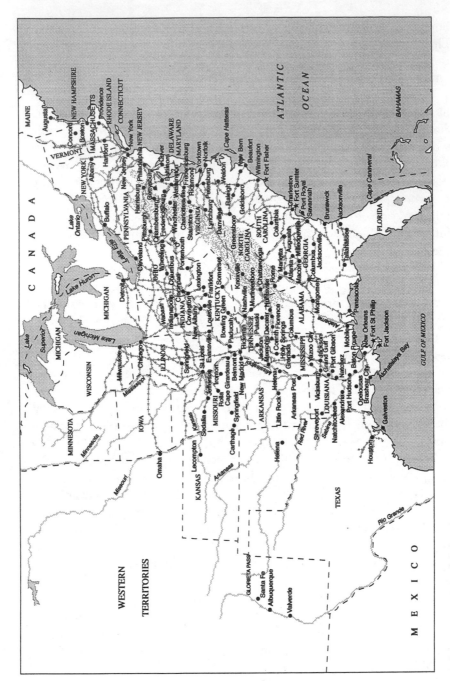

The eastern United States in 1861.

dearth of industrial resources as in the South was almost unrealizable; further, the shortage of men for the front-line regiments made it impossible to try to imitate the North, which planned to use eleven thousand men for naval construction.[36]

A careful analysis of records shows that, at least in the beginning, Mallory did not fully grasp the total interdependence (better, the symbiosis) between land and sea warfare. Mallory originally saw coast defense as an ordinary problem. The same misunderstanding had occurred before in the Joint Committee on Naval Affairs in Montgomery.[37] Yet he immediately understood that the only—and greatest—advantage the Confederacy had was to use the revolutionary technology that was upsetting maritime warfare throughout the world.

Lacking a fleet, the South was not hindered by the need to use obsolete and worthless ships. Instead, it could try to obtain ships as new and modern as possible. Compelled to fight against the enemy's crushing superiority in numbers, it could avail itself of more advanced and revolutionary warship designs and seek to defeat quantity by means of quality. Armored ships, steam, rifled guns, even the new and still veiled submarine weaponry were the arms the Confederacy should use to overcome its shortcomings and turn the tables in the war at sea. Still, not all of these ideas simultaneously entered the minds of Confederate naval leaders, and it was very difficult to foresee immediately the most correct and fruitful use of each of them.

Nine days after President Davis had offered letters of marque to privateers and only seven days before the Union announced its blockade, on 26 April 1861, Secretary Mallory sent a report of primary importance to the president. In it he detailed the first phase of naval strategy to be followed by the Confederacy. This report showed clearly that the secretary understood the revolution that was taking place in naval warfare and fully intended to exploit its effects. The United States, he wrote, had "built a navy: we have a navy to build: and if in the construction of the several classes of ships we shall keep constantly in view the qualities of those ships which they may be called to encounter we shall have wisely provided for our naval success." The point Mallory stressed was indeed revolutionary: "I propose to adopt a class of vessels hitherto unknown to naval service," he wrote.[38]

After observing that the perfect warship must combine the best possible speed, strongest armor, and maximum firepower, he underscored that at the time Great Britain and France, which had pursued this aim with great devotion and lavish spending, had not succeeded in reaching the objective. Mallory explained his first proposal: "Vessels built exclusively for ocean speed, at a low cost, with a battery of one or two accurate guns of long range, with an ability to keep the sea upon a long cruise and to engage or to avoid an enemy at will, are not found in their [i.e., of England and France] navies, and only to a very limited extent in that of the United States, the speed and power of whose ships are definitely known." Mallory stated that he had been actively engaged in seeking "steam vessels which can be most advantageously employed against commerce," adding that the Confederacy was already arming two auxiliary cruisers, the *Sumter* and the *McRae.* Still, proper cruisers could not be obtained except from overseas: he had already hinted at this in the early lines of his report.[39]

Even before submitting his report, while Mallory busied himself with trying to equip at least a pair of auxiliary units to begin cruiser warfare, on 9 May 1861 Commander James D. Bulloch, one of the most able men in the Southern navy, left the Confederacy for Europe. His primary duty was to purchase or have built several fast cruisers, "which offers the greatest chances of success against the enemy's commerce." Modern commerce-destroying warfare thus was about to appear for the first time in history.[40]

What Mallory was planning would be a sensational innovation. Operations against enemy trade on the high seas could no longer be pursued by the obsolete, almost antediluvian system of privateering but might well be undertaken by powerful and fast steam cruisers equipped by the regular navy. As their objective, these vessels would not seek to capture enemy cargoes but to destroy them. This new kind of sea warfare was bound to cause tremendous changes in the conduct of naval operations, fraught with momentous consequences for the future. It was the precursor of the *Emden* and other German raiders of both world wars, as well as commerce destroying by submarines and the "wolf packs" of the Second World War.

In the same paper Mallory delineated still another project, one that also broke with the naval tradition of the United States and put the Confederacy in the vanguard of progress: "Rifled cannon are unknown to naval warfare; but those guns having attained a range and accuracy beyond any other form of ordnance, both with shot and shell, I propose to introduce them into the Navy." In addition, he foresightedly saw the advent of "small propeller ships with great speed, lightly armed with these guns," which "must soon become, as the light artillery and rifles of the deep, a most destructive element of naval warfare." Caught in the coils of a terrible war, compelled to fight uphill against the blows of an overpowering enemy, Mallory would never succeed in realizing his program except in small part. Yet he provided a vision of light craft that would become an essential part of forthcoming fleets.[41]

Meanwhile, Mallory was already playing his third card: armored ships. The first to support his strategy was John Mercer Brooke, who quickly became the deus ex machina for the practical realization of innovation in the Confederate navy. The energetic naval secretary was already moving in the same direction. It has correctly been said that, in his mention of "a class of vessels hitherto unknown" and later hints about attempts by Great Britain and France to produce protected but fast ships, he was surely thinking of armored vessels.[42] In an early report Mallory hinted at the ultimate solution of the ironclad warship, which would realize an optimal equilibrium between speed and protection (that would be the obstacle that for many more years would trouble planners and constructors of ironclads, at least until the days of Benedetto Brin or even Cuniberti).[43] Yet his plans for armored ships were undoubtedly as innovative as those of commerce destroying or rifled guns afloat, all forerunners of the future.[44]

On 10 May, in a letter to the president of the Committee on Naval Affairs, Charles N. Conrad, after a detailed description of progress made in Great Britain and France in the field of armored warship building, Mallory stated:

> I regard the possession of an iron-armored ship as a matter of the first necessity. Such a vessel at this time could traverse the entire coast of the United States, prevent all blockades, and encounter, with a fair prospect of success, their entire Navy. If to cope with them upon the sea we follow their example and build wooden ships, we shall have to construct several at one time; for one or two ships would fall an easy prey to her comparatively numerous steam frigates. But inequality of numbers may be compensated by invulnerability; and thus not only does economy but naval success dictate the wisdom and expediency of fighting with iron against wood, without regard to first cost.

The secretary continued by underscoring how, after the introduction of new, powerful naval guns, duels between wooden ships would be desperate enterprises, "simply contests in which the question, not of victory, but of who shall go to the bottom first, is to be solved." And he exhorted Congress by insisting that "not a moment should be lost" in acquiring an armored ship.[45]

From this, Mallory's naval strategy emerges clearly: armored ships together with commerce destroyers and the wide adoption of rifled guns would constitute the "technical surprise" that would enable Confederates to reverse a situation that appeared desperate.

This "technical surprise," made possible by exploiting the revolutionary changes that had recently occurred, would, it was hoped, enable the weaker power to seize the operational initiative and to overcome an enemy that seemed to cling to an obsolete heritage from the naval past and whose technological answer would presumably be slow because the conservatism of the old naval establishment would inevitably be ranged against a possible innovative policy by the Union naval secretary.[46]

Mallory's hope to win the war with a single armored ship was indeed the kind of illusion that had existed since the world began and had characterized every statesman or chieftain who, believing that he could rely on technical surprise, thinks that he possesses the ultimate weapon. Such an opinion has always proved illusory. As Admiral Lepotier correctly underscores, "In technology as in tactics, surprise is ineffective if it cannot be fully exploited from the beginning, before any effective reaction from the adversary; and it is therefore a most difficult matter, since one is working on the unknown. Meanwhile, instead, the accumulation of preparatory activities cannot pass unnoticed by the enemy." [47]

Yet, for the time being, Mallory could do nothing else, and he sought two possible solutions to the problem. The first one consisted of trying to buy or have armored ships built in Europe, as had already been done regarding cruisers. For that purpose a second agent, Lieutenant Commander James H. North, was sent on 17 May to Great Britain with an appropriation of $2 million.[48] The second solution was based on the possibility of building one or more armored vessels within the Confederacy.

There was still another weapon whose initial use remains shrouded in a haze but whose initiator, according to good witnesses, was Mallory himself: the new, elusive, and insidious submarine warfare, intended to strike even the best-protected ship in its most vital part below the waterline.[49]

The first man to be given the responsibility for directing mine (or "torpedo") warfare was Commander Matthew Fontaine Maury. Born in Virginia in 1805, he entered the U.S. Navy at a very early age and quickly revealed a bright scientific mind, more suited to research than to the hard routine of a naval life. He became superintendent of the Naval Observatory, author of *The Physical Geography of the Sea*,[50] founder of oceanography, and student of the Gulf Stream. He was universally admired and honored by all nations. In 1839 he suffered a serious accident when a mail carriage overturned, leaving him with a limp. Because of this disability, he had fallen under the ax of the Naval Retiring Board, promoted at the time by Mallory. Only after many vicissitudes was he retained in the service. Indeed, he made scientific contributions to the navy despite his infirmity. From that moment on, however, he held a deep (and unjustified) rancor against Mallory that would have consequences later,[51] for example when he attempted resentfully to exclude Mallory from the group who initially developed submarine warfare.

Maury was much more a scientist than a man of war. Unlike John Mercer Brooke, his speculations led him toward problems of a universal character, more important for the progress of mankind as a whole than to specific technological questions; and he would not resent leaving the submarine torpedo service in less ingenious but perhaps more effective hands.

The naval strategy initially developed by Mallory was based on a four-fold technical surprise: armored ships, rifled naval guns, commerce destroying, and submarine weapons. Whereas the first one, as a surprise, was only partly successful and was soon blunted by the enemy, the second and fourth had great success, but in an unforeseen way and size. The third one enjoyed spectacular success because it was totally unexpected, a lightning bolt from the blue for nations accustomed to the old-fashioned system of privateering and because it struck when merchant mariners were only just beginning to adopt steam. Therefore, according to Lepotier, "The steam commerce raider was as much formidable and fearful for sailing merchant ships as submarines would be for freighters in 1917."[52]

Soon the fast Confederate cruisers would fall like hawks upon the slow Northern merchant sailers, giving the South its first glamorous successes and showing a stunned world for the first time the flag of the new Confederate nation flying over the seas.

FIVE

The Internationalization of the Conflict and the Beginning of the War against Trade on the Far Seas

The war at sea between the North and the South began with two acts considered traditional in every past maritime conflict, especially during the age-old hostility between Great Britain and France from the days of Louis XIV to those of Napoleon I and, later, British power against the new United States: the tendering by the Confederate government of letters of marque to privateers and the Northern proclamation of a blockade against the South.

For years, Great Britain, supreme on the seas, had initiated hostile operations by proclaiming a blockade against the enemy. Though she would not admit it, these were "paper blockades" because the Royal Navy was not only selective in choosing enemy ports to block and the time for so doing but also presumed to stop neutral merchant ships everywhere on the high seas to control both the quality and the destination of the cargo. These were paper blockades also because usually, when announced, they had little or no force behind them. In time, however, they would be strengthened.

It was obvious that in the days of sailing ships it would be very difficult to act in any other way. For Britain, directly and permanently to blockade enemy coasts (such as those of France) was unthinkable. Subject to the whims of wind and sea, the ships sailing on blockade duty could not run the risk of being caught by a storm or immobilized by a dead calm while off hostile coasts. They therefore were limited to indirect observation, ready to step in whenever the wind direction made it likely that enemy ships would put to sea. Hunting down merchant ships was generally left to such light craft as frigates, while ships of the line stood ready to oppose the enemy's battle fleet if it dared to poke its nose out of its bases. It was the strategic principle of the "fleet in being," which was used with great skill by British admirals.[1]

Undoubtedly, this system tormented neutrals. Even more galling was Britain's extensive interpretation of it, capturing enemy goods carried by neutral ships and neutral goods in enemy ships and extending the list of contraband of war practically without limit, even including foodstuffs.[2]

The weaker naval power, victim of the blockade, reacted by scattering on the high seas a swarm of privateers, ships owned by private parties and hastily equipped and armed by them. They would be granted letters of marque that distinguished them from ordinary pirates, who operated on their own. Britain did not refrain from resorting to privateering to seize what hostile traffic escaped the blockade. In the city of Halifax, Nova Scotia, there still exists a district where British privateers had their own warehouses and even a bank to deposit the money earned by their "honest" toil.

Privateering was not lawless: far from it. Privateers could stop only enemy merchant ships or carriers of enemy goods. They must wage war and behave according to the articles of international law, though these were not always observed. After putting a prize crew aboard the captured ship, they must send it to a friendly or neutral port and submit it to the judgment of a prize court. Only after the captured ship had been "condemned" could it and its cargo (or part of it) be sold at auction and the privateer pocket his prize money.[3]

The issue of letters of marque, writes William M. Robinson, Jr., "had been for centuries a spark that never failed to fire the souls of the adventurous with dreams of broad, blue waters and fat prizes."[4]

Yet what nobody seemed to consider, either in the South or in the North (with the possible exception of Secretary Mallory), was that the days of privateering (as well as of the paper blockade) were over, killed by the technological revolution and by an economy that had changed and was still changing the world of navigation. Robinson wrote: "Few subjected it to analysis in the light of the changes wrought and being wrought, by the revolutionary economic developments which characterized the epoch. Privateering was a relic of a vanished civilization. Letters of marque and reprisal connoted a decentralization of power which was wholly inconsistent with the new era of rapid communications."[5]

Neither Jefferson Davis nor Abraham Lincoln seemed to have taken this revolution into account. The steps they took (which, as in the past, were of serious concern to neutrals) interfered so heavily with the network of world communications and commercial interests as to risk provoking an immediate reaction on a global scale. The world had "shrunk" while speed of communications had tremendously quickened: inside the continental heartland of the more advanced countries, railroads and telegraph lines tied together even the most remote cities. In 1858 a first attempt had been made to lay a transatlantic cable, albeit, for the time being, with indifferent results. After 1840, when Samuel Cunard founded his transatlantic line in Boston, speedy and comfortable passenger steamers linked the two shores of the Atlantic and even the cities of the Far East with Europe and America.

Even if sailing ships still prevailed among freighters, steamers dominated passenger service; indeed, the latter, together with railways, had become so regular and frequent as to inspire Jules Verne to write the unforgettable pages of his *Around the World in Eighty Days.*

The globe had become "small," enveloped by the interests of the maritime powers. The world market was now homogeneous, solidly stabilized, and unified, and the time when a continental war could remain isolated was fast disappearing. Already on the far horizon loomed the sinister shadow of world wars that would involve all nations.[6] And this would come as an aftermath (at least, predominantly) of maritime war against trade.

For many years the powers had failed to agree upon a system of well-formulated agreements and rules about blockade and privateering. But the new situation generated by the interwining of economic interests upon all seas made such a system indispensable. On 16 April 1856, during the world Conference of Paris, convened to reorganize European diplomatic relations following the Crimean War, seven powers (France, Great Britain, Russia, Austria, Prussia, the Ottoman Empire, and Sardinia) approved a declaration which stated that privateering was outlawed and forever abolished; the flag "covered the goods," that is, enemy goods on neutral ships (provided, of course, they were not war contraband) could not be seized; the same right was to be enjoyed by neutral goods (not war contraband) aboard enemy merchantmen; freedom remained to capture enemy merchantmen and enemy goods they had on board, even if not war contraband; to be acknowledged as lawful by neutrals, a blockade must be effective in keeping warships continuously and permanently along the coasts and ports of the enemy so as to obstruct access to them.[7]

Even the United States had indirectly contributed to the Declaration of Paris. In 1854, the two leading maritime powers, Britain and France, then at war against the Russian Empire, had made known that they intended to conform, on their own initiative, to the principles that would later be incorporated in the Declaration of Paris so as not to hurt the interests of the strongest neutral, the United States, and push the latter to side with Russia.[8]

Yet when the seven powers in 1856 invited the United States to join them in signing the declaration, the American Union refused unless the text was modified to include the so-called Marcy Amendment (from the name of the American secretary of state). According to that amendment, all goods, even those of the enemy, which were not contraband of war, as well as enemy freighters carrying them, must be free from seizure. Because the maritime powers were slow in answering, the United States broke off the discussions but said that, being a weak power, it would not give up privateering.[9]

All this might have gone well as long as only words were involved. But now facts had to be faced, and it seemed highly improbable that the world's big maritime powers would accept the comeback of privateering or of a paper blockade.

Indeed, from the time of secession Great Britain had begun to worry about possible harm to its maritime trade with Southern ports, from which came cotton that was indispensable for its textile industries.[10] But when news arrived in London of the bombardment of Fort Sumter and the proclamations by the two American presidents, Great Britain realized that it was compelled to act. The situation was frightening. According to the Declaration of Paris, privateering was pure piracy, and Lincoln (to whom the rules written in the Declaration of Paris now gave comfort) in his proclamation had threatened to deal with Confederate privateers as with sea outlaws. If Great Britain adopted a similar course and sided with the North, would it not risk being dragged into a general conflict? But could it suffer the affront of what looked very much like a paper blockade without reacting, thereby abdicating its status as a great power? And by reacting, would it not be in even more danger of becoming involved in war on the side of the South?

On 3 May 1862 the British foreign secretary, Lord John Russell, received from his colleague the attorney general a detailed paper on the situation. It plainly stated that there seemed to be no other way to keep out of the hostilities than by officially noticing that a state of war existed (thus recognizing the Confederacy as a de facto government) on condition that both belligerents would comply with the principle of *justum bellum* and agree to respect the rules of the Declaration of Paris. The South must thus give up privateering and the North must impose an effective blockade.[11] For this purpose on 6 May Great Britain had contacted the French government, which said that it wholly agreed with such a position and would seek to uphold it.[12]

On 14 May, Queen Victoria, by the Proclamation of Neutrality, recognized the Confederate States of America, but only as a de facto government, without any diplomatic ties. The proclamation also made explicit reference to the old Foreign Enlistment Act, forbidding Her Majesty's subjects to enlist in either of the two armies and navies, to recruit personnel for these organizations, "to equip, furnish, fit out or arm" warships for them, or to furnish licenses for these ships.[13] This might not forbid British citizens from embarking on board a privateer, but it gave them the warning that anybody attempting to do so did it at his own risk.

The French minister for foreign affairs, Antoine Edouard Thouvenel, had already sent a message to the French ambassador in Washington, Henri Mercier, to be delivered to Secretary of State William H. Seward stressing the same ideas. The government of Emperor Napoleon III issued a neutrality proclamation similar to that of the British only a few weeks later. But the step, substantially, had already been taken.[14]

Yet Seward, changing the position always held by his government, had tried, on 25 April, to start talks with the maritime powers to offer a belated acceptance of the Declaration of Paris. But after a long negotiation, his offer was rejected.

Indeed, in his proclamation Lincoln had threatened to treat Southern privateers as pirates. If the United States now signed the Declaration of Paris on that basis, Britain and France would be compelled to acknowledge that decision and therefore to risk a dangerous collision with the Confederate States, thus starting a general war fifty years before World War I. A network of trade and economic interests had so entangled the entire world that it was becoming more and more difficult to remain neutral, as would happen disastrously forty-nine years later.[15]

What conclusions may be drawn from these events?

First, the proclamations by Davis and Lincoln were issued in an environment that differed completely from those of previous wars and produced the unexpected effect of internationalizing the maritime conflict. Given the homogeneity of the world market, it could not have been otherwise.

Second, if the North really intended to maintain its blockade, it must make the formidable effort to render it effective.

Finally, the death knell was already ringing for Southern privateers. The closing to them of British ports in the Bahamas, Bermuda, and, above all, Canada, as well as French ones in the Antilles, and the tightening of the blockade so as to hinder a return to Confederate ports all rapidly made their task impossible.[16]

The time for Confederate privateers was thus short. As early as the beginning of 1862 the institution was in its death throes. As Robinson wrote: "In April, 1861, the day of privateers had passed. But this was not then apparent. . . . They achieved individual success, but the institution of privateering was obsolete and no amount of industry and valor could save it. It belonged to a vanished order of things, like the very political and social structure which the Confederate States themselves typified."[17]

Meanwhile, Mallory had been going his own way. He had already sent a letter of instructions to Bulloch on 9 May 1861. Bulloch's mandate was to acquire six steamers in Great Britain, buying them if possible, having them built if necessary. To have the qualities demanded by the naval secretary, they probably had to be built. Because paddle wheels were utterly unsuitable for fast cruisers, they had to have screws. They needed to have range so that they could remain at sea for a long time. They could not be too large but had to combine power and speed. Draft needed to be limited without compromising efficiency. They would be armed with two big guns, at least one of them rifled, and two more guns in each broadside. Each piece needed to have a supply of at least a hundred projectiles, and each ship had to be completely fitted out and equipped with ammunition, food, and other supplies.[18]

For purchasing the big guns, Mallory advised Bulloch to contact Major Caleb Huse, an expert already sent to Great Britain by the Ordnance Department of the Confederate army.[19] As always, Mallory had shown superior ability in the choice of man. Bulloch quickly revealed himself the most capable Confederate agent in Europe. Born in Savannah, Georgia, in 1823, he served in the U.S. Navy from 1839, participating in the Mexican War. He then resigned and went to work as a sea captain in merchant ships.[20]

The outbreak of the secession crisis caught him in New Orleans, in command of the steamer *Bienville,* owned by a New York shipping firm. He immediately tendered his services to the new Confederate navy, yet with a conscientious sense of duty, he brought his ship back to her owners in New York. He then left for Montgomery, where he arrived on 8 May 1861. Bulloch was then "in the prime of life, being but forty years of age, though he appeared much older, thanks to a premature baldness and long sideburns, connected by a heavy mustache, that adorned a full countenance with a strong, clean-shaved chin, a not-too-prominent nose, high forehead, and frank, open eyes."[21]

When he called on Secretary Mallory on the ninth, Bullock was greatly astonished: he was to leave at once for Europe, according to a secret letter of instructions given him, which also informed him that his financial backers there would be Messrs. Fraser, Trenholm and Company, of Liverpool.[22]

That very evening Bulloch left Montgomery aboard the night train for

Louisville, Kentucky. There he destroyed all compromising notes and papers in his possession. Taking advantage of the fact that the borders were not yet sealed, he crossed into the North and traveled as far as Detroit, Michigan, observing everywhere vigorous preparations for war. By steamboat he crossed Lake Erie, landing in Canada, and through that neutral country reached Montreal by rail. There he took passage on the steamer *North American,* which reached Liverpool on 3 June.[23]

Like Napoleon, Bulloch knew the value of time. He therefore called at Fraser, Trenholm and Company that very evening. Finding it closed, he came back the following morning. Funds were not yet available for him; however, in the firm's local agent, Charles K. Prioleau, he found a kindred spirit. The latter (as he had already done for Major Huse) assumed full responsibility for opening a line of credit that Bulloch could use.[24]

Thus began Bulloch's financial problems, which were more serious than those of Huse because the Confederate navy was considered somewhat less important than the army. That he overcame these difficulties, which shadowed him throughout his entire mission, gave proof of his endurance and resourcefulness. Within a month after his arrival he had already purchased the ample stores of weapons, ammunition, explosives, and supplies that Mallory had ordered. In addition, still in June, he succeeded in having the keel laid for the first cruiser built in England for the Confederacy.[25]

For this tremendous tour de force Bulloch had to undertake, in great secrecy, a series of difficult steps. Unfortunately, his presence in England was known, and all the consular agents of the United States were unleashed against him with the objective of denouncing his real or presumed violations of the Neutrality Proclamation to British officials.[26]

After ascertaining the impossibility of purchasing a ship already equipped, and observing the several shipyards lined up along the Mersey, Bulloch signed a contract with the firm of William C. Miller and Sons, of Liverpool, for the building of a fast steamer of about 700 tons displacement and 185 feet long. The engines would be manufactured by Fawcett, Preston and Company, also of Liverpool. To save time, the model used was that of a Royal Navy screw sloop, already built by the same yard, appropriately lengthened and enlarged and fitted with a large set of sails. Her battery would be cast by the Blakely firm, which specialized in rifled guns of high standard.[27]

To fool Union agents, Bulloch gave the ship the Italian cover name of *Oreto* and spread the word that she was being built by order of a buyer from Palermo. He also succeeded in persuading the local agent of the Thomas Brothers firm, of Palermo, John Henry Thomas, to play the part of the supervisor of her construction and to register her in his name as the owner of the presumed *Oreto*. Finally, he hired F. S. Hull, from a prominent lawyers' office in Liverpool, directing him to provide legal suggestions and advise him how not to violate the Neutrality Proclamation or, at least, how to avoid committing a true violation. Bulloch took care, too, that no weapon, not even a penknife, was placed on board the ship until she had left British waters.[28]

All these precautions obtained the desired result. The able and suspicious American minister in London, Charles Francis Adams, did not even begin to nurture suspicions about the *Oreto* until October, when she had been under construction for four months and was well advanced.[29]

At about the same time, Bulloch closed a contract with a big shipyard, the Birkenhead Ironworks, owned by the Laird Brothers, located on the Mersey opposite Liverpool and among the major shipbuilders in Great Britain, for the construction of a second steamer, a formidable cruiser of 1,040 tons, 211.5 feet long, with powerful 1,000-horsepower engines. Capable of logging 12 knots, she would in time be armed with two 7-inch rifled pivot guns and four 4.5-inch in broadsides. Fitted with a huge set of sails, with bunkers capable of holding 350 tons of fuel, all sheathed in copper and supplied with spare parts for one year, she would be among the most advanced ships in the world.

The future cruiser was designated as hull No. 290.[30] Yet the name that would make her acclaimed and feared on the high seas and go down in history and legend, frightful to the enemy but bright and cheerful to the South, would be the *Alabama*. Indeed, according to Bulloch, she was "equal to any of Her Majesty's ships of corresponding class in structure and finish, and superior to any vessel of her date in fitness for the purpose of a sea rover, with no home but the sea, and no reliable source of supply but the prizes she might make."[31]

Unlike those of William C. Miller and Sons, of which no trace remains, the Laird shipyards still rise imposingly along the river, as crowded today as in the past with ships, cranes, and service elevators. Under the name of Cammel Laird and Company, they were until recently among the most active firms along the Mersey. There, cut and built into the rock of the riverbank, one can still see the building basin where "the *Alabama's* keel was laid," as goes the poem that tells the story of the fabulous cruiser.

Yet here, too, great caution was necessary. With his customary cleverness, Bulloch carefully checked that no weapon of any sort was placed aboard the ship while she was under construction, yet without doing anything to conceal the work in progress because excessive secretiveness would have alerted the enemy.[32]

Even before giving Bulloch his instructions, Mallory realized that many months would pass before the cruisers to be built abroad could go to sea.

He had therefore begun to investigate the possibilities of hastily launching one or two raiders directly from Confederate ports so as to have them operating while waiting for the completion of the certainly better and more powerful ships from Europe. For that purpose, he sent a board of officers to New Orleans to examine the few ships available there that could be converted into auxiliary cruisers.

On 17 April 1861, Commander Semmes, who, after failing in his attempt to get weapons in the North had been nominated head of the Lighthouse Board, called at Mallory's office and offered his ideas about launching a commerce-destroying war on the high seas. From personal observation, Semmes knew that the Union's strength lay in its economic wealth and that it should be struck precisely there.[33]

Mallory wholly agreed: he felt sure that he had found his man for this task.[34] Bulloch was a prudent, taciturn, astute, and able organizer, the ideal man to be sent to Europe on the difficult mission of bearding Union agents and having the cruisers built. Semmes, a daring and fearless old hand, extroverted, aggressive, resourceful, gifted with a relish for sensational stage tricks and capable of exploiting them to the best advantage for the Confederacy, was a better choice to become a successful sea raider than the secretive and introverted Bulloch. He could also quickly start the war against enemy trade with makeshift means, exactly what Mallory needed.

Mallory and Semmes then proceeded to examine concrete possibilities. These were extremely meager. The board sent on 17 March by Mallory to New Orleans under the chairmanship of Captain Rousseau to seek some ship to convert into auxiliary cruisers had found two small ones. One, the *Habana,* was a small screw-driven ship of five hundred gross tons, seaworthy, of a good standard, and capable of being reinforced so as to enable her to carry a normal battery of four or five guns. It was said that she could log nine or ten knots.[35] Unfortunately, she could carry fuel for no more than five days and lacked room for the crew of a warship.

Semmes read the report, which Mallory had received only that morning. Then, turning to the secretary, he said: "Give me that ship. I think I can make her answer the purpose."[36] A telegram immediately ordered her purchase.[37] Then Mallory put his bureaus to work to make the necessary arrangements.

The next day, 18 April 1861, Semmes received orders relieving him of his current duty and appointing him to command the auxiliary cruiser now christened *Sumter.* His officers were some of the best the Confederacy could provide, among them Lieutenant John McIntosh Kell, until then in command of the Georgia navy. This bearded and reticent man would become Semmes's right arm throughout a career of war at sea that was fated to become legendary.[38]

Semmes had achieved one of his desires. Several days earlier, in writing to his wife about his appointment to chair the Lighthouse Board, he had said that, should war come, he wanted a command at sea.[39] Indeed, for the Confederacy to have kept a seaman of his ability on shore duty would have been a tremendous mistake, one Mallory was resolved to avoid.

Raphael Semmes was then fifty-two years old, having been born in 1809 in Maryland. He entered the U.S. Navy when seventeen years of age and earned his stripes in the hard school of warships, since the Naval Academy at Annapolis had not yet been established in 1826. Taught to brave hurricanes and gales before he met the enemy, he acquired that intimacy with the sea that characterized seamen of the age of sails. He still remembered sailers with fondness. "The sailing ship," he wrote, "has a romance and a poetry about her which is thoroughly killed by steam."[40] Steeled by the hardships of the Mexican War, he was courageous, cold, and resolute, capable of keeping any crew under control in any circumstance and facing the worst rages of the sea with skill and daring. He thus seemed to have been born to undertake the mighty endeavor Mallory entrusted to him.[41] To him would be accorded the honor of flying the Confederate flag at sea for the first time.[42]

Semmes was then living with a friend in Montgomery.[43] His wife and daughter were in Maryland, but he was already making arrangements to move them to Mobile, where they would be relatively safe, for he warned them that once he was at sea, he could communicate with them only at random.[44] He began traveling on the day he received his new orders. In Mobile, which was making itself ready for war, he met one of his prospective officers, Lieutenant Robert T. Chapman. After "a hasty leave of a young wife," Chapman went along with Semmes to New Orleans.[45]

Upon arriving at the Louisiana port on 22 April and meeting there with Rousseau, Semmes thoroughly inspected his future ship, which impressed him favorably.[46] She was "a good, small steamship."[47] True, she appeared to be only a passenger ship, halfway dismantled and encumbered with useless superstructure (such as staterooms). Yet Semmes liked her look: "Her lines were easy and graceful, and she had a sort of saucy air about her" that made her appear suitable for her daring duty.[48]

Semmes immediately assumed control of all business. He had the staterooms torn down and set workers to make the necessary modifications in both her topside and underwater works, strengthening the deck and building beneath it a mess deck for the crew, building coal bunkers, powder magazines, and other installations. Meanwhile, he urged Mallory to send him the battery, including a boat howitzer, either by rail or by sea.[49] In New Orleans he also met his chief engineer, Miles L. Freeman, who impressed him very favorably and who was already at work on the *Sumter*.[50]

Semmes soon observed that more time would be needed to convert the *Sumter* than predicted. She was in the shipyard at Algiers, a suburb on the right bank of the Mississippi opposite New Orleans. There he lost every illusion of being able to work as in earlier times when he "could go into a navy yard, with well provided workshops and skilled workmen, ready with all the requisite materials at hand." In the great Southern port, where the almost total absence of merchant ships and ceaseless transit of troops gave evidence of the cruel grip of war, almost everything was lacking and all had to be improvised. Semmes had not only to decide personally upon the alterations to be made in the ship but also to draw the plans and explain them in detail to the yard workmen, who had probably never put a hand on a warship. Further, the finished parts and the equipment were exceedingly slow in arriving. The water tanks practically had to be "invented" and built from nothing.[51]

Nevertheless, progress was made in spite of obstacles. It is interesting to speculate why Semmes, who never wasted time, postponed his plans for sailing from New Orleans for an additional two months. Only now, thanks to the perusal of his personal papers, heretofore seldom or never used, is it possible to reconstruct the two agonizing months he spent trying to overcome every imaginable problem.

After having the main deck strengthened with powerful iron beams, Semmes notified Mallory of what he considered the proper battery for his ship: a 9-inch shell gun on pivot, to be mounted between the foremast and mainmast, and four 24-pounder howitzers, each weighing 13 hundredweight, in broadsides. The local Phoenix Foundry, added Semmes, could produce them all in good time. He was ready to issue the order and felt sure that Mallory would approve it. The ordnance already ordered might be used in some other ship, perhaps in the one being converted from the *Marquis de la Habana*.

Meanwhile, problems multiplied. The ship needed a new mainmast and a full set of sails.[52] As his letter demonstrates, Semmes evidently hoped to have his artillery pieces ready before those sent by Mallory had begun their journey via the appallingly jammed Southern railways. He was sadly mistaken.

On 26 April, upon learning of the capture by Confederates of the Norfolk Navy Yard, Semmes wrote again, asking Mallory if he could send him some 8- or 9-inch shell guns and a howitzer weighing 13 hundredweight with some ammunition to overcome possible slowness on the part of the foundry.[53] On the same day, in another message, he politely declined Mallory's proposal that he use some of the old and worn-out guns from the Baton Rouge Arsenal and Fort Jackson.[54] Then, in a third message, he informed Mallory that he had not yet received an estimate from the Phoenix Foundry for the four howitzers and feared that (owing to the great difficulty in securing the bronze), the cost would be extremely high so that he had to countermand the order until he had the estimates at hand. He suggested that cannon from Norfolk be sent to him as soon as possible. He would have primers made by a local chemist.[55]

On 30 April Semmes at last received the estimate from the Phoenix Foundry. Finding the charge of eighty cents per pound for the bronze pieces exorbitant, he asked to be authorized to order cast-iron howitzers of 13 hundredweight each, or that they be sent to him.[56] Soon after, upon learning that the Norfolk Navy Yard had several days earlier shipped him the guns by rail, he sent an officer to seize and bring them to New Orleans. The guns had been abandoned along the railroad, where they had been unloaded haphazardly to make room for some other supplies.[57]

All of this meant that the guns arrived much later than foreseen and desired. As late as 7 May Semmes wrote a concerned letter to Mallory informing him that the guns sent from Norfolk were not yet at hand.[58] When he actually received them cannot be ascertained. A calculated guess would be mid-May.

When the guns at last arrived, there remained the problem of their carriages, which had to be manufactured locally. Fortunately, Semmes succeeded in finding a good mechanic who was able to make an excellent pivot carriage for the big rifled deck gun.[59] Yet, because the guns had to arrive before it was possible to start building the carriages, these were not handed over to him until 30 May and those for the broadside pieces not until 3 June, the day the ship was formally commissioned.[60]

While still endeavoring to put together the *Sumter*'s battery, Semmes had to solve many other problems. The Leeds Foundry, the largest machine shop in New Orleans, which had undertaken to build the tanks for drinking water, was still unable to supply them by mid-May.[61] Further, there were no small arms for the crew, let alone ammunition, at least 100 rounds for each revolver and 120 for each rifle, or (if Semmes himself had to order the manufacturing of the same) at least three hundred pounds of gunpowder. Lacking also were twenty-seven hundred pounds of powder for the ship's guns. No one knew where it could be obtained if the secretary of the navy did not order its seizure.[62]

Semmes at last learned where the ammunition he needed was available.

On 7 May he asked Mallory to intercede with the army and seek to get what he needed from the Baton Rouge Arsenal.[63] Authorization apparently arrived quickly. With his customary determination, Semmes immediately asked Captain John C. Booth, the officer in command at the Baton Rouge Arsenal, to inform him about its availability.[64]

The hoped-for letter, copy attached, finally arrived from Mallory with an order sent via the Army Ordnance Department to Baton Rouge, asking that Semmes be given what he requested, although not in the amount he deemed necessary: only two thousand pounds of cannon powder and fifty rounds for each gun.[65]

Semmes immediately sent Lieutenant Chapman and his chief gunner to obtain the requisition.[66] The arsenal was slow in turning over the powder and sent it to the wrong place—to the state powder magazine of Louisiana rather than to that of the Confederacy. The state authorities exploited the mistake by seizing it all. A long and tiresome exchange of correspondence with the Louisiana governor followed so that the problem could not be resolved until mid-June.[67] This was the worst complication Semmes had to deal with; it wasted time when the *Sumter* was ready to sail.[68]

Fortunately, on 31 May Leeds and Company consigned the copper tanks for gunpowder and the iron one for drinking water. The latter was extremely well made and provided a supply of water on board for three months.[69]

Another problem was the crew. Semmes at first had thought that 84 men, including 12 marines, would suffice. Later he determined that he would need 107 officers and men. At last, realizing that there was more room on board than originally believed, he asked for 20 rather than 12 marines, as Mallory had proposed. So, exclusive of officers, the crew numbered 92.[70]

Enlisting men had posed no problems. With many good sailors in New Orleans lacking ships, there were more than enough volunteers, and it was possible to select the best ones.[71] Because of the poor communications in the South, however, time was needed for all the officers to join the ship. At last, Semmes had his muster roll. John M. Kell would be the executive officer, Robert T. Chapman the second mate, John M. Stribling the third, and William C. Evans the fourth.[72]

On 3 June Semmes finally had the Confederate flag hoisted on his cruiser, his officers and men came aboard, and the ship was towed into the river. Still, two more weeks passed before the ship could move. Semmes used the time for testing his engines and guns.[73]

On 12 June, after two months of frantic work and uninterrupted battles to overcome all manner of troubles, Semmes was able to send a message that the next day he would drop downriver and seek a favorable laying-up position from which to run the blockade. At the time, the enemy blocked both passes of the Mississippi with two large warships, the steamers *Brooklyn* and *Powhatan,* either of which could smash the little *Sumter* with a single broadside.

On 13 June Semmes tested his engines again, but the ship, weighed down with heavy ordnance and reserve ammunition, water, and coal, had a draft of about thirteen feet and was unable to log more than ten knots. Her armament was composed of an 8-inch rifled gun and four 32-pounders, each weighing 27 hundredweight.[74] At the time, Semmes did not know that a quarrel with the state of Louisiana was about to start over the delivery of the powder, which still further retarded his leaving.

At last, Semmes was able to communicate that all was ready and that he was prepared to inflict the greatest damage to the enemy in the shortest time. Further, he sent to Richmond a copy of *Reed's English Dictionary,* which would serve as a code book[75] and a copy of the muster roll of his crew, stating that the latter were of the highest quality and with a bit of drill at the guns would become excellent shots.

But now two more problems appeared. First was that of pilots, who were civilians and more often than not likely to find a thousand excuses to avoid the dangers involved in piloting a man-of-war. Yet Semmes immediately threatened to arrest any who were reluctant.[76]

Second was the increasing difficulty of running the blockade. During the two months in which he had worked feverishly to equip and man the *Sumter,* the U.S. Navy had blocked the passes of the Mississippi with still more powerful forces which the little cruiser could not confront. The only solution was to wait, concealed inside the delta, for an opening through which to avoid the Northern fleet and escape to sea.

Worrisome days followed in the infernal climate of the delta, the men tormented by a pitiless sun and swarms of fierce mosquitoes[77] in a game with the enemy that lay in wait for the Confederate ship but did not dare come up the river to capture her. Semmes had ordered lighthouse lights extinguished and beacon buoys removed. Of course, the Union commanders would not try to sail blindly up the treacherous waters of the delta, fearing perhaps that their own ships, with a draft deeper than that of the *Sumter,* might run aground and become easy prey for the daring Semmes.[78]

The last day of June was a Sunday. The *Sumter's* crew was preparing to enjoy a day of rest when a fisherman in a small oyster boat came alongside to say that the *Brooklyn,* the more feared enemy ship because faster (the *Powhatan* was a relatively slow paddle wheeler), had gone in search of a suspected sail.[79] Firing up, clearing the ship for action, and beating to quarters took but a flash for Semmes and his crew, all eager to get away from inactivity.[80] In short order the *Sumter* seemed to jump over the water, pushed by a fiercely turning screw, while from her funnels poured clouds of black smoke that, alas, also indicated her presence to the enemy.

Like an arrow, the cruiser passed close to a merchant ship from Bremen that had run aground, bypassed a little house on the riverbank where a small party of proud Southern women were waving their handkerchiefs to hail the men going to battle, and was beyond the bar. At last, the Confederate flag was flying at sea.

Yet now the *Brooklyn* suddenly appeared almost within range. The big enemy steamer had merely moved out a few miles and was hurrying back. Only the swift current had enabled the *Sumter* to reach the open sea before the Union cruiser could block the mouth of the river.

Now a race began. The *Brooklyn* headed for the *Sumter* on a collision course while stokers in both ships feverishly shoveled coal into their furnaces. The *Brooklyn* was then seen to unfurl all her sails to the wind. The *Sumter* immediately followed suit, while Semmes had the speed checked: nine knots. Because the Union ship could make at least thirteen knots, the situation for Semmes looked desperate.

Yet now began a duel in which Semmes, the old hand of sailing ships, felt altogether at ease. Not for nothing had he, while in New Orleans, modified all his sails and yards to be able to sail as closely to the wind as possible. And this he did, even at the risk of coming within range of enemy guns. Unable to match Semmes because she was less weatherly or her crew less skilled, the *Brooklyn* found herself against the wind and had to furl her sails.

Semmes's maneuver had been extremely risky. The *Brooklyn*, a giant compared with the *Sumter*, looked so dangerously close that Semmes expected her to open fire at any moment. But the wind began to freshen and the chief engineer coaxed a few additional turns out of the *Sumter*'s engines. With the wind foul, the *Brooklyn* began to fall astern to starboard. With his consummate skill in handling sails, Semmes had performed a true masterpiece of seamanship.[81]

Now the *Sumter* was sailing on the high sea. Semmes recalled: "The evening of the escape of the *Sumter* was one of those Gulf evenings, which can only be *felt*, and not described. The wind died gently away, as the sun declined, leaving a calm, and sleeping sea, to reflect a myriad of stars. The sun had gone down behind a screen of purple and gold, and to add to the beauty of the scene, as night set in, a blazing comet, whose tail spanned almost a quarter of the heavens, mirrored itself within a hundred feet of our little bark, as she ploughed her noiseless way through the waters."[82]

A History of the Confederate Navy

Three days later, not far from Cuba, the *Sumter* captured her first prize, the Union merchant ship *Golden Rocket*. Her crew was safely taken aboard the raider and then landed in Cuba; the ship, in ballast, was burned.

In the dark of the night the fire seemed to take on gigantic dimensions. The Confederate seamen looked silently at the scene. Semmes recorded: "The burning ship, with the *Sumter's* boat in the act of shoving off from her side; the *Sumter* herself, with her grim, black sides, lying in repose like some great sea monster, . . . and the sleeping sea, for there was scarce a ripple upon the water, were all brilliantly lighted. . . . The flames . . . now . . . could be heard roaring like the fires of a hundred furnaces, in full blast."[83]

That ominous fire that was rising over the ocean indicated not only the beginning of the ruthless war against Northern trade that would eventually drive the U.S. merchant marine from the seas but also the birth of the age of modern commerce-destroying warfare.

The news obviously raised an immense outcry in the North. Semmes was immediately labeled "a pirate." This was laughable because, unlike the old privateers (who, strictly speaking, were not pirates), no desire for prey animated Semmes's men, who were legally enlisted sailors. But anyone who introduces innovations in the bloody business of war inevitably becomes the target of insults by the enemy, who, as soon as possible, rushes to put into practice the same methods he had condemned.

The *Sumter* proceeded first across the Caribbean Sea, went almost as far as the Brazilian coast, escaped under the nose of the Union sloop *Iroquois,* which tried to block her inside the port of St. Pierre, Martinique, and then crossed the Atlantic.

On 4 January 1862 she was in sight of the Spanish port of Cadiz, after capturing sixteen freighters during her cruise. Of these, six were burned after taking off their crews;[84] the other ten ships carried goods belonging to neutrals. Not transporting contraband of war, they were bonded, that is, the captain and owners solemnly swore in writing that they would pay a fine at the end of the war.[85]

During her cruise, the *Sumter* had half a dozen Union cruisers snapping at her heels,[86] but their chase was in vain. In Cadiz, however, Semmes learned how fear of the great naval power of the United States paralyzed Spanish authorities. At first, he was ordered to leave within twenty-four hours; then, after he asked that he be granted the rights of a belligerent, he was allowed to remain longer, land his prisoners, and make some urgently needed repairs to his ship.[87] Yet he finally had to agree to leave, whereupon he sailed toward Gibraltar.

During that trip, while in full view from the famed rock, Semmes stopped two Northern merchant ships. He bonded one carrying neutral goods. The second, however, carried fifty tons of sulfur, which was contraband of war because it was used in making gunpowder. Semmes therefore burned her "in the sight of Europe and Africa"[88] while on the rock of Point Europe hundreds of people watched the spectacle through telescopes and binoculars.[89] So the *Sumter* raised the number of prizes to eighteen, of which eight had been destroyed.[90]

Semmes's reception in Gibraltar was very different from that in Cadiz. All the rights of a belligerent were fully granted to the little cruiser that flew the colors of the Confederacy.[91]

Trouble soon began, however. Not strongly built, the *Sumter* had suffered greatly from spending so much uninterrupted time at sea and braving the wrath of the ocean. She had begun leaking badly even before reaching European waters,[92] and her engines were in such a sad state that she could not raise more than twelve pounds of steam, not enough to put to sea.[93] Further, three fast and formidably armed Northern warships now blocked her exit.[94]

In addition, thanks to the clever plotting of the U.S. consul at Gibraltar, no private firm would sell her coal except at exorbitant prices.[95] Nor was it possible to obtain it from the neutral British government. When Semmes sent a paymaster to Cadiz on a neutral ship to try to buy coal there, the ship called at Tangier and the Moroccan authorities, intimidated by Union pressure and in open violation of international law, had him arrested, put in irons, and turned over by the office of the local U.S. consul to a Union warship that would take him to the United States as a prisoner.[96]

At this point, it was clear that the *Sumter*—her engines out of order and beyond repair and her bunkers empty—could not confront three adversaries, each of which was capable of blowing her out of the water. Her short and amazing career was over. It was a hard battle for Semmes, who wrote that "I . . . felt as if I would be parting forever with a valued friend. She had run me safely though two vigilant blockades, had weathered many storms, and rolled me to sleep in many calms."[97]

Moreover, the crew, which during the cruise had become like the commander's family, must be discharged—a very sad task for a seaman.[98] The ship was put out of commission while the crew was paid off and temporarily freed. Semmes and his officers left for London.[99] The former commander of the *Sumter* never imagined that his career as a commerce raider had just begun.

On balance, the *Sumter's* activity had been positive, revealing how farsighted Mallory had been in unleashing this new and unheard-of form of maritime war. By Semmes's calculation, the little cruiser had cost the

Confederacy less than $28,000 while the financial damage inflicted upon the enemy was more than ten times as much.[100]

Yet this was not the only result she brought. In addition to having for the first time flown the Confederate flag at sea, she had terrorized enemy merchant shipping. A wave of panic arose that impelled Northern owners to begin selling freighters to foreigners, a step that inflicted a worse blow to the Union merchant marine than if it had been sunk.[101]

Further, the U.S. naval secretary had been compelled to dispatch half a dozen of his best warships to hunt down the small cruiser, thus taking them away from blockade duty. The little *Sumter* had forced the enemy to pursue her with a naval force disproportionate to her effective power and in this way also inflicted great damage upon Northern naval operations.

Almost coincident with the *Sumter*'s cruise was that of another, even feebler raider. The latter's cruise, together with Semmes's, completed the first phase of commerce-destroying war.

In October 1861 the Confederacy was planning to send abroad two commissioners who, if officially accepted, would become ambassadors to London and Paris. They were James M. Mason of Virginia and John Slidell of Louisiana.[102] The ship chosen to carry them overseas through the blockade had originally been a passenger vessel, plying in prewar days between Charleston and New York and seized by the Confederates as enemy property. She had been incorporated into the Southern navy, converted into an auxiliary cruiser with little transformation, armed with a pair of small 6-pounders, and named the *Nashville*.[103]

She was a paddle wheeler, hence of little use for war purposes. Yet she was strong enough, twice as big as the *Sumter*, of 1,221 gross tons, and had very powerful engines.[104] The commanding officer would be Lieutenant Commander Robert W. Pegram, C.S.N.

After reconsideration, it was decided to send the commissioners by another route, first in the blockade runner *Gordon*, then in a neutral ship. Consequently, they were involved in the famous incident of the *Trent*, which will not be dealt with here because the Confederate navy had only an insignificant part in it.[105] The *Nashville* was also to proceed to England—to carry mail, said Pegram,[106] to distract the attention of the enemy from the *Gordon*,[107] which had the commissioners on board, say others.

The *Nashville* sailed toward Great Britain, keeping clear of the more frequented sea-lanes;[108] yet she had the stroke of luck of running into the Northern freighter *Harvey Birch* and burning it. On 21 November 1861 the *Nashville* entered Southampton. Her arrival caused a sensation; as the

Sumter would not reach Cadiz until 4 January 1862, she was the first Confederate warship to enter a port in the Old World.[109]

The ambassador of the United States, Charles Francis Adams, asked the British foreign secretary, Lord Russell, to deal with the ship as with a piratical craft (he did not, however, appear to be strongly convinced about his thesis).[110] But Lord Russell answered that the *Nashville* was a warship of a belligerent power, with a regular crew; Great Britain would follow closely the neutrality rules, which forbade substantially increasing the fighting power of any belligerent ship during her stay in a neutral seaport;[111] belligerent ships, however, might undertake any repair needed to be able to put to sea again. If ships from two opposing parties simultaneously entered the same neutral port, departure of the second ship had to be delayed forty-eight hours after the first ship put to sea.[112]

This declaration by Lord Russell was needed because the Union cruiser *Tuscarora* (which later would block the *Sumter* inside Gibraltar) was already moored at Southampton. The British authorities did not allow the *Tuscarora* to leave until forty-eight hours following the departure of the *Nashville* on 3 February 1862, after the necessary minimum repairs.[113]

The *Nashville* now carried in her hold many chests full of valuable English Enfield rifles for the army of the Confederacy.[114] So the moment of glory for the *Nashville* passed. Pegram knew how flimsy his ship was; therefore, he sailed first to Bermuda, then to Beaufort, North Carolina, after burning a second Northern freighter. Then the *Nashville* was laid up. She had destroyed merchant ships with a value far higher than her own and had compelled several Union war vessels to pursue her, carrying them away from blockade duties. Moreover, she had induced the British authorities to clarify for the first time the practical consequences of their neutrality and to deny once and for all the request by the Union that Britain outlaw Confederate warships.

The *Sumter* and the *Nashville* had played the prologue to the great drama of commerce destroying. This kind of warfare, however, would reach its climax only when the modern and powerful cruisers which Bulloch was having built in Great Britain were ready to sail.

S I X

The Ironclad Strategy:
First Phase

When Mallory planned to unleash his technological surprise of ironclad ships against the powerful Union navy, he was not indulging in utopian dreams. Even if the energetic secretary was gifted with a productive imagination, his ideas were always well grounded in facts. In this case, he was in an area already tested by recent experience.

The dramatic evolution in ordnance power had led the best ship-builders and seamen toward the idea of protecting warships with armor. Naval constructors had learned that to achieve such an objective they had to solve the extremely difficult problem of reconciling protection, speed, firepower, and seaworthiness, any one of which tended to neutralize the others. The danger existed that a compromise among these factors might not guarantee enough protection, or speed that would enable a ship to choose between fighting or not, or adequate firepower. Finally, the heavy weight of armor might affect a ship's buoyancy; this, indeed, seemed the most difficult problem of all.[1]

The two great maritime powers, Great Britain and France, had early begun to work on the problems. During the Crimean War, Napoleon III's navy had laid down a series of so-called floating batteries armed with sixteen 50-pounders located inside a casemate with slanting bulwarks, intended to deflect enemy shot. The casemate was as long as the ship and was protected by 10-centimeter (4-inch) armor. When fully loaded, displacement was about 1,700 tons; full length was 51 meters (more than 167 feet).[2]

The British rushed to imitate the French and built a number of similar craft. Some of these ships (the French *Dévastation, Lave,* and *Tonnante*) fought during the Crimean War, particularly in the Black Sea against the forts of Kinburn. They revealed not only a capacity for resisting the most terrible hammering by Russian guns but soon battered the forts into surrender.[3]

The negative side of these ships was that, in addition to not being able to make long trips except under tow, they used their own engines only to reach the site of action: they fought only while anchored and only against fixed targets, those on land. In other words, mobility had been sacrificed for protection and firepower. Clearly, anyone who wished to solve the problem of the ironclad warship had to find another way.

The spark of genius that gave a new dimension to the problem was provided by Stanislas Charles Henri Laurent Dupuy de Lôme, appointed on 1 January 1857 as the chief constructor (directeur du matériel) of the Imperial French Navy. The solution he found was simple and imaginative but consisted in part of a return to the past. He would protect ships, built in part along traditional lines, with adequate armor, balancing the weight of the latter by an increase in tonnage.

Thus was born the ironclad steam frigate in which the compromise between protection, firepower, speed, and seaworthiness seemed solved in a harmonious way. On 24 November 1859, the first of six projected ships, the *Gloire,* was launched. She displaced almost six thousand tons,[4] and her propulsion, as in contemporary unarmored ships, came from a combination of sails and steam. She carried thirty-six 30-pounder shell guns and her speed was satisfactory (more than eleven knots and more under forced draft). Her range, however, was severely limited—not more than fourteen days at eleven knots—and her general structure was that of the past.

It was nevertheless clear that the *Gloire* and ships of similar construction could sweep away all the wooden warships in the world. With this in mind, Dupuy de Lôme successfully proposed that France abandon the construction of unarmored ships. Meanwhile, Britain rushed to imitate France in December 1860 by launching the ironclad steam frigate *Warrior,* which was soon followed by several others.

At the same time there was born (or, rather, reborn) another principle, or myth, that of the ram. This had once been a formidable weapon (indeed, the best weapon of oared ships in times past). The dominance of sail seemed to sound the death knell of the ram: it was impossible to ram with ships moved by the wind and therefore lacking independent motive power or able to be conned at will. Now instead, many seamen (first the French rear admiral Nicolas Hyppolite Labrousse) held that steam propulsion, which enabled a vessel to be steered at will, called for fitting

A History of the Confederate Navy

rams to the bows of warships. The suggestion was quickly adopted by almost all the navies of the world.[5]

By 1861, then, in Europe, the two major maritime powers were well advanced in the construction of fleets of ironclads, even if they did not generally follow all the innovative conceptions they might have.

Yet the United States had not fallen behind because on 14 April 1842 Congress had accepted the proposal of a talented designer and naval constructor, Robert Livingston Stevens, to build a floating battery. The contract was granted to Stevens at a cost not to exceed $250,000.[6]

The vessel Stevens proposed to build was revolutionary. The ship, of fifteen hundred tons displacement, would be fitted with guns capable of firing cylindrical-pointed armor-piercing projectiles designed by Stevens himself; masts and sails were eliminated.[7]

The ship's potential performance is impossible to estimate. Costs escalated, and work on her was finally abandoned. Yet Mallory, recommending that ironclads be put into the line of battle, was moving along ground well tilled, so that his idea, in itself, did not constitute a surprise.

The real novelty lay elsewhere—in his proposal to rely on this kind of warship as the core of the future Confederate fleet and hence to seize the lead against a navy that had, some twenty years earlier, considered acquiring such a ship but had failed to do so. Indeed, the U.S. Navy also was planning to have some ironclads but not to use them as the bulk of its fleet and in no case as its exclusive mainstay. Meanwhile, Mallory was putting all his cards on the war of iron against wood, hoping to take off balance an enemy that would never expect to be challenged by such a daring adversary.

Although most seamen looked upon ironclads with little sympathy and considered them to be nothing better than auxiliaries or, at best, floating batteries, Mallory was determined to use them in battle.

As was true of commerce raiders, there were two possibilities: build ironclads within the Confederacy or acquire them in Europe. It appeared that the first idea had to be discarded. On 4 May Mallory had sent a letter to Captain Rousseau at New Orleans, asking him if it were possible to obtain armor for ironclads.[8] The answer could have been expected: the poor industrial structure of the South did not permit it.

Mallory's reaction was immediate: he must send an agent to Europe to acquire ironclads, as he had sent Bulloch for cruisers. On 10 May, at the secretary's request, Congress appropriated $2 million for that purpose.[9] Three days later Mallory called Lieutenant James H. North and alerted him to be ready to leave for Europe on a special mission,[10] and on the fourteenth he wrote to the secretary of the treasury asking him to put down a substantial sum from the appropriation approved by Congress.[11]

North's letter of instructions directed that he first go to France, a nation that was presumed to be friendly to the South's cause, and try to acquire an ironclad of the *Gloire* class. If he found that impossible, North must contract for the construction of two ironclads, one in France, the other in Great Britain, armed with the best ordnance available. The letter also suggested that North consult the most prominent experts in the field and specifically mentioned Captain Cowper Phipps Coles, Royal Navy, one of the most distinguished British innovators and planners. This suggestion showed that Mallory was aware of the most recent technological progress in the naval field. Mallory was clear about the kind of ship he wanted: "ships that can receive without material injury the fire of the heaviest frigates and liners at short distance and whose guns, though few in number, with shell or hot shot, will enable them to destroy the wooden navy of our enemy."[12]

Finally, the letter ordered North to collaborate with Bulloch and to give him any help he could. Given North's character, this clause would be the source of unending trouble. Indeed, in North Mallory had made a poor choice. Irresolute, lacking energy and initiative, slow in deciding and acting, feeble in imagination, stubborn, and narrow-minded, he was quite different from the energetic Bulloch, to whom he would be nothing more than a hindrance.[13]

A telegram from Mallory that North received on the day of his departure from America stated that the funds for him were late but that he should begin negotiating, obtain specifications, listen to the officers, and question shipbuilders, experts, and the like.[14] Whether this message provided North with excuses for his lack of initiative is not clear; yet in England he acted at first more like a tourist than an agent of a nation at war. After wasting much time, he limited himself to a sketchy external inspection of the ironclad frigate *Warrior,* which he found had too much draft for Southern waters.[15] He then decided to go to France.

What North accomplished in France other than acting as a tourist is not clear. No record has yet been found that can offer proof that he contacted imperial authorities in an effort to acquire useful ships. One could suggest that negotiations conducted in maximum secrecy do not leave documentary traces. Yet Bulloch, whose vigilance greatly exceeded North's, well documented after the war what he had accomplished, silently and clandestinely, in wartime. As for North, no accounts from himself or from anybody else have been located.

Only in late September did North contact Mallory in a message that was nothing more that a confession of failure: "Can do any thing in the way of building if I only had the money." [16] Mallory's reply, though formally polite, was scorching: "The Department regrets very much to learn that you were unable to purchase or contract for the construction of an ironclad war vessel, which could be invaluable to us at this time. But it is fully aware of the difficulties with which you had to contend. We will endeavor to construct such vessels in the Confederate States." [17]

Mallory had to reconsider the possibility of building ironclads at home. He had not waited until September to move in this direction. Perhaps North's silence prompted him to act. As early as the evening of 3 June 1861, after his arrival in Richmond, he had sent for Lieutenant John Mercer Brooke, to talk with him about the prospects for building an ironclad, also asking him to jot down the first calculations. [18]

According to his own testimony, Brooke immediately went to work, concentrating on planning. [19] At the same time Mallory decided to back him up with a specialized naval constructor and, after consulting one whom he found unreliable, decided (apparently with some doubt) [20] on the best. On 20 June John Luke Porter, future chief constructor, currently working in the Norfolk Navy Yard, was summoned to Richmond to call on Mallory. Similar orders went to the engineer in chief, William P. Williamson. [21]

Three days later the two arrived and met with Brooke and Mallory. Both Porter (who evidently was already aware of the problem) and Brooke had brought their own sketches and placed them on display. Also, Porter presented a model he had prepared. [22]

How the definitive project was formalized is not clear. Indeed, the question of credit for it provoked a long and acrimonious controversy between Brooke and Porter that lasted long after the war ended. [23] The attribution of proper recognition to either of them is a problem that is not yet solved and probably never will be. What can be guessed with some precision follows.

Porter, who before the war had taken an interest in ironclads, displayed his model, which, apparently, presented the same characteristics as the French floating batteries of the Crimean War and was intended mainly for harbor defense. [24] Brooke, instead, had in mind a true warship not only capable of steaming by herself but of fighting any enemy ship. [25] With such a plan in mind, he accepted Porter's model only in its generality. This included a great ironclad casemate with its sides inclined at thirty-five degrees from the deck to deflect enemy projectiles [26] and its lower parts submerged. Her hull ended (like that of the French floating batteries) abruptly at both ends of the casemate. Brooke instead proposed that the bow and stern of the hull be lengthened beyond the casemate "and shaped like those of any fast vessel, and in order to protect them from the enemy they were to be submerged 2 feet under water, so that nothing was to be seen afloat but the shield itself."[27]

This last characteristic, according to Brooke, would guarantee optimal speed and buoyancy because the hull would not only be more hydrodynamic but also be protected from enemy fire without the need to carry further heavy shielding. Therefore, the draft and displacement of the ship could be reduced substantially, a most desirable characteristic for a vessel likely to operate in the shallow waters of the South. According to contemporary mode, the ship would be fitted with a ram.

Here we may abandon the question of the credit for planning the ironclad. Enough to say that Mallory, soon thereafter, attributed the project to Brooke,[28] although Porter, five months later, writing to a friend, claimed substantially full credit.[29] Yet a scrutiny of the original draft, in the Archives of the Confederate Museum at Richmond, shows that the early Porter plans would *not* include the elongation of the bow and stern of the hull, which would have resulted in a "ship," and that Porter instead had stuck stubbornly to the idea of a floating battery, as he continued to call her.[30]

Still, all three men involved understood the urgency of their work, and the day after their meeting with Mallory, Brooke and Williamson began to look for the two prime necessities, engines and armor. It was a very difficult undertaking for the South because of its poor industrial infrastructure, yet there was a ray of hope: Tredegar. As might be expected, disappointment awaited them there. Joseph Reid Anderson, the manager of the Tredegar, told them that at the time there was not any industrial plant in the whole South capable of making the engines required.

At this point, the engineer in chief offered a proposal: at Gosport Navy Yard, near Norfolk, was the wreckage of the steam frigate *Merrimack,* which had been burned and scuttled by the enemy when they evacuated the yard and refloated by the Confederates. Why not use her engines? And because they could not be easily adapted to another ship, why not use the entire hull? Porter and Brooke were not pleased at the *Merrimack's* displacement, yet they did agree that her use would save a great deal of money and, far more important, time. So they reported to Mallory. The secretary accepted the proposal and sent Porter to Norfolk to inspect the frigate and make a sketch of her.[31] The three then would decide whether the project was feasible.[32]

The Gosport Navy Yard, located in a suburb of Portsmouth across the Elizabeth River from Norfolk, had been seized by the Virginia militia on 21 April 1861 following the bombardment of Fort Sumter and Lincoln's call for seventy-five thousand men to quell the Southern "rebellion."

A History of the Confederate Navy

The Confederacy had thus acquired a major navy yard, the only one deserving such a name, for the new Southern nation. On the night of 19 April a detachment of the Virginia navy commanded by Robert B. Pegram and Catesby ap R. Jones had taken over the powder magazine without firing a shot.[33] Yet, before leaving, the Federals had put the torch to several buildings and burned and scuttled the ships remaining in the yard, about a dozen, mostly old sailers.[34]

Among these was the frigate *United States,* so decrepit that the retreating Northerners did not bother to send her to the bottom. Rechristened the *Confederate States,* she would serve as a receiving ship. In addition to the heavy ordnance and priceless powder supply that fell into Confederate hands, there were a great walled drydock which the Federals had mined but failed to destroy;[35] about half of the buildings and offices; and the wreck, even if sunk, of the modern steam frigate *Merrimack.* She displaced 3,200 tons, was 230 feet long, and was capable of easily logging eleven knots (she had logged eighteen knots on her steam trial) and carrying forty guns.[36]

Although the *Merrimack* was among the best and most powerful ships of the old navy, she had been retired from active service and placed in the navy yard more than a year earlier, on 16 February 1860, to have her engines overhauled. Not satisfied with merely burning her, the Federals had scuttled her, but the water had saved her hull from the flames. Virginians had raised her and put her in the drydock on 30 May at a cost of $6,000. This was very little money for such a ship, for even with the great devastation she had suffered she was still estimated to be worth more than $250,000.[37]

On 25 June Brooke, Porter, and Williamson sent Mallory their report. The *Merrimack* could surely be converted into an ironclad and carry at least ten heavy guns because her hull was in good shape, as were her boilers and the largest and most expensive parts of her engines. Moreover, to build a similar ship would cost much more and take a very long time. The conversion cost was estimated at $110,000, mostly labor, for most of the materials needed were available in the navy yard.[38]

Making a more careful estimate, Mallory put the cost at $172,523. The expense of reconstructing the *Merrimack* to her original status as a steam frigate was estimated at $450,000, but a wooden ship of the traditional shape would have been incapable of facing the overwhelming enemy naval forces and thus would be useless. Converting her into an ironclad seemed an excellent solution from every point of view.[39]

After Porter inspected the wreck of the *Merrimack* again and submitted definitive plans, Mallory ordered Porter and Williamson to go immediately to Norfolk, the former to undertake construction work, the latter to supervise the overhaul and repair of the engines. Meanwhile, Brooke, who remained in Richmond, would see to the production and testing of the iron sheathing as well as the acquisition of heavy guns for the new ship.[40]

The Confederacy had detailed Captain French Forrest, an old and experienced officer, to command the navy yard.[41] Forrest immediately set about reorganizing the yard. Under his energetic leadership, the buildings were repaired, a navy hospital and pharmacy established, and the ordnance repair shops placed in working order. He also took care to send many heavy guns and powder seized in the yard to other parts of the Confederacy.[42] Moreover, Forrest was able to put not only the yard but the area around the city of Norfolk and the mouth of the Elizabeth River in a state of defense by laying obstructions, building earthworks, and placing coast pieces.[43] In this way, briefly, the whole area, including Sewell's Point, Pig Point, and Craney Island, was protected by about 196 heavy guns.[44] The navy, which during the entire war performed priceless tasks on land, serving scores of coast artillery pieces, manned another twenty-one batteries along the James River.[45]

Conditions were prime for starting work on the *Merrimack*. Porter began by removing all the burned parts of the ship. He then had her hull cut straight from stem to stern about three feet above her waterline (ship when empty). Immediately thereafter he started building the main deck, which, in the zone to be covered by the casemate, was planked and upheld by girders, whereas in the external parts, outside the casemate, was made of solid, bulky beams. This done, Porter began to raise the casemate framework. It was early August.[46]

From Richmond, Mallory (who had put more than fifteen hundred men to work on the ship) sent almost daily messages to speed the task, to insist that the work proceed at night and on Sundays, in other words, hurry, hurry, hurry. Time was worth more than money.[47]

The most worrisome job was Williamson's. The engines were in such a poor state that before the war the U.S. Navy had condemned them. Nor had their immersion in river water helped. Fortunately, to Williamson's aid came a very able officer, H. Ashton Ramsay, who had served as an engineer on the *Merrimack* before the war and would have the same billet in the future ironclad as her chief engineer. The two began to remove, repair, and overhaul the engines practically piece by piece.[48]

In Richmond, Brooke was wrestling with the problems of sheathing and casting guns. For the former he turned to Tredegar, which on 24 July accepted the challenge. The estimated cost was 6.5 cents per pound.[49] There was no rolling mill in the South capable of rolling plate thicker than one inch. At the beginning, therefore, it was decided to protect the vessel with three one-inch layers superimposed on each other.

As soon as Brooke obtained samples, he began to test them. To do so, he chose Jamestown Island, where the first English colony had been founded nearly three centuries earlier, and where his friend—and first-rate artillerist—Catesby ap R. Jones commanded the coastal batteries. The testing was a disaster. An eight-inch bolt fired from three hundred yards pierced the three sheets of iron as though they were cardboard and penetrated five inches into the solid oak planking.[50]

What could be done? Either building the ironclad must be given up, or Tredegar must manufacture plates two inches thick. Anderson went to work. It was imperative to widen the doors of the annealing furnaces,[51] install a new water wheel, put more hands into the rolling mill,[52] and slightly increase the cost—to seven cents a pound.[53] But the problem was solved. The ship would be protected by two superimposed layers of two-inch plates, which tests proved satisfactory.

Another problem arose, however, that of raw material. Tredegar had already used up its iron stock. Shielding with two-inch iron plates and other orders from the navy required almost two thousand tons of iron more than forecast.[54]

The only available solution, which later became the usual way to overcome the Confederacy's industrial weakness but which proved catastrophic in the long run, was to dismantle some railroad lines and use the rails. This created no problem when, as in this case, it involved enemy lines (those of the Baltimore & Ohio), whose tracks in the lower Shenandoah Valley General Thomas Jonathan Jackson had torn down to interrupt enemy communications, or Southern lines that were too exposed to enemy attack and indefensible, such as the one that connected Winchester with Harpers Ferry.[55] Yet even this was not enough, and appeals were made to the commander of the Norfolk Navy Yard to send posthaste to Richmond all the scrap iron he could gather. There were at the yard some 100 to 150 tons of residual iron, 1,000 or 2,000 tons of useless and obsolete guns, and 300 to 400 tons of old tools. All of this was very valuable to Tredegar.[56]

At last the plates were ready, but the poor railroad system of the South, already swamped with military traffic and short of flatcars, had no way to transport them to Norfolk. Some of the plates were dumped along the way and abandoned to give priority to other supplies, demonstrating how insignificant the navy's activity was considered.[57]

At Norfolk, Commodore Forrest was upset. He sent an officer to look for the plates, find and reload them, and try to get them to the navy yard.[58] Eventually, by a long detour, the plates were brought to Norfolk.[59] By 12 February 1862 Tredegar had at last completed its consignment of the plating, 723 tons in all, at a cost of $123,715.[60]

While worrying about the plates, Brooke and Anderson dedicated themselves to the guns. Catesby ap R. Jones, who had collaborated with Commodore Dahlgren in the U.S. Navy, recommended adopting big ten-inch Dahlgren smoothbores. Yet, as Tredegar was already producing fifty nine-inch pieces of this category for the Navy,[61] Brooke decided to place three of these in each broadside on the ironclad.

Then came the most important problem of the forward and stern heavy guns. Mallory stated clearly that he intended to have the ship fitted with the most modern rifled guns, of a new design, capable of firing either shells or armor-piercing bolts. This would be the second—yet by no means less important—technological surprise for the enemy.[62] The secretary knew (because Anderson had informed him) that Tredegar was outfitting itself to rifle cannons, something it had never done before.[63] Mallory therefore hoped that his request would be fulfilled.

Brooke's answer satisfied Mallory and, moreover, resulted in the creation of a piece of ordnance of the most modern conception, one that soon proved superior to any enemy cannon and to almost any cast in Europe, to rank among the most powerful muzzle-loading rifled guns ever built.[64]

According to Mallory, the cannon was superior "in strength, precision, and range" to any available in America.[65] Two models were projected: a 7-inch and a 6.4-inch. They were made, at least originally, of cast iron.[66] As their tremendous weight of 15,300 and 10,675 pounds, respectively, indicates, without their carriages (more than a locomotive of the time),[67] they were manufactured with a special kind of cast iron characterized by a very high specific gravity, that is, rich in iron and poor in graphite. It had exceptional resilience and tensile strength and was barely susceptible to dilating and warping because of its firing. At its breech, the gun was reinforced with six heavy wrought-iron bands, two inches thick and six inches wide, thirty-six inches in all, welded together. It could therefore fire great charges without the danger of bursting.[68]

To avoid the risk of an explosion in the muzzle (the nightmare of artillerists who used heavy cast-iron cannon), the designer invented a special kind of rifling with seven grooves. These were not alternately hollow and raised, as was customary, but made in the shape of elliptical bends, each ending in a tooth from whose apex flowed the next bend. These gave the muzzle of the gun a design similar to a saw-wheel (it was called the Brooke rifling system).[69]

Finally, Brooke designed for the gun a special kind of shell that had cogs at its bottom corresponding to the rifling of the piece. Over these was placed a sabot of bronze or copper that ensured the fitting of the projectile into the elliptical grooves and thus reduced the vibration that was the foremost cause of disastrous bursting in the muzzles of heavy guns.[70]

On seeing the plan, Mallory signed the order on 21 September. On the twenty-fourth Anderson accepted it and promised the first gun within two weeks.[71] Mallory answered by ordering more Brooke rifles; these the Tredegar promised to turn over by early November.[72]

Now Mallory made another significant decision: the formidable rifled guns of the ironclad, as well as the ship herself, upon both of which the South and he himself were placing great hopes, must be entrusted to an officer not only endowed with the highest merits but also of outstanding skill in artillery matters. On 11 November Lieutenant Catesby ap R. Jones received orders appointing him as the executive officer of the ship under construction, as well as another order to proceed immediately to Norfolk and there personally survey the testing and placing of the guns with the utmost speed.[73]

Unfortunately, Brooke and Jones made a great miscalculation in their forecast, which would have disastrous consequences. Believing that the ironclad would have to deal only with wooden ships and seeing how pressed the Tredegar was with orders, they decided to do without armor-piercing projectiles and to be content with conventional shells. The latter were fine if battle was only against old-fashioned ships but almost useless should the vessel be confronted by another ironclad. Yet in that summer of 1861, when, on 21 July, the Confederate armies were victorious on the fields of Bull Run in the first great battle of the war, as sunny days were slowly changing into the clear days of Indian summer, no one would have supposed that the technical surprise upon which Southerners were working with so much devotion might fail.[74]

Thus the building and arming of the first Confederate ironclad proceeded apace. The enemy, however, was also at work. In Washington, next to the White House on Seventeenth Street, there still is an unassuming building of gray brick, which is almost invisible between modern edifices. During the Civil War it was the heart of the Union naval power. The offices of the U.S. Navy Department were there, among them those where Secretary Gideon Welles and his deputy, Gustavus Vasa Fox,[75] meditated the moves of an as yet unclear naval strategy against the South.

Welles knew little about naval matters, but he made up for the lack with his determination and lack of pretention. Moreover, Fox possessed the know-how and experience that the secretary lacked. Lincoln, an expert on human nature, with deep insight had practically made Fox the true chief of staff of the U.S. Navy. Few realized it, but the quiet, unassuming, and careful Welles and the dynamic, genial, and strong-willed Fox would form, at the heart and brain of the Union navy, a formidable pair in which Mallory would meet his match. The duel would be dramatic.

The most extreme "fire-eaters"[76] often despised Northerners, saying that they were a nation of "shopkeepers." This might be true. Yet they were also a nation of entrepreneurs, engineers, skilled workmen, technicians, designers, and builders, not prone to let themselves be beaten on the field of technical progress. Even before the surrender of Fort Sumter, many letters asking about or offering suggestions for the building of ironclad warships had reached Welles.[77] The Americans, at the time of Stevens's project, had moved in this direction even before the French or English.

As could be expected (and as Mallory hoped), the reaction of Northern naval officers (except for the chief of the Bureau of Construction and Repair) toward innovations was rather negative and distrustful. In the end, thanks to the pleas of the scientist Dahlgren and also to the credit Lincoln gave to any technical innovation, especially ironclad ships,[78] Secretary Welles decided to ask Congress to authorize the appointment of a board of naval officers to study several ironclad projects and, if considered feasible, to build one. Upon receiving the required congressional authority, Welles on 8 August 1861 created the board, when the work of converting the *Merrimack* was already in full swing in Norfolk.[79]

Even if the Union moved relatively late, without the least intention of basing its main strategy on ironclads, it had an extremely strong and modern industrial plant. Once put in full gear, it would certainly not be slow in making its weight felt.

At the end of the summer of 1861, Southerners realized that the most immediate and potentially deadly threat to the Confederacy would not come from the East but from the West. In that vital area the enemy was unexpectedly seizing the initiative. Worse still, the Federals, compelled to operate in a zone where they too had no naval power, decided to play the card of iron against wood. Yet Mallory would be ready to answer in kind, and to rely on ironclads as well. But the industrial deficiency of the South would make it almost impossible for it to meet the challenge.

The Confederacy, eight times larger than Italy and five times larger than France,[80] looked immense, almost impossible to conquer and to force into surrender. This fear in the North grew after the Confederates at Bull Run showed their determination to fight to the last ditch. Of course, in 1861 armies did not just move on foot along muddy roads, ill-supplied by long lines of pack mules or wagons capable of carrying little. Now there were railroads, undoubtedly of immense value to the invaders, as well as to the defenders. Yet on such immense front lines to break off railway communications was, for cavalry raiders, child's play. And South-

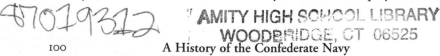

crners, being an agricultural people, had—at least in the first years of the war—an abundance of first-rate cavalry, far superior to the Northern one.

Seen therefore from the Atlantic coast, the task of Northern armies appeared (at least to skeptics) almost impossible, for the South looked boundless, a true ocean of earth, valleys, mountains, forests, and rivers. In such a landscape, the rivers appeared to be of the utmost importance. Here were the waterways that deeply penetrated the "ocean" of earth; here were the operational lines along which to "export" as far as the distant western fronts that onslaught of sea against land that slowly would take shape and in the end set up the Union naval strategy of the Civil War.[81]

In the North the first to understand this fact were landsmen, not seamen. As early as 15 April 1861, two days after the surrender of Fort Sumter, Edward Bates from St. Louis, Missouri, who had competed with Lincoln for the Republican presidential nomination and was now attorney general of the United States, had called his government's attention to the Mississippi: if a great combined army and naval force were created, it might seize control of the river in such way as to clench the noose about the South.[82]

The man who sought to give substance to such an idea was the general in chief of the U.S. Army, Winfield Scott. Old, heavy, and tormented by gout, yet still endowed with a bright mind and clear thinking, the former conqueror of Mexico City was a Virginian, but he remained loyal to the Union. From Cincinnati, General George B. McClellan, commanding U.S. forces in Ohio, had submitted to him a farfetched plan for an advance upon Richmond from the Middle West through hundreds of miles of forests that quite lacked roads.[83]

Scott answered that such a project was unfeasible. Instead, he proposed to move along rivers a great combined force of sixty thousand men in forty transports protected by twenty gunboats to seize control of the Mississippi River, down to and including New Orleans.[84]

According to Scott's estimate, such a force could be ready by 10 November 1861; meanwhile, the navy had sent west its own officer, Commander John Rodgers, who bought three riverboats, and by strengthening them extensively, converted them into gunboats.[85] It was a beginning, but Scott wanted more. In June 1861 he formally ordered the army's Quartermaster Department to build a fleet of ironclad gunboats, for which he asked an appropriation of $1,100,000.[86] The navy would equip and man them, providing the crews.

In mid-August, the Missouri engineer and entrepreneur James B. Eads, a friend of Attorney General Bates, owner of a firm engaged in raising wrecks on the Mississippi, a man of steadfast energy, boundless ability and talent, and a true organizational genius, was given a contract to build seven ironclad gunboats in sixty-four days. The formidable industrial plant of the North and its financial power made possible this—and more.[87]

Going back to St. Louis, Eads mobilized shipyard facilities. At drumbeat speed, lumber was turned out by thirteen different sawmills; three rolling mills received orders to roll iron plates 2.5 inches thick to lay over two and a half feet of oak wood. Machine shops all over the North (one was as far away as Pittsburgh) started with frenzied haste to build engines and boilers.[88]

On 12 October 1861, exactly forty-nine days after beginning work, and thus fifteen days less than estimated, the first ironclad gunboat, the eight-hundred-ton *St. Louis,* was launched.[89] The others followed.

Meanwhile, Union general John C. Frémont, the new commander in the West, on his own initiative bought two large riverboats and converted them into ironclad gunboats.[90] Thus the powerful squadron was almost ready and was commissioned at the beginning of 1862. It included nine ironclad gunboats from five hundred to a thousand tons displacement, plus three wooden ones, carrying a total of 129 guns.[91] It was a formidable force, expected to wipe out anything it met.

On 6 September 1861 the U.S. Navy had commissioned Captain Andrew Hull Foote to command the river squadron with the rank of flag officer. Foote was an energetic Yankee from Connecticut, a man who spoke sparingly, one of those Puritans who "prayed like saints and fought like devils."[92]

Because it was obvious that Southerners would build fortifications along the Mississippi, the Federal high command had had the foresight to fit out thirty-eight scows well protected by oak bulwarks, each carrying a big 13-inch mortar capable of firing 220-pound shells into any fort. Here, too, the effort to build them was astounding. Yet constructing the scows was a minor problem; far more difficult was casting thirty-eight mortars in the great Pittsburgh ironworks, as well as building from the keel up the special tugs needed to haul the mortar scows into position.[93]

It was an awesome undertaking. Had Southerners thought about it, they probably would have realized from the very beginning how ill-suited the South was to compete against the overwhelming industrial power of the North. Unfortunately, while at war, such problems are not dealt with in theory but on the battlefields, where one fights as long as a faint thread of hope remains and sometimes beyond.

Thus, suddenly, the threat of an onslaught by ironclad gunboats was extending its dark shadow over the Mississippi,[94] taking the Confederacy aback and raising in the South a feeling of deep distress.[95]

A History of the Confederate Navy

At the beginning of the war, from Montgomery and then from Richmond, New Orleans had been looked upon as a naval base from which to outfit some ships for sea. From there, the *Sumter* had been fitted out and had run the blockade. Later came the 800-ton *McRae*, armed with two 9-inch and seven 32-pounder cannons.[96]

On 5 May 1861 the *McRae*'s commander, Lieutenant Thomas B. Huger, had been ordered to spare no effort in making her ready for sea as soon as possible. Yet more than two months passed before she was ready. Even on 12 July, when she was finally given to Huger, her engines still needed several repairs. In the end, the blockade had been so tightened that she remained unavoidably trapped in the river.[97] She thus became the first unit of the New Orleans Confederate fleet.

Meanwhile, old Captain Rousseau, commanding Confederate naval forces in Louisiana, had also tried to gather some small ships. On 17 June he put into service an old but fast tug that he had purchased, furnished with some protection, renamed the *Jackson,* and converted into a gunboat by arming her with two 32-pounders.[98] Further, the navy bought and converted into gunboats two former but now idle privateers. These were the *Ivy,* which carried four small guns, and the *Calhoun,* with five. These entered service in mid-August.[99]

By this time, Rousseau had left New Orleans because on 31 July Mallory had him replaced by Commodore George N. Hollins.[100] Hollins's appointment showed that Mallory was becoming increasingly concerned about what might happen along the Mississippi. For some time there had been danger signals,[101] the last cry of alarm coming from General Gideon J. Pillow, commanding Confederate forces in Tennessee. Even though Pillow expressed faith in the impregnability of the fortifications he had built upriver from Memphis (Fort Pillow) and armed with thirty heavy guns, he insisted that the *McRae* be sent over to him because, he had to confess, the enemy, by means of a single armed tug, commanded the river and thus rendered pointless all the offensive operations he was planning.[102]

Pillow's message is extremely interesting. It summarized the tragedy of the Confederate strategy on the Mississippi: blind faith that fortifications on land would obstruct the river, yet acknowledgment that a single insignificant tug could nail fast the Southern forces by commanding the current. Moreover, Rodgers's three gunboats were nearing Cairo. Even had the *McRae* been sent, it would have arrived too late.

Meanwhile, apprehension in the West was increasing. On 24 June the Tennessee legislature asked the governor to appropriate $250,000 for naval defense. On 30 July Mallory, in a meeting with a board of officers, discussed the defensive steps which he believed had to be taken along the strategic lines he had already drafted: to build up also in the West a team of ironclads capable of operating not only along the rivers but on the high seas as well. Present at the meeting were Captains Duncan N. Ingraham and George N. Hollins, a naval constructor (most probably John L. Porter), and John M. Brooke. The latter strongly supported Mallory's ideas and sketched an organizational-operational plan for the ironclads. Clearly Mallory did not intend to stay on the defensive forever and hoped to overpower the North by turning the tables against it, forcing it to shift to the defensive.[103]

The next day Hollins, now a commodore, was sent to New Orleans. Was he the proper man? Not a young officer (he had been born in 1799), he was sixty-three years old. A veteran of the War of 1812 and the Mexican War, he had earned a reputation for recklessness, aggressiveness, and steadfastness.[104] Yet it does not appear that behind that facade there was the careful judiciousness required for his difficult task. Indeed, the commodore quickly squandered more than $250,000 for seven riverboats to be converted into gunboats. Two would serve on the lakes of Louisiana and five on the Mississippi.[105]

These were certainly not the kind of ships needed to confront the forthcoming threat, and certainly not the type Mallory wanted. Worse yet, Lieutenant Beverly Kennon, in charge of the Ordnance Department at New Orleans, had on his own account spent $146,000 instead of the $40,000 assigned to him.[106] Mallory sent the able Lieutenant Robert D. Minor to New Orleans on the pretext of reorganizing the ordnance laboratory.[107]

As soon as he arrived, Minor discontinued all unauthorized purchases, yet the expenditures had reached almost $500,000,[108] which put the Navy Department at loggerheads with the Treasury.[109] Such troubles beset Mallory at a time when he needed to concentrate fully on the problem of ironclad ships.

Even aside from the dissipation of resources that could otherwise have been used more effectively, Hollins's actions were certainly not those Mallory desired, since he had no faith in light wooden gunboats, which, furthermore, were paddle wheelers.[110] Yet the secretary accepted several contracts (mostly already closed by Captain Rousseau) for the building of three additional gunboats, two to serve on lakes and one on the Mississippi. They were similar to the earlier ones but a bit stronger and better suited for their task.[111]

In October the Mississippi Squadron was reinforced by a boat which, although of very poor quality, Hollins accepted. About a month earlier, when the illusion about privateering still had currency, a group of speculators had bought a large tug. Upon it was built a strong wooden frame covered with iron plate one inch thick so that it looked like an egg, a cigar, or a floating turtle. Christened the *Manassas* and fitted with a 32-pounder gun, the queer contrivance should have, according to the odd ideas of her builders, cruised as a privateer in the Gulf of Mexico.

As one could have foreseen, nothing came of it, and in October Hollins decided to seize it and incorporate it into his squadron. It was indeed a melodramatic event. When a platoon of Confederate sailors led by Lieutenant Alexander F. Warley arrived to seize it and her crew tried to put up a show of defiance, the determined Warley jumped upon the deck with revolver drawn. All hands scattered, and the *Manassas* entered the ranks of the Southern navy.

She was a poor vessel. Her single gun could fire in only one direction; her two engines were very old, one of them low-pressure, the other high-pressure, yet she had a solid ram forward.[112] Hollins decided to test her immediately.

Sometime earlier a division of the Federal squadron blockading New Orleans had daringly sailed up the Mississippi delta and taken a position where the river opened like a fan, at the Head of the Passes. On the night of 12 October, Hollins, with the *Manassas* in the lead, followed by the *McRae* and gunboats *Ivy, Tuscarora,* and *Jackson,* moved to attack. Disproportion of means was enormous—twenty Confederate guns, most of small caliber, against the forty-eight heavy guns of the steam sloop *Richmond,* the sailers *Preble* and *Vincennes,* and the seagoing gunboat *Water Witch.*[113] Still, Hollins trusted in the ram.

Approaching without being detected, Warley resolutely steered the ram *Manassas* toward the *Richmond.* Struck by the ram, the *Richmond*'s hull sounded like a bass drum, but a coal barge that lay alongside deflected the blow and reduced damage to a minimum. The scene that followed was worthy of a comic opera. Although both sides had daring men, neither Federals nor Confederates had yet learned the hard business of war and therefore had not bothered to send out patrols. Completely taken by surprise, the Federals crazily began firing their powerful guns in all directions. The *Manassas,* which had lost her ram and had one engine disabled, succeeded in limping away. Enemy fire had hit her funnel so that her crew risked being asphyxiated in the smoke-filled ship. Meanwhile, the Federals, fearing more attacks in such dangerous waters, hurriedly retreated to the Gulf while Hollins, concerned about facing overwhelming enemy fire, with equal speed retreated in the opposite direction.[114]

At any rate, the threat (if one admits that there was one) had been pushed back. But it was now time to think about the higher reaches of the river. There, on 3 September 1861, the farce of Kentucky's neutrality came to an end. Confederate general Leonidas Polk entered the state and

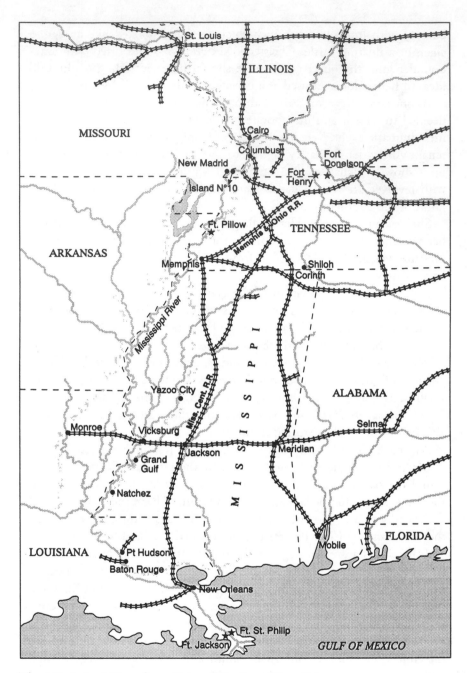

The Mississippi River from Cairo, Illinois, to New Orleans.

rushed to fortify the heights of Columbus, which afforded a good command over the Mississippi several miles south of Cairo.[115]

Thus Southerners persisted in trying to block the mighty river with land fortifications. Yet Polk, greatly concerned by the activities of Union gunboats at Cairo, soon begged Hollins for help.[116] The latter, in the late fall, sailed upriver with the *McRae*, now declassified to a riverboat, and his gunboats. Still, given the overwhelming strength of the Union squadron, he thought it wise to stay under cover of the forts and risk only occasional sallies.[117]

Yet something more was needed to face the formidable naval force the enemy was beginning to concentrate at Cairo. The Federal gunboats there were not yet ready, and at least one daring Southern naval officer thought that Hollins might have attacked Cairo and that he was excessively wary of the enemy. To this writer, this criticism seems to be poorly founded.[118]

It was, however, obvious that the construction of small wooden gunboats was only a palliative; Mallory had never nourished any illusion about them. Something else was needed to confront the enemy threat, and he was moving toward this goal.

Before mid-August, an entrepreneur from Memphis, Tennessee, John T. Shirley, was introduced to Mallory by his local congressman, John T. Currin, and by other people, including General Polk. He proposed building two ironclads in his city.[119] This seemed like manna from heaven. With J. L. Porter, Williamson, and Brooke busy working on the *Merrimack* and no navy yard available in the West, the only solution was to depend on private enterprise. Memphis was excellently situated and seemed well protected upriver by the strong ramparts of Columbus and Fort Pillow. In addition, there were men experienced in building riverboats.[120]

Events happened quickly. On 23 August, acting on Currin's proposal, Congress appropriated $160,000 for the construction of two ironclads at Memphis.[121] On the next day the president signed the law, and John T. Shirley subscribed to the contract in which he pledged to deliver the two ironclads by 24 December 1861 at a cost of $76,920 each.

They would be fitted with rams weighing no less than two tons. Their hulls would be completely shielded with railroad iron. They would be 165 feet long and their draft, when fully loaded, would not be more than 8 feet. Designs and specifications were by the chief constructor, John L. Porter.[122]

At the same time Congress also appropriated $800,000 for the naval defense of New Orleans. Mallory thereupon rushed to ask the secretary of the treasury for funds.[123]

A few days later the secretary of the navy received another substantial offer of help, probably unexpected even if coming from people who had had a close relationship with him for a long time. The brothers Asa and Nelson Tift, from Key West, Florida, had for many years been Mallory's warm friends. Prominent and able businessmen and landowners in Georgia, they had never had anything to do with naval shipbuilding even though Asa owned a maritime repair shop at Key West, and Nelson, president of a railroad company, was conversant with problems of ironwork.[124]

The brothers suggested to Mallory that they would gladly assume the task of building an ironclad warship according to new, almost revolutionary, principles. They believed that master shipwrights in the South were extremely scarce, as was properly cured timber, whereas there was an enormous amount of undressed wood. Nelson Tift had studied the possibility of employing ordinary carpenters, who abounded in a land of wooden frame houses. The ship would be built on straight lines, with flat surfaces. Its sides would be parallel, whereas the bow and stern would converge at acute angles.

The novelty (a true stroke of genius) was that there would be neither framework nor planking because the hull would be built solid by means of two-foot beams providing both strength and efficiency. The beams would be three-feet thick at the bow. The ship would be built from the keel up, and gradually caulked and painted as construction proceeded.[125] It was the principle of a self-supporting hull structure that would succeed a century later.

Nelson Tift had built a small model of the planned ship and showed it to his brother and, along the way to Richmond, to several prominent seamen both in Savannah and Charleston, among them the old and experienced Commodore Tattnall. He received general approval.

Deeply interested in the proposal, Mallory, who always encouraged innovations, had the model examined by a board of officers, including Chief Constructor J. L. Porter and Chief Engineer Williamson. They approved.[126]

On 26 August 1861 the Tift brothers sent the secretary an official letter in which they pledged to cede their invention to the Confederacy without any compensation or profit other than reimbursement for their expenses and travel costs.[127] Two days later, Mallory answered with a letter of acceptance and another stating that the two would operate not as contractors but as agents of the government.[128] The ship's plans were drafted by Chief Constructor Porter, with the help of his deputy, Joseph Pierce, and chief engineer, E. M. Ivens.[129]

The ship would be for the time almost gigantic. She would have a standard displacement of 4,000 tons and be 260 feet long.[130] She would carry twenty guns, among them four formidable 7-inch Brooke rifles. She would be propelled by three four-bladed screws, 13 feet in diameter, turned by a propulsion plant composed of three engines and eleven boilers, 30 feet long. These could develop more than 1,500 horsepower and give her a speed (remarkable for the day) of fourteen knots.[131]

Assuming that she would burn between thirty and forty tons of coal a day, the bunkers needed to have a capacity of almost a thousand tons. Her range would be almost twenty days at fourteen knots—better than the French *Gloire,* which still used auxiliary sails.[132] The armor would require a thousand tons of iron and the nuts and bolts nearly seventy-three tons.[133] The casemate of the ship would be protected by iron plates 3.5 inches thick in its most exposed parts, 2 to 1.5 inches thick in the remainder, with an angle of 30 degrees.[134]

A restless and anxious Mallory hoped that the ship could be delivered by 15 December 1861, yet he had to drop the idea of imposing any deadline and rely instead on the Tifts' ability.[135] The total cost estimate for the vessel remains unknown, yet the final cost reached $397,000 exclusive of her guns.[136] On the night of 1 September 1861 Mallory could at last write in his diary: "I have concluded to build a large ship at New Orleans upon Nelson Tift's plan, and will 'push' it."[137]

On 18 September, while the Tifts arrived at New Orleans and went to work, Mallory signed a contract for another ironclad ship with E. C. Murray, an able shipbuilder from Kentucky who had been introduced to him by General Polk and others.[138]

This ironclad, also to be built in New Orleans, would displace 1,400 tons, be more than 264 feet long and 62 abeam, and be armed with sixteen guns, among them two 7-inch Brooke rifles. It would cost $196,000 and be delivered on 25 January 1862.[139]

Mallory had indeed carried out an almost superhuman task: five ironclads were building between Norfolk and the Mississippi. The Confederates would now be able, he wrote, "with a small number of vessels comparatively, to keep our waters free from the enemy and ultimately to contest with them the possession of their own."[140]

This would be the highest objective of a small, daring navy that a few months earlier did not exist. Still, none of the formidable vessels being built had yet been launched. To reach that goal, the Southern navy must win a dreadful, deadly race against an industrially overpowering enemy. The very existence of the Southern Confederacy would depend upon meeting the challenge.

And now, all the faith, hopes, dreams—even illusions—of the South, caught as it was in the coils of an unequal struggle, revolved around the five ironclads that daring and dedicated men were building piece by piece, hoping that they might accomplish the unbelievable: reverse the situation, turning the tables against the enemy.

Meanwhile, the Indian summer was slowly yielding to cool days and the leaves were beginning to fall. October passed before work could begin in earnest in Memphis and New Orleans on the four ironclads that would operate along the Mississippi. Notwithstanding the supreme exertions of Mallory and his men, in the West the Confederates, in their race against the Federals, were more than three months late.

SEVEN

Toward the Deadline

Even though by only a bit, the Confederates were ahead of the enemy on the Atlantic front. Indeed, not until the end of August 1861 did the Ironclad Board created by the Federal secretary of the navy, Gideon Welles, send in its report.[1]

Discarding some fifteen proposals, the board recommended two. The first suggested building an ironclad steam frigate of conventional style, very similar to the French *Gloire:* 341 feet long, displacement of 3,296 tons, the future *New Ironsides.* The second was a hybrid ship, a lightly protected steam gunboat of 738 tons with broadside batteries, armor plate simply hung over her sides, and fitted with masts and sails. She would enter service as the *Galena.*[2]

These were not exciting solutions. Both were conventional ships, and their construction would require too much time, even for the powerful shipbuilding plant of the North. Moreover, they would draw too much water to sail on the shallow Southern seas, let alone sounds and rivers.[3] The board expressed many misgivings about the seaworthiness of the *Galena* and her ability to withstand severe pounding from heavy guns.

Constructor Cornelius S. Bushnell from New Haven, Connecticut, who had designed the ship, was particularly haunted by such fears. While seeking the advice of a skilled technician, he was referred to the engineer and designer John Ericsson, then living in New York.[4]

Ericsson had arrived in the United States in 1839, at the request of the wealthy, intelligent, and meddlesome Captain Robert F. Stockton. He immediately set to work to design the first screw-propelled ship of the

U.S. Navy, the *Princeton*. Launched in 1843, she was a true kaleidoscope of innovations. She was not only the first screw-steamer warship but also the first with an iron hull, with her engines situated below the waterline, working under forced draft, and fired wholly by anthracite coal.[5]

Unfortunately, during a trial on the Potomac, Stockton stubbornly insisted upon putting on board a cannon he named the "Peacemaker," a big copy of a gun drafted by Ericsson. The engineer had warned about its hurried casting, lack of reinforcements at the breech, and excessive caliber, but in vain. During the testing the gun burst, killing half a dozen spectators, including the secretary of state and the secretary of the navy. Stockton, who survived the accident, blamed Ericsson for "faults" that had produced the explosion.[6]

From that moment on, relations between Ericsson and the U.S. Navy were practically broken. The only person to speak on his behalf was Senator (and future Confederate naval secretary) Stephen Russell Mallory, who in 1853 asked that the inventor at least be repaid his costs.[7]

It was therefore with some anxiety that Bushnell sought Ericsson out. The latter listened to him, then issued his verdict on the *Galena:* she could withstand fire from a 6-inch gun, provided it was fired from a sizable distance.[8] Then the engineer displayed to an amazed Bushnell a full draft of his own: a ship, he said, that was wholly impervious to enemy fire.

Ericsson was fully aware of the strategic situation. The work on the *Merrimack* was so well advanced, he said, that the Federals would never match her if they chose to build a large ship from the keel up. The substance of the problem—a mortal race with the South—had not escaped Ericsson, who explained that the "well conceived" plan to build a large casemate on the *Merrimack* would make her a very formidable opponent, one no ordinary ship could resist. Finally, the skillful inclination of the armored shield would render the Southern ironclad impenetrable to projectiles.

Ericsson thus well understood the plan of Mallory and Brooke. Only an ironclad that was built quickly, capable of sailing shallow Southern waters, protected throughout by impenetrable iron plate, could face the extreme danger that threatened.[9]

The ship Ericsson proposed was not large. Its hull, only 120 feet long, would be entirely submerged. Above water there would be only an armored deck extending over the hull three feet on each side and about thirteen feet beyond the bow and stern, thus rendering the vessel almost impervious to ramming.[10] The anchor pit, the screw, and the rudder would be under the armored deck.

Over the deck would be fitted a revolving tower with armored walls eight inches thick, fitted with big guns and moved by an independent steam engine. The tower would be able to keep the enemy constantly under fire without the need to realign the whole ship. Toward the bow was a smaller square armored turret that would shelter the helmsman and the commanding officer. Air inside the ship would be made breathable by an ingenious system of forced ventilation activated by two auxiliary engines. A similar system would permit dispensing with the funnels during battle.[11]

Elated by the plan, Bushnell decided to take the reluctant inventor to Washington. Ericsson was cantankerous, eccentric, and proud. Yet before the Ironclad Board he gave an inspired illustration of the value of his project. At first skeptical, the board members were captured by the genius and simplicity of the proposal. On 4 October 1861 Ericsson got his contract.[12]

He had already started to work, paying no attention to skeptics or to sneers from many quarters.[13] He was playing against the South the most deadly card the Union possessed: the formidable and overwhelming power of Northern industry. A series of shops was mobilized: one would build the turret and its fittings, another the engines, while a shipyard would begin constructing the hull, and the larger Union rolling mills sprang into action to provide the armor plate. The simultaneous turning out of the several parts, with assemblage left for last, saved a tremendous amount of time. It was an advanced system of manufacturing, light-years ahead of what the poor and backward industrial plant of the South could do.[14]

Ericsson, with the tremendous industrial resources of the North at his disposal, was able to use only the most skilled workmen and first-rate equipment; work proceeded day and night.[15] On 25 October 1861, in the Greenpoint shipyard on Long Island, the keel was laid; three and a half months had passed since work had begun in Norfolk on the hull of the *Merrimack*.

At Norfolk, despite obstacles and problems, the Confederates sought to speed their work. If in the North Ericsson was the target of sarcasm and disbelief (his ironclad was labeled "Ericsson's folly"),[16] the same happened in the South, for many wiseacres were saying that the Confederate ironclad would not float, that it would capsize, that the crew inside would suffocate to death, and that the fire from its guns would deafen the men.[17] The chief engineer, Ramsay, received condolences from an officer colleague who said the ship "would soon be his coffin."[18]

As soon as he was detailed to her, Lieutenant Catesby ap R. Jones strove mightily to speed up the ship's outfitting. Already before being assigned to the *Merrimack* he had expressed keen interest in her because she appealed to his engineering instincts.[19] As a subordinate officer correctly observed, "No more thoroughly competent officer could have been selected."[20]

Nonetheless, problems escalated. Among the most disturbing was the unending difference of views between Brooke and Porter. Evidently because of his initial inexperience, Mallory had made a mistake (which he would not repeat) in not making a single ranking naval officer responsible for the construction. Although Brooke served as surveyor of the work,[21] his responsibility had not been clearly spelled out. As a result, a score of modifications were made to the ship at his initiative concerning details that evidently escaped Porter, a good constructor but not a naval officer. The thickness of the oak backing behind the armor was increased by eight more inches; at the bow and stern the casemate would have three gun embrasures rather than one so that the rifled guns could fire in almost any direction; the rudder chains were protected from enemy fire; and the number of hatches was increased to four.[22] Although necessary, these alterations required so much extra time that Porter, by his own admission, resisted them stubbornly.[23]

Not least among the problems that worried the Confederate authorities was that of security against possible sabotage.[24] Captain French Forrest issued detailed instructions for armed surveillance during the ship's construction.[25] To everybody's great relief, marines detailed to serve on board arrived on 9 December and immediately assumed guard duty.[26]

The work seemed to proceed well, even if hopes that the ironclad might be ready by January 1862, expressed in December by a young naval cadet in a letter to his mother, proved illusory. Too many obstacles remained to be overcome.[27]

Even if the ship as yet had no captain, she was soon provided with other officers. Included were some first-rate men in the C.S. Navy, among them Lieutenants Robert D. Minor and John Taylor Wood,[28] both experienced naval officers, and Hunter Davidson, the future genius of submarine warfare.

Obtaining enlisted men was more difficult. Even though the South succeeded in gathering a suitable number of officers, the same was not true for sailors. One reason was that the army, also urgently in need of personnel, had already enrolled in its ranks even those who had maritime experience.[29]

The duty of obtaining these men was assigned to Lieutenant Wood, who tackled his task with great energy. He first visited General John B. Magruder, commanding the forces defending the Virginia Peninsula between the James and York rivers, who might be more interested than any other in the quick completion of the ironclad.

Wood at first had a measure of success and selected some eighty good sailors. Yet Magruder then sent to Norfolk a number of discards. Mallory had to move personally: he wrote to his colleague in the War Department and asked that the matter be corrected.[30] Nevertheless, in February 1862 Captain Franklin Buchanan, chief of the Office of Orders and Details, lamented that the filling out of the complement was proceeding too slowly.[31]

After visiting other detachments in Richmond and Petersburg, Wood (thanks to an order by the secretary of war to military commanders to release all men with practical maritime experience) succeeded in putting together three hundred crewmen, observing with delight that they were first-rate.[32] An outstanding artillerist, Wood immediately started training the crew aboard the receiving ship *Confederate States,* concentrating on practice with the guns that Jones had carefully tested in February.[33]

Meanwhile, all the boilermakers and mechanics who could be found in Norfolk were impressed; they would complete the work on the ship's forward engine. Blacksmiths, engineers, and those skilled in fixing armor plate, with patriotic spirit, agreed to work until 8 P.M. without any increase in pay to speed the work.[34]

Yet much was still to be done: ammunition was late in coming, and coal was not yet stowed in the bunkers. In addition, there were no small arms (revolvers),[35] and not until 7 February was lubricating oil received from Richmond. Without this oil, the already poor engines would risk seizing up.[36]

On 30 January 1862 the Federal ironclad designed by Ericsson was launched on Long Island Sound and christened the *Monitor.*[37] Only ninety-five days had passed since her keel had been laid. Northern industry had performed a miracle, and the race was becoming so close that it truly hung by a thread.

Of course, the *Monitor* still had to be fitted out and armed. This process, which would take some time, granted the Southerners a short breathing space. Yet speed was essential because a new danger threatened Norfolk. In August 1861 the Federals had started a series of amphibious operations that would soon become a major danger for the South. As early as 29 August 1861 Union naval ships had broken through the Hatteras Inlet into Hatteras Sound, along the North Carolina coast. Further, on 17 November, they had captured Port Royal, in South Carolina. Several more operations followed. Then on 8 February 1862 the Federals seized Roanoke Island, opening the more northerly reaches of Albemarle Sound, as well as the canal that led to Norfolk. The enemy was now almost in the backyard of the great Confederate naval base.[38]

Southern efforts doubled. While the *Merrimack* was still in the drydock, on 11 February 1862 a young naval cadet with a special team of fifty men was sent to begin stowing aboard the foodstuffs: meat, vegetables, bread, and so on.[39] On the thirteenth, the ship was floated in the dock for a general test. Four days later the first ironclad of the young Confederate navy was launched and christened the *Virginia:* "There were no invitations to governors and other distinguished men, no sponsor nor maid of honor, no bottle of wine, no brass band, no blowing of steam whistles, no great crowd to witness the memorable event."[40] On the same day the ironclad was commissioned and her crew mustered on board.[41]

Unfortunately, even though the Confederate flag was flying over her, the *Virginia* was far from complete. Frantic work continued, with workmen and sailors standing elbow to elbow. The former hurriedly completed a series of finishing touches, while the latter, busy with coaling and loading ammunition, tried to get acquainted with their new ship and speed up her outfitting. The interior was quickly found to be uncomfortable. It was very damp,[42] possibly owing to bad ventilation and resulting condensation rather than to leaking.

Worse, what Brooke had suspected since the floating test of 13 February now became evident: because the displacement had been poorly calculated, the ship was too light so that the unprotected forward and stern parts, as well as the lower margins of the casemate, were above the waterline instead of being two feet below it. What had happened? According to one observer, Porter had mistakenly omitted in his calculations to subtract the weight of the masts, sails, and riggings of the old frigate.[43]

The ironclad had to be ballasted with hundreds of tons of scrap iron. Even so, the bow and stern were barely below the waterline and the carapace was submerged no more than six inches instead of the estimated twenty-four. Yet nothing more could be done. To ballast the ship further would jeopardize the tightness of her hull's bottom.[44] All this placed the ship at a disadvantage in the shallow waters where she must sail because her draft had been increased to twenty-two feet.

Nevertheless, the ironclad appeared to be—and was—formidable. More than 275 feet in length, amidships she had a casemate about 212.81 feet long, inclined at 36 degrees and 7 feet high. This was protected by a double layer of four-inch iron plate backed by walls of oak and pine, three feet thick. All was held together by long iron bolts almost two inches in diameter that crossed the bulwark and were secured with stud nuts and washers that were clinched and countersunk so that they would not be loosened by the report of the guns. Above the casemate, both ahead and astern, were two conical iron pilot houses, cast as a block, with walls more than a foot thick, with four loopholes each. Armament included ten guns—six 9-inch smoothbore Dahlgrens and two 6.5-inch Brooke rifles in broadside and two pivot 7-inch Brooke rifles ahead and astern. Two of the six smoothbores could fire hot shot and had their own furnace nearby. In addition to guns, the *Virginia* carried at her bow an arrow-shaped ram that weighed more than half a ton.[45]

The *Virginia* appeared to be similar to the "invulnerable ship" designed in 1855 by the Italian general Giovanni Cavalli, which also had an inclined casemate and rifled guns.[46]

Finally, on 24 February 1862 the *Virginia* had her commanding officer, whose detail came about in an odd way. Mallory wanted to commit the ironclad to someone he could fully trust, ignoring seniority of rank. Indeed, several men (among them the aged French Forrest, commanding the Norfolk Navy Yard) sought the billet. Still, Mallory decided that the only way to place the ship in the hands of a trusted person without subordinating him to senior men was to commission no commanding officer. Instead, Captain Franklin Buchanan would assume command of the James River Squadron, with the rank of flag officer, and fly his broad pennant over the *Virginia* as his flagship.[47]

Catesby ap R. Jones was understandably disappointed, for he had given his all to outfit the ship. Yet Mallory could not without raising complaints pass over all officers who were senior to Jones and who outranked him. Nor was it possible to give the duty of a flag officer to a lieutenant. Jones nevertheless did not hang back from serving the new commanding officer loyally, with discipline and sense of duty. Buchanan's commissioning, moreover, had been in the wind for some time, for at least five months, and Jones knew it.[48]

Captain Buchanan was relatively old, having been born in 1800 in Maryland. A cadet at the age of fifteen, he served in the U.S. Navy with distinction and commanded Commodore Matthew C. Perry's flagship during the historic cruise to Japan in 1855. Later he commanded the Washington Navy Yard and, after entering the C.S. Navy, served capably as head of the Office of Orders and Details, becoming Mallory's first collaborator.

In that position, he carefully surveyed all the work to outfit the *Virginia,* and it was to his credit that he detailed some first-rate officers to her. He was brave, resolute, and daring, qualities that probably motivated Mallory to select him.[49] Still, Jones (who nevertheless had the highest opinion of him) keenly observed that he had a hot temper, which in the future would cause problems.[50]

The letter of detail Mallory sent to Buchanan is worth quoting extensively for it shows the secretary's thoughts:

The *Virginia* is a novelty in naval construction, is untried, and her powers unknown, and the Department will not give specific orders as to her attack upon the enemy. Her powers as a ram are regarded as very formidable, and it is hoped that you may be able to test them. . . .

Could you pass Old Point and make a dashing cruise up the Potomac as far as Washington, its effect upon the public mind would be important to the cause.

The condition of our country, and the painful reverses we have just suffered, demand our utmost exertions, and convinced as I am that the opportunity and the means of striking a decided blow for our Navy are now for the first time presented, I congratulate you upon it, and know that your judgement and gallantry will meet all just expectations.

Action—prompt and successful action—now would be of serious importance to our cause, and with my earnest wishes for your success of yourself, officers and crew, I am.[51]

This letter is of interest for several reasons. First, it shows how much Mallory counted on ironclad ships to implement his strategy, persuaded that it was the "ultimate weapon" that by a single blow could win the war. This was an illusion. Second, Mallory requested a cruise to Washington, which was impossible because of the enormous draft of the ship. Still, the "ultimate weapon" must deliver an "ultimate blow." Several days later Mallory would ask for even more. Finally, there was the urgency for action. Four days earlier the Union secretary of the navy, Welles, had ordered Lieutenant John L. Worden, commanding the *Monitor*, to head for Virginia's waters.[52]

Meanwhile, Mallory had not forgotten the situation on the western waters and was counting on the four ironclads being built along the Mississippi River and especially on the gigantic one under construction at New Orleans. There, adversities had arisen that made those faced by the builders of the *Virginia* look insignificant. Moreover, in the West the enemy had the advantage of time.

At Memphis, Tennessee, constructor Shirley had to start by putting up a shipyard. He chose a place a bit south of the city, called Fort Pickering.[53] He then repaired the engines of two sawmills and put them to work. It was now possible to begin transporting timber there. Pine had to come more than one hundred miles by rail, while oak was acquired from five different sawmills, fortunately situated within a range of about six miles. Iron was obtained in part from Memphis, in part from the other bank of the Mississippi, in Arkansas. Railroad iron had to be used because there was no other source. Even this was not easily acquired. Confederates who were trying to armor the steamer *Eastport* on the Tennessee River diverted part of it so that the worried Shirley had to make up what he lacked by scrounging small pieces of rail here and there, each weighing between sixty and a hundred pounds.[54]

Meanwhile, Shirley vainly sought shipwrights in Memphis and New Orleans but they were nowhere to be found. He had no success with his requests for such from the local commander, General Polk, who sent him half a dozen when he needed hundreds, even though Mallory bombarded the general with messages asking him to fulfill Shirley's requests. As Mallory put it, "The completion of the ironclad gunboat(s) at Memphis by Mr. Shirley is regarded as highly important to the defense of the Mississippi. One of them at Columbus would have enabled you to complete the annihilation of the enemy." Mallory concluded by stating that the failure to send workers from the army would cause "ruinous delays."[55]

The shafts for the two projected ironclads were ordered from Leeds and Company of New Orleans, which would make them by reworking and modifying some old ones recovered from riverboats. Yet the company thus hindered the other naval constructors who were working in the Crescent City: the Confederates were arguing and struggling among themselves over scant resources.

Given this situation, one must not wonder that the construction work on the two ironclads at Memphis, which in the fall of 1861 were christened the *Arkansas* and the *Tennessee,* would not begin until October of that year and that Shirley, after trying to build both of them at the same time, had to give up and speed the work on the *Arkansas,* leaving the *Tennessee* behind.[56]

And over all this, the squadron of U.S. ironclad gunboats that the enemy was fitting out at Cairo was casting an ominous shadow.[57] Mallory had begun to worry about them during the summer and had sent to General Polk, commanding the Southern forces along the upper Mississippi, an able and resourceful naval officer, Lieutenant Isaac N. Brown, with the duty of supervising the coastal defense of the mighty river.

Born in Kentucky but later a citizen of Mississippi, Brown, almost fifty years old, was a quiet yet enterprising man, gifted with uncommon organizing ability and great daring, as proved during the Mexican War.[58] He had sailed all the world's seas from the Cape of Good Hope to Australia, twice circumnavigating the globe, and had served in the Naval Observatory under Maury, who had taught him both science and engineering. On the Mississippi he would fast become a key man for the C.S. Navy. Polk could not have received more valuable help from Mallory.

Brown had started by sending west all the heavy guns still to be found in Norfolk, some fifty of them. "No time is to be lost with regard to our river fortifications," he wrote,[59] feeling the threat growing. With practicality and timeliness, he prodded General Polk to procure the lumber with which to make ramrods for the cannons. He suggested the possibility of manufacturing the carriages speedily in Tennessee and Alabama and informed Polk that, in agreement with Maury, he was preparing to unleash torpedo warfare in western waters.[60]

After Confederates entered Kentucky, Brown committed himself to strengthen and make impregnable both the fortress at Columbus and Fort Pillow. He first had to reinforce the breeches of old guns and have special light shells manufactured for them so that they could be fired without bursting. While procuring ammunition, he sent on more cannons and carriages.[61]

Unfortunately, powder was scarce. Further, the boat carrying supplies for building river obstructions was diverted to other duties.[62] Brown nevertheless succeeded in putting up two small shell-making shops, sent fourteen 32-pounders to Columbus, had gun carriages built, and set to work to prepare underwater mines, or "torpedoes." At his request, Maury had sent torpedoes to lay around Columbus and elsewhere, together with two tanks full of explosive.[63] If Columbus and Fort Pillow became formidable fortifications, which would fall only when flanked because of operations on other fronts and not because of a direct attack, this was owing mostly to the navy and its able officer.

In New Orleans, meanwhile, the Confederates strove to complete the two great ironclads. The Crescent City certainly did not lack shipbuilding facilities. Across the river, in the suburb of Algiers, there were no less than eight shipyards with skilled workmen.[64] Yet these were already busy building small river gunboats. Besides, their location on the bank opposite New Orleans meant that materials had to be shipped across the river. For that reason both the Tift brothers and Edward Murray decided to locate their shipyards on the left bank of the Mississippi near New Orleans, in a place called Jefferson City. There, however, the yards had to be built from scratch.

Alongside the Tift shipyard, on 15 October Murray began building his 1,400-ton ironclad. First he had to write contracts through which to obtain about 1.7 million cubic feet of lumber,[65] then he busied himself acquiring engines, boilers, and shafts. Rather than building new engines, which was almost impossible, he bought the river steamer *Ingomar* whose four engines he planned to transfer to the ironclad.

These engines would power a mixed propulsion system including two screws and two paddle wheels of different diameter amidships, one abaft the other.[66] From the same riverboat, Murray recycled two Kentucky-built driveshafts about 24 feet long and 13 inches in diameter. He bought the others—19 feet long and 6.5 inches in diameter—from Kirk and Company of New Orleans. Yet these did not fit in the hull, and Kirk had no steam hammer capable of working them. In the end Murray persuaded Kirk to build one, although the driveshafts could not be placed until April 1862, when the enemy was tightening its coils about the great river city.[67]

Acquiring iron for armoring the ship was, if possible, still more worrisome. Murray had originally contracted with an ironworks on the Cumberland River in Tennessee. Yet the ironclad gunboats of the Federal squadron soon barred the river route, and the venture evaporated. Even the Clark rolling mill of New Orleans, after pledging to produce the armor for the ship (and cashing a fat advance of $5,000 from Murray's pocket), stated that it could not do so. Murray resorted to a desperate Southern resource—railroad iron. At Algiers he found a stock of about five hundred tons that had been seized by the Confederate government and purchased it for $65 a ton.[68]

The battery for the ironclad was the most motley imaginable: two 7-inch rifles, three 9-inch and four 8-inch smoothbores, and seven 32-pounders. These guns, observed engineer James Hamilton Tombs, would have to fire from embrasures so poorly designed that they could not reach a proper angle of elevation. The engines appeared to him quite unreliable.[69]

Yet Mallory placed all his hopes on the giant ship being built in the shipyard alongside Murray's. Upon arriving on 18 September, the Tift brothers, after finding a suitable place, began to build a sawmill, a blacksmith shop, huts for workers, and the building berth for the vessel. As usual, the South had to start building shops before it could construct ships.

The brothers thus faced their first difficulty—acquiring lumber. They immediately contacted all producers within a range of one hundred miles, and the timber (of which almost 2 million cubic feet was needed) slowly began to appear.[70]

On 14 October the first section of the keel was laid. On the twenty-seventh the able deputy constructor of the navy, Joseph Pierce, sent by Mallory, arrived in New Orleans.[71] Pierce's duty was to proceed with building the hull of the big ironclad. Well acquainted with his ability, Mallory had sent him to New Orleans with rigorous instructions: "The work in which you are to cooperate is of great interest and importance and I regard the early completion of the vessel of vital consequence." The ship, Mallory added, must be completed as soon as possible.[72]

Upon arriving in New Orleans and reporting to the Tift brothers, Pierce went to work. Obstacles were tremendous. Trees had to be felled, worked, planed, and transported more than 160 miles by rail to the ship. Nevertheless, in 30 days the bottom of the hull was ready; in 30 more it rose to a height of three feet; in 110 days it was complete and the boilers had been installed. Never in history had a ship of such size been built in so short a time. Even with the great ability of its shipyards, the United States had taken fifteen months (450 days) to build the hull of the steam frigate *Colorado,* which was almost the same size. Pierce explained that this result had been made possible not only by the speedy working pace (he had put six hundred men to work) but also by the distinctive self-supporting structure, which permitted the quick and smooth building of the hull.[73] This was done in spite of a strike by the carpenters demanding (and receiving) a sizable pay increase.[74]

Far more severe was the problem of the mechanical and metal parts: engines, shafts, screws, nuts and bolts, and armor plate. Here again (and in a far more grim way than for shipyards) the builders were hindered by the South's Achilles' heel, the veritable reason for its final defeat: the flimsiness and inferiority of its industrial plant.

The first headache concerned the engines. Originally, the largest mechanic shop of New Orleans, Leeds and Company, agreed to build them for $65,000. Yet, being overwhelmed with work and poorly organized, the owners asked for a delay of four months before delivering them. This being too long, in the end the contract was given to the firm of Jackson and Company, owner of the Patterson Iron Works, which pledged to produce the engines in ninety days for $45,000 plus a bonus of $5,000.[75]

At this point the Tift brothers decided that they needed a competent engineer because the one sent by Commodore Hollins, one Brough, turned out to be unsatisfactory. They turned to the skillful engineer E. M. Ivens, a civilian who happened to be in New Orleans as an agent of the Tredegar from Richmond.[76]

Meanwhile, Mallory, in whose thoughts the big ironclad was supreme, arranged to send the most capable chief engineer in the C.S. Navy, James A. Warner, without delay to New Orleans on an inspection trip.[77]

Ivens and Warner immediately realized that the propulsion power estimated for the ironclad was inadequate. The number of boilers, each thirty feet long with a diameter of more than forty-two inches, had to be increased to sixteen, the furnaces had to be improved and augmented in number, and the length of the ironclad was extended by twenty feet.[78] Jackson and Company immediately raised its price to $65,000 and postponed delivery until 31 January 1862.[79]

Now obstacles proliferated. There was not in New Orleans a single skilled workman capable of shaping the mold for casting the propellers. An appeal had to be made to Mallory, who sent one from the Norfolk Navy Yard together with two pattern makers and a blacksmith.[80]

The Tifts had to buy nuts and bolts from throughout the South, from

Macon, Atlanta, Mobile, and Chattanooga. As for the armor plate, after strenuous exertions to obtain railroad iron, Nelson Tift went on 15 November 1861 to the rolling mill of Schofield and Markham in Atlanta, which agreed to turn out a thousand tons of armor plate at a cost of six cents a pound.[81] From a technical viewpoint, this was the best solution. Yet it implied a further waste of what Confederates lacked most: time. The Atlanta firm could not start working until it had modified its machinery so that it could roll plate in the desired thickness, which was not before December.[82] When ready, the plates had to be transported to New Orleans via the disrupted and overburdened Southern railways. The result was that the outfitting of the ironclad proceeded with exasperating slowness.

There was also the problem of the driveshafts. These had to be wrought by steam hammer. Yet nowhere in the Confederacy, not even in Richmond, was there a shop with the capacity for working the big central driveshaft. The builders succeeded in getting Ward and Company of Nashville, Tennessee, to provide the lateral shafts at a cost of $3,000. Still, even this firm had to build an adequate blast furnace and steam hammer before it could begin working. Then, Ward and Company suddenly decided that it was unable to do the work. Distressed, the Tifts turned to the shop of John Clark and Company in New Orleans, whose owners said that one way or another they could manufacture the two shafts. Yet here again construction of a furnace and steam hammer was required. Not until 10 February 1862 could the Tifts state that the work on the lateral shafts would begin "at the earliest moment."[83]

Because the South was incapable of producing the central shaft, a makeshift solution was necessary. Therefore, recourse was made to one shaft that had been salvaged from the steamer *Glen Cove,* which had burned near the Virginia shore.[84] The Tredegar of Richmond said it would try to adapt it.

Yet even the Tredegar lacked a steam hammer of the size required to work such a shaft, which had been produced in the North. The work had to be handmade, with fifty mechanics working day and night, even on Sundays. It was also necessary to build annealing furnaces and cranes capable of supporting the weight of the enormous piece. As luck would have it, the Tredegar received the colossal shaft on 29 January 1862 and began to work on it. With exhausting toil, the shaft had been removed from the wrecked ship, then transported with great difficulty to Richmond by ox-drawn wagons along muddy roads.[85]

The shafts were now the greatest cause of worry. On 10 February the Tifts insisted that Mallory demand early delivery of the great central shaft.[86] On the fourth work started in New Orleans on the lateral ones and the next day the builders again pressed Mallory to provide the central shaft.[87] On the same day Robert D. Minor noted that the engines were still a long way from being installed.[88]

All this work seemed to proceed with exasperating slowness, in part because of financial problems besetting the Confederacy. Evidently foreseeing these, Mallory had decided to send to New Orleans one of the best paymasters of the navy with the special duty of disbursing officer for any expenditure relating to building the ironclads.[89] For this duty he chose one in whom he had deep personal reliance, Felix Senac.[90]

The arrival of Senac did not mean that all would go smoothly. The situation at New Orleans was already difficult before Senac arrived. Purveyors wanted to be paid in specie and refused treasury notes.[91] During the fall the issue worsened. When the purveyors finally agreed to accept notes, the Treasury Department, still strapped, instead of notes sent bonds that nobody would accept.

On 3 December a worried Mallory asked the Treasury Department for cash. On 22 February 1862, alarmed, he stated that the job of the Navy Department in New Orleans was made particularly difficult because of the slowness in forwarding funds. A few days later he underscored how this seriously damaged naval policy. At last, on 28 March, he sent the secretary of the treasury a strong letter. After remarking that the treasury bonds that the navy tendered as payments had been rejected, he stated that "having informed you that when we require bonds I would call for them—and that in all other cases we require Treasury notes—you insist that you will pay our requisitions in bonds whether we can use them or not, or, in other words, that our contracts in New Orleans must be paid not according to the stipulations of our Disbursing Agents and the rights of our creditors, but as you may dictate." Mallory said that he understood the problems the Treasury Department faced and would not discuss its policies. Yet he noted that these had seriously paralyzed the navy's ability "to build and equip vessels and to conduct its operations."[92]

Busying himself to the utmost, Senac succeeded in averting the danger that the purveyors would stop deliveries to the navy; yet he had to face imposing obstacles caused by the fluctuation of prices, in turn generated by rampaging inflation.[93]

After Federal gunboats made threatening raids up the Tennessee and Cumberland rivers, pushing as far as Forts Henry and Donelson (built by the Confederates to protect these watercourses, lest their control enable the enemy to threaten the heart of the state of Tennessee),[94] Mallory, pushed by Nashville's mayor, decided to transfer there the able and resourceful Lieutenant Isaac Brown, taking him away for the time being from General Polk's command and assigning him the duty of acquiring

A History of the Confederate Navy

some boats (pointed out by the mayor himself) to be converted as quickly as possible into auxiliary warships.[95]

Displaying his usual drive, Brown set to work to armor the steamer *Eastport* and began fitting out four more riverboats, but too late. On 6 February the Union ironclads under Flag Officer Foote battered Fort Henry into surrender with a hailstorm of shot and shell. The gunboats *Tyler, Conestoga,* and *Lexington* then immediately sailed up the Tennessee and captured the unfinished *Eastport* (which was then commissioned into the Union fleet, a bitter lesson that Southern sailors would never forget), while the Confederates burned or blew up the other ships. The enemy gunboats then carried their raid as far as Muscle Shoals, Alabama.[96]

Worse still, on 17 February 1862 (the day the *Virginia* was launched), Fort Donelson, which had been under attack for three days by land and by river from General Grant's troops and Foote's ironclad gunboats, sur-rendered—leaving in enemy hands 14,623 prisoners, sixty-five cannons, and two generals and throwing the heart of Tennessee wide open to the invaders. The capital, Nashville, fell on 25 February, the day after Captain Buchanan, in Norfolk, had assumed command of the *Virginia*.[97]

Now Columbus, threatened with flanking, became untenable; its for-bidding ramparts had to be evacuated on 28 February. The defense of the Mississippi rested on Island No. 10, which the enemy was already rushing to invest with General Pope's divisions and Foote's ironclad gunboats.[98]

The threat Mallory had felt coming was now grimly visible. In the West the enemy had about a three-month start over the Confederate navy and was taking advantage of it in a remorseless and uncompromising way.

To be in time to oppose the enemy with ironclads (the only weapon capable of turning the tide of battle), the Confederacy had first to hamper, slow down as much as possible, and perhaps stop the adversary's pressure and second to make every exertion to speed up the building of the great armored ships.

Stop the enemy? How? And where? Mallory, together with the other Confederate leaders, now had to make a strategic choice upon which much, possibly all, depended. The danger from the upper river had been clear from the beginning. The Federals' construction of a formidable fleet of ironclad gunboats was all too evident. Secret Confederate agents who had infiltrated the North's naval shipyards at St. Louis had sent report after report about an imminent attack in force by enemy naval vessels with New Orleans as their final objective.[99]

The Confederates could not know what the Federals' real purpose was. Since 7 November 1861 the most brilliant man among Northern naval leaders, Gustavus Vasa Fox, had conceived the daring plan to break through the Mississippi Delta and attack New Orleans by sea. In a secret top meeting on the fifteenth, President Lincoln and Union general in chief George B. McClellan had approved the plan. On 9 January 1862 Captain David Glasgow Farragut had been detailed to command a new, powerful Gulf Blockading Squadron, including twenty-six warships and twenty-one mortar boats fitted with big 13-inch mortars capable of crushing any defensive work. Nor could the Confederates know that Farragut had hoisted his pennant of flag officer on the first-rate steam sloop *Hartford*, nor, in the end, that his task, once his forces were assembled at the mouths of the Mississippi, was to break through and take New Orleans.[100]

On 24 February Farragut was advised that seventeen blue-water gunboats would be added to his squadron.[101] He now could begin the slow, wearisome work of bringing his fleet across the bar into the delta.[102]

This did not greatly concern the Confederate leaders, who had seen Union ships undertake such a move to tighten the blockade. Yet somebody in New Orleans was frightened and raised the cry of alarm. Indeed, at the end of January local newspapers expressed concern over the great naval array under Farragut. Yet the latter's objectives still did not look clear.[103] Even General Mansfield Lovell, commanding Southern forces in New Orleans, as late as 27 February believed that the threat of the Union naval forces gathering at the Mississippi's delta would not be directed against the great port city.[104]

To face the twin dangers that were gathering, the C.S. Navy could enjoy the major strategic edge of interior lines, which would enable it to concentrate against whichever of the two threats looked closer. Yet such a concentration of force (or, better, of weakness) could do nothing more than retard the enemy's pace and so allow the Confederates to hold their own until their ironclads entered service. Given the frantic Confederate struggle against time, even a modest delay of the enemy's advance seemed vital.

In such a situation, it seems clear that Mallory considered the impending threat from upriver substantially more urgent, and he acted accordingly. He was also persuaded (and not without reason, even if it came back to the illusion of the "ultimate weapon") that the two big ironclads being built in New Orleans, once commissioned, would sweep every enemy ship from the Gulf "in ten days."[105] Moreover, the Union fleet was composed of wooden ships wholly unable to stand up to an ironclad.

The attack from the northern side had to be stopped or slowed down. As early as 13 November 1861 Mallory had detailed to New Orleans another able naval officer, Captain John K. Mitchell, to take charge of the small squadron that was then near Columbus.[106] Yet at the end of January

1862, with the situation worsening, Hollins personally assumed command of the forces on the upper river and left Mitchell in temporary command at New Orleans.[107]

The Confederacy had made remarkable efforts to put a flotilla together. Hollins could now marshal the gunboats *McRae, General Polk, Ivy, Jackson,* and *Calhoun,* with some twenty guns. To these were added the *Pontchartrain, Maurepas,* and *Livingston,* which were commissioned between the end of January and the end of February 1862.[108]

Moreover, in August 1861, trying to seek ways to prevent the enemy naval forces from descending the river, the Confederates had decided to convert two large drydocks anchored near New Orleans into floating batteries that could be towed upriver and placed in some strategic position.[109] The work had begun in earnest in September 1861. When the first, christened the *New Orleans,* carrying twenty guns, was finally ready, she was given to Lieutenant John J. Guthrie as commanding officer, with nine other officers and twenty-five men. On about 10 December, after being towed upriver, she was anchored near Island No. 10.[110] The other floating battery, the *Memphis,* was being converted so slowly that she would probably never be able to leave New Orleans, for as late as the end of 1861 she was still unmanned.[111]

The navy contributed to the building and fitting out of these floating batteries and put them into commission, as well as the gunboats already mentioned. They all might be useful for a delaying action that would both slow down the enemy and buy time to outfit the ironclads.

Yet one must question how much this all might have contributed to worsening both the delays and the obstacles that harassed the builders of the big ironclads; also, if diverting a sizable part of the dwindling resources of the South did not in the end cause more losses than gains; and, finally, if this was not, in fact, an example of a detrimentally dispersive policy.

Interference by the army into naval matters came from the new commander of land forces at New Orleans, General Lovell, who on 7 October 1861 had relieved General David E. Twiggs. Lovell had usually cooperated with the navy. For some time he had sought to coordinate land and naval forces; yet both President Davis and the secretary of war had repeatedly told him that he had no authority over the navy.[112]

Still, under pressure from local congressmen, the House had on 14 January 1862 approved the organization of a corps "for special and temporary services on Western Waters." On the same day the secretary of war ordered Lovell to seize fourteen riverboats.[113] The secretary then told Lovell to put together with them a naval force that would have no connection with the navy; it would be wholly dependent upon the army and recruit its crews from riverboatmen. The boats would be strengthened forward by iron rams and fitted with a heavy gun: in other words, they would be ram-gunboats. Commanding officer of the flotilla, designated the River Defense Fleet, would be river captain James E. Montgomery.[114]

To complicate matters further, the governor of Louisiana fitted out two small state-owned gunboats. The cost to equip the River Defense Fleet was fantastic: $1,363,000, at a time when the navy, which was progressing in fitting out the only ships that might effectively confront the enemy, was complaining of a shortage of funds.[115]

Still, Captain Montgomery's ram-gunboats would be met by their counterpart. In the North, Charles Ellet, Jr., an engineer, inventor of suspension bridges, and prophet of the ram, had been detailed by Secretary of War Edwin M. Stanton to perform a similar task. On 27 March 1862 Ellet was commissioned to build a flotilla of battering rams, to be constructed by converting seven riverboats. They would carry no guns, yet, strengthened by three gigantic beams fitted from bow to stern, they would be able to deliver blows that Montgomery's could only dream about. As in the South, the rams were assigned to the army, not to the navy, and Ellet was commissioned to command them with the rank of colonel.[116]

All these threats stimulated the Confederates to quicken the fitting out of the only ships that could turn the situation—the ironclads. Of the two under construction in New Orleans, Murray's seemed almost ready. At the end of January she had been christened the *Louisiana*. Lieutenant Robert D. Minor, then chief of the Naval Ordnance Laboratory in the Crescent City, wrote Mallory on 31 January 1862: "The *Louisiana* will be launched on Monday or Wednesday the third or fifth of February—no machinery in—but all ready to be put on board." He stated that the casemate had not yet been armored but that, as soon as she was launched, she would be shielded with double layers of railroad iron. He concluded optimistically: "In three weeks she will be ready for her armament. Has great capacity for fuel, water, and provisions." He added that the vessel was two-thirds completed.[117]

On 6 February the *Louisiana,* though largely incomplete, was launched. She slipped smoothly into the water, impressing a huge crowd to whom she appeared very powerful. Unfortunately, she still lacked her armor, engines, and all of her weapons, and her shafts were not ready.[118] On 2 March Mallory detailed Commander Charles F. McIntosh to be her captain.[119] Upon arriving in New Orleans, the latter immediately started working to overcome the great obstacles that still hindered her completion.

In his diary Robert D. Minor noted that he had several misgivings about the other and larger ironclad because she depended too much for buoyancy amidships, while her bow and stern tended to pull downward, threatening to separate the ship into three pieces. Yet he had already prepared a correction—the application of strong tie beams. According to his calculations, the draft of the ironclad would be no less than fourteen feet three inches, perhaps more. He then pointed out the true problem: the foundation bearing slab for the engines, the boilers, and the supports for the driveshafts had been installed thirty days earlier, yet the Tifts lamented that everything else—engines, shafts, guns—was slow in coming in.[120]

The guns involved complication after complication. Originally, Mallory on 14 October 1861 had written that the ironclad should have sixteen guns, with the two forward and those in the stern being extremely powerful rifles. All the pieces would be cast in New Orleans.[121] Upon learning that rifled guns cast there were not reliable,[122] on 25 January the secretary had directed that only the twelve broadside smoothbores, as well as their carriages, would be made in New Orleans. All this bouncing to and fro had greatly retarded the provision of the weaponry. Resolved that the ironclad must have the maximum destructive power, Mallory decreed that she should have not two but four bow and stern guns and that they would be powerful 7-inch Brookes weighing six tons each.[123]

The manufacture of the carriages for the four great rifles began on 17 February.[124] On the twenty-fourth Mallory brought pressure to bear on Captain Mitchell to have both the other guns and all the carriages ready as soon as possible even if night work were necessary.[125]

Both in New Orleans and in Memphis the struggle against time was becoming frantic and agonizing. At Jackson, Mississippi, General Beauregard, commanding the Confederate troops in Mississippi, always sensitive to naval problems, began to worry about the level of completion of the *Arkansas* and the *Tennessee*. Like constructor Shirley, he knew that the two ironclads had greater value for the Confederacy than "many regiments."[126] He therefore sent one of his officers, Captain John J. Guthrie, to inspect the conditions of the two vessels in Memphis.[127] Some days later Guthrie reported that only the keel and framework of the *Tennessee* had been completed and estimated that she would not be ready for at least six weeks; his most optimistic forecast was late April. The *Arkansas* was more advanced.[128]

A few days later the *Arkansas* received her executive officer, Lieutenant Henry Kennedy Stevens, transferred from Charleston to speed up work on her as much as possible.[129] His first impressions were not good. Work on the ironclad progressed slowly, and speeding it up looked very difficult.[130] Yet, fighting against many obstacles, he succeeded in rushing the work toward completion of the ship.[131]

Meanwhile, on 6 March, the Union ironclads and mortar boats had started a destructive bombardment against Island No. 10.

Yet, first in the minds of everybody was the giant ship being built in New Orleans. The *Virginia* had proved her mettle against the Union navy, and Mallory was led to believe that the New Orleans ironclad would be able to sweep every Gulf port clear of enemy ships in ten days—again the illusion of the "ultimate weapon."[132]

Nevertheless, on 15 March Mallory felt compelled to utter a cry of agony: "The Tredegar Works has disappointed us terribly," he wrote to the Tifts. "The shaft is not ready and, although promised from day to day, may not be ready for a week." He asked that a substitute be found immediately; still, he knew well that it was impossible to do so. He then prodded the Tifts to "work night and day to get your ship done without regard to expense."[133]

On the next day, the bombardment of Island No. 10 began. On the seventeenth Mallory telegraphed that the big driveshaft would leave Richmond in two days.[134] On the twentieth, however, he telegraphed again to say that it would leave two days later.[135]

Meanwhile, a new and distressing problem had to be solved. Although the shaft was completed on 22 March, there was no railroad car in the South that could transport the gigantic fifty-foot piece.[136] A special car had to be built, which caused the loss of still more time, so that it was not until the twenty-fourth that it left for New Orleans. "A beautiful piece of work," Mallory telegraphed, adding: "Strain every nerve to finish ship. Expend money to encourage mechanics if essential to speedy completion. Work day and night."[137] In the meantime, work on the lateral shafts proceeded doggedly at New Orleans.[138]

Mallory had taken a series of extremely important steps. First, on 21 March he ordered Commander Arthur Sinclair to leave Norfolk and proceed to New Orleans to assume command of the great ship. "This will, it is expected, prove a very formidable vessel," the secretary wrote, "and every possible exertion must be made to complete her at the earliest moment."[139] He directed Sinclair to ready her guns, ammunition, supplies, and coal so that she might move as soon as possible. Sinclair reached New Orleans on 3 April. On the fifth the ship was christened by Mallory with the name that would go down in history: the *Mississippi.*[140]

On 29 March, the secretary had detailed a new commanding officer to the New Orleans naval base: Captain William C. Whittle. Hollins was busy with the flotilla upriver, so, temporarily, Mitchell served as Whittle's deputy.[141] While George Minor, chief of ordnance, pushed the sending of the guns to New Orleans,[142] Mallory was writing to Whittle: "Work day and night to get the *Louisiana* and the *Mississippi* ready for action. Not an hour should be lost. Spare neither men nor money. Put the best officers you can get on board if those we sent don't arrive in time. Strike a blow at the enemy yourself, should Captain Hollins be absent when ready."[143]

On 9 April, at last the great driveshaft arrived in New Orleans. Yet Island No. 10 had fallen to the Federals three days earlier. Now only Fort Pillow still defended Memphis. A wave of panic swept the Tennessee city. From Richmond, Mallory directed that urgent steps be taken so that the ironclads being built there would not fall to the enemy. He sent a telegram about this to Commodore Hollins and an even more beseeching one to Commander Charles H. McBlair, recently detailed to Memphis to assume command of the *Arkansas:* "Get your boat to New Orleans and complete her as soon as possible if she is in danger in Memphis."[144]

Fortunately, either because McBlair was not in the habit of acting briskly, or because he had not lost his coolness, he was late in executing the order, and the ironclads did not leave Memphis. Indeed, the Federals needed time to reorganize after the battle for Island No. 10 and were not able to launch an attack quickly even though they were extremely worried about the ironclads the Confederates were building there.

The race was now in its last stages. Fitting the great central shaft to the *Mississippi* began on 17 April.[145] On the next day, 18 April, Commander David D. Porter's U.S. fleet of mortar boats began bombarding the forts that defended New Orleans south of the city. On the nineteenth the *Mississippi* was launched. She was fully covered with iron plates to the waterline, yet her upper works still had to be armored. The great central shaft carried its propeller but was not yet connected to the engines, which were not fully installed. Still lacking were the two lateral shafts, casemate armor, and all the guns, several of which had not yet arrived in New Orleans.

Work proceeded hastily, with the Tifts confident that she would be ready by 10 May.[146] Would the enemy grant the indispensable time? This was the agonizing question that worried all the men who worked frenziedly on the great vessel.

Certainly the ship looked imposing—and legend began to grow about her even before she was fitted out—a legend in great part accurate. According to Louisiana's governor, she was worth more to the Confederacy than fifty thousand soldiers and could have swept the whole Federal fleet from the river.[147] She was the largest and most powerful warship in the world; never had anything similar been built. So held Commodore Hollins[148] and even the Tifts, who quoted the opinion of all the officers and sailors who saw her.[149] Her captain, Sinclair, considered her to be the most fantastic warship he had seen in his lifetime and held that she could not only clear the Mississippi of enemy ships but also drive all blockaders away from Southern ports.[150]

The *Mississippi* also deeply troubled the enemy. General Henry W. Halleck, commanding Union forces in the West, had written Flag Officer Foote to put him on guard.[151] The future admiral David D. Porter considered her strong enough to drive off the whole Union fleet. As he put it, the ironclad was "the most splendid specimen . . . the world had ever seen (a sea-going affair), and had she been finished and succeeded in getting to sea, the whole American Navy would have been destroyed."[152]

Admiral Farragut, commanding the Union squadron that would soon be moving against New Orleans, knew that the *Mississippi*, "a magnificent vessel," would have operated against his wooden ships like a bull in a china shop. Still, he was ready to play with cool daring the only trump card he had in his hands: beat the Confederates in time.[153] Having kept informed about the progress of the Confederate ironclads' construction, he knew well that the *Mississippi* would be "the terror of the seas."[154]

And now, while the Federals remorselessly clamped their grip along the great river from north and south, while their forces were still overwhelming and the Confederates desperately struggled to overcome their inferiority by trying to complete their ironclads, the *Mississippi* was looming larger and larger in the perspective of the naval war and towering, dark and supreme, over New Orleans. As the days went by, she seemed to occupy center stage, to become the protagonist whose presence or lack thereof would decide the outcome of the imminent battle. Enormous, powerful, formidable, she increasingly dominated minds and thoughts. She was the object of almost mad hope on the one hand, of irrational terror on the other.

She, it was deemed, would be able, were she to be completed during her desperate race against the clock, to emulate what her sister ship, the ironclad *Virginia,* had achieved: stunning the world in battle on the far shores of the Atlantic Ocean.

E I G H T

The Battle (I)

Captain Buchanan had pondered early about what strategic goals the iron-clad *Virginia* could accomplish. Knowing that Mallory expected him to strike the enemy with a daring attack based on technological surprise, he asked himself how, through her, he could obtain maximum results.[1] As soon as he became a flag officer he showed that he had a precise, knowledgeable, and circumstantial plan suitable for the occasion, which he had been elaborating in great detail at least since January 1862.[2]

The waters below Norfolk, where the *Virginia* must first move, were those of Hampton Roads. There, between two rivers, the James to the west and the York to the east, extends for several hundred miles, in a northwest-southeast direction, the great peninsula of Virginia. Upon it some of the first English colonists had settled; on its western coast, along the bank of the James River, Jamestown was founded, their first city. Historic Williamsburg is not far away, and old, stately mansions still stand, among the most venerable patrician abodes of the Old Dominion. Upriver was the Confederate capital, Richmond.

At the southern tip of the Peninsula, dominating the roadstead, stood Fortress Monroe, which was in Federal hands. Under its guns the powerful U.S. blockading squadron lay at anchor; yet for a military and naval base, this was a poor location; it was precarious, lacked drinking water, and had no space for an army to gather. For these reasons, Union general Benjamin Butler had, on 27 May 1861, in a successful surprise attack, seized (right under the nose of general John B. Magruder, commanding

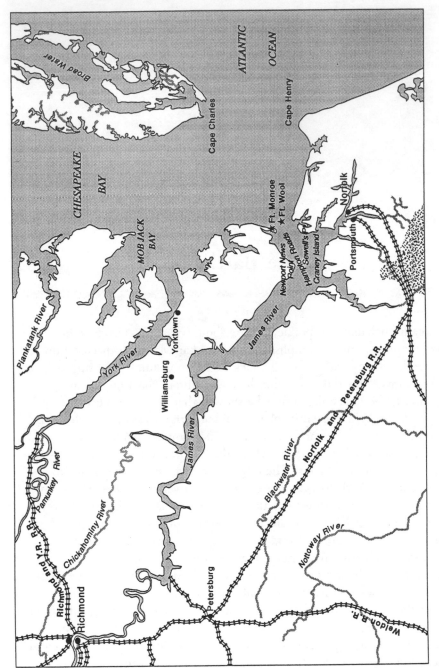

The Virginia Peninsula.

Confederate forces) the good port of Newport News, to the southwest of Fortress Monroe.[3]

Newport News was a fine base: springs provided plenty of drinking water; there were two piers along which ships of any tonnage could be moored; it had ample room for an army camp. Moreover, the town was built on hilly ground where Butler immediately organized a large entrenched camp and placed artillery, which, interrupting the communication between the James River and Hampton Roads, cut off the waterway to Richmond. Thus the Federals had an excellent starting point for future movements against the Southern capital, using the river as an easy line of operations.[4]

When Buchanan assumed command at Norfolk, the situation did not look changed in any important way. Still, during the months of artificial quiet that followed the Union defeat at Bull Run (21 July 1861) a man was appointed general in chief in Washington who, in spite of several flaws, had a keen understanding of operational lines, at least of that along the James (which during the war would be of outstanding importance) and who rushed to make use of it.

George Brinton McClellan, initially under Scott's orders, then as his successor as general in chief of the Union army,[5] had earlier dedicated his remarkable organizational talent to putting together a solid and coherent army capable of fighting the long and difficult war that was now expected even by those who had refused to see it come. Then he began to make plans for using his forces against the enemy.

In all likelihood, McClellan was impressed and stimulated by the enterprises that the Blockade Board of the navy (or, better, the clever Gustavus Vasa Fox) had organized following the suggestions of Alexander Dallas Bache, head of the U.S. Hydrographic Survey.[6] The board had started working even before the battle of Bull Run. From its studies there emerged for the first time a strategic orientation that would in time give birth to the doctrine of amphibious warfare, that is, the use of sea power to operate (together with the army) against the extensive, vulnerable, and (at least for the time being) poorly defended seacoasts of the Confederacy, in other words, sea against land.[7]

Like victory in the pages of Tacitus, amphibious strategy, which was one of the decisive elements in defeating the South, had "many fathers." One cannot deny, for example, that old General Scott's earliest idea of strangling the Confederacy by blockading it along the Atlantic coast, the Gulf of Mexico, and the rivers, even if basically a passive one, had at its base an intuition of a new use of combined naval and land power.[8] The Blockade Board went further, planning and putting into practice an active (i.e., aggressive) use of sea power. Yet, for the time being, the objective was limited to making the blockade more effective.[9]

General McClellan (even though he found an able advocate in the late Rowena Reed),[10] had a more complex role. It is not necessary to repeat well-founded criticism aimed at him from many sides.[11] Enough to recall that the general, wishing for several reasons, among them perhaps some valid ones, to avoid a direct engagement with the Confederate forces on the Virginia front and convinced that a threat directed at Richmond would throw the Confederates off balance, after toying with several projects of landing along the Virginia coast, in the end proposed moving the entire Army of the Potomac in a big naval convoy to the mouth of the Rappahannock River near Urbanna. From there he estimated that he could fall upon Richmond in two days, stealing a march on the Southern divisions of General Joseph E. Johnston entrenched at Bull Run, well to the north. The necessary condition for the success of such an operation was to maintain control of the crucial logistical-strategic line of operations of the James River, already controlled by the Union troops at Newport News.[12] On 27 February 1862 McClellan drafted the orders for the preparation of the convoy and embarking operations.

On the Peninsula, since January General Magruder had feared an attack of this kind and had sounded the alarm to President Davis.[13] The matter was deferred to the authorities in Richmond, first of all to the navy.[14]

The Federals, well aware of the importance of controlling the James River, had moved to its mouth two old but powerful ships—the sloop *Cumberland* (1,726 tons, 24 guns) and the large frigate *Congress* (1,869 tons, 50 guns)—with orders to collaborate with the land batteries at Newport News and seal up the river. Even if these were sailing ships,[15] their firepower was so imposing as to dissuade the light Confederate craft along the river from making any attempt to reopen the passage.[16]

Buchanan had a sharp mind and an outstanding perception of naval strategy. He well knew, as stated by John D. Hayes, that "he who would use navigable waters for military purpose must first be able to deny these waters to the enemy" and that "control of navigable waters gives a powerful freedom of action to its possessor."[17]

The waters to be conquered from the enemy lay ahead: the mouth and course of the James River, which, if left to Northerners, would play in their favor, according to Lepotier, "a role far more important than that of the Tagus river during the Napoleonic war in Spain." It could become "the unhealable maritime sore in the side of the land power and cause a mortal infection." Worse still, for the South, the effect would be far more lethal than in Spain "because this sore would be exceedingly close to the vital center of the Confederacy."[18]

A History of the Confederate Navy

The *Virginia* now offered a unique possibility of healing the sore, snatching (hopefully forever, or at least for a long time) its control from enemy hands. Buchanan foresaw a three-pronged action: escorted by the small gunboats *Beaufort* and *Raleigh,* the ironclad would strike from Norfolk toward the mouth of the James; the small James River Confederate squadron would sail downriver to join her; and, most important, General Magruder would move overland against the enemy positions at Newport News.

Buchanan arrived at Norfolk on 25 February. On 2 March he wrote to Magruder specifying his plan and expressing his intention to move with the ironclad within five days. But she was not altogether ready. She still lacked 18,200 pounds of powder, and her armored gunports had not yet been installed. Yet the powder was being loaded, and he was resolved to go to sea anyway.

His plan (which he neatly outlined in a couple of sentences) was first to eliminate the two large ships that blocked the river, then turn and silence the coastal batteries. "I sincerely hope," he concluded, "that, acting together, we may be successful in destroying many of the enemy." [19]

Unfortunately, Magruder, who clearly did not trust the *Virginia,* and who, in any case, showed a very poor understanding of sea power,[20] had already hurriedly written Richmond a letter in which he begged off from the game and, alleging the bad state of the roads (which was not wholly untrue), categorically refused to collaborate.[21]

Buchanan was unimpressed. He knew from Northern newspapers that the *Monitor* was approaching. The new Union ship (sought by every local U.S. commanding officer, afraid that at any moment the fearsome Confederate ironclad might fall on them) was approaching with great difficulty through a stormy ocean, revealing her limited seaworthiness.[22]

Therefore, Buchanan, without delay, on 3 March sent his operational order to John R. Tucker, commanding officer of the James River Squadron, composed of an auxiliary cruiser that would later become the schoolship *Patrick Henry* (ten guns) and two small gunboats, the *Jamestown* and the *Teaser* (two guns each). Tucker was to descend the river and join him. Buchanan confirmed his intention of sinking the two large Union ships *Cumberland* and *Congress* and silencing the coastal batteries at Newport News. He also underscored the hope and the confidence of the Confederate nation in the ironclad and the ships that would fight alongside her.[23]

In a letter of 4 March to Secretary Mallory, Buchanan first politely explained that the enormous draft of his ship precluded any possibility of sailing up the Potomac and attacking Washington, as Mallory had suggested. Moreover, he continued, she still lacked her gunport shutters, as well as deck howitzers to drive back boarders.

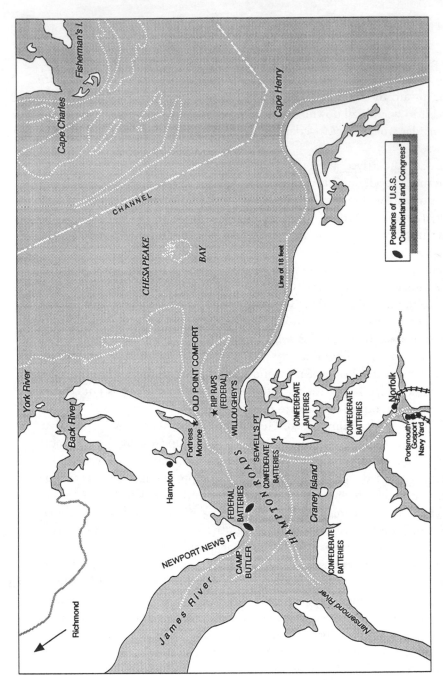

Hampton Roads and the Chesapeake. The limits of shallow water are indicated, as well as the positions of the USS *Cumberland* and *Congress*.

Still, he added that he would have makeshift shutters installed hoping to have the last supplies of gunpowder and shells aboard by 6 March. He planned to move against the enemy during the late night of 6 March to give battle on the seventh. "I feel confident," he concluded, "that the acts of the *Virginia* will give proof of the desire of her officers and crew to meet the views of the Department as far as practicable."[24]

Yet, to Buchanan's great annoyance, it was impossible for the ship to move either during the night of 6 March or on the day of the seventh. A fierce gale was whipping the eastern coast of North America, the one that, during these hours, almost sank the *Monitor.* Moreover, the pilots refused to carry such a large vessel with such deep draft downriver at night.[25]

Unfortunately, the *Virginia* needed calm waters. Her turning circle was enormous: she required thirty to forty minutes to make a complete turn.[26] Therefore, action had to be postponed to 8 March. On the day of compulsory idleness the last of the powder was brought aboard.[27]

The dawn of 8 March 1862 arose clear over a calm sea. A little before eleven o'clock Buchanan had his flag officer's pennant hoisted on the ironclad and ordered all workmen, who were frenziedly putting the finishing touches to her, to clear. The stokers fired up, and the *Virginia* unmoored and began, at first slowly, to descend the Elizabeth River toward the enemy. At that moment, the advantage she had over the U.S. Navy had been narrowed to a single day—yet that would be enough.

The ironclad quickly increased speed and, contrary to pessimistic forecasts of the evening before, was soon logging six to eight knots.[28] News that she was sallying out, escorted by the gunboats *Beaufort* and *Raleigh,* spread like lightning. Thousands of people crowded the banks or crammed themselves into small boats.[29] Yet there were no shouts or cheers; it seemed that an eerie silence had fallen over the land. Many others, who had not come to the riverbanks, were kneeling in churches, praying for their kinsmen, for their country. Everybody understood how momentous was the hour, how awesome the event.[30]

For the first time in naval history an ironclad, rather than being limited to acting as a floating battery, was giving battle to an enemy fleet. And no witness failed to realize the drama that was about to be played out and to understand how much was at stake.[31]

In announcing to his crew that they were going into battle, Buchanan added, "The whole world is watching you to day." He then informed the commanding officers of the two gunboats that followed that a specific signal would mean "Sink before you surrender."[32]

It was a calm, clear day.[33] The area around the beautiful Hampton Roads looked like an immense arena accommodating almost the entire world. Moreover, thousands of Union and Confederate soldiers on the opposite shores and Federal sailors on board their ships were watching the awesome scene. Among the audience were also the crews of the French warships *Gassendi* and *Catinat*, in addition to reporters from many countries.

Upon reaching the mouth of the Elizabeth River, where the water was very shallow, the ironclad had to call upon the gunboat *Beaufort* to help her, by means of a towing hawser, to turn ninety degrees to port. Once freed, she headed directly toward the mouth of the James River.[34] It was 12:30.

Fifteen minutes later the enemy ships sighted the *Virginia* and beat to quarters.[35] To Federal sailors, she appeared like a house sunk in the water up to the roof gutters, with dense smoke billowing from the chimney.[36]

Sailors aboard the *Cumberland* and the *Congress*, who were doing their Saturday laundry, scurried to clear the decks while the general quarters was being sounded.[37] In the Union array, other than the *Cumberland* and the *Congress*, whose sides, bristling with guns, barred the James River, there were in the roadstead, moored near Fortress Monroe, the steam frigates *Minnesota* (forty-seven guns) and *Roanoke* (forty-six guns), both twins of the *Merrimack*. With her engines broken down, the *Roanoke* could move only by sail or under tow. Then there was the sailing frigate *St. Lawrence*, of the same class as the *Congress*.[38]

The three ships immediately moved toward the ironclad, the *Minnesota* by her engines, the *Roanoke* and the *St. Lawrence* slowly, under tow. Eight miles farther, the *Minnesota* ran aground. Because the two other ships had already grounded, the *Cumberland* and the *Congress* were to face the ironclad alone.[39]

The Confederate squadron of the James had descended the river in time for the rendezvous of 7 March. Upon learning that the operation had been postponed for a day, it had anchored six miles upriver from Newport News[40] in plain view of the Union sailors on the *Cumberland*.[41] Now Commander Tucker ordered the crew to weigh anchor and move toward the sound of the guns.

The Federals opened fire first, without appreciable results.[42] The *Virginia* continued to move ahead without bothering to answer. Then at fifteen hundred yards she opened fire, and her rifled bow gun knocked the *Cumberland*'s stern pivot gun and its crew out of action.[43] The curtain had been raised on the drama.

At that point Confederate sailors saw through the gunports to starboard an imposing ship: it was the *Congress*, in front of which the ironclad was now passing. The sight lasted for only a second because the powerful Union frigate suddenly was covered with flashes—a formidable broadside of twenty-five guns fired at the Confederate ship. Yet shot and shell bounced as harmlessly against her carapace as if they were tennis balls. The *Virginia* answered with point-blank fire,[44] which had a devastating effect on the wooden ship. Walls caved in, pieces of artillery were dismounted and thrown aside like twigs, large fires erupted aboard, and dead and wounded were everywhere.[45]

Without bothering further with the *Congress,* the ironclad moved toward the *Cumberland* like "some devilish and superhuman monster or the horrible creation of a nightmare," or even "a huge half-submerged crocodile,"[46] meanwhile keeping up a lively gun duel with the sloop. The *Cumberland*'s missiles usually bounced off the ironclad's armor, but the *Virginia*'s began to smash the Federal ship, littering her decks with so many dead and wounded that blood stained everything and even ran through the scuppers.[47]

In the meantime, the crew of the *Virginia* felt a great shock, as though the ship had grounded. Minutes later Flag Lieutenant Robert D. Minor passed the word: "We have sunk the *Cumberland.*"[48] In fact, the ironclad had rammed the sloop on the starboard side of her bow. As it hit, the ram, which first broke through the antitorpedo obstructions surrounding the *Cumberland,* made a rumble clearly heard above the din of the guns,[49] opening in her side, under the waterline, a hole large enough for a wagon to pass through. She began to take on tons of water and to settle very rapidly.[50] The action was so sudden that observers could not believe their eyes when they saw the topmasts of the *Cumberland* incline to more than forty-five degrees.[51]

The Federal sailors, nevertheless, continued firing until the water reached the upper deck. With all her flags flying, the *Cumberland* foundered, an object of admiration even to her enemies.[52]

Yet before she sank, the sloop inflicted the only damage the *Virginia* would suffer in two days of battle. Aside from the ram, which was broken off when it hit, remaining embedded in the side of the sloop and causing some minor leaks in the *Virginia*'s bow, the *Cumberland*'s gunners, firing steadily at point-blank range, succeeded in tearing away the muzzles of two broadside guns, knocking them out, and repeatedly hitting the tall funnel of the ironclad, which caused smoke to fill her casemate and reduce her draft, diminishing her speed.[53]

Now the ironclad, freeing herself from the sinking enemy ship, steamed several miles up the James River and with the fire of her guns silenced and knocked out the coastal batteries, which throughout the engagement had fired unavailingly at her. She also blew up a transport ship moored near the coast and sank another one. Then, having been joined by Tucker's squadron, she steamed toward the *Congress.*[54]

Her captain, having been called to sit on a court-martial, was not aboard the ship; yet the officers on board realized immediately that their big ship was doomed. There being only one thing to do, they did it: beach her to save her from sinking and get her into such shallow waters that the dreadful ironclad could not get close enough to ram her. The small gunboat *Zouave* was ordered to take the *Congress,* already seriously wounded, with several fires raging aboard, under tow to the shore.[55]

Buchanan warily came as close as possible to the Union frigate and, aided by his five gunboats, started to dismantle her with an accurate fire from his guns. In a short while, on the *Congress,* acting captain Lieutenant Joseph B. Smith fell. There were 136 killed and wounded aboard; the frigate was a heap of wreckage devoured by fierce fires; her guns were silent.[56] The officers remaining on board therefore decided to lower the flag.

Buchanan ordered the gunboats *Beaufort* and *Raleigh* to go alongside to receive the surrender and help rescue the wounded. Just as this was being done, two companies of Union soldiers, supported by a section of field artillery, wildly opened fire from shore, wounding and killing several Confederate officers and sailors as well as some Northern prisoners that were being taken aboard.

A scene of awful confusion followed. The *Beaufort* steamed away (according to Buchanan, without being authorized and without explaining to him what she was doing). Buchanan, recklessly going up to the iron-clad's deck, in the open, to consider the situation, saw his flag lieutenant, Robert D. Minor, who had volunteered to sail in a small boat to blow up the wreck, fall wounded as he neared the *Congress.*

Until that moment the flag officer had behaved with great coolness and wisdom. Yet now he was seized by one of those temper tantrums that according to Catesby ap R. Jones were his main flaw. In a towering rage, he not only ordered whatever remained of the *Congress* destroyed by incendiary shells (which was an explainable reaction, even if the murderous enemy fire came from troops ashore and not from the ship); he also, instead of seeking cover, lingered on the upper deck fully exposed to enemy fire coming from shore.

A few moments later he fell seriously wounded by a rifle bullet which, hitting one of his legs, injured the femoral artery.[57] Command of the ironclad devolved upon Catesby ap R. Jones, whom Buchanan trusted completely.[58]

It was now 5 P.M. Immediately Jones steered the ironclad toward the *Minnesota.* That splendid steamer, pride of the U.S. Navy, lay grounded, powerless, already the target of incessant fire from the C.S. gunboats. Lit up by the sinister glare of the burning *Congress,* she looked like an enormous monster in dire straits, surrounded by her enemies.[59]

A History of the Confederate Navy

Unluckily for the Confederates, the grounded steam frigate could not be closed by the *Virginia* because of the latter's deep draft. The ironclad nevertheless directed upon her brisk and accurate shooting, causing great damage and some fires.

Then, after night fell, when sighting guns became impossible and pilots began to fear grounding in the shallows, she broke off contact, leaving the destruction of the *Minnesota* to the next day.[60]

Mooring for the night near Sewell's Point, the *Virginia* left behind a scene of devastation and terror: three ships sunk, another dismantled and turned into a gigantic funeral pyre by whose glaring light the fifth ship, the *Minnesota,* lay crippled and disabled, motionless like a wounded titan awaiting the mortal blow. About three hundred Union officers and men had been killed.[61] The other Union ships had fled from the "monster" and cleared out of Hampton Roads. There was panic and fear everywhere. "It was a great victory. . . . The IRON and the HEAVY GUNS did the work," wrote an elated Robert D. Minor from his hospital bed.[62]

On the Union side was dismay and dejection.[63] Yet at 9 P.M. the *Monitor* had at last arrived, and a dog-tired Captain Worden moored her near the *Minnesota.*[64]

The Confederates had caught a glimpse of the *Monitor* but either did not identify her or did not fathom her significance.[65] What now attracted their attention was the *Congress,* which, after burning for some time, soon after midnight exploded with such a deafening, terrible crash that windows miles away trembled, sending a gigantic plume of flames to an incredible height, like the eruption of a volcano.[66]

Soon after 6:30 the following morning the *Virginia* was again ready to move under Catesby ap R. Jones's command. Her objective was to give the coup de grace to the *Minnesota.* But when the ironclad came within two thousand yards of the ship and opened fire, the *Monitor,* which had already fired up and cleared for action, made for her. About to begin in Hampton Roads was the first battle between ironclads ever recorded in the world's history. A witness wrote: "With the first gun, fired by the *Monitor,* that quiet Sunday morning the combined navies of the world passed over into the scrap heap of useless and forgotten things. The ships of England, France, Austria, Spain; all were so hopelessly out of class as the Spanish Armada. A new type of fighting ship had been born and before noon had proved its worth. Two great war machines, each radically different from the other, had come into being unknown to each other, and from them both arose the modern battleship."[67] There was about to begin "a battle which, revolutionizing as it did in an instant the whole science of naval warfare," would become "more memorable than any seafight of history."[68]

All eyewitnesses agreed that meeting the *Monitor* was a surprise for the Confederates. Through the gunports, the *Virginia* sailors saw a strange mechanical contrivance similar to a "cheesebox on a tray."[69] There was no time to be in awe, for the *Monitor* moved resolutely against the Confederate ironclad and the battle began.

For four hours the two ironclads traded shot and shell, firing broadsides that would have reduced to splinters any other ship in existence and closing from one hundred to fifty yards, still without noticeable effect. The lack of damage to the *Monitor* was due in part to the fact that the *Virginia* had only explosive and incendiary shells. When producing her guns, Brooke had given priority to projectiles capable of destroying the wooden ships he expected her to meet; the encounter with an ironclad had not been anticipated, at least not so soon.[70] On her side, the *Monitor* with her enormous guns (two 11-inch Dahlgrens) fired round shot weighing 168 pounds—yet they were ineffective against the *Virginia's* carapace.[71]

No one can say how the battle would have gone if the opponents had had projectiles capable of piercing armor plate such as those Brooke was at that very time manufacturing and which, according to the inventor, would have been able to batter the *Monitor's* turret to pieces in a few minutes.[72] For the time being, the armor had bested the gun.

Realizing the futility of gunfire, Jones decided to try the weapon Worden feared above all else: the ram. Either because of the *Monitor's* promptness in steering clear so as not to receive the full impact or because the *Virginia's* ram had been broken the day before against the *Cumberland,* the blow inflicted no damage on the *Monitor.*[73]

Shortly thereafter the Confederate ship grounded, and it was her turn to be at the mercy of her enemy. Yet at that very moment, when the Union ironclad was closing to within a few yards of the *Virginia,* a lucky shell succeeded in hitting the slit in the *Monitor's* pilot house and temporarily blinding Worden (later one eye was saved). Worden's executive officer, Samuel Dana Greene, was so upset that he took the *Monitor* into water so shallow that the *Virginia* could not possibly follow her.[74]

At this point the *Virginia* could again have tried to finish off the *Minnesota,* but the tide was falling quickly and the pilots feared that she might not be able to go back to her base. Persuaded that the *Monitor* had "thrown in the towel," Jones ordered the battle suspended.[75]

So ended two days that saw a new era in the world's naval history. But who had won? Naturally, both sides claimed victory. It is therefore necessary to analyze the events dispassionately. Many analyses have been made, but the best (and keenest) remains that of Robert W. Daly. It is substantially correct except in a few particulars.[76]

Notwithstanding the resounding echo that the event raised throughout the world and its great importance in naval history, the battle between the ironclads of 9 March 1862, from the viewpoint of maritime strategy in the Civil War, was substantially an anticlimax: the decisive day was the preceding one, 8 March.

Indeed, on 9 March the *Virginia* had come out merely to "complete her job," destroy the *Minnesota.* If that was the Confederate aim, whereas that of the *Monitor* was to save the steam frigate, then it seems correct to say that on that day the *tactical* victory belonged to the *Monitor.* Captain Worden handed over this success to history when, from his hospital bed where he lay blind, he asked: "Have I saved that fine ship, the *Minnesota?*" and, upon receiving an affirmative reply, had answered, with the plainness of an ancient Roman: "Then, I don't care about myself."[77]

Nevertheless, despite Worden's gallantry, the decisive battle had been fought the day before, and the far more important *strategic* victory lay indisputably with the Confederates. Indeed, not only had the enemy fleet, after suffering crippling losses, been driven from the roadstead, not to return while the *Virginia* dominated the waters (even the *Monitor* after 9 March would never again risk action there), but the vital strategic line of the James River and the waters thereof were now firmly in Confederate hands. This looked crystal clear to General McClellan, who had to give up his best line of operation along that river ("now closed to us") and try to use the York, "although less promising."[78] From his side, the commanding officer of the U.S. Corps of Engineers, General John G. Barnard, said straightforwardly: "The *Merrimac* . . . proved so disastrous to our subsequent operations."[79]

Worse still, McClellan, although using the York as an operational line, had to move all of his supplies by land along slow, muddy routes. This was because Flag Officer Louis M. Goldsborough, commanding Union naval forces, was compelled to deny the general any naval support (except for a token two warships) on the York because he had to keep all of his vessels well concentrated against "the monster" that might appear at any moment.[80]

Obviously, the success of its first ironclad in battle against enemy warships excited and thrilled the South. Buchanan, as he deserved, was promoted to admiral, the first and only one to carry such a rank in the C.S. Navy. Jones, who, after Buchanan was wounded had assumed the duty of "lieutenant commanding," became a commander.[81]

Moreover, Mallory, without delay, wrote personally to Jones praising him for his accomplishment in what (he keenly observed) above all else had contributed to make the *Virginia* so superior to the enemy: the outstanding way in which her excellent guns and their crews had been prepared, drilled, and engaged. The letter demonstrated Mallory's deftness in judging men and matters of the sea, his skill in choosing cadres, and his understanding of matters that were "rarely named in reciting and recording the triumph, and usually meet with no public recognition."[82]

The Confederate Congress voted an address of thanks to the officers and men of the *Virginia*.[83] Meanwhile, at Norfolk the ironclad and her crew were receiving the triumphal apotheosis of the winners. Thousands of people applauded passionately, shouted "hurrahs," and waved handkerchiefs and flags from the piers. Whistles of ships that had raised their great bunting piped happily while the *Virginia* slowly steamed up the Elizabeth River.[84] It was an unforgettable hour.[85]

The next day a moving thanksgiving ceremony was held on the ironclad's gun deck.[86] Then, on Buchanan's order, Lieutenant John Taylor Wood hurried by the first train to Richmond to bring Secretary Mallory and President Davis the first report of the future admiral and the flag captured aboard the *Congress*. Wherever he went, there were cheering crowds, to whom he had to tell the events of the battle. In Richmond he was personally escorted by Mallory to meet President Davis, who had with him the new secretary of state, Judah P. Benjamin, and many military leaders. Davis questioned Wood at length and expressed his strong desire that the *Virginia* be repaired as soon as possible.[87]

Of course, the illusion of having the "ultimate weapon" at hand had by no means disappeared. Indeed, Mallory wrote Buchanan a letter in which he proposed nothing less than an attack on New York. Upon reaching there, he said, the ironclad would "shell and burn the city and the shipping," and "such an event would eclipse all the glories of the combats at sea . . . and would strike a blow from which the enemy could never recover. Peace would inevitably follow. Bankers would withdraw their capital from the city. The Brooklyn Navy Yard and its magazines and all the lower part of the city would be destroyed, and such an event, by a single ship, would do more to achieve our immediate independence than would the results of many campaigns."[88]

On 19 March Admiral Buchanan answered from his hospital bed in a thoughtful letter. After underscoring that the *Virginia* was still an experimental ship, that in battle she had showed herself to be by no means invulnerable, and that the *Monitor* was her equal, he continued by saying that the ironclad could possibly leave Hampton Roads. Yet she then would have to face the fire of some of the heaviest known coastal guns, to whose projectiles she had not yet been exposed. But worse would follow: "Should she encounter a gale or a very heavy swell, I think it more than probable she would founder." Also, the *Monitor* and other major enemy vessels would follow her, battering her with their heavy guns. Then, it was most improbable that pilots could be found off New York, and it would be impossible for a ship of her draft to cross the bar while under fire from forts mounting very heavy guns. If the *Virginia* were able to reach the city she would create havoc and inflict much damage upon its houses and ships. Yet the enemy would bottle her up in the roadstead and she would be lost. The admiral concluded: "I consider the *Virginia* the most important protection to the safety of Norfolk, and her services can be made very valuable in this neighborhood, taking her opportunity to make a bold dash at some other point."[89]

This sensible advice included a realistic evaluation of the enormous power of the ironclad if correctly used. The *Virginia*'s crew never suffered from the illusion that she could have passed unhurt by the enormous guns of Fortress Monroe, which could hurl four-hundred-pound projectiles.[90]

While elation spread throughout the South, and its newspapers rushed to daydream about how the *Virginia* could achieve the most stunning successes,[91] the North succumbed to an unreasonable panic. Even statesmen, who should have kept cool heads, ascribed apocalyptic capabilities to the Confederate ironclad.[92]

Although the arrival of the *Monitor* had restored some confidence, indications were not lacking that even the new ironclad, although able to challenge the "monster," was by no means her superior, that the *Monitor* should gird for a deadly fight, and that she must not be exposed to undue risk and particularly must not sail into waters dominated by the hostile ironclad.[93]

During these frantic days, U.S. Naval Secretary Welles was bombarded with letters presenting harebrained proposals for countering the *Virginia*.[94] Even if most of these were not worthwhile, many undertakings were being decided upon in the North, the most important ones in secrecy. Such fervid activity should not have been underrated by the South because it was a signal of the unconquerable fighting will of the North.

Some proposals edged on the absurd. Nurturing little trust in the navy as a whole and in the *Monitor* in particular, U.S. Secretary of War Edwin Stanton decided to consult Commodore Cornelius Vanderbilt, owner of a transatlantic fleet. He asked the latter to have his best and fastest ship, the *Vanderbilt*, sent to Fortress Monroe to be used as a battering ram against the *Virginia*. With commendable patriotism Vanderbilt gave the ship to the Union as a gift. Yet one wonders what a wooden ship might have done against the frightful ironclad.[95]

Meanwhile, Gustavus Vasa Fox and John Ericsson were secretly meditating about other strategies. The North was already mobilizing its great industrial plant. Within a few days, Ericsson got contracts for building six more ironclads of the *Monitor* class, which soon would increase to twenty-seven.[96]

Secretary Welles wanted the sum appropriated by Congress for the building of ironclads increased to $30 million, while Fox was at work to make the new ironclads enormously more powerful than the *Monitor.* After debating the possibility of fitting them with huge 20-inch Dahlgren guns as well as a ram[97] (the latter proposal being accepted by Ericsson),[98] he more realistically decided to go along with Ericsson's recommendation of 15-inch smoothbores,[99] still, however, studying and testing together with Dahlgren the monster 20-inch gun.[100]

The duel between gun and armor was fully under way. Still, Welles, Dahlgren, and Fox persisted in leaning on the past as long as they sought to rely on smoothbores of still greater size, whereas in the South Mallory and Brooke, with their rifled guns, were showing the way to the future, which indeed should have appeared clear from the great efficiency of the *Virginia's* guns.

The first, historical battle between ironclads had also produced deep emotion across the Atlantic. The London *Times,* upset, observed that, out of the 149 first-class ships in Her Majesty's navy, only two were still useful—the ironclads *Warrior* and *Black Prince.* It was as though the two American vessels had sunk at one blow all the world's wooden ships.[101]

The Duke of Somerset, First Lord of the Admiralty, speaking in the House of Lords on 3 April 1862, neatly delineated the substance of the formidable change that had closed an era in naval history. It was certain, he said, that everyone already realized the impossibility of wooden ships surviving a fight against an ironclad; yet merely knowing this was not enough. It was mandatory to change the naval strategy of the British Empire and be ready to use ironclads (until then reserved for the Home Fleet) in every corner of the globe. Theoretical truth, in other words, had been transformed into a political and strategic fact of the greatest importance, and naval warfare had changed forever.[102]

Meanwhile, at Richmond, the energetic Mallory, to speed up the foreseen repairs, had on the very day of the battle ordered new armor plate produced.[103] He had quickly freed himself from the illusion of the "ultimate weapon" and returned to sound, concrete policy.

First, the *Virginia* must be docked while work was speeded up on building a new ironclad to accompany her. Together, they would be most formidable. The keel of the second vessel was laid soon after the battle of Hampton Roads, and she would be named the *Richmond.* She was sketched by John Luke Porter from a model he had built several years earlier: overall length of more than 172 feet with 11 foot draft. She would have a great armored casemate and carry four of Brooke's best 7-inch rifled guns as well as two smoothbores.[104]

The *Virginia* entered drydock on 10 March.[105] Mallory directed that no labor or money be spared to make her ready as soon as possible.[106] He insisted to Commodore French Forrest, commanding the Norfolk Navy Yard, that in the construction of the new ironclad "a moment must not be lost." As many men as possible should be put to work day and night to build her and her engines. The secretary concluded his pressing request by saying, "One such vessel would be worth a fleet of wooden vessels to us."[107]

This exhortation might mean that old Forrest was not yet entirely persuaded, or so Mallory thought. At any rate, on the next day the secretary came back to the issue in a concerned tone and with a lecture: "Sir: The work of getting the *Virginia* and the iron-plated gunboat (in course of construction at Norfolk) ready for sea at the earliest possible moment is the most important duty that could devolve upon a naval officer at this time, and yet this Department is ignorant of what progress is being made upon either. I am not advised that a day's work has been done upon the *Virginia* since she went into dock." Mallory continued by asking that the department be informed *daily* about the work done on her and offered to send additional officers if needed.[108]

Three days later an urgent telegram reached Forrest asking him if the *Virginia* was ready for sea: "If not, when will she be?"[109] On the next day, clearly disappointed by the way Forrest was handling the work, Mallory appointed Captain Sidney Smith Lee as the new commanding officer of the Norfolk Navy Yard.[110]

The secretary soon began prodding Lee to push work to the utmost, to keep him well aware of the progress made on the ironclad, and to hasten the production of the armor-piercing projectiles to be provided her. In the same letter Mallory informed Lee that he had appointed a new flag officer for the Norfolk Squadron: Captain Josiah Tattnall.[111]

Relieving Buchanan was certainly not an easy decision for Mallory to make, yet he had no choice. Buchanan's wound healed very slowly; two months passed before he could begin to walk with crutches, and still in June the wound bothered him, giving him great pain.[112]

On 21 March Mallory had telegraphed Tattnall, commanding the Savannah Squadron, to proceed immediately to Norfolk and assume command of the naval forces in Virginia's waters. The official letter of detail followed on 25 March. Tattnall was directed to hoist his broad pennant on the *Virginia*.[113]

Born near Savannah, Georgia, in 1795, Josiah Tattnall was now sixty-seven years old. Tall, with an imposing presence, he had been described by one of his colleagues as the *beau ideal* of a naval officer. He had fought against the British and the Mexicans and in China. Daring, able, and experienced, he was naturally unselfish, modest, and gentlemanly. Even if he did not possess the strategic flair of Buchanan, he was, under the circumstances, a first-rate selection.[114]

On the same day that he detailed him, Mallory sent Tattnall his confidential instructions. The secretary had guessed the enormous importance of the psychological pressure that the ironclad exerted on the enemy and intended to exploit it to the full. Tattnall was therefore to make the *Virginia* appear as destructive and fearsome to the enemy as possible. The Federals believed the *Virginia* more heavily damaged than she really was; a surprise attack on the *Monitor* thus might be possible.

Such a conclusion seemed warranted because it was hoped that the new armor-piercing projectiles could penetrate the *Monitor*'s armor and a new ram almost twelve feet long could do the same. Enclosing a copy of the *Monitor*'s design from the *Scientific American,* the secretary designated her as the obstacle to be removed. To this end, he recommended that Tattnall consult with Buchanan and place full trust in Catesby ap R. Jones.[115]

Everybody now eagerly awaited the *Virginia*'s return to action. A restless naval cadet in her crew wrote to his mother: "In a few days you will hear more of the *Virginia,*"[116] and Buchanan, who from the hospital carefully followed the refitting of the ironclad, told Mallory that she was almost ready for sea.[117]

She finally left drydock on 4 April. In announcing that event, Tattnall emphasized that she was in better condition than when she had left it the first time for the battle at Hampton Roads. A new steel ram twelve feet long had been installed.[118] Under the place where the armor ended, the unprotected hull had been covered with 440 iron plates, 2 inches thick and 3.5 feet high, extending from her bow for 160 feet, thus providing better protection for both the magazines and the engines; also the roof of the casemate had been strengthened.[119] Moreover, other repairs had been made: a new funnel added, several armor plates and two damaged guns replaced, and the like.

Yet the ironclad's officers were unhappy. Nothing had been done to protect the propeller or rudder, which remained the most vulnerable parts of the ship. The iron reinforcement added to the casemate's roof was poor because of bad workmanship by both the constructor and shipyard workers.[120] The engines were still inadequate.[121]

Yet, even though the strengthening had deepened her draft, the ironclad had never looked so formidable.[122] Only the port shutters for her guns were still lacking, Tattnall lamented. Yet Mallory, acting with customary energy, succeeded in solving the problem.[123] He now grew restless: the *Virginia,* he telegraphed to the commanding officer of the navy yard, must be ready for action whenever Tattnall decided.[124]

And it was high time for action. On 2 April General McClellan had landed at Fortress Monroe, where he had already concentrated sixty thousand men and one hundred guns; another twenty-five thousand men were to follow soon.

Now the Union Army of the Potomac began to march slowly up the Peninsula. Because the two lines of operations by the James and the York rivers were barred—one was closed, the other was unsafe—nothing else could be done. On the fifth, the Federal divisions arrived in front of the defense line near Yorktown, where General Magruder barred the Peninsula; they stopped there.[125]

General Robert E. Lee, who coordinated Confederate military operations under President Davis's authority, fearing a Union naval presence on the York, forwarded a request to Mallory: could not the *Virginia* pass during the night under the guns of Fortress Monroe (and of the Union squadron) and attack the Federal ships (if any) along the York? It would be of the utmost importance that she first strike the enemy transports that were landing troops and supplies for McClellan.[126]

The secretary of the navy, who could better evaluate naval warfare problems, disagreed. The dangers would be enormous, and the loss of the *Virginia,* caught between the big guns of Fortress Monroe, of the other fort at the Rip-Raps island, and those of the enemy squadron, would be certain. Moreover, her absence would expose Norfolk to the enemy. Much better objectives were the approximately two hundred transports that were unloading. As for the enemy, Mallory wrote, "A wholesome fear of the *Virginia* has . . . induced him to abandon his plans of crossing his troops from Newport News and Old Point to attack Norfolk." Now addressing Tattnall, Mallory concluded: "Could you destroy his transports, you would scatter his army to the winds."[127]

On 10 April Tattnall learned that the enemy, confident that the *Virginia* still remained in her dock, had risked sending several transports into the roadstead to land troops at Hampton, south of Fortress Monroe, because there were very few moorings at the fortress. Tattnall's plan was quickly formulated: he would sortie with his squadron and attack the transports. He thus hoped to provoke the *Monitor* into a decisive battle. Of course, he continued, had he been ordered to do so he would try to reach the York River, yet he agreed with Mallory that this would be a hopeless attempt.[128]

At 6 A.M. on 11 April, the *Virginia,* followed by the smaller craft, sortied and steered for the enemy's transport fleet. For a few seconds, nothing happened. Then the transports stampeded. Like chickens sighting a hawk, they flew out of the roadstead and sought safety under the guns of Fortress Monroe.[129] Only three remained trapped near Hampton.

Yet, to Tattnall's great annoyance, the *Monitor* did not move from the channel between the forts. This was part of a well-conceived plan that Tattnall understood. Alongside the still fearsome *Monitor* there was now the smaller ironclad *Naugatuck* fitted with a long-range rifled 100-pound Parrott gun. Moreover, there were some half dozen larger ships, among them the *Vanderbilt*. The latter, fitted with a ram, was supposed to run like a forlorn hope on the *Virginia* and sink her.[130] The enemy squadron had about two hundred guns, not including those of the forts.

The *Virginia* advanced to almost within firing range. All about, onlookers waited eagerly. In addition to the two French warships there was the British *Rinaldo,* whose officers observed that the Confederate ironclad steered with surprising ease and made more than seven knots, much better than the old *Merrimack*.[131] The ironclad advanced to within two hundred yards of the foreign ships. An exchange of signals followed, then the latter moved a bit to the south and out of range. The stage for the battle was clear—if only the *Monitor* would accept the challenge.

Yet the new captain of the Northern ironclad, Commander William N. Jeffers, who desired to fight Tattnall, was under strict orders. He was to lure the *Virginia* into a trap and avoid being enticed into the snare Tattnall was setting for him—that is, to draw the Federal ironclad under the Confederate guns at Sewell's Point. In the end, Tattnall resorted to open provocation. The gunboat *Jamestown* entered Hampton's waters and, under the nose of the Federals, captured the three transports that had sought refuge there and towed them away. Finally, after a long-range artillery duel with the *Naugatuck,* and firing a last shot in disdain, the *Virginia* at nightfall returned to her mooring.[132]

From the viewpoint of a Monday morning quarterback, it might be said that had Goldsborough resolutely moved against the *Virginia* with all of his ships, the Confederate ironclad would have found herself in dire straits, as later happened to the *Tennessee* at Mobile Bay. Still, as somebody observed, Goldsborough was Goldsborough and not Farragut, and few Farraguts and Nelsons are born.

One must add the awe that the *Virginia* inspired and the fact that the improvements made to her and her guns (which the Federals most certainly knew about) would have cast doubt on the success of the *Monitor* in a new duel. For the *Monitor*'s crew, who were eager to engage the *Virginia,* their first calm, clear, and near view of the "monster" made her appear "a formidable looking thing," as an officer of the *Monitor* wrote, adding: "I had but little idea of her size and apparent strength till now."[133]

Mallory praised Tattnall's daring and prudence and told him what he believed was the key to the situation: as soon as the *Richmond* was ready, he would include her in Tattnall's squadron next to the *Virginia*. The situation would then change, and Mallory urged that the work on the new ironclad be pushed to the utmost. About ten days earlier the secretary had insisted to Commodore S. S. Lee that not a single hour be lost and that Lee should seek additional workmen in North Carolina if necessary.[134]

Now Hampton Roads was again dominated by the *Virginia,* which for several days following took her ease because there was not a single enemy ship therein. Union transports were again compelled to unload at the limited and narrow space at Fortress Monroe.

Yet, on the same day the *Virginia* made her successful sally, McClellan had arrayed 118,000 men in front of the Yorktown defense line. Still, the Union general felt unhappy because the loss of his best line of operations along the James River and the complete mastery of Hampton Roads by the Confederate navy were hindering him and compelling him to advance at a snail's pace.[135]

And this was not the only help that the small Confederate navy granted to General Magruder, defender of Yorktown: on 18 April, Tattnall sent three gunboats, the *Jamestown, Raleigh,* and *Teaser,* under Lieutenant Commanding Joseph N. Barney, up the James River to protect the right wing of Magruder's forces with their fire;[136] a few days later the flag officer added to this squadron the remaining small ships, the gunboats *Patrick Henry* and *Beaufort,* putting everything under the orders of Commander John R. Tucker.[137]

The small fleet carried out in a remarkable way its task of protecting and helping the Confederate land forces, bombarding the enemy troops with an effective fire, and receiving high praise from the supreme command of the army.[138]

Yet the *Virginia* remained alone to defend Hampton Roads, Norfolk, and the James's estuary. This was a very difficult task, as Tattnall clearly told Mallory. Even if fear of the frightful ironclad was still holding back the enemy, to protect everything with a single ship was very risky.[139]

The secretary was perfectly aware of the situation. The *Richmond* must be ready as soon as possible. Thus began another desperate race against time. Moreover, the enemy, outside the roads, had gotten another reinforcement: the ironclad *Galena,* six guns. From Richmond Mallory was pressing the issue: organize on the *Richmond* new gangs of carpenters to work at night;[140] run any risk because the enemy was at the gate with overwhelming strength and the outlook was the loss of Norfolk in twenty days. No effort should be spared.[141]

The secretary's plans thus began to take shape. The *Virginia,* clearly, must be ready to play the ultimate card: leave Hampton Roads and try to deliver a forlorn-hope attack against the ships on the York River that were supplying McClellan[142] (even though Tattnall, who doubted such a possibility, tried on the same day to dissuade the Confederate military authorities).[143] Under such circumstances, only the *Richmond* would remain to defend and save Norfolk. To her would fall the honor and the onus of driving the *Monitor* back while the *Virginia* would sortie for her ultimate undertaking.[144] On 1 May Mallory, who felt the situation coming to a head, peremptorily ordered that the *Richmond* be launched at once.[145]

Two days later, General Joseph Johnston would order the Confederate forces to evacuate the Yorktown line and retreat up the Peninsula toward Richmond. After much soul-searching, the general, caught in the predicament of saving either Norfolk or Richmond—and persuaded that he was not able to defend both—decided upon this strategy.[146] Therefore, preparations would be made for the excruciating sacrifice: giving up the naval base. Mallory had already sent orders to abandon Norfolk and carry away all important supplies.[147]

And so that the great movement which both the land and naval forces of the Confederacy were to undertake would succeed, the highest military and naval Confederate authorities requested that the *Virginia* make a supreme effort.[148] An almost impossible task was asked of her: "We look to the *Virginia* alone to prevent the enemy from ascending the James River," Mallory telegraphed Tattnall. And on the next day: "Please endeavor to protect Norfolk, as well as the James River."[149] This was mandatory, lest the Confederate forces of General Benjamin Huger, protecting Norfolk to the northeast, were to be left hopelessly trapped.

Both officers and men aboard the *Virginia* felt that the supreme moment was approaching. The Confederacy again trusted in its small navy at one of the most difficult hours of its short existence.

N I N E

The Battle (II)

Those ominous last days of April 1862 threatened disaster for the Confederacy in the West, along the Mississippi River. The forts protecting New Orleans were under a hailstorm of shells, to which they answered with some success.[1] In Richmond the naval secretary was faced with a challenging choice. Though threatened from both north and south, the Confederate navy on the Mississippi had the great edge of interior lines. Yet the question was, Against which of the two enemy groups should its forces be concentrated?

The Confederate army had already decided: advancing from the north were not only the Union ironclad gunboats but also the powerful armies of the Tennessee and of the Cumberland commanded by Generals Grant and Don Carlos Buell; therefore, General Beauregard, who must stop them, needed any available reinforcement. There was no choice: the Southern high command at Richmond decided that General Beauregard would not only keep the troops "lent" him by General Lovell but that Lovell should send him posthaste another six of the best regiments taken from those defending New Orleans.[2]

Mallory had from the beginning considered the northern threat the more serious; so did President Davis. Along the lower Mississippi, Mallory argued, the threat was from wooden ships that the forts should be able to deal with. From the north, however, ironclad ships were coming, and against these the iron of the *Louisiana* and eventually the *Mississippi* must be used.[3]

Commodore Hollins, commanding the upriver flotilla, however, drew different conclusions from the same situation. After convincing himself of the impossibility of opposing the Union ironclad gunboats with his own wooden ships, on 9 April he proposed that his flotilla be sent to fight the enemy south of New Orleans. He repeated the suggestion on the eleventh. It appears that, understanding the folly of leaving the waters of the upper Mississippi open to the enemy, he halfheartedly proposed that Mallory send the *Louisiana* to the northern sector, maintaining with great optimism that she would be ready in three days.[4]

Mallory thoroughly agreed that Confederate ironclads were needed to fight those of the Union. Yet he could not help seeing the irresponsibility of Hollins's proposal to abandon the upper river to the enemy before Southern ironclads were ready. He at once answered that the commodore should not move his flotilla and at all costs should use it to prevent the enemy from advancing downriver. He hoped that the *Louisiana* would join him promptly, followed as soon as possible by the *Mississippi*.[5]

The impulsive Hollins, however, evidently accustomed to doing things his own way, requested by Commodore Whittle to come to New Orleans because the situation there was serious, overlooked Whittle's lack of authority over him and, before drafting his messages to Mallory, decided on his own to sail instantly to New Orleans with the *McRae* and the *Ivy* without bothering to request authorization from the secretary.[6]

Hollins's telegram in which he asked for such authorization had been sent while he was already proceeding toward New Orleans and after turning over what remained of the flotilla to Commander Robert F. Pinkney. Indeed, he sent one of his telegrams to Mallory from Baton Rouge, not far from New Orleans.[7]

Hollins's conduct so verged on insubordination that he would have deserved to be court-martialed.[8] Whittle's "inducement" to Hollins showed that he, too, was unclear about the limits of his responsibilities. In Richmond the fact that Hollins generated more confusion than power was, it seems, taken into consideration because, with some hypocrisy, the decision was made to relieve him and recall him at once to the capital to chair a board of examinations for naval cadets. Meanwhile, in Tennessee, where public opinion considered him guilty of having deserted his place of duty, Hollins was being lampooned and blamed in the press.[9]

At New Orleans, the fitting out of the two ironclads was still well behind schedule. Mallory, hoping that at least the *Louisiana* could be readied in time, on 16 April ordered Whittle to send her upriver as soon as possible.[10]

By now the hailstorm of shells that threatened to blow the forts to bits had provoked panic in that city. The governor of the state frantically asked that the *Louisiana* not be sent to the upper Mississippi. So did General

Lovell, commanding at New Orleans; yet the secretary of war had already written him: "The *Louisiana* was ordered up the [Mississippi] River to meet three ironclad boats which have succeeded in passing Island No. 10." [11]

Still, after ordering Whittle to have the *Louisiana* proceed upriver, Mallory, considering the worsening situation south of New Orleans, had second thoughts; therefore, in a following message he authorized Whittle to decide for the best after consulting both General Lovell and Governor Thomas O. Moore. [12]

Whittle at once ordered that the *Louisiana* be sent to support the forts south of New Orleans and that Commander John K. Mitchell assume command of the Confederate naval forces that would defend the river against an attack by Farragut. "Impress upon the officers and men of the Navy, and the volunteers under your command that the eyes of the country are upon them," Whittle concluded. "They are expected to emulate the glorious deeds recently enacted in Hampton Roads." [13]

Yet when an attempt was made on 20 April to move the *Louisiana* downriver, the Confederates had to admit that she was in very poor condition. Armor on her forecastle, hatch coaming, and gunport shutters had not been completed, nor had that on her deck. Her guns were still unmounted, or mounted in haste, so that some were too high and others too low compared with their embrasures. Even worse, the engines that should turn her two screws had not yet been installed, leaving the ironclad to depend for propulsion only on her central paddle wheels. As a result, she was impossible to steer. Either because of the eddy made by the wheels, which neutralized the rudder, or because of the absence of her screws, which would have helped to steer her, the ironclad was being dragged helplessly downriver by the current.

She had to stop her engines and was taken under tow by two steamers; this was also necessary because her caulking had not been finished and water raised by the paddle wheels flooded the magazines. Finally, to crown the drama, sailors were lacking. They had to be substituted for by a company of artillerists from the army. [14]

In front of an eager and hopeful crowd, on sunny 20 April the ship moved. Mitchell had had embarked upon the two escort vessels that towed her gangs of mechanics, carpenters, and caulkers. As soon as the ironclad reached the forts and moored along the right bank of the river, a little north of Fort St. Philip and just out of range of Porter's mortar boats, they immediately went to work.

The ironclad's guns were mounted that night, with backbreaking labor. Yet the shape and slimness of the gunports prevented them from being elevated more than five degrees (i.e., they had to fire only slightly above

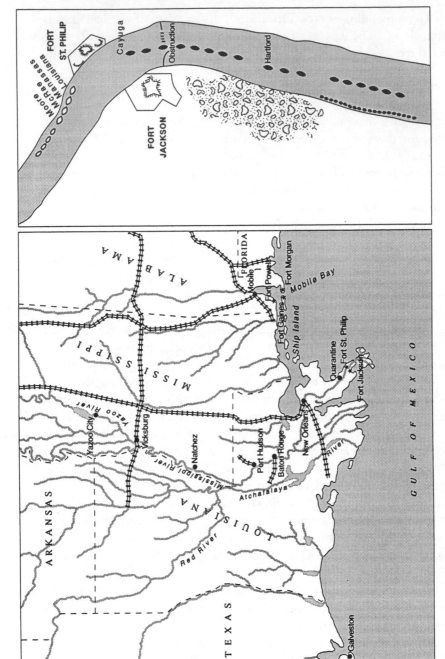

The lower Mississippi River and the positions of C.S. and U.S. warships at the beginning of the battle, early dawn of 24 April 1862.

point-blank), and they had only a very limited traverse. The result was that they could fire little more than directly ahead. Still, McIntosh did not seem disheartened: working night and day, the caulkers and carpenters succeeded in stopping the leaks; mechanics began to install the engines and to connect them to the driveshafts of the twin screws. Her crew worked tirelessly, as did several squads of sailors lent by the gunboat *McRae,* anchored nearby. And the gunners spent the nights ready at their pieces.

If the work proceeded well, Mitchell hoped that the ship would soon be able to move and attack the Federal wooden vessels. It was trusting in *spes, ultima dea.* Indeed, the enemy on the Mississippi was inexorably threatening to beat the Confederates on the brink, with respect to time.[15]

In addition to the *Louisiana,* commanded by Charles McIntosh, Commodore Mitchell had the small gunboat *McRae* (seven guns), commanded by Lieutenant Thomas B. Huger, the ram *Manassas* (one gun), still commanded by the daring and bold Alexander F. Warley; and the gunboat *Jackson* (two guns), under the orders of Francis B. Renshaw. There were also two steam launches, each fitted with a small howitzer, and half a dozen tugs and unarmed vessels. These could be useful for pushing fire rafts against enemy ships or, at the worst, could be scuttled and transformed into passive obstructions.

Further, there were two gunboats belonging to the state of Louisiana, the *Governor Moore* and the *General Quitman* (two guns each). These soon put themselves under Mitchell's orders; the commodore knew he could depend on them. One of these was commanded by Beverly Kennon, a former Confederate naval officer who had transferred to state service. He had "distinguished" himself by his bungling management of the Ordnance Bureau in New Orleans, yet he was aggressive, daring, and displayed a spirited initiative. In sum, the Confederacy had six ships carrying about thirty guns.[16]

These were all the forces Mitchell could muster. There were also six gunboat-rams of the noted (or, better, notorious) River Defense Fleet commanded by "Captain" John A. Stevenson. Yet when Mitchell sent the latter a written order from General Lovell, placing him at Mitchell's disposal, Stevenson answered that he would not take orders from the navy or from any naval officer; however, he would "contrive" to meet the "pleas" of the commodore and pledged to "cooperate." Therefore, Mitchell informed General Johnson K. Duncan, commanding the forts, that he would not bother any more about the River Defense Fleet and that he washed his hands of it.[17] Events would prove that he had made a wise decision.

On the opposite side, Farragut could array four first-class and two second-class sloops and sixteen seagoing gunboats, carrying 245 guns:[18] a ratio of 8.17:1 to the disadvantage of the Confederates. The forts mounted 126 guns, of which 115 could shell the river and the zone nearby,[19] yet the forts were (obviously) motionless so that Farragut would be compelled to endure their frightful fire for only a relatively short time.

Even including the guns on land, the ratio still remained to the Confederates' disadvantage by 3.10:1. In addition, of the *Louisiana's* sixteen guns only eight could be brought to bear on the enemy's ships, at least until she was at her mooring.

The Southern naval forces looked exceedingly disadvantaged. Yet, what about the *Mississippi,* the formidable ironclad, free from the flaws and shortcomings of the *Louisiana?* She was indeed gigantic, powerful, protected not by railroad iron but by armor plate welded in the best way and armed with extremely powerful guns. Among Farragut's wooden ships she would have been "like a bull in a china shop,"[20] yet would she be ready in time? Work on her proceeded with frantic bustle, without a second of respite, in a distressed effort to stop time that seemed to be slipping through everyone's fingers. The builders estimated that ten to fifteen more days were needed to complete her.[21] Would Farragut allow himself to be beaten in such a dreadful challenge?

Every exertion was needed to complete the *Louisiana.* Yet Commodore Mitchell complained that General Duncan was disturbing the works by pressuring him immediately to tow the unfinished ironclad near the forts, where she might possibly hit and disperse the enemy mortar boats or at least compel them to withdraw. The commodore answered in a well-reasoned letter, saying that though he was fully aware of the impending threat, he could not subject the *Louisiana* to enemy fire before the most urgent work on her had been finished, certainly not while she lacked motive power. He specified that he now had fifty mechanics at work in addition to her own crew and men from other ships.[22]

On 23 April Duncan repeated his urgent request. He was supported by General Lovell, who was backed up by Commodore Whittle, who, in turn, brought pressure to bear on Mitchell. Buttressed by the advice of all his ship captains, Mitchell repeated the same day that it was impossible to shift the *Louisiana* near the forts in her present condition. He added, however: "We have an additional force of mechanics from the city this morning, and I hope that by to-morrow night the motive power of the *Louisiana* will be ready, and in the meantime her battery will be in place and other preparations will be completed so to enable her to act against the enemy."[23]

"To-morrow" would be too late. During that very night of 24 April, Farragut unleashed his attack.

From the ramparts the Confederates were keeping a sharp watch.

Around 3:40 A.M., when gigantic shadows were sighted moving upriver, they opened fire, which was answered immediately and formidably by the Union warships.[24] Instantly General Duncan sent a last, urgent plea to Mitchell for help: "You are assuming a fearful responsibility if you do not come at once to our assistance with the *Louisiana* and the fleet."[25]

The commodore did not deserve such a rebuke. The *Louisiana,* still unable to move, could do nothing but wait for the enemy at her mooring; but the smaller ships had already stoked the fires, steering at once for the enemy squadron that, after a fearsome artillery duel with the forts, was passing them.[26]

As foreseen, no substantial help came from the gunboat-rams of the River Defense Fleet. Evidently believing that discretion was the better part of courage, they fled and ended up ingloriously destroyed.[27]

Because the gunboat *Jackson* had been sent to defend the canals to the north of the forts from enemy troops that might land from the sea, the Confederates were able to deploy, other than the immovable *Louisiana,* only the ram *Manassas,* gunboat *McRae,* and two Louisiana state gunboats. Commander Warley daringly steered to attack with the *Manassas* and, although subjected to dreadful enemy fire, succeeded in ramming in succession the two large sloops *Mississippi* and *Brooklyn.* The first reported extensive damage to her external planking but not enough to spring leaks. The second, well protected by chains wound about her as an improvised yet effective shield, sustained the blow without any remarkable damage. After attacking other ships, the gallant Warley, subjected to a withering fire and with his only gun disabled, had to beach the *Manassas* and scuttle her.[28]

Steering bravely into battle, the *McRae* was immediately surrounded by enemy ships so that she could fire in any direction, almost always hitting the mark, particularly the U.S. sloop *Iroquois,* which was struck by accurate fire from the Confederate ship. Yet, in the end, crushed by the overwhelmingly more numerous enemy, almost shot to pieces, ablaze, and with her captain, Thomas B. Huger, mortally wounded, she was compelled to retreat. Lieutenant Charles W. Read, now commanding, tried very hard to salvage the ship that was taking water from all sides; yet later he could not stop her from sinking.[29]

The major Confederate success was attained by the Louisiana state gunboat *Governor Moore.* After a fierce battle with the seagoing gunboat *Varuna,* she succeeded in ramming and sinking her. Soon afterward, the small Southern vessel, reduced to a wreck, ablaze, and with fifty-seven dead men aboard (more than half of her crew), had to be scuttled.[30]

The *Louisiana* was the target of fire from several Union ships, which hurled at her many a fierce broadside. Yet these had no effect on her rmor, while shells from the six guns that her crew succeeded in manning pierced the sides of Federal ships as though they were made of papier mâché. Yet the enemy vessels could move and the *Louisiana* could not so that soon they were able to withdraw from her fire. Unfortunately, Captain McIntosh, standing on the upper deck, which was imperfectly protected by a weak iron bulwark, fell mortally wounded. Command of the ironclad passed to Lieutenant John Wilkinson.[31]

Except for the *Louisiana,* at the end of the day the Confederate flotilla had been smashed to pieces and Farragut was proceeding toward New Orleans, which he planned to reach on the twenty-fifth, to receive its surrender. Meanwhile, General Lovell's Confederate troops rushed to evacuate the city because the Union troops of General Butler, coming from the sea and landing upriver from the forts, were approaching.

Still, what of the *Mississippi?* The armor plate needed to protect her casemate (the only part not yet covered) had finally arrived but still on railroad cars. The two lateral driveshafts had also arrived a few days before and workmen had carried them aboard. The central shaft was aboard but not yet connected with the engines, which still required some work. The second of the two lateral shafts had been placed on board two days earlier, on 22 April. The two lateral screws were still ashore on the pier. The two 7-inch rifled guns had also arrived, but the others were still in Jackson, Mississippi.[32]

Two more weeks and the fearsome ironclad would be ready for action.[33] Yet Farragut was approaching New Orleans. The Confederates had not overcome their handicap in the deadly race with the Federals. Was it still possible to salvage the big ironclad or, at the worst, to prevent her capture by the enemy?

Early on 24 April, before Farragut's ships arrived off New Orleans, Commodore Whittle summoned Sinclair, commanding the ironclad, and issued him the necessary instructions. Sinclair was given two river steamers, the *St. Charles* and the *Peytona,* to tow the ironclad.

The two boats had taken their time, however, and did not arrive until around 8:00 in the evening. Sinclair loaded everything he could on the *Mississippi* and then tried to have her towed upriver. It then appeared that both steamers lacked enough power to tow the heavy ship against the swift, strong current; indeed, they as well as the *Mississippi* were being slowly pushed backward.

After repeatedly trying throughout the night, Sinclair decided to go to New Orleans in a hopeless search for other steamers, but there he was confronted by a nightmare. Captains and crews of commercial steamers had fled. Confusion, panic, and a sense of defeat were everywhere. And now Farragut's ships hove into view.

There was not a minute to waste. Lieutenant James I. Waddell, executive officer of the *Mississippi*, put her to the torch.[34] After the fire had eaten away her mooring lines, the *Mississippi* began to float slowly with the current, appearing to the appalled Federals "formidable even in her expiring flames." Farragut summarized the meaning of his historic victory in a single sentence: "We were too quick for them."[35]

The shocking loss resonated through the South. At Norfolk, a young naval cadet from the *Virginia* wrote that the *Mississippi* would have been worth a dozen "Merrimacks" to the South.[36]

Yet on the *Louisiana*, tied up near the forts, the Confederate flag still flew and, under her commanding officer, Wilkinson, work on her was breathlessly pursued. To what end? Perhaps to attack the enemy as soon as she was ready because the forts were still in Southern hands. Perhaps to try to reach the sea and then the Confederate base at Mobile, Alabama, or go upriver and attack Farragut's fleet.[37]

On 27 April, at last, after extreme exertions, the engines were connected to the screws and the ironclad would be ready to move on the morrow. Yet fate dictated that the Confederates would again be defeated by a twenty-four-hour delay. On the twenty-seventh, disaster struck, albeit from factors not under naval control. The garrisons of the forts, who had fought stubbornly and bravely, resisting an unending day and night bombardment, were almost entirely composed of volunteers from New Orleans. Upon learning that the city was in enemy hands, the soldiers became disheartened and concerned about their dear ones.

During the night of the twenty-eighth the garrison of the most important fortification, Fort Jackson, mutinied, spiked the guns (possibly to prevent their falling intact into enemy hands), and deserted. General Duncan could do nothing but surrender both forts.

Now bereft of support from the forts, the *Louisiana*, trapped in the river and deprived of any base, was lost. She had on board only ten days worth of supplies and would not have been able to go to sea, where the powerful blockading enemy fleet would have seized her (provided that she could have forced her way out, which was improbable). All her officers agreed with Mitchell: she had to be scuttled.[38]

The Confederate officers and men still on board quickly set fire to the ironclad. Like the *Mississippi*, with her mooring gone she sailed downriver until the flames reached the magazine. Then she blew up with a deafening roar and a huge column of white smoke. It was 28 April 1862.[39] The two ships in which Mallory and the whole South had placed so many hopes had ceased to exist.[40]

Meanwhile, the situation was also worsening in Hampton Roads. Yet Mallory was coolly playing the few cards remaining to him. On 3 May he issued his orders: important supplies still at Norfolk must be moved. Captain Richard L. Page would at once transfer the workshops to North Carolina. Ordnance and engineering equipment would be sent either there or to Richmond. The ironclad *Richmond* must be launched immediately; the strong iron sides of the *Virginia* would guarantee protection. On the same day Commander Tucker was ordered to leave without delay for Norfolk with the *Patrick Henry* and the *Jamestown* and tow the *Richmond* upriver to the head of the James.[41]

Tucker received Mallory's order on 5 May. That night he sailed toward Norfolk and on the next night was able to come back upriver. The *Patrick Henry* towed both the *Richmond* and the little unfinished gunboat *Hampton;* the heavy guns and ordnance supplies of the new ironclad were in a brig towed by the *Jamestown.* By the seventh, the ironclad was safe in Richmond at the new Rocketts Navy Yard, near the southern end of the city.[42] In this case, at least, fast action and initiative by the Confederate naval authorities had guaranteed good luck.

The *Richmond* had been salvaged literally under the enemy's nose. On the fifth the president of the United States, Abraham Lincoln, had unexpectedly arrived at Fortress Monroe. There he had shared his remarkable strategic instinct with the Union's military leaders.[43] His innate propensity for action and his daring contrasted strikingly with the caution and wavering of McClellan and Goldsborough.

The president was not slow in discerning the Achilles' heel of the Confederates: the *Virginia,* even though formidable, was alone and could not protect everything. Further, a deserter had brought news that Norfolk was about to be evacuated. The president did not hesitate. He instantly ordered that the whole Union squadron enter the roadstead and attack the Confederate coastal batteries at Sewell's Point while the ironclad *Galena* and two other gunboats would undertake a raid up the James River. Unable to repel both attacks, the *Virginia* must choose one or the other.[44]

The raid up the James River began on the night of 7 May.[45] It was led by one of the most daring Union sailors, Commander John Rodgers. At dawn of 8 May the U.S. ships entered the mouth of the James; the Confederates had narrowly succeeded in salvaging the *Richmond,* just ahead of the enemy raid. Yet the line of operations represented by the James was again in Union hands.[46]

Only the *Virginia* might have tried to regain control. Mallory had ordered her to protect the river's mouth.[47] Yet General Huger, fearing that he must abandon his forts and guns to enemy hands if the ironclad did not protect them, obtained a modification of her orders.[48] Indeed, on the same day, 8 May, as Rodgers's flotilla surged up the James, the major

Union squadron approached Sewell's Point and began bombarding it.[49] Lincoln's two-pronged plan was in action.

Without delay, the *Virginia* steered for the enemy. What else could she do? It was necessary to abandon the James River and counter the more serious threat. It would be her last battle.

At the approach of the ironclad, the Union ships scattered like chaff in the wind. Still unwilling to engage her, they hoped to lure her toward Fortress Monroe. Tattnall again avoided the trap; again the waters of Hampton Roads were incontestably dominated by the *Virginia.* Yet Rodgers was already up the James River, where the Confederate ironclad, because of her enormous draft, could not reach him.[50]

Yet Lincoln was still disappointed by the way his commanders were conducting operations. He would not stand passively by while Southern forces retreated. Rather, he thought, it was necessary somehow to land troops on the Virginia shore, on the opposite side from Fortress Monroe, to trap the enemy. Consequently, he took the trouble to find a landing place outside of the roadstead, on the coast facing Chesapeake Bay, where the *Virginia* could not interfere, either because she would be attacked by the whole Union squadron or because of shallow waters.[51]

On the morning of 10 May, four Union infantry regiments landed on the Virginia coast, near Ocean View, northeast of Willoughby Point.[52] General Benjamin Huger, commanding Confederate forces in Norfolk, was so overwhelmed by panic that he speeded up the evacuation already under way—and forgot to notify Tattnall.[53]

That same morning the *Virginia,* nearing Sewell's Point, observed that no flag flew over Confederate positions. Tattnall immediately realized that the Southern troops had evacuated and that the ironclad alone faced an enemy who now commanded both sides of Hampton Roads and was at Norfolk's very gate. What to do? There was only one solution, and after conferring with his officers, Tattnall took it: immediately sail up the James River before the enemy could arrive at its estuary overland, attack and destroy Rodgers's flotilla, and then help defend the Confederate capital, Richmond.[54]

Pilots who were questioned said that this was possible if the ironclad was lightened so that her draft would not exceed eighteen feet. Her crew immediately went to work and threw overboard everything but her guns and ammunition. Yet, at 1 A.M. the pilots changed their minds. To sail up the James, they said, would be possible if an easterly wind blew against the current and raised the water's level. At the time, the wind was westerly and the water was too shallow.[55]

Cowardice? Treason?[56] There was no time to think about such things.

The *Virginia* had been rendered unable to confront the enemy. At least two feet of her unarmored hull were above the waterline, as were her screw and rudder. She now faced a danger immensely greater than her destruction: her capture and use by the enemy. No doubt was possible: better to destroy her.

With heavy hearts, the *Virginia*'s sailors beached her near Craney Island. There forty years earlier Tattnall, as a young naval cadet, had had his baptism of fire, fighting against the British under a flag that now belonged to his enemy. Because the ironclad was too big and there was water between her and the shore, her boats had to shuttle to and fro to land all her three hundred crewmen safely.

Catesby ap R. Jones and John Taylor Wood were the last to leave, after spreading flammable matter everywhere and setting the fuses. In short order, while her sailors walked away sadly through the woods, the *Virginia* became a huge funeral pyre. Then her cannons began to discharge. At about 4:30 in the morning of 11 May 1862 she blew up with a fearsome explosion.[57]

The loss of the *Virginia* upset the South. General Robert E. Lee wrote to his wife that her destruction distressed him so much that any other problem was pushed into the background.[58]

Now that the frightful ironclad was gone, on 12 May the *Monitor* sailed up the Elizabeth River to Norfolk and anchored where the *Virginia* had been moored.[59]

It was now the North's turn to fall under the illusion of the "ultimate weapon." By order of the president, who was in Norfolk, Commodore Goldsborough directed that the ironclads *Monitor* and *Naugatuck* join the *Galena* on the James and together sail up the river as far as Richmond "to bomb the city into surrender."[60]

Seven miles south of Richmond, on the right bank of the James, are the heights of Drewry's Bluff that rise about fifty feet above the river level. There Confederates had begun to build a fort. The keen eye of Robert D. Minor had detected the bluff's importance in preventing enemy ships from sailing up to Richmond, and at his suggestion, engineers began to strengthen the fort with railroad iron.[61]

The work had lagged behind because the *Virginia* was protecting Richmond. Then the situation had changed for the worse. Now the *Virginia*'s sailors, almost all of them first-rate gunners, were directed there; Tattnall had correctly considered them the most important part of the ironclad to save for the Confederacy, rather than foolishly throwing them against the enemy in a ship that would be doomed to destruction.

These men had traveled through the night, first on foot, then by train, and were dog-tired. They found Richmond under martial law; troops were everywhere, preparing to confront McClellan's approaching divisions. Yet another, much closer and deadly threat were the Union ironclads that were sailing upriver. Commotion reigned.[62]

The *Virginia*'s men immediately hurried to Drewry's Bluff, took up positions next to the other Confederate troops, and like them began to mount some heavy guns that had been sent there in great haste. It was raining. For two days, in the mud, the ironclad's crew, together with that of the gunboat *Jamestown* (which had been scuttled to obstruct the channel in front of the fort) and with some men from the *Patrick Henry*, built big earthworks strengthened with logs. According to Scharf, the fort mounted nine big naval guns, eight of them Brooke rifles, and a 10-inch Columbiad.[63]

At 7:30 A.M. on 15 May, Confederate lookouts saw the gray outlines of the Union ships. Then a midshipman from the *Virginia* pulled out the old ragged flag of the ironclad that he had brought with him in his knapsack, at the cost of throwing his reserve clothing into the water, and loosened it to the wind.[64]

With cool boldness, Rodgers anchored the *Galena* in the middle of the river and opened fire. The battle soon leaned in the Confederates' favor. The *Monitor* and the *Naugatuck* had great trouble elevating their guns so that they could hit the fort, and the *Galena* showed the flimsiness diagnosed by Ericsson. Under the accurate fire of the Southerners—to which the artillerists from the *Virginia* gave a remarkable contribution—the weak armor of the ironclad was pierced several times until Rodgers, after more than three hours of fearful pounding, ordered a retreat. He had thirteen killed and eleven wounded on board.[65]

The Confederate capital had been saved just in time. Contrary to myth, the *Virginia*'s crew was not the whole (possibly not even the majority) of the defenders; yet their presence, in addition to the know-how of these seasoned fighters, gave a symbolic meaning to the Southern victory. By land and by sea the small but spirited Confederate navy was always present, fighting often in dire situations and making a valuable—sometimes decisive—contribution to the defense of the South, despite the pessimists and the detractors.

At the same time, on the Mississippi River, where the enemy was threatening to strike a fatal blow, it was the small Southern navy that once again helped save the Confederacy from another catastrophe. After the fall of New Orleans, President Lincoln wanted and intended that the final blows be given the South along the Mississippi, which he called "the backbone of the rebellion."[66]

With the Crescent City taken, Farragut and Butler could not rest or allow the Confederates time to recover. The president, himself a westerner who knew the river well from personal experience, had discerned the key point, the only one that would grant command of the river along its whole course and split the Confederacy in twain: Vicksburg.[67] Therefore, Farragut was ordered to proceed from New Orleans without delay to take Vicksburg.

Vicksburg, Mississippi, was strategically crucial for several reasons. First, the riverine city was linked to the east by a trunk line to the great Memphis and New Orleans Railroad; toward the West, by ferry, it was tied to another railroad which, from the suburb of De Soto, across the river from Vicksburg, led to Shreveport, Louisiana, and from there to Texas, providing the only great transverse railway that linked the eastern part of the Confederacy to the trans-Mississippi states, source of substantial food supplies, especially meat.[68]

Second, the city rose upon a hill some two hundred feet above the river level, toward which the slope descended gradually. Therefore, its position was excellent for firing down with a sweeping or raking fire toward the stream.

Finally, the river before Vicksburg made a double horseshoe bend; any ship trying to sail there would be exposed thrice to devastating fire. Especially deadly would be shooting at the second bend, where a water battery might hit with raking fire throughout her whole length any ship rash enough to pass.

To make it impregnable, the city of Vicksburg was protected to the north and south by streams and swamps that would prevent any attempt to approach her, whereas the eastern hilly ground which extended several miles inland also permitted an easy defense by means of earthworks.[69]

General Beauregard had been the first to understand Vicksburg's importance, even before New Orleans fell. On 21 April 1862 he ordered Vicksburg fortified at once with some twenty guns.[70] Among these were the first-rate ones from Jackson that had been intended for the ironclad *Mississippi*. Together with others from New Orleans, they were forwarded by General Lovell.[71]

Again the guns of a scuttled Confederate ironclad would put an insuperable obstacle in front of the enemy naval forces. Captain of Engineers D. B. Harris, detailed by Beauregard, placed eighteen heavy guns in such a way that the batteries could strike the river with raking fire. Then, on Lovell's order, on 12 May General Martin Luther Smith arrived in Vicksburg and assumed command.[72]

There was not a minute to lose. Farragut (who would soon be promoted to rear admiral,[73] the first in the U.S. Navy to be awarded that rank) on 2 May had sent a strong advance guard from his squadron toward Vicksburg, preparing to follow it immediately with his heavy ships. The latter in turn were joined by two transports carrying twelve hundred soldiers commanded by General Thomas Williams.

On the ninth Farragut reached Baton Rouge, Louisiana's capital, which had already surrendered to the advance group. On the twelfth, the day General Smith arrived in Vicksburg and twenty-four hours after the *Virginia* blew up in Hampton Roads, the city of Natchez was captured without firing a shot. In it were some of the most splendid residences of planters from Louisiana and Mississippi.[74]

On the eighteenth the Federal ships reached Vicksburg, but there the scene changed. Just in time, the Confederates had succeeded in fortifying the city, and now they turned down any summons to surrender. As the ships had great trouble hitting Vicksburg's forts from the river and General Williams could not attack the city with only twelve hundred men, Farragut left near Vicksburg an observation flotilla of six seagoing gunboats and returned temporarily to New Orleans. The Confederates had earned some respite—but not for long.

Meanwhile, on the upper reaches of the Mississippi, the River Defense Fleet, composed of the eight remaining gunboat-rams, had succeeded, on 10 May, through a stroke of luck, in surprising and ramming the two Union ironclad gunboats *Cincinnati* and *Mound City* anchored near Plum Point Bend, above Fort Pillow. Only shallow water saved them. Yet there would be no more such successes because the Northerners quickly recovered.

Unfortunately, General Beauregard, who faced Union forces in northern Mississippi, had to evacuate Corinth, which caused Fort Pillow to fall and opened the road to Memphis to the enemy. On 6 June 1862, the River Defense Fleet, emboldened by its recent success at Plum Point, attacked before Memphis the U.S. squadron of ironclad gunboats, now commanded by Commodore Charles H. Davis, and Ellet's rams. The outcome was a disaster for the Southerners: only one of their boats, the *General Van Dorn,* managed to survive by fleeing. All the others were either destroyed or captured.[75]

Now the whole Mississippi looked open to the Union navy. On 18 June Farragut's squadron, followed by Porter's seventeen mortar boats (which would immediately shell the Confederate positions) and by an expeditionary corps of forty-five hundred men and ten fieldpieces under General Williams, was again before Vicksburg. From the north the rams had preceded the ironclad squadron and now got in touch with Farragut. On the twenty-eighth he gallantly forced his way under Vicksburg's guns and joined the rams' flotilla, now commanded by Alfred Ellet. South of the city he had left the large first-class sloop *Brooklyn,* two seagoing gunboats, and the still-firing mortar boats.

Because Farragut and Williams had decided that it would be impossible to assault Vicksburg, defended by more than ten thousand Confederates,[76] Williams's troops landed on the De Soto peninsula, where they soon began to dig a canal that would cut through to the bend of the river to divert its course and leave the city dry.[77] The attempt failed.

On 1 July Commodore Davis's squadron with the ironclad gunboats and six of his mortar scows reached Farragut. The Federals were clearly in earnest and the crucial fortress was now in a viselike grip.

Still, taking it would not be easy. General Earl Van Dorn, who on 27 June had relieved Lovell as commanding officer of the department encompassing south-central Mississippi and what remained of eastern Louisiana, had at once grasped the situation. The army could resist stubbornly; yet, if left to fight alone, it might not save the fortress, which (as even General Beauregard feared) would in the end be lost: "Boats now below city" will come up "unless beaten back by superior force. Foot by foot the city will be sacrificed." Only the navy could change this grim outlook and prevent the whole course of the river from being lost to the Confederacy, with appalling consequences.[78]

The navy had no more than one card to play; but it was of the greatest value. And the navy was ready to play it with cool resolution. Through all this time the Confederates had doggedly worked on the two ironclads being built in Memphis. Unfortunately, the military authorities had not shown a great understanding of the situation's urgency and had been slow in sending workmen. Yet the constructor had employed hands who were not naval carpenters. At last, on 25 April, when New Orleans fell, the *Arkansas* was complete, except for the officers' quarters. Armor was in place almost up to her deck. Her engines were on board, ready to be installed. On the *Tennessee,* planking was being nailed; other equipment was on shore nearby, except for deck fittings, which had not yet been moved from the railroad warehouse, and the iron, which was on the other side of the Mississippi.[79]

In a few days, at least one of the two ironclads would therefore have been ready to defend Memphis.[80] But panic seized Commander McBlair when he learned of the fall of New Orleans, and he hastily decided to tow away the *Arkansas* that very night, leaving the unfinished *Tennessee* to her fate. She would be burned and destroyed on her slipway the night before Memphis, too, fell.[81]

The rest of the iron and other equipment necessary to complete the *Arkansas* were hastily loaded on barges. McBlair ordered that both the ironclad (whose engines were not yet installed) and the barges be taken in tow by the steamer *Capitol* and hauled up the Yazoo River, which

A History of the Confederate Navy

emptied into the Mississippi a bit north of Vicksburg, and moored about fifty miles upstream from its mouth.

A little later, upon learning from the governor of Mississippi that Farragut's powerful squadron was again sailing upriver, the unfinished ironclad was towed up the Yazoo another hundred miles as far as Greenwood, a small, sleepy town of the Old South. All this jolting about was not good for the ship. A barge with four hundred iron bars, ready to be used to armor her casemate, sank in the river; the engines were dismounted and then placed back on board amid great chaos.[82]

It seemed most possible that the ironclad would end up rusting in that remote part of the South. It also appeared that Charles H. McBlair was not the right man to spare her such a fate. Officers and men were depressed.[83] Then, the most prominent citizens of Greenwood expressed their concern to the authorities in Richmond; finally, General Beauregard, upon learning that the work on the *Arkansas* was lagging behind, asked flatly that the secretary of the navy relieve McBlair of command.[84]

Mallory himself was so concerned that he needed little prompting. On 24 May 1862 McBlair was relieved by Lieutenant Isaac Newton Brown, who proceeded immediately to Greenwood, climbed aboard the ironclad, and assumed command.[85] Brown was among Mallory's happiest choices. This modest and reserved Kentuckian had served in the U.S. Navy for twenty-eight years, fought in the Mexican War, then sailed around the world in U.S. warships from the Cape of Good Hope to the Straits of Magellan, Japan, and the Mediterranean. In the C.S. Navy he painstakingly and capably collaborated in the defenses of Columbus, Island No. 10, and Fort Pillow. Sent to the Tennessee River, he began to put up a flotilla which, unfortunately, following the surrender of Fort Donelson, had been scuttled or captured by the enemy. Ever since, serving under the Confederate flag, he had to solve the most irksome problems with scarce means, yet none would be more exacting than what now confronted him on the *Arkansas*. Years later one of his best officers, who had served under him on the ironclad, said that Brown alone deserved credit for fitting out the ship. Another observed that he was indeed the right man in the right place.[86]

When Brown went aboard on 9 May, the condition of the *Arkansas* was enough to dishearten anyone. Yet Mallory's orders were clear: "Finish and equip that vessel without regard to expenditure of men or money."[87] It was then the flood season so that the ship was four miles from shore. McBlair's inefficiency and ineptitude so overwhelmed Brown that he considered the behavior of that officer almost treasonous.[88]

The iron armor reached only one foot above the waterline. The other

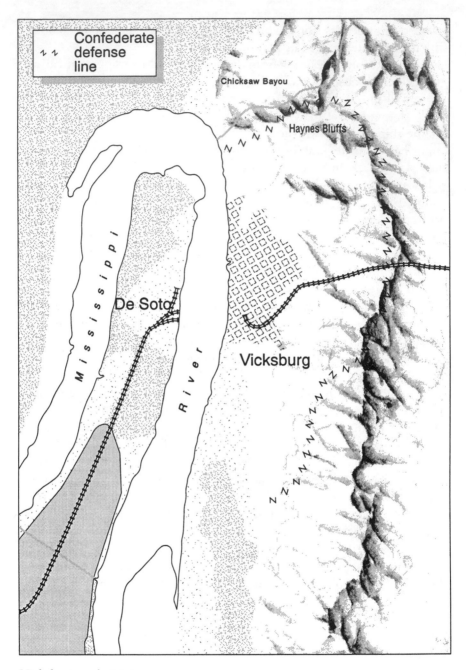

Vicksburg and vicinity.

iron necessary to continue the work was at the bottom of the river, apparently lost. The gunports had not yet been cut in her casemate, and the guns themselves, without carriages, were scattered about the deck. There was neither shell nor shot.[89]

Constructor Shirley, who had sailed on the ship to Greenwood, was pessimistic. The engines needed repairs which would take ten days before they could be installed correctly and put in motion. There was an immediate need for at least twenty-five carpenters and five mechanics, as well as an officer and twenty-seven men to protect the yard.

Brown did not waste a minute. He got a diving bell with which to fish up the iron plate from the river's bottom. This done, on the next day he had the ship towed back to Yazoo City, where the high riverbank would not be subject to flooding and where better shops were available to complete the work.[90]

At Yazoo City, the situation improved. The patriotic local people let Brown dispense with armed guards. The steamer *Capitol,* tied up alongside the *Arkansas,* served as a receiving ship for workmen. Moreover, her engine, which powered her loading cranes, was used to activate a drill that made the holes for nuts and bolts in the iron bars. Local planters were requested to send all the hands they had, and in a short while two hundred men (mostly from nearby military detachments) were at work.

Fifteen blacksmith shops were set up on shore after an appeal to local blacksmiths, who began to work energetically.[91] The agrarian South, poor and almost destitute of an industrial plant, was undertaking the building of an ironclad by mobilizing its one asset: skilled craftsmen. Work proceeded day and night, without respite. Under the hot Mississippi sun, working hours went from 5:00 A.M. to 7:00 P.M.;[92] at night, in more hospitable air, work continued by lantern light.

Much of the iron still needed was scraped up in the local area. It was then transported and unloaded in the only railway station and from there carried by wagon some twenty-five more miles to Yazoo City. Original planning of the ironclad called for six guns, but Brown found four more and still other equipment in gunboats down the Yazoo that could no longer serve any purpose.[93]

Still lacking were gun carriages, which had never been manufactured in Mississippi. At last, Henry Kennedy Stevens, the able executive officer, discovered that two citizens of Jackson were willing to produce them. When they asked for drafts, Lieutenant George W. Gift traced them by means of two simple set squares. Everybody was delighted when, some days later, Stevens appeared at the head of a convoy of wagons pulled by oxen, carrying the much desired carriages.[94] The projectiles were made mostly in Jackson, and some powder could be manufactured in Yazoo City.[95]

Meanwhile, there had arrived downriver, not very far from Yazoo City, the last two surviving gunboats of Hollins's hapless flotilla, the *Livingston* and the *Polk,* as well as the ram of the late River Defense Fleet, *General Van Dorn.* Fleeing from the disaster at Memphis, these had been moored in a place called Liverpool's Landing, near the mouth of the Yazoo, where they found shelter near a floating obstruction formed by a large lighter. Yet because of the obstruction, the three small ships had to remain downriver. Luckily, two guns that had been saved from Fort Pillow were placed near them on land to protect the mooring.[96]

At once Brown sent there one of his best officers, Lieutenant Charles W. Read. Read commanded the *McRae* after Thomas B. Huger had been mortally wounded; then he was sent by the Navy Department to Memphis to serve on the unfinished ironclad *Tennessee,* which was never completed.[97] He was then transferred to the *Arkansas.*

Brown's orders to Read were to strengthen the defense of the small vessels, to turn them bows-on, and to keep steam up so that they would be able to ram any enemy ship that might appear. Yet Commander Pinkney (who had relieved Hollins), would not hear of it. Commodore William F. Lynch was being sent by Mallory to assume command of all naval forces on the Mississippi, and upon him devolved any decision.[98]

Lynch, upon arriving some days later and inspecting the *Arkansas,* telegraphed Mallory that she was "very inferior" to the *Virginia.* And it was, alas, true. Still, Brown had accomplished something akin to a wonder, for the ironclad appeared to be formidable in many ways. When she had been towed up the Yazoo, she was little more than a hull. In five weeks she had been fitted out, her crew had been mustered, and her engines were ready for trial.[99]

The ironclad was 165 feet long and had a draft of 11.5 feet. The walls of her casemate outboard were 1 foot thick, while at both ends the thickness was up to 1.6 feet. They were protected by armor composed of railroad iron 4.5 inches thick. The top of the casemate, which served as upper deck, was covered by half-inch plate. This, however, was not enough because it made the ship vulnerable to plunging fire.

Unfortunately, not enough time had been available to bend railroad rails to form adequate protection for the pilothouse, which was armored throughout only with double iron bars two inches thick (much less strong than the "T" beams made from iron rails). This appeared to be the weakest point of the ship, along with her stern, which was covered with boilerplate, just for appearance's sake. The quarter deck, practically in the open, was over the pilothouse, and communication between it and the rest of the ship was by voice pipe.

She carried ten guns, among them two first-rate 8-inch Columbiads forward. Thanks to their perfect fit in the bore, their projectiles had very little "windage." They therefore had a remarkable penetrating force and did not need to be elevated much (otherwise Columbiads could not have been used aboard a ship). There were also two rifled 6-inch guns aft and three more guns on each broadside, among them two 100-pounder Dahlgrens (one on each side).[100]

She was fitted out while the presence of the enemy was imminent. Once again these men were fighting (as was by now the rule in the Confederate navy) against time, against the lack of almost any means, against overwhelming obstacles. The enemy warships were at a distance of no more than six hours' sailing.

On 26 July Lieutenant Colonel Ellet, with two rams, reconnoitered the Yazoo. Not considering it timely to try to break the floating obstruction at Liverpool's Landing, he retreated. Still, his action caused Captain Pinkney to panic and order the three small ships set afire, thus scuttling them and denying Brown his only remaining escort.

There was, however, one positive result: to avoid collision with the burning wrecks, Ellet turned about and went back to Vicksburg. There from 27 June the Union heavy guns were incessantly battering the city and its fortifications. Their deep thunder was plainly heard at Yazoo City, a dark threat to the handful of brave men working without rest on the *Arkansas*. They were well aware that the Federal ironclad gunboats were only six hours away and that between them and their ship there was only the floating obstruction at Liverpool's Landing.[101]

Brown had more problems. To bring the crew up to two hundred men was not easy. Luckily, the captain could rely on a first-rate group of officers; the problem was the shortage of noncommissioned officers and enlisted men.

At first, it appeared that he might be able to recruit the crews of the defunct River Defense Fleet. These men, however, had resigned and left, some of them (Brown surmised) going over to the enemy.[102] Then, by a stroke of luck, one hundred men were obtained from the gunboats scuttled at Liverpool's Landing. For the remainder, it was necessary to convert about a hundred soldiers into improvised sailors. Of these, sixty were transferred from the Missouri regiments of General Jeff Thompson. They were good artillerists even if they had never manned heavy naval guns. The other forty were volunteers from Vicksburg and were drawn from some Louisiana regiments. The latter were lent to the navy: indeed, they had to be sent back to their regiments when the ironclad reached the port of Vicksburg.[103]

And now the myth of the "ultimate weapon" once again seemed to carry the Confederates away, who indeed, at Vicksburg had their backs to the wall. On 14 June President Davis, pointing out the disaster that threatened the Confederates both up- and downriver from Vicksburg, had asked what progress was being made in fitting out the ironclad which he believed was their last hope.[104]

Then, on 24 June General Van Dorn, foreseeing the fall of fortress Vicksburg, telegraphed the president asking that the *Arkansas* be put under his orders. Davis answered in the affirmative, adding that he had sent appropriate instructions to Commander Brown.[105]

Brown nourished no illusions about miracles. As an old salt, he correctly appraised the possibilities of his as-yet-unfinished ship. Several days earlier he had conceived a more limited yet more realistic strategy for the ironclad. What he had in mind was for her to share in a combination of hit-and-run attacks against enemy ships, both from afloat and ashore, to make it impossible for them to navigate the Mississippi. The *Arkansas* would also protect the Yazoo and its tributary streams, keeping them safe for transportation of Confederate supplies, which were of the utmost importance to the defenders of Vicksburg.[106]

This was similar to the strategy Buchanan and Tattnall had followed with so much success in Hampton Roads and at the mouth of the James River, which the *Virginia* might have continued indefinitely if not for the fall of Norfolk. The *Arkansas,* according to Brown's strategy, would threaten the Union squadrons, acting as a "fleet in being" and making the waters of the Mississippi so unsafe for them as to compel them either to concentrate in a single place, like a besieged fleet, or retreat from Vicksburg.

Placing the ironclad under General Van Dorn's orders was the wrong decision because it subordinated a naval vessel to a man who, even if daring, had no knowledge of naval matters and, still worse, unrealistically overrated the ship's possibilities. This was made apparent in a telegram in which he requested that the *Arkansas* sally and attack single-handedly the enemy's combined squadrons. Van Dorn added that it was "better to die game and do some execution than to lie by and be burned up in the Yazoo."[107]

Brown was incensed at such an idea; moreover, he understood that his proposed plan had been rejected. Therefore, he answered that he had not yet moved because the fitting out of his ship was not complete. He said that as soon as she was ready she would be used in a worthy way, adding that if the army would engage in as extreme an effort as was required from the navy, the war would soon be over. He concluded, "The difficulties are only known to those engaged in it." [108]

What was being asked of the *Arkansas* was clear: she was about to enter the second battle in history between ironclads. And this time the enemy had an overwhelming numerical superiority. On the twentieth the ironclad left Yazoo City and anchored off Liverpool's Landing, a clear confirmation of Brown's aggressive intent. [109]

Because the rivers were rapidly falling, speed of action was essential. On 4 July the *Arkansas* ended her engines' trial, and they were found to be satisfactory. She logged eight knots in slack water and four when sailing upstream. Unfortunately, if one of her screws stopped, she tended to yaw despite the efforts of the helmsman. She therefore had to go back to Yazoo City for modifications. [110]

On 14 July the *Arkansas* passed the obstruction and began to descend the Yazoo. [111] At dawn of the fifteenth, with her crew at general quarters, she made for the Mississippi. Her orders were to break through the Union squadron that was attacking Vicksburg from the north side. After a short stop near the city, she must sweep away the enemy naval forces to the south, then try to make for the sea to reach the Confederate port of Mobile, Alabama. [112] This required almost a superhuman effort.

Meanwhile, the Federals near Vicksburg had begun to feel ill at ease; on the same day, therefore, they had sent a naval patrol composed of the ironclad gunboat *Carondelet,* gunboat *Tyler,* and ram *Queen of the West* up the Yazoo to reconnoiter. As soon as they sighted the *Arkansas,* the Union ships wisely reversed course, firing as they did. In the artillery duel the *Arkansas* immediately took the upper hand. Her guns pierced the *Tyler's* hull eleven times and that of the *Carondelet* at least thirteen times, forcing her to run ashore and knocking her out of action. Federal losses amounted to almost sixty men killed, wounded, and missing. [113]

Unfortunately, flaws in the *Arkansas's* structure caused her considerable damage. A shot that entered the poorly protected pilothouse mortally wounded the chief helmsman and seriously injured his deputy. The funnel was severely damaged, reducing draft and, consequently, speed. Yet in the main, enemy projectiles bounced off her carapace, which, as a whole, held well. [114]

Now the ironclad entered the Mississippi twelve miles upriver from Vicksburg, where two Union squadrons were anchored: four rams, eight of Farragut's seagoing warships, five ironclad gunboats, and several small vessels. All these ships were caught unready; their boilers were cold or had inadequate steam pressure. [115] Once again, the daring displayed by the men of the small Confederate navy was rewarded with a prize, for the enemy had been totally surprised.

After an eerie lull, all the Northern ships opened fire with an awful roar, which grew in violence. The *Arkansas* answered forcefully. Her fire blew up the boilers of the ram *Lancaster,* which was disabled and knocked out of action, and landed many hits on the enemy vessels. While firing quickly, she steamed through the whole enemy squadron.

The ironclad needed about thirty minutes to reach Vicksburg and anchor there, seeking safety under the fortress's batteries. It was high time to do so: several enemy projectiles had pierced her weak armor, exploding inside, and her deck was running with blood and littered with dead bodies.[116] Her flag had been knocked down, yet young Midshipman Dabney M. Scales, under heavy fire, scampered to the open deck and raised it again.[117]

Vicksburg's whole garrison and civilians—more than twenty thousand people—had anxiously observed the fierce battle from the clifftops. Generals Van Dorn, John C. Breckinridge, and Stephen D. Lee had climbed up the courthouse tower to get a better view. Soon they saw the river covered by an immense cloud of thick smoke, from which came the deafening thunder of gunfire. Only when the ironclad moored at Vicksburg could they realize the appalling trial to which she had been subjected.

Most enemy shot and shells had failed to pierce the casemate, which, in the main, had resisted well; yet those that did had damaged gun carriages and guns, showered wooden or iron splinters everywhere, and killed or wounded several men so that the deck was slippery with blood.[118] Throughout the battle, the ironclad had never been more than seventy-five yards from the enemy, firing continuously. She had lost ten killed and fifteen wounded, but she had inflicted much heavier losses and damage to the enemy and had thrown the Union squadrons into panic.[119]

Van Dorn at once sent a victory message to Richmond.[120] But the enemy, aghast at the danger and angry over its setback, was hurriedly preparing to act. The *Arkansas,* which had lost several men and had to return many more to their own regiments, had to gird for her third battle in a single day.

Farragut decided to bring his eight seagoing vessels downriver from Vicksburg: he could not abandon Porter's mortar boats, leaving them exposed to raids by the awesome ironclad. Yet the admiral had also ordered that, in passing, his ships attack the *Arkansas.* Federal fire was withering, but darkness made it difficult for the Union artillerists to sight their target. A huge bolt penetrated the *Arkansas's* hull, killing another two men and wounding three.[121]

The ironclad answered in kind, landing many shells on the Union ships, inflicting severe damage and many losses. The seagoing gunboat

Winona, repeatedly hit below the waterline, was at risk of foundering and was at last towed to safety only by a stroke of luck and with great difficulty.[122]

At dawn of 22 July the Federals made a last-ditch effort to sink the *Arkansas.* The big ironclad gunboat *Essex,* of more than five hundred tons, engaged the Confederate vessel at close range, while the *Queen of the West* tried to ram her. Even though she was caught with her boilers cold and workers on board, the attempt failed. Two large projectiles from the *Essex* pierced her armor, killing or wounding another five men, but in the end the Union ships got the worst of it.[123]

All attempts to eliminate the worrisome ironclad had failed. She loomed like a nightmare over the two Union squadrons, which, not knowing when she might come out to fight, had to keep their fires ceaselessly stoked and their steam up despite the unbearably hot July sun. Keeping the furnaces on board the Union ships stoked meant that the coal supply would be burned up quickly. Further, the river was rapidly falling and Farragut had very little time to continue playing the game of blind man's bluff.

On 24 July, with his whole fleet, the mortar boats, and transports that had taken on board General Williams's troops, he retreated to New Orleans. Only the ironclad gunboat *Essex,* former Confederate ram *Sumter,* and three seagoing gunboats remained, based at Baton Rouge.[124]

Once again, with great daring, the little Confederate navy had earned a dazzling success. Edwin C. Bearss writes: "With one ironclad, a handful of guns . . . the Confederates had regained control of 250 miles of the Mississippi. The failure of Halleck and his Generals to grasp the strategic significance of what was happening on the Mississippi had cost the Union dearly. The first major campaign against Vicksburg had failed. . . . The successful defense of Vicksburg and the recovery of the reaches of the Mississippi between Port Hudson and Vicksburg was a great victory by Confederate arms which had been largely bypassed by military historians."[125]

Yet there would be an anticlimax when, unfortunately, Van Dorn persisted in nurturing his illusion that he had found the "ultimate weapon." While Captain Brown was on sick leave and repair work on the *Arkansas* was still far from complete, Lieutenant Henry Kennedy Stevens, temporarily in command of the ironclad, received orders to sail at once in support of a land attack directed by General Breckinridge against Baton Rouge.[126]

From Grenada, Brown telegraphed Stevens not to move while his ship was still not fitted out, but to no avail. General Van Dorn appealed to

Commodore Lynch, who took on himself the responsibility for giving the ill-advised order. At 2:00 A.M. on 3 August the ironclad silently hoisted anchor for her last cruise.[127]

Breckinridge moved against Baton Rouge overland. Again the ironclad was requested to perform wonders by sweeping away the *Essex* and three seagoing gunboats Farragut had left to protect the city. Unfortunately, Stevens had been compelled to leave his ailing chief engineer, Charles W. City, a first-rate professional, behind in a hospital. Although he did his best, City's relief was probably not good enough.[128]

The *Arkansas*'s engines, heavily strained, had to be stopped at least three times for repairs. In the late afternoon of the fifth, Breckinridge, who had not succeeded in overcoming Union defenses in spite of the fall in battle of their general, Thomas Williams, and whose troops were being mercilessly shelled by the heavy guns of Federal ships, not attacked by the *Arkansas* as had been hoped, disengaged and decided to retreat.

Only the next day was the *Arkansas* able to move. When she arrived in front of the *Essex* and the other enemy ships, both of her engines failed and she drifted. Nothing more could be done: the last Confederate ironclad had to be scuttled, lest she be captured.[129] Commander Henry Kennedy Stevens, last to abandon her, had to swim to land.

The *Essex* and the other Federal ships kept at a safe distance while the blaze devastated the *Arkansas,* which her crew had abandoned with heavy hearts. When the fire reached her guns, they began to discharge in succession. The scene was appalling: it looked as though the ironclad still wanted to fight on, alone and with no crew on board, against her enemy. Then there was heard only the deep rumble of the enormous conflagration. The blaze seemed to consume the dreams and hopes that the Confederate navy could win the war through the technical surprise.[130]

T E N

The Second Phase of Confederate Naval Strategy

While the sultry August of 1862 passed and on battlefields of the Civil War great armies were arrayed against each other in a deadly fight, the young Confederate navy seemed to hit its nadir of defeat and disgrace. All the South's dreams had failed: Mallory's impressive and daring strategic plan to deal the enemy a decisive and lethal blow by means of technical surprise seemed to have ended in nothing. None of the five ironclads initially built in the South was still afloat. After so many illusions, the awakening was bitter. The attempt to defeat the North on its own ground—technological power—appeared (and, in a sense, had been) quixotic and utopian.[1]

Yet Mallory had allowed himself to be under an illusion for only a short while, always keeping a cool mind and a clear sight. Nevertheless, he risked becoming the scapegoat for the frustrations of many who had allowed themselves to be deluded, as well as by his political enemies. A few days after that fateful 6 August, when the *Arkansas* had to be set ablaze, on the twentieth, the chairman of the Joint Committee on Naval Affairs, Charles M. Conrad, who was envious of Mallory, introduced a resolution to Congress asking that the prospect be discussed of suppressing the Navy Department, transferring its tasks to the secretary of war.[2]

Soon thereafter, Representative Henry Stuart Foote, a bitter and angry opponent of both President Davis and Secretary Mallory, introduced the proposition that the House vote its lack of confidence in Mallory. Answering the motion, Ethelbert Barksdale, a supporter of Mallory, in an attempt to stave off such scheming which might be fatal to the Confederacy, introduced his own resolution, asking that the conduct of the Navy Department be investigated by a joint committee.[3]

The approval of this proposition on 27 August 1862 was followed by the designation of the committee. It was now evident that the proposals by Conrad and Foote could not be debated until the committee reached its own conclusions. If these were favorable to Mallory, both the proposition to abolish the Navy Department and the motion of lack of confidence would be doomed.[4]

For some time Mallory had understood that "ignorance and presumption" were fostering the senseless claim that he had been incapable of building a navy, whereas he had done everything within human power using the poor means at hand. He had a clear conscience and was ready to confront the investigating committee.[5]

That his most rabid enemies would participate on the committee, together with others who supported him, attested to the reliability of the inquiry and made him confident of his ultimate vindication.[6] He knew that he had carried out a true revolution in naval warfare which had astonished the world, and he felt sure of the verdict of the committee and—more important—of history.[7]

Until 24 March 1863 Mallory would be subjected to the inquiry; at last, the committee would end its work without acknowledging any of the charges leveled against him. For the secretary, certainly it was no small success. Yet, while he had to strive to put together records and testimony for the inquiry to give the lie to insinuations and indictments, he was heavily burdened with the need—which could not be put off—to confront the relentless and mighty pressure from the enemy.[8] Such pressure, at the very moment when the Navy Department was being subjected to indictment in Richmond, had assumed such a new and lethal perspective as to threaten disaster for the South.

The idea of amphibious warfare had slowly grown and become clearer in the minds of Northern leaders (first among them the resourceful and clever Gustavus Vasa Fox) by reading and digesting the reports of that invaluable organism of the U.S. Navy, the Blockade Board.

From such reports, it emerged clearly that the blockade, which, under the new rules imposed by the Declaration of Paris must be "effective" (i.e., enforced by means of ships permanently positioned along enemy coasts), was impossible. One can wonder if this was not exactly what the authors of the declaration secretly hoped for. The Federal Blockade Board understood quickly that such a blockade might not be enforced without at least seizing some base along the enemy coast to serve as a point of support. This, indeed, turned out to be indispensable because of the hur-

A History of the Confederate Navy

ricanes that, between May and November, beat the Atlantic shores of North America with unbelievable fury.[9]

The U.S. naval strategists, moving along unexplored paths toward a new and more effective blockade, stumbled, by trial and error, upon the decisive discovery that command of the sea—which the Union navy enjoyed—could be used for opening new land fronts along the miles and miles of Confederate coasts and its inland waters so that they could set up a true invasion by sea, a second front.[10] This would be a grand strategy that American amphibious forces would in the future carry to successes never before seen. Far away, beyond the horizon, lay hidden in the future the shores of Sicily, Normandy, and Korea.[11]

The first operation had been commanded by Commodore Silas H. Stringham some time earlier, on 29 August 1861, against Hatteras Inlet, which leads into Pamlico Sound on North Carolina's coast. Heavily bombarded by Union naval forces, Forts Hatteras and Clark, which protected the inlet, had been forced to surrender. Over them were raised the Stars and Stripes. The whole garrison, including Flag Officer Samuel Barron, C.S. Navy, in charge of coastal defenses of Virginia and North Carolina, was taken prisoner.[12]

The people of the South were dismayed. A few days later, when a Union expedition from the new base at Fort Hatteras seized and destroyed another Confederate work that protected Ocracoke Inlet and landed troops near the small town of Portsmouth, they found that the local people had fled. Overwhelmed by fear, they had made a mass exodus.[13]

But worse for the South was yet to come. On 29 October 1861 a great amphibious expedition of fifty-one ships (fifteen war vessels and thirty-six transports), commanded by Flag Officer Samuel F. Du Pont and carrying on board General Thomas W. Sherman with an expeditionary corps of 12,653 soldiers, had set sail for South Carolina. The expedition (with ships already earmarked to compose the new South Atlantic Blockading Squadron) appeared off Port Royal, South Carolina, on 5 November.

After a heavy bombardment, Forts Walker and Beauregard fell, and on the seventh the small town of Port Royal was taken by Union troops. On the ninth Beaufort was seized.[14]

During the night of 11 January 1862 another great expedition set sail. It was composed of seventy warships and transports under Commodore Louis M. Goldsborough, commanding the North Atlantic Blockading Squadron. Aboard there was a corps of fifteen thousand soldiers, commanded by General Ambrose Burnside. They belonged to a special Coast Division Burnside had organized.[15]

On 7 and 8 February the expedition seized Roanoke Island, where in the sixteenth century the first English colony in North America had been

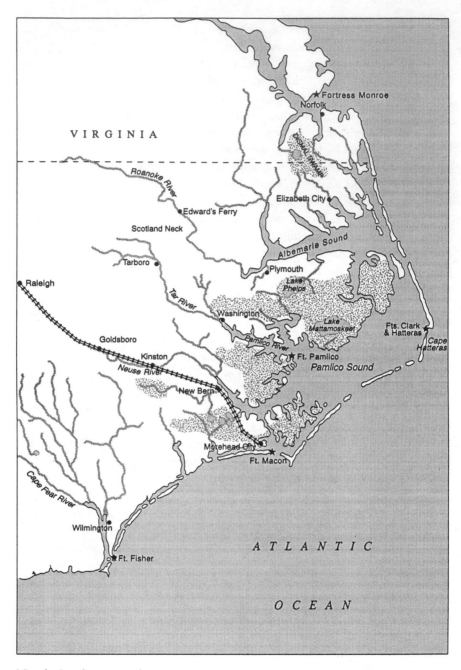

North Carolina coastal waters.

settled and whose possession opened the way to Albemarle Sound. On the ninth, the diminutive Confederate flotilla of seven small gunboats commanded by Commodore William F. Lynch and derisively called the "mosquito fleet," which had already lost two ships near Roanoke, was destroyed near Elizabeth City by the powerful Union ships.

Only the *Beaufort* and *Raleigh* managed to escape up the navigable canal (which they then obstructed) and reach Norfolk, where they would bravely fight alongside the ironclad *Virginia.*[16]

On 14 March, Federal troops seized the city of New Bern on the Neuse River, thus threatening the very heart of the state of North Carolina and panicking its people.[17] On the previous 24 November the Federals had landed on Tybee Island, Georgia, near the estuary of the Savannah River, provoking a similar wave of distress and fear.[18]

Nearby is the great port of Savannah, ancient capital of Georgia. To protect it, the U.S. government had built on little Cockspur Island, situated to the north of Tybee, a great walled fort begun in 1829 and christened with the name of General Casimir Pulaski, Polish hero of the American Revolution. Its ramparts were 7.5 feet thick, and it mounted forty-eight guns.[19] Everybody in Savannah (and, indeed, in the United States) considered it impregnable.[20]

This was not the opinion of General Quincy A. Gillmore, U.S. Corps of Engineers. He had placed on Tybee Island, with the approbation of his superior, General David H. Hunter, a series of siege batteries, including thirty-six guns. One of these batteries was composed of heavy rifled guns: five Parrotts and a 48-pounder James. Soon, fire from the great rifled pieces, which had a range of up to fifteen hundred yards, began piercing the walls of the fort as though they were cardboard. On 11 April Fort Pulaski surrendered; with it, all the old fortifications with brick walls were swept away from the stage of war and the techniques of siege warfare surged ahead. Moreover, the Federals had won an excellent base from which to threaten Savannah, even though the city was still protected by other formidable works.[21]

On 3 March 1862 Union troops landed at Fernandina, Florida, soon afterward seizing St. Augustine and Jacksonville. It was Mallory's home state.[22]

As a whole, amphibious operations conducted by the Union along the Atlantic coast had given them great success and resulted in disaster for the South, not to speak of those on the Gulf of Mexico, where New Orleans, the major port and largest city of the Confederacy, had also been lost. The repercussions upon Southerners were overwhelming. They now, writes James M. Merrill, "knew that the Yankees controlled the seas and could strike swiftly, mercilessly, and without warning against Confederate shores. Entire neighborhoods, terrified and panicky, packed belongings and high-tailed it for the interior."[23]

The outcome of the opening of a new front, arising unexpectedly from the waves, was catastrophic for the South. Almost the whole Atlantic coast, from Virginia to the Carolinas, Georgia, and Florida, had been invaded by the enemy. Everywhere, masses of frightened civilians, distraught with panic, dragging behind them the aged, the children, and the few belongings they had been able to gather on carts, were abandoning homes, fields, cities, and birthplaces.

The exodus assumed impressive proportions from the beginning in North Carolina, hit first and most deeply by Union amphibious forces. "How differently had this Valentine's Day been passed from the last!" a North Carolina woman wrote in her diary. "Then I was peacefully planting fruit trees at Hascosea. Today, in the face of a stern reality am I packing up my household goods to remove them from the enemy." She went on to say that on 15 February 1862 she had found her father's house full of strangers: "As we stopped at the door we were surprised to see the windows of the Dining Room crowded with little faces watching our descent from the carriage. On entering the Drawing Room two strange ladies sprang up and met us with the exclamation: 'Where did you come from?' We soon found that they were Refugees. . . . Poor people, they have been driven from their homes by the advance of the enemy and are now seeking an asylum, a shelter for their heads." With them were other women "and children and Grandchildren, to the number of nineteen whites and seventy negroes, all homeless and houseless . . . they brought sad accounts from below. The inhabitants of Edenton were leaving panic stricken. . . . It is pitiable to see the fright of the inhabitants. The roads are crowded with Refugees in vehicles of every description, endeavoring to move what of their property they can, to save it from the grasp of the invader."[24]

Everywhere the fugitives presented a pitiable scene of misery and sorrow: "The scene there beggars description," would write some time later another diarist from Louisiana: "crowds of Negroes of all ages and sizes, wagons, mules, horses, dogs, baggage and furniture of every description, very little of it packed. It was just thrown in promiscuous heaps—pianos, table, chairs, rosewood sofas, wardrobes, parlor sets, with pots, kettles, stoves, beds and bedding, bowls and pitchers, and everything of the kind just thrown pell-mell here and there . . . everybody and everything trying to get on the cars."[25]

In South Carolina, people had hastily left plantations located along the coast as no longer safe;[26] in Georgia those who still tilled the land did so

A History of the Confederate Navy

with anguish over the possibility of abandoning their harvest. In every case, they had started sending away women and children.[27]

The sea power of the North now seemed to loom large on the horizon, like a threatening giant capable of emerging at any moment from the waves and moving by titanic and devastating strides to invade the South.

For the Confederacy this threat required urgent and exceptional decisions. On 5 November 1861, when Du Pont's squadron appeared in Port Royal Bay, General Robert Edward Lee assumed command of a new military department encompassing South Carolina, Georgia, and the Atlantic side of Florida.[28]

The keen mind of the great general quickly grasped both the substance and the extreme danger of the situation. Decisions soon followed: all coastal works, except those of the major port cities, were evacuated and Confederate troops retreated to an inland defense line out of range of the big naval guns that gave the Federals so much of their superiority. Waterways had to be obstructed to check their penetration by Union ships. The rivers Stono, Edisto, and Combahee were barred by fortifications with heavy artillery, built well inland from their mouths.

Other works were built in front of Hilton Head and on the Broad and Salcatchie to protect Savannah by land. The same was done at Charleston. The railroad through Pocotaligo and Coosawhatchie that joined Charleston with Savannah was equally well protected. This would permit Southerners to shift their forces speedily toward any threatened point.[29]

The strategic rationale upon which this defensive structure was founded was so well conceived that it did not fall until almost three years later, when it was taken from the rear by troops coming overland, whereas the so-called German Atlantic Wall, based on the idea of last-ditch defense on the seashore, fell to the first formidable blow from the sea.

If this problem was solved, another remained. The most important ports—Wilmington, North Carolina; Charleston, South Carolina; Savannah, Georgia; and Mobile, Alabama, on the Gulf of Mexico—as well as the capital itself, that is, the gates to the South, opening toward the sea, of course had to remain points of contact with enemy naval forces and thus were exposed to direct threats. Withdrawal from them was impossible; to keep them was a question of life or death to the Confederacy. Even if protected by land, they were still extremely vulnerable by sea. Therefore, they could not be defended without a substantial contribution from the navy. Here was the worrisome problem: what could the navy do?

Bit by bit, in the keen mind of Mallory, well before those of any other Southerners, the vague contours of what was in essence a new, deadly

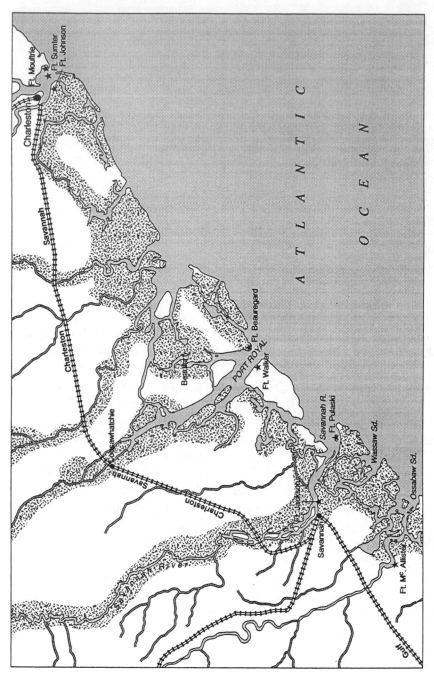

The seacoast between Charleston, South Carolina, and Savannah, Georgia.

threat from the sea against the land, was taking shape. Without caring about the malice of the inept and slanderers, the secretary was already plotting the new strategy that, in close cooperation with land forces, would solve the fearful problem.

That strategy was based on several remarks about recent naval events that required considerable farsightedness and therefore had escaped the careless critics of the Navy Department. Indeed, if one can see beyond the failures sustained by the C.S. Navy, one must acknowledge that the first sally of the Confederate ironclads had earned a series of successes.

No ironclad had succeeded in breaking the blockade. Yet, after a bit of elation, when even Mallory himself had fallen under the illusion of the "ultimate weapon," the secretary had soon become aware of the hard facts, and the battle experiences of the first Southern ironclads had helped him to grasp the essence of the problem.

He held that among the primary objectives of the young Confederate navy was to break the blockade (as he had clearly stated), but this must be done by seagoing ironclads to be built in Europe.[30] Henceforth, this would become one of the capstones of his naval strategy. Needed was a review and reassessment of the policy of shipbuilding in Europe, giving the major impetus to the creation of a squadron of seagoing ironclads that alone might challenge the enemy fleet on the high seas with a good chance of success.

Still, the results achieved by homemade armored ships had been sizable. In addition to battering and scattering a whole squadron, thus showing the entire world the impotence and obsolescence of wooden warships, the *Virginia* had for more than a month dominated the waters of Hampton Roads, causing McClellan's amphibious plan to fail and substantially contributing to saving Richmond and, perhaps, the Confederacy itself. As French Admiral Lepotier correctly observes, she had so frightened the enemy that she alone played the part of a fleet-in-being. She indeed, according to Robert W. Daly, "in her awkward but mighty casemate personified that silent, corrosive, deadly pressure of sea power so eloquently explained by Mahan."[31]

Even more stirring had been the success of the *Arkansas*. She, too, had caused an impending Federal amphibious operation to fail; moreover, she had faced two fleets, defeated them, and saved for the Confederacy the formidable base of Vicksburg as well as three hundred miles of the Mississippi River. In so doing, she had prevented the enemy from splitting the Confederacy in twain, granting it a full year of respite.[32]

One must also consider what might have happened if the other three ironclads being built along the great river of the West, mainly the formidable *Mississippi,* had been ready in time. New Orleans would have been saved and Farragut's expedition would have ended in disaster.

From this viewpoint, it was evident that the home-built ironclads had made a major contribution to checking the formidable onslaught that the enemy, with its new and deadly strategy of unleashing against the South a veritable invasion from the sea, had attempted by means of amphibious operations on a scale heretofore unknown.

It was becoming evident to Mallory that he must soon organize naval defense starting from such considerations, before the South would be delivered a lethal blow, a harsh reality that many of his fellow countrymen (and some later historians) seemed unable to understand.

Yet the priceless experience of the Southern ironclads, their impressive performance against enemy warships (including the *Monitor* herself), and their proven unseaworthiness[33] pointed the way. Any Confederate seaport must have a squadron of homemade ironclads, which, putting aside the reveries of those who dreamed that they could break the blockade, would, according to Mallory, instead operate in coastal waters as true "moveable forts—with formidable batteries capable of destroying any ironclad in the world." Their presence in harbors, rivers, and roadsteads would check the enemy navy, which had proved capable of passing land forts but had not yet been able to overcome such floating fortresses.[34]

An able and daring Confederate naval officer had stated this truth when, after underscoring that the enemy ships at Vicksburg had been driven back by the guns of the *Arkansas* and not by the shore batteries, said: "Do not underrate ironclads: in them alone is our dependence for harbor defence."[35]

This, henceforth, would be the new ironclad strategy. Yet these ships could not be built in the old yards exposed to enemy attacks. To be safe from the foe's raids, both the yards and other naval plants had to be moved inland as much as possible; indeed, coastal zones had now become front lines. Therefore, with unbelievable efforts, they were transferred to the interior, either to the deepest roadsteads or, better, along rivers.[36] Also the Pensacola Navy Yard, now utterly useless because it was blocked by the enemy, had to be evacuated.[37]

The new locations of the Confederate naval logistic system were discussed in Chapter 3. Undoubtedly, this was an able and brilliant solution to the problem; still, new problems arose, mostly because of the distances between the several centers or because of deteriorating railroad communications.[38] This was the price paid so that building new ironclads might proceed in relative safety.[39]

Yet it was not enough. Under the devastating fire from Stringham's and Du Pont's cannons, the forts built by the Confederates had been smashed as though made of cardboard. But they were destroyed not so much because of flaws in the works as the inadequacy of their weapons, mainly old smoothbores, or obsolete guns, rifled in some way. Their modest throw weight and weak power of penetration had rendered them altogether unable to compete with the powerful ordnance of Union ships.[40]

Clearly, heavy rifled guns of large caliber and of great initial muzzle velocity were needed, as Mallory understood. The navy, indeed, had already solved the problem, thanks to the powerful gun invented by J. M. Brooke, who was already at work to improve it and make it still more powerful. Collaboration with the Ordnance Department of the army was close and permanent.[41] A growing number of Brooke guns, more often than not served by naval crews, were provided to forts.

In the army, one of the most staunch supporters of the new gun was General Beauregard.[42] Indeed, it is even possible that the new defense line created by the genius of General Lee could not have been held without support from such naval guns, which were capable of keeping enemy warships at arm's length.

Of course, the grimmest problem relative to port defense that concerned Mallory and Brooke was the threat represented by enemy ironclads, and Brooke was already at work to meet it. The first solution (albeit not the only one) was to make the rifled guns still more powerful. The 6.4-inch cannon was strengthened by a double banding at the breech; the 7-inch received a similar double, then triple band. Guns 12 and 18 feet long, weighing about 15,000 pounds, could fire projectiles up to 240 to 300 pounds.[43] Later, Brooke would turn out smoothbore 10- and 11-inch pieces built by the same method. These were evidently intended to exploit at minimum distance the great initial speed consistent with the absence of rifling.[44]

Starting in May 1862, the Tredegar of Richmond had cast thirteen 6.4-inch, thirty-nine 7-inch, and one 8-inch rifled and six 10-inch and two 11-inch smoothbores, all Brookes.[45] Yet because it had to work at its maximum for the army, the Tredegar obviously could not satisfy all the needs of the navy (see Chapter 3). For this reason, there arose the plan to create the Naval Cannon Foundry at Selma, Alabama, which went into full production on 1 July 1863, when Catesby ap R. Jones assumed command of it. Fortunately, in the interim, the Tredegar managed some production for the navy.

The foundry at Selma had a long story. Colin J. McRae, beyond realizing the importance of Selma for producing naval equipment, had also at hand the type of iron the C.S. Navy was requesting from him: "The iron from which our best cannon(s) are made is a strong, coarse grained n° 1 cold blast charcoal iron, of the first fusion. In the pig, its fracture is a dark gray with coarse crystals in the center, growing finer toward the edges. It is irregular in its structure and very difficult to break, its density is about 7.3 and its tenacity about 25,000 lbs to the square inch."[46]

To produce such pig iron, the furnace must be loaded with about fifteen thousand pounds of iron ore and two tons of coal; the fusion required about five hours. McRae knew that he could obtain such pig iron from the furnaces of Bibb County, Alabama, especially from one named Brierfield, capable of producing twenty-five tons of first-rate pig iron a day.[47] McRae hoped to get coal from Phineas Browne.[48]

For several reasons, McRae never succeeded in getting the foundry under way.[49] His correspondence with Mallory throws light on the problems that bedeviled the Confederacy. To begin with, McRae had not been able to muster skilled workmen, even though he sent recruiting agents to Rome, Chattanooga, Atlanta, Charlotte, and Richmond. Then, the buildings of the factory were in such bad shape that he had to put his pattern makers and foundrymen to work doing repairs. Further, it even seems that the need to concentrate on casting heavy guns was not clear to him, as he was talking of producing plates for ironclads and even naval engines.[50] Finally, at the beginning of 1863, McRae turned the foundry over to the government.[51]

Major Nathaniel R. Chambliss, who, by order of General George W. Rains had assumed command of it, tried very hard to get the plant into operation.[52] Yet very soon the management of the foundry was taken over by the navy, which entrusted it to Commander Catesby ap R. Jones.

On the day he assumed command, Jones wrote to Brooke explaining the extreme difficulties that had to be overcome if the foundry were to operate.[53] First was the shortage of skilled workmen and machinery, part of which had been transferred elsewhere, thus greatly impairing the effectiveness of the plant. Then, the cooling pit was full of water, which meant that a steam pump had to be put to work day and night to dry it. Neither patterns nor molds had been prepared for casting heavy guns, except for 10-inch Columbiads. Very few forges were ready to operate. There was no room for a gun carriage shop, which meant that additional land had to be obtained.

Still, Jones was not a man to limit himself to grievances. In the same long letter he also listed steps already taken. The production of molds to cast heavy guns had begun; if one hundred pounds of cement were quickly sent to him, he would repair the pit by stopping the water from running in.

In reviewing the personnel situation, he had found that there were at the foundry about one hundred white workers and a large number of blacks whose pay was gravely in arrears. The army (responsible for this situation) must be pressured to give the workers their due, which amounted to between $30,000 and $40,000. Still more urgent was to send copper, tin, and steel.

In the same letter, Jones also said that on the advice of General Rains, the services of an able English technician, George Peacock, had been obtained. Although the army had pledged to pay Peacock $3,000 a year, Jones, if necessary, was ready to increase his pay. Hence another expert offered his outstanding brain to the Confederate navy. Born in 1823 in Yorkshire, Peacock had begun working in a foundry as a youth, soon acquiring great skill. Gifted with a lively and bright mind, he then went to work as an independent engineer in Liverpool. There he attracted the attention of John Ericsson, upon whose advice he moved to the United States in 1848. In America he was technical manager of several metallurgical shops and introduced into the manufacturing of metal pipes a new process that would revolutionize the production system. He was also a scholar, a scientist, and a man of genius of international fame. During the first months of the war he was superintendent of a foundry at Columbiana, Alabama, already working for the Confederate government. It was from there that Jones sought to entice him to Selma. Still, he did not budge until Congress created specially for him the office of superintendent of the naval foundry at a pay double that of Jones, that is, $4,000 a year, as Jones later told Brooke in a letter dated 5 June.[54]

Other than Peacock, there was needed another highly skilled engineer, a Mr. Tucker, whose task would be to organize the blacksmith shops and put into place the steam hammers, cranes, and the like; Jones urgently requested him.[55]

Yet, the pit was still in bad condition; if cement did not come soon, it would remain useless.

But the basic personnel plan for the foundry was ready: a commanding officer, an executive officer, a chief of ordnance, a paymaster, a surgeon, a chief engineer, a civilian engineer, three clerks, and one designer. The departments were foundry, rolling mill, toolroom, patterns warehouse, blacksmith's shop, carpenter shop, bricklayers, and diggers.

A few days later, Jones was able to inform Brooke that he was bargaining for a plot of land on which to extend the plant, at a cost of $100,000. He also proposed to provide an incentive for the skilled workmen with a suitable increase of pay, which was granted in the amount of $1 a day.[56]

Soon Jones achieved wonders. As early as 13 June he was ready to ask Brooke for the pattern of a 7-inch rifled gun of the type cast at Tredegar; on the twenty-fourth he asked for the immediate delivery of 111 tons of cast iron for cannons and another 25 tons for sundry factory work, adding that in July he would need another 450 and 150 tons, respectively. At the same time he was writing this letter, he was able, at last, to have work begun on the pit, trusting that it would be ready in fifteen days so that the first heavy 7-inch cannon could be cast by mid-July.[57]

Alas, here, too, the Confederate navy had to contend against heavy odds because of the poor technical equipment of the South. Not until 28 June did the pattern for the 7-inch gun arrive in Selma, where the pit was already being walled, in the hope that it would be ready for casting to begin within a week.[58]

Yet, when the week ended, water continued to leak into the pit, rendering it useless. Still, Jones was not a man to give up: he would have four small temporary pits dug and then wholly remake the larger one.[59]

In the end, his stubbornness was rewarded. He had overcome all obstacles and on 1 August he was able to announce that the first experimental 7-inch cannon had been cast. A few days later the foundry manufactured four hundred shot and shells for the navy and (even more meaningful) thirty-two hundred artillery projectiles for the army. The cast iron used had come from the Brierfield Furnace of Bibb County, Alabama.[60]

On Mallory's special order, Peacock made a careful chemical and mechanical test of the several kinds of cast iron available, concluding that the Brierfield Furnace's was best suited to cast cannons, whereas the others, from the Shelby Iron Company and the Cane Creek Furnace, were better for rolling (the latter furnace had provided the iron used to make the plates for the *Virginia*).

Peacock ordered the casting together at one time for eight hours fifty thousand pounds of pig iron in air furnaces, fed with highly resinous pine stumps, thereby obtaining a 30 to 40 percent increase in the tensility of the metal. He also suggested that the Brierfield Furnace be enlisted to work full-time for the navy.[61]

Peacock's and Jones's method of lengthening the fusion process in air furnaces accentuated the decarbonization of the metal, converting it into an extremely resistant, steel-like cast iron.[62]

Notwithstanding major constraints and limitations caused by its lack of industrial plant and skilled workmen, the Confederacy succeeded in casting heavy naval guns that were probably the most powerful in the world, according to Ethel Armes: "The great guns, from 2 to 3 feet in diameter through the breech, were from 10 to 18 feet long, and heavier than locomotives . . . massive, tough and indestructible." The Selma Foundry was regarded as the best in existence.[63]

During its lifetime it produced and delivered seventy-two heavy guns—seventy Brookes and two Parrotts—yet the total cast reached more than one hundred if experimental pieces are counted. It should be stressed that the manufacturing was very complex (and that there was a chronic shortage of labor): a single Brooke required about three months of work, day and night.[64]

Yet Brooke had not dedicated his genius only to granting its best rifled guns to the navy, according to Mallory's wish. Indeed, without proper armor-piercing projectiles the hoped-for results would never be achieved in the fight against enemy ironclads, which, after the *Monitor*'s experience, had the thickness of their turrets' armor increased from five to eleven inches.[65]

One day Brooke, while observing at the Tredegar the process of punching armor plates to make the holes for screws, noted that a punch with a flat, not a pointed, end, by a single stroke made holes one and one-quarter inches in diameter through two-inch plate. The reason was clear to Brooke: the flat point transferred the total impact of the mass at the same moment on a single point of the surface, whereas in a pointed punch the mass released its own kinetic energy gradually. Therefore the latter was gradually arrested by the resistance of the plate, which absorbed, still gradually, the stroke without being pierced. Thus originated the solid shot with a flat point designed by Brooke.

Yet he soon observed that cast iron had a tendency to shatter upon impact, thus annulling its perforating power. Wrought iron lacked the required hardness. Brooke brilliantly solved the problem by slightly tapering the cylindrical mold of the projectile toward the top so that the major compression of metal there increased its hardness.[66] Still, it was always necessary for the projectile to strike the enemy armor perpendicularly. But it was a good solution, at least until the advent of shaped-charge projectiles.

The Confederate navy, therefore, was now providing for its ironclads both heavy guns and armor-piercing projectiles, which would no longer permit the enemy such easy successes as those at Hatteras Inlet or Port Royal, as the U.S. Navy leaders would soon discover to their great discomfort.

Indeed, on 6 January 1863 the Federal secretary of the navy, Gideon Welles, sent to Rear Admiral Du Pont, commanding the South Atlantic Blockading Squadron, the big ironclad frigate *New Ironsides* as well as four more ironclads of the *Monitor* class, with the objective of forcing their way into the harbor of Charleston "and demand[ing] the surrender of all its defenses."[67] Welles, to increase further Du Pont's fleet power, sent him two more ironclads of the *Monitor* class and also the *Keokuk,* which had fixed turrets.[68]

It was a massive array, carrying at least twenty-seven heavy guns. On 7

April 1863 the ironclad armada weighed anchor and steered for Charleston Harbor. Soon firing began in earnest on both sides. The battle lasted until 5:30 P.M., at which time the Union ships had to withdraw. All Federal vessels had been hit; two ironclads of the *Monitor* class had been so heavily damaged that they had to be drydocked. The *Keokuk* fared even worse. Hit by armor-piercing projectiles from two Brooke guns placed at Fort Sumter, she began to founder and, despite the gallant exertions of her crew, sank to the bottom. Her guns were later salvaged by a Confederate naval officer.[69] Twenty days later, General Beauregard and his staff awarded the merit for the victory to the outstanding power of Confederate heavy guns, above all to the rifled Brookes.[70]

The formidable heavy rifled artillery that the farsighted Mallory had wanted and the genius of Brooke and his collaborators (above all, Catesby ap R. Jones) had created, greatly increasing the power of Confederate coastal defense, represented the second pillar of the new Confederate naval strategy in that dreadful struggle between land and sea.

Soon, the brave Union sailors had to notice, to their great chagrin, that the time when Southern forts, weak and poorly defended by old, second-rate cannons, fell easy prey to Federal ships had passed for good.

Finally, in addition to ironclads and formidable rifled guns, the third pillar of the new Confederate naval strategy would be represented by the enormous increase in power of a futuristic, terrible weapon now used systematically on a larger scale than in the past—the frightful submarine ambush: "Thanks to progress in technology and to the genius of their scientists," writes Admiral Lepotier, "the Confederates in a few years would make gigantic strides in such war tools."[71]

Indeed, from the primitive system of fixed obstructions, the Southerners soon passed to deadly explosive barrages and then to a more complicated and sophisticated system—the successful attempt to deliver explosive devices directly against enemy hulls, attacking them in the most vulnerable and least protected place, their underwater works.

Still, before such daring strategy would be realized, another obstacle had to be put overcome. The Confederate navy had started its life with an excess of older officers, which quickly became a worrisome problem.[72] Many among the less young (for example, Buchanan or Semmes) had been shown to possess daring and the will to fight and had backed up Mallory's innovative ideas. Yet others (not to say the majority) had turned out to be slow, lacking in imagination and initiative, opinionated, dull, and even worse, incapable of understanding (if not openly hostile to) the new and revolutionary methods Mallory sought to introduce.[73]

It was very like the situation that Mallory had faced in the U.S. Navy in 1853 at the time of the Naval Retiring Board. In many cases, the old officers who now appeared as obstacles were the same whose retention had been put into question by the board.

In the North, Mallory's antagonist, Secretary Welles, had solved the problem by confining the older or less able men to unimportant billets or sinecures. Yet the C.S. Navy, enmeshed in a war for survival, could not do likewise or enjoy the luxury of creating a host of useless bureaucrats. Mallory therefore began to think about a parallel organization, to last for the duration of the war, which could possibly outflank the exacting standards for promotion and detail based on seniority and instead give billets for ability or merit.

The first possible solution probably came at the beginning of 1862, when the navy had to face the problem of reabsorbing what remained of the "privateers" into the regular forces. Mallory had then proposed to the president the creation of a volunteer navy parallel to the regular one, to be joined by anybody who had already armed—or planned to arm—a "private" vessel to engage in commerce raiding. Officers and petty officers of such a volunteer navy would be given a "provisional" rank for the duration of the war, wear the regular uniform, draw government pay, and serve according to all naval regulations. It was, indeed, a way to give a final nudge to the liquidation of privateering.

Yet it is interesting to see how Mallory used (perhaps by a *lapsus*) the expression "provisional navy" that possibly was turning about in his mind.[74]

The volunteer navy was created by a law of 18 April 1863, when indeed it was no longer needed because privateering had died a natural death, and there remained at sea only raiding cruisers of the regular navy.[75] The volunteer navy remained an organization apart and would also have some important tasks, but it had nothing to do with the later provisional navy except that the name (and with it, probably, the intuition of a way to solve an ever more pressing problem) occurred to Mallory for the first time in his letter to President Davis about the volunteer navy.

Mallory had already explored other avenues. First, in 1862, he had obtained from Congress a law authorizing him to commission two captains, five commanders, and fifty lieutenants for the duration of war, without regard to seniority. Soon thereafter, another law stipulated that all admirals and a substantial number of other officers would be commissioned only for gallantry in war.[76]

This arrangement, however, met stubborn opposition from those who were devoted to seniority and who sought in any possible way to scuttle it (and in fact continued such attempts for the whole war).[77]

Mallory then took a final step: in May 1863 Congress, at his prodding, created the provisional navy.[78] The law stated that all the personnel and naval ships of the regular navy might be transferred to the provisional one at the president's judgment. The officers would be transferred to the provisional navy in the number considered necessary. There they could be commissioned, without any limitation as to age or seniority, to the rank that "the needs of the service" would indicate as necessary.

This system, of course, would last only for the duration of the war. Yet if the Confederacy could survive it, the ranks would be reexamined and possibly confirmed. It replaced seniority with merit and skill.[79]

In addition, it was made clear that only officers transferred to the provisional navy could serve afloat. The others would be limited to land duty. Yet particularly brave officers would be detailed to such important duties as chiefs of the several bureaus of the Navy Department or receive billets overseas.[80]

Thus, as the year 1862 ended, the Confederate navy was at last ready to meet what now appeared to be the most deadly threat from the sea: amphibious attacks that were threatening to overwhelm the South and bottle up its vital seaports.

As Admiral Lepotier correctly observes, "The operations coming from the sea, after neutralizing the outside offensive power and the supplies of the adversary, can move against the very heartland, considered as a great besieged fortress, opening breaches, making diversionary attacks, wearing down the defender on such points of the defense line which are accessible and along which the attacker enjoys superiority of manoeuvre; lastly, if the circumstances warrant, to break the defense line itself."[81]

To Mallory and his able collaborators must be given credit for fathoming the main issue of naval strategy in the Civil War: that of sea against land. As will be seen, the contributions of the Confederate navy to such a deadly struggle would be of vital importance and as a whole successful.

E L E V E N

The New Ironclad
Strategy: First Phase

Mallory became increasingly persuaded that the new ironclad strategy of the C.S. Navy had to be two-pronged and that it was imperative to build seagoing ironclads in Europe. Indeed, despite Lieutenant North's fiasco, he had never wholly given up the idea.[1] Who might be able to resume such an enterprise with any probability of success if not the able, trustworthy, resourceful Bulloch?

After work began on the two cruisers in the Mersey shipyards, Bulloch had decided that his constant personal supervision of the work was neither necessary nor advisable because it would draw the suspicion of Northern agents, who were buzzing around everywhere. Experience had made him aware of many problems relative to the projects he must carry out in Europe, first of all the question of finances, and this all required a full review with Mallory.[2]

Yet while Bulloch was thinking of going back for a short while to the Confederacy, he wanted to seize the occasion to bring with him a ship loaded with war supplies, thus showing the reward that the Confederacy would gain from running the blockade in its own ships instead of depending on foreign traders.

On 22 June 1861, together with North, there had also landed in Great Britain an agent of the Confederate army, Major Edward C. Anderson.[3] He had been sent to control the activity of Major Huse, about whom many slanders had been circulating; Anderson soon became convinced of Huse's honesty.[4] Therefore, he dedicated himself to helping acquire war supplies for the army while waiting to go back home. Bulloch proposed to him that the navy and army share the cost of buying a swift steamer to be loaded with war supplies and on which they could make the trip to the South. The suggestion was submitted to Prioleau, who approved.[5]

Bulloch had also informed one of the Confederate commissioners in Europe, A. Dudley Mann, of the project.[6] The tireless naval officer soon bought the first-rate iron-hulled steamer *Fingal,* which in time would play an unexpected part in the history of Southern armorclads. The *Fingal* was almost new, speedy (thirteen knots), 185 feet long, with a gross tonnage of 800 tons; hence she had very good stowage area.[7]

On board the *Fingal* Bulloch loaded four rifled naval guns (two 4.5-inch and two 2.5-inch landing ones) with carriages and eight hundred projectiles; one thousand short Enfield rifles with bayonets; five hundred revolvers with ammunition; a great number of sailors' uniforms; and no less than four hundred powder barrels.[8]

With her cargo complete, the *Fingal* sailed secretly from Grenock. On board was a man trusted by Bulloch, the second mate, Captain John Low, born in England yet a Georgian by choice. He soon would prove among the ablest seamen of the Confederacy.[9] On 15 October 1861, during a storm, the *Fingal,* after approaching Holyhead to take aboard Bulloch and Anderson, began her ocean trip.[10]

Behind him, Bulloch left an angry and disappointed James North, who had sought in vain to be given charge of all plans and funds for the ships being built in England, receiving instead a polite yet categorical denial.[11]

The crossing was made without any circumstances worthy of note except that the *Fingal* had to approach the island of Terceira, in an isolated nook of the Azores, to take on water. Bulloch took good note of the place, which later would be invaluable for cruiser warfare.[12]

The *Fingal* was eagerly awaited in Savannah, Georgia. Old Commodore Tattnall (still in command there) had issued the necessary orders so that the blockade runner might enter the Savannah River without any hindrance. This would be easy because Fort Pulaski was still in Confederate hands. He also had sent the small gunboat *Sampson* with pilots to help the ship.[13]

Everybody was thrilled at Fort Pulaski when the *Fingal* appeared with the Confederate flag flying at the topgallant. The crossing had gone well, and at 4:00 P.M. on 12 November 1861 Bulloch moored at Savannah.[14]

From there he proceeded immediately to Richmond to meet Mallory. The following days would be significant for the future Confederate program of building seagoing ironclads in Europe. After the failure of North's mission, Mallory had given up such a program, at least for the time being, and had concentrated on homemade armorclads.

Yet the so-called *Trent* Affair, known in Richmond four days before the

Fingal would anchor at Savannah, had boosted Southern hopes (at least until 8 January 1862, when news reached London and Paris that the U.S. government had released the two Confederate commissioners); the Confederates were hopeful that Great Britain would intervene in the conflict or grant diplomatic recognition to the Confederacy.[15]

These prospects, for a little while, led Mallory to reconsider the possibility of having armorclads built in Europe; in such a case, Bulloch would be involved. Mallory first hinted at this idea on 11 January 1862.[16]

Three days later, the Confederate naval agent got a clear order in writing: because North "has not been able to do anything with it," Bulloch should see to the construction of an imprecise number of seagoing ironclads in France or England. Attached to the letter were detailed plans prepared by Chief Constructor John L. Porter and by Engineer in Chief W. P. Williamson. As always, Mallory was betting on innovations: low armored decks, free from hindering accoutrements, and guns capable of firing in any direction. These would evolve later into revolving turrets.[17]

As ill luck would have it, the Union fleet tightly blockaded the *Fingal* inside the river, whereupon Bulloch, now commissioned a commander,[18] had to leave his ship and go back to England aboard a blockade runner; he landed in Liverpool on 10 March 1862. Two days earlier the *Virginia* had achieved her great success in Hampton Roads, giving birth to the fleeting impression that European-built armorclads were not needed.

Moreover, as soon as he reached Great Britain, Bulloch was busy with the challenging problem of arranging for the escape to sea of the two commerce raiders being built on the Mersey. Thus he could not fully concentrate on the ironclads until June 1862.[19]

Meanwhile, New Orleans had fallen, the *Louisiana* and the *Mississippi* had been scuttled almost without firing a shot, and the *Virginia* had to be blown up to avoid capture by the enemy. Of the homemade ironclad fleet, only the *Arkansas* remained, and Mallory was gradually developing his new naval strategy in which ironclads built in Europe would take first place. Yet it was the inept North who would arrange for laying down the first Confederate ironclad in Great Britain. This is a tangled story.

At Richmond, Mallory had been acting with customary speed on behalf of Bulloch. On 11 April the Confederate Congress, at his behest, authorized contracts for building six ironclads to be paid for with cotton.[20] Mallory wrote to inform Memminger that the appropriation was for $2 million and should immediately be made payable in Great Britain.[21] The secretary of the treasury was willing to act, but as usual he had to accept disastrous exchange rates: $1,453,145 to obtain £93,933 and 8,000 French francs. In any case, the sum was soon sent to Fraser, Trenholm and Company in England.[22]

For a number of reasons, it took much time for the money to reach Europe. North was depressed; then in May Fraser, Trenholm and Company gave him about £30,000 (nearly $500,000). Of course, he thought the money was for him, whereas it was really part of an earlier appropriation to cover the cost of the future raider *Alabama*.[23]

With this money (which he should not have had), North proceeded to carry out a project that had come up unexpectedly and on which he had already begun to busy himself. During his travels, he had met Edward P. Stringer, an agent of the prominent London bank of W. S. Lindsay and Company. William S. Lindsay, member of the House of Commons and shipowner, was a warm sympathizer with the Southern cause[24] and was, incidentally, trusted by Emperor Napoleon III.[25]

It was Stringer (probably backed by Lindsay) who had introduced North to George Thomson, Glasgow shipbuilder, who had shipyards along the Clyde. Thomson, trusting the Lindsay bank, declared that he was ready to take an order.

Following an exchange of ideas, North had sent the builder a letter formally asking him to prepare a plan.[26] The Confederate officer then sent a frantic message to Mallory asking for £200,000.[27] Thus when Fraser, Trenholm and Company gave him £30,000, he thought the money was for him, in reply to his request.

North (who on 5 May was commissioned a commander yet ranked junior to Bulloch, which greatly annoyed him)[28] received on 20 May from the brothers James and George Thomson the specifications for the armorclad to be built and on the next day signed the contract.[29] On 7 June, in a coded message announcing the beginning of work on the ship, North urgently requested that Mallory send him £200,000 to cover expenses.[30] The total cost was £182,000, to be paid in nine installments. The ship should be ready in one year.

Simply designated by the Thomsons as "No. 61" and variously given the names *Glasgow* or *Santa Maria* by the Confederates, she would go down in history with the fanciful nickname of "Scottish sea monster." The ship laid down in the Clyde shipyard from which many of the best British vessels had gone to sea was a formidable ironclad frigate 270 feet long and of 4,747 tons displacement. She would be powered by two engines totaling 500 horsepower and fitted with a strong ram. The plate (which would protect the hull over the waterline) would be 4.5 inches thick, but thin to 3 inches aft. The armor would be backed by teak 18 inches thick. Her battery would be of twenty guns, disposed, according to the old system, in broadsides. Yet some of the guns would be powerful rifled Whitworths.[31]

Certainly the "Scottish sea monster" would be extremely powerful, superior to any vessel in the Union navy, yet the ship had some flaws. The gunport lids would be hinged above rather than below, with the risk that if they were hit by enemy fire they might close during battle. There would be no device to raise the screw propeller from the water, which would seriously impair her speed when under sail and require her to burn a lot of coal. Worst of all, her draft of twenty feet would make it impossible for her to enter Southern coastal waters, condemning her to wander forever, far from the homeland, like a ghost ship. Her draft, concludes Frank J. Merli, would hinder her access to Southern ports "far more effectively than any Federal Squadron could do." [32]

Even if up to his neck with getting his two cruisers to sea, Bulloch found time to carry out Mallory's order to concern himself with the building of ironclads and pointed out to North such shortcomings, as well as the lack in the contract of a penalty reservation warranting against late delivery or seizure of the ship. [33]

Even if the first cruiser, the *Florida,* was able to sail only on 22 March, and the *Alabama* could not do so until 22 July, Bulloch unstintingly involved himself in the ironclad program. Unlike North, who seemed to be careless, he was perfectly aware of the predicaments he must overcome: more than anything else, possible interference by the British authorities, under heavy pressure from the Union to forestall building ships that could not be passed off as merchantmen.

Indeed, Bulloch was already finding it extremely difficult to get the two cruisers to sea. Therefore, after thoughtful consideration, he suggested to Mallory that the wooden parts of the ironclads be fitted in the Confederate States. If Mallory would send him scale drafts and accurate plans, he would have all the armor plates, hardware, and the like produced in Great Britain and number the parts and ship them to the South for assemblage, a solution that would meet practically no obstacle from the British government. [34] He was proposing building prefabricated ships a century in advance of their time.

Yet nothing came of it, for two reasons. As Bulloch himself put it, Richmond trusted too much in the British sympathy for the Southern cause, [35] and, most likely, the poor industrial plant of the South was overburdened and unable to undertake such work.

In his reply, after saying that he had sent Bulloch $1 million and had requested an appropriation of another million, Mallory insisted that the initiative be taken in England with great urgency. [36] Bulloch became involved in this job even before the second cruiser was at sea.

The Confederate naval agent was familiar with the Laird brothers' shipyards and admired their skill, uprightness, and reliability. Therefore he informed them of his exigency. Unlike North's, his mind was clear and determined. The ships to be built must be of a size and draft that would enable them to enter Southern ports and to sail and steer even in narrow and shallow waters. But they must be genuine seagoing ships, capable of facing the ocean and crossing it without problems and giving battle on it. They must also carry the heaviest armor and most powerful guns to be superior to any major enemy ship; yet they must be capable of the highest speed.

Therefore, a series of difficult equations had to be solved to coordinate moderate size, great power, and major protection with handiness and speed. To such ends, it would greatly help if only a few but extremely powerful guns, sheltered in armored turrets, were put on board. Weight would be concentrated amidships so as not to weigh down the sides with stiffeners.

The letter in which Mallory told him about the $1 million appropriation did not reach Bulloch until 10 June. Meanwhile, he had, on his own initiative, turned to the Laird shipyards, but without being able to make any financial commitment. The Lairds trusted him, and when he was able to ask officially for a contract, they had already prepared both scaled plans and specifications. On 4 July 1862 Bulloch was at last able to send Richmond a coded message announcing the signing of a contract for the building of two ironclads.[37]

The Lairds' plans met Bulloch's hopes. The two ships would have the following characteristics:[38] 1,896 tons displacement, 235 feet in length, 42 feet beam, full load draft of 17.6 feet. The armor, to begin 3.5 feet under the waterline, would be 4.5 inches thick, though it would decrease to 2 inches at bow and stern. The plates would be backed by teak bulkheads 9 inches thick that tapered to 5 inches at both ends.[39] The 350-horsepower engines would provide a speed of 15.5 knots.[40] The twin screws could operate independently, thus permitting the ship to turn very tightly.

The two ironclads would cost £93,750; by ordering both of the same type, Bulloch got a discount of £2,500. Fitting out time called for the first to be ready in eight months (March 1863) and the second in ten months (May 1863).[41]

The problem of armored turrets was still to be solved. The best prototype existing was that designed by Captain Cowper Phipps Coles, Royal Navy;[42] yet because it appeared that the British Admiralty had bought all of Coles's patents, it was uncertain whether it would be available.[43] The Laird brothers arranged a meeting with Bulloch and Coles,[44] which resulted in the signing of a contract on 5 December 1862 that authorized the use of the Coles turrets for both Confederate ironclads.[45]

The ships would be fitted with three revolving turrets (later reduced to two), each protected by 5.5 inches of armor, backed by teak 12 inches thick. Unlike those that Ericsson put on the *Monitor,* Coles's turrets would not be cylindrical but shaped like truncated cones. Mallory, who had studied the matter for years, had suggested, as optimal, an inclination of 38 degrees.[46] Only their top part would emerge from the armored deck, thus reducing by half of its height the portion of the turret exposed to enemy fire. This also would eliminate worry about the need to make the base of the turret so tightly closed to the deck as to stop leakage; it would thus be possible to fit it on roller bearings to make it revolve much more easily and speedily than in the Ericsson model.[47] Each turret would have two powerful rifled guns: indeed, the Confederate ironclads would be true monocaliber ships, anticipating Cuniberti's by almost half a century.

According to usual shipyard practice, the Lairds named the ships Nos. 294 and 295. Bulloch never used the numbers and always designated them as "armorclad ships." Yet the people at large began to call them rams, perhaps because many were impressed by the fact that each (as was the fashion) had at her bow what looked like a formidable beak, six to seven feet long,[48] or because the name "ram" made the ships seem more threatening and devastating. Yet this definition was used ill-naturedly by enemy propaganda and passed into the work of historians. The designation "armorclad ships" is better because it was used by Bulloch and also because it better describes their true strategic aims.

Those aims were perfectly clear to Gustavus Vasa Fox. The U.S. Navy, he correctly thought, had neither ships nor guns capable of countering such ironclads; therefore, to check their completion by the Confederates would become for the Union a matter of life or death.[49]

Bulloch indeed feared more than anything else the heavy pressure that the Union government might bring to bear upon the British, mainly through the action of the skillful U.S. ambassador at the Court of St. James, Charles Francis Adams.[50]

Mallory was insisting that the ironclads be fitted out as soon as possible. On 8 August, while communicating gloomy news about the destruction of the *Arkansas,* he wrote Bulloch: "I must impress upon you the great importance of completing [the] ironclad vessels at any earliest moment." He also suggested that the naval agent pay a bonus to hasten the work: "Not a day, not an hour must be lost in getting these ships over, and money is of no consequence in comparison to the speedy accomplishment of this work." He predicted that, should the two ironclads be fitted out and equipped, the reconquest of New Orleans and of the Mississippi would be feasible.[51] This was the offensive strategy he was planning for the armored ships being built in Europe.

Unfortunately, besides unending worry about what the British government might do, Bulloch faced several other problems. Of these, two were particularly harrowing. The first was that of funds. Even if in August President Davis, at Mallory's urgent request, had approved an appropriation of $3.5 million for building the ironclads overseas, and in September the secretary of the navy had requested $4 million more for the same purpose, it soon turned out that the foreign exchange available in the Confederacy (to which there must be added bonuses of 100 percent and more, whereas the bonus on gold did not exceed 30 percent) was running out.[52]

Mallory then discovered that he could finance the construction in Europe by means of cotton certificates issued by the secretary of the treasury to be tendered for sale to English cotton manufacturers, at a rate of eight cents per pound of cotton.[53] At the end of the war (or as soon as favorable conditions existed), the holders of the certificates could exchange them for cotton in any Confederate port at the current price, hence netting handsome profits.[54] Thanks to the produce loan, the Confederacy had in stock about 417,000 bales of cotton. At eight cents per pound the cotton would be worth $16 million. At the beginning of 1863 Mallory asked the secretary of the treasury for $3 million in cotton certificates.[55]

The second problem Bulloch had to face (which was never wholly solved) came from one of Mallory's worst mistakes. Eager to put to sea the fleet of seagoing ironclads upon which so much of his new strategy depended, or perhaps even trying to "extend the target," so as to make it more difficult for the British authorities to seize the ships, he signed contracts for building ships in Europe with private speculators (or with their lobbies). Once a contract had been signed, those people had nothing else to do with the navy; it was presumed that they would arrange on their own account to have the ships contracted for, built somewhere, and delivered.

Upon arriving in Europe, those people sought financing. To get credit, they boasted that they had the backing of the Confederate government. They thus shattered the secrecy Bulloch believed was indispensable for success because such unwanted advertising only increased Union pressure and made the British authorities more wary.[56] No speculator ever succeeded in building anything.

The case of Lieutenant George T. Sinclair (one of the seven Sinclairs who served in the C.S. Navy) was different. He arrived in Great Britain not as a civilian but with a specific mission from Mallory. He needed to have built a large commerce raider, protected by armor plate along her sides, then assume command of her.[57] Bulloch was to help him and assist him financially.

Because he had no money, Bulloch gave Sinclair a copy of the designs of the *Alabama* and consigned him to God's mercy. It was Sinclair who, to raise funds, with the help of the Confederate commissioner in Great Britain, James M. Mason, and of banker Lindsay, first had the idea of marketing cotton certificates.[58]

Sinclair was able to sign a contract with the Thomson brothers' shipyard in Glasgow, where the "Scottish sea monster" was being built. At a cost of £51,250 the Thomsons would build a cruiser similar to the *Alabama* but larger (231 feet long). The sides would be partially protected by plates, and she would carry three 8-inch pivot guns fore and aft and four more guns in broadside. She was given the conventional name of *Canton,* then of *Pampero,* to fool Northern agents, who, indeed, would not be fooled at all.[59]

Meanwhile, Bulloch stubbornly pushed to have his ironclads built. Work proceeded on them in bad weather and at night, by gaslight. He already thought that the time was ripe for Mallory to send their officers, not to England but to Madeira or some other place. He also flattered himself that he would assume command of one of the two mighty vessels.[60]

After much deliberation, he had chosen the battery for both ironclads. Of course, the guns would not be put on board. Bulloch did not even want to have powder magazines built on the ships. Nothing must even hint at the presence of any weapon. The battery would be fitted later, outside of British waters.

The guns would be powerful 9-inch rifled Blakelys, with steel bores, set in pairs, two in each turret. They would each weigh one ton and be able to fire 240-pound projectiles. In addition, each ship would have two rifled 70-pound 5.5-inch Whitworths, one on the bow, the other aft, behind metal shields. These would have the task of hitting small ships. Bulloch thought that once the ironclads were at sea, they would be able to sweep away the whole enemy fleet that blockaded the South.[61]

During the first months of 1863, the new Confederate naval strategy linked to the seagoing squadron of ironclads to be built in Europe was thus taking shape. There was only one threat looming on the horizon: the dogged attempts by the Union government to stop their building. These, Mallory wrote, "have caused me great anxiety."[62] Indeed, this would be the first, fierce struggle that the Southern ironclads in Europe must face— one in which their formidable war power would be of no avail.

Luckily, the building of homemade ironclads and heavy guns for defending the seacoasts and inland waters of the Confederacy presented no such problems. The South did, however, face unending enemy pressure. As always, Mallory would try to squeeze time to the utmost.

The new armored home fleet already had a ship, the *Richmond.* She had been built in Norfolk and been towed up the James River to safety before the enemy arrived. She was now being fitted out in Rocketts Navy Yard, near the Confederate capital. Criticism circulated about her: her engines were weak; she would not make more than five knots; she would not be ready until late in October 1862.[63]

Actually, however, by the middle of September she was fitted out and ready to receive her battery: three 7-inch Brooke rifles weighing fourteen thousand pounds each, cast especially for her at Tredegar.[64] On 1 October the guns were delivered and she was ready to be commissioned.[65] To the Brookes were added two smoothbores, one for each side; then one more rifled Brooke, a formidable one with triple banding at the breech, designed expressly by John Mercer Brooke, was added to her battery and placed in the embrasure at the bow on 1 November 1862.[66]

The *Richmond* was covered with 4-inch plate backed by oak and pine bulwarks 22 inches thick. She was 172.6 feet long. Her structure (like that of all ironclad vessels built henceforth) was similar but not identical to that of the scuttled *Virginia*. Indeed, the ends of her casemate had a rectangular rather than round shape, and her forward and stern sections were not submerged.

As the vessel was being prepared in Richmond, in Charleston, South Carolina (a city which, more than any other, had reasons to feel threatened by an enemy attack from the sea), either through the impetus of the commanding officer of the naval squadron, old Commodore Duncan N. Ingraham, or its patriotic people, impressed by the achievements of the *Virginia,* the *Daily Courier* had opened a ladies' collection of money for the building of an ironclad.[67]

The initiative might have been funny or even pathetic if not for the incredible response it obtained. Offers of money came from everywhere, including children and even black slaves. Those who had little or no money sold or auctioned off family objects and goods. In the end, enough money to build an ironclad was raised and sent to the governor. Confederate soldiers and sailors could be proud of the support their women gave to their struggle. Even the flag of the new ship was sewn by a Charleston woman.[68]

In March 1862, when the deeds of the *Virginia* stunned the world, the keel of the new ship was laid in the Marsh and Son shipyard.

A few days later, when news arrived that the naval secretary was willing to pay for building the ironclad, the Executive Council of South Carolina decided to construct a second one. The work was entrusted to J. M. Eason.[69]

Work at the Eason yard, located on the Cooper River, proceeded quickly, and the second armorclad was launched first, on 23 August 1862, seventeen days after the destruction of the *Arkansas*. Fitted out in record time, in September she was christened the *Chicora* and put into commission.[70]

Work on the ship that should have been fitted out first proceeded more slowly. Lieutenant Alexander F. Warley, the superintendent of construction (who had been captured at New Orleans but returned after an exchange of prisoners), felt disheartened.[71] At last, launched on 11 October 1862, the ship was named the *Palmetto State*. In the presence of the governor, General Beauregard (now commanding Confederate forces in South Carolina), and a host of the women at whose initiative the ship had been built, she was solemnly christened. At that moment, the other ship, the *Chicora,* with all flags flying, slowly approached and saluted her twin, amid great enthusiasm.[72]

Of the same class as the *Richmond* and designed by John L. Porter,[73] the two ironclads were 150 feet long and protected by 4-inch armor plate backed by oak bulwarks 22 inches thick. The *Palmetto State* carried four guns (of which two were rifled Brookes), the *Chicora* six. The latter cost $262,829, the former a bit more. Commanding the first was Commander John Rutledge; the second, Captain John R. Tucker.[74]

General Beauregard, more than many other army officers, well understood the character of the war being fought between land and sea. Yet, unfortunately, he began to ponder a plan intended to break the blockade by means of a surprise attack from the new ironclads. He was in part moved to do so because the local press had begun to grumble about a "do-nothing fleet."[75]

On the night of 30 January 1863, therefore, the two ironclads silently slipped out to sea. Having raised his pennant upon the *Palmetto State,* Commodore Ingraham personally commanded the action.

At 4:30 next morning, at high tide, the two vessels were able to cross the bar and reach the open sea. Their lights were out, their crews at general quarters. Thousands of soldiers watched them anxiously in silence from the slits in the forts.[76] It was the first time, after the stirring actions of 1862, that Confederate ironclads offered battle to the enemy.

Their dim gray-blue paint well concealed the two iron "monsters" so that they fell upon an enemy who did not become aware of them until they were at close quarters. When the crew of the Union ship *Mercedita* sighted the *Palmetto State,* it was too late. The ram of the ironclad hit the side of the vessel, opening a large hole. In the meantime, the rifled gun on the bow of the Confederate fired a shell into the engine room of the enemy, bursting her boilers. Immobilized and disabled and at first appearing about to sink, the *Mercedita* lowered her flag.[77]

The two ironclads should have been followed by steamers, carrying fifty soldiers to take care of the prisoners. Yet for some unknown reason, these did not succeed in crossing the bar. Ingraham, therefore, paroled the Union crew.[78]

The *Chicora,* which had steamed farther, had resolutely engaged another large Federal ship, the *Keystone State.* The latter was soon hit by a shell which started a fire and killed and wounded several men. After the fire was put out, the *Keystone State* spiritedly resumed fighting; though her projectiles barely scratched the plating of the *Chicora,* the latter's shells created havoc on board the Union ship, disabling the engines and causing more loss of life. In the end, the *Keystone State* also decided to surrender, then changed her mind and succeeded in limping away with twenty dead and as many wounded on board.

The slowness of the ironclad did not permit her to pursue the fleeing enemy; therefore, the *Chicora* turned against another ship, the *Quaker City,* sending a shell into her engine room and partially disabling her.[79]

The Union squadron had been scattered, but the two ironclads, built for the defense of inland waters, could not pursue the enemy because of their slowness and unseaworthiness. Indeed, this flaw was so serious that the sortie had been possible only because the sea was flat calm; otherwise the two Confederate ships would have risked sinking.[80]

The enemy had been hit very hard, yet this was a victory without follow-up. Only seagoing ironclads, built in Europe, could have truly swept the blockade. Thus the attempt by Confederates to open the port of Charleston failed.[81]

Still, a victors' welcome rightly awaited the two ironclads at Charleston. They had disabled two Federal ships, damaged two more, and inflicted serious casualties on the enemy: twenty-four dead and as many wounded, as well as putting a whole squadron to flight. At 8:45 A.M. the two ironclads anchored near the bar and waited for high tide to enter the harbor.

The battle had lasted four hours. After waiting for the tide another seven hours, at 4:00 P.M. they entered the harbor amid hurrahs from the garrison of the forts and moored at Charleston. There the wharves were packed with hundreds of people who cried, laughed, and applauded with an enthusiasm not seen since the surrender of Fort Sumter.[82] Such rash actions by ironclads designed and built only for harbor defense, however, would soon lead to a serious letdown for the Confederacy.

After her arrival from Europe the steamer *Fingal* had remained trapped in the Savannah River. Because she was unable to get out, it was decided to use her hull to build an ironclad (as had been done with the *Merrimack*). The transformation work was entrusted to the Tift brothers, builders of the *Mississippi.*[83] Soon the hull was cut down almost to the waterline and covered with a deck three inches thick. Over this was built a heavily armored casemate, covered with plates made by rolling out railroad iron and backed by strong bulkheads of oak and pine.

Getting the rails for armoring the ship had not been easy. Forty-seven citizens from Savannah had sent a petition directly to President Davis asking for the rails seized by the navy from warehouses of the Georgia and Gulf Railroad. Davis turned the letter over to Mallory and told him to see what he could do. The secretary answered that armoring the former *Fingal* required six hundred tons of iron.[84]

The ship was large. She displaced more than 1,000 tons, was 204 feet long, and was armed with four heavy rifled Brookes cast at Tredegar: two 7-inch pivot guns fore and aft and two 6.4-inch in broadside. Her main flaw was her draft of 17 feet when under full load.[85]

During her fitting out, the ironclad had been an object of particular care. To be sure her engine was effective, Chief Engineer James H. Warner had been summoned.[86] The work had long been under way in the spring of 1862, but it stretched out, probably because of obstacles encountered in finding iron. Finally, in early August 1862, the ironclad, christened the *Atlanta*, underwent her engine trial. Then another four months passed before she could be commissioned, simultaneous with Mallory's formulation of his new naval strategy. The ship looked powerful. Yet the living quarters and conditions aboard were poor because of leakage from the points of junction between the new deck and the old hull and the shabby finishing of the interior.[87]

On 5 January 1863, Tattnall, now commanding the Savannah Squadron, began to move the ship downriver; but the Corps of Engineers failed to open a passage through the obstructions in time, and the ironclad had to go back. It took much time to open a passage through which the *Atlanta* could move. It was 19 March, and Tattnall was planning to go to sea and attack the nearby Union base at Port Royal, South Carolina, which was protected only by wooden ships, hoping to repeat Ingraham's success at Charleston. Unfortunately, two deserters warned the enemy and the project had to be canceled. The ironclad moved again on 30 March but grounded because of her deep draft.[88]

Still, even if nobody realized it, with her movements the ship was worrying the enemy and forcing him on the defensive. Rear Admiral Du Pont, commanding the South Atlantic Blockading Squadron, considered the *Atlanta* "formidable"[89] and was much worried because (as Tattnall already knew) he had moved from Savannah all his armorclads, slated for the action against Charleston.

Knowledgeable in naval strategy, General Beauregard had telegraphed from Charleston pointing out the hazardous situation of that part of the

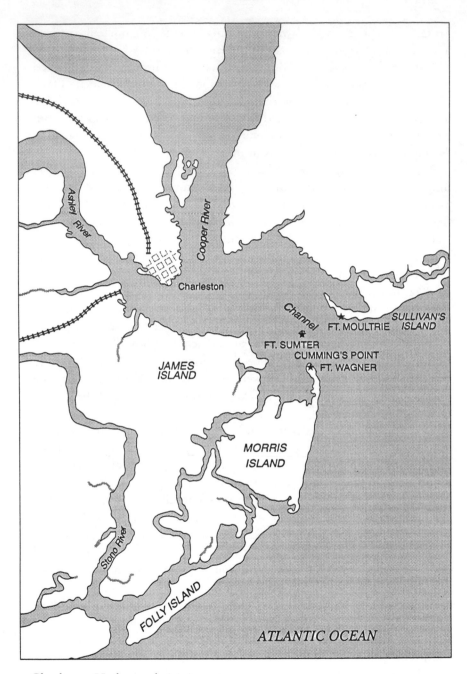

Charleston Harbor and vicinity.

Union squadron that remained between Savannah and Port Royal without a single ironclad, and Mallory who, catlike, was watching enemy movements, had suggested seizing the opportunity: "Can you not strike the enemy a blow . . . while his ironclads are off Charleston?" he telegraphed Captain Richard L. Page, who had assumed command of the Savannah Squadron, while Tattnall (who had conceived the daring plan others would implement) had been limited to commanding the naval station, to his great chagrin.[90]

Tattnall, who was an expert on ironclads because he had commanded the *Virginia,* had told Mallory that the *Atlanta,* because of her deep draft, which not only made navigation difficult in shallow waters but hindered steering, might not be counted on to face enemy ironclads of the *Monitor* class at close quarters.[91]

To crown all the problems, the *Atlanta* had trouble with her bow gun, the one most necessary in battle.[92] Therefore, Brooke was requested to send a substitute from Richmond, which could not be done until late in May.[93] Meanwhile, Du Pont, increasingly worried, had regained some of his ironclads and wisely placed two of the *Monitor* class, the *Weehawken* and the *Nahant,* to watch the exits from which the feared Confederate vessel might appear. Moreover, he put in command of them one of the best and most experienced ironclad officers in the U.S. Navy, Captain John Rodgers.[94]

At Savannah, changes continued to wrack the Confederate naval command. After Tattnall's authority had been limited to the naval station, the squadron had been entrusted first to Richard L. Page, then, possibly because Page was not sufficiently resourceful, to Commander William H. Webb, who during the battles at Hampton Roads had ably guided the small gunboat *Teaser.*[95]

Perhaps overly confident and too daring, Webb soon decided to make for the sea and attack the two Federal ironclads.[96] Unfortunately, it was a bad idea. Yet the fatal decision had been made. On 28 May 1863 the obstructions were ordered opened,[97] and on the thirtieth the *Atlanta* got under way.

Because Federal forces in Fort Pulaski had closed every exit, Webb had to pass through a tangle of canals that linked the two large parallel rivers of the area, the Savannah and the Ogeechee, then to follow the narrow and winding St. Augustine Creek to get out into the Wassaw (or Warsaw) Sound. Secretary Mallory had doubted the success of the venture. Another ironclad, the *Savannah,* was being built. Could not Webb wait until she, too, was ready? Webb impatiently disregarded the advice. Like others who did not fully understand the strategic situation, he wanted to break the

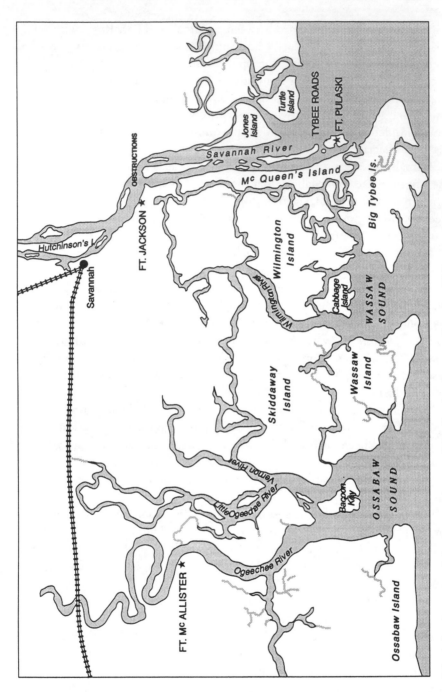

The inland waters of the Savannah zone. The floating battery *Georgia* still lies on the bottom of the Savannah River in front of Fort Jackson.

blockade along the entire coast between Savannah and Charleston. At least, this was his dream.[98]

At the crack of dawn on 16 June 1863, after toiling along the shallow waters of the narrow and winding reaches of the river and losing several days, first because of running aground, then because a boiler's valve had to be replaced,[99] the *Atlanta* advanced into Warsaw Sound and was immediately sighted by the Federals.

Rodgers steered to attack with both of his ironclads. Unfortunately for the Confederates, the *Atlanta* grounded and heeled enough to make it impossible to use her guns. The *Weehawken,* followed by the *Nahant,* closed to three hundred yards and began to pound the inert, immobile ship with their huge 15-inch and 11-inch Dahlgrens. It was no longer a battle: it was target practice that would fast become an execution.

The effect of such mighty blows was frightful. The concussion of the first shot threw down all the Southern sailors; then splinters and bolts in the interior began to fly about, wounding many men. Much of the internal oak bulwark was wrecked, then the pilothouse was ripped off and in part destroyed while the two helmsmen fell mortally wounded. It was clear that in a few more minutes the armor plating would be knocked off.

The *Atlanta* tried to fight, but after firing seven rounds that found no target, she had to lower her flag.[100] The battle, if it may be considered such, had lasted for only a few minutes. Thus the first Southern ironclad fell into enemy hands.

News of the capture stunned the South. Admiral Buchanan, who had commanded the *Virginia* in the battle of Hampton Roads, in a confidential letter expressed his astonishment. The event looked incredible to him because he had known Webb to be a daring officer.[101] This was perhaps Webb's greatest flaw: he lacked not bravery but good sense. For many years after the war, able and experienced Southern naval officers criticized his conduct, Bulloch in a somewhat veiled way, Parker more openly.[102]

At Richmond, all criticisms fell upon Mallory.[103] And perhaps rightly so. Prisoner of his effort to replace older with younger officers held to be more aggressive, he had in this instance committed an error in his choice and evidently had not firmly opposed the rash initiative. This had been a major mistake because he should have shown the strictness on basic strategic problems that a leader must always follow.

Fortunately, Savannah did not remain undefended. In October 1862 another armorclad, the *Georgia,* had been launched. She was 250 feet long and armed with ten guns. Yet her engines were so poor that she could not breast the current. She was therefore reclassified as a floating battery and anchored before Fort Jackson, downriver from Savannah. There, crossing her fire with that of the fort, she for the following years provided the main active obstacle to the enemy's attempts to sail up the river—and she is still there, on the bottom of the Savannah River, where she was scuttled at the end of the war.[104]

Mallory stubbornly continued to develop his program. Four ironclads were being built in North Carolina; another one, the *Savannah*, was almost ready in the city that was her namesake; a powerful one had been laid down in Charleston. At least seven had been laid down in Alabama to protect Mobile and several others along the Mississippi.[105]

On the James River, a second ironclad was started in the navy yard. The *Richmond* was performing her duty as a strategic threat to the enemy. Thought had been given at the army's request to have her cross the obstructions to support a land attack against Suffolk, but the Corps of Engineers, concerned about the safety of the capital, had refused to open the passage so that nothing came from the proposal, even though Mallory was not wholly against an attempt.

Of course, the *Richmond* might have succeeded; yet she might also have ended like the *Atlanta* and then the enemy ships, crossing the opened obstructions, might have appeared in front of the Confederate capital.[106]

The first experiences of the new phase, in which attempts were still being made to clarify the strategy, confirmed the events of 1862. As the new ironclads were commissioned, the ports and waterways of the South would be tightly sealed to the enemy. Meanwhile, the powerful squadron being built in Europe would, if hopes materialized, have the task of attacking the enemy fleet from the rear.

T W E L V E

The Zenith of Commerce Destroying on the Far Seas

Upon returning to England after his trip aboard the *Fingal,* the tireless Bulloch had devoted his full energy to the fitting out and putting to sea of the two cruisers being built on the Mersey before thinking about ironclads.

It was not an easy task. The wily Confederate had found in Thomas H. Dudley, U.S. general consul in Liverpool, a worthy adversary: resolute, bold, and shrewd, he was fully engaged in seeking to checkmate the Southern initiatives. To this end he had unleashed on Bulloch's heels an array of private detectives and spies. Even if such means were disgusting to the honest Dudley, he believed that the game was worth the candle.[1]

Bulloch's absence had not been good for the cause; but when at 4:00 P.M. on 10 March 1862 he detrained at Liverpool, he immediately brought the situation back under his control.

The first of the two cruisers, disguised under the name of *Oreto,* had already been launched and fitted out and had successfully passed her engine trial. Bulloch therefore found her ready for sea and decided that she must leave England as soon as possible.[2]

On 22 March 1862 she set sail under command of a British master mariner, James A. Duguid, with a local crew. Her papers showed that she would make for Palermo. Yet her officers (and only they) knew that such a destination was false. On board, as "passenger," was John Low.

The U.S. ambassador, Charles Francis Adams, after being informed by Dudley, had done everything in his power to delay her departure and even to have her seized. But the Liverpool port authorities (hence the Foreign

Office) had decided that although the *Oreto* had been built as a warship, she had on board nothing that might be used for war purposes, no explosives, no ammunition, no weapon of any kind.[3]

Who would command the cruiser raised many entangled questions. After a series of qui pro quo with the hardly astute North,[4] who had repeatedly been tendered command of the raider and declined on the ground that she had no weapons aboard (the reasons for which apparently escaped him),[5] Bulloch decided otherwise. With his usual speed and wisdom he had already identified the man he needed: Lieutenant John Newland Maffitt.[6]

Born in February 1818, Maffitt was forty-three years old. His whole life had revolved around the sea. He had entered the world while his mother was sailing to meet her husband, a Methodist minister. When not yet thirteen he returned to sea as a midshipman in the U.S. Navy.[7] Since 1843 he had commanded ships engaged in the suppression of the illegal slave trade, and he had distinguished himself in chasing the slavers.

At the time of secession, having grown up and been educated in North Carolina, he immediately headed south. At the time he was in Mobile Bay, commanding a U.S. naval ship, the *Crusader,* and felt honor bound to return her to New York and to the U.S. Navy, which owned her and had entrusted her to him. In Mobile there were men who plotted to board the *Crusader* and seize her for the Confederacy, but Maffitt tersely announced that he would shoot anyone who tried to do so. After several minor assignments in the Confederate service, he was commissioned to command a blockade runner, the *Nassau,* based in the port bearing the same name, in the British Bahamas.

Bulloch thought highly of Maffitt. He knew that, having served in the Coast Survey, Maffitt was well acquainted with American waters. He also correctly gauged Maffitt's daring, boldness, initiative, and stern sense of duty. Therefore, he ordered that the cruiser, whose true name was the *Florida,* proceed to the Bahamas; there Low would turn her over to Maffitt. All the implements of war, guns with their carriages, ammunition, individual weapons, and the like (equipment that did not fall under the ban of the British neutrality laws) would be shipped separately aboard the steamer *Bahama* and transferred to the *Florida* in waters free of danger.[8]

The *Florida* (as Bulloch proudly emphasized) was therefore the first warship "built under contract" for the C.S. Navy. She was a small ship, like the other still building in England, and could do very little to change the course of the war. Yet these vessels could at least "illustrate the spirit and energy" of the Southern people and, at the same time, "repay upon the enemy some of the injuries his vastly superior force alone has enabled him to inflict upon the States of the Confederacy."[9]

Unfortunately, Maffitt was at sea when, on 28 April 1862 (the same day, on the faraway Mississippi, that the *Louisiana* and the *McRae* had to be scuttled), the *Florida* arrived at Nassau, after an ocean crossing in which she had showed first-rate seagoing qualities, logging up to twelve knots.[10] Low had to wait for Maffitt a rather long time. Meanwhile, the local U.S. consul, Samuel Whiting, unleashed a campaign asking that the ship be seized for violating British neutrality laws.

When Maffitt arrived on 4 May, Whiting's proceedings were well advanced and the ship was seized until a local admiralty court absolved her and ordered her release.[11] All this consumed an enormous amount of time; it was August when the ship was at last freed.[12]

The next step was to transfer the equipment and weapons and to do so hurriedly because U.S. authorities had not yet thrown in the towel. Because the transfer could not take place in Nassau Harbor, the full cargo of the *Bahama* was quickly transshipped to the schooner *Prince Alfred*,[13] and on 7 August the two ships sailed separately for their rendezvous. The day before, on the Mississippi, the Confederates had been compelled to blow up the *Arkansas.*

After skillfully eluding chase by the U.S. warship *Cuyler*, which was watching her closely, the *Florida*, taking in tow the *Prince Alfred*, proceeded to anchor near an islet off the beaten track.[14]

Transferring the cargo required almost superhuman effort because the *Florida*, hindered in enlisting men by the unending watch by Northern agents, had on board only 22 sailors instead of the normal 130 and just a few officers. Luckily, among the latter was Lieutenant John M. Stribling, who had already served aboard the *Sumter.* He had journeyed to Nassau on board the *Bahama* on his way to the South, where he would meet his young bride. Upon learning of the *Florida*'s situation, he volunteered to serve on the cruiser. With a sigh of relief, Maffitt billeted him as his executive officer.[15]

The *Florida*'s numerically insignificant crew had to transfer eight extremely heavy guns and their carriages, as well as tons of projectiles, powder, rigging, and the like. In a torrid tropical climate and under the hammering of the August sun, officers and men stripped to the waist and earnestly went to work.

On the second day a sailor fell ill; in eight hours he was dead. It was a frightening occurrence. Shortly before the *Florida* sailed from Nassau, a yellow fever epidemic had broken out. That may have been why the skin of the dead man looked so yellow. Was the deadly epidemic on board?

Anguish seized Maffitt, yet he kept calm, not wishing to spread panic. After all, the man, while in port, had given himself up to heavy drinking. Could not that have been the cause of his death? Meanwhile, work went on unceasingly. Eight days of backbreaking labor were required, but finally all the weapons were loaded, the guns placed, ammunition was in the magazines, and the *Florida* could officially be commissioned in the Confederate navy.[16]

But the ship had barely weighed anchor when a desperate cry from Stribling startled Maffitt. In the hurried transfer of equipment from the *Bahama* to the *Prince Alfred*, indispensable tools had remained aboard that ship and were not retrievable. Lacking were the rammers and the sponges necessary for loading the guns. Also missing were their sights, locks, beds, and quoins for aiming, tools without which it would be impossible to fire the guns. The ship was thus wholly unarmed.[17]

Yet worse was still to come. When an inventory was taken, it was discovered that during her seizure at Nassau several thefts had occurred and many valuable instruments were missing. Worse yet, suddenly three crewmen were struck with yellow fever. "The pestilential tyrant of the tropics had invaded the *Florida*." Every attempt to conceal it was in vain because in a short while almost half the crewmen were stricken.[18]

There being no surgeon on board, the captain had to try to nurse the sick men. Already concerned with his ship's condition, Maffitt was compelled to postpone warlike actions, thereby disappointing the great expectations that had been held for him. Moreover, he had to steer for the nearest neutral port. On 19 August he took his vessel into Cardenas, on the island of Cuba.[19]

No sooner had temporary clearance been obtained from the Spanish authorities to remain in their waters as long as necessary than Lieutenant Stribling left for Havana to find a doctor.[20] Then Maffitt noticed that he himself was beginning to shiver from the deadly fever. It was 20 August. For at least ten days he hovered between life and death before he began to recover. Meanwhile, he had received the bitter news that his stepson, sixteen-year-old John Laurens Read, aboard as a midshipman, had died. So had the third assistant engineer, John Seeley, and three sailors.[21]

Fortunately, Stribling had been able to find in Havana a citizen from Georgia, Dr. R. H. Barnett. Upon seeing the conditions on the ship, Barnett gave up the practice he enjoyed in the Havana hospital to volunteer aboard the *Florida* as the acting surgeon. Stribling also succeeded in covertly enlisting eight sailors and four stokers.[22]

Maffitt, still very feeble, badly needed time for convalescence, but this was impossible. Now the Spanish governor general, Francisco Serrano, telegraphed him that Northern warships, called by the local U.S. consul, were blockading the bay and that the *Florida* was in a dangerous situation, risking a neutrality violation by the Federals. Therefore, he invited him to proceed immediately to Havana.

At 8:30 A.M. on 31 August the Spanish packet boat, sailing toward Havana, was fired at by a U.S. ship that mistook her for the cruiser. Thus the *Florida* was able to slip away unseen and on 1 September to enter the port of Havana.

There it turned out that enlisting men or getting needed implements was impossible. Though polite, the Spanish hosts stuck strictly to neutrality. Therefore, Maffitt decided that there was nothing to do but try to get to a Confederate port. He chose Mobile Bay, on the Gulf of Mexico, which, according to his information, was watched by a single enemy ship. At nightfall of the same day, the *Florida* quietly slipped to sea and, hugging the coast, eluded the cruising Federals and made for Mobile.[23]

During the passage, the yellow fever continued to rage on board, striking those newly enlisted. Luckily, only one enemy ship was sighted far off.[24]

At 3:00 P.M. on 4 September 1862 the entrance to Mobile Bay was in sight, as well as two blockading Federal warships. These were the seagoing gunboats *Oneida* and *Winona,* each carrying ten guns, enough to break the defenseless *Florida* into shivers by a single broadside. What to do? The *Florida* drew too much water to risk an approach by night; moreover, the Confederates on land had extinguished the beacons. The only choice was to play the fox.[25]

Maffitt raised an English flag and, at 6:00 P.M., steered directly for the *Oneida,* commanded by one of his old comrades in arms, Commander George Henry Preble. This vessel was compelled to reverse engines and go astern to avoid colliding (therefore giving way to the *Florida,* which was running daringly at her and so bypassed the *Oneida*).[26] Now Preble, faced with a British flag (and perhaps remembering the recent *Trent* Affair), fired a warning shot, then a second one, before delivering a full broadside. This, however, was fired off hastily and inaccurately because, by another ruse, Maffitt had aimed his heavy but useless guns at the *Oneida,* thus forcing the Union warship to fire hurriedly to anticipate the still puzzling vessel.[27] The *Oneida's* broadside, therefore, was imprecise and too high and damaged only the running and standing rigging of the Confederate cruiser.

Yet now the *Winona,* followed by the mortar boat *Rachel Seaman,* rushed in, and the *Florida* became the target of such a withering fire that Maffitt almost lost hope. Fortunately for him, the *Oneida's* engines were in very poor shape, and one of her boilers was out of commission[28] so that she could make only a few knots, and the Confederate ship began to open distance. With a skillful turn of the helm, Maffitt succeeded in putting the two major enemy ships in line with each other so that one of them, the *Winona,* had to cease firing temporarily so as not to hit her sister vessel.

Yet the Federal ships had succeeded in dealing the *Florida* some devastating blows. One 11-inch shell from the *Oneida* had entered through the coal bunker and struck a boiler, wounding nine men and killing a petty officer. Had it exploded (which fortunately it did not) there would have been a slaughter. Another shell, from the *Winona,* had pierced the pantry and galley. Still another, exploding near the starboard gangway, had severely damaged the ship. In the meantime, shrapnel, exploding among the masts, destroyed the standing rigging and wounded other men, one mortally.[29] At least her great speed enabled the cruiser to open distance from the enemy. Finding herself in shallow waters, the *Oneida* had to give up the chase.[30] The *Florida,* safe at last, sailed up the channel amid the cheering of the garrison of Fort Morgan and anchored in Mobile Bay.

In addition to severe damage caused by enemy fire, yellow fever still raged on board the *Florida.* In Mobile the deadly disease dealt the ship its most cruel blow—the death on 12 September of the able and gallant executive officer, John M. Stribling.[31] Maffitt himself was still so feeble that merely writing a letter to his daughter was an exertion.[32]

The *Florida,* which had to be quarantined, had a small steamer put alongside to serve as a hospital. Nevertheless, Admiral Buchanan, commanding the Mobile Squadron, went personally aboard to tender Maffitt and his gallant crew his compliments and those of Secretary Mallory.[33]

Only on 3 October, when quarantine was lifted, could needed repairs start on the vessel. Still, such work proceeded slowly. The deep draft of the *Florida* forced her to remain in the middle of the bay. This meant that parts to be repaired frequently had to be dismounted, brought to land, repaired there, then returned on board. Even though the yellow fever epidemic was over, the workers made it an excuse and unwillingly went on board. Moreover, bad weather often limited or stopped work, mainly that involving the repair of standing and running rigging.[34]

In the meantime Maffitt was quietly enlisting and training men and appointing officers. Among these was Lieutenant Samuel W. Averett. A man of fine character even if inexperienced, he was billeted as the executive officer, replacing Stribling. Maffitt was also happy to receive on board the young Lieutenant Charles W. Read, whom he had specifically asked for. Well known for his daring, Read had a distinguished service record aboard the *McRae* and the *Arkansas.*[35]

Mallory, eager to see the cruiser in operation against the enemy, had already sent Maffitt his directions, which left him ample freedom to judge actions and means, except for careful deference to neutral rights.[36] On 10 January 1863 the *Florida* was at last completely refitted, had her full complement of officers and men, and her guns were ready to operate: two heavy 7-inch Blakelys forward and aft and six 6-inch Blakelys in broadside. Admiral Buchanan had extended all the help in his power by filling up the *Florida's* coal bunkers even at the cost of giving up almost the whole stock of coal at the Mobile station.[37]

What the vessel needed now was a favorable night to escape, for outside the bay the Union squadron greedily awaited its prey. During the preceding days, Mallory's impatience had reached its limit. Restlessness is a poor adviser, and it led Mallory to plunge into one of his worst mistakes. On 30 December he had summarily relieved Maffitt from command of the *Florida,* ordering his replacement by Lieutenant Joseph N. Barney.[38]

Fortunately, Admiral Buchanan, a good judge in the matter of gallantry and skill, had immediately written to the secretary explaining the reasons for delay (among them was the disposition from Richmond "to await further orders") and praising Maffitt.[39] Moreover, Buchanan had turned to President Davis, who happened to be in Mobile and who soon telegraphed Richmond. Maffitt was thus restored to his command.[40] The only outcome was Maffitt's bitter anger toward Mallory, which, among other things, revived ancient grudges because Maffitt had been one of the officers who had run the risk of falling victim to the notorious Naval Retiring Board.[41]

The long wait had heavily taxed everybody's endurance. Buchanan had instructed Maffitt to have the hull of his cruiser painted gray to make her less visible.[42] The *Florida* approached the bar twice and twice was grounded. Her crew, with the help of the gunboats *Morgan* and *Gaines,* had to unload her guns, ammunition, and coal to refloat her.[43]

At last, on 19 February 1863, Buchanan was able to inform Mallory that on the night of the sixteenth the *Florida* had gone to sea during a fierce northeaster, fast disappearing into the darkness. No gunfire had been heard, which should mean that the cruiser had escaped.[44]

Indeed, the *Florida* had made it. The night had been truly dreadful. With pelting rain and visibility reduced to a mere twenty yards, the pilot had waited until 2:00 A.M. before awakening Maffitt. At 2:20 A.M. the ship had got under way, crossed the bar, passed silently as a ghost near an enemy vessel that failed to see her, and reached the sea.

Until then, the skillful chief engineer of the *Florida,* Charles W. Quinn, had been able to burn coke. Now, with the supply burned out, he had to use lower-quality fuel. Soon, a flare from the funnel, owing to dusty coal, gave the alarm. While blue and red running lights suddenly appeared on the enemy ships and their drums beat to quarters, "half a dozen rampaging Federals" loosed themselves in chase. All in vain: the speedy cruiser had wasted no time in opening distance.[45]

During the day the *Florida* sailed through the storm. The large U.S. steam sloop *Brooklyn* suddenly appeared straight ahead, dismaying everybody, yet she paid the *Florida* no attention. Mistaking her for another Federal ship (the speedy cruiser *Cuyler,* the only one that Maffitt feared because her speed was almost as good as his own), the *Brooklyn* was deceived by the *Florida's* furling her sails and heaving to as night fell.

Bad weather ended on the morning of the seventeenth in bright sunshine; along the whole horizon nothing could be seen but sky and sea.[46] The *Florida* now steered for the ocean. Her hunt for Union merchant shipping had begun.

Meanwhile, the other cruiser built through Bulloch's exertions was already in action on the high seas. Initially, this had not been foreseen. When the *Florida* (still under her cover name of *Oreto*) had left Liverpool, the second ship was still indicated only as No. 290 and was not yet ready to be launched.[47] Bulloch had the work speeded up so that on 15 March 1862 the 290 was at last launched with the false name of *Enrica.*

It was now indispensable to find an experienced and reliable master mariner of English nationality to take her out of British waters. Bulloch found his man in Matthew J. Butcher, of the Cunard Line, whom he had met some years earlier in Havana. This choice turned out to be a very happy one, both because of Butcher's ability and because of his prudence and loyalty.

The ship was soon able to undergo her engine trial.[48] Sure of being given command of the cruiser, Bulloch was ready to leave with her. But Mallory sent him a message telling him that he must remain in England to see to the building of ironclads. Command of the new ship would devolve upon Captain Raphael Semmes, who, by this time, had given up any hope of recovering the *Sumter.*[49]

Unfortunately, mail exchanges between the Confederacy and its agents in Europe were subject to delays because of the need to filter them through the blockade. Therefore Mallory, not yet aware that Bulloch had detailed Maffitt to command the *Florida,* again directed that she be assigned to North,[50] which was by now impossible. In the meantime, Semmes, not knowing this, had left England for the Confederacy together with his executive officer, John M. Kell, on the steamer *Melita,* loaded with war supplies for the South and making for Nassau, Bahamas.[51]

When he arrived there on 13 June, he found a message in which Mallory informed him of his new duty.[52] He soon answered the secretary and got ready to go back to England.[53]

According to Frank J. Merli, Mallory, in choosing Semmes, "again demonstrated his knack of matching men and missions. . . . The *Alabama*'s career under his spirited direction is a legend of the sea a century after man and ship disappeared." [54]

Semmes, with his usual drive, had lost no time; while still in Nassau he had already commissioned some of his old officers: Lieutenant John M. Kell, Surgeon Francis L. Galt, and lieutenant of marines Becket R. Howell, all designated to duty on the *Alabama,* were ordered to proceed immediately to Liverpool. [55]

There Bulloch was becoming restless. The ship (under the name of *Enrica*) now had coal aboard and all her provisions (except, obviously, any weapon or warlike equipment). He must hasten her departure. The U.S. ambassador, Charles Francis Adams, was bombarding Lord Russell with requests to seize her. [56] Now the Northerners, not wanting to get nowhere again as in the case of the *Florida,* had hired an outstanding British attorney, the future queen's solicitor Robert P. Collier, who on 26 July submitted a formal request for her seizure. [57]

Yet Bulloch was not a man to be easily circumvented. The wily commander had his own "mole" in the Foreign Office (a secret so well kept that even today only vague suppositions can be made about who he might have been), [58] from whom he learned on the same day that, if he wanted to avoid seizure, he must sail within forty-eight hours. When, on the twenty-ninth, the British government issued the order to stop the *Enrica,* it was too late. The ship was gone. [59]

No sooner had he received the alarming message from his "mole" than Bulloch had rushed to the Laird shipyard and asked to take advantage of his right to make a third trial of the ship's engines. He had to hurry because from another secret agent he had in Southampton he had learned that the USS *Tuscarora* had arrived in that area, evidently with the charitable intention of "fishing up" the defenseless cruiser when she entered the Atlantic.

During the day of the twenty-eighth, while extra loads of coal were put on the ship, the invaluable John Low went aboard together with Bulloch to help Captain Butcher, who had been informed of the situation. The vessel, ready at anchor, had ornamental flags flying and even some guests on board, formally invited to witness the "trial." At dawn of 29 July 1862 (the day the British government issued the seizing order), the ship, escorted by the tug *Hercules,* steamed out from the Mersey, leaving the British agents, who soon arrived, dumbfounded.

When on the open sea Bulloch politely informed his guests that he desired to keep the ship out for the whole night; therefore, he brought them back to Liverpool in the tug, after mooring the *Enrica* in the lonely Moelfra Bay, on the Welsh coast. The following morning, the tireless

Bulloch rejoined his ship by means of the *Hercules,* which also had on board forty or so men, who filled out the cruiser's complement.[60]

During his short time in Liverpool, Bulloch (who, thanks to his impressive network of secret agents, was following the activity of the enemy) had received a telegram from one of his men stating that the *Tuscarora* had left Southampton and was sailing toward the mouth of the St. George's Channel; therefore, he took the daring decision to have his ship sail north, go around northern Ireland, and enter the Atlantic from there.[61]

Luckily, he had hired one of the most experienced pilots in Liverpool, George Bond. At 2:30 A.M. on 31 July, while a fierce gale mixed with showers of rain blew across the Irish Sea, the ship came out briskly from the bay and started her hazardous trip. Indeed, the awful weather should have suggested that she seek shelter; but the storm provided the best protection.

At 8:00 A.M. the Isle of Man was sighted through sheets of rain, and the ship soon entered the North Channel and proved herself a first-rate sailer, logging 13.5 knots, a very high speed for the time. At 6:00 P.M. a fisherman was hailed near the mouth of the channel and Bulloch with Bond went ashore, while the *Enrica,* in Butcher's and Low's skillful hands, disappeared in the squall and steered for the Atlantic.

The two men found lodging for the night in a small local hotel. Bulloch later wrote: "During the evening it rained incessantly, and the wind skirled and snifted about the gables of the hotel in fitful squalls. Bond and I sat comfortably in the snug dining-room after dinner, and sipped our toddy, of the best Coleraine malt; but my heart was with the little ship buffeting her way around that rugged north coast of Ireland."[62]

The next day, by ferryboat and railroad, the two went back to Liverpool, where Bulloch learned that the *Tuscarora* had peeped into Moelfra Bay, missing the *Enrica-Alabama* by only a few hours.

By this time the Confederate cruiser was in the vast Atlantic and sailing at full speed toward that little, lonely bay at Terceira in the Azores that Bulloch had by chance discovered during his trip in the *Fingal.*

The ship must now receive her battery and her officers. Bulloch had already taken care of the first. While the vessel was still in the yard, her guns had been ordered from an outstanding English manufacturer: a smoothbore 8-inch Blakely and a rifled 7-inch 100-pounder to be placed on pivots forward and aft and six 32-pounders for the broadsides. Orders had also been made for their projectiles, both shot and shells; powder; loading and sighting equipment; revolvers and rifles with bayonets; cutlasses, ammunition, uniforms for 150 men; hammocks; and the like. All had been inventoried, packed, numbered, stored, and kept ready for shipping.

Meanwhile, Bulloch had managed to buy a fine sailer, a jigger-masted

A History of the Confederate Navy

bark of 450 tons, that was renamed the *Agrippina* and moored without being noticed near the London docks. For her, Bulloch was able to find a good master mariner of oceangoing ships, Alexander McQueen, who later would long serve as the coal supplier for the *Alabama.*

When it was clear that the *Enrica* had to sail from Liverpool at the earliest moment, Bulloch immediately telegraphed his agents to load the *Agrippina* without delay and put her on the way to Terceira, under sealed orders to be opened at sea by the captain.[63] Upon coming back to Liverpool, Bulloch was informed that the sailer was at sea and had already crossed the Pas de Calais.

The problem of officers remained. Bulloch hoped Semmes would arrive in London in a few days.[64] Semmes was indeed approaching. He had embarked with his small staff on the steamer *Bahama,* which was returning to Europe.[65] In Liverpool, Bulloch, understanding this, had already hired the same *Bahama* to carry Semmes and his officers to Terceira, together with two 32-pounder guns and some more men for the crew.[66] Semmes arrived on 8 August. On the thirteenth, the *Bahama* got under way again with him aboard together with all the officers and Bulloch himself, who intended to escort them.[67]

On 20 August the steamer entered Terceira Bay and everybody on board was elated to see both the *Alabama* and the *Agrippina* already anchored there. Work of transferring cargo began immediately and in two days all the guns were aboard and properly mounted; the magazine was full; the coal was stored; and the bark could leave.[68]

Semmes thereupon put on his proper uniform, relieved Butcher, and assumed command. The *Alabama* (which was now her name) and the *Bahama* slowly left the bay. Then, outside of Portuguese waters, in front of the whole crew and officers in dress uniform, the Confederate flag was raised for the first time above the cruiser. It was hailed by three hurrahs from the crew while the small band played *Dixie.* It was 24 August 1862. At midnight Bulloch wished Semmes godspeed and left the *Alabama* to return to England. The sky was full of stars, and a bright comet was shining to the northward.[69]

On 5 September the *Alabama* captured and burned its first prize, a whaler named *Ocmulgee.*[70] By the end of 1862 the raider had destroyed eight Union merchantmen and bonded two more.[71] The farseeing Bulloch had kept in his service the bark *Agrippina,* which could tender coal to the *Alabama* during meetings arranged on the high seas.[72]

Yet the long cruise was not always smooth. On 16 October, the *Alabama* had the fearful experience of sailing through a hurricane. Abruptly, night had fallen in full daylight; low black clouds covered the masts while a fierce wind tore those sails that had not been furled in time and gigantic waves cascaded over the ship as though they would crush her to the bottom of the ocean.[73] Then, suddenly, came a sinister, funereal calm while the waves turbulently climbed over each other, growing to a peak without any direction. The cruiser was in the hurricane's eye and was crossing it at incredible speed, only to find herself instantly in a full storm again. Now the wind, because of the rotary motion of the hurricane, blew from the opposite direction with frightening rumblings.

Only by putting out lifelines was it possible to avoid having someone thrown overboard or crushed against the bulkheads. A launch, torn loose from its davit, was dashed into splinters.[74] Those two hours seemed like two centuries to the crew, and for four hours more, after the passing of the hurricane, towering waves rose to frightening altitudes. Yet in the end the small ship passed the awful test and showed her seakeeping qualities.

Later, in wintertime, the cruiser entered the Gulf of Mexico and steered for the port of Galveston, Texas, at a time when it appeared that Union forces were organizing an expedition to land a large number of troops there. This project was abandoned because Galveston (already in Federal hands) had been retaken by Confederates.

Upon nearing Galveston on 11 January 1863 with the aim of attacking some enemy troop transports, Semmes sighted no transport but five Union warships, precluding any possibility of attack by him. Yet the skillful sailor managed to let himself be sighted at a fair distance. The Federals thereupon dispatched the auxiliary cruiser *Hatteras* to seek him out. It was exactly what he wanted.[75]

The *Alabama* began to pull away slowly. Her aim was to draw the enemy where the sound of gunfire could not be heard by the rest of the U.S. squadron. The *Hatteras* meanwhile was approaching with her crew at general quarters. Night was falling. Now the Union warship, at a distance of two hundred yards, asked the *Alabama* to identify herself by showing her pennants. Semmes answered that she was "an English ship" and in turn asked for the pennants. As the *Hatteras* showed her colors, Semmes suddenly had the battle flag hoisted, signaled, "This is C.S.S. *Alabama*," and ordered his guns to open. The *Hatteras* spiritedly answered in kind, even if her battery (two rifled 30-pounders, one 20-pounder, and four smoothbore 32-pounders) was far less effective than that of the Confederate. When the Federal tried to come to close quarters for boarding, the *Alabama*'s greater speed enabled her to steer clear.[76]

In a short while, the Southern cruiser's guns started several fires on board the enemy ship and disabled her engines. Soon thereafter water began to pour through holes in her hull, the vessel could not be steered, and she began to founder. The Union captain was compelled to lower his flag and ask for assistance—which was immediately granted. Officers and men were rescued and taken aboard the *Alabama* as prisoners of war. The battle had lasted only thirteen minutes.[77]

The engagement with the *Hatteras* was extremely important because it showed that Confederate cruisers could not be taken lightly. After paroling and landing the officers and crew of the sunken warship at Jamaica, the *Alabama* continued her cruise. In May 1863 the Confederate raider destroyed another sixteen enemy merchantmen and bonded four.[78]

The *Florida,* after leaving Mobile, had also started her cruise and by 6 May 1863 had destroyed eleven merchantmen.[79] On that same day the Confederate cruiser captured the bark *Clarence,* from Baltimore, loaded with coffee.

Maffitt had already detached, as his auxiliary ship, another captured sailer, the *Lapwing,* for use as a collier. As a result, a daring plan grew in the enterprising mind of Lieutenant Charles W. Read. Would Maffitt entrust him with the *Clarence?* He had high hopes of entering Hampton Roads by stealth and there boarding and seizing an enemy ship or burning the merchantmen moored at Baltimore.[80] It seemed like a crazy idea, yet Maffitt, knowing his man, agreed and gave Read a dozen sailors and a small boat howitzer.[81]

Thus began one of the most incredible adventures of the Civil War. Read soon realized the impossibility of entering Hampton Roads and also that the *Clarence* was a very poor sailer, slow and clumsy. Yet he succeeded in capturing and destroying three merchantmen. Then, on 12 June, after seizing the bark *Tacony,* a much better vessel than the *Clarence,* he burned the latter and transferred his crew and howitzer to the former.[82]

Now he started on a raiding cruise with a sailer, in the age of steamers. Jim Dan Hill, almost a century later, nicknamed him "the Confederate von Lückner."[83] Keeping near the American coast (where no one believed that Southern raiders dared to intrude), deceiving enemies time after time by the innocuous look of his sailer or scaring them with dummy wooden guns, Read succeeded in capturing and destroying another thirteen merchantmen and bonding five.[84]

Read's forays, perhaps even more than those of the major raiders, spread panic along the Northern coast. Naval Secretary Gideon Welles, unwilling to take any ship from blockading duty, had to send a dozen vessels to hunt down the ghostlike raider. Still, this was not enough. From all sides frantic requests rained on Welles to send more ships to join the chase. Panic spread and seemed to envelop the Union secretary himself. "Send out anything you have," he telegraphed Rear Admiral S. P. Lee at Newport News; and to Rear Admiral Hiram Paulding at New York: "Send what vessels you can on pursuit" (it being understood that he meant pursuit of the *Tacony*).[85]

The source of all this uproar paid no attention and, unconcerned, went on with his devastating cruise. On 23 June, after capturing the fisherman *Archer,* because the supply of ammunition for his howitzer had been expended, Read, during the night, scuttled the *Tacony* and transferred with his crew to the little ship, then sailed on undisturbed, while the pack of chasers, now grown to almost forty regular and auxiliary warships,[86] went on frantically hunting for the bark, which lay on the bottom of the sea.

Read did not intend to stay put. On 26 June he boldly entered the port of Portland, Maine, piloted by two fishermen who had mistaken his crew for an excursion party. Upon arriving there and anchoring, at 1:30 A.M., he surprised and captured the revenue cutter *Caleb Cushing* and tried to take her out to sea. The flat calm betrayed him. Pursued by two auxiliary warships and three tugs loaded with soldiers and carrying several guns, Read resolutely prepared for battle. But the little cannon of the *Caleb Cushing* had only five rounds. When these had been spent, he had no choice but to scuttle his ship and be captured by the enemy. Soon thereafter the *Archer* was found by Union troops.[87]

The incredible adventure had ended (but not Read's, who tried, unsuccessfully, to escape from prison). Still, the daring idea of operating along the enemy coasts would not be without consequences in the future of the Confederate navy.

During the summer and fall of 1863 the activity of the raiding cruisers became a drumfire. The *Alabama,* too, detached a captured sailer, the *Tuscaloosa,* commanded by John Low, in September 1863. On 27 December this ship, after entering St. Simon's Bay in South Africa, was seized by local authorities according to the principle that a prize, which she originally was, could not be taken into neutral waters. During her cruise she had destroyed only a single merchantman,[88] yet this (as Low well understood) indicated the tremendous impact the raiders had had on Northern sea trade.

On 23 August 1863, meanwhile, the *Florida,* needing both hull and engine repairs, had to seek refuge in the French port of Brest. It would be the beginning of a long stay. Yet up to that moment the cruiser, together with the sailers *Clarence, Tacony,* and *Archer,* had destroyed thirty-seven merchantmen and bonded another nine.[89] Since 5 August 1863 the *Alabama* had destroyed another six ships, bonded one, and transformed still another into the auxiliary *Tuscaloosa.*[90]

On that 5 August the Confederate raider reached the South African coast and entered Cape Town. The welcome she received was enthusiastic and showed how the *Alabama* (and, on a smaller scale, the other Southern raiders) had already entered into legend, awaiting an everlasting place in history.[91]

Semmes spent several days between Cape Town and Simonstown to supply and repair his ship. Then, on 24 September 1863, he took his leave of South Africa and sailed into the Indian Ocean.[92]

He persisted in following his procedure of securing and reading carefully all the newspapers found aboard the ships he captured. From these he was able to fathom with great accuracy where enemy ships sent to hunt him down were, as well as merchant ships. Such information determined his course. He now intended to move to the Far East to strike the U.S. traffic in the straits between Java and Sumatra and in the China Seas.

He well knew that the Federal cruiser *Wyoming* operated there and that she usually anchored under the shadow of ominous Krakatoa. Succeeding in eluding her, he crossed the Sunda Strait, destroyed a number of enemy merchantmen, and on 2 December reached Pulo Condore, in Cochin China. From there he steered for Singapore, where he arrived on 21 December 1863.[93]

There Semmes found at least twenty Union merchantmen, lying unemployed at anchor. He correctly surmised that others in the same condition were rotting in the ports of Canton, Shanghai, Bangkok, and in the Philippines.[94] Such was the fear inspired by Southern raiders!

In 1863, which may be considered the year when the Confederate commerce-destroying war reached its zenith (even though it would be carried on with remarkable success in 1864), the *Florida* and the *Alabama* were not alone. There were, of course, the auxiliary ships armed by them. But on 13 May 1863, when the *Alabama* lay at anchor at Bahia (today Salvador) in Brazil, another ship flying the Confederate flag entered the port. She was CSS *Georgia* under Commander William L. Maury.[95]

During the fall of 1862 the Confederacy had sent another agent to England, the famed oceanographer Matthew Fontaine Maury. His central mission was to acquire implements for submarine warfare. Secretary Mallory, always eager to escalate the commerce-destroying war, had also charged him with finding a good ship to be fitted out as a cruiser and operate alongside the raiders already at sea.[96] In March 1863 Maury bought for that purpose a brand-new iron-hulled screwship, just fitted out at Dumbarton, along the Clyde, and named the *Japan*.[97]

Even if the relentless Dudley was not late in realizing the questionable side of the business, the *Japan* was indeed a true merchantman and sailed from Grenock untroubled on 1 April 1863. That same night, in a dangerously rough sea, the little tug *Alar*, carrying guns and ammunition, as well as officers and part of the crew for the would-be cruiser, hoisted her anchor.[98]

The stormy waters of the English Channel were certainly not the best place for transshipment; yet eventually, two 24-pounders and two 22-

pounders were aboard with the other accoutrements, and the ship became the CSS cruiser *Georgia*, commanded by William Lowndes Maury, a cousin of the oceanographer and a distinguished naval officer, who had succeeded in reaching England after a risky trip.[99]

As a raider, the *Georgia* was not the best. Her iron hull required much more maintenance than a wooden one. Nevertheless, during her crossing of the Atlantic she managed to capture and destroy nine merchantmen.[100] The climax of her cruise was her arrival in Bahia and meeting the *Alabama*. It was the first time that two Confederate warships were together in a neutral port.[101]

After sailing as far as Cape Town and then recrossing the Atlantic, the *Georgia*, on 29 October 1863, had to enter Cherbourg, France, for repairs.[102] Unlike the *Florida*, which would go to sea again for another cruise, she would not leave. The small ship was inadequate for carrying out the mission she had bravely undertaken.[103]

The results obtained by the Confederate cruisers in 1863 were appalling for Northern maritime trade. The raiders not only sank many U.S. merchantmen, they also spread such a panic that the cost of freight and insurance skyrocketed.[104]

In addition to blocking ships in seaports to rot, the raiders produced an exodus of shipowners toward neutral flags. Even if sales were fake more often than true, shipowners had to concede that their ships were unable to defy the threat of the raiders.[105]

Indeed, the strategy of commerce raiding, unleashed by the genial Mallory, had opened a new era in maritime warfare. In the age of steam and of submarine cables, commerce destroying was no longer (as in the privateers' era) isolated from the global network of naval operations. Against an enemy who could wield overwhelming sea power, it took on the character of a "minor counterstroke," a maritime partisan warfare and, at best, a strategic side attack (the U.S. Navy was compelled to send as many as eighty warships, at different times and places, to hunt down commerce raiders).

As worldwide communications were becoming more and more vital, commerce raiding was now part of the operational system. Only sailing in convoys would have worked for eluding raiders; during both world wars, the Allied navies had to resort to convoys so as not to be strangled by raiders, both surface and submarine. Yet had the Union organized convoys, it would have been compelled to give up the blockade to escort them. The U.S. Navy, even if overwhelming, could not marshal strength enough for both needs.

Here also, Mallory played his favorite card, that of technical surprise. In the era of transition from sail to steam, the Southern raiders could avail themselves of both means to save coal and outspeed the enemy. Another problem for the Union was that while hunting the raiders scattered about the oceans, they ran the risk of meeting them with inferior ships (as in the case of the *Hatteras*).

At the same time, cruiser warfare stressed the focal zone for this kind of war: the Atlantic, between Cape San Roque and the Rio de la Plata, main theater of the frightful battles of the Atlantic in World Wars I and II.[106]

Still, the surprise that the handful of daring Confederate sailors were preparing in their war against trade was far from over. The campaign of 1864 would show new initiative intended to inflict heavier blows to Northern commerce.

T H I R T E E N

The Unleashing of Submarine Warfare

The prospect of striking enemy warships beneath the waterline so as to deal them a mortal blow had obsessed the minds of strategists and scientists from the earliest days of the war at sea. After the introduction of the shell gun and the answer to it—the ironclad—and the invention of the underwater screw propeller, this need became urgent. Still, few had noticed and no one had ever thought of making it a weapon of primary importance to use on a large scale. In a short time the Confederates would make submarine warfare an extremely important and feared tool of war.[1]

It had long been known that an underwater offensive could be developed in three ways: by inert obstructions, explosive obstructions, and hitting enemy hulls directly by means of submarine boats carrying explosive devices. The first method would lead to a variety of obstructions; the second to what are called today mines and in Civil War times torpedoes; the third to submersible boats.

Passive underwater obstructions were as old as the world. Torpedoes, however, were developed after the invention of explosive powder. The Italian engineer Federico Giambelli was probably the first to make use of such contrivances when, defending Antwerp in 1588 against the Spaniards, he loosed on enemy ships small floats filled with explosives and provided with a time device, which would be brought into contact with ships by the current of the Scheldt.[2]

His devices, however, could at best strike a ship at the waterline. A true underwater mine was invented by the American David Bushnell, from Connecticut, about 1771. It would be carried beneath the enemy hull by a small submersible boat (also invented by Bushnell) and attached to the enemy ship by a sort of auger. The explosion was caused by a time device. Using one of these, in 1777, during the War for Independence, he succeeded in blowing up a schooner.[3]

It is clear that at the beginning no one had conceived of an explosive obstruction. Instead, attempts were made to solve the problem of a direct attack by a submersible boat. In Napoleon's era, Robert Fulton, inventor of the steamboat, also sought the same aim. Although he had built a much more advanced submarine, he failed to generate interest in it either by the French (who did not understand it) or the British (who understood it too well and therefore tried to suppress it).[4] Fulton named the underwater explosive contrivance a "torpedo" after the name of a fish capable of paralyzing its prey with an electrical shock. It was to be an apt name.

The development of submarine navigation would proceed very slowly, while that of explosive obstructions made notable progress. Underwater ignition was the basic problem, and for this, owing to the limited means at the time (it was, let us remember, the age of stone flintlock), there seemed to be no answer.

Therefore, Fulton had no other solution than to use a time device, which would cause an explosion in a very short while, and to transport the torpedo beneath the enemy ship. This is why both he and Bushnell were interested in the concept of the submarine boat.

Yet soon technological progress offered two inventions that would open the way to the awesome destructive power of the torpedo: chemical primers and electrical devices.[5] The first was based on a primer with fulminate of mercury (ignited by percussion) or the use of two glass pipes enclosed in a waterproof tube made of thin sheet brass. One glass pipe contained potassium, the other sulfuric acid. When the pipes were broken by the bending or smashing of the container tube, the chemicals ignited and fired the powder. Both devices made it possible to produce the contact torpedo, which would explode when struck by a hull.[6]

The second solution was revolutionary. In 1777 Alessandro Volta (who in 1800, by inventing the battery, laid the cornerstone for future progress in electrical science) experimented with an underwater device that exploded by lighting a mixture of gas with an eudiometer.[7]

Thereafter the pace of development quickened. In 1836, Samuel Colt, the inventor of the revolver, by using a Voltaic battery, built the first electrically commanded torpedo. He had also proposed a solution for the major problem that hindered the use of this kind of device: insulation of the electrical cable.[8] His system would permit the device to be exploded at will. Unfortunately, he ran up against the conservatism and disbelief of the military establishment. With his maniacal tendency to conceal the secret of his invention, he contributed to the distrust. For the time being, his proposal had no success in the United States.

Torpedoes nevertheless began to appear in other areas. In 1848, ignoring Colt's previous invention, a German engineer, Walter von Siemens, laid torpedoes to defend the port of Kiel during a war with Denmark; in 1859 the Austrians laid torpedoes to defend Venice; finally, during the Crimean War, the Russians used them in both the Baltic and the Black seas.[9]

Like the ironclad, therefore, the torpedo (and the submarine as well) was not invented by the Confederates. It had already been used in war. Yet its use had been sporadic, with limited results, and had hardly influenced naval operations. Only the Confederate navy would make it a pillar of its strategy and use it on such a scale as to revolutionize the methods of warfare and not only at sea.

Unlike the strategy of the ironclads, commerce destroyers, and rifled naval ordnance, the origins of Confederate submarine warfare are clouded in uncertainty and mystery. This is understandable because of the caution necessary to thwart the strenuous efforts of Northern agents to penetrate the secrecy of a weapon that soon revealed its frightful power.[10] Unfortunately, the absence or vagueness of documents on the subject makes speculation difficult.

Hunter Davidson, formerly a commander in the C.S. Navy, who had served as the head of the Submarine Battery Service, in 1874 sent former president Davis a letter with an enclosed pamphlet, printed in March of that same year, in which he stated that "the first idea of using torpedoes on the Confederate side, originated I believe with the Hon. S. R. Mallory, Secretary of the Navy, and he directed the distinguished Captain M. F. Maury, LL.D., to make experiments with a view to their general employment if practicable." Further, "the Hon. S. R. Mallory . . . always believed in the success of the undertaking from the first."[11] Two years later, in June 1876, Davidson again published the text of his pamphlet in the *Southern Historical Society Papers*.[12]

In 1898, R. O. Crowley, formerly the electrician of the Confederate torpedo service, repeated the text in which Davidson gave Mallory credit for thinking up the idea of torpedo warfare and for assigning the task to Maury.[13]

To establish who were, under Mallory, the most important leaders of this branch of naval service, one must note what former president Davis said in 1881. He (who in 1867, together with General Lee, had, at the request of Davidson, highly rated both the outstanding merits and the relevant functions of the latter)[14] now gave the lion's share of the credit to General Gabriel J. Rains, head of the torpedo service.[15]

In 1887, J. Thomas Scharf impartially gave credit to Rains, Davidson, and Lieutenant Beverly Kennon. He also quoted—but without attributing to him a primary role—Matthew F. Maury and gave credit to the navy as a whole, that is, to Mallory.[16]

Later, biographers of Maury gave the great oceanographer complete credit for torpedo warfare and suggested that Mallory had been hostile to such a form of war. According to these writers, Davidson, Rains, and Kennon had been imitators or, at best, followers.[17]

Matthew Fontaine Maury was outstanding not only in American history but also in the science of the world. He was led in 1825 to join the navy in part because of his older brother, a naval officer, whom he idolized. In the service, he soon showed a much greater disposition for experimental science than for purely military matters.

Gifted with an outstanding speculative mind, he studied oceanic phenomena during three long cruises. From then on, he pursued a scholarly career. He revolutionized the science of oceanography and navigation.

The serious accident of 1839, which crippled him for life, probably contributed (in addition to his own merit) to his detail in 1842 as superintendent of the navy's Depot of Charts and Instruments, which became, in 1854, the U.S. Naval Observatory and Hydrographic Bureau. Thanks to his outstanding scientific production, he received honors, medals, decorations, and acknowledgment from almost every nation in the world as among the major scientists of the century.[18] It would be interesting to try to understand how much his growth to world stature—in contrast to the infirmity that, as a naval officer, he must have felt humiliating—contributed to his extreme touchiness.

When in 1855 Maury fell under the scrutiny of the Naval Retiring Board, he was not struck from the navy list but placed in the reserve. This was not so much because of his bodily defect (which was a major obstacle to active duty) as because of his indisputable vocation. His great contribution to the navy came from his scientific activity, not from service on a quarterdeck, where his scientific genius would have been wasted. Further, by the express wish of the secretary of the navy, he retained the superintendency of the Naval Observatory.[19]

The decision undoubtedly had some validity, even if it may have been inappropriate. Yet Maury considered it an unbearable abuse and insult, and he let loose a resounding and angry campaign against the board, mobilizing politicians and prominent men (especially those of the Whig party) against the decision and personally against Mallory, giving his polemics a personal character and using extremely bitter and sour words.

Maury, despite his many virtues (in his private life, he was a very nice human being), had some flaws in his nature that hindered people from reaching an easy understanding with him in public and scientific life. He tended to think of nautical studies as his personal preserve. Because of this he fell out first with his fellow scientist Alexander Dallas Bache, head of the Coast Survey and formerly a friend of his, then with Senator Jefferson Davis (a Democrat like Mallory), who had supported Bache.

Maury also tended to consider opinions that disagreed with his as personal insults. Therefore, he nurtured an everlasting hatred against those who he felt had done him an offense.[20]

At last, in 1858, Maury was restored to active duty. After secession he resigned his commission and served first Virginia, then the Confederacy. His mood is easy to imagine when one remembers that the president was Jefferson Davis (about whom he gave at once a venomous opinion),[21] and that his naval superiors included Mallory and two of his closest aides, Captains Barron and Buchanan, both of whom had been members of the hated Naval Retiring Board.[22]

That Maury busied himself with torpedoes seems certain. There is also a famous account of experiments he made with small explosive devices in a bathtub at the home of his cousin Robert H. Maury while he was his guest.[23] Among those present apparently was Lieutenant Hunter Davidson, who became and remained a warm friend of Maury's and later wrote that these experiments had been carried out by Mallory's order, which does not seem unlikely.[24]

All the records at hand, in which Maury claimed priority in having invented torpedo warfare (and particularly the electrical torpedo) were written after the war.[25] There remains no document contemporary with the events.

Maury was never capable of giving a balanced opinion of Mallory, seeing him only through the distorted lens of rancor and contempt, even going so far as to attack the secretary openly in a newspaper (although he attempted to conceal his authorship by using a pen name).[26]

Moreover, because Davidson always showed only respect, sympathy, and warm friendship toward Maury, it seems reasonable that the case is best expounded by Davidson and Crowley, who had no reason to lie and so hurt Maury.

Secretary Mallory, who was much more dispassionate and capable of considering men according to a cool rationality,[27] had seen in Maury (probably knowing the opinions he had expressed on the subject) the ideal man to begin the difficult job of torpedoes and gave him the duty.

It is certain that Maury dedicated himself to the matter, for in mid-June 1861 he was ready to perform a practical proof in Mallory's presence by exploding a submarine percussion torpedo near the Rocketts Navy Yard on the James River. The secretary immediately created a half-secret organization named the Bureau for the Defense of Coastal Waters and Rivers as part of the Office of Ordnance and Hydrography, with Maury as its head and many able naval officers as aides, and asked Congress for an appropriation of $50,000 for it.[28]

The first submarine attack on Union shipping at Hampton Roads was made on 7 July 1861 by means of contact torpedoes, supported by floats that kept them about twenty feet underwater and carried by the current toward the enemy vessels. No explosion resulted, either because some water leaked in or because the primer (which had been set for a depth of thirteen feet) did not work at twenty because of excessive water pressure.[29]

The bitter truth was that torpedoes were far from flawless and very hard to improve. Would electrical ignition give a better outcome? Maury may have gotten the idea of trying an electrically ignited torpedo by remembering a meeting he had had with Samuel Colt in 1842, when the inventor had done research at the Naval Depot of Charts and Instruments that Maury then directed. This is only a conjecture, yet it should not be discarded out of hand because Maury, a first-rate oceanographer, had never done electrical research except incidentally when called upon to suggest the best sounding for laying a transatlantic cable.[30]

At any rate, for the time being he employed either percussion or friction torpedoes. He was already thinking of other projects, thus leaving the immediate responsibility for a new attack to Robert D. Minor.[31] The action, conducted under Minor's direction on 11 October 1861, again failed.[32]

Since summer, meanwhile, the Union threat along the Mississippi had grown, and Maury busied himself with its water defense. Initially, it appears that he told Lieutenant Isaac N. Brown (who would later command the *Arkansas*) that he would personally go west to supervise minelaying. The trip never materialized, but Maury found in Brown an able officer ready to use underwater weapons and to answer the request by General Polk for an expert in this field.[33]

With danger increasing and winter approaching, the demand to use torpedoes to defend western waters became pressing, even from civilians.[34] Brown was already working on this problem in Memphis, Tennessee, when Maury sent him two torpedoes, loaded with powder, adding that he had more ready to forward, if required, to defend the fort at Columbus. Brown telegraphed his request to Mallory because he had found the torpedoes to be of good quality and easy to handle. Therefore, he suggested to General Polk that their laying be entrusted to an able river captain, C. Hesling, who lived in Columbus.[35]

Maury saw to the sending of another twenty torpedoes to be delivered to Columbus by his son Richard, also a naval officer.[36] But Brown had already been transferred to the Tennessee River in the frantic attempt to create a naval squadron there and was succeeded by Commander Washington Gwathmey.[37]

By this time others were working to produce torpedoes. In December, the last nineteen out of a lot of fifty, made by A. T. Saunders (possibly by Brown's order), were sent to Columbus and Memphis. Of the percussion type, they contained twenty-five pounds of powder.[38] It seems also that Lieutenant Beverly Kennon (at the time chief of ordnance in New Orleans) produced some and sent them to Brown. Even land torpedoes were planted around Columbus.[39]

Unfortunately, all the activity undertaken between December 1861 and the first months of 1862, which may be considered the first use of torpedoes on a large scale by the Confederacy, ended in nothing. After the fall of Fort Henry, Union gunboats moved with lightning speed up the Tennessee River, and the torpedoes the tireless Brown was preparing to lay in it had to be exploded on 7 February, together with the steamer *Samuel Orr* that carried them, to prevent their capture by enemy gunboats.[40] In Columbus, evacuated in March 1862, many torpedoes were seized intact by Union troops, who, it seems, overlooked the ominous warning.[41] The first phase of underwater warfare appeared to have ended in failure.

Radical changes occurred toward the end of 1862, primarily because of the ability of the Southerners to learn from experience and the new naval strategy following the destruction of the *Arkansas*. The new course also came about through a radical reorganization of the cadre. Among the new leaders, two stood out: Lieutenant Hunter Davidson and General Gabriel James Rains.

From the beginning, others in addition to Maury had begun on their own initiative to use torpedoes. On 7 July 1861, when Maury conducted his first unsuccessful attack with explosive devices against the enemy fleet on the James, another officer, Lieutenant Beverly Kennon, still in Virginia, unknown to Maury, tried another action with torpedoes of his own invention against the USS *Pawnee*. It also failed.[42] Kennon was then transferred to the Mississippi, where he made an important contribution to torpedo warfare, although he never became preeminent in this field.

The case of General Gabriel J. Rains was different. Born in 1803 in North Carolina, he was the brother of another prominent Confederate general, George W. Rains, head of the Nitre and Mining Bureau, organizer of the production of explosives for the Confederate army, and founder of the great powder works at Augusta, Georgia. Gabriel had already had a brilliant career in the U.S. Army. From 1839 to 1842, during the Seminole War in Florida, he experimented with a land mine. Upon becoming a Confederate brigadier general in 1862, he got command of a division that was part of the army engaged in stopping the advance of General McClellan up the Virginia Peninsula.[43]

To protect the retreat of his forces, Rains used pressure land torpedoes (or subterra shells, as they were then called) during the evacuation of both Yorktown and Williamsburg, mainly to stop enemy cavalry.[44] He achieved three results. First, the enemy, which suffered severe losses, protested, claiming that this was a "barbaric" method of warfare and making reprisals (which were far more "barbaric" because, unlike the use of mines, they violated the laws of nations; for example, McClellan compelled Southern prisoners of war to remove the torpedoes "at their own risk").[45]

Second, Confederate military leaders were sharply divided. Although General Daniel H. Hill considered any means to destroy "our brutal enemy" to be "lawful and proper,"[46] the corps commander, General James Longstreet, opposed the use of subterra shells. Even the army commander, General Joseph E. Johnston, disapproved of land torpedoes.[47]

Third, and most important, the secretary of war, George W. Randolph, made aware of the problem, though not in principle opposed to the use of land torpedoes, concluded that such weapons were lawful when used at sea.[48]

Therefore, General Rains was transferred to the Submarine Defense, initially on the James and Appomattox rivers. Any interested military authority was ordered to assist him.[49] What had happened to General Rains should not astound us. The common destiny of all who introduce new weapons in warfare is to be branded as "barbarians," "inhumane," and the like. A year earlier Maury had met opposition in his own family. Although he was shocked by the thought of using torpedoes, he overcame his distaste by thinking about the decision of the Northern government to include medicinals in the list of war contraband,[50] a cruel decision that resulted only in increasing needless suffering for the wounded in the hospitals (among them Northern war prisoners) because of the dearth of analgesics.

Rains's new assignment coincided with the formulation of a project by Maury that would increasingly distract him from torpedo warfare. For some time he had been proposing a plan to build many very fast, small steam gunboats, each fitted with two heavy rifled guns, "nothing but floating gun carriages," to hurl against the enemy in Hampton Roads. He thought a hundred could be built for $1 million.[51] The project had some merit. Even if in a clumsy form, it portended the idea of the light warship, destined for a bright future. Yet, at the moment, to snatch control of

Hampton Roads from the enemy, the Confederates were preparing something else: the ironclad, whose purpose Maury appears not to have understood. Indeed, he had opposed it.[52]

Maury, with the support of Virginia's governor and of the chairman of the Committee on Naval Affairs, Charles M. Conrad, succeeded in obtaining from Congress approval of his plan and an appropriation of $2 million. The main shipyard to be used was that at Fluvanna, Virginia.[53]

The project turned out to be a utopian dream. First, given the industrial deficiencies of the Confederacy, fitting out a hundred steamships was impossible, even if Mallory did his utmost including the idea of seizing railroad locomotives for their engines. Yet the plan was killed by the appearance of the Union ironclad *Monitor*. It was now clear that "Maury's gunboats" could not face the overwhelming enemy. None of the ships projected by Maury was ever built. Both Congress and the president decided instead to concentrate on the construction of ironclads.[54]

By June, Maury had at last succeeded in laying down along the James several obstructions made of electrical torpedoes activated by batteries. The small gunboat *Teaser* was permanently assigned to torpedo service.[55] The dearth of insulated electric cable had plagued the Confederates until, by a stroke of luck, they succeeded in getting about ten thousand feet of submarine telegraph cable lost by the enemy in Chesapeake Bay. Believing that he could make better use of it, Maury sent it to the secretary of war.[56] On 30 June he ceded command of the torpedo service to Lieutenant Hunter Davidson.[57]

The great oceanographer would soon leave for Europe. In August, the Confederate Congress decided to send him across the Atlantic to obtain electric cable and other equipment indispensable to torpedo warfare. He was also to get a pair of cruisers to sea for commerce raiding.[58]

In Europe Maury would also serve as a de facto Confederate ambassador. He had entrée to the First Lord of the Admiralty and to princes and scientists, who admired and respected him. He could defend the Southern cause by writing in the London *Times*. With his country at war, he would be a hundred thousand times more useful in Europe than if he remained in an obscure duty at home.[59]

During the fall of 1862 the new Confederate naval strategy was in full bloom. In October of that year, Congress decided to create three organizations: the Confederate States Submarine Battery Service, the Torpedo Bureau, and a Secret Service Corps.[60] With such acts, the Confederacy had at last decided to adopt the submarine weapon openly as a legitimate tool of war.[61]

Although the Secret Service Corps—ubiquitous, invisible—had practically no limits to its field of action, the duties of the Submarine Battery

Service and the Torpedo Bureau were well defined. The first was specifically in charge of defending the vital waters approaching the Confederate capital, Richmond (the wide and deep James River particularly), as well as those of Wilmington harbor, the favorite port for blockade runners. The Torpedo Bureau had other responsibilities, especially land torpedoes to be used to prevent landings along the Southern coasts[62] and to protect against inland threats to the Confederate forts whose guns dominated the waters.

Yet, because it was impossible to draw a fine line between land and sea along the Confederate coasts, the services ended up by operating jointly, harmonizing their functions.[63] The Confederacy thus unintentionally stumbled onto a system of interforce cooperation, which, despite inevitable friction, resulted in a practical organization of remarkable efficiency and flexibility, transforming torpedo warfare into an ubiquitous and crafty tool of war, truly frightful to the enemy.

The Secret Service Corps mustered no more than twenty-five officers and men, commanded by Captain Thomas E. Courtenay. It originally had as a theater of operations the area beyond the Mississippi as well as the river itself, although it later operated everywhere.[64] It would attack the enemy not only with torpedoes but also and above all with explosive devices in acts of sabotage.

It was composed mainly of volunteers, enlisted (with their ranks) in the volunteer navy and operating according to the law of privateering, which awarded them 50 percent of the value of enemy property destroyed.[65] Attacks would be made only on water and along the Confederate railroads seized by the enemy. Strictly forbidden was any action against ships flying a flag of truce, enemy passenger liners on the high seas, or passenger trains in enemy territory. Only enemy military targets, broadly defined, were to be attacked.

After undergoing many trials and modifications, the law was approved in final form by Congress in secret session, signed by the president on 17 February 1864, and formalized in March by Secretary of War James A. Seddon. The Secret Service Corps had already been operating for at least one and a half years.[66]

Perhaps the most successful and deadly weapon used by the Secret Service Corps was the so-called coal torpedo made of an explosive device enclosed in a block of cast iron molded so as to look like a large piece of coal and imitating it so well as to deceive anybody. A sample was shown to President Davis, who thought it amazing.[67]

The device was to be introduced surreptitiously into fuel destined for Union warships. It is impossible to know how many ships were destroyed by such an infernal machine. Perhaps the most important victim was the troop transport *Greyhound,* sunk on 27 November 1864 in the James River by the explosion of such a device in her furnace.[68] The coal torpedo would be discovered by the Union soldiers only after the war, when they found a sample in Richmond, possibly the same one that had been shown to President Davis.[69]

Another infernal machine was invented by Captain John Maxwell, also of the Secret Service Corps. This was a time bomb hidden in a wooden military chest, filled with candles, which would be inserted into the cargo of enemy ships.[70] On 9 August 1864, Captain Maxwell, together with another agent, succeeded in planting one of his devices on board a large lighter full of explosives at City Point, Virginia, the major logistical base of Union armies. Maxwell set the timer so that it would explode the bomb only after a nearby passenger ship had left for Baltimore and while many of the wharf workers, busy unloading ships, would be at mess. He then walked away.

The explosion was frightful. Warehouses nearby were set on fire and blew up; two transport ships were smashed to pieces; fifty-eight men were killed and forty wounded; and the Union general in chief, Ulysses S. Grant, could have been hit. Unfortunately, there were some civilian casualties, even though the Confederates had tried to spare them.[71]

The Submarine Battery Service dedicated itself to developing electrical torpedoes. Unfortunately, the small gunboat *Teaser,* which should have provided a floating base for the service, was captured by Union ships on 4 July 1862, together with torpedo designs, plans, and equipment.[72] But Davidson soon obtained a new, small, fast ship, appropriately named the *Torpedo,* in which he organized a laboratory, entrusted to the skillful electrician R. O. Crowley.[73]

Compared with Maury's first attempts, the system of electrically ignited torpedoes developed by Davidson and Crowley was far more advanced and innovative. Torpedo cases were usually manufactured at Tredegar;[74] the electric cable started arriving from Europe; and the primers were made of electrical resistors of platinum inserted in a rod of fulminate of mercury. The resistor, heated red by the current, caused the explosion.[75]

Discarding the old, cumbersome Wollaston battery row, Crowley projected a new power supply, made by a row of Boynton batteries, modified so as to make them smaller and portable without reducing their power. This device could be carried and activated by only two men. Torpedoes would be exploded usually at two fathoms depth from five hundred yards away by using a thousand yards of cable.[76] In a short while, using torpedoes of seventy-five to two hundred pounds and even more, Davidson succeeded in planting twelve thousand pounds of explosives in the James River.[77]

The arrival from England of the Wheatstone exploder greatly increased the power of electrical torpedoes. This was an electromagnetic device weighing thirty-two pounds and containing as many as three magnets arranged in series, which, by the action of a crank, generated alternating current at high voltage. It permitted the simultaneous ignition of as many as twenty-five torpedoes joined together by means of several circuits.[78]

In Great Britain Maury was studying this system.[79] Toward the end of the war, the scientist at last succeeded in developing a torpedo controlled by two operators who would ignite it only when both saw the target over it at the same time. The operators could communicate with each other by a telegraph which used the torpedo cable itself, for the telegraph, being battery powered, used continuous low-voltage current, whereas the explosive device responded only to the high voltage of the magnet.[80] Unfortunately, this system came too late for the Confederacy.

The activity of Davidson and his team contributed remarkably to the defense of the James River. On 1 January 1863, with the system completed, President Davis, Secretary Mallory, and General Robert E. Lee inspected it. It looked so powerful that Mallory considered its contribution to closing the James to Union penetration and defending Richmond at least equal to that of a whole naval squadron or an army. The Confederate leaders even considered withdrawing a large number of troops from that district to employ them elsewhere.[81]

Yet the first great success of torpedo warfare did not take place on the James River but on the western waters. General Gabriel J. Rains, head of the Torpedo Bureau, had started working immediately. He was not only an organizer but also a prophet of torpedo warfare: "It is said that ironclads dominate the world," he wrote, "but torpedoes dominate ironclads."[82]

After giving up his command in the Peninsula, Rains had been for a while in the Bureau of Conscription. There he was able to set out his extensive studies of torpedoes in a full and detailed manuscript with sketches, data, and the like and send it to President Davis.[83] The finding of this manuscript, believed to have been lost, among the holdings of the Confederate Museum at Richmond, Virginia, permitted the reconstruction of the techniques followed by Rains with a breadth and a thoroughness heretofore not possible.[84]

It was Rains's belief that torpedoes could "scatter a blockade and destroy the ships; close the Mississippi river; check the advance of an army; stop raiders; destroy cavalry; burn a city." He even projected such futuristic weapons as a torpedo boat with no crew that might "be navigated by a wire from shore but rolled on a cylinder there, so fixed that positive electricity will turn the rudder one way and negative another way so as to steer." The fire would be kept up by oil or turpentine dropping gradually from a barrel to the living coal. To burn down a city, he proposed launching small balloons with fire bombs, ignited by a time device.[85]

On such assumptions, Rains had set to work to create infernal machines of various descriptions. Experiments he conducted persuaded him that water acts like a cushion protecting vessels against nearby explosions from outside. It was therefore necessary to have the torpedo explode directly against a ship's hull. "It is," he later wrote, "the secret of my great success with torpedoes."[86] Because of this, even though he had invented several kinds of electric torpedoes, Rains preferred to work with contact ones, in which field he became a wizard. When nothing else was available, he used tarred wooden kegs (so-called keg torpedoes).[87]

Moreover, to cause the explosion, he invented a very sensitive fuse capable of exploding under a pressure of only seven pounds. The explosive mixture Rains invented for this fuse was made of 50 percent potassium chlorate, 30 percent antimonium sulfate, and 20 percent glass powder.[88] The fuses projected by Rains were considered such a secret and so risky that he personally experimented with them, at the cost of being wounded by an accidental explosion.[89] By tireless work, Rains succeeded in planting 101 torpedoes in the Roanoke River in North Carolina. These were laid by one of his best collaborators, J. R. Fretwell, from Texas, himself a torpedo inventor.[90]

Another device invented by Rains was the submarine mortar battery. It was composed of shells attached to wooden floats, just under the surface of the water. Near Charleston, Rains laid twenty-five of these batteries to close access to the Stono River.[91] In short order, the great South Carolina port was protected by torpedoes everywhere.[92]

In the western theater, the task of protecting the Mississippi at Vicksburg was given by the Torpedo Bureau to Lieutenant Beverly Kennon, already experienced with torpedoes. He had two members of the Torpedo Bureau sent to the Yazoo River, Zedediah McDaniel and Francis M. Ewing. They would work under the direction of Captain Isaac Brown, of *Arkansas* fame, who was also a torpedo expert.[93] The Yazoo River was soon mined with the fearful devices. There the Confederacy would at last score its first success in underwater war.

It was 12 December 1862. A Union squadron, composed of two ironclad gunboats, two protected ones, and one ram, began to sail up the Yazoo. They were part of a large action attempted by Rear Admiral Porter, in cooperation with General Sherman, to get around Vicksburg's fortifications through watercourses to the north.[94]

Upon reaching Drumgould's Bluff, where Confederate entrenchments reached to the river and which was a pivotal point in the defense of

Vicksburg, the Union sailors soon noticed the presence of many underwater devices; still, they proceeded. A few minutes later, the ironclad gunboat *Cairo*, of more than five hundred tons, in quick succession struck two torpedoes. After a deafening double explosion that blew her guns, weighing many tons, into the air, she sank in twelve minutes. The crew was rescued and the squadron retreated. At last, after months of experiments and frustration, for the first time the Confederate underwater weapon had entered the war, showing its frightful power.[95]

Meanwhile, Fretwell was planting torpedoes in Mobile Bay[96] in collaboration with another Texan, E. C. Singer, who in private life had been a gunsmith (he was also related to the inventor of the sewing machine). He, with Fretwell, had invented a percussion torpedo considered to be among the best.[97] Singer, of course, also sent his devices to defend the waters of Texas.[98]

Rains was not satisfied with simply sending out his best agents; he was personally everywhere, laying torpedoes in the waters of the naval base at Augusta, Georgia, on the Savannah River; at Charleston; at Mobile. From still-existing records, it is possible to follow his activity.[99] He laid other torpedoes on the James and the Cape Fear River in the Wilmington area.[100]

Yet the important base of Charleston was uppermost in his mind. As head of the Office of Submarine Defense, he had sent there a most capable officer, Captain Martin M. Gray, with thirty-one noncommissioned officers and men. General Beauregard (who better than anybody else in the army understood the blend between sea and land war) had ordered that any help and as much labor as possible be put at his disposal.[101]

Since assuming command in Charleston, the general had decided, on his own account, on 30 September 1862, to use torpedo warfare. He initially gave charge of this to Captain Francis D. Lee, who, in civilian life, had been an engineer and who would busy himself with contact torpedoes.[102] In Charleston an attempt was made to use electrical devices. These had a double polarity. Contact with the iron hull of enemy ships would close the circuit and generate the explosion. The electrical work was entrusted to Lieutenant Charles G. De Lisle and to a civilian, M. J. Waldron. When this system failed, they went to work on contact torpedoes.[103]

Still, it was Rains who gave the greatest impulse to scattering explosive devices in the waters, sounds, inlets, and waterways all around Charleston,[104] planting about 110 devices in the harbor and the Stono River.[105]

Soon torpedo warfare became more successful. On 28 February 1863 the ironclad *Montauk*, of the *Monitor* class, after failing to bombard Fort McAllister, Georgia, into surrender, steering back on the Ogeechee River, struck a torpedo and, just in the nick of time, was towed away before sinking; she had to be put in drydock with serious damage.[106] On 13 July 1863, on the muddy waters of the Yazoo, the large ironclad gunboat *Baron De Kalb* (eighteen guns) hit a torpedo and sank in fifteen minutes.[107] This great success was the result of the ceaseless activity of Captain Isaac Brown and Fretwell, who had laid fifty torpedoes of the Singer model in the waters of the area.[108]

On the James River, on 8 August 1863, an electrical torpedo exploded under the bow of the gunboat *Commodore Barney*. A great column of water arose, and the ship was shaken like a leaf; forty crewmen were thrown overboard. Fortunately for the Federal ship, the explosion had been premature and she escaped, although with serious damage.[109]

Not so lucky the following year would be another large gunboat, the *Commodore Jones*. On 4 May 1864 the Union forces had started a major amphibious operation intended to take the Southern fort at Drewry's Bluff, on the James River, where in 1862 they had been repulsed by Confederate artillerists. On 6 May the *Commodore Jones* struck an electrical torpedo loaded with two thousand pounds of powder. The ship, which displaced 542 tons, was tossed into the air as though she were a feather while a gigantic column of water shot up. For a while it was possible to see her propellers spinning crazily in the air. Then she broke into pieces, and what remained of her disappeared beneath the water of the river together with almost a third of her crew.[110]

Although this was a great success, it also showed a weakness in the use of electrical torpedoes, compared with contact ones. Soon after the explosion, Union troops succeeded in landing and killing or capturing the men who had operated the device and, after questioning one of them, neutralized other torpedoes.[111] This would have been impossible had contact torpedoes been used.

Deeply concerned with the terrible power of Confederate infernal machines, the U.S. Navy had John Ericsson design and build a device called the "alligator" or the "devil." This machine consisted of a raft pushed by a ship. In front the raft had a half-submerged comb designed to engage the cables that anchored the torpedo. When these cables were cut, the device would automatically explode, still far from the ship.[112]

Rains, however, soon invented a counter in the form of a device he called "the circumventor of the devil." This was made by a wooden torpedo held on the bottom by a cable knotted in a special way. The cable ended at the surface of water in a float that would become engaged in the teeth of the "devil." The traction exerted on the cable would loosen the knot. The wooden torpedo (lighter than water) would bounce to the surface and strike the ship's hull. This was a major success for the Confederates, for it made the "devil" practically useless. One such device, discarded by Union sailors, fell into Southern hands and was displayed to a crowd in Charleston.[113]

Thus in 1863 torpedoes became a great terror for the Federals. Mallory considered them as powerful as an army corps.[114] Warships of any description, ironclads, steamers, gunboats, and troop transports, were destroyed by the fearful submarine explosions.

How many? General Rains said fifty-eight, a number President Davis confirmed in his narrative. Scharf gives a much smaller number, only thirty sunk and nine damaged. The historian of torpedoes Milton F. Perry lists twenty-nine ships sunk and fourteen damaged.[115] Thus it may be said with reasonable certainty that torpedoes destroyed or disabled some fifty Union warships, a fleet equal (at the time) to about thirty thousand tons of shipping. Never during the conflict did any other Confederate naval weapon cause such havoc in the Union navy.

Yet far more important was that the torpedo, together with ironclads and heavy Brooke guns, made a major contribution to sealing up Confederate ports and inland waters against enemy amphibious operations.

The Confederates' inventive genius did not end here. They planned an "active" torpedo war, carrying the devices directly against enemy hulls, either by submarines or torpedo boats employed for the first time in naval history.

FOURTEEN

Submarines and Torpedo Boats Enter the War

The idea of a submarine boat was conceived in America by David Bushnell. Yet only thanks to Robert Fulton did underwater navigation occur in earnest.

Robert Fulton had started an engineering career after dedicating several years of his life to fine arts.[1] His most remarkable invention would be the steamboat. Yet earlier, in 1797, he had gone to Paris while the war of the First Coalition in Europe was being fought and Great Britain was strangling France with her overwhelming naval power. He started working on a project for a submarine boat and created interest in building it.[2]

Fulton's first contacts with the French navy were disappointing, but after the coup d'état of 18 Brumaire, the first consul, Napoleon Bonaparte, paid him more attention.[3] On 24 July 1800, the submarine, christened with a name of destiny, the *Nautilus,* was launched in Paris and tested in the Seine River.[4] Successive trials, held at Le Havre and Brest, proved even better.

She was built of wood, with iron ribs, and was completely covered with copper. She was driven by hand-cranked propellers. Diving and rising were made possible by flooding special tanks, then expelling the water by means of a pump. Major problems included poor propelling force and lack of visibility during immersion because lighted candles soon consumed her air reserve. Yet Fulton anticipated the snorkel by fitting his boat with a small breathing pipe that enabled her to remain submerged for up to six hours.[5]

Fulton's boat dove and rose quite well; it had an underwater speed of one knot. Unfortunately, the minister of the navy in Paris was succeeded by a devotee of the old school who was hostile to innovation. Then, the signing of the Peace of Amiens with England ended interest in the submarine. Moreover, it appears that the French navy considered the vessel simply an oddity.

The Peace of Amiens was short-lived. The English then sought to obtain Fulton's services. If Ministers Pitt and Castlereagh were enthusiastic, Admiral Lord St. Vincent, First Lord of the Admiralty, saw more clearly and further into the future. As he put it, it would be crazy "to encourage a mode of war which they who commanded the sea did not want and which, if successful, would deprive them of it." In the end, depressed and rewarded with only £15,646.14.2 to cover his costs, Fulton returned home in 1806. There he died nine years later. He left to his fellow countrymen and to the whole of mankind his last invention, the steamboat.[6]

Yet the race to build a submarine had begun. After a series of attempts more or less successful and more or less scatterbrained, it fell to a professor of mathematics and design of the Nantes Lycée, Brutus de Villeroy, to build a submarine boat. Made wholly of sheet iron, it was tested successfully in the Bay of Noirmoutier on 15 August 1832. In 1859 the inventor moved to Philadelphia, Pennsylvania. There in 1861 he began working on a new submarine, arousing the suspicion of the local police, who mistook him for a Confederate agent. Fortunately for him, his predicament attracted the attention of Rear Admiral Du Pont, who summoned the Frenchman and entrusted him with building a submarine intended to destroy the feared ironclad *Virginia*.[7]

Northerners were therefore the first to envision a submarine in the Civil War. They even built some, including the one that can be seen today in the Washington Navy Yard, named the *Intelligent Whale*. It was not completed in time to operate during the war.[8]

The U.S. Navy in that era never did more than toy with such an idea. It never seriously tried to put submarines to practical use; indeed, it never considered doing so. The U.S. Navy, as Lord St. Vincent had tersely stated, commanded the sea, therefore it had no interest in or need to develop the submarine weapon.

The most important submarine created (even if indirectly) by Brutus de Villeroy was built not in a shipyard but in the lively imagination of a writer. Among his students at the Nantes Lycée had been a youth named Jules Verne. It would be Verne who would "launch" his famed submarine in the unforgettable pages of *Twenty Thousand Leagues under the Sea*. With a keen sense that seemed to join the experience of a recent past to the dawn of an unbelievable future, he named it the *Nautilus*. But his novel appeared in 1867, after the American Civil War. It cannot be doubted that the awesome destructive power attributed to Captain Nemo's ship owed much to the overwhelming impression made upon the writer by what the Confederates, alone and first, had been able to realize.

There is ample evidence that the Confederates had earlier begun to think about building a submarine. As early as October 1861, several voices had warned Flag Officer Goldsborough, commanding the U.S. naval forces blockading Hampton Roads, of this fact.[9] After the war, the detective Allan Pinkerton, who in 1861–62 headed McClellan's secret service, affirmed that a submarine had been built in Richmond by Tredegar and that one of his agents was present during the boat's trials.[10] Milton F. Perry questions Pinkerton's testimony.[11] Yet the Tredegar records in the Virginia State Archives at Richmond contain indisputable evidence of the submarine built in Richmond and therefore provide incontestable proof.

Indeed, on 26 November 1861, J. R. Anderson sent to W. G. Cheeney, agent of the naval secretary, a detailed estimate about the building of an iron submarine, specifying that the cost of construction approached $6,000, with another $200 for erecting a shed over her so that workers would be protected from prying eyes.[12]

Commodore Goldsborough's fears were therefore not wholly unfounded even if the building of the boat was slower than the Federals feared. As late as March 1862, Tredegar was still making alterations in her construction.[13] Records fail to tell us the fate of this boat or even if she was ever commissioned. It appears that her inventor was James Jones from Richmond, who in 1863 had decided to operate her in Texas waters (or was ordered to do so). Part of his projects, with pertinent designs, fell into Union hands while a messenger was trying to deliver them to Texas. Jones may have succeeded in reaching Texas and having at least one submarine built in Houston and four more in Shreveport, Louisiana.[14] Of their operations, if any, nothing is known.

Greater success followed a project started in New Orleans while the Crescent City port still remained in Confederate hands. The idea came from a riverboat captain, James R. McClintock, who had been born in Cincinnati, Ohio, in 1829, and Baxter Watson. These men owned a pressure gauge plant in New Orleans. Money came from Horace L. Hunley, a wealthy sugar dealer born in Tennessee in 1828.[15] To this project Hunley would devote his full support, his energy, his money, and, in the end, his life.

The submarine was built in the McClintock-Watson shop, 2 Front Street, New Orleans, and tested in Lake Pontchartrain in the fall of 1861. Because she sailed poorly, a second boat, named the *Pioneer*, was built. This one, so small that she had room for only three crewmen, was launched in February 1862. She proved satisfactory and destroyed a floating target with an explosive device. Her builders therefore asked for a letter of marque that would qualify her as a privateer.[16] This occurred early in April 1862 while Congress was creating the volunteer navy; therefore, it may be said that the *Pioneer* would be commissioned in that navy.

The submarine was of about four tons displacement (her builders do not say whether surfaced or submerged). She was thirty-four feet long with a diameter of four feet. She was fitted with steering and diving rudders and propelled by hand-powered screws.[17]

Her major problem was that when she was underwater, her compass seemed to go crazy, forcing her to surface frequently to check her course. The instrument was replaced, but results were poor. Only the invention of the gyroscopic compass, which would come many years later, would have solved the problem.[18]

Nevertheless, her builders and financial backers were satisfied. Their application was approved, and they got their tiny boat qualified as a privateer.[19] A few days later New Orleans fell into Farragut's hands. The submarine was scuttled in Lake Pontchartrain. There she lay forgotten until 1909, when she was found in the bottom sand and recovered. She is now on display before the Cabildo, in Jackson Square, New Orleans.

McClintock and Hunley sought housing in Mobile. There they again took up their project, which assumed greater dimensions. The authorities in Mobile allowed them to use a good machine shop owned by Thomas Parks and Thomas B. Lyons, located in Water Street.[20] There, work started immediately on a new boat.

Today in Mobile, because of the demolition of the old port district, no vestige remains of the small shop that was so important in the history of submarine warfare. Yet for several decades it remained intact, and I had the good fortune to see it. It still looked as it must have been when a handful of daring and imaginative men worked to turn the submarine dream of the Confederacy into reality.

The first step they took was way ahead of their time. Disappointed in manual propulsion, the inventors thought of the energy source of the future: electricity. This would be provided by large batteries mounted in series so as to produce the highest possible voltage. The engine to be activated would be "magnetic."[21] Apparently the inventors considered using a "magnetic engine," something that had never been attempted on such a scale. Indeed, the device had been invented in 1829 by a scientist whose mind and outstanding capability were now serving the North: Joseph Henry. This "engine" was a sort of reverse magnet, which, instead of converting mechanical energy into electrical (as in exploders), did the opposite. It was a forerunner of the electric engine that would appear many years later. An expert electrician was called from New Orleans to mount it.[22]

Unfortunately, the magnetic engine turned out to be a failure. A long time would pass before technology could provide reliable electrical propulsion for submarines. Handpower still had to be depended upon.[23] The unfortunate attempt by McClintock and his friends was applied at least on board one submarine, which, however, "sailed" only through the fantasy of mankind and not on the sea; most probably, Jules Verne was inspired to describe the propulsion system of his *Nautilus* as a "magnetic engine" energized by enormous batteries in series based on what was known to the public about Confederate experiments.

Construction work proceeded. The new submarine was no longer qualified as a privateer, even though she was built and manned by private hands (who, however, now might be considered members of the volunteer navy). Unfortunately, during an attempt to attack an enemy ship near Fort Morgan, she failed to overcome rough seas and foundered. Her crew was rescued.[24]

Admiral Buchanan, General James E. Slaughter, and local authorities extended help to the builders. New financing was obtained, and finally a fourth submarine was ready.[25] This one, christened the *Hunley*, was forty feet long, four feet wide, and five feet high. Hatches were located on two low conning turrets fitted with thick glass portholes that were at the height of the faces of the commander and the first officer. The commander controlled the surface and diving rudders; the first officer controlled the water taps and the pump that expelled water from the tanks. Two small iron ladders provided access from the interior to the hatches. A mercury level gauge measured depth. In addition to providing a bit of light, a candle would indicate lack of oxygen. Finally, a segmented cast-iron keel could be disconnected from inside if quick rise was called for. The crew consisted of nine men, including two officers. Eight of them worked at the cranks that moved the screw. The submarine could make up to five knots.[26]

The explosive device the submarine would carry against the enemy was a copper torpedo with ninety pounds of powder, fired by percussion. Originally it was planned to tow the torpedo beneath the target. It was then discovered that the waves might push the explosive contrivance toward the submarine, with catastrophic results. Therefore, a twenty-foot spar was fitted to the bow, with the torpedo at its end. The device had clamps and a second pulling ignition system. This arrangement allowed the torpedo to be fastened to the hull of an enemy ship so as to explode it from a safe distance.[27]

A simple snorkel located between the conning turrets brought air into the interior when the submarine was on the surface or just below the waterline.[28] Had the inventors studied Fulton's projects more closely, they might have—as he had—included cylinders containing compressed air; McClintock may have thought of this, yet in the Confederacy of 1863 it was difficult to find such contrivances.

Another serious fault (one that Fulton had obviated) was the excessive weight of the keel. This meant that the boat would emerge a very few inches above the water, at risk of being flooded and foundering if the ports were kept open. As will be seen, this is exactly what happened.[29] Last, the ballast tanks, located forward and aft, were made like tubs, that is, open at their tops (perhaps to obtain quicker immersion by reducing air resistance). This meant a serious danger of flooding when the boat moved sharply away from the horizontal.

The submarine, however, satisfactorily passed a series of tests in Mobile Bay. Yet Admiral Buchanan observed that the shallow water there hindered her maneuverability. He so informed Secretary Mallory.[30] Therefore, as Hunley proposed, the boat was sent to Charleston, where the enemy squadron, including many ironclads, threatened the city.[31] Moreover, in command there was General Beauregard, a supporter both of land and sea cooperation and of using every new war tool. Indeed, he eagerly brought pressure to bear upon railroad directors to have the submarine transported as quickly as possible.[32]

The boat was taken apart and loaded upon two flatcars and forwarded to Charleston, where she would pass into history. McClintock went along with her; Hunley planned to join her later and recommended absolute secrecy.[33] The enemy must be surprised and defeated.

Everyone in Charleston hoped that Confederate naval weapons would succeed in striking the enemy fleet hard; the firm of John Fraser and Company posted a prize of $100,000 to anyone who sank the feared U.S. ironclad *New Ironsides* or the powerful steam frigate *Wabash* and $50,000 for each *Monitor*-class ironclad sunk.[34]

There was no need to spur Confederate submariners. Lieutenant John Payne, C.S. Navy, volunteered to serve on the boat, as did seven sailors. The will to act was great, so after some hasty exercises, the little boat sortied at night to attack the *New Ironsides*. It was a serious mistake. The *Hunley's* crew should have had long and careful training. Enthusiasm alone was not enough; the sortie was fatal. The submarine's hatches were closed too late. A large ship passing by sent a wave that flooded the interior and sent her to the bottom in a few seconds. Lieutenant Payne, with half his body outside the hatch, managed to jump into the sea after ordering that the ship be abandoned and was saved, but the crew perished.[35]

The second tragedy occurred because of another gross error. The boat, moored near Fort Johnson, got under way before casting off her lines, and again her hatch was open. Lieutenant Payne tried frantically to retrieve the snarled hawser. His action caused a sudden movement of the diving rudder, and the little boat, diving with her hatches open, sank. Payne and two crew members were rescued; the others were lost.[36]

Charleston's citizens were distraught. Rumors spread of a "floating coffin," of a "deadly trap by a crazy inventor," and the like. Truly, both accidents had been caused by gross human mistakes. It was still not understood that one could not become a submariner overnight and that sailing such a ship required long experience.[37]

Beauregard nevertheless continued to trust the submarine. Hunley then arrived in Charleston with a team of men who had served on the boat in Mobile. Among them was Second Lieutenant George E. Dixon, of the Twenty-first Alabama Infantry, evidently lent to the navy. He would command the submarine while Hunley, as he had done in Mobile, would handle administrative matters.

Experienced and careful, Dixon had already been aboard the *Hunley* several times in Mobile and now firmly stressed the need for lengthy training. Yet during his absence, he could not prevent Hunley, guided more by enthusiasm than good sense, from taking out the little boat that bore his name. Another disaster resulted. Hunley lacked experience in handling a supremely sensitive craft that reacted suddenly to the slightest provocation and required getting used to. The boat was made to dive too quickly. She sank like a stone by the bow at a thirty-five-degree angle[38] and embedded herself in the muddy depths. Then the water in the open-topped tanks cascaded into the interior because the ship was tilted at such a sharp angle.

As the positions of the corpses revealed when they were recovered, in his distressing situation Hunley lost control and forgot to close the diving valve while using the pump. All those aboard, including Hunley, perished.[39]

Lieutenant Dixon was now free to begin the methodical training that was needed. There was no lack of volunteers despite the terrible accidents, even when the men were informed about the extreme danger of the undertaking.

In a place called Mount Pleasant, on Sullivan's Island, Dixon organized what Milton F. Perry calls the first submariners' school ever created on American soil (and, we may add, in the world).[40] There Dixon started the systematic training of his men. W. A. Alexander, his executive officer, wrote a terse narrative about events of the fall of 1863. From that and from some other sources,[41] we learn that the training proceeded methodically. Mornings were devoted to learning in detail about the structure and peculiar characteristics of the submarine so as to teach the proper behavior to the crewmen when conning the boat. After 1:00 P.M. came practical drill. This was sometimes extended into the night, when the boat came so close to enemy ships that the submariners could clearly hear the Union sailors talking and singing. In each case the submarine, now operated by experienced hands, performed well, even if she appeared temperamental, difficult to handle, and did not forgive the slightest thoughtlessness or error.

It was then decided to experiment with a prolonged immersion. As W. A. Alexander tells the story:

> It was agreed by all hands, to sink and let the boat rest on the bottom, in the Back Bay, off Battery Marshall. . . . It was also agreed that if anyone in the boat felt that he must come to the surface for air, and he gave the word "up," we would at once bring the boat to the surface.
>
> It was usual, when practicing in the bay, that the banks would be lined with soldiers. One evening . . . Dixon and myself and several of the crew compared watches, noted the time and sank for the test. . . . Each man had determined that he would not be the first to say "up." Not a word was said except an occasional "How is it," between Dixon and myself, until it was as the voice of one man, the word "up" came from all nine. We started the pumps, but I soon realized that my pump was not throwing. From experience I guessed the cause of the failure, took off the cap of the pump, lifted the valve, and drew out some seaweed that had choked it.
>
> During the time it took to do this the boat was considerably by the stern. Thick darkness prevailed. All hands had already endured what they thought was the utmost limit. Some of the crew almost lost control of themselves. It was a terrible few minutes. . . . We soon had the boat to the surface and the manhead opened. Fresh air! What an experience! Well, the sun was shining when we went down, the beach lined with soldiers. It was now quite dark, with one solitary soldier gazing on the spot where he had seen the boat before going down the last time. He did not see the boat until he saw me standing on the hatch combing, calling to him to stand by to take the line. A light was struck and the time taken. We had been on the bottom two hours and twenty-five minutes.[42]

Well worked, with caution, the submarine had passed her test. Now, as everybody in Charleston (and the submariners above all) desired, she should move against the enemy. General Beauregard issued orders on 14 December 1863.[43] All that was needed was a favorable occasion.

Unfortunately, on 5 February 1864 Dixon lost his able executive officer, W. A. Alexander, who was summoned to Mobile to take charge of the production of a quick-firing gun.[44] This showed, if there was need to do so, that the highest authorities, even those favorable to submarines, did not yet understand how much professionalism and training were needed to operate them. Otherwise they would not have taken his most able collaborator from Dixon, especially for a mission of such importance.

Dixon decided to act. He was becoming restless. He was clearly self-confident and trusted his boat.[45] At dusk on 17 February 1864, while the sea was flat calm, the submarine left her mooring and steered silently for the enemy—and toward an everlasting place in the annals of submarine warfare.

With the moon shining, the officer of the deck on the Union warship *Housatonic,* a steam sloop of 1,240 tons, fitted with thirteen cannons, discerned something that looked like a wooden plank floating just underwater and speedily approaching the ship. It was 8:45 P.M. General quarters was immediately beaten, the anchors were hoisted hurriedly, and the ship got slowly under way. But in less than two minutes a fearful explosion blew the vessel out of the sea while cascades of water washed over her deck. The big ship then rolled violently on her side and sank in a few minutes. Her stern had been disintegrated by the explosion.

Still, thanks to the calm water, the crewmen saved themselves. Only five men were wounded. The powerful vessel was now lying on the bottom.[46] For the first time in world history a submarine had sunk a warship.

The night passed, dawn came, but the *Hunley* did not come back.[47] General Beauregard still had hope and was preparing to honor the brave submariners.[48] Then, as hope began to fade, he telegraphed Richmond, saying that from questioning several prisoners of war, he had learned the name of the Federal ship sunk and that no trace had been found of the Confederates.[49] He at last had to acknowledge that the submarine had gone to a watery grave together with her victim, which had dragged her down into the deep of the sea.[50]

Why? Let us try a hypothesis that seems reasonable. When Dixon launched his attack, the *Housatonic* was riding at anchor. Yet in the clear moonlight, the Federals could see the shadow of the submarine and began to move their ship. Meanwhile, the *Hunley* had succeeded in fastening her torpedo to the hull of the enemy. The movement of the ship prematurely pulled the lanyard before the *Hunley* could sail away to a safe distance. Struck by the wave of the explosion, she sank, together with her victim.[51]

Nevertheless, evidence had been given of the fearful power of the submarine and that nothing could counter it. The pages of Jules Verne will help us fully appreciate this fact. Reading them, we can hear the formidable echo of the Charleston episode throughout the world, as well as the fear of coming disasters.

The first to understand the implications were the Union sailors. A wave of panic swept them. What impressed them most was that the attack had come like a thunderbolt after only a few minutes' warning. Hurriedly, all anchored vessels were fitted with antitorpedo devices (forerunners of antitorpedo nets). Those at sea were ordered to move constantly. The burden placed on their engines and fuel consumption can be easily imagined.[52]

Before the *Hunley* sailed on her final mission, the Confederates had started to use another futuristic weapon—the torpedo boat—near Charleston. The idea first took shape in the mind of General Beauregard, following a suggestion by his young, brilliant engineer, Captain Francis D. Lee.[53] It took a long time to convince the authorities of the wisdom of such a project. Finally it reached Mallory's desk. The secretary gave his full approval.[54] Beauregard also assured Mallory that the new weapon would remain under the control of the navy.[55]

Work began immediately under the direction of Captain Lee. The navy sent the chief naval constructor, John L. Porter, who allotted the work to the shipyard of F. M. Jones. Cameron and Company had charge of the engines, supplied by the navy, which also provided the hull of an unfinished gunboat abandoned in Charleston.[56]

Work proceeded with satisfactory speed, even though the local authorities could not provide much of the equipment requested.[57] By Christmas 1862 the hull was almost complete; by the beginning of 1863 the engines were ready to be placed on board; and during January the boilers were installed.[58]

Now trouble began, owing to the usual chronic dearth in the Confederacy—there was no iron to sheathe the little ship.[59] Beauregard, in distress, even thought of having such boats built overseas, an idea later adopted by Mallory.[60] In the end, on 11 July 1863, the small boat was launched without sheathing.[61] She was painted gray and was so low in the water as to appear almost submerged. So that she would give off little smoke, her engines were fired by the best anthracite coal.[62]

In the end, the still unfinished little boat, named the *Torch,* was commissioned and entrusted to Captain James Carlin, who had previously commanded a blockade runner. With an improvised crew, on the night of 21 August 1863, Carlin moved against the big enemy ironclad *New Ironsides.* He failed. The crew was a ragtag gang. Probably when the order to attack was given, a series of mistakes sent the *Torch* on the wrong course: instead of striking the enemy vessel perpendicularly, she lay alongside. Worse, at that very moment, the defective engine stopped, and the boat, without sheathing, was leaking badly everywhere. By a stroke of luck, Carlin managed to start the engine and steam away while the Union crew, taken by surprise, fired crazily in all directions.[63]

The *Torch* turned out to be almost useless. It had been a bad decision to send her into action hastily and with an untrustworthy crew. The idea itself, however, was excellent. The proof was the panic that her ghostlike appearance aroused and continued to create aboard the great enemy iron-clad.[64]

The conception was therefore potentially fruitful, and it was not given up. A true torpedo boat, the first one in history, would soon be created. The initiative sprang from a civilian plant in Charleston that manufactured explosive devices, the Southern Torpedo Company, managed by Theodore Stoney, a Charlestonian, and St. Julien Ravenal.[65] They began to build an assault boat in the shipyard of David C. Ebaugh, located along the Cooper River. The work was supervised by Captain Lee, based on a plan drafted by Ross Winan from Baltimore, a Southern sympathizer.[66]

The resulting boat was fifty-four feet long and five feet six inches wide. Shaped like a cigar, it was lightly protected by metal plating and open only in its center, where lay a powerful steam engine, which, however, because of the backwardness of Southern industry, had to be obtained from a railroad works. A high iron armored funnel assured good draft.

She was fitted with tanks like those of submarines. At the moment of the assault, these caused her to lie low in the water, leaving only a part of her deck above it. An explosive device at her bow was fastened to a spar fourteen feet long. The spar was movable and controlled from inboard. When contact with the enemy occured, it would be lowered so as to strike the target beneath the waterline. The powder charge weighed one hundred pounds. The explosive contrivance was made of copper and fitted with four supersensitive contact primers.[67]

It was the first assault boat in the world's naval history, an early ancestor of the assault boats used by the Italian navy that would shock its enemies in both world wars.[68]

The torpedo boat was transported overland on a railroad flatcar from the Cooper River to Charleston Harbor and launched near the western end of Broad Street. Well ballasted and painted a gray-blue color to make her almost invisible, she barely broke the surface of the water. Christened the *David,* perhaps because she must contest with the "Goliath" of the U.S. squadron, she was officially commissioned into the C.S. Navy.[69]

To command her, an able and daring naval officer who had volunteered, Lieutenant William T. Glassel, was chosen.[70] The executive officer was one of her builders, Stoney, but a substitute for him was provided so that he would not be hindered in preparing other assault boats. The chief engineer was James H. Tomb, an outstanding torpedo expert. The helmsman, coming from the crew of the ironclad *Palmetto State,* was the competent and brave J. Walker Cannon. The stoker was sailor James Sullivan. The orders were to attack the major enemy vessels as soon as possible.[71]

After long training, in which the *David* showed that she could log seven knots, she steered for the enemy on the night of 5 October 1863. Weather conditions were at their best: the water was calm under a covering light fog.[72] The target was once again the formidable *New Ironsides,* of 3,468 tons, whose eighteen big guns could fire a broadside heavier than all the ships of the *Monitor* class put together.[73]

Unseen by friend or foe, the *David* slipped silently out of the harbor. Soon the impressive Union fleet was visible to the four daring men who steered the small torpedo boat. In the early darkness, they could clearly hear signals by trumpet and drums aboard the ships and see the campfires of enemy infantry along the shores of Morris Island. Motionless, the *David* waited. Then, at 9:00 P.M., the signal for "lights out" was heard. Glassel took the helm and steered the *David* directly for the Northern ironclad.[74]

When she was three hundred yards from the *New Ironsides,* Union sentries gave the alarm and cried "stop!" At forty yards the Federals opened fire. Glassel answered with a shot that hit the deck officer. Now the *David* raced like lightning upon the enemy, and a few seconds later a frightful explosion shook the ironclad and made her joints quake as though she was breaking up. Cannons weighing tens of tons were tossed aside like twigs, and a huge column of water more than one hundred feet high washed over both ships.[75] The *David* was brutally shaken, and the hurricane of water put out her fires, stopping the engine dead. Believing that she would sink, Glassel ordered "abandon ship."

Not long afterward, while being carried away in the strong current, he was fished out by a Federal ship and made prisoner together with stoker Sullivan. Tomb, who had remained near the *David,* climbed aboard and, with helmsman Cannon, succeeded in starting the engine. Threading their way through enemy ships that fired wildly at them in the darkness, they returned unharmed to Charleston. In addition to words of praise, Mallory proposed that both Glassel and Tomb be promoted.[76]

The ironclad nevertheless remained afloat. The explosive contrivance had struck her just over seven feet beneath the waterline and (unfortunately for the Confederates) along a dividing bulkhead that helped dampen the force of the explosion.[77]

For a moment the Union sailors were happy. Then, with coal removed, they made a careful inspection inside the hull and learned that the iron-clad had suffered severe damage; indeed, her structure was almost disrupted. A big beam was badly split. The framing of the engine room had cracks four feet long. Moreover, her side had been pushed inboard four to five inches for a length of forty feet. The internal overheads seemed to be pushed from their sides by ten feet and many leaks were discovered.[78] And this was just the damage above the keel. The only solution was to place the ironclad immediately in drydock, lest she sink.[79]

The *New Ironsides* was towed to Port Royal, South Carolina. It was soon discovered that the damage could not be repaired there. She was therefore sent to Philadelphia and remained disabled for more than a year. Yet, as happened eighty years later, when the British battleships *Queen Elizabeth* and *Valiant* in 1941 were almost mortally blasted by Italian assault boats in Alexandria, Egypt, harbor,[80] now the Northerners kept tight secrecy about the serious damage to their powerful vessel. Only after the war did the Confederates learn the details. Yet the disappearance of the fearsome ironclad from the enemy line confirmed the success of the first mission in history by an assault boat.[81]

On 5 May 1864 the *David*, now commanded by James H. Tomb, attacked the USS *Memphis* in the North Edisto River, near Charleston. Her spar torpedo fully struck the enemy twice, but in neither case did it explode, and the *Memphis*, firing crazily and uselessly, succeeded in fleeing.[82]

Captain Francis D. Lee held that Tomb, against his better judgment, had used a defective weapon.[83] Yet other cases in which no explosion occurred caused some to fear sabotage.[84] Indeed, the most prominent scholar on Northern espionage, Meriwether Stuart, has proved indisputably that at least two of the most dangerous Northern secret agents succeeded during the war in infiltrating the Confederate torpedo service. Surely the enemy would have spared no effort to strike this awesome branch of the Confederate navy.[85]

A short time later the *David* moved against the large U.S. steam frigate *Wabash*. Only a very rough sea saved the powerful ship from at least three attacks.

Meanwhile, the C.S. Navy, with the help of General Beauregard, proceeded painstakingly to develop the new deadly weapon. The building of more torpedo boats was started.[86] Soon two were ready for launching in Charleston.[87] The program was extended to such other ports as Wilmington, North Carolina, and Mobile, Alabama. In the latter base, the job was entrusted to the able Lieutenant Colonel Victor von Scheliha, commanding the engineers in the Gulf of Mexico.[88]

Still other boats were being built in Savannah, Georgia. Here the Confederates had, as usual, to overcome many difficulties, mainly enemy raids that frequently disrupted railroads, causing the suspension of work when just two tons of coal would have allowed it to proceed. Yet at least one torpedo boat was launched.[89]

Elsewhere, in Virginia waters, near Newport News, the torpedo boat *Squib*, thirty-five feet long, with an explosive device of fifty-three pounds of powder, commanded by Hunter Davidson, successfully attacked the big steam frigate *Minnesota* during the night of 9 April 1864, damaging her so seriously that she was disabled and put out of commission for some time.[90]

Engines presented the most challenging problem in building assault boats. In despair, Mallory sought to acquire them and their boilers in England. He turned once again to Bulloch, asking him to have a dozen built and shipped as soon as possible. Soon thereafter the secretary pressured Bulloch to have six complete boats built and sent over either fitted out or dismantled. He enclosed to this end the projects of Constructor William A. Graves and Engineer in Chief Williamson.[91]

No record shows whether either the boats or the engines were ever sent to the Confederacy. With his usual vigor, Bulloch undertook the task, yet he had so many requests to satisfy that the work on the assault boats lagged behind. Only on 26 January 1865, when the South was near defeat, could he write that all six boats were ready and that he would try to ship them. It was too late.[92]

The exact number of torpedo boats put to sea by the Confederates remains unknown. After Charleston fell, Rear Admiral John A. Dahlgren wrote that he had found nine of them and had refloated two that had been scuttled by the Confederates.[93]

Despite all these obstacles, the Confederates succeeded in making the torpedo boats effective and greatly feared by Union sailors. Officers and men in Federal ships, even if protected by antitorpedo nets, were haunted by the deadly boats that hung about them in the darkness, like vultures in search of prey.[94]

Rear Admiral Dahlgren, a feared foe of the Confederates, perceived the tremendous importance and the future prospects of the assault weapon. Himself an inventor, the able seaman threatened to prosecute Lieutenant Glassel and stoker Sullivan for using a weapon "not recognized by civilized nations." Privately, he informed Secretary Welles that Glassel was a most experienced officer in this kind of warfare.[95] Among the enemy inventions of which he was aware, he had seen none work so well in its first use. He added: "The secrecy, rapidity of movement, control of direction, and precise explosion, indicate, I think, the introduction of the torpedo element as a means of certain warfare. It can be ignored no longer. If 60 pounds of powder, why not 600 pounds?" He concluded by suggesting to Assistant Secretary Fox that it was of the utmost importance that the U.S. Navy in turn acquire assault boats as soon as possible.[96]

Even if with less luck than they perhaps deserved, once again the Confederates had played with skill and daring the card of technical surprise in naval warfare. The consequences would go far beyond the Civil War, changing forever the strategy and methods of war at sea.

Stephen Russell Mallory, Secretary of the Navy, C.S.N. (National Archives, Washington, D.C.)

The Great Seal of the Confederate Navy Department. (Courtesy Lee A. Wallace, Jr.)

Commander Raphael Semmes aboard CSS *Sumter,* sitting between his officers. Executive Officer John M. Kell is standing behind him; others (from
left to right): Surgeon Francis L. Galt; First Lieutenant William F. Evans;
Lieutenants John M. Stribling and Robert T. Chapman; Chief Engineer
Miles J. Freeman; First Lieutenant of Marines Beckett K. Howell. (Courtesy
of the Confederate Museum, Richmond, Virginia)

The famed 7-inch Brooke rifle, now on the Battery at Charleston, South
Carolina. (Courtesy E. Milby Burton)

First Lieutenant Edward Crenshaw, wearing the uniform of the C.S. Marine Corps. (Courtesy Lee A. Wallace, Jr.)

Confederate 10-inch seacoast Columbiad (model 1862), now on the Battery at Charleston, South Carolina. (Courtesy E. Milby Burton)

An 11-inch Union Dahlgren, salvaged by the Confederates from the relic of the U.S. ironclad *Keokuk,* sunk by Confederate batteries during the failed Federal attempt to enter Charleston Harbor, now on the Battery at Charleston, South Carolina. (Courtesy E. Milby Burton)

Confederate ironclad, possibly the *Richmond,* on the James River. She might be instead the *Muskogee* on the Chattahoochee River. (Courtesy U.S. Naval History Division)

The CSS ironclad *Atlanta* on the Savannah River, possibly before her capture by U.S. ironclad monitors. (National Archives)

Left: Lieutenant Charles W. ("Savez") Read, among the most daring Confederate naval officers. (Courtesy U.S. Naval History Division) *Right:* Commander John Newland Maffitt. (Courtesy U.S. Naval History Division)

The CSS *Florida* on the Atlantic Ocean. (Courtesy U.S. Naval History Division)

Captain Raphael Semmes on the deck of the CSS *Alabama*. Executive Officer John M. Kell is in the background. Note the big Blakely pivot gun and the gray uniform worn by the two officers. (Courtesy U.S. Naval History Division)

The CSS *Georgia*, off Cherbourg, France. (Courtesy U.S. Naval History Division)

Confederate torpedo invented by General Gabriel Rains. This is a percussion one as used for the submarine mortar battery. (Courtesy E. Milby Burton)

Matthew Fontaine Maury. (Courtesy Lee A. Wallace, Jr.)

A Confederate torpedo boat of the *David* type, abandoned on the South Carolina shore after the evacuation of Charleston. (Courtesy U.S. Naval History Division)

The CSS *Albemarle* after the U.S. Navy refloated her to be sold for scrap. (National Archives)

The CSS *Stonewall* after her surrender to Spanish naval authorities in Cuba. (Courtesy Lee A. Wallace, Jr.)

Another picture of the CSS *Stonewall* after her surrender. (National Archives)

The CSS *Shenandoah* in the Bering Sea. (Courtesy U.S. Naval History Division)

FIFTEEN

The New Ironclad Strategy:
Second Phase

Bulloch was apprehensively following the building of the ironclads in Great Britain. There was serious concern that the British government might obstruct their delivery, bypassing the law with an order in council. Thus the Confederate naval agent in January 1863 had for the first time suggested shifting additional new ship orders from British to French shipyards.[1]

Now the question was, What were the possibilities for the Confederacy of shipbuilding in France? In October 1862 Emperor Napoleon III, in a long talk at St. Cloud with the Confederate commissioner in France, John Slidell, had suggested to Southerners the possibility of building warships in French shipyards, disguising them as being built for Italy.[2] Because the Confederates considered the French government autocratic, the imperial will de facto represented the law.[3]

Napoleon's proposal fired lively hope in Slidell, even though, some days later, the emperor, probably on the advice of his minister of the navy, Prosper Chasseloup-Laubat, had his secretary's office negate the idea. Still, that Slidell was right in not despairing turned out to be true only three days later, on 7 January 1863, when Lucien Arman, member of the Corps Législatif, confidant of the emperor, and leading French shipbuilder, contacted him and manifested a desire to build war vessels for the South in his shipyards. He added that he was "authorized" to make such an offer.[4]

Unfortunately, Bulloch, who was immediately informed by Slidell, had no money. All available funds were being used for the construction of the four vessels in the shipyards on the Clyde and the Mersey. Yet the solution to his financial problems soon came from France itself. There Slidell was in close touch with Emile Erlanger, a wealthy French banker and financier, director of the Paris office of the firm of Erlanger and Company from Frankfurt, whose son was engaged to Slidell's daughter. Perhaps enticed by the fat dividends that could be netted by means of the cotton certificates,[5] Erlanger had proposed that the Confederacy float a large loan based on cotton bonds in the major European financial markets.[6]

The terms requested by Erlanger soon appeared excessive. It was clear that he would have banked handsome profits, while the Confederacy would receive not more than 61 percent of the proceeds; it would have to put down about 520,000 cotton bales to cover the amount of the loan of $25 million at par.[7] Yet, in dire need, the Confederates had to bow. On 18 March 1863 subscriptions were officially opened in the stock exchanges of London, Liverpool, Paris, Frankfurt, and Amsterdam.[8]

Ultimately, on a face value of the bonds of £3 million, the Confederates received no more than £1,780,000, equal to $8,900,000.[9] Still, for them this was good news. The proceeds would be paid by Erlanger to the Confederacy in eight installments; on 24 March they received the first one, or, better, an advance on it that amounted, according to the prudent reckoning of Secretary of the Treasury Memminger, to £30,000, or $400,000.[10]

Even before receiving the official letter from Memminger, Mallory had prepared an estimate of costs to build ironclads "in Southern Europe," that is, in France.[11] The Confederate Congress secretly appropriated a total of $5,200,000 for them. Yet, because of the rate of exchange, it had to raise the figure to more than $10 million, even though it was not clear how the Confederacy could ever obtain the appalling difference in relation to the rates of the Erlanger loan.[12] These rates, however, were better than Memminger estimated because Mallory was soon able to send $26,000 to North and $630,137 to Bulloch.[13]

Bulloch was already at work. An emissary from Arman, Henri Arnous de la Rivière, had come to Liverpool to meet him and invited him to France. There Bulloch visited the Arman shipyards at Bordeaux and was greatly impressed by them. It was there that some of the famed French floating batteries used in the Crimea had been built.

Bulloch asked several questions about the French neutrality law. Arman reassured him, saying that he would proceed with the consent of both the emperor and the minister of trade, Eugène Rouher. Bulloch thereupon signed a contract for four fast cruisers of about fifteen hundred tons with four-hundred-horsepower engines, each armed with twelve or fourteen 6-inch rifled guns. It was decided to use the *canons rayés de trente* of the French navy because they could be obtained locally.[14]

Despite these favorable signs, a suspicious Bulloch still did not feel at ease, either because of the neutrality problem or the financial one. When, however, the French minister of the navy, Chasseloup-Laubat, authorized Arman to arm the ships (they would allegedly be built to sail in pirate-infested Chinese waters), Bulloch was cheered.[15]

Meanwhile, General Colin J. McRae had left the Selma Foundry when he was appointed financial agent for Europe with the duty of consolidating the administration of Confederate funds abroad, with those of the Erlanger loan his first priority. He arrived in Paris on 14 May and immediately took over all financial issues, to Bulloch's great relief.[16] Yet the latter soon realized that McRae's arrival was only a start, even if an important one, of a long and complicated process.

With the Confederates obviously in a hurry, Arman decided to build in his Bordeaux shipyard only two of the cruisers for the South and entrust the others to the care of a distinguished engineer and iron founder, J. Voruz of Nantes, who was also a member of the Corps Législatif. Voruz would have two hulls built in his city, respectively in the shipyards of Jollet and Babin and of Dubigeon, under his supervision, and assume personal charge of the ordnance for all four ships.[17] Now Bulloch could think about ironclads, a problem he had not given up since his first contact with Arman.

Unfortunately, the South, after the elation of the Erlanger loan had passed, still had money problems. At Richmond Mallory was distressed by the difficulty of raising the $5,200,000 appropriated by Congress for building ironclads in France. "We have now assurance," he wrote Memminger, "that French builders are prepared to construct vessels of any class for us, and to arm, equip and deliver them upon the high seas or elsewhere." If the secretary of the treasury was not able to obtain the required money immediately, he should at least put at the navy's disposal an appropriate amount of cotton on which to issue certificates.[18] When news of the appropriation reached him after considerable time—Bulloch did not receive Mallory's letter until 30 June—he acted without delay.[19]

At the time the South's fortune seemed at its zenith. A few weeks before, a great victory had been won on the battlefield of Chancellorsville, Virginia. Now the invasion of Pennsylvania by Lee's army had lifted Southern morale and hopes. No one seemed to understand that the great Southern general was playing an almost hopeless card or that in the West, along the Mississippi, the powerful fortress of Vicksburg, which in the past year the brave ironclad *Arkansas* had helped to preserve, was now near surrender.

Both Mallory and Bulloch understood the need to grasp the opportunity. "I deem of great moment that the construction of ironclad ships of war shall be commenced in France at once," wrote the secretary.[20] Meanwhile, Bulloch, his fears about the delivery of the British ironclads to the South allayed for the moment, was drafting their strategic objectives. On 4 July the first of the two, built in the Laird shipyards, the 294, had been launched, and it looked formidable. From Paris Arman had sent plans for another ironclad.[21]

Bulloch said he would be able to enlist local engineers, stokers, and enough gunners to serve at least a single cannon on board each ship. Even in such a condition, he held, the ironclads could successfully confront any wooden fleet. He proposed that they sail for Wilmington, North Carolina, and there, appearing suddenly at break of dawn, sweep away the blockading squadron. The ironclads would enter that port and enlist full crews composed of Southern sailors. They could then sail along the Atlantic coast taking a terrible toll on the enemy, reopen the Mississippi, and, by reversing the blockade, put Northern ports under contribution. Bulloch indicated the first objectives: Portsmouth, New Hampshire, and Philadelphia, Pennsylvania.[22]

Neither the defeat of Lee at Gettysburg nor the surrender of Vicksburg could now stop the Southern seamen. The longed-for objective seemed to be at hand—why wait? Bulloch left Paris on 14 July. In Bordeaux on the sixteenth he and Arman signed a contract for two ironclads at a cost of 2 million francs (or £100,000, or, at the ruinous rate of exchange the Confederates had to submit to, $500,000) each.[23]

The two ships would be of 171.10 feet length and 32.8 feet beam; when fully loaded, draw 14.4 feet; have three-hundred-horsepower engines; have two independent screws; displace a thousand tons; and have a speed of twelve knots when under full load. They would be protected by plates 5 inches thick in the central section, decreasing fore and aft to 3.5 inches. They would be armed with one large 10-inch 300-pounder Armstrong in a bow casemate and two 6-inch guns in a turret astern. All equipment would be like that of the French imperial navy. Time until delivery was ten months.[24]

Yet the Confederates did not put their trust only in France. Mallory had not forgotten the powerful squadron that was being fitted out in Great Britain. "I regard," he had written, "the acquisition of an adequate naval force as of so much importance to the best interests of the Country" as to feel compelled to ask for the help of President Davis in solving the irksome problem of money. It thus became possible to finance the building of naval vessels overseas through cotton certificates.[25]

Still, Bulloch, to carry out his tasks—mainly those in France—had been compelled to beg for advances from Erlanger, who had applied an exorbitant rate of interest to them.[26]

Toward mid-July the awesome naval squadron that should destroy the Union blockaders was at last taking shape. At that time the Confederates had in Europe at least five powerful ironclads in different stages of building or fitting out. This force needed a commanding officer. On 30 August 1863 Mallory detailed, with the rank of flag officer at sea, Commodore Samuel Barron, who on the next day started the long trip overseas with his officers.[27]

Yet destiny was beginning to turn against the Confederates. After the victory at Chancellorsville, the defeats of Gettysburg and Vicksburg cast dark shadows.

Bulloch feared that the British authorities might interfere with his program of naval construction. While hunger for cotton, as well as his policy of intervention in Mexico, had made Emperor Napoleon III solicitous of Confederate goodwill, the situation was far different in Great Britain. The huge investment of British capital in the Northern states, the blackmail indirectly exerted by the Union of a potential threat to Canada, and the unending, implacable diplomatic pressure brought to bear by the U.S. ambassador, Charles Francis Adams, especially after the havoc visited upon Northern maritime trade by the *Florida* and the *Alabama,* had compelled the British government to reconsider its neutrality policy.

Indeed, the Neutrality Proclamation was vague. For its executive side, British authorities referred to an old law of 1819. This was the Foreign Enlistment Act, passed to prevent too-open participation of British subjects in Latin American rebellions against their Spanish ally.[28] The problem was to clarify whether this law should be considered a purely domestic one, as originally designed, and therefore having as its only aim stopping British citizens from engaging in foreign wars. In this case, it could be argued only that ships built for the Confederacy must not have aboard British arms, ammunition, or sailors.

If instead the act was part of international law, it would imply a much wider and more sweeping interpretation. Times had changed greatly since 1819. The world had shrunk, and every action undertaken—or permitted to be undertaken—by a major power ran the risk of internationalizing the war, making it general and dragging everybody into it. Faced with such an appalling prospect, Her Majesty's government balked.

The event that had generated Bulloch's greatest fear happened well before the question had been raised of building warships in France, in April 1863. At that time, either to appease the Union or to determine how much the law might be stretched without breaking it, the British authorities had decided to seize a small ship recently launched at Liverpool, the *Alexandra.*[29] She had been launched on 7 April 1863 by the Miller and Son Shipyard, where the *Florida* had been built. Constructed at the expense of Charles J. Prioleau, christened with the name of the Princess of Wales, she should, as intended by the financier, become the property of the Confederacy as a gift. Moreover, she had no warlike characteristics except, perhaps, the unusual sturdiness of her sides. Yet the case had been chosen for political purposes, as the matter dealt with a ship effectively and openly built for the South.[30]

Bulloch hired some of the best British attorneys, but the battle in the court did not start until 22 June 1863. Meanwhile, all other Confederate naval construction in Great Britain had slowed down or been suspended because of the fear of government action. This caused delay that would, in the long run, be fatal.[31]

On 20 June 1863, however, the *Alexandra* was acquitted. It looked like a triumph for the Confederates, but it was not. The test simply persuaded the British government that the law of 1819 did not help it to get disentangled from the awkward predicament in which it felt involved; therefore, if it wished to avoid the anger of Union authorities, it must have direct recourse to executive action, leaving aside the Foreign Enlistment Act. The common economic interests as well as the military and naval power of the North could not be challenged with impunity, especially after the Confederate defeats at Gettysburg and Vicksburg. In other words, *les gros bataillons ont toujour raison.*[32]

Determined not to give up the ironclads, Bulloch sought a way to save them. In Paris, Arman had introduced him to brothers François and Adrien Bravay, owners of the Bravay and Company trading house. They would "buy" both ironclads from the Lairds on the pretense of reselling them to the khedive of Egypt. Instead, while in France, they would be "resold" to the Confederacy. The deeds of sale were made in a regular way and with the utmost observance of the law; yet the Lairds were kept unaware of this undertaking so that they might sell the two ships in good faith.[33] The ships were even given Egyptian names: *El Tousson* and *El Munassir.*

All aspects of the transaction had been carefully weighed. Unfortunately, as is often said, the devil is concealed in inponderables. And these took the form of a blunder committed by the British ambassador in Paris, Lord Cowley. Asked by the foreign secretary, Lord Russell, to inquire about Bravay and Company, he hastily and carelessly answered that such a firm did not exist. He was wrong.[34] The existence of the firm was then ascertained, but the British government had become alarmed. Meanwhile, pressure from the United States became heavier and more relentless, and pro-Northern Englishmen were becoming paranoid. Even while holding Adams at bay, Lord Russell began to think that perhaps he should delay the delivery of the ships until their status was clarified.[35]

The U.S. government, however, had not the least intention of temporizing. On 5 September 1863 Ambassador Adams had penned and sent to Lord Russell a fateful letter which hastened the crisis: "One of the ironclads is about to leave. . . . It would be superfluous in me to point out to your Lordship that this means war."[36] Lord Russell had decided a day earlier to act. He was prodded to do so because the new khedive of Egypt had told the British ambassador that he was not interested in the two ships, although he admitted his late father's connection with Bravay.[37]

An order sent to the customs officer at Liverpool forbade the delivery of the ironclads pending proceedings to ascertain their legal status. It seemed that the case of the *Alexandra* would be repeated. But this time, putting aside the law, Lord Russell decided to prevent an act that could generate appalling consequences. No lawsuit was begun, and a week later, a detachment of royal marines was sent aboard and a British gunboat sealed the exit from the Mersey.[38]

The Confederacy had lost the two powerful ships in which it had placed so much hope. The British government's offer to buy the two vessels from Bravay for the Royal Navy and the £180,000 the Confederates pocketed were bitter solace.[39]

On 26 October, the day the ironclads passed into British hands, the *Canton* was also seized. This was the big cruiser Commander Sinclair was building along the Clyde. Soon thereafter the ship passed into ownership of the British investors who had underwritten the cotton certificates and from them to the government. The fate of the ship that should have become the Confederacy's "super *Alabama*" also befell the "Scottish sea monster," which North was compelled to sell to the kingdom of Denmark for £240,000. History does not say how much of this money ended in the pockets of the Thomson brothers. It seems that the Confederacy got only crumbs.[40]

Thus ended the dream and hope of the South of putting afloat a formidable battle fleet built in Great Britain. Bulloch's genius, ability, and exertions had failed to preserve it.

There was still another chance, however, in the ships being built in France. On 16 October 1863, Flag Officer at Sea Samuel Barron and his officers left for Paris, where they took quarters at 30, rue Drouot. This would be the headquarters of the C.S. Navy in Europe, from which, it was hoped, the commodore would raise his pennant over the two ironclads that were taking shape in the shipyards of Bordeaux.[41]

Things were going better at home. There Mallory, after deciding upon the new ironclad strategy, had steadily pushed construction. Mention has already been made of the *Richmond, Chicora,* and *Palmetto State,* as well as of their operations, and of the unlucky *Atlanta.* Yet for Mallory these were just a beginning. His aim now was to build as many ironclads as possible in Southern yards.[42]

The first place where it was necessary to act, because of the enemy threat, was the Mississippi and its tributaries. There the loss of the *Arkansas* had been a true disaster. Yet 1863 had begun with a very favorable event, even if it occurred in Texas and not in the Mississippi Valley. There, in the preceding fall, Union naval and land forces had, in a surprise landing, seized the port city of Galveston. On New Year's Day, however, Confederates had retaken the city in a surprise attack, driven off the enemy naval squadron, and captured the gunboat *Harriet Lane*. Another, the *Westfield,* had been blown up by Union sailors to prevent her falling into Southern hands. It had been an army, not a navy, success, yet it provided some hope.[43] Moreover, off Galveston a few days later the *Alabama* sunk the *Hatteras*. And this time it was a Confederate naval victory.

Mallory was already thinking about building new ships along the Mississippi. Because it was becoming increasingly necessary to exploit the tributaries of the big river in areas enemy ships could not reach, the secretary had arranged for the construction of two ironclads on the Yazoo, in the old navy yard at Yazoo City, and of one on the Red River.[44]

For shipbuilding at Yazoo City, Mallory had the right man at hand: the energetic Captain Isaac Brown, who had commanded the *Arkansas* and organized torpedo warfare in the West. The building supervisor was Commodore Lynch, commanding Confederate naval forces in the West. At Yazoo City workmen had already began to convert the gunboat *Mobile* into an ironclad. Together with her would be laid down a big paddle-wheel ironclad, projected by John L. Porter. Efforts had immediately begun to secure railroad iron, engines, and ordnance stores. This ship would be "formidable and useful," and Brown received ample discretionary power in her building.[45] The original appropriation was for $300,000.[46]

The task of building an ironclad on the Red River at Shreveport, Louisiana, was entrusted to Lieutenant Jonathan H. Carter.[47] As early as 1 November 1862 Carter, on behalf of the navy, had signed a contract that called for the delivery of such a ship in six months at a cost of $336,000.[48]

Yet this was not enough. Mallory was already projecting the construction of a pair of ironclads on the Cumberland and Tennessee rivers. He had entrusted that duty to Commodore Barron before sending him to Europe.[49] An attempt to launch ships on two rivers fully exposed to raids by enemy war vessels was too risky, however, and the idea was given up.[50]

Better progress was being made along the Yazoo and Red rivers. At the first place, Brown—who soon relieved Lynch as commander of the naval forces in the West—had immediately put to work his capable collaborator,

Lieutenant Henry Kennedy Stevens, who soon was busy looking for coal, anchors, and chains and seeking ordnance from the Confederate works on the Big Black River. At Shreveport, Carter had sent an agent to Jefferson, Texas, to inspect the ironworks and local coal mines there.[51]

Had the time come for the Confederates to resume operations on the Mississippi and in the West generally? On 12 December the Union ironclad gunboat *Cairo* had struck a torpedo in the Yazoo. Then, between 14 and 24 February 1863, Southerners succeeded in trapping and capturing the Federal ram *Queen of the West* and the ironclad gunboat *Indianola*, which had recklessly descended the river beyond Vicksburg.[52] Yet the capture, made by Confederate soldiers rather than sailors, accomplished nothing. On the next day, Confederates panicked when they sighted a "powerful ironclad" (it was a fake) the Union sailors had sent down the great river and hurriedly scuttled the *Indianola*.[53] So this comedy of errors ended to the detriment of the South.

Meanwhile, Brown at Yazoo City and Carter at Shreveport fought doggedly against all odds: time, labor shortages, and lack of equipment, that is, against the well-known curse of the South, the crude and backward industrial plant.

Moreover, the enemy stranglehold around Vicksburg was becoming tighter and more threatening. In addition, iron from the Shelby Iron Company, already contracted for and to be delivered at Yazoo City,[54] was transferred to the nearly finished ironclads being built at Selma, Alabama. It was the tragedy of the South once again: the Confederates lacked everything, and the several programs were fighting each other for the scanty resources available.[55]

It was no longer possible to continue. The construction of the two ironclads at Yazoo City had to be abandoned.[56] All the Confederates could do was to destroy the hulls of the two unfinished vessels lest they fall into enemy hands. On 4 July the fortress of Vicksburg surrendered. The battle for the Mississippi was over; the South had lost.

Yet on 14 April, shortly before Grant attacked, Carter had launched his ironclad at Shreveport. Together with the ram-gunboat *Webb* (which had played a notable part in the capture of the *Indianola*) and some minor units, that was all that was left to the Confederates in the West. Of course, the new ironclad had no hope of taking the offensive or of reaching the Mississippi; still, it could surely help protect what was left of Louisiana and effectively oppose further enemy penetration toward the West.[57]

Carter had spared no effort in fitting out the ship that Mallory had christened the *Missouri*. He had succeeded in acquiring railroad iron, paying $100 a ton for it, and had pushed work even though the army had refused to detach the naval carpenters he needed.[58] Evidently railroad iron was not enough, for Carter, apparently a resourceful man, managed to build a blast furnace of twelve to thirteen thousand pounds capacity and insisted that the government seize the ironworks at Jefferson, Texas, and send officers capable of managing them. In the end, he compromised by using the rails of the Vicksburg, Shreveport and Texas Railroad.[59]

Still, something went wrong. The ordnance for the *Missouri* was seized by the army for the forts at Grand Gulf. There, they would do excellent work on U.S. ironclad gunboats.[60]

In the end, instead of six guns, the ironclad received but two Dahlgrens of different calibers (an 11-inch and a 9-inch) and an old siege gun. She never obtained more. The ironclad made her engine trials on 17 June, logging up to six knots, and on 12 September was put into commission. She was 183 feet long with a casemate of 130 feet. Her propulsion was by a single large wheel located in the casemate astern. Three rudders assured stability.[61]

If the time necessary to fit out and commission the *Missouri* was longer than foreseen, elsewhere time lags were even worse. In Richmond two more ironclads, sister ships of the *Richmond,* had been laid down. Yet it appeared very clear that they would not be ready in 1863 for one reason: iron for their armor was lacking. Still, other works proceeded quickly. In June 1863 the *Virginia II* was launched in the presence of a cheering crowd, as was the *Fredericksburg;* but then work slowed down because of the lack of iron; the Tredegar had enormous difficulty in finding it.[62]

The same happened with five other ironclads laid down in North Carolina. Two of these, the *Raleigh* and the *North Carolina,* were in the shipyard at Wilmington, the most important port of entry for blockade runners. Although threatened by the enemy, the Confederacy was determined to defend it.[63] Work on the two ships proceeded. Mallory had transferred Commodore Lynch from the West so that he could supervise the building of the ironclads in North Carolina.[64]

It seems, however, that Lynch failed to get along either with the local military commander, General William H. C. Whiting, or with the governor of the state, Zebulon B. Vance.[65] Vance was a spirited, able, and talented former Union man. After secession, he cast his lot with the South. A war volunteer and a gallant soldier, he was elected governor in 1862. A staunch defender of states' rights, he had had a series of clashes with President Davis and with the Richmond authorities. He nevertheless understood the requirements of war—especially of the defense of his state—and was an excellent politician and organizer.[66] Yet Lynch failed to get along with him, forcing Mallory to intervene personally many times.

Still, the work at Wilmington proceeded. On 14 May 1863 Lynch could inform Vance that the *North Carolina* had been launched, fitted out, had her battery aboard, and was ready to be put into commission, which eased his concerns about defending Wilmington.[67] She was of the *Richmond* class: 150 feet long, with four cannons. The *Raleigh,* which went into commission later, was similar.[68]

If the port of Wilmington—heavily protected by formidable fortifications and torpedoes—was now safe, the zone in North Carolina that caused the main concern was that facing the sounds. There, major Union amphibious operations had struck hard and deep before the Confederates had been prepared to react. The enemy had sailed many miles up the great rivers and taken possession of the cities of New Bern, Washington, and Plymouth, respectively on the Neuse, Tar, and Roanoke rivers, as well as the localities of Edenton, Winton, and Beaufort. At any moment the enemy might try to push to the heartland of the Confederacy, a prospect General Lee considered with deep anxiety.[69]

To protect this vital zone, Mallory had decided to build three ironclads, one on each of the major rivers. The first, to be constructed by Howard and Ellis, was laid down in the shipyard at Whitehall, a small village on the Neuse River, and appropriately named the *Neuse.*[70]

For the second and third ironclads, shipbuilders Martin and Elliott, from Elizabeth City, North Carolina, were employed. They, especially the young and spirited C. Gilbert Elliott, had several months earlier worked for Mallory on the unlucky attempt to build gunboats to escort the famed *Virginia.* Now they signed a contract for an ironclad to be built at Tarboro, on the Tar River, for $40,000 and to be launched by 1 March 1863. Her name was not specified.[71]

Soon thereafter, Martin and Elliott wrote Mallory that the shipyard at Tarboro, located a mere eighteen miles from the Roanoke River, could and must be protected against indirect attacks from the enemy sailing up that river. They therefore proposed building a third ironclad on the Roanoke, at a place called Tillery Farm (better known as Edward's Ferry). They pledged to launch it by 12 April 1863.[72]

The proposal was approved by Mallory, and they soon received the contract. The third ironclad would be named the *Albemarle* and, according to the plans of Chief Constructor John L. Porter, would be of the same class as the other two. Among the three projected, she would be the only one to win a place in history.[73]

The dangerous bridgehead established by the enemy in North Carolina soon made its power known. On 11 December 1862 a large Union expeditionary force moved along the Neuse River toward Goldsboro, advancing about sixty miles. Heavy fighting with Confederate forces soon followed. Yet the latter could not stop Union cavalry that appeared before the ship-

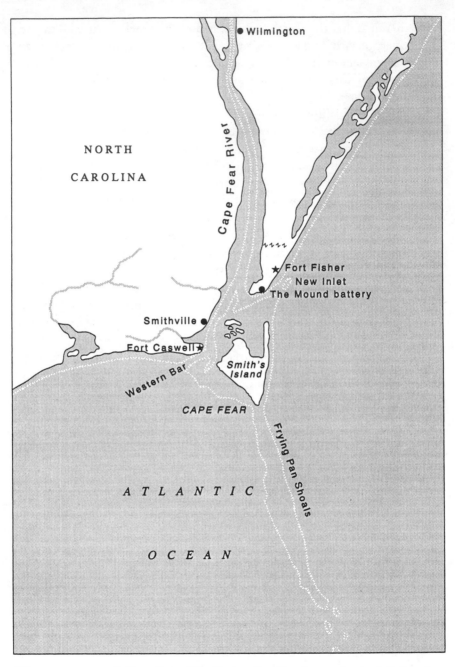

The waters around Cape Fear. The Frying Pan Shoals are clearly delineated.

yard at Whitehall and shelled the hull of the *Neuse,* then under construction there.[74]

Finally, the enemy was driven back after fierce fighting and retreated toward their base at New Bern, leaving behind a scene of devastation and plundering. The hull of the *Neuse* was soon repaired and towed to nearby Kinston to be fitted out.[75]

Unfortunately, the situation would be even worse at Tarboro. After long inactivity, on 18 July 1863 the enemy let loose a new raid, this time along the Tar River, with the usual sad outcome of violence and destruction against the local people. On 20 July the Federal raiders entered Tarboro and found the ironclad under construction. They depicted her later as "fine" and with "frame very heavy and solid" and set her afire. The first of the three new ships was gone without ever having touched water.[76] Work must be pushed on the other two ironclads, for they could threaten the main Union bases at New Bern and Plymouth. From Richmond General Lee urged speed.[77]

Yet another problem arose, worse than enemy danger: the lack of iron for plates. The inadequacy of the agricultural South was making itself felt again. The only solution was the usual, unfortunate one: rip up the railroad tracks that were less used or rendered practically useless by enemy threat. Earlier, Mallory had asked the secretary of war to grant him the rails of the Portsmouth and Weldon or of the Norfolk and Petersburg lines.[78] The results were disappointing. Although the removal of the rails was ordered, enemy pressure made the operation impossible.[79]

Another solution had to be found. The secretary of the navy decided to detail Lieuteant Commanding James Wallace Cooke to North Carolina to superintend the building of the *Albemarle* with what iron could be acquired locally.[80] Cooke was the officer who would give the Confederacy its last naval victory. Born in Beaufort, North Carolina, in 1812, at sea since 1828, Cooke had fought with the Confederate "mosquito" fleet against the Federals in the sounds, showing energy, ability, coolness, and daring. A quiet, active, unassuming, and stubborn man, he would be among the best choices Mallory made.[81]

Cooke soon discovered that Governor Vance had a large stock of railroad iron and so informed Mallory, who immediately wrote to ask that it be sent to the Tredegar to be converted into two-inch plate, to be then installed in two courses so as to make a four-inch armor. Vance agreed to cooperate and ordered that the rails of the Atlantic and North Carolina Railroad, which were on the part of the line nearest to the enemy, be given for plating the *Neuse.* For the other ships, he suggested that rails from the Seaboard and Roanoke Railroad be used. These were in part owned by an "alien enemy," hence could be seized.[82]

Still, iron was scarce at the beginning of 1863[83] and continued to be for several months so that Cooke, in June, flatly stated that if the problem was not solved, the project must be given up. Mallory contacted Vance again, making it clear that he knew iron was available in his state.[84]

Opposition to handing over the rails came less from Vance than from the railroad companies. Commodore Lynch had written Vance that the *Albemarle,* in cooperation with the army, could sweep the enemy from the sounds as the *Virginia* had done at Hampton Roads. Vance therefore put pressure on the railroad companies, and in the end four hundred tons of rails were obtained.[85]

All this had taken much time, yet work on the two ironclads went on steadily. Work on the *Albemarle,* particularly, was an almost titanic undertaking. There was no shipyard at Edward's Ferry, not even one under construction. There was only a cornfield, chosen by Elliott because it was high enough above the river not be flooded by freshets. There the workers, led by Cooke, started literally from scratch. Nothing better signified the industrial indigence of the South. With the help of local people, some country blacksmiths were gathered and three small sawmills were put together. One sawmill was located near the hull, the others in forests nearby where trees were felled, cut, sawed, and planed into lumber. The work proceeded under the endless threat of enemy raids: the workmen were compelled, with the help of some blacks sent from nearby plantations, to dig entrenchments around the yard and to mount on them a couple of field guns.[86]

At last, in October 1863, the *Albemarle* was ready for launching. On the night of 3 October, taking advantage of an exceptionally high tide and a clear moon, the hull was pushed—or, better, dragged—into the river. Unfortunately, a little "jump" into the water resulted in a little bending, or "hogging," of the keel. Mallory sent the chief constructor, John L. Porter, to control the damage, which turned out to be small and did not cause any leaks.[87]

The ironclad was then towed to Halifax, about a mile upriver, where her fitting out began. On 30 November 1863 Mallory could officially state that both the *Neuse* and the *Albemarle* had been launched and were being fitted out.[88]

Work at Charleston, South Carolina, proceeded more rapidly, for on 16 October 1862 a contract for a large ironclad had been signed with F. M. Jones and J. M. Eason.[89] Her keel was laid down in November. The ship would be 180 feet long, named the *Charleston,* and armed with four rifled Brooke guns (two on each broadside) and two 9-inch smoothbores ahead and astern. Covered by more than six hundred tons of armor plates, she would be the most powerful and swift Confederate ironclad in South Carolina waters. She was completed toward the end of 1863.[90]

In Savannah, Georgia, the capture of the ironclad *Atlanta* by the enemy caused panic.[91] The navy, however, was already looking ahead. In that city there was an able naval constructor, Henry Frederick Willinck, born there in 1825. At seventeen years of age he had gone to a large New York shipyard, where he worked for nine years and thoroughly learned his job.[92] Immediately after the outbreak of the war he put himself in the Confederate navy's service and signed a contract to build two gunboats. When he then proposed to Mallory that he build an ironclad, he received a positive answer.[93]

The contract was speedily closed. In August 1862 work aboard what would become the *Savannah* was already in full swing, and it was proposed that Willinck build a second vessel.[94] The contract for the ship that would become the *Milledgeville* was signed on 13 December 1862. Her hull should be ready in six months. The navy would provide plates and hardware, and she would cost $160,000.[95] Unfortunately, this ship, which was to be 175 feet long, would never be completed.[96]

Work on the *Savannah* proceeded very quickly. Her armor plates were turned out by the Atlanta Rolling Mill and then cut and drilled at Savannah.[97] Her engines were built in Columbus, Georgia, by the Naval Iron Works, which shipped them to Savannah on 6 November 1862.[98] The usual time lag followed because of the lack of skilled workmen, constantly taken away from work on the ship for other duties,[99] and slowness in delivery of the plates by the Atlanta Rolling Mill, whose small size made fulfilling all the orders difficult.[100]

At last the *Savannah* was launched on 4 February 1863. A bit more than four months later, on 30 June 1863, she was commissioned into the navy by Captain William W. Hunter, who, after Webb's capture aboard the *Atlanta,* had assumed the duty of flag officer of the local squadron.[101] Hunter hoisted his pennant over his new flagship and, after speed trials, stated that she made at least 6.5 knots, had no engine problems, and appeared to be satisfactory.[102] She was indeed an excellent ship, well built and solid.[103]

Alas, solving its problems would never be easy for the small Southern navy. On 3 August one of the *Savannah*'s engines, under heavy strain, was disabled when both the piston and cylinder broke. Hunter decided to send the defective engine back to the Naval Iron Works at Columbus, which had built it. Estimated time for repair was a month.[104] Fortunately, at Columbus Chief Engineer J. H. Warner performed miracles: in less than fifteen days the engine was repaired and returned to Savannah.[105]

The ironclad was at last able to operate without problems. She was among the best built by the Confederacy. Of the *Richmond* class, she was 150 feet long with a draft of 22 feet. She had a battery of four 6.4-inch Brookes and was fitted with four air blowers to make service aboard more bearable.

The Confederates had also busied themselves along the western boundary of the state of Georgia, where the Chattahoochee River flows. There the city of Columbus had been converted, by immense effort, into a center of war production. At its end the river empties into Apalachicola Bay, Florida, where lies a city of the same name. This had soon become a target of Northern amphibious operations so that the Confederates had to evacuate it.[106] There the U.S. Navy first learned about another ironclad being built in a shipyard near the Columbus Naval Iron Works.[107]

It was a big ship, of the *Fredericksburg* class, 180 feet long, first named the *Muscogee,* then the *Jackson.* Work on her was being pushed energetically. Her battery would include five or six guns, and she would be truly powerful.[108] Installation of her engines began in mid-June. Still, the lack of iron for her armor and the difficulty in finding skilled labor took so much time that she could not possibly be launched until the end of 1863.[109]

Meanwhile, Mallory was worried about the port of Mobile, Alabama, on the bay of the same name, which was more than thirty nautical miles long. After the fall of New Orleans, Pensacola, and Apalachicola, Mobile was the only Confederate port of significance on the Gulf of Mexico, and it must not be lost. Cries of alarm were coming from Alabama's governor, who feared that enemy ships might sail up the Alabama and Tombigbee rivers.[110]

Steps had already been taken to defend Mobile. Under the direction of the able von Scheliha, great torpedo fields were being laid down, leaving a channel 450 yards wide to enable friendly ships to get in and out, which would turn out to be fatal. There were also two forts, Fort Morgan (capable, when finished, of mounting forty-five cannons) and Fort Gaines, with a battery of twenty-six cannons; both of them could fire on the channel.

In the spring of 1862, the state of Alabama obtained an old river tug, the *Baltic,* armored her, fitted her with six guns, and delivered her on 12 May to the Confederate navy, which put in command Lieutenant James D. Johnston, an able and experienced officer. The ship looked powerful; she was 186 feet long, armed with two Dahlgren guns and two other 32-pounders and two minor ones; but her paddle-wheel propulsion system was obsolescent, she was slow, could not steer easily, and had very poor crew quarters.[111]

Fortunately, about two hundred miles from Mobile lay the town of

Selma. There, as at Columbus, the Confederacy had organized one of its industrial centers. Colin J. McRae, while still busy with the Selma Cannon Foundry, had located near the city a place adaptable for a navy yard.[112] From there he had introduced to the naval secretary Henry D. Bassett, from Mobile, who was engaged in naval construction.[113] Mallory acted with his usual speed: on 1 May 1862 Bassett signed a contract for the construction of two floating batteries at a cost of $100,000 each. The navy would provide armor and hardware. Time of delivery, respectively, was sixty and ninety days.[114]

Actually, building the two ships took much more time. Named the *Huntsville* and the *Tuscaloosa* and originally planned as ironclads of the *Albemarle* class, they ended up being used as floating batteries because their engines were inadequate; with a speed of no more than two to three knots and lacking enough power to move upstream, they could not have been used as anything else.[115]

Much more was needed at Mobile to fulfill Mallory's new ironclad strategy. First, Mobile required a resourceful, able, and authoritative commanding officer. Mallory had been considering Admiral Buchanan, but he was still ailing because of the wound received at Hampton Roads, which forced him to walk with crutches.[116] Not until August 1862 was he able to reach Mobile and assume command, just in time to greet the raider *Florida* under Captain Maffitt, which entered the bay on 4 September.

Buchanan found the small naval squadron there in flawless order, but the danger was serious. If the enemy, he argued, attacked with ironclads, they could probably destroy the city because the Confederate gunboats would not be able to counter them. The forts had some batteries ready, their men were well drilled, resolute, and well led, yet still lacking were many heavy cannons that would have completed the other batteries. There was one positive note: cooperation between the navy and the army looked excellent to the admiral.[117]

Painstakingly, Mallory tried to solve the problems besetting Buchanan. He was already closely following the building of the two floating batteries entrusted to Bassett at Selma.[118] On 1 August 1863 he had detailed, from Richmond, Commander Ebenezer Farrand, and from Columbus Chief Engineer Warner, with the duty of thoroughly inspecting the situation.[119] On 2 September Farrand was entrusted with the task of starting new ironclad building at the most suitable place along the Alabama River.[120] He must operate under Buchanan's orders.

Among the several contracts closed by Farrand, two were to succeed. The first one was for a large paddle-wheel ironclad (the future *Nashville*) to be built at Montgomery. The second was a powerful screw ship to be laid down in the Selma Navy Yard.[121]

So began the manufacturing process that would end with the launching of one of the most powerful and famed Confederate ironclads, the *Tennessee*.[122] The Selma Navy Yard had been built from nothing, making use of a four-acre field located on the riverbank at the entrance to the city along the main street just beyond the bridge. Today a small monument with an inscription is all that remains of the yard where there was built, among others, a vessel fated to go down in history.

As soon as the work began, the usual distressing fight against time and the scarcity of everything from skilled labor to guns and engines also started. Yet it was imperative to put into commission as soon as possible some ships capable of confronting the enemy. Buchanan saw that there was no other solution than to attack the enemy ships as soon as they succeeded in passing the forts. These (and also the Spanish Fort, situated at the extreme northeastern corner of the bay to protect the mouths of the rivers) were in good condition in October, although many batteries and the powder magazines were still far from completed.[123]

The Selma Cannon Foundry was not yet in operation, and Buchanan lamented that he lacked guns for all the ships under construction. Hoping that Richmond would be able to provide them, for the time being, he could use six pieces of several types, furnished by the army. Meanwhile, the Naval Iron Works at Columbus was asked to send carriages.[124]

The work on the two floating batteries was slowing down. Still, the admiral had only them to count on in case of an enemy attack.[125] With great exertion, two rifled Blakely guns and their carriages could be obtained from Charleston;[126] and—not without great difficulty—three hundred tons of coal were found.[127] But now arose the usual nightmare: lack of iron. The Atlanta Rolling Mill said it could not deliver the needed plate. Could the Shelby Iron Company provide it? Or could a surrogate, perhaps, be found in railroad iron?[128]

At last, the iron arrived, some from Atlanta, more from Shelby, and the two floating batteries, the *Huntsville* and *Tuscaloosa*, were launched on 8 February 1863.[129] The two ships could now make their engine trials, and the results were, as expected, poor: 2.5 knots for the *Tuscaloosa*, 3.5 for the *Huntsville*, which, even at that limited speed, trembled and quivered excessively.[130] It being clear that such ships could never confront the enemy in open battle, they would be used as designated, as floating batteries.

Thus matters went ahead amid almost insuperable obstacles: shortage of crewmen, medicinals, surgical instruments, skilled labor, and coal. Fortunately, the forts had been greatly improved and the men had been well drilled, but heavy cannons still had to be delivered.[131]

Now all hope was staked on the *Tennessee*. At the end of February 1863 the ironclad was ready for launching. It was a touching occurrence for all who relied so much upon the powerful vessel. An eyewitness wrote that, upon the firing of a signal gun, the great ship descended into the water like an arrow. The tide in the river was so high that she demolished a semisubmerged warehouse with her cutting ram. Then, taken in tow by the beautiful steamer *Southern Republic,* whose calliope cheerfully played *Dixie,* the great ship descended the river amid the cheers of enthusiastic crowds gathered on the riverbanks.[132]

In May 1863 the ironclad was ready to receive her engines. Because Columbus, swamped with orders, could not build them, they were taken from a riverboat.[133] The mounting of armor, provided by Shelby and the Atlanta Rolling Mill, began in July.[134] By September this work was almost finished. To the contrary, work on the *Nashville,* although her engines were installed, was slowed down because there was not enough iron. In October the *Tennessee* was ready for her battery.[135] Finally, in December Buchanan held a series of trials that proved her most satisfactory. Still lacking were cannons, crew, and commanding officer. For this billet, Buchanan was thinking of James D. Johnston, a first-rate officer, who at the time commanded the *Baltic.*[136]

A most important problem was at last nearly solved. Commander Catesby ap R. Jones now had the Selma Cannon Foundry well in hand. On 20 December he was able to send to Mobile the first heavy gun and, in answer to Buchanan's pressing demand, started to cast the battery for the *Tennessee.*[137]

The year 1863 was ending, and in Mobile the Confederates had succeeded, by great exertions, fighting above all against the backwardness of their industrial plant and underdeveloped economy, to make possible— even if only in part—Mallory's strategy. In a few days, the great ironclad *Tennessee* would be commissioned and ready to oppose her iron sides to the enemy threat.

S I X T E E N

Crisis of the Blockade, The Climax of Confederate Naval Strategy, and The Battle of Plymouth

At the beginning of 1864, a truth some already knew became clear. The most serious logistical problems for the Southern war effort were caused not so much by the Northern naval blockade as by the haphazard system (or absence of any system) by which the Confederacy spent its money in Europe and conducted blockade running (or abandoned it to conduct itself).

The scanty resources of the South were being siphoned off by unscrupulous speculators;[1] cotton that the Confederacy had to sell for six to ten cents a pound was sold by them on European markets for fifty to sixty cents. Toward the end of 1863 those people had banked approximately $20 million.[2] Had the Confederacy instead exported cotton on its own account, according to Frank L. Owsley, it would have "dispensed with foreign loans, bought its warlike stores at the lower cash rates and supplied its citizens with commodities of prime necessity."[3]

The businessmen, mostly British but also local men and even Northerners, netted handsome profits from running the blockade; yet the goods they preferred to carry were often useless to the Confederacy and, indeed, created a dangerous financial drain. These included goods of small bulk and light weight that could be sold at the highest prices: French champagne, Paris perfumes, silks, and other luxuries. Of course, it was far less dangerous to run the blockade with such cargoes than to carry explosives and weapons.[4]

The navy, which suffered more than any other Confederate agency from this situation, had early indicated a solution to the second problem: organize a state-owned fleet of blockade runners manned and commanded by naval personnel. Bulloch had given an example as early as 1861 by acquiring and accompanying the blockade runner *Fingal* to the Southern port of Savannah. Then at the end of 1863, he bought another good seven-hundred-gross ton ship, the *Coquette,* and entrusted her command to an able officer of the C.S. Navy, Lieutenant Robert R. Carter.[5]

The success of this enterprise stimulated Bulloch to suggest to Mallory that they put into operation a "fleet of formidable swift light-draft steamers" that would enable the navy to "control all the shipments" running the blockade.[6] Bulloch had in mind the example provided by the army, which, at the initiative of Huse, already had five steamers transporting warlike equipment and weapons, and also the enterprising Governor Vance of North Carolina, who had sent a state-owned ship, the *Ad-Vance,* to sea for the purpose.[7]

Yet even Bulloch was unable to have the necessary number of steamers built. Faster and more daring measures were needed. One who saw the matter clearly was Colin J. McRae, who wrote from Europe: "Not a bale of cotton should be allowed to come out of the Country, not a pound of merchandise go in, except on Government account."[8] He had been appointed general agent for all the Confederacy's financial operations in Europe.[9]

On 6 February 1864, under strong pressure from President Davis, Congress approved two bills. The first forbade the importation of any unnecessary goods; the second forbade exporting any cotton, tobacco, sugar, molasses, or rice, as well as army and navy stores, except by special authorization from the president.[10] In addition, any ship that sailed out or in must put half of her cargo space at the disposal of the Confederate government and provide lists of her officers, crew, and passengers, all of whom must have regular passports. Moreover, the cargo must be available for inspection, and sea freights were to be set by the government. Within the Confederacy, all dealings in cotton must be centralized in the hands of a government agent, Colonel Thomas L. Bayne, at whose disposal the government put $20 million. He alone could decide what cotton would be shipped overseas in payment for goods supplied. Ships that refused to submit to these new rules were excluded from trade. All foreign trade of the Confederacy was thus nationalized.[11] To quote Richard P. Lester: "King Cotton was at last to be dethroned and made to work for his people."[12]

Returns were immediate. Confederate credit in Europe increased by leaps and bounds. The bonds of the Erlanger loan, which, after the defeats of Gettysburg and Vicksburg had been down to 42 per share, rose to 77, and Bulloch at last had the money to undertake his program of building six torpedo boats.[13]

Of still greater importance, the national blockade runners, in large part manned by naval officers and hands, shuttled cotton to Europe and war supplies to the Confederacy. Despite the utmost exertions by the Union navy, archival records show indisputably that blockade running was at its best, indeed reached its apex, in 1864. In that year, 19,503 bales of cotton left Wilmington and 5,900 left Charleston for a total of 25,403 bales, or almost 13 million pounds. Of these, 8,001 were shipped to Nassau, Bahamas, 1,954 to Bermuda, 164 to Halifax, Nova Scotia, 193 to Havana, and the rest elsewhere, but all eventually were destined for Europe.

In ten months, twenty-three ships left Wilmington, twenty-three from Charleston, and nine from other ports for a total of fifty-five trips with the loss of only five ships captured.[14] An estimate for the whole year raises the figures even higher. No accurate tally exists of the number of ships entering Confederate ports during the same period with priceless cargoes of war supplies, yet it appears that they can be reckoned at about the same number. By 25 October 1864, 1,400,000 pounds of lead, 1,850,000 pounds of saltpeter, 136,382 rifles, 420,000 pairs of shoes, and 292,000 blankets had been brought in,[15] as well as 53 cannons and more than 2,000 boxes of medicinals.[16]

In July 1864 George Alfred Trenholm succeeded Memminger as secretary of the treasury. Trenholm, the important Charleston merchant and businessman, had fully supported the Confederacy and kept at sea a fleet of blockade runners devoted to Confederate interests, to which he himself was totally dedicated. Upon assuming office, he resigned from all his business charges, including the celebrated Fraser, Trenholm and Company, and went to work in earnest for the government. This was a step in the right direction, even if it came too late.[17]

All these decisions—to be praised both for their foresight and for their daring—would not, in the end, retrieve the Confederacy's fortunes. Not the blockade but its backward agrarian economy doomed the South. The most deadly cause of the dearth that starved the soldiers on the front line was not the blockade but the collapse of the Southern railroad system. For this reason the armies were hungry "while foodstuffs rotted in the lower South,"[18] the inevitable consequence of the primitiveness and backwardness of Southern industry.

The near failure of the blockade as a weapon to win the war quickly was now admitted, albeit privately, by the Union secretary of the navy, Gideon Welles: "Wilmington seems to be almost an open port," he confided to his diary on 30 August 1864; and (an ominous sign for the Confederacy) he turned his mind again to the most deadly weapon of the U.S. Navy: amphibious attacks against the South.[19]

At the beginning of 1864, thanks to great efforts, labor, and the stubbornness of Mallory and his collaborators, the tools for the new strategy he had masterminded after mid-1862 were at last ready. It may well be said that in the first half of 1864 (and to an extent in the following months of that year) the small Confederate States Navy reached its peak, both as an effective force and in its successes.

On the far seas, the *Alabama* was operating along the Malabar Coast in the Indian Ocean. In Europe the *Florida,* after her repairs at Brest, returned to sea on 10 February for her second cruise.[20] Maffitt was no longer her captain. After recovering from the lingering effects of his long and severe illness, he had been detailed to command a blockade runner. The *Florida* was now entrusted to Lieutenant Commanding Charles Manigault Morris, a South Carolinian, rated by the *Florida*'s most prominent historian as experienced and competent, yet lacking Maffitt's daring and imagination.[21] The two most feared Confederate cruisers had resumed in earnest their commerce-destroying war, provoking panic among Northern shipowners. A few days later, on 17 February, the submarine *Hunley* sank the *Housatonic.*

It was in the area of ironclads, however, that Mallory's strategy reached its zenith. With unending exertions, he had succeeded in putting a considerable ironclad fleet afloat, at least in American waters, for in Europe another mishap threatened to kill any hope that the Confederate flag would fly over a squadron of seagoing armored vessels.

In France, indeed, all seemed well under way when a clerk in the Voruz firm, introducing himself as a certain Trémont (almost certainly a cover name) stepped into the office of the U.S. ambassador in Paris and offered to provide him documentary evidence that the vessels building in the shipyards at Bordeaux and Nantes were for the Confederate navy.[22]

Ambassador William L. Dayton sent the informer to John Bigelow (then general consul and later ambassador in Paris as a successor to Dayton), and Bigelow concluded the bargain with "Trémont," who asked for a "refund" of 20,000 francs ($5,000). Bigelow settled with him for 15,000 francs.[23]

Dayton then went to see the French foreign minister, Edouard Drouyn de Lhuys, and disclosed what the latter already knew: that Arman's two ironclads (which purportedly were being built for Egypt and already had their fake names of *Cheops* and *Sphinx*) were being constructed for the C.S. Navy. Drouyn de Lhuys feigned indignation, then began to argue.[24] In the end, Emperor Napoleon III, retreating from his previous stance, ordered that the four sloops not receive any weapon[25] and be sold (perhaps by a fake sale) to some neutral and that the two ironclads be denied the right to sail. It was a fierce blow, and Bulloch, for a while, gave way to despair.[26] Then he recovered and began to seek any possible way of getting his hands on the ships. He would, in the end, succeed in obtaining at least one ironclad on which to hoist the Confederate flag, but it would be too late.

Yet in American waters Mallory's unceasing activity was finally being rewarded. On the James River, two more ironclads, the *Fredericksburg* and the *Virginia II*, were put into commission in March 1864 and joined the *Richmond*.[27] Soon thereafter, at the Richmond Navy Yard, the keel was laid for a fourth powerful ironclad 217 feet long that would be named the *Texas*.[28]

The three ironclads already commissioned formed a powerful squadron, and the Union sailors feared their being put into action. In Washington, Gustavus Vasa Fox actually thought of employing the famous submarine of Brutus de Villeroy, the *Alligator*, against them, but that proved impossible.[29]

The 1864 campaign had brought the armies of Generals Grant and Butler to the shores of the James.[30] Moreover, the U.S. Navy had assured them protection by a powerful squadron commanded by Acting Rear Admiral S. P. Lee. Among other ships, he had four *Monitor*-class ironclads, fitted with 15-inch guns which could have destroyed the Confederate armored ships (with the possible exception of the *Virginia II*); he also had the former Confederate ironclad *Atlanta*. Nevertheless, the Union ships did not dare risk showing themselves along the middle stretch of the James and were protected with elaborate obstructions.[31]

On his side, Mallory was thinking about using his squadron offensively. Commodore John K. Mitchell, who soon relieved French Forrest as flag officer of the James River Squadron, had similar thoughts.[32]

On 6 May 1864 the Confederates scored another major success by sinking the U.S. gunboat *Commodore Jones* with an electrical torpedo. Mallory's strategy was becoming increasingly effective. He insisted that the squadron take the offensive. Although the engineers were slow in removing the obstructions,[33] at last on 24 May the Confederate ironclads descended the river and anchored near Chaffin's Bluff. From there, they proceeded to take a position a few thousand yards from the enemy fleet.[34]

Two days later shots were exchanged with the Union navy. Then, in cooperation with land forces, the Confederate squadron went into action several times, effectively bombarding enemy troops. In several cases, as when it drove the enemy from the important position of Signal Hill and during General Lee's offensive against Fort Harrison, its participation was decisive.[35] Mallory had good reason to be satisfied with such success. Almost for the first time, Union troops had been defeated and scattered by fire from the heavy guns of a Confederate ship, not vice versa.

Even Charleston Harbor now appeared safe. At the beginning of 1864 the local squadron had been strengthened by the addition of the powerful ironclad *Charleston*. She became the flagship, commanded by an ironclad veteran, Captain Isaac N. Brown, of *Arkansas* fame.[36] It was hoped that the squadron, now led by Flag Officer John R. Tucker, would be joined by a fourth vessel, one of the most powerful ironclads built by the South, the *Columbia*, 216 feet long, with six heavy cannons and 6-inch armor. Her engines were being built by the Naval Iron Works at Columbus, Georgia.[37]

At Wilmington, the ironclad *North Carolina* had at the beginning of 1864 been joined by her sister ship, the *Raleigh*. At Savannah, Georgia, the *Savannah* was operating to Mallory's satisfaction, but it was Mobile, Alabama, and the North Carolina sounds that concerned the secretary.

Mobile Bay was not easy to defend, and the city, which before the war had been a major port for cotton trade and now was engaged in active blockade running, was a likely Union target. Yet the Confederate building program that should have placed a sizable ironclad squadron afloat slowed because of the usual reason: the lamentable industrial backwardness of the South. Iron was lacking,[38] labor was lacking. Although men worked day and night, work slowed down.

The ironclads being built in the Mobile area (excluding the two floating batteries already launched) numbered six. Of these, the *Tennessee* waited for her guns and crew; the *Nashville*, launched the previous June at Montgomery, had been towed to Mobile to be fitted out. She was 271 feet long and looked powerful. An observer said she was "a tremendous monster. . . . The *Tennessee* is insignificant compared with her."[39] Iron for her armor was lacking, however, and Buchanan was compelled to suspend work on her and give priority to the *Tennessee*.[40]

As for the other four ironclads, the second laid down at Selma (which would have been a twin of the *Nashville*) was abandoned because her launching went wrong.[41] Work on the other three, building on the Tombigbee, was slow. The site chosen for the shipyard, at Owen Bluff, was unhealthy, supplies were slow in coming, and labor was scarce. One of the three was launched at the end of 1863, thanks to workers sent from the army.[42] It was clear that the great squadron planned for the defense of Mobile Bay would be limited to the *Tennessee*, at least for the first months of 1864.

Work continued in earnest on the *Tennessee*. In January she received her battery, provided by the Selma Naval Foundry.[43] Now two problems had to be solved: enlist the crew and officers, and get her over the bar so that she could ply the bay's waters.

Buchanan wanted a commanding officer who was active and energetic and who would prefer the hardships aboard the ironclad to the leisure of life ashore.[44] At last he succeeded in securing the able, experienced, and daring Lieutenant Commanding James D. Johnston as well as several officers. In most cases these—unlike Johnston—were young and inexperienced,[45] a defect that would become apparent later, at crucial moments.

Thanks to the good services of Secretary of War Seddon, of General Dabney H. Maury, military commander of the district, and of General Leonidas Polk, commanding forces in Alabama, 110 men were transferred to the navy.[46] Buchanan, who was a strict disciplinarian, had to transform those landsmen into sailors.

Last to be solved was how to get the *Tennessee* over the bar. This was no trifle. The estuaries of the rivers that flow into Mobile Bay had never had more than 9.5 feet depth of water, whereas the ironclad's draft was 13 feet. When loaded with coal, supplies, water, and ammunition, she would draw up to 14 feet. Yet Buchanan had been compelled to mount her cannons aboard even though their weight increased the draft by more than 4 inches because the work required was so complicated that it could not be done far from land. Meanwhile, the new sailors, who had never seen a big gun before, had to be drilled.[47]

Should the enemy try to enter Mobile Bay before the *Tennessee* had passed the bar, Buchanan had decided to offer battle wherever the ship was. Everybody in Mobile, throughout Alabama, and elsewhere in the South hoped that a single ship could defeat a fleet (the old delusion of the South); therefore, thought the admiral, an attempt must be made. Otherwise the sailors aboard would be pilloried for the rest of their lives.[48]

Before the ironclad would reach navigable water, she must sail down the bay for some twenty nautical miles. Caissons called "camels" in sailor lingo were therefore built. Attached to her hull and filled with air, they would lift her. It was neither a speedy nor a simple undertaking. The first "camels" were inadequate, the second ones were destroyed by fire in the shop. At last, on 18 May 1864, the *Tennessee* reached the water of the bay.[49]

The ironclad anchored ten miles from Fort Morgan together with the two gunboats *Selma* and *Morgan,* and on 22 May Admiral Buchanan hoisted his pennant over the *Tennessee.* The ship had been put into commission on 2 April.[50] She greatly improved the defenses of Mobile Bay. Her enemy Farragut called her "formidable." Alfred Thayer Mahan termed her "the most powerful ironclad built, from the keel up, by the Confederacy."[51]

She displaced 1,273 tons, was 209 feet long with a 48-foot beam, and was fitted with a casemate 79 feet long. The internal structure of the latter was of yellow pine 18.5 inches thick, plus 4 inches of oak; 1.5-inch bolts were driven through her entire shield (both inward backing and iron plates 5 inches thick, increasing to 6 inches forward) and riveted inside. Her outer decks were armored with 2-inch sheet iron. The lower reaches of the casemate descended under the waterline and formed a solid angle that would make it very difficult to ram the ship. She carried a formidable battery of six rifled Brookes: two of 7.5 inches forward and astern, pivoted so that they could be fired either from a porthole in front of them or from two ports on the sides. She carried the other four, of 6 inches, in broadsides. The plate, made of iron provided by Alabama mines, cast by Shelby, and rolled in Atlanta, could withstand the most terrible pounding by enemy cannons.[52]

Nevertheless, the *Tennessee* had some serious flaws that would impair her at critical times. First, even though in her engine trials she had logged eight knots, when fully loaded she would barely make six. Second, her port shutters, five inches thick, were hinged high so that under enemy fire they might fall and obstruct the portholes.[53] Last and most serious, through some unbelievable oversight, the tiller chains passed over the deck astern and were therefore fully exposed to enemy fire. Attempts to remedy this defect had failed.[54]

She was a very powerful ironclad—but she was alone. This was a far cry from Mallory's plan for the defense of Mobile Bay, which could not be wholly implemented for the reasons already stressed. Nevertheless, the *Tennessee* was a formidable obstacle which the enemy would find across its path on the day it decided to attack.

The other area of concern was the sounds of North Carolina.[55] There the Federals had conducted their first amphibious operations, and now they threatened the heart of the state. To check these dangers—and possibly to reverse a situation that had become dangerous—General Robert E. Lee considered a great combined sea-land operation in which the main burden would fall upon ironclads. His letter of 2 January 1864 was the starting point of a plan that, overcoming extreme obstacles and even failed attempts, would finally result in the last great Confederate naval victory.[56]

Amid a thousand hindrances, work along the Neuse and Roanoke rivers proceeded without a break. To save time, Mallory detailed Commander James W. Cooke and Assistant Naval Constructor William A. Graves to assume direct responsibility for the fitting out of the *Albemarle;* Cooke would command the ironclad.[57] Lieutenant Benjamin P. Loyall was commissioned to command the *Neuse.*[58]

As usual, the problem was the late arrival of iron. At the beginning of

February 1864 Mallory sent Lieutenant Robert D. Minor to Kinston and Edward's Ferry. He reported that the *Neuse*'s engines had been installed, but her armor was incomplete. Although in an advanced stage, the *Albemarle* still lacked her guns and part of her armor.[59] There was also interference by the army, which was monopolizing railroad cars, thus leaving the iron in Wilmington for lack of transportation.[60] All this caused an enormous slowdown that would prove fatal for at least one of the two ironclads.

As was now customary, crews were made up of soldiers who, transformed into sailors, were to serve big cannons.[61] This time the army had willingly sent enough volunteers: it needed the help of the ironclads for an attempt to retake New Bern and Plymouth.[62]

Meanwhile, the rivers were falling by almost twelve inches daily.[63] It was clearly a question of now or never. On 12 April the general headquarters of the Confederate army ordered Brigadier General Robert F. Hoke to assume command of the forces that would operate against Plymouth[64] with the understanding that because the *Albemarle* was almost ready whereas the *Neuse* was not, the simultaneous attack on New Bern would be canceled. General Hoke planned to move against Plymouth with three brigades, about seven thousand effectives, and some thirty field guns.[65]

Naval support was required because the enemy had made Plymouth into a formidable fortress. Garrisoned by about three thousand Federal soldiers[66] commanded by General Henry W. Wessells, with many guns including a dozen heavy ones, the small town was completely surrounded by a trench system with ditches and chevaux-de-frise. There were also many redoubts and forts, of which Fort Williams, located at the center, was the strongest, capable of firing on any approaching road.[67]

On its river side the fortress was protected by a naval squadron composed of the gunboats *Miami* (eight guns), *Southfield* (six guns), and *Ceres* and *Whitehead* (four guns each): a total of twenty-two heavy guns, among them 9-inch Dahlgrens and 100-pounder Parrotts that could rain a withering fire on the attacking troops.[68]

On 16 April General Hoke went to Hamilton on the Roanoke River, where the *Albemarle* was being fitted out, and begged for Cooke's help. On board the ironclad men were still at work; Cooke had succeeded in gathering the necessary iron, even requisitioning scraps from nearby farms (which earned him the nickname of "ironmonger captain").[69]

The most valuable help had been given him by Peter Evans Smith, who owned the cornfield where the ironclad was being built and who was a loyal Confederate. To be sure, the South had no modern industry; yet it possessed several *bricoleurs,* well endowed with ingenuity and initiative, masters of the art of improvising. Smith was one of them. He had put together the sawmills and blacksmith shops; he now invented a kind of "helicoidal puncher" that made it possible to drill the armor plates in four minutes instead of twenty so that they might be quickly bolted to the ship.[70]

Thus except for some details, the ironclad was ready for action and capable of helping the army. She looked imposing; a Southern lady from nearby said she appeared bulky. The ship was 152 feet long, propelled by two engines of two hundred horsepower each and twin screws, with a draft of nine feet of water. Her battery consisted of two Brooke 8-inch rifles on pivots, which, through several portholes, could fire in any direction. The framework of the ship was made of solid pine, eight to ten inches thick with armor four inches thick. From her prow, built solid for eighteen feet of strong oak, the armor protruded, forming a powerful ram.[71]

Hoke was truly impressed by the ironclad and asked Cooke to collaborate on the attack planned for Plymouth. The captain at first hesitated. Then, upon considering the importance of his ship in the difficult action ahead, he answered that, finished or not, she would take part in the battle. It was the night of 16 April 1864.[72]

At about 2:00 P.M. on the seventeenth, General Hoke's gray battalions arrived in front of Plymouth and made contact with the enemy, which immediately opened an intense artillery fire.[73] The next day, the eighteenth, Hoke attacked along the whole front. Under an infernal fire, the Confederates advanced slowly. Although they captured one of the forts, the isolated Fort Wessells, their losses were heavy and included the colonel commanding the column. Elsewhere the Confederates received such a hailstorm of bullets, shot, and shell that they were pinned to the ground.[74] Even worse, the U.S. naval squadron battered the Confederate battle line with its heavy guns—with terrible effects. Where was the ironclad? And why did she not arrive?[75]

The Federals (who were aware of the *Albemarle*) were very concerned lest the awesome ship might arrive at the scene of battle. The U.S. squadron was commanded by a young, daring officer, Commander Charles W. Flusser, who anticipated that the ironclad could arrive at any moment; he had resolved to fight her and give no quarter. In him, Cooke would meet a worthy opponent.[76]

Cooke had wasted no time. On the night of the seventeenth he had put the *Albemarle* into commission and had immediately weighed anchor.[77] Work was still under way aboard. The ship was towing a raft fitted with a blacksmith shop. While the crew completed their drill at the guns, workers placed and bolted the last armor plates.

Unfortunately, the ironclad's engines had been installed by the *bricoleur* method, and toward 10:00 P.M. the bolts that held the main joint of the central propeller folded. The ship stopped. Men went frantically to work to repair it, but six hours were lost. The ironclad moved only to have the head of the rudder post break, causing another delay of four hours.[78]

At last, after having lost ten hours, at dawn on the eighteenth, the ironclad could move while last-minute work was done aboard. At 10:00 P.M. of that day she dropped anchor three nautical miles above Plymouth. There the battle raged, and the thundering report of heavy guns filled the air.[79]

Cooke sent an officer to explore the obstructions placed by the U.S. Navy. The answer was disappointing: it was impossible to overcome the tangle of torpedoes, poles, and sunken boats that blocked the channel. Fortunately, Gilbert Elliott, the young and energetic constructor who had started building the ironclad, had asked to be authorized to come down with Cooke as a volunteer aide. He now asked for, and got, permission to examine the obstructions and in the darkness of the night moved to do so in a small boat with three sailors.

Elliott has left us a valuable record of that nighttime enterprise. With their oars muffled, and scarcely breathing, the four moved silently in the dark. They kept the boat in the shadow of the riverbank to avoid being sighted by enemies they could see close by, who were busy evacuating noncombatants by boat. They managed to pass unseen by a Union battery of heavy guns, including a 200-pounder Parrott that would have been able to smash the small boat into splinters. Using a rod, Elliott and his crew began to probe the obstructions, at the risk of causing an explosion that would have blown them up. With great joy they noticed that the night had brought a considerable freshet which had raised the level of water about ten feet over the obstructions.[80]

The ironclad could just pass over them as long as it stayed in the middle of the current. Cooke immediately roused the crew and ordered general quarters. At 2:30 A.M. of the nineteenth the ironclad steered silently toward the enemy.

At sunrise she passed Fort Gray, which fired its heavy guns at her—among them a 200-pounder—with the only effect on the powerful ironclad that of a rain of pebbles.[81] Without bothering to answer, the ship steamed forward. It did not take her long to reach the stretch of water before the city. There, with his array of ships, Commander Flusser awaited the Confederates. The Union commanding officer had used loose chains to fasten his flagship, the *Miami,* to the *Southfield.* He hoped to entice the slower ironclad as though between the sides of pincers and smash her by having his big guns fire point-blank at the *Albemarle.*

Yet Cooke was not a man to be caught. Quickly turning, he shot the

Albemarle ahead at full steam and struck the *Southfield* with her sharp ram amidships. With an awful roar, the bow of the ironclad crashed almost ten feet into the hull of the enemy ship, which rapidly began to sink, dragging with her the *Albemarle,* which had not yet succeeded in disengaging, so that water poured into the ports of the casemate. In this grim situation, Cooke kept his crew calm until the enemy ship touched the bottom of the river and turned over on its side, freeing the ironclad.

Now a fierce artillery fight began with the *Miami,* whose projectiles bounced off the *Albemarle*'s armor while she inflicted frightful damage and losses upon the enemy. When the gallant Flusser fell dead, the *Miami* with the two minor gunboats fled down the river.

Cooke had won, but he did not pursue. He had much else to do. Now the ironclad began to pound the enemy fortifications on the reverse side with her heavy guns.[82] She continued her merciless firing all day of the nineteenth and through the following night. At dawn of the twentieth the Confederate infantry moved to attack while the *Albemarle* supported them by bombarding the Union troops. Fighting was still very heavy, yet now only Fort Williams, where General Wessells was in command, still resisted. The Confederate artillery fire (especially by the two heavy guns of the ironclad) made it impossible for the Federals to man the ramparts. At 10:00 A.M. of the twentieth, with a heavy heart, General Wessells raised the white flag.[83]

Into Confederate hands fell almost three thousand prisoners, twenty-eight cannons, five thousand rifles, seven hundred barrels of flour, and a large amount of supplies and ammunition. Most valuable for the navy were three hundred tons of coal. Moreover, the Confederates had taken the naval base of Plymouth from which they hoped their ironclads might move to drive the enemy from the sounds.[84]

It was a major victory, one, as the enemy correctly observed, in which Plymouth would not have been taken had not the Confederate ironclad been present.[85] Again, as at Hampton Roads and Vicksburg, Confederate navy men had shown themselves masters at planning and conducting combined operations in which the power of the ironclad, so strongly asserted by Mallory, had been the decisive factor. Richmond and the Confederacy exulted. Congress voted a solemn address of thanks and named Hoke a major general and Cooke a commander.[86]

On the front line, however, nobody was resting on his laurels. On 26 April Hoke was already marching toward the other Union base at Washington, North Carolina, and on the twenty-seventh the enemy evacuated it.[87] Loss of sea power in the zone made it impossible for Union forces to hold the base. With only one ironclad, used with imagination and daring, the Confederates had won a dazzling victory. Unfortunately, it would be their last.

Hoke now thought of eliminating the last and strongest base of the bridgehead: New Bern. For this operation the other ironclad, the *Neuse,* should cooperate.[88] She, too, was ready, and on 22 April she weighed anchor and began to descend the river that was her namesake. Unfortunately, she had waited too long: the river had fallen so much that after half a mile she ran fast aground on a sandbank. This was a terrible blow to the Confederate authorities. President Davis demanded that supreme efforts be made to refloat her.[89] Confederate sailors tried every way they could to free her—in vain. The water had fallen seven feet in four days and continued to fall. The ship could not move until the water began to rise again.[90]

General Beauregard, who had recently assumed command of all forces operating in southern Virginia and North Carolina,[91] did not want to give up the opportunity. It was high time for action: if the *Neuse* was inoperable, use could be made of the victorious *Albemarle.*[92]

The ironclad was to embark on a very risky venture. She must leave the Roanoke River for the sea, cross the sounds infested by enemy ships, then sail up the Neuse estuary, which was full of obstructions. Yet the stakes were so high that Cooke decided to play the dangerous game. He knew that there were no enemy ironclads in the sounds and believed that the other ships could not stand up against the *Albemarle,* or at least could not damage her severely.[93]

The U.S. Navy feared the ironclad. Unable to send her own armored ships into the sounds (their draft prevented their crossing the Hatteras Inlet, even if Gustavus Vasa Fox was thinking of this and had therefore consulted Ericsson),[94] Fox had concentrated many gunboats inside the sounds and had detailed to command the squadron a gallant officer, trained by Farragut, Captain Melancton Smith.[95]

Smith was not one to fall back without a fight. His squadron was composed of four large gunboats: the *Mattabesett,* ten guns (among them two rifled 100-pounder Parrotts); *Sassacus,* twelve guns; *Wyalusing,* fourteen guns; *Miami,* eight guns; and three smaller ones: *Whitehead,* four guns; *Commodore Hull,* six guns; and *Ceres,* two guns. The total of fifty-six cannons included eight rifled 100-pounder Parrotts.[96] Those ships were not armored, but they were a formidable array against the *Albemarle,* which had only two guns.

Upon hoisting her anchors at noon on 5 May 1864 the ironclad moved, followed by two small tenders, the *Cotton Plant* and the *Bombshell,* and steered for her second battle. The latter, a Federal ship, had been sunk during the battle of Plymouth, then raised. About three hours later the

Albemarle passed by the Union advanced post, which gave the alarm. Smith immediately ordered his squadron forward, the four big gunboats in line ahead, the minor ones in another line, protected by the larger ships. His order was to engage the ironclad as closely as possible and open fire at point-blank range, with the objective of crushing her with the enormous superiority of his metal.[97] At 5:00 P.M. the *Albemarle* opened fire at about eight hundred yards. The battle had begun.[98]

The ironclad's second shell struck the flagship *Mattabesett,* destroying part of her rigging and wounding some of the gunners forward. At this point, the second Northern gunboat in line, the *Sassacus,* fired a broadside from her big guns at close range at the ironclad. It had no effect. When the *Albemarle* then tried to ram the *Mattabesett,* the latter, with superior speed, managed to avoid what could have been a mortal blow.

Meanwhile, the *Sassacus,* which had opened distance to capture the small tender *Bombshell,* turned to starboard and suddenly steamed at full speed toward the ironclad and with a blow that "seemed an earthquake" drove her prow against her side and made her heel fearfully. Many of the crew, among them the captain, were hurled to the floor, water entered the portholes, and the lights went out. Cooke's calm voice heartened his crew, and Confederate gunners fired point-blank at the rammer a shell that crashed into her and caused one of her boilers to burst. The gunboat had already suffered severe damage during the ramming: the sides of her bow had been wrecked, together with some of her stanchions. The explosion of a boiler disabled her for good. Unable to steer, she drifted helplessly downriver.[99]

The battle raged. The ironclad now targeted the enemy ships with well-aimed shell and shot, until the *Wyalusing,* almost sinking, withdrew. Fighting was suspended at 7:30 P.M. The Union sailors had had enough. Their ships had suffered serious damage; the *Sassacus* and the *Wyalusing* were disabled, the first reduced almost to a wreck. Their losses were five dead and twenty-four wounded.

Still, the *Albemarle* could not continue her cruise. Her smokestack was almost destroyed, causing pressure to fall to near zero, thus risking her being immobilized while under enemy fire. Only by throwing oil and greasy materials on the fires did Cooke succeed in raising the pressure to the minimum necessary to permit the ship to move.

The vulnerability of their funnels was one of the weakest points of Confederate ironclads. This problem had seriously hindered the action of the first *Virginia* and in the future would have even more serious consequences. Moreover, one of the *Albemarle*'s cannons had had its muzzle shot away, thus reducing the firepower of the ironclad to a single gun. A respite was needed.[100] Cooke, therefore, had his ship anchor off Plymouth for repairs. He was still determined to move on New Bern as soon as possible. Cooke's failure to arrive in front of New Bern did not affect the campaign, however, because it had been called off by direct order from President Davis.[101]

What had happened? On 4 May General Hoke had invested the fortress and demanded its surrender. If this were not accepted, he was ready to attack and was sure of success.[102] But other serious events were occurring. Indeed, on the same day, the enemy loosed a gigantic offensive on all fronts. In northern Virginia General Grant had crossed the Rapidan with more than one hundred thousand men. Worse, the Union Army of the James, commanded by General Butler and escorted by formidable naval forces, had sailed up the James River to threaten the Confederate capital.

General Beauregard was therefore compelled to order Hoke to call off his offensive and quickly take most of his troops toward the new front, leaving the zone protected by only a handful of men.[103] The appalling dearth of fighting men compelled Confederate headquarters to face the threat in North Carolina with scanty troops so as to divert all manpower available to the main fronts.

To oppose any possible attack by the enemy, there remained the *Albemarle.* As long as she was at Plymouth, no attempt by the Federals to resume their invasion from the sea could succeed. Protected by her iron sides, the people of tidewater North Carolina could enjoy relative peace. Moreover, the Confederate soldiers, fighting against heavy odds on the Virginia front, could be sure that no enemy could come from the Carolina sounds.[104]

Mallory's new naval strategy was at work, and it now extended along the whole maritime front, from the James River to Louisiana waters. Twelve ironclads were in commission, an almost insuperable obstacle for the enemy. Even though the *Albemarle* had been compelled to give up her attack against New Bern, the battle of 5 May had shown that she was supreme in those waters and that the enemy squadron had had to yield to the ironclad.

In the meantime, probably with the objective of supporting the action of the *Albemarle,* another ironclad had gotten under way during these same days. On the late afternoon of 6 May, escorted by two small gunboats, the *Yadkin* and the *Equator,* the ironclad *Raleigh* had sailed out of Wilmington. It was a risky enterprise because there, too, the river was falling and the ship drew too much water so that it had been necessary to lighten her considerably to cross the bar.[105]

Around 8:00 P.M., the ironclad suddenly appeared in front of two Union blockading vessels, the *Britannia* and the *Nansemond.* The *Britan-*

nia was the first to open fire. Then, seeing that her projectiles had no effect on the carapace of the *Raleigh*, she wisely decided to move out and disappeared. Nightfall protected her as well as the *Nansemond*, which exchanged shots with the *Raleigh* at about 11:45 P.M. At dawn all but four of the Union ships were gone, and the battle with them resumed. The USS *Howquah* was hit in her funnel and saved herself from destruction by fleeing. Seeing that their shot and shell were useless, the *Nansemond*, the *Kansas,* and the *Mount Vernon* reversed course and retreated toward the high sea. The fight had taken place at a fairly great distance for the day's ordnance, which was why the slower ironclad did not get close enough to sink the enemy ships.

Now the *Raleigh* practically commanded the sea around her. About 8:00 A.M., she reversed course and steamed back to Wilmington. Unfortunately, on reentering the river she ran hard aground on a falling tide and could not be refloated. Stuck fast, she broke her back and was lost. The Confederates succeeded in rescuing only her guns and armor plates.[106]

It was an unlucky incident, most probably caused by the weakness of the hull. Yet to the U.S. Navy, which ignored the misfortune the Confederates had suffered, the appearance of the ironclad left a deep and lasting impression. All the commanders of ships who had had anything to do with her agreed in characterizing her as "formidable and dangerous." That fear certainly contributed to keeping the Union ships at a safe distance from the port that was so important for blockade running. In this sense it may be said that the *Raleigh* was not lost in vain.[107] The effect produced on the U.S. Navy was such that fifteen days later it was still studying plans to "destroy" the *Raleigh* by a surprise attack, wholly ignorant that she was already disabled.[108]

The activity of Confederate ironclads was indeed rewarding. In June, a concerned commander of U.S. naval forces on the James River asked for more ironclads of the *Monitor* class because the Confederate ones had been firing with telling effect on his ships.[109]

In sum, it may be said that the Confederate ironclads, overcoming great obstacles, had succeeded in implementing the defense strategy that Mallory had assigned them. Elsewhere, however, the C.S. Navy was also undertaking daring offensive actions.

SEVENTEEN

The Commandos of
the Confederate States Navy

It was difficult for the Confederate Navy to conduct offensive operations. After the possibility of obtaining ironclads from Europe faded, it had to fight under conditions of overwhelming inferiority and increased enemy pressure. The loss of any hope of turning the tables on the high seas shifted the emphasis to new initiatives that would surprise the enemy and make him more circumspect.

Mallory and his collaborators began to embrace the concept of partisan warfare at sea, the weapon of the feeble against the stronger. From this idea would emerge for the first time in history what in World War II would be commando warfare, waged by Confederate amphibious raiders.

Occasional attacks on enemy ships had been made in Chesapeake Bay,[1] but the effective organization of commando operations was the work of two men: Commander John Taylor Wood and Acting Master John Yates Beall. Wood served aboard the ironclad *Virginia,* then was detailed to the coast batteries at Drewry's Bluff, where, after the fight against Union ironclads he found service boring.[2] Wood, therefore, went to Mallory with a plan for the organization of sea-raiding patrols. Small, fast boats, no larger than a small wherry, capable of carrying fifteen to twenty men and their weapons and food supplies for one week would be needed, as well as wagons to transport the boats overland. They would be put into the water only near the place of a planned attack.[3] The tactics Wood proposed were described by Admiral Lepotier: "The attack and the reaction are so much more rapid and brutal as the theater is reduced; and, in such a case, surprise cannot be achieved except during the darkness of the night."[4]

Wood's raiders made their first surprise attack on the night of 7 October 1862, capturing and destroying the U.S. steamer transport *Francis Elmore* on the Potomac.[5] They had moved covertly. Wood had chosen some fifteen sailors from the James River Squadron and had with him a couple of his boats on wagons, as well as an ambulance. The quick and stealthy action opened up the possibilities of commando operations.[6]

Wood soon decided to strike again. On 28 October 1862, by night, he and his raiders boarded, captured, and destroyed the Federal merchantman *Alleghanian*.[7] This new exploit dismayed the enemy. Secretary Welles urged all in the Union navy to be vigilant and alert.[8]

Wood meanwhile had been commissioned a colonel in the C.S. Army.[9] A Confederate law allowed any navy or army officer to hold commissions in both services, and the amphibious character of his operations qualified Wood for such dual status. He planned another surprise attack, this time against an enemy warship. To assist in the operation he chose Second Lieutenant Francis L. Hoge, who would soon become a most capable commando leader.[10]

On the night of 19 August 1863 Wood's raiding party, composed of eighty-two officers and men, moved silently out of Richmond. The operation had been prepared with such secrecy that not even Secretary Mallory knew its objectives or the exact time of departure.[11] Four boats were carried on wagons. Among the raiders were engineers, stokers, gunners, and naval surgeons so that if the attempt were fully successful, Wood could put a full Confederate crew aboard the enemy ship they seized.[12]

The enemy had been warned about these secret operations since the end of July.[13] Yet when a series of untoward events compelled Wood to delay his coup for a day or so, the enemy may have slackened his watch.[14]

Finally, Wood established a base along a stream that flowed into the Rappahannock River and there, on 21 August, he met Colonel Thomas L. Rosser, commanding the Fifth Virginia Cavalry Regiment, which, by secret orders, had been sent to support the raiders.[15] It was decided that the Confederate cavalrymen would base themselves in the small village of Urbanna, on the Rappahannock, and be ready to help Wood.

Wood moved on the night of 23 August. The weather was bad: heavy clouds darkened the moon, the wind howled among the big, black trees on shore, and high waves shook the small boats like straws. On that stormy night it seemed that all the powers of nature were colluding with the enemy to thwart the operation. Suddenly, by the gleam of lightning bolts, the bows of two enemy gunboats at anchor were sighted about four hundred feet ahead. They were the *Satellite,* armed with a 32-pounder gun and a 12-pounder howitzer, and the *Reliance,* carrying a rifled 30-pounder Parrott and a 24-pounder howitzer. Each ship's crew numbered about forty men.[16] The ships were so close together that the attack had to be simultaneous. Wood with two boats made for the first, while Hoge with the other two steered for the second. Although the alert was given by Union sentries, it came too late because of the darkness. The raiders were swiftly on board engaging in a fierce fight with the crewmen who, half awake and half dressed, rushed from their berths grasping whatever weapon was at hand. When the Union midshipman Rudolph Sommers, who led the resistance, fell seriously wounded, the crew surrendered, and the Confederates took possession of the *Satellite.*[17]

The fight on the *Reliance* was fiercer, either because Hoge fell seriously wounded upon reaching the deck or because the Federal captain, Henry Walters, led an immediate counterattack. Finally, when Walters was wounded, Midshipman H. S. Cooke, who had replaced Hoge and received two bullets in the side, succeeded in overcoming the Northerners just as a supporting boat sent by Wood approached through the waves. The Union lost four dead and four wounded; the Confederate victory cost three wounded.[18]

Assuming command of both ships, Wood locked the prisoners in the holds and steered for his base at Urbanna. There he turned the prisoners over to Rosser and gave shelter to the wounded of both sides. Rosser gave him thirty sharpshooters to complete the crews.

Wood decided to use the captured gunboats to attack enemy shipping. Unfortunately, the engines of the *Reliance* were out of order, perhaps sabotaged by Northerners during the fight, and the bunkers of both ships were almost empty. Therefore Wood took only the *Satellite* and a few hours later again plowed into the rough waters of the bay. On the second day he captured three enemy sailing merchantmen, the schooners *Golden Rod,* *Coquette,* and *Two Brothers,* the first of which was loaded with valuable coal, and towed them to Urbanna.[19]

Wood returned to the stormy waters of the bay the next day, but clouds of smoke indicating that many large warships were closing on him persuaded him to return to Urbanna. There, after setting the *Golden Rod* afire because of her deep draft, he sailed up the Rappahannock as far as Port Royal with his small flotilla, which defiantly flew the Confederate flag and was hailed by both the local people and Southern soldiers.

The enemy controlled the other riverbank, however, and the flotilla could not go back because powerful Union ships were closing the circle around it. After recovering everything valuable on board (especially the ordnance), Wood resolved to scuttle both gunboats and schooners by burning them and go back to Richmond with his small boats loaded on wagons.[20]

The gallant operation triggered great excitement in Richmond. Hoge, who was recovering from his wound, was, at Wood's recommendation, commissioned a lieutenant.[21] Wood's enterprise caused dismay and concern among the enemies, who feared him as a constant threat.

The other organizer of commando warfare, John Yates Beall, was born in 1835 at Walnut Grove, Virginia, to a family of wealthy farmers. After studying law at the University of Virginia, Beall had volunteered for the Confederate army at the outbreak of the Civil War and fought in the Shenandoah Valley in General Turner Ashby's command.[22] Severely wounded in the chest, he was discharged from the army, but he still wanted to fight for the South. His wound was slow in healing. The creation of the volunteer navy offered him the opportunity to rejoin the service.

Secretary Mallory, to whom he explained his plans, gave him the warrant of acting master in the navy, and he enlisted a small commando of volunteers, some twenty men with two boats: a white one called the *Swan* and a black one named the *Crow*.[23]

Beall was suffering from tuberculosis, and he did not intend to waste time. On the night of 18 September 1863, after several minor actions, he captured the U.S. sailing merchantman *Mary Anne* in Chesapeake Bay and then, during a fierce hurricane that almost sank his two small boats, the schooner *Alliance*. On the next night three other schooners fell into his hands: the *Horseman, Pearsall,* and *Alexander.*

Beall transferred his raiders to the *Alliance* and tried to run the blockade during the night and bring her into Southern waters. Unfortunately, the ship ran aground and had to be scuttled, but part of the valuable cargo was salvaged and taken to Richmond, while three enemy gunboats vainly chased the raiders.[24]

Around 10 November 1863 Beall put his boats back into the water and that very night captured a schooner near the enemy coast. But at daylight, the enemy, rushing in from land and sea, captured him and his men. The Union rejoicing was immense: at last, the "notorious" commander Beall was in their hands.[25] In violation of the law of nations, Union authorities had Beall and his men, all of whom were regularly enlisted in the Confederate navy, put in irons and planned to try them as pirates. They would have done so but for the reaction of the Richmond authorities. President Davis had an equal number of Union prisoners, officers and sailors, placed in irons and threatened reprisal against them for any treatment contrary to the laws of war visited upon Beall and his officers and sailors. On 5 May 1864 Beall and most of his men were exchanged with Northern prisoners.[26] Upon returning to Richmond, Beall began planning new and daring actions.

John Taylor Wood meanwhile had moved his center of operations along the coast of North Carolina, in part at the request of President Davis and General R. E. Lee, who commanded that area, as well as Virginia,[27] and, above all, of Secretary Mallory, who kept the commandos ready, drilled, and well organized.[28]

In the preceding chapters, I have stressed the strategic importance of the North Carolina seacoast where the penetration of U.S. amphibious forces was particularly threatening and dangerous. Mallory thought that the two ironclads *Neuse* and *Albemarle* would solve the problem. The *Albemarle* proved his claim by quickly sweeping away the enemy forces. Yet construction on the ironclads had proceeded slowly.[29] Lee therefore decided to strike a blow at New Bern without waiting for the ironclads. This would turn out to be a serious mistake. In January 1863, Generals D. H. Hill and J. J. Pettigrew had made an attempt to drive the enemy from New Bern without support from the C.S. Navy. The two Union gunboats in place had bombarded the Confederate troops with their heavy guns, forcing them to retreat. Now Lee, without waiting for the ironclads, trusted in Wood's raiders. If they could seize one of the enemy naval vessels, perhaps the expedition would succeed.

Whatever Mallory might have thought about this plan, he agreed to cooperate. On 16 January 1864 he had Hoge sent to Wilmington, North Carolina, to begin preparing the boats required for the operation.[30]

Hoge's was the first party of raiders to be put in motion. But Wood decided, along with the secretary, that Hoge (who had specialized in torpedo service)[31] should be assigned the difficult task of choosing and organizing all the raiding parties. The Wilmington party would be put under the command of Lieutenant George W. Gift.[32]

Hoge was busy organizing the second party at Richmond: forty-five men picked carefully from among the sailors of the James River Squadron, together with four midshipmen. Hoge saw to it that each man was armed with rifle, revolver, and ax, dressed in the best-quality clothes including a sailor's pea coat, and provided with a blanket, three days' food rations, and forty cartridges.[33] The party would be commanded by Lieutenant Benjamin P. Loyall,[34] who would soon thereafter command the ironclad *Neuse*.

The third party was formed in Charleston and would come over together with that from Wilmington. In all, including a group of marines commanded by Captain Thomas S. Wilson,[35] the commando unit contained 33 officers and 220 enlisted men. Because the commandos' movements had to be speedy and secret, they usually traveled by night. This time the boats were loaded on railroad cars.

The parties were to meet at Kinston, North Carolina, on the Neuse River, where the ironclad of that name was being built. Upon arriving there, Wood was unpleasantly surprised to find neither the party from Wilmington nor that from Charleston. Gift had had great difficulty obtaining boats, crews, weapons, and supplies.[36]

At last, he too arrived in Kinston and met Wood, who had let his boats sail a few miles downriver because he did not want them to be too conspicuous in Kinston. Now the whole commando was united. It had twelve boats and two large launches (brought by Gift), each of which could carry up to forty-five men and a 45-pounder field howitzer. It was the evening of 31 January 1864.[37]

Dividing his flotilla into two groups, Wood chose Lieutenant Loyall as his second in command. Then the boats began to move silently. Because of their size, Gift's launches required a lot of time to be unloaded from the railroad cars and put into the water. Gift remained behind with eighty men and the order to join Wood on the morrow.[38]

The distance between Kinston and New Bern is about thirty miles as the crow flies. Because of the meandering of the river, the boats had to cover double that distance. Everything was silent except the swash of the oars. When the night shadows fell, Wood realized that he had arrived a bit upriver from New Bern; therefore, he had the boats beached and sent the men ashore on a small island in the river, where they could smell the salty air from the sea. After the men had eaten, he told them for the first time about the daring operation they were to undertake.[39]

Late at night the boats moved forward silently, but no enemy ship appeared on the river. Wood therefore turned back with his party and once again put them into bivouac on a lonely riverbank.[40]

At dawn of 1 February, while they ate a cold breakfast, the men heard the thunder of gunfire together with the intense rattle of fusillade. It was General George E. Pickett, launching a land attack against New Bern. A little later Gift arrived from Kinston with his two launches and joined Wood. Gift, hearing the noise of the battle, had feared that the other party was already engaged without waiting for him.[41] Actually, the raiders could not move before sunset.

To protect New Bern, the U.S. Navy had three large gunboats: the *Lockwood, Hull,* and *Underwriter,* the last most powerful. The flotilla was commanded by Second Lieutenant George W. Graves. As soon as the battle began, General Innis N. Palmer, commanding the Union forces at New Bern, ordered Graves to send the *Underwriter* and the *Hull* upriver to support the Federal troops with their heavy guns. The *Hull* immediately ran aground, and the *Underwriter* proceeded alone while Graves, with the flagship *Lockwood,* steamed toward the Trent River, which empties into the Neuse downriver from New Bern, to protect the city against attacks from the rear.[42]

At nightfall of 2 February, Wood and Loyall, with two boats, carefully advanced to reconnoiter. Soon, ahead of before them in the darkness, they sighted the outline of the *Underwriter,* moored near the right bank of the river so as to be part of the Union fortifications. "Here she is!" the two officers exclaimed together. After carefully scanning her through his binoculars, Wood decided she would be the objective of the raiders.[43]

Back at his emergency base, Wood gathered his officers and ordered that the attack be made between midnight and 4:00 A.M. Several anxious hours passed. Looking at the stars that shone among the clouds through the cold winter night, a young cadet wondered how many of the raiders would still be alive at dawn the next day. The *Underwriter* was a formidable enemy. She displaced 341 tons, was 186 feet long, had 800-horsepower engines, and carried five heavy guns: a 20-pounder Parrott rifle and four 32-pounder Dahlgrens. A single broadside from her cannons would turn the raider flotilla into ashes.[44] She had a crew of eighty-four officers and men, all seasoned sailors.

Shortly after midnight the raiders' boats were readied. First, they were divided into two groups of six each, one commanded by Wood himself, the other by Loyall. The plan was to try to catch the gunboat between them. The two launches commanded by Gift would follow. All moved downriver.

Wood then gathered his officers and men about him and uttered a fervent prayer that God would preserve them during their dangerous mission. "It was a strange and ghostly sight," wrote Thomas J. Scharf years later, the event still alive in his memory. "The men resting on their oars with heads uncovered; the commander also bareheaded, standing erect in the stern of his boat; the black waters rippling beneath; the dense, overhanging clouds pouring down sheets of rain, and, in the blackness beyond, an unseen bell tolling as if from some phantom cathedral." Four tollings: it was the bell of the *Underwriter* ringing out two o'clock.[45]

The commando moved. Suddenly, no more than three hundred feet away, the powerful and threatening shape of the gunboat emerged from the darkness and rang out with the rough call: "Boats ahoy!" They had been discovered, and on the deck of the enemy ship the signal calling all hands to quarters echoed. Wood did not hesitate: "Give way boys, give way!" It was a frightful moment. If the enemy opened fire on the boats with its big guns, all was lost.

The light boats seemed to jump over the water, but the enemy sailors, understanding that they had neither enough time nor space to aim their cannons, quickly manned the rails and opened an infernal rifle fire upon the raiders. The Confederate marines tried to answer from their boats. Wood, who gallantly stood up in the stern of his skiff and exhorted his rowers in a calm voice, seemed to possess a charmed life though all around him men fell. His helmsman was struck by a bullet in the forehead.

Now the boats were closing up around the enemy vessel and the Confederates bravely began to board under a hailstorm of bullets. Fierce fighting occurred on deck. Engineer Emmet F. Gill, who had been designated to take charge of the gunboat's engines after her seizure, fell, hit by four bullets, and some five raiders were also killed. Yet the others, led by Wood, succeeded after fearful hand-to-hand fighting in driving the Union sailors down the ladder to the wardroom and then to the coal bunkers. Some escaped by jumping overboard, but about thirty were captured. The gunboat's commanding officer was dead. Amid the tumult, Wood's voice was heard: "The ship is ours!"[46]

Had the Confederates been able to move the gunboat, their victory would have been complete: the *Underwriter* was the most powerful vessel in that zone, and they would have commanded the waters. Engineers worked frantically to get the ship under way, but the task proved impossible. The fires were almost out, and there was hardly any pressure. Hours would have been needed.

Suddenly a frightful jolt shook the gunboat: from land, the artillerists of the Federal fort were firing on her at almost point-blank range with their heavy guns.[47] The ship, immobile under the hail of shells, might become a deadly trap for the raiders. With a heavy heart Wood ordered the *Underwriter* abandoned after setting her afire, taking with him the dead, wounded, and prisoners.

The duty of burning the ship fell to Hoge, but when he approached Wood, the latter expressed fear that the fire had not caught. Hoge went back to the *Underwriter* to inspect her. Enemy shells rained upon the ship, exploding everywhere, and the magazine might at any moment blow up beneath his feet. Still, Hoge descended into the hold and started a new fire. The ship was now burning like a torch, floodlighting Hoge's small boat. While the raiders rowed upriver, the *Underwriter* continued to burn, illuminating the estuary. At about 5:00 A.M., a gigantic flare was followed by an awful explosion: the gunboat had blown up. The action cost the Confederates eight dead and twenty-two wounded; the Union lost nine dead, eighteen wounded, and twenty-two prisoners.[48]

The next day, lacking the expected support from the gunboat, General Pickett decided to give up the attempt to retake New Bern.[49] Not until the ironclad *Albemarle* sailed to battle would the Confederates succeed in driving the enemy from the coastal towns of North Carolina.

Still, the commando operation had been a major success. On 15 February 1864 the Confederate Congress approved a resolution of thanks and encomium for Wood and his men.[50]

Yet the highest praise for the Southern raiders came after the war from a foe of the Confederate navy, Admiral David D. Porter: "This was rather a mortifying affair for the Navy," he wrote about the *Underwriter*'s capture, "however fearless on the part of the Confederates. This gallant expedition was led by Commander John Taylor Wood of the Confederate Navy. . . . It was to be expected that, with so many clever officers who had left the Federal Navy and cast their fortunes with the Confederates, such gallant actions would often be attempted."[51]

From Washington, Gustavus Vasa Fox fully appraised the importance and above all the political impact of the operation by the Confederate commandos and expressed his determination to create such an organization in the U.S. Navy.[52]

Raiding parties evoked great enthusiasm and were becoming almost a standard part of the C.S. Navy. There were many who bravely planned to follow the daring examples of Wood and Beall, and squadron commanders advocated the creation of such groups.

Perhaps the most prominent operation by a raiding party occurred on the night of 2–3 June 1864 in waters near Savannah, Georgia. There, Confederates had observed that a good seagoing enemy gunboat, the *Water Witch*, of 378 tons displacement, armed with four cannons, had rashly sailed up Ossabaw Sound, one of the tangled waterways that surround the old Georgia city. She had at first been supported by the ironclads that had vainly tried to reduce Fort McAllister, but now she was alone.[53]

The enemy gunboat's risky location did not escape the notice of young Lieutenant Thomas Postell Pelot, a South Carolinian, commanding the floating battery *Georgia*. Perhaps inspired by the recent daring operation of Wood's commando, Pelot submitted a plan to Flag Officer William W. Hunter, commanding the Confederate Savannah Squadron, and got authorization to proceed.[54]

The raiding party was to be composed of 12 officers and 115 men picked from the crews of the floating battery *Georgia*, ironclad *Savannah*, and gunboat *Sampson*. Pelot would personally lead them. His second in command was Lieutenant (junior grade) Joseph Price. The best and most trustworthy Confederate pilot in the expedition was the free black Moses Dallas.[55]

The boats moved secretly on 1 June 1864, but finding the gunboat among the tangled channels was far from easy.[56] At last, on the night of the third, the *Water Witch* was sighted and the raiders moved to board her under an extremely heavy fire from the enemy, who had immediately discovered them. Pelot was killed in the attack. Next to him, fighting

A History of the Confederate Navy

gallantly, fell pilot Dallas. Price assumed command. Though severely wounded, he succeeded, after a short but fierce fight, in compelling the enemy to surrender.[57]

The Confederates lost six dead and eleven wounded, the Federals, two dead, twelve wounded, and seventy-seven prisoners.[58] It was a great victory for the raiders, the greatest achieved to that time, even if paid for at a very high cost by the death of the able and gallant Pelot. Captured intact, the *Water Witch* was commissioned into the C.S. Navy. Detailed to command her was Lieutenant Alexander F. Warley.[59] Elation for the success—even if tempered by sorrow for the losses—swept the Confederacy. Congress voted an address of praise, and Price was promoted to commander.[60] The battle flag of the ship was solemnly presented to Secretary Mallory.[61]

The commandos were now famous in the South. John Taylor Wood was considering a new operation. For some time he had been working on a plan to launch a surprise attack on the Federal prison camp at Point Lookout on the Potomac. He would free the Confederate prisoners, arm them, and lead them to cooperate in an attack that General Jubal Early would launch toward Washington in the summer of 1864. When it was learned that the enemy was aware of the enterprise, it was called off.[62]

Yet Wood and his raiders would not stay still for long. They became involved in a plan that Mallory had been developing, intended to strengthen commerce destroying. He needed "a light draft, fast steamer" and added: "I perceive that a new class of such vessels with two propellers, had been successfully devised."[63]

The British, indeed, had already sent to sea such vessels and used them successfully as blockade runners. Among the best was the *Atalanta*. Designed by an expert in the Royal Navy and fitted with twin screws powered by two 100-horsepower engines that moved them at 120 revolutions per minute, she was 220 feet long and had a draft of only 9 feet. Displacing 700 tons, she was painted light gray, which made her almost invisible. Moreover, thanks to the independent action of the two engines, if one were reversed, she could turn about, around her own center. She could log seventeen knots, which made her perhaps the fastest steamer then plying the seas.[64]

The ship had made two trips as a blockade runner. Attempts by Union cruisers to find her had failed.[65] Five days after Wood gave up his expedition against Point Lookout, Mallory bought her for £25,000 without cargo, even though her real value was £17,000.[66]

The secretary's plan was to unleash against enemy trade in nearby coastal waters a new kind of cruiser characterized by very high speed and manned by a crew of daring naval raiders.[67] Southern cruisers based their movements on the slowness with which news about their location reached enemy naval forces, despite the efforts of U.S. consular agents. Progress in communications (which would be fatal to the *Alabama*) was compelling the Confederates to pass from cruising to raiding. Progress might be exploited not only by the defenders but also by the offenders. The outcome would be, as Admiral Lepotier wrote, "as a whole, a general acceleration of operations, a more spirited drive." [68]

Mallory, knowing that the immensity of the oceans, which had been the most important shield for Southern cruisers, was shrinking, planned to use speed instead of space to his advantage in commerce destroying. In addition, action in coastal waters would greatly alleviate the pressure of the blockade by compelling the enemy to send more vessels to hunt down the raiders. It would, finally, make Northerners conscious of the presence of war at their own door. [69]

The *Atalanta* was quickly converted into a cruiser, commissioned with the new name *Tallahassee,* and armed with three guns: a rifled 32-pounder, another, also rifled, 110-pounder, and a heavy Parrott aft. [70] The crew of 120 officers and men was picked carefully. The executive officer would be Lieutenant William H. Ward; in charge of the marines would be Captain Edward Crenshaw. [71]

Wood did not spare money from his small allowance to ensure that the ship was fitted with everything required. [72] Mallory, perhaps foreseeing that the vessel would not be able to return to a Confederate port, ordered Bulloch to have £10,000 ready for Wood. [73] The training of the commando was speedy and accurate.

On 4 August 1864 the *Tallahassee* was ready to sail from Wilmington. During that same night she slipped silently downriver and neared Fort Fisher. All her lights were extinguished except that over her steering compass. Yet the weight of her guns, ammunition, supplementary coal supply, and abundant crew had increased her draft to 13.5 feet and, in the darkness, she grounded at least twice.

Finally, on the night of 7 August, she succeeded in scraping over the bar. There was no moon, and the daring cruiser sailed between two enemy ships, which opened fire in the dark. Their aim was good, yet the Confederate ship escaped unhurt, thanks to her lower board, and her powerful engines soon took her far away in the night. [74]

But danger was not yet over. The next day the *Tallahassee* had to run the external blockade belt, made up of the best and most powerful (and most dangerous) enemy ships. Thanks to her speed, she succeeded in escaping from at least five enemy vessels. On 11 August, when only eighty nautical miles from Sandy Hook, she captured her first prize, the sailer *Sarah A. Boyce.*

A History of the Confederate Navy

Now Wood pushed forward until he was barely twenty miles from New York. There he captured a pilot boat and, putting his own men aboard, used it to guide toward him enemy merchantmen steaming toward the great Atlantic port. They usually ignored the snare and, one after another, fell into the trap he had set for them.[75]

Meanwhile, he was contemplating a daring raid into the port of New York to set it afire. For this he hoped to bribe—or compel to guide him—some pilot he had made prisoner. Yet nobody agreed, and, after capturing and burning the large ship *Adriatic,* he sailed toward the New England coast.

Panic swept the North. No Union warship was at hand to operate in the New York zone. Who could ever have imagined that an enemy cruiser would dare appear right in the heart of the Northern port system? A pack of naval ships was sent out to hunt the "pirate."[76]

Her powerful engines took the *Tallahassee* far away, up the Northern coast, capturing and destroying any enemy merchantman that fell to hand. On 18 August, the *Tallahassee* entered the neutral port of Halifax, Nova Scotia, Canada. There she was welcomed by the garrison and the people, but the local British authorities were aloof. The North was daily becoming stronger, and strength inspires respect. At least, it was possible to load eighty tons of coal and change a damaged spare mast for a new one.[77]

Then, on the night of 20 August, after having gained the service of a first-rate Canadian pilot, Wood silently left for the sea, all lights out, and at 2:00 A.M. was on the ocean and sailing south. Deceived by word that Wood was still in Halifax, the enemy steered northward seeking him where he was not.[78]

The *Tallahassee* continued southward undisturbed and on the night of 25 August entered Wilmington by running the blockade after a brisk exchange of cannon fire with the enemy squadron. At 10:00 A.M. on the twenty-sixth she moored at the pier. Her raid had lasted twenty days and had seriously alarmed the enemy, frightening the port cities of the North. She had eluded and mocked the powerful Union squadrons and captured thirty-three merchantmen, of which twenty-six were destroyed, two released, and five bonded.[79]

Summoned to Richmond for duty there, Wood suggested that the ship be prepared for sea service. The *Tallahassee* again left port on 26 October. She was now commanded by Wood's executive officer, Lieutenant William Ward. To deceive the enemy, the vessel was rechristened the *Olustee.* During her second cruise she captured another six merchantmen along the Delaware coast. Upon coming back to Wilmington, she was reconverted into a blockade runner with the (suitable) name of *Chameleon.*[80]

By this time she was too well known to the enemy, and changing her name would achieve nothing. She had to change her operating area and activities.

A third raid was carried out by another fast cruiser, the former blockade runner *Edith,* renamed the *Chickamauga* and fitted with three light rifled cannons. Captain John Wilkinson, an able and experienced blockade runner, was detailed to command her. She reached the ocean on 28 October and during her cruise (which lasted until 19 November) destroyed half a dozen enemy merchantmen.[81]

Meanwhile, John Y. Beall, back from prison, had resumed his activity. Much earlier, either in February or March 1863, when joining the navy, he had presented Mallory with an extremely daring plan: to enter Canada by stealth with a Confederate commando, seize some Union ships on the Great Lakes, and use them to conduct bold raids either against Northern shipping or against such enemy cities as Detroit, Toledo, Buffalo, and Chicago. Moreover, he would try to free Confederate prisoners at Johnson's Island on Lake Erie.[82]

The same plan was submitted to Mallory by another naval officer, Lieutenant William H. Murdaugh. Mallory, President Davis, and other authorities found the proposals feasible but decided against implementing them so as not to annoy neutral Canada (and, needless to say, Great Britain).[83]

By October 1863, the situation had changed, and Mallory reconsidered the project. Beall was then a prisoner in the enemy's hands, and Murdaugh had given up the plan and was serving overseas.[84] The planned coup on Lake Erie was therefore entrusted to a commando composed of about fifteen officers and sailors and placed under the orders of Robert D. Minor. Among others, the latter had with him Benjamin P. Loyall and George W. Gift and had been given a sum equivalent to $111,000 in gold, consisting of $35,000 in specie and 450 cotton bales, as well as turpentine worth about another $100,000. He also had with him two secret agents, one of them a Catholic priest.

The commando boarded the swift naval blockade runner *R. E. Lee,* commanded by Lieutenant John Wilkinson, who also would survey the expedition. The ship left Wilmington on 7 October 1863 and arrived at Halifax, Nova Scotia, on the sixteenth. There Wilkinson gave the *R. E. Lee* to another officer, and the party divided and rejoined quietly in Montreal. Yet just when the operation seemed to be going well, U.S. Secretary of War Stanton, alerted by a secret agent, informed the governor-general of Canada about the matter. Abiding by neutrality, the governor stopped the enterprise. The Confederates had to return to the South. Even worse,

Wilkinson's successor in command of the *R. E. Lee* proved inept and let the ship fall into enemy hands.[85]

In 1864 Beall was back, and it was up to him. The operation had to be reorganized on a new basis. The Confederate government already had in Canada a small party of secret agents who worked under the cover of Commissioners Clement C. Clay and Jacob Thompson, who represented the Confederacy there.

Beall started from zero. With some of his raiders, he secretly crossed Northern territory and reached Canada. There, on 18 September 1864, at Sandwich, on Lake Erie, they boarded the U.S. ship *Philo Parsons,* which normally plied between Detroit and Sandusky Bay and already had on board—or would soon have—the other raiders. At 2:00 P.M. on the nineteenth Beall forcibly seized the ship and raised the Confederate flag. There was no resistance by either the crew or passengers.[86]

The daring coup seemed to have begun well. Beall had succeeded where the previous commando had failed. When the ship neared Kelley's Island, Beall surprised and seized a second ship, the *Island Queen.* Aboard he found many Union soldiers about to be discharged. They were paroled, as were the civilians found on both ships, but the *Island Queen* was in bad shape and had to be scuttled.

It was now necessary to proceed toward Johnson's Island and capture the U.S. gunboat *Michigan,* whose crew should already have been immobilized by another Confederate agent, Captain Charles H. Cole of the army. But Cole had been betrayed and arrested, and Beall, who certainly could not confront a gunboat with a passenger ship, had to scuttle the *Philo Parsons* and give up the operation.[87]

Thus failed, on the threshold of success, what might have been the most daring action of the Confederate raiding parties. Yet panic once again gripped the North. For days, Union authorities worked frantically to concentrate military forces and to commission auxiliary gunboats on the Great Lakes.[88]

Beall remained in Canada, but his story would end in tragedy. The Confederate raiders who operated there were planning operations against the big cities of the North, Chicago, New York, and Philadelphia.

On 15 December 1864 the possibility arose of attacking a train in Northern territory to free seven Confederate generals who were prisoners. Beall would be the leader, and a secret base was established at Buffalo. Unfortunately, the daring raider, perhaps betrayed, fell into Union hands. It soon was clear that the Federals would not acknowledge his status as an officer in the C.S. Navy and would try him as a "spy" for "violations of the laws of war."

Mallory sent to Thompson in Canada a copy of Beall's commission as a Confederate naval officer to attest to his military position.[89] It was in vain. Beall was charged with planning to set fire to Northern cities. Southerners answered that Union troops had just burned Atlanta to the ground. The South, however, was now losing the war, and the North felt strong enough to impose its own interpretation of the law.

A court-martial, meeting at Fort Lafayette, rejected evidence produced by the defense and on 8 February 1865 sentenced Beall to death by hanging.[90] Many Union men in the North were horrified by the sentence. Even fiery enemies of the South such as Thaddeus Stevens, Governor John Andrew of Massachusetts, former senator Orville Browning of Illinois, and many U.S. congressmen, pleaded for a pardon. Yet Lincoln was adamant. Beall was hanged on 24 February 1865.

When facing death he was firm and calm. The enemy soldiers who attended the execution were moved by his demeanor. One cannot escape the impression that the sentence and execution amounted to something like legal murder.[91]

During those weeks, the Confederacy was nearing its end. The scaffold on which Beall died seemed to loom tragically against that bloody twilight like a symbol of the unequal fight by a small navy against the overwhelming strength of a powerful enemy that no exertion, no desperate gallantry, could overcome.

EIGHTEEN

The Crisis

The Confederacy's first serious naval setback occurred on the far seas while at home Mallory's strategy was enjoying success. At the beginning of June 1864 the cruiser *Alabama* was approaching the English Channel.[1] During a long cruise that had taken her around the world, she had destroyed fifty-five enemy merchantmen and bonded ten more. She had also sunk the USS *Hatteras* in battle.[2] No other Southern raider could boast such a record.

Yet now the *Alabama* was in wretched condition and in dire need of repairs. Her boilers were "roasted" and her engines badly needed overhauling. Her joints screeched, and her copper sheathing was torn and bent.[3] She must find a port and be placed in drydock. Furthermore, the men, especially Captain Semmes, were worn out from years of sailing almost without respite through dreadful storms and torrential rain, changing from freezing climates to tropical ones. They were also worried about the future of the South.[4]

At 12:30 P.M. on 11 June 1864 the *Alabama* entered the French port of Cherbourg.[5] It would be her last call. Cherbourg was then a base of the French Imperial Navy, and all the drydocks were the property of the government. The *Alabama* therefore needed the emperor's authorization to be admitted there for repairs. Emperor Napoleon III, however, was at Biarritz and would not be back in Paris for several weeks. Had the cruiser entered Le Havre, where there were several private dockyards, she would have been accepted immediately.[6]

This delay sealed the *Alabama*'s fate. At the same time, the U.S. cruiser

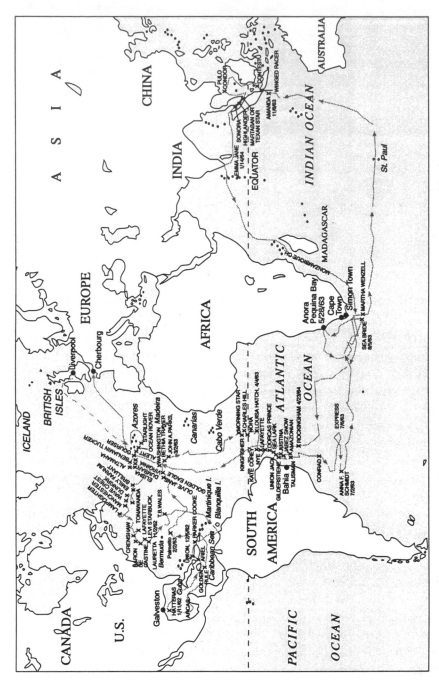

The CSS *Alabama*'s cruise around the world with the names and places of ships sunk or captured.

Kearsarge was off Flushing, Holland, watchful in the event of a Confederate attempt to put a new raider to sea. In November 1863, through a middleman, Matthew Fontaine Maury had bought the former HMS *Victor* in England. She sailed on 24 November 1863, was rechristened the *Rappahannock,* and was commissioned into the C.S. Navy. Soon thereafter her engine bushings failed and she was compelled to seek refuge at Calais and enter a drydock.[7] The ship had caused Mallory great concern, which was increased by the arrival of the *Kearsarge* in the Pas de Calais area while the Confederate cruiser was being repaired.[8]

The *Kearsarge* was moored in the Schelt, before Flushing,[9] when, on 12 June 1864, a telegram from the U.S. ambassador at Paris, Dayton (who had been notified by the American consul at Cherbourg), informed her captain of the presence of the *Alabama.*[10] The Northern cruiser immediately sailed and on the fourteenth entered Cherbourg, mooring at some distance from the Confederate ship. Her declared purpose was to take aboard the prisoners the *Alabama* had landed. The French minister of marine denied her this (at Semmes's request) because a belligerent could not increase her own crew in a neutral port. At the same time, however, the minister denied the Southern cruiser permission to enter a drydock and authorized her only to coal and make a few urgent repairs.[11]

Semmes and his officers had carefully scanned the enemy vessel with powerful telescopes but had not noticed a cunning device the Union sailors used to increase their ship's protection. The *Kearsarge* had along her sides a sort of armor made by many lengths of anchor chain. These strips, attached to the hull, were hidden by wooden boards painted the same black as the hull.[12]

Semmes sent for his reliable executive officer, John M. Kell, telling him bluntly: "Kell, I am going out to fight the *Kearsarge.* What do you think of it?" The two discussed the features of both ships. The Northern cruiser was the stronger, having been built for battle, whereas the *Alabama*'s main asset was speed. But because her hull had deteriorated, the ship might not be faster than the enemy. The hands on board were almost equal in number: 163 on the *Kearsarge,* 149 on the *Alabama.* The Confederate had one more gun: eight in all, a rifled 7-inch Blakely, an 8-inch smoothbore, and six 32-pounders, against the *Kearsarge*'s seven (two 11-inch Dahlgrens, four 32-pounders, and a rifled 28-pounder). Yet the weight in metal of the Union vessel's broadsides (thanks mainly to the two heavy Dahlgrens) was greater.[13]

Kell had qualms because the *Alabama*'s powder was of doubtful quality after long exposure to humidity.[14] But Semmes had decided to fight, and Kell proceeded to clear the ship for action as best he could.[15]

Semmes made a spectacular gesture: through the Confederate consular agent he gave the captain of the *Kearsarge* notice that he intended to leave Cherbourg and give battle.[16] Thus the die was cast. Semmes expected to succeed, even though a Confederate officer who had called on him had warned him of the power of the *Kearsarge*'s big cannons.[17]

Three questions arise more than a century after the event. Why did Semmes offer battle? Did he know how the enemy vessel was protected? If he did know, why did he give battle?

The answer to the first question is simple. Semmes has told us that if the *Alabama* had entered a port where private shipyards were available or if the emperor had not been absent from Paris, she would immediately have been put into drydock, her crew would have been discharged with several months of leave, and the battle with the *Kearsarge* would never have occurred.[18]

Under cover of darkness the *Alabama* could have tried to slip out of the port. Captain John Ancrum Winslow, commanding the *Kearsarge*, was concerned that she might do so, and he had enlisted the help of the local U.S. consul to place observers at the mouth of the harbor. For the Confederate to escape by stealth was therefore impossible.

Perhaps Semmes had run out of patience. He would show the enemy that the *Alabama* was not a pirate, as Union propaganda proclaimed, but a warship capable of fighting. Even the enemy cruiser's crew understood his intent.[19] His letter of challenge was self-explanatory: Semmes must not allow the enemy to claim that the Confederate vessel had been attacked while seeking to avoid battle. Nor could he wait because other U.S. ships would soon have joined the *Kearsarge* and bottled up the Confederate cruiser. The powerful steam frigate *Niagara*, 4,582 tons and thirty-six guns, which with a single broadside could have blown the *Alabama* to pieces, had been ordered to rush to Cherbourg.[20]

More controversial is the matter of the armor. In his official report Semmes stated that had he known the *Kearsarge* was an "ironclad," he would never have given battle. He confirmed this in his *Memoirs*, as did his executive officer, the honest and straightforward Kell.[21]

Still, many years later, Lieutenant Arthur Sinclair, an officer aboard the *Alabama* whose devotion to Semmes was unquestioned, asserted that the Confederate captain had been told of the armor by a French naval officer.[22] This revelation caused a bitter controversy between Sinclair and Kell (Semmes had died), which solved nothing.[23]

It seems impossible now to determine the truth, though the statements by Semmes and Kell appear to be the more reliable. Yet it seems clear that even if Semmes knew about the armor, he could not turn back after the letter of challenge. He probably hoped that his gunfire might detach the protective chains from the sides of the *Kearsarge*.

The dawn of Sunday, 19 June 1864, rose bright and clear, without a cloud in the blue sky of Cherbourg. The *Alabama* had lighted her fires at 6:00 A.M. The decks and brasswork of the cruiser were clean and polished. Officers and men had donned their best uniforms, and the Confederate flag fluttered at the peak.[24] Never had the ship looked more beautiful and bright than on that deadly morning.

She weighed anchor, then passed in front of the French ship of the line *Napoléon,* which had her crew at quarters and her band playing *Dixie* in honor of the men who were ready to fight and perhaps die so far from their country. A huge crowd was gathering on the docks, along the shores, and on board small boats to witness the impending battle. In one such boat, unknown to most, was the great painter Edouard Manet, who would draw a most impressive image of the fight.

Followed by the French ironclad frigate *Couronne,* whose duty was to check that the neutrality law was respected, the *Alabama* sortied. All of her hands were at battle quarters. Out of the harbor the *Kearsarge,* which had sailed several hours before, was waiting for her. While the *Couronne* veered and began to sail back, the Confederate left French territorial waters and steered resolutely for the *Kearsarge,* which immediately steamed toward her at full speed. At eighteen hundred yards the *Alabama* opened with her heavy 100-pounder Blakely. Aware of the edge that his powerful guns gave him at close quarters, Winslow tried to close with the enemy. But Semmes was not one to be easily taken in. The two vessels began to steer in circles at a distance of about five hundred yards, exchanging shot and shell. Semmes soon noticed that his projectiles hit the sides of the *Kearsarge* without damaging them and that the quality of his powder was poor. The powder probably cost Semmes the battle. Even though his gunners, lacking regular drill, were much less accurate than their adversaries, they did place a 100-pound shell in the sternpost of the Union ship, which embedded in the rudderpost. Had it exploded, the Northerner probably would have been sunk. But the shell was a dud.[25]

Now the three advantages of the *Kearsarge*—better rate of fire, the hull protected by chains, and shells that exploded—began to tell, and after sixty-five minutes the *Alabama* had holes in her sides large enough to let a cart through, and she began to sink to the bottom. To save the wounded lying on the deck, Semmes lowered his flag and then sent a small boat to the enemy to ask for assistance and to transfer the most seriously wounded to the *Kearsarge.*[26]

The Union men were slow to act. Apparently they suspected some trick by Semmes, whom they feared even after they had defeated him. At Winslow's request, the private British yacht *Deerhound,* owned by John Lancaster, which had come to witness the battle, helped to rescue the survivors, including Semmes, Kell, the captain of marines Becket K. Howell, and several others, thus saving them from captivity.[27]

At 12:24 the *Alabama*'s bow rose high and she sank in forty-five fathoms of water. There were no cheers, only deep silence on board the *Kearsarge*.[28]

The battle had cost the U.S. cruiser one man killed and two wounded. The losses on the *Alabama* were much higher: twenty-six dead (of whom seven fell on the deck and nineteen drowned when she sank) and twenty-one wounded, among them Semmes himself, who got a painful but not serious wound in one hand. Among the dead were shipboy David Henry White and stoker Andrew Shilland, two of the several black men among the fighting and fallen Southerners.[29]

The loss of the *Alabama* was a severe blow to Southern morale. Yet in Confederate waters the C.S. Navy was still potent, and commerce destroying on the far seas continued. Indeed, on 10 February 1864 the other famed cruiser, the *Florida,* her repairs completed, had sailed from Brest, resuming her hunt for enemy merchantmen under a new commanding officer, Lieutenant Commander Charles Manigault Morris, a South Carolinian, who, though he lacked the daring and drive of Maffitt, was a competent officer.[30]

The battle off Cherbourg, therefore, was an isolated episode, albeit an ominous one. The first signal of the impending crisis came later, during the sultry summer of 1864, when the Union armies of General Ulysses Grant were engaging the Confederates in a deadly fight on every front.

Even before becoming general in chief of the U.S. Army, Grant had been aware of the strategic importance of the port city and communication network center of Mobile, Alabama, and had decided to attack it from its land side.[31] After assuming command of all the Union armies, he included in his master plan for the 1864 campaign three basic objectives: the capture of Richmond, Atlanta, and Mobile, the last to be attacked concurrently by land and sea.[32] In addition, Admiral Farragut, another prime strategist, had in mind taking Mobile ever since his capture of New Orleans.[33]

Fortunately for the Confederacy, General Nathaniel P. Banks, who, with some thirty thousand men,[34] should have attacked Mobile from inland in the spring, was deflected by orders from Washington to conduct an almost senseless campaign toward Texas, along the Red River, so that the threat to Mobile was delayed.[35]

During this time the Confederates put into commission the mighty ironclad *Tennessee.* They were just in time because Farragut, back in the Gulf of Mexico since the end of January 1864, was thinking of attacking Mobile on his own. The Union admiral, who in the past had expressed some mistrust of ironclads,[36] was now worried by those the Confederates were putting into commission and alerted the U.S. naval secretary: "Without ironclads we should not be able to fight the enemy's vessels of that class," inasmuch as the operation against Mobile must be an amphibious one, with the cooperation of at least five thousand men from the army to attack the Confederate forts.[37] Naval authorities in Washington did not want to divert ironclads from other duties, and the soldiers were engaged under Banks in the dismal Red River campaign. But Farragut had not lost his fighting spirit, and he proceeded to prepare his ships and men for the attack.[38]

The Union delays should have given the Confederates enough time to ready themselves. But again their backward industrial plant was unable to meet the demands placed on it.

The first problem was the *Tennessee*. Although powerful, she was too slow because her engines, recovered as described earlier from a river paddle-wheel boat, had been patched together and adapted by a system of connecting gears to give her screw propulsion. This, of course, resulted in a great dissipation of power, and she could make no more than six knots under the best conditions.

Even worse, the South held absurdly high hopes for her, believing again that a single ship could defeat a dozen. Moreover, under the pressure of public opinion, Buchanan had no choice: if he and his men on the *Tennessee* did not act, they would be pilloried for the rest of their lives.[39]

Yet the most serious deficiency was that there was only one ironclad. The *Nashville*, launched at Montgomery, had been towed to the estuary of the river a year earlier; she looked formidable, a "tremendous monster," which made the *Tennessee* seem insignificant by comparison.[40] Yet in the spring of 1864 she was still very far from completion because of lack of iron for armoring her and lack of guns. Early in May 1864 work could barely begin to armor the bow of her casemate.[41]

The same situation existed with respect to the two ships launched on the Tombigbee and towed to the deltas, for they were completely unarmored.[42] In Selma, Jones had his few men in the naval foundry working day and night to cast the guns for the *Nashville*. Because the walls of her casemate were more inclined than usual, she required cannons with longer barrels, thus complicating the work.[43] Only in May was Jones able to inform Buchanan that he had cast the first four of the seven 7-inch Brookes the ironclad needed.[44]

As the spring of 1864 gave way to summer, the *Nashville* and the other two ships remained above the bar, mostly incomplete. With them were the two floating batteries, the *Huntsville* and the *Tuscaloosa*, unable to meet the enemy in open waters because of their extreme slowness; they were barely able to move against the weak current in the bay.[45] Therefore, if Farragut attacked, Buchanan would be compelled to confront the whole enemy squadron with only the *Tennessee.*

Farragut meanwhile was waiting for ironclads and land troops. At last, when he wrote to Secretary Welles that the fearsome *Tennessee* had appeared at the mouth of the bay and repeated his requests for an ironclad and at least three thousand soldiers, the U.S. secretary took action. On 7 June 1864 the ironclad *Manhattan* was ordered to proceed to the Gulf and report to Farragut.[46] On 3 July a second ironclad, the *Tecumseh,*[47] was ready to leave Norfolk. On 9 July, Admiral Porter was ordered to send Farragut two light-draft ironclads from the Mississippi Squadron: the *Winnebago* and *Chickasaw.*[48]

All were formidable vessels of the *Monitor* class but much more powerful than the famed prototype. The *Manhattan* and *Tecumseh,* newly built in New York and launched in the fall of 1863, had been constructed in light of the experiences drawn from the *Monitor* and from the other such ships that had fought in the failed attack on Charleston. They displaced 2,100 tons, were 225 feet long, and had much stronger armor than used earlier. Their most important asset was their ordnance: each had two gigantic 15-inch Dahlgrens—the same caliber used by the 40,000-ton battleships of World War II—capable of firing projectiles weighing more than 430 pounds. These were the guns that had almost demolished the Confederate ironclad *Atlanta,* compelling her to surrender.

The *Winnebago* and *Chickasaw,* although built to operate in shallow inland waters (they had a draft of only six feet), would prove themselves, as Farragut said, extremely efficient. They were 229 feet long, displaced 1,300 tons, and had two turrets with four 11-inch Dahlgrens. This was the caliber used by the *Monitor* in her battle against the *Virginia,* as well as by the German "pocket battleships" of World War II.[49]

At last the soldiers arrived. On 17 June General Edward R. S. Canby, commanding Union forces in the West, conferred with Farragut,[50] and on 3 July sent him General Gordon Granger with twenty-four hundred men.[51]

Admiral Buchanan expected this increased enemy force to attack at any moment.[52] In addition to the *Tennessee,* he could deploy three small gunboats: the *Gaines, Morgan,* and *Selma,* with a total of 22 guns. This small squadron faced an enemy who had at least eighteen ships (of which four were ironclads) with 147 guns.[53] The Federal admiral, however, had first to sail up the channel that led into the bay, under fire from Fort Morgan, which mounted thirty-eight cannons (of which seven were in the water battery and therefore the most effective), and pass through extensive torpedo fields.

Mobile Bay, about thirty nautical miles long and generally of shallow depth, has several entrances. The main one is between the long promontory of Mobile Point that protrudes from the extreme end of the eastern coast of the bay and Dauphin Island and is about three nautical miles wide. A shoal almost two miles long projects from the island, narrowing the navigable channel to little more than a mile near Mobile Point.

On the point rises the great pentagonal walled Fort Morgan. Built in 1818 as part of the coastal defense program undertaken by the U.S. government after the disastrous British landing in the War of 1812, it rises on a site indicated as early as 1497 on a map by Amerigo Vespucci and where successively the Spaniards, French, and British had built fortified works. Its shape is modeled exactly on the Florentine Fortezza da Basso. It covers twenty-eight acres.

Although walled, Fort Morgan was obsolete in 1864 and unable to stand up to the fire of powerful rifled guns. It nevertheless still had a tactical job to perform, that is, to protect the rear and sides of the water battery from land attacks. Its objective, therefore, was defensive. The offensive task was that of the water battery, which, with its seven guns—among them a rifled 8-inch Brooke firing perforating projectiles—would be responsible for protecting the channel.[54]

A weak point in the Confederate position was Mobile Point peninsula. Low and sandy, it presented no obstacle to the landing of troops seeking to take Fort Morgan from the rear. A minor defensive work was sited at the point of Dauphin Island, mounting some twenty-six guns and called Fort Gaines.[55] To the west of the island there is a shallow channel that also leads to the bay. There on a small island in the middle of the channel the Confederates had built an earthwork called Fort Powell that mounted six cannons. They had also barred passage through the waters on both sides by placing obstructions.[56]

Despite the fear they aroused, the obstructions were the weakest point of the Mobile Bay defenses. According to the able Confederate commander of the Corps of Engineers, Victor von Scheliha, the obstructions in the main channel (whose waters were as much as sixty-five feet deep) were built on sand and unstable gravel. Strong currents had forced the Southerners to use only torpedoes and no passive obstacles. Moreover, they had been obliged to leave a gap of at least five hundred yards between Fort Morgan and the triple torpedo barrage to the west to allow passage of blockade runners.[57] Mahan correctly observed that if the Confederates had laid electrical torpedoes, they would have been able to close the channel. Because they did not, they were limited to obstructing the western part of the channel by a triple contact-torpedo barrage that they hoped would force enemy ships under Fort Morgan's guns.[58]

Admiral Farragut, who had carefully studied the defensive Confederate organization and gathered accurate information about it,[59] had located the weak side of the enemy position: the short channel, which would permit ships a quick passage, remaining for the shortest possible time under fire by Fort Morgan and in the torpedo area. Therefore he planned to pass the batteries with his ships in two columns. Ironclads to the right would protect the major wooden ships; these in turn would cover the minor ones, lashed to them by cables which they would drop soon after entering the bay. Unarmored vessels were protected by placing anchor chains along their sides and covering the decks with sandbags (the *Richmond* alone carried a layer of three thousand sandbags).[60]

Admiral Buchanan had determined to begin the battle as soon as the Federal ships passed the channel. He had, with a single ironclad, already confronted an enemy squadron at Hampton Roads and did not despair of success.[61] The trouble was that at Hampton Roads he had faced only the *Monitor,* whereas the *Tennessee* had to confront at least four ironclads, each much more powerful and better armed than the *Monitor.* Moreover, Farragut, daring and aggressive, who had studied the preceding battles against Southern ironclads, had decided that his wooden ships would not sit and wait to be attacked but would run against the *Tennessee,* seeking to ram her and crush her with the sheer weight of their projectiles.[62] In that way they would deny the Confederate ironclad the tactical initiative.

Admiral Buchanan intended to use the power of his guns from the beginning. He therefore placed his small squadron upward of the channel so as to flank the fire from Fort Morgan and bring enfilading fire to bear on the enemy ships as they appeared.[63]

Between 1 and 2 August 1864 General Granger with twenty-four hundred soldiers joined Farragut and on the afternoon of the third began to land his troops on Dauphin Island under cover of six gunboats. On the fourth, the Union troops were in position and ready to open on Fort Gaines.[64] Farragut intended to move that same day but the late arrival of the *Tecumseh* compelled him to delay the attack for twenty-four hours.

At 5:30 A.M. on 5 August 1864 the Union squadron got under way.[65] The tide was rising, and the current helped the Federal ships sail up the channel. Moreover, a light, five-knot southwesterly wind would blow gunsmoke into the eyes of Fort Morgan's defenders. At 6:30 the ironclad *Tecumseh* opened with her monster 15-inch gun. The battle of Mobile Bay had begun.

As Catesby ap R. Jones had recommended, Confederate artillerists at Fort Morgan fired calmly and accurately at the Union ironclads.[66] At 7:30 the *Tecumseh,* mortally hit by at least two piercing shots from the rifled guns of the fort, went off course and ended up in the torpedo fields.

There was a fearful explosion, and the big ironclad, her hull smashed, sank by the bow. For a moment her propeller could be seen spinning madly in the air, then she foundered, dragging with her into the chasm her captain, Tunis Craven, and ninety-two other officers and men.[67]

While fire from the fort increased, the Confederate gunboats *Selma*, *Gaines*, and *Morgan*, protected by the *Tennessee*, delivered a raking fire on the most advanced Union ships. Perhaps because of this fire, perhaps because her captain had been warned about the torpedo fields, the sloop *Brooklyn*, leading the column of wooden ships, suddenly reduced speed, nearly causing the flagship *Hartford*, astern, to collide with her. Farragut ordered his vessel to take the lead and go forward in spite of the torpedoes.[68]

Thus the *Hartford* appeared before the *Tennessee*, which steered to ram her, meanwhile firing shells at her that killed ten men and wounded five. Yet the slowness of the ironclad and the mobility of the U.S. sloop caused the attempted ramming to fail. The Confederate ships, however, were hitting their enemies with merciless fire. From the gunboat *Morgan* the sloop *Oneida* got a shell in her engine room and had to be towed away from the action, disabled. The *Selma* repeatedly struck the *Hartford*, whose decks, according to a marine on board, looked like a slaughter pen.[69]

It was Hampton Roads all over again where the small Confederate ships, protected by the *Virginia*, had inflicted hard blows upon the Federal ships—or so it seemed. By 8:20, Farragut believed that the first part of his action had succeeded. Despite severe losses, he was inside Mobile Bay. It was now the turn of the small Confederate squadron to reverse the fortunes of the battle.

While the *Tennessee*, protected by her invulnerability, exchanged shot and shell with the enemy ships, causing them heavy damage, she again tried in vain to ram the *Brooklyn* and also the *Richmond* and the *Lackawanna*, which were at some distance from her. She was too slow, and the enemy avoided the blows.

The ironclad turned about, but her circle brought her under Fort Morgan. Farragut meanwhile had loosed his seagoing gunboats against the small Confederate ships that had temporarily been isolated from the ironclad. The *Gaines*, hit in seventeen places, leaking badly, her rudder disabled, sought refuge near Fort Morgan but foundered four hundred yards from it. The *Selma*, fighting against the powerful gunboat *Metacomet*, resisted until, almost cut to pieces and dismantled, she had to surrender. The *Morgan*, later, helped by darkness, reached Mobile, where she would soon take part in its defense.

It was now again up to the *Tennessee*. Upon nearing Fort Morgan she had been inspected and found to be undamaged. Admiral Buchanan had

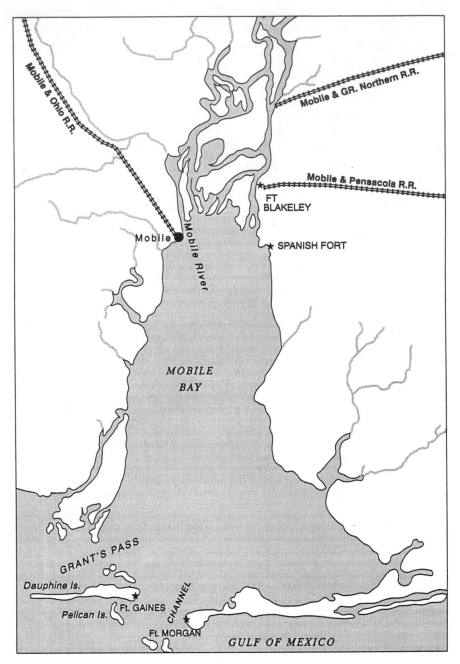

Mobile Bay and its approaches and fortifications.

to reach a decision. Obviously, he should renew action against the enemy. "Follow them, Johnston," he ordered the captain of the *Tennessee.* "We cannot simply let them go this way." As William N. Still, Jr., correctly supposes, Buchanan was counting on surprise (the enemy was preparing to anchor) to inflict the maximum damage possible upon the Union squadron, then retreat under the guns of Fort Morgan and act like a floating battery.[70]

Admiral Farragut, however, was also planning to attack. During the night he would engage the *Tennessee* with his three ironclads at close quarters so as to exploit his gigantic smoothbores.

Buchanan needed to attack during daylight. The problem for him was *how.* According to Alfred T. Mahan, the Confederate admiral should have exploited the light draft of his vessel, as well as the range of his big rifles, by staying in shallow waters far from the Federal ships and battering them with his fire from afar. If he attacked at close quarters, he would play into his enemy's hands.[71]

Mahan's view makes sense. Yet how does one explain Buchanan's decision to come to close quarters? First, if the *Tennessee* stayed in shallow waters, she could not have stopped the three U.S. ironclads (whose draft was equal to or less than hers)[72] from coming to close quarters. Second, from the whole battle as well as from his report afterward, it is clear that Buchanan (thinking, perhaps, of his experience with the *Virginia*) trusted in the ram. This hope would prove his undoing.

Experience had proven that a ship could not be rammed while in motion. Indeed, two years later at Lissa the Austrian ironclad *Herzherzog Ferdinand Max* would succeed in ramming the Italian *Re d'Italia* only after the latter, struck in her rudder, was lying still in the water.[73] The slowness of the Confederate ironclad, owing to her patched-up engines, made her faster enemies safe from her ram.[74]

When Farragut saw the *Tennessee* coming, he ordered all his ships to steer for her at once, seizing the initiative and putting the Confederates on the defensive. Immediately the *Monongahela,* the *Lackawanna,* and the *Hartford* rammed the *Tennessee.* They caused hardly any damage to her, whereas she answered with a devastating shellfire that heavily damaged the enemy vessels.

Yet the worst for the Confederate ironclad was now coming: the three Union ironclads, which had until then been detailed to exchange shots with Fort Morgan, were now rushing to take part in the battle, led by the *Manhattan.* An officer of the *Tennessee* wrote:

> The *Monongahela* was hardly clear of us, when a hideous-looking monster came creeping up on our port side, whose slowly revolving turret

revealed the cavernous depth of a mammoth gun. "Stand clear of the port side!" I shouted. A moment after a thundering report shook us all, while a blast of dense, sulphurous smoke covered our port-holes, and 440 pounds of iron, impelled by sixty pounds of powder, admitted daylight through our side, where before it struck us there had been over two feet of solid wood, covered with five inches of solid iron. . . . I was glad to find myself alive after that shot.[75]

The ironclads *Chickasaw* and *Winnebago,* placing themselves astern of the *Tennessee,* began to hit her mercilessly with their big 11-inch cannons. For more than an hour the *Tennessee* sustained the awful pounding, always answering in kind, then she tried to retreat under the protection of Fort Morgan. It was impossible; she was slower so that the enemy ironclads (and, indeed, all enemy ships) hung close to her, continuing the merciless fire.

The armor of the Confederate vessel began to crack. Then all the weak points of the ironclad began to fail: the port shutters, their chains shattered, blocked the portholes and made it impossible for the Confederate gunners to fire. The rudder chains were smashed, together with relieving tackle that had been installed. The funnel, knocked to pieces, caused steam pressure to fall to almost zero, and a suffocating smoke invaded the ironclad while the temperature in the engine room increased to 140 to 145 degrees.[76]

Incapable of steering, standing still, with water pouring in from leaks opened by repeated collisions with enemy vessels, the *Tennessee* was wholly disabled. Her casemate was being filled with dead and wounded. Admiral Buchanan himself, while seeking to have some gunports repaired, fell severely wounded with a broken leg (after the battle, it was feared that it would have to be amputated). At this point, Captain Johnston obtained authorization from the wounded admiral and made the distressing but necessary decision to lower the flag. It was 10:00 A.M.

Farragut had won a brilliant victory but at what cost? Fifty-two U.S. officers and men had been killed and 170 wounded. Adding the losses of the *Tecumseh,* the number of killed increased to 145 and the total of the losses to 315 killed and wounded. Aside from the loss of an ironclad, the sloop *Oneida* had been disabled; the flagship *Hartford* had been hit twenty times, the *Brooklyn* thirty times. Others had received serious damage except for the ironclads, which, though they had been repeatedly hit (the *Winnebago* alone was struck nineteen times) had resisted well. The Confederates lost 12 killed and 20 wounded and a number of prisoners, among them Admiral Buchanan.[77]

General Granger, who had received a two-thousand-man reinforcement, proceeded methodically to reduce the forts. Fort Morgan resisted the longest; attacked by land and sea, bombarded by the heavy guns of the squadron as well as by the army pieces, it held out until 23 August. Farragut was now in control of the bay and had closed Mobile to the blockade runners. Yet the city still had powerful defensive works. It was also protected from the bay side by what remained of the C.S. squadron, now commanded by Captain Farrand. It was still a road, railroad, and production center. Only an attack from the landward side by a large army could take Mobile.

The Confederate navy had lost the battle for Mobile because the scarcity of its industrial plant had compelled it to confront an overwhelming enemy with a single ironclad, fitted with a patched-up engine. Nevertheless, Secretary Mallory's work was bearing fruit. In the fall of 1864 there would be activity by the cruisers as well as torpedo warfare. The other Southern squadrons were still fighting bravely. While at Mobile Bay Fort Morgan was under siege, near Richmond the ironclads of the James River Squadron had operated twice, on 13 and 17 August, bombarding Union army positions with remarkable success and exchanging shots with three enemy ironclads of the *Monitor* class. The squadron operated again on several occasions, particularly on 22 October and 7 December 1864.[78] Also the *Albemarle* controlled the North Carolina sounds.[79]

Then, in October, two terrible blows struck the Confederate navy. Upon leaving Brest, the *Florida* had started her second Atlantic cruise, although repairs made in France were unsatisfactory and her engines used too much coal.[80]

Near Belle Isle (a small island located near Lorient), the cruiser had met a merchantman that transferred to her warlike materials that could not have been loaded at Brest without violating French neutrality. Then she had made for the Atlantic, dumbfounding the U.S. cruiser *Kearsarge* (which would deal with the *Alabama* a few months later). The enemy, panic-stricken by the return of the *Florida,* sent a fleet of cruisers to hunt her down.[81] The Confederate vessel was compelled during a stay at Bermuda to enlist substitutes for all of her engineers, who were ill or had quit, then continued her cruise according to Mallory's instructions.[82]

On 4 October 1864 the *Florida* entered the Brazilian port of Bahia. She had not touched land for sixty-four days and needed supplies and repairs. During her second cruise she had destroyed eleven enemy merchantmen and bonded two more.[83]

Unfortunately, already moored in that port was the U.S. cruiser *Wachusett.* Fearful that some incident might occur, the Brazilians tried to impose respect of their neutrality. Yet at 3:00 A.M. on the night of 7 October 1864,

Captain Napoleon Collins, commanding the *Wachusett,* under strong pressure from the local U.S. consul, steered silently with lights out for the *Florida,* rammed her, and demanded her surrender.

Because Captain Morris and almost all hands were ashore and the guns were unloaded, Lieutenant Thomas K. Porter, who was aboard, had to yield. Despite the firing of some useless shots by Brazilian ships and forts, the *Wachusett* took the *Florida* under tow and dragged her out to the open sea in blatant violation of the law of nations.[84]

Thus the second of the most famed Confederate cruisers was gone. According to Frank L. Owsley, Jr., Morris probably made a mistake in not accepting a challenge to fight that the Federal commander, Collins, had sent him. The *Florida* was better armed than the *Wachusett,* had rifled cannons, and, being faster, could have determined the range of battle. She might at least have avoided an inglorious end.[85] The question remains whether damage had not made her slower and less maneuverable and therefore unable to give battle in proper conditions.

The second hard blow for the Confederate navy occurred in home waters. In the sounds of North Carolina the *Albemarle* was a permanent nightmare to the enemy. Mallory hoped to have another ironclad of the same class, now being built by C. Gilbert Elliott, join her.[86] Yet the latter never came. As at Mobile Bay, the poor industrial plant of the Confederacy made the hope illusory.

The *Albemarle* was alone and would remain alone. Nevertheless, she was much feared by the enemy, who swore to destroy her. This was certainly more easily said than done until a young and daring U.S. naval officer, Commander William B. Cushing, proposed an action inspired by the South's use of torpedo boats. Gustavus Vasa Fox, who had been greatly impressed by such actions, authorized the operation, and Cushing was detailed to New York. There he got two steam barges forty-five feet long, to which were fitted spars tipped with explosive devices.[87]

On the night of 27 October 1864, Cushing, with a crew of seven men, under cover of darkness silently approached the Southern ironclad, moored near Plymouth, with one of his barges. The night was extremely dark, foggy, and rainy. Moreover, because of the usual lack of personnel, the Confederates had been compelled to reduce their guard force to the bone.[88]

They did sight the assault boat and opened a brisk fire. Cushing's jacket was torn to shreds and the sole of a shoe taken away by the bullets. The boat steered for the ironclad at full speed. A large stack of wood lighted by the Confederates so they could see the enemy helped Cushing find his target. The ironclad was protected by a barrage of floating logs, but Cushing had foreseen that they would be slimy from long immersion so his assault boat could slide over them, although it could not possibly come back.

Cushing passed over the logs and exploded his device at the exact distance he had previously calculated. It opened a great hole in the *Albemarle*'s hull that sent her down in eight feet of water to lie on the bottom. Cushing and one of his men, protected by darkness, swam to safety. Two Union sailors were killed and the others taken prisoner.[89] Denied the protection of the powerful ironclad, Plymouth was almost immediately retaken by the Union army and navy.

In spite of these blows, the small Southern navy still was able to help the Confederacy. Deadly blows often came by land, not by sea. On 2 September Atlanta had fallen into the hands of General Sherman, causing the loss of the rolling mill and other plants. Its equipment had been moved to Augusta, Georgia, and the ordnance shop was hurriedly moved to Columbia, South Carolina. Now Sherman started his famous march through Georgia, heading for Savannah and overcoming any resistance, which the Confederate army was practically incapable of offering.[90]

General William J. Hardee, commanding the Savannah area, sent a frantic appeal to the navy to cooperate in defending several strategic places.[91] The gunboat *Macon* was sent upriver to protect the railroad bridge of the vital Savannah and Charleston line.[92] The gunboat *Isondiga*, in turn, followed by the *Sampson,* was sent to cover another strategic point.[93]

Yet Hardee, tightly pressed by Sherman, compelled to defend himself with a handful of troops against an overwhelming enemy, asked if the navy could send the ironclad *Savannah* or at least the floating battery *Georgia* to protect the railroad viaduct, whose loss would be a disaster for the Confederacy.[94]

This was impossible because of the deep draft of the *Savannah*. The *Georgia* was immovable because of bad weather, and there was no way she could be towed. The *Savannah* sailed upriver as far as the city and at first lay at a strategic point at the confluence with the Ogeechee River, then near Fort Jackson.[95]

Yet the enemy was pressing mercilessly forward. To Sherman's sixty-two thousand seasoned men Hardee could oppose but some ten thousand, hurriedly assembled, to man the thirteen-mile-long fortified line between the Ogeechee and the Savannah rivers. On 13 December the commanding officer of the *Macon* was ordered, following a request by Hardee, to blow up the railroad bridge and come back to protect the extreme right wing of the line.[96] He did not succeed because enemy artillery had already closed the river below the gunboat.

After a brisk exchange of shots, the *Macon* (and also the *Sampson*) had to turn about and seek safety in the upper reaches of the Savannah, near Augusta, where they would participate in the defense of that city. The trouble was that Commodore William W. Hunter was with them so that now the ships downriver had to fend for themselves.[97] Captain Thomas W. Brent of the *Savannah* assumed temporary command of the squadron.

On 13 December the strong Fort McAllister, which had protected the Ogeechee River and often driven back the Union ironclads, fell when taken from the rear by Sherman's troops.[98] Now Sherman contacted the U.S. naval squadron and through it obtained twelve heavy siege guns with which to bombard Savannah. That he intended to place such guns "as close as possible to the heart of Savannah"[99] meant that the city would have to endure the horrors of a bombardment. Moreover, Sherman was trying to send columns beyond the Savannah River to trap the defenders by cutting off their only route of retreat. Savannah had become untenable, and General Hardee decided to evacuate it.[100]

The only escape route for the Confederates was one bridge, leading from Savannah to Hutchinson's Island. On the other side of the island, to cross the second branch of the river, it was necessary to improvise a pontoon bridge, which the Confederates, working frantically, finished by 19 December.[101] At night the sad retreat procession began: tired and ragged soldiers, wagon trains of stunned civilian refugees, with makeshift vehicles upon which they had stuffed their few, poor belongings.

Near the bridge, the navy watched. The ironclad *Savannah* and gunboat *Isondiga* manned their guns and thus ensured that the enemy would not encroach; meanwhile, they prevented the Federals from crossing troops to the other bank of the river to cut off the Confederate retreat.[102] The enemy did not meddle. The *Savannah* was now a trapped lion but still a lion and still awesome, as stated by General Sherman himself.[103]

While soldiers and refugees, bent under their loads, silently crossed the river during the cold night, the vain hopes that technological backwardness had not prevented the Confederate navy from nurturing were going up in smoke. The new ironclad *Milledgeville* (which had never received her armor) was set afire. By Mallory's order, Commodore Tattnall blew up the shipyard;[104] the floating battery *Georgia,* her guns spiked, was scuttled and sunk at her mooring. Even the gunboats *Isondiga,* which had grounded, and *Water Witch,* which had been seized so gallantly, were burned. Then, after the refugees' procession ended, the bridge was cut.

Alone, the *Savannah* defiantly remained on the river to protect the rear guard of the retreating army and permit the evacuation of the military warehouses. She was ordered to remain for two days more.[105] The Federal troops at last came within range of the *Savannah* and started shelling the ironclad, which, with her flag still flying, answered with a brisk fire.[106]

Orders from Richmond were that she was to try to reach the sea and steer for Charleston. Captain Sidney Smith Lee insisted that it would be better "for the Navy, for our cause and Country" if the ironclad "should fall in the conflict of battle" while striking the enemy "a blow that will relieve defeat from discredit" rather than surrender.[107]

Brent got ready to follow orders, a difficult task because two enemy ironclads were waiting for him at the mouth of the river.[108] When he tried to find a path through the torpedo fields, he discovered that the anchors that fastened the torpedoes had, with the passing of time, so settled in the mud that it was impossible to remove them. Moreover, in the confusion, it was not possible to find officers from the Corps of Engineers who might know of other paths. The *Savannah,* one of the best Confederate ironclads, was hopelessly trapped by the very obstructions that had been intended to protect her and the other Southern ships. On the night of 21 December 1864, at 11:00 P.M., the ironclad, taken near the South Carolina coast, was set ablaze and, a little later, burst. It was such a frightful explosion that it lighted the sky all around and shook buildings miles away.[109]

This was a scene of disaster. Yet it was certain that the evacuation of Savannah and the salvaging of the defending army were owed to the small Confederate navy, which had held to the bitter end. The Savannah Squadron had not been defeated: the enemy had reached the city from land behind it, not by sea.[110]

N I N E T E E N

The Flag Still Flies

For the Confederacy conditions at the end of the year 1864 looked ominous. Only a single success relieved the gloom. On 24 December the Federal navy had unleashed an amphibious operation against Fort Fisher, which defended Wilmington, North Carolina, the most important port for blockade runners.

More than fifty warships, commanded by Rear Admiral David Dixon Porter, convoyed a great expeditionary force directed by General Benjamin Butler. Despite the failure to hurl a ship full of explosives against the fort, the Union fleet subjected the mighty Confederate work to one of the most fearful bombardments in history. Yet it accomplished nothing. Fort Fisher held, and the Federals were compelled to give up in humiliation. It was a happy Christmas for the Southern defenders. But it would be the last.[1]

On 13 January 1865, the Federals made another attempt. The inept General Butler had been replaced by the able Alfred H. Terry, and Porter remained in command of the naval force. Terry used means less glamorous but more effective: under cover of night, he succeeded in landing eight thousand soldiers. Meanwhile, the ships kept up such a heavy fire that the defenders were unable to oppose the landing. Protected by a deadly fire from the warships, the Union soldiers attacked, and on 15 January, after a bloody fight, Fort Fisher was taken. The Northern fleet had fired more than fifty thousand projectiles, or about a thousand pounds for every linear yard of the fort. The modern and efficient industrial plant of the North had been able to produce the tremendous number of shells required and much more. Nevertheless, the battle had been hard-fought and had cost the Union more than a thousand casualties.[2]

For the Confederates, the loss of Fort Fisher was a disaster. It was the port for almost all blockade-running trade. The Southerners evacuated the estuary of the Cape Fear River after blowing up all the remaining works. Yet, as at Mobile, the city of Wilmington remained in their hands.

Wilmington's situation was worse than that of Mobile. Even though it was protected by an unbroken line of entrenchments commanded by an able officer, General Robert F. Hoke, it no longer had any naval support. Mention has already been made of the fate of the ironclad *Raleigh*. The *North Carolina*, patched together with scraps, had never been able to move. Her draft was too deep to allow her to cross the bar, and her engines, recovered from a riverboat, gave her little power. In September 1864, the hull, which was not protected by copper sheathing, had been so eaten away by worms that the poor ship sank while at her mooring.[3]

For the Federals to seal Wilmington's port had required two gigantic amphibious expeditions. Yet for the Confederates it was a military, not a naval, defeat. Mallory was indeed planning an offensive operation. Taking advantage of the absence of enemy warships because they were engaged at Wilmington, the James River Squadron would move to attack the great enemy base at City Point, with the objective of compelling Grant to give up the siege of Petersburg.[4]

Unfortunately, Commodore Mitchell, commanding the squadron, was neither a Buchanan nor a Farragut. He evidently failed to understand the need to strike quickly. Mallory began to lose patience. On 21 January he wrote Mitchell an urgent letter: did the commodore not realize that a unique occasion had arisen? Then the order: move on the next morning.[5] On the same day at 9:00 P.M. Mallory sent another message: "Unless you act at once, action will be useless." He also sent Mitchell a team of daring and able officers, among them Robert D. Minor and Charles W. Read (returned from prison), with three torpedo boats, to attack the enemy ships with explosive devices.[6]

Finally, the squadron moved. The ironclad *Fredericksburg* succeeded in passing the obstructions, but the *Richmond* and the *Virginia II* grounded. At dawn the Confederate ships faced extremely heavy fire, not only from the forts that the Federals had built along the riverbanks but also from the ironclad *Onondaga*, which, with one of her monster 15-inch guns, struck the *Virginia II* with a shot that cracked her 6-inch armor, splintered the internal wooden backing, killed one sailor, and wounded two.

The gunboat *Drewry* (whose crew had previously been transferred to an ironclad) blew up with a terrible blast after being hit by enemy fire.

When the ironclads that had grounded were again afloat, Mitchell tried to resume the action, but the funnel of the *Virginia II,* damaged by a 15-inch projectile from the *Onondaga,* was pouring smoke and steam into the interior of the casemate. Mitchell needed no more justification to give up the action, even though the daring Read suggested going ahead with only two ironclads.[7]

Mallory, in disgust, decided to replace Mitchell. Because Raphael Semmes, now a rear admiral, had returned from England, the secretary on 18 February 1865 detailed him to command the James River Squadron. John M. Kell, the executive officer of the *Alabama,* now a commander, was already in command of the ironclad *Richmond.*[8]

Even Semmes, although daring and aggressive, could do little. The enemy had reinforced its squadron with the powerful ironclads originally sent against Fort Fisher, and the small Confederate squadron was hopelessly outnumbered. Any idea of offensive operations, therefore, had to be given up.

Even though it had overwhelming superiority, the enemy navy did not attack. Like Richmond and Savannah, Charleston remained invulnerable from the sea. Admiral Dahlgren, partly at General Sherman's request, had often sent his ironclads to test Charleston's defenses. On the night of 15 January 1865, the great ironclad *Patapsco,* 1,875 tons, struck a torpedo. The powerful ship sank in less than a minute with the loss of 62 men of her crew of 105.[9]

After crossing the Savannah River, Sherman advanced across South Carolina. Another city impregnable from the sea was about to fall to enemy columns arriving from the interior. On 14 February General Beauregard decided that Charleston should be evacuated. Once again, it was of the utmost importance to prevent the few irreplaceable Confederate troops from being trapped by the enemy.[10]

The unconquered naval squadron had no way to escape. It had played a vital part in sealing up the port to the enemy naval force, but now it was doomed and had to be scuttled.

On 12 January 1865 the ironclad *Columbia,* among the most powerful built by the Confederacy, had joined the three already at Charleston. She was covered by 6-inch armor, was 216 feet long, and carried six heavy guns. Unfortunately, during her first trial in the harbor she struck a submerged wreck and was now half sunk.

The others were in good condition. During the night of 17–18 February, while the army and a destitute crowd of refugees evacuated the city amid the deafening noise of exploding military warehouses, locomotives, shipyards, and two ironclads still being built, the Confederate sailors proceeded to scuttle the squadron.

There were three successive explosions: the *Palmetto State,* the *Chicora,* and the flagship *Charleston,* for which at least twenty tons of powder had to be used and whose explosion was so fierce that it shook the city, already wrapped in flames, and even the Union warships at a distance. Gigantic hunks of red-hot iron fell everywhere.[11] Many small torpedo boats were also scuttled.

Disaster was imminent, and the navy was being swept away in the defeat of the Southern land forces. On 22 February 1865 the city of Wilmington fell to the Union army. Yet the small Confederate navy was still damaging the enemy: on 1 March Dahlgren's flagship, the *Harvest Moon,* hit a torpedo and sank.

Meanwhile, Federal columns spread throughout North Carolina. The Confederate ironclad *Neuse* was cornered because of the defeat on land. In the fall of 1864 she had finally been put afloat and had helped protect the river that was her namesake, as well as the countryside around, from enemy raids. Now, Confederate military authorities, nearly surrounded by Sherman's divisions, begged the navy to sacrifice the ironclad to protect the retreat of Confederate forces. The *Neuse,* now alone to face the enemy, went into action, dispersing with the fire of her powerful guns several troops of Federal cavalry until she, too, isolated, had to be scuttled on 13 March 1865 to prevent her capture.[12]

Now it was Richmond's turn. Throughout the winter General Ulysses Grant had been tightening the noose about the Confederate capital. One after another, the railroads vital to the life of the city and to Lee's army had been cut. On 2 April the Southern government abandoned Richmond and began the general evacuation of the area.

Thus the end was in sight for the James River Squadron. That very night Admiral Semmes ordered that the three ironclads and minor ships be burned and blown up. At midnight the vessels were set afire and a series of frightful explosions rocked the city, now aflame, with shocks like those of earthquakes. The shells in each ship's magazine, thrown high in the dark sky, exploded in bunches at different times. It was a hellish pyrotechnical spectacle.[13]

As long as the three ironclads had defended the James, the enemy had not attempted to take Richmond from the water side. The vessels had been a formidable obstacle that no naval force would have dared to challenge and perhaps could not have overcome.[14]

Now Semmes hoped that the crews of the squadron might join their comrades from other ships that had been scuttled earlier. These men had been organized into a naval brigade, composed entirely of sailors, who fought in the trenches together with army soldiers, contributing to the last-ditch defense of the capital and now retreating in good order.

Amid the catastrophic scene, Semmes and his sailors found a locomotive and some railroad cars. Naval engineers had no problems in tending land engines, and the group was soon under way toward Danville, Virginia. The story of the Confederate States Navy, begun aboard a train, was ending in a railroad convoy.

At Danville, Semmes found the president and his cabinet. Mallory ordered him to form his sailors into an artillery brigade. For ten days they held the trenches assigned to them. Then, on 9 April, General Lee surrendered at Appomattox. The surrender of General Johnston followed at Bennett Farm on 1 May. Now Semmes had to dissolve and muster out his command. The naval brigade had followed the retreat of General Lee from Richmond. Always on the front line, it had protected the retreat, driving back enemy attacks. At the moment of surrender, it still held the section of the front assigned to it together with two hundred marines.[15]

The same day that Richmond was evacuated, Federal cavalry occupied Selma, Alabama. Retreating Confederates had already destroyed the Naval Cannon Foundry and other plants there, which they were planning to set afire in case of danger.[16] From Selma, General James H. Wilson, commanding the Union cavalry troops, proceeded toward Columbus, Georgia. There the Confederates were compelled to scuttle the almost completed ironclad *Jackson* (former *Muscogee*).[17]

Only Mobile's defenses remained. In January and February 1865 General Canby, commanding Union forces in western Mississippi, had begun to receive reinforcements at an accelerated pace and was able to muster an army of 45,200 men. He started his march on 17 March.[18] According to his plan, they would move up the bay along its eastern coast and be supported by the naval squadron commanded by Rear Admiral Henry K. Thatcher.[19]

Confederate general Dabney H. Maury had about ten thousand men in Mobile.[20] At the point where the enemy attack was expected, Mobile was protected by Spanish Fort and Fort Blakely, located about four miles apart along the Appalachee River near its confluence with the Tensaw (two branches of the wandering delta of the Alabama and the Tombigbee). On the river side the forts were covered by the naval squadron, commanded by Flag Officer Ebenezer Farrand. In turn, the vessels were protected by strong torpedo fields. The forts were well manned by artillerists with powerful 11-, 10-, 7-, and 6.25-inch Brookes.[21]

On 26 March 1865 Canby invested Spanish Fort and started his bombardment; on the thirtieth he attacked Fort Blakely. It was now up to the navy, and the Confederate ships supported the forts by shelling the Union troops. The Federal forces, under continuous naval fire, began to suffer grievously. Broadsides came from the ironclad *Nashville,* the floating battery *Huntsville,* and—very effectively—from the small gunboat *Morgan,* which had escaped the destruction of Confederate ships at Mobile Bay.[22]

Foreseeing this naval strength, General Canby had repeatedly requested support from the U.S. Navy, and Rear Admiral Thatcher, who had overwhelming forces, provided it.[23] On 27 March, Thatcher, who had forged ahead with his five ironclads, sent one of them, the powerful *Milwaukee* (1,300 tons, two turrets with four heavy 11-inch Dahlgrens), to fire on Confederate steamers supplying Spanish Fort. Late in the afternoon, after compelling one transport to flee, the big ironclad struck a torpedo and sank in three minutes in ten feet of water but without loss of life.[24]

It was the first of several episodes that gave the Confederate navy its last victories in home waters. Action by Union naval forces was becoming increasingly necessary, and Thatcher began minesweeping.[25] Now Canby requested that the ironclads support him by firing on both the forts and the Confederate ships.[26]

When Thatcher believed that the minesweeping was completed, he again pushed forward with his four ironclads. At 2:00 P.M. on 29 March, another ironclad, the *Osage,* struck a torpedo and sank with the loss of six men.[27] Finally, on 1 April, the gunboat *Rodolph* was blown up by a submarine explosive device.[28]

The doomed Confederate navy was exacting a terrible toll from the enemy. Even after the Confederates evacuated Mobile, at least another five ships of various types would be sunk by torpedoes.[29]

Yet the enemy, strong because of overwhelming numbers and a massive superiority in artillery, was now investing Spanish Fort by regular approaches. General Maury decided to evacuate the fort, which was becoming untenable, and on 10 April fell back on the city of Mobile. Fort Blakely had to be abandoned on the eleventh. Finally, on 12 April 1865, the city of Mobile was handed over to the enemy and Maury retreated northward with the remainder of his troops.[30]

Again a Confederate squadron, undefeated by the enemy, was trapped because of events of the land war. Commodore Farrand decided not to give up his ships. The floating batteries *Huntsville* and *Tuscaloosa,* unable because of the weakness of their engines to breast the current, were scuttled. The other vessels, led by the *Nashville,* sailed several miles up the Tombigbee River, anchored, and kept the enemy at bay.[31]

Early in April, Carter, the captain of the ironclad *Missouri,* had taken her down the river to near Alexandria, Louisiana, to support the soldiers who were defending what remained of that state.[32] There he was joined by Lieutenant Charles W. Read, sent by Mallory. Read—a man who would never yield—had asked the secretary to detail him to command the ram *Webb,* which had a speed of up to twenty-two knots. Read proposed sailing her down the Red River into the Mississippi and then to sea to resume commerce destroying.[33]

On 31 March, with Carter's blessing, he assumed command of the ram. It took three weeks to put together a crew and to get ammunition, food supplies, and coal. Finally, on 22 April, about two weeks after the surrender at Appomattox, the *Webb* was ready to go.[34]

The first part of the expedition went well, for the *Webb* reached New Orleans, eluding the guard of Union ships mostly by false signals and destroying the telegraph lines. At New Orleans the enemy squadron was at her heels, and the *Webb* was hailed by a blast of cannon shots. A few miles ahead a big steam frigate barred the river. The daring enterprise had failed. Read could do nothing but set his ship afire and blow her up.[35] The last daring action of the Confederate navy gave Northern naval authorities a serious scare.[36] It was 24 April 1865.

Two days later the last Confederate forces in the East surrendered. On 2 May Secretary Mallory, who had followed President Davis on his retreat across the Carolinas and Georgia, wrote him a letter, stating sadly that the miserable condition of his family prevented his following Davis into exile and begged him to accept his resignation.

The president accepted the resignation "under the circumstances," then, remembering that Mallory had been a member of his first cabinet and expressing deep regret for the separation, he wrote:

> We have passed together through all the trials of the war and the not less embarrassing trials to which the Congress has of late subjected the Executive. Your minute knowledge of naval affairs and your counsel upon all important measures have been to the Administration a most valuable support. For the zeal, ability and integrity with which you have so long and so constantly labored, permit me who had the best opportunity to judge, to offer testimonial and in the name of our country and its sacred cause to return thanks. I will ever gratefully remember your uniform kindness and unwavering friendship to myself; and will fervently pray for your welfare and happiness in whatever position you may hereafter be placed.[37]

The organization of the Confederate navy thus ceased to exist. Gathered along the Tombigbee River, however, the Mobile Squadron still flew its flag. On 8 May Commodore Farrand signed surrender terms and turned over his ships.[38]

Only the ironclad *Missouri* remained. On 3 June 1865, one month after the acceptance of Mallory's resignation, Commander Carter surrendered. The Confederacy no longer existed.

Yet at sea the flag of the Southern navy still flew. Bulloch had achieved his last two missions. One dealt with commerce raiding, the other with seagoing ironclads.

As early as 18 July 1864 Mallory had begun working to replace the lost raider *Alabama*.[39] Even though the *Rappahannock,* acquired by M. F. Maury, had ended by being hopelessly trapped at Calais,[40] Bulloch had not given up. He had decided that it was no longer possible to have ships built for the Confederacy in France or Great Britain. Ships would have to be bought.

For some time he had eyed a fast steamer, built in Glasgow for the Indian Ocean, of 1,160 tons displacement, 850-horsepower engines, covered with teak wood, 222 feet long, capable of running like a swallow. She was appropriately named the *Sea King*.[41] In the late fall of 1864 Bulloch had succeeded in acquiring the ship for £15,000 through a British agent who had provided him cover. This man, named Richard Wright, was the brother-in-law of Charles Prioleau, the faithful agent of Fraser and Trenholm. The ship went to sea on 8 October 1864. Union spies were always vigilant, but on this occasion they did not guess that Richard Wright was really acting for Bulloch.

Hard on the heels of the future cruiser came the transport *Laurel,* carrying the officers, part of the crew, ordnance (four 8-inch cannons and two 32-pounder Whitworths), small arms, uniforms, food supplies, and coal.[42]

On 19 October the *Laurel* had joined the cruiser, now rechristened the *Shenandoah,* at Madeira. The transfer of weapons and supplies had taken place, the ship was put into commission, and Lieutenant Commanding James Iredell Waddell, C.S.N., had assumed command and hoisted the flag. This would be the last Confederate ensign to be lowered. Waddell was tough, energetic, and daring.[43]

On 30 October the cruiser captured her first prize, but her real objective was the northern Pacific Ocean, where the great Union whaling fleet worked untroubled.[44] After rounding Africa and destroying several enemy merchantmen, she proceeded through the Indian Ocean and on 25 January 1865 reached Melbourne, where the Australian people and authorities admired both the clean and impeccable uniforms of officers and men and the flawless discipline on board the Confederate cruiser.[45]

On 1 April the cruiser sighted Ascension Island and on the fourteenth came within sight of the Kurile Islands. There she arrived five days after the surrender of General Lee at Appomattox. On the tenth she had destroyed her first whaling ship and started hunting others.[46]

Bulloch had undertaken another enterprise. In France, shipbuilder Arman had been compelled to sell the ironclads built for the Confederacy, the *Sphinx* to Denmark and the *Cheops* to Prussia. In October 1864 they

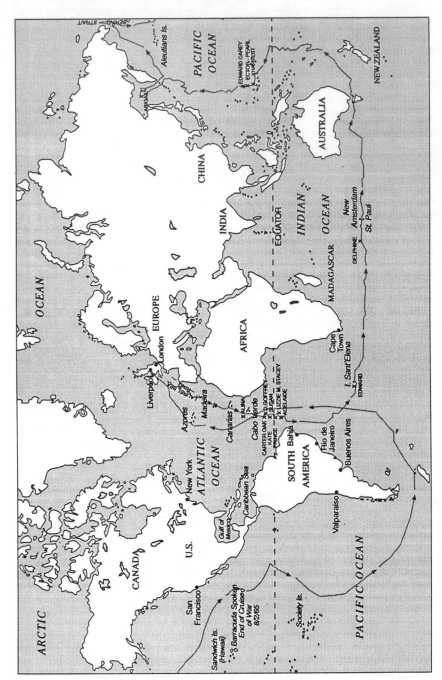

The "last flag": The CSS *Shenandoah's* cruise around the world.

were still moored at Bordeaux. The wily Arman had managed to sell the two ironclads to two belligerent countries that could not, under the neutrality laws, acquire them. Only after the war between Prussia and Denmark in 1864 was the *Sphinx* sent to the Danes, who then did not know what to do with her.[47] Arman turned to Bulloch. Did he still want the ship?

Bulloch knew that matters for the Confederacy were going from bad to worse. Its port cities were falling one after another. Any possible help was needed, and surely the arrival of a powerful ironclad from Europe might spread panic among Union seamen. Therefore, Bulloch decided to buy the ship. Arnous de la Rivière, Arman's agent, immediately set the sale in motion together with a Danish banker named Puggard. The deal cost Bulloch more than 450,000 French francs (375,000 pocketed by Arnous de la Rivière and 80,000 by Puggard), but on 7 January 1865 the Confederate States Navy finally acquired its first and only ironclad built in Europe.[48]

Her commanding officer was a Virginian, Captain Thomas Jefferson Page. Daring, brave, and experienced, Page was an excellent choice.[49]

Leaving Copenhagen with a provisional crew under a Danish captain and the cover name of *Olinda,* the ironclad, with Page on board, sailed toward the English Channel, where she should meet the blockade runner *City of Richmond* that was carrying the crew (mostly former sailors from the *Florida*) and supplies.[50] All went wrong from the start. A gale of unheard-of violence compelled the supply vessel to seek shelter at Cherbourg, while the *Olinda* sought safety in the Norwegian port of Kristiansand. It had soon become clear that she was a poor sailer, with a worrisome propensity of failing to rise from the wave troughs. At last, Page succeeded in persuading the frightened crew to move, and on 24 January 1865, near the French island of Houat, the ironclad met the *City of Richmond* and took aboard crew and supplies. This gave rise to the usual protest by the Federal chargé d'affaires, but the French minister Drouyn de Lhuys paid no attention. The ship was commissioned into the Confederate navy and renamed the *Stonewall.*[51]

There were still more delays. At Houat, near Quiberon, because of a heavy sea, the *Stonewall* was unable to take enough coal aboard. Page decided to enter the Spanish port of El Ferrol to complete his coaling. It was 12 February 1865. The ship was not in good condition and needed repairs; her officers raised a strong protest so that Barron and Bulloch rushed to the scene to avoid what looked like a mutiny.[52]

This problem solved, the Spanish port authorities had to be placated.[53] Finally, after coaling and repairs, Page was able to move on 19 March. But now the vessel could not sail because of the rough sea.[54] Meanwhile, the

Federals had sent the large steam frigate *Niagara,* which had twelve 150-pounder rifled Parrotts, commanded by Captain Thomas T. Craven, together with the smaller *Sacramento,* to intercept the ironclad. Page was unconcerned: he would fight.

On 24 March 1865 the ironclad went to sea. Yet Craven did not dare to confront a vessel about which a myth of invincibility had grown and prudently kept his distance. For the whole day, from 10:30 A.M. to 8:30 P.M., Page, with the Confederate flag flying, sailed to and fro in full sight of the Union ships, which being faster, kept out of range. At nightfall, the ironclad steered southward and, after coaling in Lisbon, on 28 March left European waters for America.[55]

The *Stonewall* coaled at Tenerife on 1 April. On 6 May, upon reaching Nassau, Bahamas, the Confederate sailors got dismal news: all Southern forces had surrendered or were about to.

Like a ghost ship, the *Stonewall* left the Bahamas for Cuba. The U.S. Navy was ready to hunt her down. She had spread panic in Washington and along the coasts, and now ironclads and vessels of all descriptions were mobilized to confront the fearsome ship, which was soon blockaded in Cuban waters. Page nevertheless resolved not to let the enemy take his ironclad. He turned the *Stonewall* over to neutral Spain, which gave him some $16,000 with which to pay off his crew. It was 19 May 1865. The ironclad had kept the Confederate flag high for almost a month after the end of the Confederacy.[56]

The *Shenandoah* was still operating in the Sea of Okhotsk, inflicting serious losses upon Northern whalers. On 2 August 1865 Waddell learned from a British merchantman that the last Confederate forces had long since surrendered. He decided to disarm his ship and sail for Great Britain. The trip was a long one: the *Shenandoah* reached Liverpool on 6 November 1865 and was turned over to British authorities.[57]

The Confederate States Navy had thus flown the country's flag for almost four months after Appomattox and for more than two months after the last armed resistance ceased. It was the last to challenge the enemy. Its ships were the last to give up. And the navy as an organization never surrendered.

Some Final Remarks

The great archaeologist Sir Leonard Woolley, in a delightful book, paradoxically held that the best thing for one who studied an ancient city was the presence nearby of a volcano, which, having buried the urban area in just a few minutes, would have preserved intact the records for his use and for that of other scholars. He added that "unfortunately" this rarely happens.

The same can be said for historians. Is there one of them who does not desire to run across some beautiful and complete manuscript collection, perfectly preserved, that would transmit intact the entire documentation of an event or an epoch?

One who reasons this way should dedicate himself to the history of the victors because the vanquished not only "have no history" but normally have no archives except by the tender mercy of the winner, who might have picked up some debris here and there; and those, at best, have big (and often irreparable) gaps.

In the final collective disaster that befell the Southern Confederacy at the end of the Civil War, the naval archives were almost all burned in Richmond and Charlotte, North Carolina.

The lack of a central documentary collection, in addition to discouraging many historians, helped to foster a plethora of prejudices, legends, and myths about the strategic objectives of the Confederate States Navy, which took the place of truth and sometimes were transmitted from one book to another.

According to the most deep-rooted myth, the strategic objective of the

Confederate States Navy was to break the blockade. Because it failed to do so, the Confederate navy was considered a failure. The truth is that, at first, Mallory nurtured the illusion not only of being able to break the blockade but also of seizing command of the sea by means of the ultimate weapon, which he believed he possessed. His ability to learn from experience quickly prevailed. Experience taught him about the true, immediate, and deadly danger represented by U.S. amphibious operations, which were threatening the heart of the South. From that moment on, his objective and that of his able and valiant collaborators was to make the Confederacy safe from the invasion by sea that was being steadily developed by the Federals in such an ubiquitous way and on such a scale as to become a series of major interforce operations.

In meeting this threat, the success of the small Confederate navy was remarkable: for four years it protected the rear of the Southern armies fighting on several fronts and contributed substantially to retaining control of the port cities through which vital supplies arrived for these armies. In the end, it was the collapse of the land fronts that directly or indirectly caused defeat. Of the six coastal cities (Richmond included) finally seized by the enemy, five fell for this reason.

If one remembers that to reach its ends the Confederate navy had to start literally from zero, one must admire the accomplishments of men operating under extreme difficulties. The Confederates showed an outstanding sagacity not only in creating new war tools but in using them in exceptional and creative ways so as to transform them from technical curiosities into tested elements that would change radically and forever the conduct of war at sea.

Ingenuity was not lacking; one remains astonished by how much there was of it. The true, formidable obstacle was what I consider to be one of the basic reasons for the defeat of the South—perhaps, *the* basic one. Like any old-fashioned, agrarian nation, the South had an outstanding intellectual elite, a true intelligentsia. Although brilliant, it was numerically small. And the war being fought was not the last conflict of the Napoleonic era but the first of the industrial age.

The North might have been, as some Southerners said contemptuously, a nation of "shopkeepers," but it was also one of mechanics, technicians, and engineers. And the North had lots of them. A John Mercer Brooke was not enough to offset the thousands who ran the industrial plants of the North. This is the characteristic feature of industrial as well as technological warfare. A few brilliant brains are not enough to win. Indispensable is a gigantic and modern industrial machine capable of hurling against the enemy more iron, more lead, more cannons, more ships, more shells, more locomotives, more railroad rails than he can put together. All this must be done in the most efficient way and in the shortest time. Otherwise defeat is inescapable.

The South's problem was not only a quantitative one. The Confederates, by extreme exertions, managed to put into commission twenty-nine ironclads, whereas the North not only commissioned almost sixty but sold ironclads abroad (the two ironclad steam frigates of the Royal Italian Navy which fought at Lissa, the *Re d'Italia* and *Re di Portogallo,* were built in New York in 1862).

The production plant of the South lagged well behind the Northern one. The problem was that the Southern industrial plant was that of a pre–industrial revolution society. It was substantially composed of old-fashioned manufactures, run by old-fashioned labor systems, not by modern industrial concerns. No Southern industry, not even the Tredegar (as Charles B. Dew demonstrated) had, before the war, the ability to compete on the market with the modern Northern plants.

In the North, industry was becoming more and more the dominant factor in the economy; in the South, manufacturing was subordinated to the needs and economic and political aims of agriculture, exactly as it had been for centuries in any civilized European state and even in the North before the industrial revolution. Moreover, in the South the ruling class was still in the main agricultural.

Hence the basic problem was a qualitative one, which cannot be solved by statistics. The South lacked a mass of skilled workmen, which the North had.

One cannot but admire the incredible exertions of the South; yet a comparison of the building of the *Virginia* with that of the *Monitor* or the story of the *Louisiana* and the *Mississippi* contrasted with the creation of a big ironclad gunboat fleet on western waters shows the difference. The North had the advantage of a strong, modern, rational, and efficient industrial concern, enjoying a wide array of skilled workmen, technicians, and engineers; in the South industry was a work of *bricoleurs,* of a few men endowed with genius but children of a bygone technical era. From this viewpoint, the South had lost the war even before a single cannon shot had been fired.

The truth is that after the industrial revolution (which changed not only the quantity but the quality of social production) no agricultural, underdeveloped community could ever defeat an industrial one, and the South was no exception. It is useless to argue whether Southern manufactures, blacksmith shops, and plantations were or were not efficient in their own way. Maybe they were, but that is not the point. The point is that its social, economic, and technological structures made the Southern community, as a whole, incapable of competing against the terrible onslaught from the modern industrial North.

The Navy is the technical armed force; by studying its history, the dreadful inferiority of the South emerges in its full tragic meaning. Yet Mallory never gave up his struggle for command of the sea. To this end, he continued with extreme doggedness to develop his program for building ironclads overseas. British technology was certainly not underdeveloped; it was the most advanced in the world. Could not the South make use of it to reverse the fortunes of the war at sea?

Here appears another factor that must not be overlooked. In the age of industrial warfare, the idea of fighting and winning a war without possessing an advanced war industry is sheer illusion. Too many imponderables are at work. First is the fear of enemy strength among possible foreign producers. One who dreams of waging a war without a strong and modern industry has lost before starting to fight.

In spite of obstacles, what the Confederate navy succeeded in doing was astonishing. With the exceptions of Cherbourg and Mobile Bay, as well as in the initial engagements in which the mosquito fleets did all they could against an overwhelming enemy, the navy ended the war without being defeated. It was the collapse of the Confederate armies that dragged the naval forces into the general disaster. Almost everywhere the navy survived after the defeat of the land armies; it actually survived the very Confederacy that had created it.

After the war, the victorious Union navy did not forget amphibious warfare. One must start from Confederate shores to understand the achievements of World War II from Sicily and Normandy to the Pacific, as well as of the Korean War. The able and efficient actions the Southerners devised to counter the enemy's deadly operations fell into oblivion: neither Germans, Japanese, nor North Koreans learned anything from the defensive experiences of the Southern navy and probably did not study them.

The Confederate States Navy found in Secretary Mallory a leader of outstanding competence, foresight, and talent. If the main tasks of a commander in chief are the correct formulation of strategy, the selection of cadres, and control of execution, Mallory did not fail in any category. His strategic ability was excellent. In selecting cadres, he showed a keenness, an understanding of men, and an ability to weigh them that were the secret of many a success. Buchanan, Semmes, Bulloch, Brooke, Jones, Wood, the two Minors, Howell, Warner, Brown, Read, and many others formed an elite rarely found in naval history.

Less brilliant were Chief Naval Constructor John Luke Porter and Engineer in Chief William P. Williamson, but they were the best the South could offer. As for control, one need merely glance at the records to see that Mallory's was continuous, omnipresent, and, in the end, even harassing.

Mallory paid the cost of his isolation with some major blunders that a better organization of command certainly would have avoided. In the selection of cadres his errors were few, but some had serious consequences, for example, the choice of Lieutenant North for the mission to England and that of Webb to command the Savannah Squadron. Elsewhere, his most serious error was probably in trusting too many people for overseas shipbuilding. It would have been better had he left the task to Bulloch. Perhaps he thought that more results might be achieved by more people. If so, he erred. Worse was that he trusted speculators who brought the Confederacy discredit and not a single ship.

Many of Mallory's mistakes stemmed from the Confederate navy's command system. Mallory had few to assist him: no chief of staff, no commander in chief of the fleet, no organization of command and control, no board of admirals. One may object that the U.S. Navy operated in the same way because such was the system by which the old, small antebellum navy had been directed and that both sides did nothing but follow it. Still, the Federals had the invaluable Gustavus Vasa Fox and the Blockade Board, which amounted to a sort of chief of staff and an operations bureau.

There remains to be discovered whether the methods Mallory followed were a result of lack of time to create, in addition to a navy, a new command system or to Mallory's personal leaning toward centralism, not rare in men as efficient and active as the Confederate secretary of the navy.

In the long run this lack of an efficient command system proved the Achilles' heel of the small Southern navy. One should not, however, be too severe: the great and powerful U.S. Navy (as well as the army) did not adopt a truly modern command structure until years after the war. Indeed, this did not come until the end of the century.

President Davis had the great merit of fully evaluating Mallory's outstanding qualities and of leaving him alone. Mallory was the only member of the cabinet (except for Postmaster General Reagan, of minor importance) who carried out his duties for the duration of the war.

All in all, the Americans were wise; it can be proved that the Northern enemies of the Confederate navy carefully studied the innovations it introduced and after the war adopted them in their own service. So, they were, basically, the testamentary executors of a small navy that showed a higher genius and a stronger heart than destiny would allow it.

Abbreviations

(With short titles; full titles to be found in the Bibliography.)

AMV: Archives de la Marine, Chateau de Vincennes, France
AS/T: Accademia delle Scienze, Torino, Italy
ASDAH/MA: Alabama State Department of Archives and History, Montgomery, Ala.
AW: The Annals of the War
BL: Battles and Leaders of the Civil War
CLCA/LGB: Cammel Laird Company Archives, Liverpool, Great Britain
CLS/CSC: Charleston Library Society, Charleston, S.C.
CM/RV: Confederate Museum, Richmond, Va.
CNM/CG: Confederate Naval Museum, Columbus, Ga.
DUL/DNC: Duke University Library, Durham, N.C.
EUL/AG: Emory University Library, Atlanta, Ga.
FHSC/TF: Florida Historical Society, Tampa, Fla.
GHS/SG: Georgia Historical Society, Savannah, Ga.
GSA/AG: Georgia State Archives, Atlanta, Ga.
JC: Journal of the Congress of the Confederate States of America
LC: Library of Congress, Washington, D.C.
LSU/BRL: Louisiana State University, Baton Rouge, La.
MDAH/JM: Mississippi Department of Archives and History, Jackson, Miss.
MdHS/BM: Maryland Historical Society, Baltimore, Md.
MM/NNV: Mariners Museum, Newport News, Va.
MUL/OO: Miami University Library, Oxford, Ohio
NA/W: National Archives, Washington, D.C.
NARG: National Archives, Record Group
NCDAH/RNC: North Carolina Department of Archives and History, Raleigh, N.C.
NHD/W: Naval History Division, Washington, D.C.
NHF/W: Naval Historical Foundation, Washington, D.C.

NHSL/NY: New York Historical Society Library, New York
NPL/NV: Norfolk Public Library, Norfolk, Va.
NPL/NY: New York Public Library, New York
OR: Official Records, Armies
ORN: Official Records, Navies
PMHSM: Papers of the Military Historical Society of Massachusetts
PRO: Public Record Office, London
RUL/HT: Rice University Library, Houston, Texas
SCDAH/CSC: South Carolina Department of Archives and History, Columbia, S.C.
SCHS/CSC: South Carolina Historical Society, Charleston, S.C.
SCL/CSC: South Caroliniana Library, Columbia, S.C.
SHC/CHNC: Southern Historical Collection, Chapel Hill, N.C.
SHSP: Southern Historical Society Papers
TUL/NOL: Tulane University Library, New Orleans, La.
UAL/TA: University of Alabama Library, Tuscaloosa, Ala.
UFL/GF: University of Florida Library, Gainesville, Fla.
UGL/AG: University of Georgia Library, Athens, Ga.
USMHI/CP: U.S. Army Military History Institute, Carlisle Barracks, Pa.
USNA/AM: U.S. Naval Academy, Annapolis, Md.
UVL/CV: University of Virginia Library, Charlottesville, Va.
VHS/RV: Virginia Historical Society, Richmond, Va.
VMU/RV: Valentine Museum, Richmond, Va.
VSA/RV: Virginia State Archives, Richmond, Va.
WM/W: William and Mary College Library, Williamsburg, Va.

Notes

CHAPTER ONE

1. On Semmes's physical appearance, see Gamaliel Bradford, *Confederate Portraits* (Boston, 1914), pp. 217ff; D. Macrae, *The Americans at Home,* new ed. (New York, 1952), pp. 378–79; and the photograph of Semmes in *The Photographic History of the Civil War,* ed. F. T. Miller and R. S. Lanier, 10 vols. (New York, 1911), 6:287.

2. About the definitive regulation on ranks of officers in the Confederate navy, see below, Chapter 2. Originally it used the same ranks as the U.S. Navy.

3. The correspondence between Semmes and the Union naval secretary, as well as the invitation from Montgomery to Southern naval officers to place themselves at the disposition of the Confederacy, was published by Semmes in his *Memoirs of Service Afloat during the War between the States* (New York, 1869), pp. 75ff. This is the first (and more reliable, because nearer the events) edition of Semmes's memoirs.

4. Commander Semmes had already written on 11 December 1860 to Senator Alexander Stephens of Georgia, the future vice-president of the Confederate States, politically a moderate, expressing his own opinions and doubts about the situation and asking advice. Stephens answered on 20 January. See Semmes to Stephens, 11 Dec. 1860, Stephens to Semmes, 20 Jan. 1861, in Admiral Semmes Papers, ASDAH/MA. On 24 January Semmes had written to the Hon. I.L.M. Curry, a Confederate congressman, to assure him that he was ready to place himself at the disposition of the new Confederacy. Curry answered on 1 February, saying that he would submit Semmes's name to the new authority. Curry to Semmes, 1 Feb. 1861, Semmes to Curry, 6 Feb. 1861, with advice about the organization of the future navy, Semmes Papers, ASDAH/MA.

5. Semmes, *Memoirs,* pp. 81ff.

6. See Raimondo Luraghi, *Storia della Guerra Civile Americana,* 5th ed., rev. (Milan, 1986), as well as the Introduction to *La Guerra Civile Americana,* ed. Raimondo Luraghi (Bologna, 1978); Raimondo Luraghi, *The Rise and Fall of the Plantation South* (New York, 1978).

7. Charles S. Sydnor, *The Development of Southern Sectionalism, 1819–1848* (Baton

Rouge, 1948); Avery O. Craven, *The Growth of Southern Nationalism, 1848–1861* (Baton Rouge, 1953); Jesse T. Carpenter, *The South as a Conscious Minority, 1789–1861: A Study in Political Thought* (New York, 1930); D. M. Potter and D. E. Fehrenbacher, *The Impending Crisis, 1848–1861* (New York, 1973).

8. See Avery O. Craven, *Civil War in the Making, 1815–1860* (Baton Rouge, 1959); Thomas P. Kettell, *Southern Wealth and Northern Profits* (New York, 1860); Luraghi, *Rise and Fall.*

9. Dwight L. Dumond, *The Secession Movement, 1860–1861* (1931; reprint, New York, 1963); Frank E. Vandiver, *Their Tattered Flags: The Epics of the Confederacy* (New York, 1970); Emory M. Thomas, *The Confederate Nation* (New York, 1984).

10. Lincoln to L. Trumbull, 10 Dec. 1860, in *The Collected Works of Abraham Lincoln,* 8 vols., ed. Roy P. Basler (New Brunswick, N.J., 1953), 4:149–50; Lincoln to E. Washburne, ibid., 1:151, and to Alexander Stephens, ibid., p. 160.

11. Vandiver, *Their Tattered Flags.*

12. That is, Virginia, Tennessee, Arkansas, and North Carolina, which would later join the Confederacy; Maryland, Delaware, Kentucky, and Missouri, which instead would remain in the Union.

13. *OR,* Ser. 4, 1:1.

14. Original draft of the Provisional Constitution of the CSA, CM/RV. It is printed in *OR,* 4, 1:92ff.

15. *JC,* 1:44.

16. See the Provisional Constitution of the Confederate States.

17. *JC,* 1:42, 44.

18. Ibid., pp. 48, 51.

19. J. Thomas Scharf, *History of the Confederate States Navy from Its Organization to the Surrender of Its Last Vessel* (New York, 1887), p. 28.

20. *ORN,* Ser. 2, 2:41ff.

21. Southern officers in the U.S. Navy who resigned made it a point of honor to return their ships to Union ports. See, e.g., Felix Senac, *Saga of Felix Senac, Being the Legend and Biography of a Confederate Agent in Europe,* ed. Regina Rapier (Atlanta, Ga., 1972). But see the opinion of Confederate president Jefferson Davis in his *Rise and Fall of the Confederate Government,* 2 vols.; reprint, ed. Bell I. Wiley (New York, 1958), 1:313ff.

22. John E. Johns, *Florida during the Civil War* (Gainesville, Fla., 1963), p. 49, says that the base was completely neutralized by the presence of such Federal forces.

23. *ORN,* Ser. 2, 2:42ff.; but there is a more complete text in Alfred Roman, *The Military Operations of General Beauregard in the War between the States, 1861 to 1865,* 2 vols. (New York, 1884), 1:422. This book was ghostwritten by Beauregard. The Drummond lights, or "calcium lights," used to illuminate a stage (called "limelights," literally, "lights of lime"), were made by lamps in which a piece of spent lime was made incandescent by flaming jets of hydrogen and oxygen. They gave a soft and very bright light. It appears that Beauregard was the first to think of using them for military purposes. He later made use of them when a general, in Charleston Harbor during the bombardment of Fort Sumter. Yet in the same harbor the Federals used them even more effectively. See *OR,* Ser. 1, 1:294.

24. *ORN,* Ser. 2, 2:42.

25. E. Milby Burton, *The Siege of Charleston, 1861–1865* (Columbia, S.C., 1970), pp. 8–9.

26. Report from Col. Charles Allston, Jr., 23 Jan. 1861, Confederate Navy Papers, SCDAH/CSC.

27. Minutes of the Annual Message addressed to the Legislature of South Carolina by Governor Pickens, 11 Jan. 1861, SCDAH/CSC.

28. Report from steamer *Seabroock,* 23 Dec. 1860, signed by Walter Gwynn, Major, Corps of Engineers, SCDAH/CSC.

29. Scharf, *Confederate States Navy,* p. 658.

30. Journal of the South Carolina Executive Council, 1861, SCDAH/CSC.

31. Scharf, *Confederate States Navy,* pp. 24ff. He, however, admits that those data are approximate.

32. Lieutenant of Engineers P. E. Prims to General J. G. Totten, 30 Jan. 1861, *OR,* Ser. 1, 1:329.

33. Guy Frégault, *Pierre le Moyne d'Iberville* (Montreal, 1969), pp. 193ff.

34. Z. H. Burns, *Ship Island and the Confederacy* (Hattiesburg, Miss., 1971), p. 16.

35. C. Monet to Governor Pettus, 2 Jan. 1862, in Governor's Correspondence, li, MDAH/JM; Jefferson Davis to General D. E. Twiggs, 25 May 1861, *OR,* Ser. 1, 53:690; D. E. Twiggs to L. P. Walker, 6, 7 July 1861, ibid., p. 707, S. R. Mallory to L. P. Walker, 10 July 1861.

36. Scharf, *Confederate States Navy,* pp. 23ff.

37. *JC,* 1:67–68.

38. Johns, *Florida,* pp. 26ff.; Scharf, *Confederate States Navy,* p. 21. Incidentally, here the Confederates got the only naval vessel seized by them: the side-wheeler gunboat *Fulton,* of 698 tons displacement, armed with four 32-pounders. The *Fulton* was a wreck, which the Confederates put into a drydock. Her refitting never ended and the *Fulton* never saw service (see "Confederate Forces Afloat," Naval History Division, *Civil War Naval Chronology, 1861–65,* 6 vols. (Washington, D.C., 1961–66), 1:230.

39. Scharf, *Confederate States Navy,* p. 21.

40. Munroe d'Antignac, *Georgia Navy* (Griffin, Ga., 1945), p. 7.

41. John McIntosh Kell, *Recollections of a Naval Life, Including the Cruises of the Confederate States Steamers* Sumter *and* Alabama (Washington, D.C., 1900), p. 181.

42. Georgia Navy Ledger, GSA/AG; Wayne to Tattnall, 28 May, 5 June 1861 in Adjutant General Office, Naval Matters, ibid. See also J. M. Kell to N. C. Munroe in d'Antignac, *Georgia Navy,* p. 12.

43. Naval History Division, *Civil War Naval Chronology,* 6:298.

44. Claims for Guns, 1861–62, Adjutant General Office, Naval Matters, GSA/AG; Wayne to Morris, 20 Feb. 1861, ibid.

45. John D. Winters, *The Civil War in Louisiana* (Baton Rouge, 1963), p. 44.

46. Scharf, *Confederate States Navy,* pp. 24ff.

47. *JC,* 1:40.

48. Jefferson Davis, Acting Secretary of the Navy, to Commodore Charles Stewart, Commanding Navy Yard, Philadelphia, 4 Oct. 1853, Brockman Private Collection (courtesy of Charles J. Brockman, Jr.), Athens, Ga.

49. John H. Reagan to Jefferson Davis, 21 May 1867, in *Jefferson Davis, Constitutionalist: His Letters, Papers and Speeches,* 10 vols., ed. Dunbar Rowland (Jackson, Miss., 1923), 7:106.

50. Mallory to his son Buddy, 27 Sept. 1865, in Stephen Russell Mallory Diary, SHC/CHNC.

51. Mallory Diary, 1 Aug. 1862, SHC/CHNC.

52. *OR,* Ser. 4, 2:1046.

53. David D. Porter, *Incidents and Anecdotes of the Civil War* (New York, 1885), p. 10. According to a prominent member of the Confederate navy, Captain John Newland Maffitt, however, Davis had wholly underrated the naval needs and, moreover, did not favor the building of ships. See the private diary of J. N. Maffitt in Emma M. Maffitt, *The Life and Services of John Newland Maffitt* (New York, 1906), pp. 220ff.

54. Davis to Semmes, 21 Feb. 1861, *OR,* Ser. 4, 1:106ff. The original of the letter is found in Records Relating to Confederate Naval and Marine Personnel, NARG 109.

55. Only later, after his nomination as secretary of the navy, did Mallory send a letter to Semmes asking him to purchase in New York two or more fast steamers of small draft and capable of carrying at least one heavy cannon of 8 or 9 inches and possibly also a pair of 32-pounders. These, acting as speedy patrol boats, should be able both to engage and to flee. Semmes failed to find any such ships. See Mallory to Semmes, 13 Mar. 1861, Admiral Semmes Papers, ASDAH/MA (printed also in Semmes, *Memoirs,* p. 87).

56. J. M. Matthews, ed., *The Statutes at Large of the Provisional Government of the Confederate States of America, from the Institution of the Government, February 7, 1861, to Its Termination, February 18, 1862, Inclusive, Arranged in Chronological Order, Together with the Constitution of the Provisional Government, and the Permanent Constitution of the Confederate States* (Richmond, 1864), p. 33.

57. *JC,* 1:85, 105ff. The opposition came from the two representatives from Florida who considered Mallory too lukewarm toward secession.

58. Davis, *Rise and Fall,* 1:314. If one is to believe General Josiah Gorgas, chief of the Ordnance Bureau of the Confederate army, however, Davis would level much criticism toward the navy and its secretary. See *The Civil War Diary of General Josiah Gorgas,* ed. Frank E. Vandiver (University, Ala., 1947), pp. 58–59.

59. This has been correctly understood by Burton J. Hendrick, *Statesmen of the Lost Cause: Jefferson Davis and His Cabinet* (New York, 1939), pp. 363ff.

60. Mallory Diary, vol. 2, SHC/CHNC. This document, the second part of the diary, unpublished as is the first one, was written by Mallory during his postwar prison term and includes ample and interesting autobiographical data. Unless otherwise indicated, constant reference to Mallory's diary is made in this chapter. The most complete (even if not wholly satisfactory) biography of Mallory to date is Joseph T. Durkin, S.J., *Stephen Russell Mallory: Confederate Navy Chief* (Chapel Hill, 1954). See also P. Melvin, "Stephen Russell Mallory: Southern Naval Statesman," *Journal of Southern History* 10 (1944): 137ff.

61. Craven, *Civil War in the Making,* pp. 89ff.

62. See H. D. Langley, *Social Reform in the United States Navy, 1789–1862* (Urbana, Ill., 1967).

63. M. F. Maury to J. H. Otley, 21 Sept. 1865, Folder 5, Matthew Fontaine Maury Papers, LC. In this letter appears the rabid protest of the great oceanographer, a future officer of the Confederate States Navy, who had fallen under the ax of the Naval Retiring Board because he limped. The question was later resolved in his favor, yet he always held a stubborn animosity against Mallory. See Frances L. Williams, *Matthew Fontaine Maury: Scientist of the Sea* (New Brunswick, N.J., 1963).

64. The British had always considered American frigates as "ships of the line in disguise." See Alfred T. Mahan, *From Sail to Steam: Recollections of a Naval Life* (New York, 1907), pp. 32–33.

65. Robert L. Stevens's project had been considered by the secretary of the navy since 1842, but it never was completed. See James P. Baxter III, *The Introduction of the Ironclad Warship* (1933; reprint, Hamden, Conn., 1968).

66. *The Statutes at Large of the Provisional Government*, p. 53.

67. *JC*, 1:124ff.

68. The Rope Walk was the only navy institution that did not operate at a loss. See *ORN*, Ser. 2, 2:751–52.

69. The head had the rank of surgeon general, as in most naval services.

70. The officers of this bureau had the ranks of paymasters and assistant paymasters.

71. See John D. Hayes, "Captain Fox: *He* Is the Navy Department," *U.S. Naval Institute Proceedings* 95 (Sept. 1965): 64ff.

72. This Blockade Strategy Board (whose tremendous importance has been underrated by many a historian) met for the first time on 27 June 1861. It had been organized by Gustavus Vasa Fox under the suggestion of Professor Alexander D. Bache, prominent scientist and superintendent of the Coast Survey of the United States. See G. V. Fox to S. F. Du Pont, 22 May 1861, in *Samuel Francis Du Pont: A Selection from His Civil War Letters*, 3 vols., ed. John D. Hayes (Ithaca, N.Y., 1969), 1:71. Special attention should also be given to Admiral Hayes's perceptive introduction, esp. pp. lxviiiff.

73. Scharf, *Confederate States Navy*, does not mention him.

74. "An Act to Provide for the Organization of the Navy," "Laws of the Navy," in *Register of the Commissioned and Warrant Officers of the Navy of the Confederate States to January 1, 1864* (Richmond, 1864), pp. 59ff.

75. *JC*, 1:156ff.

CHAPTER TWO

1. See, as an example, the opinion of the military expert J.F.C. Fuller, *Grant and Lee: A Study in Personality and Generalship* (Bloomington, Ind., 1957), pp. 39ff.

2. *JC*, 1:173ff.

3. Stephen R. Mallory Diary, SHC/CHNC. The attacks of "gout" (most possibly instead an inflammation to the sciatic nerve) appeared just a few days after his arrival in Richmond.

4. Thomas C. De Leon, *Four Years in Rebel Capitals; an Inside View of Life in the Southern Confederacy from Birth to Death* (1890; reprint, New York, 1962); William H. Russell, *My Diary North and South*, ed. Fletcher Pratt (New York, 1954), p. 88; J. H. Shofner and W. W. Rogers, "Montgomery to Richmond: The Confederacy Selects a Capital," *Civil War History*, 10 June 1964, pp. 155ff.

5. William H. Parker, *Recollections of a Naval Officer, 1841–1865* (New York, 1883), p. 205.

6. *The City Intelligencer or, Stranger's Guide* (Richmond, 1862), pp. 3–4.

7. *Le Opere di Raimondo Montecuccoli*, ed. Raimondo Luraghi, 2 vols. to date (Rome, 1988–), 2:301.

8. Joseph T. Durkin, S.J., *Stephen Russell Mallory: Confederate Navy Chief* (Chapel Hill, 1954), p. 145.

9. Mallory to Memminger, 22 Feb. 1862, Letters Received by the Confederate Secretary of the Treasury, Treasury Department Collection of Confederate Records, NARG 365; James D. Bulloch, *The Secret Service of the Confederate States in Europe, or, How the Confederate Cruisers Were Equipped*, 2 vols. (1884; reprint, New York, 1959), 1:52ff. and 99ff.

10. Christopher G. Memminger, born in 1803 in Germany, emigrated to America with his mother when he was a baby, hence he grew up totally American. After a successful career as a lawyer, he served for twenty years as chairman of the Finance Committee of the South Carolina legislature. As secretary of the treasury of the Confederacy, he enjoyed the full trust of President Davis. Honest and energetic, he was nevertheless a rather narrow-minded man, perhaps because of his legalistic mentality. See the basic biography, H. D. Capers, *The Life and Times of Christopher G. Memminger* (Richmond, 1893).

11. Douglas B. Ball, "Confederate Finance, 1861–1865: Economic Policy Making during the American Civil War" (Ph.D. dissertation, University of London, London School of Economics, 1974), pp. 38, 501. Ball calculated the specie reserves and foreign exchange stored in Southern banks at $27,200,000, a sum quite close to that of $26 million offered by John C. Schwab, *The Confederate States of America, 1861–1865: A Financial and Industrial History of the South during the Civil War* (New York, 1901), p. 142.

12. Schwab, *Confederate States,* p. 144. Ball, "Confederate Finance," p. 200, table 30, says $1,700,000. E. Merton Coulter, *The Confederate States of America, 1861–1865* (Baton Rouge, 1950), p. 151, agrees with Schwab, yet Ball seems to offer more current data. According to him, p. 533, the composition of the total sum would be as follows: (a) confiscated enemy goods, $200,000; (b) from the mints, $500,000; (c) from customs deposits, $700,000; (d) from post offices, $300,000; total, $1,700,000. If one subtracts (c) and (d) (which Schwab possibly did not take into account), one arrives at the sum of $700,000, more or less Schwab's conclusion.

13. Total estimate of expenses, *ORN,* Ser. 2, 2:50.

14. Albert Gallatin, cited in Ball, "Confederate Finance," pp. 128ff.

15. Eugene M. Lerner, "The Monetary and Fiscal Program of the Confederate Government, 1861–1865," *Journal of Political Economy* 62 (Feb.–Dec. 1955): 50ff. Ralph L. Andreano, "A Theory of Confederate Finance," *Civil War History* 2 (1956): 21ff., underscores (p. 23 n. 6) how Memminger tried but partially failed to float a specie loan. See also Ball, "Confederate Finance," p. 533, where the total sum of specie and foreign exchange gathered by the Confederate government through the entire war is set at $8,964,000. See also Frost to Memminger, 1, 4 Apr. 1861, Denegre to Memminger, 21 Dec. 1861, Letters Received by the Confederate Secretary of the Treasury, Treasury Department Collection of Confederate Records, NARG 365; Memminger to Denegre, 4 Dec. 1861 (the answer to the letter is quoted above), Treasury Department, Secretary of the Treasury, press copies of letters sent, War Department Collection of Confederate Records, NARG 109; Trenholm to Davis, 18 Jan. 1865, Treasury Department Collection of Confederate Records, NARG 365. Last, see L. Schweikart, "Secession and Southern Banks," *Civil War History* 31 (June 1985): 111ff.

16. Ball, "Confederate Finance," p. 502.

17. *Historical Statistics of the United States, Colonial Times to 1970,* 2 vols. (Washington, D.C., 1975), 1:518. The average cotton bale weighed five hundred pounds.

18. T. F. Kettell, *Southern Wealth and Northern Profits,* ed. F. M. Green (University, Ala., 1965), p. 21.

19. Harold D. Woodman, *King Cotton and His Retainers: Financing and Marketing the Cotton Crop of the South, 1800–1925* (Lexington, Ky., 1968), p. 19; Andreano, "Theory of Confederate Finance," p. 24, n. 10.

20. *JC,* 1:186–87.

21. Hammond to Memminger, 11 July 1861, and to Trenholm, 5, 18 June 1861, James H. Hammond Papers, LC.

22. Memminger to Dubuisson, 3 Oct. 1861, Letters Sent by the Confederate Secretary of the Treasury, NARG 365.

23. Richard C. Todd, *Confederate Finance* (Athens, Ga., 1954), p. 35, gives the data provided by James D. B. De Bow, who directed the financial proceedings of the loan. The wise decisions were at last taken by the Confederate authorities in 1864. See Raimondo Luraghi, *The Rise and Fall of the Confederate Government* (New York, 1968), passim.

24. Ethel S. Nepveux, *George Alfred Trenholm and the Company That Went to War, 1861–1865* (Charleston, S.C., 1973), p. 25.

25. C. K. Prioleau to Beauregard, 25 Sept. 1880, in Alfred Roman, *The Military Operations of General Beauregard in the War between the States, 1861 to 1865,* 2 vols. (New York, 1884), 1:59–60.

26. Memminger to Davis, 25 Sept. 1877, in *Jefferson Davis, Constitutionalist: His Letters, Papers and Speeches,* 10 vols., ed. Dunbar Rowland (Jackson, Miss., 1923), 3:25ff.

27. According to General Beauregard, this happened during the first ten days of May (Roman, *Military Operations,* 1:52ff.).

28. See note 26.

29. Trenholm to Memminger and to Beauregard, 18 Sept. 1878, in *Jefferson Davis, Constitutionalist,* ed. Rowland, 3:30ff.

30. Richard C. Todd, *Confederate Finance* (Athens, Ga., 1954), p. 26.

31. Frank L. Owsley, *King Cotton Diplomacy: Foreign Relations of the Confederate States of America* (Chicago, 1959), pp. 18ff.

32. Ball, "Confederate Finance," p. 474.

33. Eugene M. Lerner, "Inflation in the Confederacy," in *Studies in the Quantitative Theory of Money,* ed. Milton Friedman (Chicago, 1955), pp. 163ff. Inflation started quickly in the South; a year after the bombardment of Fort Sumter, in April 1862, the ratio of devaluation was already 1:80. See the "Table of Confederate Inflation," Richmond, Va., Civil War Centennial Commission, 1961.

34. Mallory to Memminger, 11 May 1861, Letters Received by the Confederate Secretary of the Treasury, Treasury Department Collection of Confederate Records, NARG 365.

35. Ball, "Confederate Finance," p. 559.

36. Durkin, *Mallory,* p. 146.

37. General Estimate of Expenses, *ORN,* Ser. 2, 2:44ff.

38. J. K. Mitchell to Mallory, 28 Apr. 1864, *ORN,* Ser. 2, 2:639ff.

39. L. Y. Beall to Mallory, 30 Oct. 1864, ibid., pp. 749ff.

40. *Historical Statistics,* 1:837ff.

41. Welles to Fourth Auditor, 22 May 1861, U.S. Department of the Treasury, "Confederate Navy," NARG 56.

42. J. Thomas Scharf, *History of the Confederate States Navy from Its Organization to the Surrender of Its Last Vessel* (New York, 1887), pp. 32–33.

43. Governor Letcher to Commodore French Forrest, 18 Apr. 1861, Confederate Navy Records, 24770/ab, VSA/RV.

44. Mallory to W. B. Preston, 16 Aug. 1861, Naval Records Collection of the Office of Naval Records and Library, CS Navy: Subject File, NARG 45.

45. Mallory to President Davis, 16 June, 18 July 1861, ibid.; see also *ORN,* Ser. 2, 2:76ff.

46. Mallory to J. Benjamin, 22, 23 Jan. 1862, *ORN,* Ser. 2, 2:153.

47. *Register,* 1864, pp. 73–74.

48. Scale of Rank in Service, *ORN,* Ser. 2, 2:58.

49. Law of 28 Dec. 1861, *Register of the Commissioned and Warrant Officers of the Navy of the Confederate States to January 1, 1864* (Richmond, 1864), p. 72.

50. *Register,* 1864, p. 87.

51. Mallory to President Davis, 30 Apr. 1864, *ORN,* Ser. 2, 2:149ff.

52. William H. Parker, "The Confederate States Navy," in *Confederate Military History: A Library of C. S. History in Twelve Volumes,* ed. Clement A. Evans (Atlanta, Ga., 1899), pp. 96ff. (There is a reprint which lacks the additional vol. 13.)

53. *Register,* 1864, p. 83.

54. *Elements of Seamanship,* prepared as a textbook for the Midshipmen of the C.S. Navy, by Wm. H. Parker, Commanding C.S. School-ship *Patrick Henry,* Richmond, Va., 1861.

55. *Regulations for the Interior Police of the Confederate States School-ship* Patrick Henry (N.p., n.d. [Richmond, 1863]).

56. Parker, *Recollections,* pp. 349ff.

57. *A Digest of the Military and Naval Laws of the Confederate States from the Commencement of the Provisional Congress to the End of the First Congress under the Permanent Constitution,* analytically arranged by W. W. Lester and W. J. Brownell (Columbia, S.C., 1864), pp. 197ff.

58. Mallory to Pinckney, 3 Nov. 1864, Charles A. Anderton Papers, NCDAH/RNC.

59. Buchanan to Mitchell, 2, 5 Apr. 1863, and Order of the Day, 17 Apr. 1863, signed by J. K. Mitchell (head of the Office of Orders and Details, whose duty it was to enforce rules about the uniforms), John K. Mitchell Papers, VHS/RV; *Register,* 1861, p. 84.

60. Raimondo Luraghi, *Storia della Guerra Civile Americana,* 5th ed., rev. (Milan, 1986), p. 232.

61. Mallory to J. Benjamin, 10 Jan. 1862, *ORN,* Ser. 2, 2:127.

62. Ibid., p. 53.

63. *Digest of Military and Naval Laws,* pp. 215–16; *JC,* 5:445.

64. Mitchell to Hunter, 23 Feb. 1864, Savannah Squadron Papers, EUL/AG.

65. S. S. Lee to Hunter, 16 Oct. 1864, William W. Hunter Papers, DUL/DNC.

66. Ralph W. Donnelly, *The History of the Confederate States Marine Corps* (Washington, D.C., 1976), p. 2. See also J. E. McGlone, "The Lost Corps: The Confederate States Marines," *U.S. Naval Institute Proceedings* 98 (Nov. 1972): 68ff.

67. J. E. Johnston to R. E. Lee, 25 May 1862, *OR,* Ser. 1, 2, pt. 3:543, in which the Confederate general considers Colonel Beall as "eminently qualified for the grade of Brigadier General." Ralph W. Donnelly, *Biographical Sketches of the Commissioned Officers of the C.S. Marine Corps* (Alexandria, Va., 1973), pp. 2ff.

68. Beall to Mallory, 14 Aug. 1862, *ORN,* Ser. 2, 2:251; *Register,* 1864, p. 71.

69. Donnelly, *History,* p. 2.

70. Mallory to Van Benthuysen, 30 Mar. 1861, Van Benthuysen Papers, TUL/NOL.

71. Mallory to Van Benthuysen, 17 Mar. 1861, ibid.

72. Donnelly, *History,* p. 17. According to Donnelly, the best officers of the C.S. Marines were, in addition to Colonel Beall, Lieutenant Colonel Henry B. Tyler, Major H. Terrett, Major Israel C. Greene, and Major Algernon S. Taylor, all formerly of the U.S. Marine Corps. See also Donnelly, *Biographical Sketches,* passim.

73. Mallory to Van Benthuysen, 27 Apr. 1861, Van Benthuysen Papers, TUL/NOL.

74. McGlone, "Lost Corps," pp. 59ff.

75. Mallory to President Davis, 27 Feb. 1862, *ORN,* Ser. 2, 2:149ff.

76. Williamson to Mallory, 15 Aug. 1862, ibid., pp. 240ff.

77. President Davis to Governor Joseph E. Brown (circular), 19 Sept. 1864, in *The Confederate Records of the State of Georgia,* 6 vols., ed. A. D. Chandler (Atlanta, Ga., 1909), 3:622. Of these, five volumes were printed irregularly, starting in 1909, by C. P. Byrd, state printer; a sixth one remained in manuscript and is preserved in the GSA/AG.

78. President Davis to Beauregard, 28 Dec. 1864, in *Jefferson Davis, Constitutionalist,* ed. Rowland, 6:429.

79. Mallory to Brown, Governor Brown's Letterbook, GSA/AG.

80. *Register,* 1861, 1863, and 1864.

81. See the appraisal of him by Paymaster De Bree in *ORN,* Ser. 2, 2:643.

82. De Bree to Mallory, 14 Nov. 1863, ibid., pp. 552ff.

83. W. F. Howell to De Bree, 25, 31 Aug. 1863, ibid., pp. 557ff.

84. J. A. Semple to Mallory, 18 Oct. 1864, ibid., pp. 762ff.

85. Mallory to President Davis, 5 Jan. 1876, Jefferson Davis Papers, DUL/DNC.

86. Mary E. Massey, *Ersatz in the Confederacy* (Columbia, S.C., 1952), pp. 72ff.

87. *ORN,* Ser. 2, 2:763.

88. Mallory to President Davis, 5 Jan. 1863, Jefferson Davis Papers, DUL/DNC.

89. De Bree to Mallory, 18 Apr. 1861, *ORN,* Ser. 2, 2:642ff.

90. Mallory to Ware, 4 Apr. 1861, Paymaster Ware's Papers, Naval Records Collection, NARG 45.

91. De Bree to Ware, 24 Aug. 1863, 17 Mar. 1864, ibid.

92. S. Gonzales to Ware, 21 Aug. 1863, and R. S. Stockton to Ware, 28 Aug. 1863, ibid.

93. J. S. Barton to Ware, 2 Sept. 1863; R. S. Stockton to S. Gonzales, Sept. 1863; W. F. Howell to Ware, 1 Oct. 1863, ibid.

94. De Bree to Ware, Sept. 1863, where it is stated that Howell had "agents everywhere"; W. F. Howell to Ware, 23 July 1864, ibid.

95. Mallory to Van Benthuysen, 17 May 1861, Van Benthuysen Papers, TUL/NOL.

96. Mallory to Bulloch, 9 May 1861, *ORN,* Ser. 2, 2:64ff.

97. Bulloch to Mallory, 9 May 1861, ibid., pp. 83ff.

98. Bulloch to Mallory, 13 Aug. 1861, ibid., pp. 542ff.

99. Flory C. Corley, *Confederate City: Augusta, Georgia, in the Confederacy* (Columbia, S.C., 1965), p. 49.

100. De Bree to W. W. Hunter, 3 Nov. 1863, W. W. Hunter Papers, TUL/NOL.

101. *ORN,* Ser. 2, 2:763.

102. W.A.W. Spotswood to Mallory, 1 Nov. 1864, *ORN,* Ser. 2, 2:758ff.

103. W.A.W. Spotswood to Mallory, 30 Nov. 1863, ibid., pp. 559ff.

104. *Instructions for the Guidance of the Medical Officers of the Navy* (Richmond, 1864).

105. J. Benjamin to Mason, 13 May 1863, *ORN,* Ser. 2, 3:757; *Register,* 1864, p. 86.

106. See the several flags in *ORN,* Ser. 2, vol. 3.

CHAPTER THREE

1. Report of the Secretary of the Navy, 26 Apr. 1861, *ORN,* Ser. 2, 2:51ff.

2. James R. Soley, *The Blockade and the Cruisers* (1883; reprint, New York, 1963), pp. 12ff.; Charles B. Boynton, *The History of the Navy during the Rebellion,* 2 vols. (New York, 1867), 1:99ff.

3. *ORN,* Ser. 2, 1:262.

4. J. Thomas Scharf, *History of the Confederate States Navy from Its Organization to the Surrender of Its Last Vessel* (New York, 1887), p. 369.

5. Investigation of the Navy Department, *ORN*, Ser. 2, 1:431ff.

6. *ORN*, Ser. 2, 1:791ff.

7. William N. Still, Jr., *Confederate Shipbuilding* (Athens, Ga., 1969), p. 7.

8. *ORN*, Ser. 2, 1:791.

9. G. Lebergott, "Labor Force and Employment, 1800–1960," *Studies in Income and Wealth* 30 (1966): 131ff.

10. "Population," in U.S. Department of Commerce, Bureau of the Census, *Sixteenth Census: 1940* (Washington, D.C., 1942), 1:20.

11. Fabian Linden, "Repercussions of Manufacturing in the Antebellum South," *North Carolina Historical Review* 17 (Oct. 1940): 313ff.

12. Harold D. Woodman, *King Cotton and His Retainers: Financing and Marketing the Cotton Crop of the South, 1800–1925* (Lexington, Ky., 1968), pp. 152ff. Much of the capital invested in Southern industries was in Northern hands.

13. Eugene D. Genovese, *The Political Economy of Slavery* (New York, 1966), pp. 155ff.; Raimondo Luraghi, *The Rise and Fall of the Plantation South* (New York, 1978), pp. 55ff. For more particulars, see Eugene D. Genovese, *The World the Slaveholders Made* (New York, 1969), and, with Stanley L. Engerman, *Race and Slavery in the Western Hemisphere* (Princeton, 1975). See also two works that have become classics: Ulrich Bonnell Phillips, *Life and Labor in the Old South,* new ed., ed. C. Vann Woodward (Boston, 1963), and Avery O. Craven, *The Growth of Southern Nationalism, 1848–1861* (Baton Rouge, 1953). In addition, see Robert S. Starobin, *Industrial Slavery in the Old South* (New York, 1970), and R. C. Wade, *Slavery in the Cities* (New York, 1964).

14. See the list, with details of ships built, in Scharf, *Confederate States Navy,* p. 25, n. 1.

15. William N. Still, Jr., "Facilities for the Construction of War Vessels in the Confederacy," *Journal of Southern History* 31 (1965): 285ff.

16. Soley, *The Blockade and the Cruisers,* p. 35.

17. W. H. Petters to the Governor of Virginia, John Letcher, 19 Oct. 1861, *ORN*, Ser. 2, 2:107ff.

18. *BL,* 1:712n.

19. Still, "Facilities for the Construction of War Vessels," pp. 285–86.

20. "Manufactures of the United States in 1860," U.S. Census Bureau, *Eighteenth Census, 1860* (Washington, D.C., 1865), pp. 716–17.

21. Still, "Facilities for the Construction of War Vessels," p. 286.

22. Walter Chandler, "The Memphis Navy Yard: An Adventure in Internal Improvement," *West Tennessee Historical Society Papers* 1 (1947): 68ff.

23. T. P. Kettell, *Southern Wealth and Northern Profits,* ed. F. M. Green (University, Ala., 1965), pp. 85ff. The original 1860 edition referred to data for 1850. Even Kettell, however, lists eighty-eight shipyards in the South that were not available to the Confederacy. Of those he listed, therefore, only fifty-seven were usable by the Confederates.

24. Still, *Confederate Shipbuilding,* p. 45.

25. See Still, "Facilities for the Construction of War Vessels," pp. 290ff.; James M. Merrill, "Confederate Shipbuilding at New Orleans," *Journal of Southern History* 28 (1962): 87ff.; Ralph W. Donnelly, "The Charlotte, North Carolina, Navy Yard," *Civil War*

History 5 (May 1959): 72ff.; William N. Still, Jr., "Confederate Shipbuilding in Mississippi," *Journal of Mississippi History* 30 (Nov. 1968): 291ff.

26. Still, "Facilities for the Construction of War Vessels," p. 290.

27. Still, *Confederate Shipbuilding*, p. 290.

28. Bern Anderson, *By Sea and by River: The Naval History of the Civil War* (New York, 1962), p. 290.

29. D. W. Knox to Mrs. V. P. Thompson, 21 Jan. 1943; Gideon Welles to J. L. Porter, 17 Apr. 1861, ZB File, John Luke Porter Papers, NHD/WDC.

30. See John W. H. Porter, *A Record of Events in Norfolk County, Virginia, from April 19th, 1861, to May 10th, 1862, with a History of the Soldiers and Sailors of Norfolk County, Norfolk City, and Portsmouth Who Served in the Confederate States Army or Navy* (Portsmouth, Va., 1892).

31. J. L. Porter to Mallory, 10 Sept. 1862, Naval Records Collection, Area File 7, NARG 45, also reproduced in *ORN*, Ser. 2, 2:271ff.; Mallory to A. G. Brown, same date, ibid.

32. See, e.g., Tom H. Wells, *The Confederate Navy: A Study in Organization* (University, Ala., 1971), pp. 97ff.

33. See the favorable opinion of such a severe man as John M. Kell, *Recollections of a Naval Life, Including the Cruises of the Confederate States Steamers* Sumter *and* Alabama (New York, 1907), p. 130.

34. Willink Papers, EUL/AG; Miscellaneous Papers, CM/RV; William Francis Martin Papers, SHC/CHNC; Confederate Navy Records, VSA/RV; Project of the ironclad *Virginia*, MM/NNV; NARG 19, 45, 109. All contain many original construction plans signed by J. L. Porter. For example, in CM/RV, MM/NNV, and VSA/RV can be found several successive developments of the plan for building the ironclad *Virginia*, the original one being in CM/RV. Plans of the cruiser *Alabama* built in England are in NARG 109. The plans for an ironclad to be built in Europe, among other material, are in MM/NNV.

35. J. L. Porter to Moore, 4 Nov. 1861, Miscellaneous Papers, CM/RV.

36. James D. Bulloch, *The Secret Service of the Confederate States in Europe, or, How the Confederate Cruisers Were Equipped* (1884; reprint, New York, 1959), 1:448.

37. *ORN*, Ser. 2, 1:448.

38. Still, *Confederate Shipbuilding*, p. 59.

39. See Roberto Lenti, "Per una storia della cantieristica genovese nel xvii secolo: La costruzione della *San Giovanni Battista*" (M. A. thesis, University of Genoa, 1970), pp. 51ff.

40. Manlio Calegari, "Legname e costruzioni navali nel cinquecento," *Miscellanea Storica Ligure* 3 (1964): 79ff., 135ff.

41. J.G.S. Hutchins, *The American Maritime Industry and Public Policy, 1789–1814* (Cambridge, Mass., 1941), p. 205.

42. Bibliothéque Nationale, Paris, Ms. Français 21339, *Mélanges Colbert*, Mémoire concernant la Marine de Hollande (written by Seignelay). This also appears in *Lettres, instructions et mémoires de Colbert*, ed. Pierre Clement (Paris, 1865), 3, pt. 2, "Instructions au Marquis de Seignelay." Among other important things, this manuscript says, "Ayant examiné les vaisseaux que j'ai trouvés sur le chantier, tant à Amsterdam qu'ailleurs, j'ai remarqué . . . qu'ils n'ont pas assez d'égard au bois qu'ils employent, parce que, comme ils vont toujours au bon marché . . . ils le mettent en oeuvre aussytost qu'il est venu de chez le marchand, sans examiner s'il est sec ou s'il est vert."

43. Robert G. Albion, *Forests and Seapower: The Timber Problem of the Royal Navy, 1652–1862* (Cambridge, Mass., 1926), p. 13.

44. Ibid., pp. 370ff.

45. Hutchins, *American Maritime Industry,* pp. 79ff.

46. J. E. Defebaugh, *History of the Lumber Industry in North America,* 2 vols. (Chicago, 1906), passim.

47. "Historical Statement on the Use of Live Oak Timber for the Construction of Vessels in the Navy. . . ," 14 Dec. 1832, in *American State Papers: Documents Legislative and Executive of the Congress of the United States,* Vol. 4: *Naval Affairs* (Washington, D.C., 1861), pp. 191ff.

48. Hutchins, *American Maritime Industry,* p. 79.

49. "Historical Statement," p. 92.

50. Albion, *Forests and Sea Power,* p. 34; *De Bow's Review,* 26 (6 Dec. 1859): 710ff.

51. Still, *Confederate Shipbuilding,* p. 47.

52. *Manufactures of the United States in 1860,* compiled from the original returns of the Eighth Census, under the direction of the Secretary of the Interior (Washington, D.C., 1865), p. clxxxiii, which indicates for the states of the North and West an annual extraction of 908,700 tons, saying nothing about the South.

53. Ethel Armes, *The Story of Coal and Iron in Alabama* (1910; reprint, New York, 1973), pp. 156ff.

54. G. Elliott to Vance, 11 May 1864, Letter Book and Correspondence of Governor Zebulon B. Vance, NCDAH/RNC; Milton to D. L. Yulee, 30 May 1863, Governor John Milton Letterbook, FHSC/TF; George Reid to Gilbert Elliott, 15 Nov. 1861, William Francis Martin Papers, SHC/CHNC; Mallory to Davis, Jefferson Davis Papers, MUL/OO; Mallory to Brown, Governor Brown Papers, GSA/AG. But see Still, *Confederate Shipbuilding,* passim.

55. Report of Secretary Mallory to the President, 16 Aug. 1862, *ORN,* Ser. 2, 2:246. Iron was imported both as finished products and engine parts. See Still, *Confederate Shipbuilding,* p. 50.

56. General Order No. 59, 16 June 1863, *OR,* Ser. 4, 2:594ff.

57. *ORN,* Ser. 2, 2:244.

58. *Manufactures of the United States,* p. clxxviii.

59. Ibid.

60. Luraghi, *Rise and Fall of the Plantation South,* pp. 123ff.; Lester J. Cappon, "Government and Private Industry in the Southern Confederacy," in *Humanistic Studies in Honor of John Calvin Metcalf* (Charlottesville, Va., 1941), pp. 151ff.; Charles H. Ramsdell, "Control of Manufactures by the Confederate Government," *Mississippi Valley Historical Review* 8 (Dec. 1921): 231ff.; Robert C. Black III, *The Railroads of the Confederacy* (Chapel Hill, 1952), esp. pp. 95ff.; *OR,* Ser. 4, 2:160ff.

61. Still, *Confederate Shipbuilding,* p. 55.

62. J. M. St. John to Seddon, 6 Oct. 1864, *OR,* Ser. 4, 3:695ff.

63. Benjamin to President Davis, 12 Mar. 1862, *OR,* Ser. 4, 1:987ff.; Mallory to A. G. Brown, 11 Apr. 1862, *ORN,* Ser. 2, 2:183; Mallory to President Davis, 24 Sept. 1862, ibid., p. 264.

64. *Register of the Commissioned and Warrant Officers of the Navy of the Confederate States to January 1, 1864* (Richmond, 1864), passim.

65. Wells, *Confederate Navy,* p. 47.

66. George M. Brooke, Jr., "John Mercer Brooke, Naval Scientist," 2 vols. (Ph.D. diss., University of North Carolina, 1956). This work is based on a rare collection of John M. Brooke Papers, in possession of the estate. I must here express my appreciation to the late director of the Southern Historical Collection, Aaron Copland, through whose good offices I obtained permission to consult the dissertation.

67. J. R. Anderson to Mallory, 8 Aug. 1861, J-31, Letterbook, Outletters May 1–Aug. 24, 1861, Tredegar Company Records, VSA/RV. See also Larry J. Daniel and Riley W. Gunter, *Confederate Cannon Foundries* (Union City, Tenn., 1977), pp. ivff. (a basic work).

68. Charles B. Dew, *Ironmaker to the Confederacy: Joseph R. Anderson and the Tredegar Iron Works* (New Haven, 1966), pp. 2ff. I saw what remained of the Tredegar several years ago, when the debris were in an almost complete state of neglect. Today the remains of the greatest metallurgical plant of the South have been in part restored and transformed into a historical park, a meritorious enterprise that saved what remained of the ruins from the ravages of time.

69. He again donned the uniform in the fall of 1861 with the rank of Confederate brigadier general and served until the summer of 1862, when, wounded, he left the army to dedicate himself totally to the Tredegar. See ibid., pp. 94ff.

70. Contract Book, July 1859–Apr. 1865, pp. 146–47, copy of prices left with Secretary Mallory of the Confederate States Navy, Tredegar Company Records, VSA/RV.

71. Eugene M. Mitchell, "Atlanta: The Industrial Heart of the Confederacy," *Atlanta Historical Bulletin* 1 (May 1930): 20ff.; James M. Russell, *Atlanta, 1847–1890* (Baton Rouge, 1988), p. 95. One of the owners, William Markam, was an alien enemy (Northerner) so he was compelled to give up his share.

72. Elizabeth Bowlby, "The Role of Atlanta in the War between the States," *Atlanta Historical Bulletin* 5 (July 1940): 177ff.

73. Report by G. Minor, 12 Aug. 1862, *ORN,* Ser. 2, 2:248ff. Yet the navy had to authorize the army to use the rolling mill for a large number of working hours. See Mallory to D. P. McCorkle, 8 Sept. 1863, VMU/RV.

74. Frank E. Vandiver, "The Shelby Iron Works in the Civil War: A Study of Confederate Industry," *Alabama Review* 1 (Jan. 1948): 12ff.; (April 1948): 111ff.; (July 1948): 203ff.

75. J. S. White to A. T. Jones, 9 Aug. 1861, in Shelby Iron Company Papers, UAL/TA.

76. Articles of Agreement, 18 Mar. 1862, ibid.

77. C. McRae to H. H. Ware, 18, 22 Mar. 1862, ibid.

78. A. T. Jones to Lynch, 4 Sept. 1862, Mallory to A. T. Jones, 10 Sept. 1862, ibid.

79. Frank E. Vandiver, "Industry in the Confederacy: Shelby Ironworks Typified the Independent Manufacturer," *Army Ordnance,* July–Aug. 1948, pp. 71ff.

80. A. T. Jones to Catesby ap R. Jones, 27 July 1862, Shelby Iron Company Papers, UAL/TA.

81. William N. Still, Jr., *Iron Afloat: The Story of the Confederate Armorclad* (Nashville, Tenn., 1971), pp. 191ff.

82. A. T. Jones to Mallory, 9 Dec. 1862, Shelby Iron Company Papers, UAL/TA.

83. Bowlby, "The Role of Atlanta in the War," p. 186.

84. See Dew, *Ironmaker to the Confederacy,* and Armes, *Story of Coal and Iron in Alabama,* passim. See also Kathleen Bruce, *Virginia Iron Manufacture in the Slave Era* (1931; reprint, New York, 1968), a work of basic importance.

85. G. T. Sinclair to Mallory, 22 Apr. 1861, *ORN,* Ser. 1, 4:306.

86. Exactly 333,000 pounds, or 151.72 tons. This calculation results from considering

the powder keg as having a capacity of 10 gallons, which was the usual amount for such containers. On this subject see W. B. Taliaferro to Governor of Virginia John Letcher, 23 Apr. 1861, *ORN,* Ser. 1, 4:307ff.

87. Commander William H. Parker, C.S.N., gives a total of 1,195 heavy cannons. See "Confederate States Navy," in *Confederate Military History: A Library of C. S. History in Twelve Volumes,* ed. Clement A. Evans (Atlanta, Ga., 1899), 12:30. The authoritative Daniel and Gunter, *Confederate Cannon Foundries,* p. iv, say "about 1,750 guns," but they also include light ones.

88. W. F. Lynch to A. B. Fairfax, 28 Apr. 1861, *ORN,* Ser. 1, 4:402–3; A. B. Fairfax to A. M. Gibbs, 24, 29 Apr. 1861, ibid., p. 404; D. French Forrest to R. L. Page, 8 May 1861, ibid., p. 406.

89. Daniel and Gunter, *Confederate Cannon Foundries,* p. iv. The size of cannons expressed in pounds gives the weight of the solid shot that the gun can fire. Yet the same indication is given when the same piece fires exclusively (or prevailingly) shells, which evidently weigh less. Such indication of size was used (but not always) for smoothbores and far more infrequently for rifles, whose caliber is normally given in inches.

90. Report by General J. Gorgas, 20 Apr. 1861, *OR,* Ser. 4, 1:277ff.

91. William H. Parker, *Recollections of a Naval Officer, 1841–1865* (New York, 1883), p. 207.

92. *Civil War Naval Ordnance* (Washington, D.C.: Navy Department, Naval History Division 1969), p. 5; Warren Ripley, *Artillery and Ammunition of the Civil War* (New York, 1970), pp. 17ff.

93. J. Gorgas to Seddon, 15 Nov. 1863, *OR,* Ser. 4, 2:955; Richard I. Lester, *Confederate Finance and Purchasing in Great Britain* (Charlottesville, Va., 1975), pp. 113ff.; Jac Weller, "The Confederate Use of British Cannon," *Civil War History* 3 (June 1957): 135ff.

94. The Tredegar's share was 1,099. Figures supplied by Dew, *Ironmaker to the Confederacy,* p. 111. Bruce, *Virginia Iron Manufacture in the Slave Era,* p. 461, gives a total of 1,048. See also Order Book, Tredegar Company Records, VSA/RV.

95. Daniel and Gunter, *Confederate Cannon Foundries,* p. 24.

96. Ibid., pp. 85ff.

97. Diary of R. D. Minor, 6 Nov. 1861–8 Feb. 1862, entry of 30 Jan. 1862, Minor Family Papers, VHS/RV.

98. Armes, *Story of Coal and Iron in Alabama,* pp. 134ff.; Maurice Melton, "The Selma Naval Ordnance Works," *Civil War Times Illustrated* 14 (Dec. 1975): 19–20; William N. Still, Jr., "Selma and the Confederate States Navy," *Alabama Review* 14 (Jan. 1962): 19ff.

99. Charles S. Davis, *Colin J. McRae: Confederate Financial Agent* (Tuscaloosa, Ala., 1961), pp. 27ff.

100. McRae to President Davis, 19 Feb. 1862, Letterbook, Colin J. McRae Papers, ASDAH/MA.

101. G. Minor to McRae, 25 Mar. 1862, ibid.

102. Still, "Selma and the Confederate States Navy," p. 21.

103. "Contributions to the History of the Confederate Ordnance Department," in *SHSP,* 12:66ff.

104. Special Order No. 1, dated 20 Feb. 1862, which announced the acquisition of the foundry. The name of Naval Foundry instead of Government Foundry appears for the first time on 13 June 1863. After 18 June, correspondence is regularly signed by Captain

Catesby ap R. Jones, Commanding the Naval Foundry. See Naval Foundry Letterbook, Naval Gun Foundry Papers, NARG 45.

105. Letterbook 1, Naval Gun Foundry Papers, NARG 45. The particle "ap" before the middle initial is of Welsh origin and is more or less equivalent to the Spanish "de."

106. Still, "Selma and the Confederate States Navy," p. 23.

107. E. Farrand to Governor Shorter, 7 Feb. 1863, Governor's Papers, ASDAH/MA; Mallory to President Davis, 30 Apr. 1864, ORN, Ser. 2, 2:630ff.

108. Gun Shop Book, 2 vols., 2: entry of 19 Nov. 1864 with the casting of heavy cannon no. 125, Naval Gun Foundry Papers, NARG 45. It is possible that a third volume of the Gun Shop Book, barely under way, was lost. It might have indicated that more than 125 heavy guns had been produced. See Daniel and Gunter, *Confederate Cannon Foundries*, pp. 81ff.

109. Account Book, Sept. and Nov. 1864, Naval Gun Foundry Papers, NARG 45.

110. Diffie W. Standard, *Columbus, Georgia, in the Confederacy: The Social and Industrial Life of the Chattahoochee River Port* (New York, 1954), p. 43.

111. Account Book, 31 July 1863, Naval Gun Foundry Papers, NARG 45.

112. Mallory to President Davis, 5 Jan. 1865, Jefferson Davis Papers, DUL/DNC.

113. Mallory to President Davis, 18 July 1861, ORN, Ser. 2, 2:76ff.

114. Mallory to S. S. Lee, 15 Aug. 1862, ORN, Ser. 1, 1:780.

115. W. P. Williamson to Mallory, 15 Aug. 1862, ORN, Ser. 2, 2:240ff.

116. Donnelly, "The Charlotte, North Carolina, Navy Yard," pp. 72ff.

117. Wells, *Confederate Navy*, p. 55.

118. H. Ashton Ramsay to J. M. Brooke, 5 May 1864, OR, Ser. 4, 3:521ff.

119. R. D. Minor Diary, 30 Jan. 1862, Minor Family Papers, VHS/RV.

120. D. P. McCorkle to J. M. Brooke, 7 May 1864, OR, Ser. 4, 3:522.

121. Flory C. Corley, *Confederate City: Augusta, Georgia, in the Confederacy* (Columbia, S.C., 1965), p. 49.

122. J. M. Brooke to J. Gorgas, 11 Apr., 9 May 1863, in Records of Confederate Naval and Marine Personnel, War Department Collection of Confederate Records, NARG 109.

123. Bulloch, *Secret Service*, 1:448.

124. Mallory to Bulloch, 30 July 1862, ORN, Ser. 2, 2:230; Bulloch to Mallory, 24 Sept. 1862, ibid., p. 274.

125. Bulloch to Mallory, 7 Nov. 1862, ORN, Ser. 2, 2:291; Mallory to Bulloch, 7 Jan. 1863, ibid., p. 332. An accurate, if concise, description of the weapon is in B. R. Lewis, *Small Arms and Ammunition in the United States Service, 1776–1865* (Washington, D.C., 1960), p. 64.

126. Standard, *Columbus, Georgia, in the Confederacy*, p. 38.

127. Mallory to Bulloch, 20 June 1864, ORN, Ser. 2, 2:673ff. This letter is not the only example of such a project by Mallory.

128. Guncotton, i.e., nitrocellulose explosive, was obtained by drenching cotton in a strong solution of nitric and sulfuric acids, then washing it with water. Its explosive power was enormously superior to that of black powder; only half of it produced the same effect as a given black powder charge. In Civil War days, the procedure of slowing down the ignition of guncotton by colloid action was not yet known. Still, Mallory tried to use it for submarine torpedoes.

129. Still, *Confederate Shipbuilding*, p. 44.

130. Mallory to Hollins, 18 Dec. 1861, *ORN,* Ser. 2, 1:517.

131. R. D. Minor Diary, 30 Jan. 1862, Minor Family Papers, VHS/RV. Ninety thousand pounds of powder were to arrive in New Orleans from Texas. Because part of it had deteriorated, the usable quantity was reduced to forty thousand pounds. Of the latter, half was seized by army units operating in Texas, which meant that the navy could count on only twenty thousand pounds, or nine metric tons.

132. Ammunition, Powder, Box 10, Vouchers of Naval Bases, C.S.N. Subject File BA, Naval Collection, NARG 45.

133. Mallory to Walker, 6 Sept. 1861, Letters Received by the Confederate Secretary of War, War Department Collection of Confederate Records, NARG 109.

134. Bulloch, *Secret Service,* 1:112.

135. Mallory to Bulloch, 28 Sept. 1861, *ORN,* Ser. 2, 2:95.

136. Frank E. Vandiver, *Ploughshares into Swords: Josiah Gorgas and Confederate Ordnance* (Austin, Tex., 1952), p. 74; George W. Rains, *History of the Confederate Powder Works* (Augusta, Ga., 1882).

137. G. Minor to Mallory, 15 Aug. 1862, *ORN,* Ser. 2, 2:250.

138. J. M. Brooke to Mallory, 25 Nov. 1863, ibid., p. 755, and 4 Nov. 1864, ibid., pp. 755ff.

139. F. G. Barnes to R. D. Minor, n.d. [29 Apr. 1862]; R. D. Minor to Governor of Virginia Letcher, 6 Mar. 1862, in Ammunition, Powder, Box 10, Vouchers of Naval Bases, C.S.N. Subject File BA, Naval Collection, NARG 45.

140. R. D. Minor to F. B. Renshaw, 2 Dec. 1861, *ORN,* Ser. 2, 1:777; G. Minor to Mallory, 15 Aug. 1862, ibid., p. 250.

141. Mallory to President Davis, 27 Feb. 1862, ibid., pp. 149ff.

142. *Register,* 1864, pp. 73ff.

143. Communication to the author by the late Bell I. Wiley, who had Tom H. Wells as a student before the latter died in a car accident. See Wells, *Confederate Navy,* pp. 107ff.

144. Mallory to Bulloch, 29 Dec. 1863, *ORN,* Ser. 2, 2:560ff.; Bulloch to Mallory, 19 Mar. 1864, ibid., pp. 611ff.; 29 Sept. 1864, ibid. pp. 728ff.; 20 Oct. 1864, ibid., pp. 735ff.; 26 Nov. 1864, ibid., pp. 774ff. See also Bulloch, *Secret Service,* 2:229ff.

145. R. D. Minor Diary, 30 Jan. 1862, Minor Family Papers, VHS/RV, which notes that the shop, owned by a man named Kirk, could produce engines for the ironclad *Mississippi* but not the driveshaft, which had to be made by Tredegar.

146. *Yearbook of the City of Charleston, 1883,* pp. 550ff., SCHS/CSC; Ernest M. Lander, Jr., "Charleston: Manufacturing Center of the Old South," *Journal of Southern History* 26 (1960): 330ff.

147. Contract Book, July 1859–Apr. 1865, p. 161, Tredegar Company Records, VSA/RV; contract dated 27 Jan. 1862 with W. P. Williamson for two engines with 10-inch by 24-inch cylinders, complete with boilers and driveshafts for each of the two gunboats under construction, at a total cost of $22,500, Order Book, 13 Aug. 1861–27 Nov. 1862; R. D. Minor to J. R. Anderson, 19 Sept. 1862, ibid., acknowledging the supplying of the engines for the ironclad *Richmond.*

148. Bruce, *Virginia Iron Manufacture in the Slave Era,* pp. 296ff.

149. Report dated 25 Apr. 1862 by Commander W. Radford, Construction at Richmond, C.S.N. Subject File, Naval Collection, NARG 45.

150. W. P. Williamson to W. F. Martin, 10 Oct. 1861, and Talbott & Bros. to G. Elliott, 4 Nov. 1861, William Francis Martin Papers, SHC/CHNC.

151. Still, "Facilities for the Construction of War Vessels," pp. 285ff.

152. Standard, *Columbus, Georgia, in the Confederacy,* pp. 11ff.

153. Ibid., p. 43.

154. Letterbook of J. H. Warner, Chief Engineer, Columbus Naval Iron Works, CNM/CG. This very important manuscript was at the Buffalo and Erie Historical Society, Buffalo, N.Y., where I studied it carefully. It was later given to CNM/CG, where it may be found today. The first letters sent are dated September 1862 (for the first one, the date is unreadable, the second is September 13).

155. Standard, *Columbus, Georgia, in the Confederacy,* p. 43.

156. Warner to Mallory, 15 Oct. 1862, J. H. Warner Letterbook, CNM/CG.

157. Standard, *Columbus, Georgia, in the Confederacy,* p. 69, n. 22.

158. J. L. Porter to Mallory, 1 Nov. 1864, *ORN,* Ser. 2, 2:750ff.

159. John Gibbon, *The Artillerist's Manual* (1860; reprint, Greenwood, Conn., 1971), p. 54.

160. St. John to Randolph, 31 July 1862, *OR,* Ser. 4, 2:26ff.

161. Ralph W. Donnelly, "Confederate Copper," *Civil War History* 1 (Dec. 1955): 355ff.

162. Ibid., p. 357.

163. Peet to Mallory, 29 Aug. 1861, *ORN,* Ser. 2, 2:93ff.

164. "Statements of Contracts Made by the Navy Dept.," ibid., pp. 93ff.

165. Donnelly, "Confederate Copper," p. 364.

166. Vandiver, *Ploughshares into Swords,* p. 201.

167. It is worth trying to clarify if the true cause of the dismal state in which Confederate warships' hulls were generally found by the U.S. Navy (leaking) was caused more by the lack of copper sheathing than the use of raw wood in their construction.

168. Bulloch to Mallory, 17 Mar. 1864, *ORN,* Ser. 2, 2:606ff.; Mallory to Bulloch, 20 June 1864, ibid., pp. 673ff.

169. J. M. Brooke to Mallory, Brooke Letterbook, War Department Collection of Confederate Records, NARG 109.

170. Ralph W. Donnelly, "The Confederate Lead Mines of Wytheville County, Virginia," *Civil War History* 5 (Dec. 1959): 402ff.

171. Ibid., p. 404.

172. "Importation of Lead Articles at Charleston and Wilmington since November 1, 1863," *OR,* Ser. 4, 3:930ff.

173. *Manufactures of the United States,* pp. clxxiii–xxiv. See also R. F. Munn, *Coal Industry in America: A Bibliography and Guide to Studies,* University of West Virginia Library, Morgantown, W.Va., n.d.

174. Bruce, *Virginia Iron Manufacture in the Slave Era,* p. 109.

175. Armes, *Story of Coal and Iron in Alabama,* pp. 149ff.

176. D. French Forrest to Mitchell, 10 Sept. 1862, J. K. Mitchell Papers, VHS/RV.

177. General Order No. 85, 16 June 1863, *OR,* Ser. 4, 2:594ff.

178. S. S. Lee to Mallory, 31 Oct. 1864, *ORN,* Ser. 2, 2:753ff.

179. Catesby ap R. Jones to Warner, 15 Oct. 1864, Subject File, C.S.N., Naval Collection, NARG 45.

180. Ware to Brown, 26 Aug. 1862, Paymaster Ware's Correspondence, and Contract dated 10 Aug. 1863 between Commander Farrand and I. D. Spear, agent of the Mobile and Selma Mining Company, ibid., NARG 45. The latter said he would procure half of the output of his mines.

181. J. N. Barney to General Magruder, 3 May 1863, Records of Confederate Naval and Marine Personnel, War Department Collection of Confederate Records, NARG 109.

182. J. DeBree to Mallory, 11 Aug. 1862, *ORN,* Ser. 2, 2:249ff.

183. Draft of contract of imprecise date, C.S.N. Records, VSA/RV. It remains unknown if the contract was fulfilled.

184. J. DeBree to Mallory, 11 Aug. 1862, *ORN,* Ser. 2, 2:249ff.

185. Buchanan to Mallory, 15 Oct. 1862, Admiral Buchanan's Letterbook, Franklin Buchanan Books, SHC/CHNC. This collection of Buchanan's books was until recently included in a different collection, named Buchanan-Screven Papers.

186. Browne to Mitchell, 26 Feb. 1863, Phineas Browne Papers, ASDAH/MA.

187. J. H. Warner to D. H. Hunter, 27 Aug. 1862, Savannah Squadron Papers, EUL/AG.

188. J. A. Doah to Buchanan, 18 Sept. 1862, Paymaster Ware's Correspondence, Naval Collection, NARG 45.

189. W. H. Blake, "Coal Barging in Wartime, 1861–1865," *Gulf States Historical Magazine* 1 (1901): 409ff.

190. Buchanan to Mitchell, 25 Oct. 1862, Admiral Buchanan's Letterbook, Franklin Buchanan Books, SHC/CHNC.

191. Circular letter dated 1 Oct. 1863, Savannah Squadron Papers, EUL/AG.

192. J. P. McCorkle to Tattnall, 22 Aug. 1863, ibid.

193. Percival Perry, "Naval Stores Industry in the Antebellum South, 1789–1861" (Ph.D. dissertation, Duke University, 1947).

194. Mallory to President Davis, 30 Nov. 1863, *ORN,* Ser. 2, 2:520ff.

195. Scharf, *Confederate States Navy,* p. 51.

196. S. W. Corbin to R. D. Minor, 16 Apr. 1863, Minor Family Papers, VHS/RV.

197. S. S. Lee to Mallory, 31 Oct. 1864, *ORN,* Ser. 2, 2:753ff.

198. Lewis C. Gray, *History of Agriculture in Southern United States to 1860,* 2 vols. (1932; reprint, Gloucester, Mass., 1958), 2:822.

199. Mallory to President Davis, 29 Feb. 1862, *ORN,* Ser. 2, 2:148ff.; ibid., p. 159, Enclosure 9.

200. Scharf, *Confederate States Navy,* p. 51.

201. Mallory to Memminger, 26 Nov. 1864, with a request for an extraordinary appropriation of $75,000 to transfer and put the Rope Walk back into operation, Letters Received by the Confederate Secretary of the Treasury, Treasury Department Collection, NARG 365.

202. Mallory to President Davis, 26 Apr. 1861, *ORN,* Ser. 2, 2:51ff.

203. Scharf, *Confederate States Navy,* p. 31. To corroborate his information that lumber still had to be cut, see *ORN,* Ser. 2, 1:542.

204. Soley, "The Union and Confederate Navies," in *BL,* 1:611ff.

205. Scharf, *Confederate States Navy,* p. 44.

206. Bulloch, *Secret Service,* 1:52ff.

CHAPTER FOUR

1. Alfred Thayer Mahan, *From Sail to Steam: Recollections of a Naval Life* (New York, 1907), p. 3.

2. H. Moyse-Bartlett, *From Sail to Steam* (1946; reprint, London, 1968), p. 5.

3. Bernard Brodie, *Sea-power in the Machine Age* (Princeton, 1943), p. 3.

4. Mahan, *From Sail to Steam,* pp. 25ff.

5. See Ruth White, *Yankee from Sweden: The Dream and Reality in the Days of John Ericsson* (New York, 1860); William C. Church, *The Life of John Ericsson,* 2 vols. (New York, 1890).

6. Another inventor, Francis Petitt Smith, an Englishman, constructed a screw propeller at the same time as Ericsson. Indeed, his patent was granted six weeks before the Swede's. The latter, however, had been working on his model since 1833. Ericsson developed it and brought it to definitive development in the United States while Smith did so in England. See James Phinney Baxter, *The Introduction of the Ironclad Warship* (Cambridge, Mass., 1933), pp. 12ff.

7. Brodie, *Sea-power in the Machine Age,* pp. 35ff.

8. This was the case even if the major artillery piece then in naval use, the 32-pounder, weighing more than two tons and served by a crew of four men, was not a weapon to be overlooked. See Baxter, *Introduction of the Ironclad Warship,* pp. 181ff.

9. Louis Napoléon Bonaparte and Général Favé, *Etudes sur le passé et l'avenir de l'artillerie,* 6 vols. (Paris, 1846–71), 5:33ff. In 1794 and 1795 the Committee of Public Safety resumed experiments with naval cannons at Meudon. These were most secret (only members of the committee itself and twelve high-ranking army and navy officers could assist), but the projectiles continued to burst inside the barrel in disturbing proportions. Some time later, to stop the longitudinal rotation of the round sphere inside the gun, which could drive the fuse against the bore of the piece provoking the premature explosion of the shell, a new committee, created by the Directory to which belonged none other than Borda, Laplace, and Périer, accepted the solution of putting the shell on a so-called sabot of wood, cylindrical and fixed to it by metal strips. This gave the projectile an approximately cylindric-conical shape, impeding the longitudinal rotation. Finally, in 1802, a report from a new naval committee concluded that the metallurgical problem had not been well solved, with the result that both the guns and the projectiles were defective and the latter fell apart in the barrel; fuses were bad, and at sea they were damaged by dampness and therefore the shells either failed to explode or did so immediately upon leaving the piece (fuses had therefore to be improved); metal strips that held the shells at the sabots became useless from rust and fell off. Nothing could be accomplished unless substantial progress were made in the casting of pig iron, in the making of fuses, and in shielding the shells from humidity (ibid., pp. 40ff.).

10. The full title is *Nouvelle Force maritime, ou exposé des moyens d'annuler la force des marines actuelles de haut-bord, et de donner à des navires très pétits, assez de puissance pour détruire les plus grands vaisseaux de guerre* (Paris, 1821). The second edition, which appeared a year later, stated in its long title that the work dealt with *"une espèce nouvelle d'artillerie de mer, qui détruirait promptement les vaisseaux de haut-bord."* Paixhans later developed his ideas in other writings: *Expériences faites par la Marine française, sur une arme nouvelle. Changements qui paraissent devoir en résulter dans le système naval, et examen de quelques questions relatives à la marine, à l'artillerie, à l'attaque et à la defense des cotes et des places* (Paris, 1825); *Force et faiblesse militaires de la France* (Paris, 1830).

11. Napoléon and Favé, *Etudes,* 5:156.

12. Baxter, *Introduction of the Ironclad Warship,* p. 25. Paixhans, *Force et faiblesse de la France* pp. 401ff., states that the experiment was done at Brest between 1823 and 1824 and that the British, Swedes, and Russians immediately imitated it.

13. AMV, 7DD1, 65, and BBB 1109, 1110, 1111, and 1113. Enclosed here are the minutes

of the meetings of the Conseil des Travaux, all of the utmost importance to understand the development of the ideas of both Paixhans and the first great builder of ironclads, Stanislas Dupuy de Lôme. See also Baxter, *Introduction of the Ironclad Warship*, passim.

14. Let us consider two artillery pieces of the same caliber, one rifled, the other smoothbore, which would fire two projectiles of the same weight with equal charges. It can be proved that their initial muzzle speed will be the same, yet the one fired by the rifled gun would have a speed at impact three times greater than that fired by the smoothbore and therefore (supposing an equal mass) a far superior kinetic energy. (Remember that kinetic energy is equal to half mv squared.) As for the cylindrical-conical projectile, one must remember that the projectile fired by a smoothbore gun, because of major attrition on its inferior part caused by gravity, leaves the gun with a rotary movement along its trajectory. If it is spherical, however, that is unimportant; but if it is cylindrical-conical, having its barycenter near its base, it will tend to arrive on its target base rather than point first. Rifling gives the projectile an axial rotary movement, neutralizing this. It is interesting to observe that Leonardo da Vinci first posed the problem and, lacking rifling for stabilizing, designed a shell with its base deeply excavated in order to raise the barycenter toward the point. The designs may be seen in the Museum of Technology, Milan, Italy. As for "shrapnel," named after its inventor, the British Colonel Henry Shrapnel, who designed it in 1802, it is a projectile exploded by time fuse; it is full of round balls that scatter like rain.

15. The prototypes of Cavalli's cannon are at the Artillery Museum of Turin, Italy. It is very interesting to observe that to solve the problem of forcing the projectile into the barrel, so as to be sure that it became engaged in the rifling, Cavalli sought to find the correct solution by means of breechloading. Yet, because closing devices were still far from perfect (pig iron, easily overheated, would expand and let the gas escape), after Cavalli a general return had to be made to muzzle loading. The indispensable forcing of the projectile into the rifling was obtained through "rings," or "clogs," or "socks," or "sabots," made of lead, copper, or other soft metal, generally put around the base of the projectile. This method (still used for some cannons of World War I) did not prevent the "rattling" of the projectile inside the barrel, which frequently caused disastrous explosions inside the gun, making it burst. See Napoléon and Favé, *Etudes,* 6:91ff., and *Scritti inediti del Generale Cavalli,* 4 vols. (Turin, Italy, 1910).

16. Napoléon and Favé, *Etudes,* 6:369.

17. Emanuel Raymond Lewis, "The Ambiguous Columbiad," *Military Affairs* 28 (Winter 1964): 111ff.

18. H. L. Scott, *Military Dictionary* (New York, 1861), pp. 164ff., does not provide the precise date. Even John Gibbon, *The Artillerist's Manual* (New York, 1860), avoids the problem. Baxter, *Introduction of the Ironclad Warship*, p. 22, says "during the War of 1812." E. R. Lewis, who has made the most thorough study of the subject, in "The Ambiguous Columbiad," p. 114, gives the date 1811 and states that it concerned a 50-pounder cannon and that during the War of 1812 it was produced with different calibers from 18- to 100-pounders but that Bomford never sought patents. Later, Lewis returned to the subject in his *Seacoast Fortifications of the United States: An Introductory History* (Washington, D.C., 1970), p. 33, and said that the idea was "developed about 1810 or 1811." This appears logical because Bomford was thinking about the matter for some time even if there is no certain evidence of the casting of a Columbiad before 1811. On the last point, see the authoritative Warren Ripley, *Artillery and Ammunition of the Civil War* (New York, 1970), p. 71, who

ascribes to 1811 the invention of the Columbiad and even calls the first to be cast "model 1811."

19. See Robert E. Spiller et al., *Literary History of the United States,* 2 vols. (London, 1969), 1:168. Bomford was Barlow's brother-in-law and tied to him by strong family bonds. According to other sources, however, this name was given to all guns cast by the Columbia Foundry, owned by Henry Foxhall, of Georgetown, Maryland. See Lewis, *Seacoast Fortifications of the United States,* p. 32 n. 34. Yet, given the ties between Barlow and Bomford, the last account seems to be the least possible despite the authoritativeness of Lewis.

20. For an example of use on shipboard, see Chapter 9.

21. The chamber, by concentrating the effect of the propellent along the longitudinal diameter of the sphere (that is, on the center of the projectile), permitted the use of less charge, hence the firing of shells eliminating (at least in part) the danger of an explosion inside the barrel.

22. The process lasted for twenty hours, using 50 liters (11 gallons) of water a minute, or a total of 187 cubic meters (613.36 cubic feet), and keeping the external part warm. By this means, the bore of the gun was made by the best-tempered (i.e., most hard) iron, whereas the external part remained more flexible. See Napoléon and Favé, *Etudes,* 6:379. Rodman also invented a device to check the pressure of gases inside the bore and shaped his Columbiad according to the gradual decrease of inside pressure (ibid., 6:317). He invented new kinds of gunpowder, called "compressed." Black powder was pasted together and shaped into hexagonal prisms pierced by cylindrical holes. The ignition was gradual, the inherent strength of the explosive developing gradually to produce the best action for pushing a projectile out of the gun. The basic idea of Rodman was that the pressure implemented by the explosive powder inside the bore of the gun in a given time diminishes proportionally to the increase of the dimension of grains of powder and that this occurs in a proportion higher than the corresponding initial speed squared. He succeeded in this way to moderate the dangerous intrinsic tendency of black powder to ignite too quickly, which was good for causing explosions (torpedoes, shells, etc.), but not for throwing projectiles out of a gun. See J. T. Rodman, *Reports of Experiments on the Properties of Metals for Cannon, and the Qualities of Cannon Powder* (Washington, D.C., 1861).

23. See Raimondo Luraghi, *Storia della Guerra Civile Americana,* 5th ed., rev. (Milan, 1986), pp. 244ff. Several authors (among them Lewis, "The Ambiguous Columbiad," pp. 120ff.) deny that Rodman's cannon could qualify as a Columbiad, given the difference in their building. But the current use prevailed; it cannot be denied that Rodman's gun corresponded with the ultimate development and tasks of the Columbiad, had the same ballistic characters, and was so considered by expert foreigners (see Napoléon and Favé, *Etudes,* 6:396ff.).

24. Ralph Earle, "John Adolphus Dahlgren (1809–1870)," *U.S. Naval Institute Proceedings* 3 (1925): 427ff. Vittorio Cuniberti, a chief naval constructor of the Royal Italian Navy, projected in 1903 the first monocaliber warship (armed with twelve 8-inch guns) and then published a modification of his project in the 1903 issue of *Jane's Fighting Ships* under the caption "The Ideal Ship." There he proposed for his warship eight 12-inch guns in four revolving towers. Admiral Sir John Fisher liked the idea and decided to build a ship starting from Cuniberti's plans. Such was the origin of the famous *Dreadnought.* See Admiral Franco Micali Baratelli, *La Marina militare italiana nella vita nazionale (1860–1914)* (Milan, 1983), pp. 324ff.

25. Ripley, *Artillery and Ammunition of the Civil War*, p. 91.

26. Ibid., pp. 109ff.; J. N. Paulding, *The Cannon and Projectiles Invented by Robert Parker Parrott* (New York, 1879), passim. Also E. D. Morgan to Simon Cameron, 24 July 1861, *OR*, Ser. 3, 1:347; J. Lesley, Jr., to E. D. Morgan, 2 Aug. 1861, ibid., p. 379. Although very good, Parrott cannons had not yet overcome the metallurgical problems, at least those of large calibers (the fieldpiece was quite reliable) because they had a dangerous tendency to overheat and to burst at the muzzle. Nevertheless, the Confederates, other than using captured ones, also built some Parrotts themselves, mostly for the army.

27. Adolphe Auguste Marie Lepotier, *Les Leçons de l'histoire, 1861–1865: Mer contre terre* (Paris, 1945).

28. Ibid., p. 32.

29. Alfred T. Mahan, *The Gulf and Inland Waters*, vol. 3 of *The Navy in the Civil War* (New York, 1883), p. 3.

30. Lepotier, *Les Leçons de l'histoire: Mer contre terre*, p. 10.

31. *OR*, Ser. 3, 1:67ff.

32. *ORN*, Ser. 2, 3:96ff.

33. *OR*, Ser. 3, 1:89ff.

34. Charles Boynton, *The Story of the Navy during the Rebellion* (New York, 1867), 1:83ff.

35. Joseph T. Durkin, S.J., *Stephen Russell Mallory: Confederate Navy Chief* (Chapel Hill, 1954), p. 158.

36. Lepotier, *Les Leçons de l'histoire: Mer contre terre*, p. 45.

37. Tattnall to Kennard, 14 Aug. 1861, Kennard to Tattnall, 17 Aug. 1861, UGL/AG; Report of the Committee on Naval Affairs, Feb. 1861, *ORN*, Ser. 2, 2:41ff.

38. Mallory to Davis (Report of the Secretary of the Navy), 26 Apr. 1861, *ORN*, Ser. 2, 2:51ff.

39. Ibid.

40. Mallory to Bulloch, 9 May 1861, *ORN*, Ser. 2, 2:64–65; Mallory to Conrad, 9 May 1861, ibid., p. 66, wherein the sum to be given Bulloch for buying or contracting for six ships and purchasing other naval stores was set at $1 million (James D. Bulloch, *The Secret Service of the Confederate States in Europe, or, How the Confederate Cruisers Were Equipped*, 2 vols. [1884; reprint, New York, 1959], 1:47ff.).

41. *ORN*, Ser. 2, 2:53.

42. George M. Brooke, Jr., "John Mercer Brooke, Naval Scientist" (Ph.D. dissertation, University of North Carolina, 1956), 2:760; J. M. Brooke to Mallory, 6 May 1861, ibid. See the resolution offered to the Confederate Congress by Representative William Chilton of Alabama on 27 Feb. 1861, *JC*, 1:90. On this question see Baxter, *Introduction of the Ironclad Warship*, passim; yet the most authoritative study of Confederate ironclads is William N. Still, Jr., *Iron Afloat: The Story of the Confederate Armorclad* (1971; reprint, Columbia, S.C., 1985), esp. p. 11.

43. Benedetto Brin, one of the greatest naval constructors, was the first to put on board of Italian ironclads the enormous Armstrong guns of one hundred tons, realizing the maximum of both protection and speed; for Vittorio Cuniberti, see above, note 24. See also F. Micali Baratelli, *La Marina italiana* (Milan, 1983), pp. 176ff., 354ff.

44. Still, *Iron Afloat*, p. 11.

45. *ORN*, Ser. 2, 2:67ff.

46. Adolphe Auguste Marie Lepotier, *Les leçons de l'histoire: Les Corsaires du sud et le pavillon etoilé: de l'*Alabama *à l'*Emden (Paris, 1936), p. 176.

47. Ibid., p. 177.

48. Mallory to North, 17 May 1861, *ORN,* Ser. 2, 2:70ff.; "Estimate of the amount required for the purchase or construction of one or two steamers in England or France fully armed and equipped," ibid., p. 72.

49. According to Commander Hunter Davidson, who brought the Confederacy's underwater weapon to its greatest effectiveness, Mallory planned its first use (*SHSP,* 2:1ff.).

50. New York, 1855. The book was translated into many languages. The Italian translation was printed in Rome in 1872; it had been made by naval lieutenant Luigi Gatta.

51. Frances Leigh Williams, *Matthew Fontaine Maury: Scientist of the Sea* (New Brunswick, N.J., 1963), pp. 270ff.

52. Lepotier, *Les Leçons de l'histoire: Les Corsaires du sud,* p. 177.

CHAPTER FIVE

1. At London, on the top of the Old Admiralty building, there was a wind vane. Whenever this indicated that the wind was blowing toward the French coast, the British fleet rushed to sea, sure that French ships were out. The latter indeed tended to move when they could sail leeward to be ready to return to their own bases as soon as required. In their turn, the French blockade runners, coming in from the high seas, chose the same moment to try reaching French ports because the favorable wind would speed them and the French battle fleet was out and could protect them. See E. B. Potter and Chester W. Nimitz, eds., *Sea Power: A Naval History* (Englewood Cliffs, N.J., 1960), pp. 36ff.

2. Geoffrey Best, *Humanity in Warfare: The International Law of Armed Conflicts* (London, 1980), pp. 70ff. The definition of "contraband of war" was always difficult. Grotius classed goods transported by ships into three categories: those that were clearly war contraband (weapons, ammunition, uniforms, military accoutrements); those that were dubious; and noncontraband. Controversies began because the blockading power tended to consider "dubious" (hence subject to confiscation) many of the goods of the third list, e.g., foodstuffs, so long as they helped the enemy to resist.

3. See Charles La Mache, *La Guerre de course* (Paris, 1901). Of great help has been the textbook by Admiral Giovanni Clara, *Appunti di diritto bellico marittimo* (Livorno, Italy, 1983), and the M.A. thesis of Giorgio Macino, "Il concetto di neutralità nella sua strutturazione giuridica e nella sua evoluzione storico-politica. Connessioni e sviluppi della preda marittima" (University of Genoa, Italy, 1973). As for prey, one must remember that it is "normally untouchable private property" but that "wartime maritime law permits its seizure," whereas, what is public property of the enemy (ships, accoutrements, and so on) is fair prize, for which recourse need not be made to a prize court. See Clara, *Appunti,* p. 77.

4. William M. Robinson, Jr., *The Confederate Privateers* (1928; reprint, Columbia, S.C., 1991), p. 1. This is the standard work on the privateers of the American Civil War.

5. Ibid., p. 3. When communications were difficult and slow and notices and orders carried by sailing ships could take months to reach their destination, the issue of letters of marque and reprisal provided privateer captains the authority without which they could not have operated.

6. See George R. Taylor, *The Transportation Revolution, 1815–1860* (New York, 1951).

7. The Declaration of Paris was published in the languages of the seven contracting powers. I have made use of the Sardinian (i.e., Italian) version, in *Raccolta dei Trattati e delle Convenzioni fra il Regno d'Italia e i Governi Esteri* (Turin, Italy, 1862). On blockade, see Julius W. Pratt, "The British Blockade and American Precedent," *U.S. Naval Institute Proceedings* 46 (1920): 1789ff., and Sally W. Mallison and Thomas Mallison, Jr., "A Survey of the International Law of Naval Blockade," *U.S. Naval Institute Proceedings* 102 (1976): 44ff.

8. Ephraim D. Adams, *Great Britain and the American Civil War,* 2 vols. (New York, 1925), 1:139. Of course, the old method of warfare was now impossible.

9. Because the Marcy Amendment would have covered not only enemy goods that were not contraband but the enemy merchant ship itself, the war at sea would have been limited to battles between warships because no private freighter would any longer carry contraband of war. The American proposal was approved by minor powers that were not signatories of the declaration.

10. Adams, *Great Britain and the American Civil War,* 1:65ff.

11. Ibid., p. 86. On 4 May Lord Russell wrote to the British ambassador at Washington, Lord Lyons, along these lines. See Lord Russell to Lyons, 4 May 1861, PRO, FO, 5/755/121.

12. Lynn M. Case and Warren F. Spencer, *The United States and France: Civil War Diplomacy* (Philadelphia, 1970), pp. 54ff.

13. Adams, *Great Britain and the American Civil War,* 1:94ff.

14. Case and Spencer, *The United States and France,* pp. 54ff.

15. The best analysis of the negotiations is ibid., pp. 86ff.

16. There was no doubt that Confederate privateers might enter some neutral ports; yet, in any case, neither the British, the French (because these powers did not permit prizes to enter their ports), nor the Spanish, because Spain, early in the war, took the same position toward the naval war as Britain and France did. In other neutral ports, however, they would be subject to the same limitations that were placed on belligerent warships, i.e., strict time limits that would have hindered the sale of prizes, which involved very long procedures. See Robinson, *Confederate Privateers,* pp. 27ff.

17. Ibid., p. 343. The North also launched several privateers, which captured some Southern merchant ships that were not quick enough to seek refuge in port (ibid., pp. 303ff.). There were also, among New England sailors, some who shamelessly declared themselves ready to request letters of marque from the South to wage privateer warfare against the Union to which they belonged (S. Kingsbury to Mallory, 29 Apr. 1861, *ORN,* Ser. 2, 1:333ff.). Mallory, who had no authority over privateering and did not believe in it, evidently said nothing about the matter or washed his hands of it. From this viewpoint, the accusation directed by the South toward Northerners, that they were willing to seek money and be ready to take any action to get it, does not lack some support. Interesting also, for the status of Confederate privateers, is what was written by the former president of the Confederacy, Jefferson Davis, in *SHSP,* 11:181ff.

18. Mallory to Bulloch, 9 May 1861, *ORN,* Ser. 2, 2:64–65.

19. James D. Bulloch, *The Secret Service of the Confederate States in Europe, or How the Confederate Cruisers Were Equipped* (1884; reprint, New York, 1959), 1:53ff. About Huse, see his thin book of recollections, Caleb Huse, *The Supplies for the Confederate Army: How They Were Obtained in Europe and How Paid For* (1904; reprint, Dayton, Ohio, 1970). See

also Samuel B. Thompson, *Confederate Purchasing Operations Abroad* (Chapel Hill, 1935); Richard J. Lester, *Confederate Finance and Purchasing in Great Britain* (Charlottesville, Va., 1975).

20. Jon L. Wakelyn, *Biographical Dictionary of the Confederacy* (Westport, Conn., 1977), pp. 117–18. The best portrait is that by Jim D. Hill, *Sea Dogs of the Sixties* (1935; reprint, New York, 1961), pp. 63ff. Bulloch's sister, who married a Roosevelt, was the mother of the future president of the United States Theodore Roosevelt. Bulloch was therefore the latter's uncle. See also William F. Roberts, "James Dunwoody Bulloch and the Confederacy," *North Carolina Historical Review* 24 (1947): 315ff.

21. Hill, *Sea Dogs of the Sixties,* p. 66. When Bulloch sailed to Europe, he was thirty-eight years old, having been born in 1823.

22. They were the English agents of the George Alfred Trenholm Company, of Charleston, South Carolina.

23. Bulloch to Mallory, 13 Aug. 1861, *ORN,* Ser. 2, 2:83ff. In his *Secret Service,* 1:48, Bulloch instead says that he landed in Liverpool on the fourth. The third of June seems more probable because it appears in a contemporary document, whereas the memoirs were written twenty years later. The exact date is a matter of no consequence.

24. After underscoring Huse's energy and ability, Bulloch writes: "I have always felt that the safety of Richmond at the time of General McClellan's advance from Yorktown up the peninsula, in the spring of 1862, was largely due to the efforts of Mr. Charles K. Prioleau and Major Huse, because the former furnished the credit, and the latter bought and forwarded the rifles and field artillery without which the great battles of Seven Pines and the Chickahominy, could not have been successfully fought" (Bulloch, *Secret Service,* 1:53).

25. Ibid., p. 54.

26. Secretary of State William Henry Seward to the Ambassador of the United States in London, Charles Francis Adams, August 1861 (no day), in U.S. Instructions—Great Britain, Diplomatic Correspondence, vol. 17, General Records of the Department of State, NARG 59.

27. On this vessel, the future cruiser *Florida,* there is a very good study: Frank Lawrence Owsley, Jr., *The C.S.S. Florida: Her Building and Operations* (Philadelphia, 1965). Even if neither Bulloch nor Owsley cites this fact, the final specifications and plans for the *Florida* were made by John Luke Porter (see Chapter 3, note 34).

28. Bulloch, *Secret Service,* 1:56ff.; Owsley, *C.S.S. Florida,* pp. 19ff.

29. Adams to Seward, 18 Oct. 1861, in U.S. Legation, Britain, Despatches, vol. 77, Diplomatic Correspondence, General Records of the Department of State, NARG 59.

30. Bulloch, *Secret Service,* 1:225.

31. Ibid., p. 62. A book on the Confederate raider *Alabama* (or, better, it seems, on its captain) was announced when the final editing of the present book was already taking place so that this writer was not able to make use of it: John M. Taylor, *Confederate Raider: Raphael Semmes of the Alabama* (McLean, Va., 1994).

32. William Laird to Captain Jansen, 6 June 1869, in *Alabama* Letters, CLCA/LGB.

33. Semmes to Mrs. Semmes, from Detroit, 21 Aug. 1860, Admiral Semmes Papers, ASDAH/MA, in which he voices his admiration for the wealth of the Northwest and the rise of big cities there.

34. Notices about this colloquy are in Raphael Semmes, *Memoirs of Service Afloat during the War between the States* (New York, 1869), pp. 92ff.

35. "Narrative of Service aboard C.S.S. *Sumter*," William P. Brooks Papers, GHS/SG. William P. Brooks, the second engineer of the *Sumter*, had served on board the ship when she was a passenger vessel plying between New Orleans and Havana. He tells us that she had been built in Philadelphia and gives her gross tonnage as 499 tons. See also Semmes, *Service Afloat*, pp. 93ff.

36. Semmes, *Service Afloat*, p. 93.

37. The sum for the payment, $45,000, was requested from the Treasury Department on 20 April. Another $35,000 was requested on the twenty-fourth to purchase the second steamer indicated, the *Marquis de la Habana*, that would become the auxiliary cruiser *McRae* (Mallory to Memminger, 27 June 1861, in Letters Received by the Confederate Secretary of the Treasury, Treasury Collection, NARG 365).

38. Mallory to Semmes, 18 Apr. 1861, *ORN*, Ser. 1, 1:613.

39. Semmes to Mrs. Semmes, 15 Apr. 1861, Admiral Semmes Papers, ASDAH/MA.

40. Semmes, *Service Afloat*, p. 149.

41. The best biography of Semmes is the short yet authoritative one by William J. Robinson, Jr., in *Dictionary of American Biography*, 22 vols. (New York, 1946), 16:579ff. See also the sketch by Gamaliel Bradford, *Confederate Portraits* (New York, 1914), pp. 217ff. See also Raimondo Luraghi, *Storia della Guerra Civile Americana*, 5th ed., rev. (Milan, 1986), p. 311. Edward D. Boykin, *Ghost Ship of the Confederacy: The Story of the* Alabama *and Her Captain, Raphael Semmes* (New York, 1957), is in many ways unsatisfactory.

42. Semmes to Mrs. Semmes, 18 Apr. 1861, Admiral Semmes Papers, ASDAH/MA.

43. Semmes, *Service Afloat*, p. 95.

44. Semmes to his daughter, 3 May 1861, Admiral Semmes Papers, ASDAH/MA.

45. Semmes, *Service Afloat*, p. 95.

46. Semmes to Mallory, 22 Apr. 1861, Semmes to Mrs. Semmes, 25 Apr. 1861, *Sumter* Letterbook 1, Admiral Semmes Papers, ASDAH/MA. The letter to the naval secretary is also printed in *ORN*, Ser. 1, 1:614.

47. Semmes to his daughter, 3 May 1861, Admiral Semmes Papers, ASDAH/MA.

48. Semmes, *Service Afloat*, p. 96. A good book about the *Sumter* is that by Charles G. Summersell, *The Cruise of the C.S.S.* Sumter (Tuscaloosa, Ala., 1965). Summersell, however, did not use the extremely important Semmes Papers.

49. Note by Semmes, *ORN*, Ser. 1, 1:613; Semmes to Mallory, 22 Apr. 1861, Admiral Semmes Papers, ASDAH/MA; account of expenditure of the *Sumter* approved by Semmes for a total of $19,174.94, Paymaster Ware Papers, Naval Collection, Confederate Subject File SC, NARG 45.

50. Semmes to Mallory, 25 Apr. 1861, in *Sumter* Letterbook 1, Admiral Semmes Papers, ASDAH/MA.

51. Semmes, *Service Afloat*, p. 102.

52. Semmes to Mallory, 25 Apr. 1861 (second letter of the date), *Sumter* Letterbook 1, Admiral Semmes Papers, ASDAH/MA.

53. Semmes to Mallory, 26 Apr. 1861, Admiral Semmes Papers, ASDAH/MA.

54. Semmes to Mallory, 26 Apr. 1861 (second letter of the date), ibid.

55. Semmes to Mallory, 26 Apr. 1861 (third letter of the date), ibid.

56. Semmes to Mallory, 30 Apr. 1861, ibid.

57. Semmes, *Service Afloat*, p. 99.

58. Semmes to Mallory, 7 May 1861, *Sumter* Letterbook 1, Admiral Semmes Papers, ASDAH/MA.

59. Semmes, *Service Afloat,* p. 99.

60. Private Journal of the Commander of the C.S.S. *Sumter,* Admiral Semmes Papers, ASDAH/MA. The manuscript bears the motto *"Deo Adjuvante!"* If one thinks of the great exertions Semmes had to make to put the little craft to sea, it is a good motto. An extract of the journal is included in Semmes, *Service Afloat,* passim. Other extracts are to be found in *ORN,* Ser. 1, 1:691ff.

61. Semmes to Mallory, 16 May 1861, *Sumter* Letterbook 1, Admiral Semmes Papers, ASDAH/MA.

62. Semmes to Mallory, 1 May 1861, ibid.

63. Semmes to Mallory, 7 May 1861, ibid.

64. Semmes to Booth, 10 May 1861, ibid.

65. Semmes to Mallory, 16 May 1861, ibid. Herein acknowledgment is made of the receipt of a letter written by Mallory to Semmes on 11 May, with a copy of the order enclosed.

66. Semmes to Chapman, 20 May 1861, in Semmes, *Service Afloat,* p. 102.

67. Semmes to Governor Moore, 16 June 1861, *Sumter* Letterbook 1, Admiral Semmes Papers, ASDAH/MA. The controversy ended only after a direct meeting between Semmes and the governor, who pledged to solve the problem. See Semmes's note at the end of his letter of 17 June, ibid.

68. Semmes to Mallory, 16 June 1861, ibid.; Invoices dated 14 and 15 June 1861 for providing the *Sumter* with shells, shots, powder, etc., Confederate Subject File BA, Naval Collection, NARG 45.

69. Private Journal of the Commander of C.S.S. *Sumter,* Admiral Semmes Papers, ASDAH/MA.

70. Semmes to Mallory, 29 Apr., 1, 10 May 1861, *Sumter* Letterbook 1, ibid.

71. Semmes, *Service Afloat,* p. 101.

72. Semmes to Mallory, 23 May 1861, *Sumter* Letterbook 1, Admiral Semmes Papers, ASDAH/MA.

73. Private Journal of the Commander of C.S.S. *Sumter,* Admiral Semmes Papers, ASDAH/MA; also in Semmes, *Service Afloat,* p. 104.

74. Semmes to Mallory, 14 June 1861, *Sumter* Letterbook 1, Admiral Semmes Papers, ASDAH/MA, also printed in *ORN,* Ser. 1, 1:615.

75. According to the method of indicating words by three numbers: page, column, word. Evidently Semmes had another copy. Semmes to Mallory, 14 and 16 June (two letters) 1861, *Sumter* Letterbook 1, Admiral Semmes Papers, ASDAH/MA.

76. Semmes to the Chief Pilot of the Mississippi, 22 June 1861, *ORN,* Ser. 1, 1:616; Semmes to Mallory, 15 June 1861, *Sumter* Letterbook 1, Admiral Semmes Papers, ASDAH/MA. Semmes observed that most pilots were Northerners (as were most sailors). This explained their unwillingness to work for the Southern cause. Semmes, however, found an apparently Southern pilot who with skill and daring piloted the *Sumter* as far as the bar before returning ashore (Semmes, *Service Afloat,* p. 109ff.).

77. "Narrative of William P. Brooks," Brooks Papers, GHS/SG.

78. Semmes to Mallory, 24 June 1861, *Sumter* Letterbook 1, Admiral Semmes Papers, ASDAH/MA. The decision to eliminate both lights and beacon buoys, even if it made Semmes relatively safe (totally safe in nighttime), also hindered his running the blockade by night. See Semmes to Mallory, 30 June 1861, ibid. The two letters are also printed in *ORN,* Ser. 1, 1:617–18.

79. Semmes, *Service Afloat*, pp. 112ff.

80. "Narrative of William P. Brooks," Brooks Papers, GHS/SG.

81. Throughout this narrative, I have relied on the extraordinarily graphic account by Semmes in *Service Afloat*, pp. 114ff. It has been checked against Semmes's Private Journal of the Commander of C.S.S. *Sumter*, Admiral Semmes Papers, ASDAH/MA, and "Narrative of William P. Brooks," Brooks Papers, GHS/SG. The latter holds that Semmes was resolved to blow up his ship rather than surrender. From the other side, the report by Commander C. H. Poor, commanding the *Brooklyn*, to Flag Officer Mervine, commanding the Gulf Blockading Squadron, is in *ORN*, Ser. 1, 1:34.

82. Semmes, *Service Afloat*, pp. 120–21. The comet seen by Semmes might perhaps be that of Encke.

83. Ibid., p. 129.

84. Private Journal of the Commander of C.S.S. *Sumter*, Admiral Semmes Papers, ASDAH/MA; Semmes to Mallory, 16 Jan. 1862, ibid. (also printed in *ORN*, Ser. 1, 1:654ff.). The system Semmes used to salvage the crews of ships he destroyed was to land them if a coast was very close. Otherwise he would keep them on board the *Sumter* until he was able to transfer them to some freighter passing by or land them in a neutral port. He treated his prisoners with the utmost humanity. For example, he never put them in irons, and they ate the same food his crew did.

85. How much these pledges would be respected no one can say. The *condicio sine qua non* for collecting payments was that the Confederacy would win the war, which did not happen. The ransom bond was in itself questionable, in part because it was a leftover from the privateer era. See Clara, *Appunti*, p. 76.

86. Semmes, *Service Afloat*, p. 305.

87. The voluminous correspondence between Semmes and the Spanish authorities is to be found in *Sumter* Letterbook 1, Admiral Semmes Papers, ASDAH/MA (it is printed only in part in *ORN*, Ser. 1, 1:652ff.).

88. Semmes, *Service Afloat*, p. 308.

89. Semmes to Mallory, 23 Jan. 1862, *Sumter* Letterbook 1, Admiral Semmes Papers, ASDAH/MA, printed in *ORN*, Ser. 1, 1:654ff.

90. Private Journal of Commander Semmes, Admiral Semmes Papers, ASDAH/MA, printed in *ORN*, Ser. 1, 1:744ff.

91. Private Journal of Commander Semmes, Admiral Semmes Papers, ASDAH/MA.

92. Report by Officers of the *Sumter* to Semmes, *ORN*, Ser. 1, 1:666–67.

93. "Narrative of William P. Brooks," Brooks Papers, GHS/SG.

94. They were the steam sloops *Tuscarora*, *Kearsarge*, and *St. Louis* (*ORN*, Ser. 1, 1:356ff.).

95. Captain of the *Kearsarge*, C. W. Pickering, to the Union Secretary of the Navy, Gideon Welles, 12 Mar. 1862, *ORN*, Ser. 1, 1:358.

96. Semmes to Mallory, 24 Feb. 1862, *Sumter* Letterbook 1, Admiral Semmes Papers, ASDAH/MA; Semmes to J. P. Mason, Commissioner of the C.S.A. in London, 26 Feb. 1862, ibid. These letters are also printed in *ORN*, Ser. 1, 1:664ff. In addition, Semmes gives a detailed account in *Service Afloat*, pp. 329ff.

97. Semmes, *Service Afloat*, pp. 342–43.

98. Ibid.

99. Semmes to Mason, 30 Mar. 1862, *Sumter* Letterbook 1, Admiral Semmes Papers, ASDAH/MA.

100. Semmes, *Service Afloat,* p. 345. The *Sumter* had really cost more because $45,000 had been appropriated only for buying her. But she had inflicted much greater damage upon enemy trade than her cost.

101. George W. Dalzell, *The Flight from the Flag: The Continuing Effect of the Civil War upon the American Carrying Trade* (Chapel Hill, 1940), pp. 30ff.

102. See Frank L. Owsley, *King Cotton Diplomacy: Foreign Relations of the Confederate States of America,* 2d ed. (Chicago, 1959). Also see the Confederate Secretary of State R.M.T. Hunter to Mason, 23 Sept. 1861, *ORN,* Ser. 2, 3:257ff., and to Slidell, same date, ibid., pp. 265ff.

103. *Report of Evidence Taken before a Joint Special Committee of Both Houses of the Confederate Congress, to Investigate the Affairs of the Navy Department* (Richmond, 1863), p. 200. Dealt with here are the proceedings of the Joint Congressional Committee to inquire about the secretary of the navy, a matter discussed at some length later. It is printed in *ORN,* Ser. 2, 1:430ff., yet without any enclosure. When questioned by the committee, Pegram, commanding the *Nashville,* stated that his ship had been brought into service for the specific purpose of carrying Commissioners Mason and Slidell to Europe; that unlike the *Sumter,* no changes had been made in her structure; and that because her decks had not been strengthened, she could carry only two small 6-pounders (this contradicts what is said in *ORN,* Ser. 2, 1:126, according to which the ship would have been fitted with a number of 26-pounders, which appears impossible if the deck was only two inches thick, as stated by Pegram). The steamer *Nashville* was brought into the C.S. Navy owing to a certain Trescott, who pointed to the ship, observing that it was still idle, whereas a party of local merchants would have sent her to run the blockade to Liverpool (see W. Henry Trescott to Hon. R.M.T. Hunter, 6 Aug. 1861, Confederate Navy Papers, LC). The Confederate government accepted the suggestion yet decided to use her differently (Mallory to Ingraham, 19 Sept. 1861, *ORN,* Ser. 2, 2:94). To purchase and fit out the *Nashville* cost $120,000, plus an appropriation of $30,000 for purchasing weapons in Europe (Mallory to Memminger, 21 Sept. 1861, Letters Received by the Confederate Secretary of the Treasury, Treasury Collection, NARG 365).

104. I had occasion to see part of the engines of the *Nashville* in the Fort McAllister Park Museum of the Georgia Historical Commission, on the Ogeechee River near Savannah, Georgia, and to notice how mighty they were. The ship was sunk by a Union ironclad in the river. Before being hopelessly closed in, the ship had become a blockade runner, renamed the *Rattlesnake.*

105. The commissioners left the South on a small passenger ship, the *Gordon,* which during the night of 12 October 1861, taking advantage of pitch-black darkness and a rain shower, ran the blockade to the Bahamas. There they took passage on the British packet *Trent* to Europe. The U.S. cruiser *San Jacinto* stopped her on the high sea and, in violation of the law of nations (and also of British neutrality), arrested both of them and carried them as prisoners to the North. One can imagine the uproar from the British lion: for a while, the United States feared (and the Confederacy hoped) that the United Kingdom would intervene in the conflict. In the end, however, the moderation and ability of President Lincoln and of Secretary of State Seward prevailed. The two commissioners were transferred to an English ship and reached their destination safely, whereupon the matter ended. See Luraghi, *Storia della Guerra Civile,* pp. 380ff., and bibliographical note.

106. *ORN,* Ser. 2, 1:631.

107. Warren F. Spencer, *The Confederate Navy in Europe* (University, Ala., 1983), p. 28.

108. Pegram to Mallory, 10 Mar. 1862, *ORN,* Ser. 1, 1:745.

109. William C.. Whittle, Jr., to W. C. Whittle, Sr., 2 Mar. 1862, William C. Whittle Papers, UVL/CV. William Conway Whittle, Jr., was the third mate of the *Nashville.*

110. Adams to Seward, 2 Jan. 1862, vol. 78, Department of State, Diplomatic Correspondence, Great Britain, NARG 59.

111. Pegram to the Duke of Somerset, 24 Jan. 1862, Confederate Area File 4, Naval Records Collection, NARG 45, together with copies of the correspondence exchanged between the commander of the *Nashville* and the port authorities of Southampton. In the letter, Pegram futilely insisted that he be allowed to strengthen his deck so that it might support cannons (of course, bigger ones). His request was turned down by the British authorities because fulfilling it would have violated the neutrality laws.

112. Lord Russell to Adams, 28 Nov. 1861, vol. 78, Department of State, Diplomatic Correspondence, Great Britain, NARG 59. Spencer, *Confederate Navy in Europe,* calls attention to the importance of this exchange of letters because in it the British conception of neutrality with respect to the naval side of the American Civil War was first clarified. With it begins the jurisprudence of the Neutrality Act. Lord Russell's policy toward the American war is clearly described by Frank J. Merli, *Great Britain and the Confederate Navy, 1861–1865* (Bloomington, Ind., 1970).

113. *ORN,* Ser. 1, 1:747.

114. "Narrative of the Cruise of the *Nashville,*" William Robert Dalton Papers, *Civil War Times Illustrated* Papers, USMHI/CP.

CHAPTER SIX

1. The problem is admirably discussed in James Phinney Baxter III, *The Introduction of the Ironclad Warship* (1933; reprint, Hamden, Conn., 1968), pp. 69ff.

2. The exact displacement was 1,668.68 tons. See *Devis d'armement* of the floating batteries, AMV 7, DD1.

3. Baxter, *Introduction of the Ironclad Warship,* pp. 69ff.

4. The exact displacement was 5,617.93 tons. See ibid., pp. 109ff.

5. Ibid., pp. 337ff., discusses the return of the ram.

6. *Statutes at Large of the United States of America,* 5:472.

7. Baxter, *Introduction of the Ironclad Warship,* p. 49.

8. *ORN,* Ser. 2, 1:791.

9. *ORN,* Ser. 2, 2:66–67, Act of Congress. For the estimate Mallory forwarded to Congress with President Davis's approval see ibid., p. 72.

10. James H. North Diary, SHC/CHNC. The manuscript belongs to J. North Fletcher, of Warrenton, Virginia, whom I thank for the use of it.

11. Mallory to Memminger, 14 May 1861, Letters Received by the Confederate Secretary of the Treasury, Treasury Department Collection of Confederate Records, NARG 365.

12. Mallory to North, 17 May 1861, *ORN,* Ser. 2, 2:70–71.

13. Warren F. Spencer, *The Confederate Navy in Europe* (University, Ala., 1983), pp. 29ff.

14. Mallory to North, 24 May 1861, North Diary, SHC/CHNC.

15. North to Mallory, 16 Aug. 1861, *ORN,* Ser. 2, 2:87. Spencer, *Confederate Navy in Europe* (p. 221, n.s), observes that the letter must have been written by North some days before August 16 because on that day he was traveling in France and was in Cherbourg.

16. North to Mallory, September 1861 (no day), *ORN,* Ser. 2, 2:87. The difficulties in sending money were now over because on 30 July Mallory had sent North $600,000,

taking it from the appropriation made for Bulloch (see Mallory to Memminger, 30 July 1861, Letters Received by the Confederate Secretary of the Treasury, Treasury Department Collection of Confederate Records, NARG 365). Had North possessed minimal initiative, he would have obtained the necessary credit from Fraser, Trenholm and Company, as Bulloch had done.

17. Mallory to North, 27 Sept. 1861, *ORN*, Ser. 2, 2:95ff. The secretary insisted that North should make "every exertion to ascertain the practicability of building or buying an ironclad war sloop" and that he must stay in Great Britain until otherwise ordered.

18. J. M. Brooke to wife, 19 June 1861, in George M. Brooke, Jr., "John Mercer Brooke, Naval Scientist" (Ph.D. dissertation, 2 vols., University of North Carolina, 1956).

19. Ibid.

20. John Mercer Brooke, "The *Virginia* or *Merrimac [sic]* Her Real Projector," *SHSP,* 19:3ff., where he wrote that he suggested initially that Mallory call Porter and Williamson; yet the secretary preferred a "practical mechanic" whom he called from Norfolk. This man turned out to be inept for the task. Probably Mallory did not want "two roosters in the henhouse," thus foreseeing the differences between Brooke and Porter. If this was the case, one may ask why Mallory did not at once make Brooke responsible for the whole project, a lack of decision that, perhaps, derived from inexperience. See *ORN*, Ser. 2, 1:783.

21. French Forrest to J. L. Porter, 20 June 1861, and to W. P. Williamson, same date, Gosport, Va., C.S. Navy Yard, Order Book, 22/4–15/10 1861, VSA/RV.

22. Brooke later wondered whether Porter might have rushed to prepare his model according to information supplied by the "practical mechanic" earlier called to Richmond (and who was one of his employees). Yet, since that man had been ordered to be absolutely unobtrusive, he would not betray the details of the sunken bow and stern to Porter, and Porter, for this reason, was not able to put it in his model (Brooke, "The *Virginia* or *Merrimac,*" pp. 24ff.).

23. Ibid. Also see J. M. Brooke, "The Plan and Construction of the *Merrimac,*" *BL,* 1:715ff., which contains Brooke's postwar arguments. See also John W. H. Porter, *A Record of Events in Norfolk County, Virginia, from April 19th, 1861, to May 10th, 1862, with a History of the Soldiers and Sailors of Norfolk County, Norfolk City, and Portsmouth Who Served in the Confederate States Army or Navy* (Portsmouth, Va., 1892). Herein Porter's son sustains the position of his father who had already briefly described it in *BL,* 1:716ff., and also in many letters to newspapers. All the correspondence is printed, with great objectivity, in Brooke, "The *Virginia* or *Merrimac.*"

24. Baxter, *Introduction of the Ironclad Warship,* pp. 226ff.

25. William N. Still, Jr., *Iron Afloat: The Story of the Confederate Armorclad* (1971; reprint, Columbia, S.C., 1985), p. 14. Another basic study of the ironclad, Robert W. Daly, *How the* Merrimac *Won: The Strategic Story of C.S.S.* Virginia (New York, 1957), pp. 25ff., inclines to support Porter's reasons but does not plumb the matter to its bottom.

26. It appears that Porter's initial proposal was to incline the casemate's walls at forty degrees from the deck. Later, observing that a greater inclination would have increased protection without interfering with the firing of the guns, he brought it (apparently on his own initiative) to thirty-five degrees from the deck. See Porter, *Record of Events in Norfolk County,* p. 334. It is unclear on what basis the usually accurate Still (*Iron Afloat,* p. 24) speaks of "about 36 degrees."

27. *ORN*, Ser. 2, 1:784.

28. Report of the Secretary of the Navy, 29 Mar. 1862, *ORN*, Ser. 2, 2:174–75.

29. J. L. Porter to Reverend J. S. Moore, 4 Nov. 1861, P-689, CM/RV: "I have converted the *Merrimac* into a floating battery, and she is said to be the eighth wonder of the world, no nation has ever attempted anything of the kind on so large a scale." He enclosed a very detailed draft, in which decks aft and astern are shown to be two feet underwater, as in Brooke's project, now adopted by Porter. Note the stubborn use of the expression "floating battery," which not only countered the plan adopted but also Mallory's purposes about the tactical and strategic use of the ship.

30. In the original draft, signed by Porter, the ship appears without any lengthening of the hull beyond the casemate. This first draft, which was the original one by Porter, seems to solve the controversy in Brooke's favor ("*Merrimack*-gun deck," C.S. Navy Papers, CM/RV).

31. "U.S.S. *Merrimac*—June 1861 and 1862," signed by "J. L. Porter, Naval Constructor," ibid.

32. *ORN*, Ser. 2, 1:784.

33. Catesby ap R. Jones to R. B. Pegram, 29 July 1876, Confederate Area File 7, Naval Collection, NARG 45. The action had not yet been authorized either by the governor or the navy of Virginia. See Narrative of Captain Samuel Barron, in command of the state naval forces, W. P. Palmer et al., eds., *Calendar of Virginia State Papers,* 11 vols. (Richmond, 1875–93), pp. 166ff.

34. W. H. Petters to Virginia Governor Letcher, 19 Oct. 1861, *ORN*, Ser. 2, 2:107ff.; G. T. Sinclair to Mallory, 22 Apr. 1861, ibid., Ser. 1, 4:306ff.; W. B. Taliaferro to Governor Letcher, 23 Apr. 1861, ibid., 306ff.

35. It was a petty officer of the U.S. Navy who disconnected the primers of the mines to avoid blocks of granite thrown by the explosion upon the houses of Portsmouth. See Daly, *How the* Merrimac *Won,* p. 13; Porter, *Record of Events in Norfolk County,* pp. 14–15.

36. *ORN*, Ser. 2, 1:141ff.

37. French Forrest to R. E. Lee, 30 Mar. 1861, *ORN*, Ser. 1, 5:801; Mallory to President Davis, 18 July 1861, *ORN*, Ser. 2, 2:76ff. About the *Merrimack,* see Greville Bathe, *Ship of Destiny: A Record of the U.S. Steam Frigate* Merrimack, *1855–1862* (St. Augustine, Fla., 1951).

38. The incomplete report is in *ORN*, Ser. 2, 2:174ff. This can more usefully be integrated with the text printed in *SHSP,* 19:11ff.

39. Mallory to President Davis, 18 July 1861, *ORN*, Ser. 2, 2:76ff.

40. Mallory to French Forrest, 11 July 186[1] (which is the correct date, even if the *SHSP* says 1862), *ORN*, Ser. 2, 1:784, 2:175, and *SHSP,* 19:12–13.

41. Mallory to French Forrest, 11 June 1861, Daybook of French Forrest, C.S. Navy Records, VSA/RV.

42. French Forrest, Order Book, C.S. Navy Yard, VSA/RV.

43. F. Forrest to Spotswood, 6 May 1861, French Forrest Letterbook, ibid.

44. French Forrest, Order Book, ibid.

45. Mallory to Memminger, 9 July 1861, Letters Received by the Confederate Secretary of the Treasury, Treasury Department Collection of Confederate Records, NARG 365.

46. J. Thomas Scharf, *History of the Confederate States Navy from Its Organization to the Surrender of Its Last Vessel* (New York, 1887), p. 152.

47. Mallory to President Davis, 27 Feb. 1862, *ORN*, Ser. 2, 2:149ff.; see also *ORN*, Ser. 2, 1:802.

48. Ramsay to Tattnall, 5 Apr. 1862, *ORN,* Ser. 1, 7:752; H. Ashton Ramsay, "The Wonderful Career of the *Merrimac,*" *Confederate Veteran* 25 (Apr. 1907): 310ff.

49. Anderson to Mallory, 24 July 1861, Letterbook, Tredegar Company Records, VSA/RV.

50. *ORN,* Ser. 2, 1:785–86; Catesby ap R. Jones, "The Ironclad *Virginia,*" *Virginia Magazine of History and Biography* 49 (1941): 297ff.

51. Charles B. Dew, *Ironmaker to the Confederacy: Joseph R. Anderson and the Tredegar Iron Works* (New Haven, 1966), p. 116.

52. Anderson to Mallory, 8, 26 Aug. 1861, Letterbook, Tredegar Company Records, VSA/RV. Another difficulty was that, whereas the holes for the bolts could be made in one-inch plate by a punching machine, those two inches thick had to be drilled, which required far more work.

53. Anderson to Mallory, 3 Aug. 1861, Anderson to Ingraham, 11, 13 Sept. 1861, ibid.

54. Anderson to Mallory, 8 Aug. 1861, ibid.

55. Anderson to Major T. R. Sharpe, 17 Sept. 1861, Anderson to the Secretary of War, 19 Sept. 1861, ibid.; Angus J. Johnston, *The Virginia Railroads in the Civil War* (Chapel Hill, 1961, p. 23).

56. Anderson to Mallory, 5 Oct. 1861, Letterbook, Tredegar Company Records, VSA/RV.

57. Anderson to March, 16 Nov. 1861, ibid. Dew, *Ironmaker to the Confederacy,* pp. 117–18, probes the question deeply, while William C. Davis, *Duel between the First Ironclads* (Garden City, N.Y., 1975), offers a very good overall view.

58. F. Forrest to W. J. Webb, 21 Nov. 1861, French Forrest Letterbook, C.S. Navy Papers, VSA/RV.

59. Anderson to R. D. Minor, 30 Nov. 1861, Letterbook, Tredegar Company Records, VSA/RV.

60. Anderson to Mallory, 28 Oct. 1861, ibid.; Tredegar Company Journal, Feb. 1862, ibid.; VIII-4, Sales, Rolling Mill, Feb. 1862, ibid.; Mallory to Memminger, 9 Dec. 1861, Letters Received by the Confederate Secretary of the Treasury, Treasury Department Collection of Confederate Records, NARG 365.

61. Contract Book, Tredegar Company Records, VSA/RV; C. ap R. Jones to R. D. Minor, 9, 16 Sept. 1861, Minor Family Papers, VHS/RV. In the latter, Jones insists that ten-inch smoothbores would be fitted to the ironclad under construction. In another letter to Minor, 22 Sept. 1861, ibid., Jones appears not yet wholly converted to rifled cannon. See Dew, *Ironmaker to the Confederacy,* p. 112.

62. Mallory to Davis, 29 Mar. 1861, *ORN,* Ser. 2, 2:174–75.

63. Anderson to Mallory, 3 July 1861, Letterbook, Tredegar Company Records, VSA/RV.

64. Walter W. Stephen, "The Brooke Gun from Selma," *Alabama Historical Quarterly* 20 (1958): 462ff.

65. Mallory to Bulloch, 30 Apr. 1862, *ORN,* Ser. 2, 2:186ff.

66. According to Stephen, "The Brooke Gun from Selma," p. 463, the Brookes produced at Tredegar were instead of wrought iron. This is contradicted by the Foundry Book, Tredegar Company Records, VSA/RV, and by Brooke himself (see Brooke, "John Mercer Brooke," vol. 2, where Brooke, writing to his wife on 22 Sept. 1861, tells her that the gun had been cast). Later, certainly, at Selma Brooke guns would be perfected through a better quality of metalworking. For the time being, however, Brooke made use of a particularly strong cast iron.

67. Brooke, "John Mercer Brooke," vol. 2, noted that in Brooke's own diary the weight of the guns is given as 14,500 and 9,000 pounds, respectively, yet today the exact weight of the guns still available, calculated by technicians of the U.S. Navy, is 15,300 and 10,675 pounds. See *Civil War Ordnance* (Washington, D.C., 1969), p. 20; Warren Ripley, *Artillery and Ammunition of the Civil War* (New York, 1970), pp. 128ff.

68. Later, Brooke would place over the original banding a second one, formed by three more bands seventeen inches wide, and then a third one. When a new seven-inch piece fired in battle was mistakenly given a double charge, it successfully resisted an explosion of twenty-eight pounds of powder. See Mallory to Bulloch, 30 Apr. 1862, *ORN*, Ser. 2, 2:186–87.

69. Ripley, *Artillery and Ammunition of the Civil War*, pp. 128ff.

70. Designs of shells signed by Brooke, Records of the Bureau of Ordnance, Louisville Bureau Papers, NARG 74. See also *Civil War Ordnance*, p. 19. The best description of the projectile is in the authoritative Sidney G. Kerksis and Thomas S. Dickey, *Heavy Artillery Projectiles of the Civil War, 1861–1865* (Kennesaw, Ga., 1972), pp. 84ff.

71. Anderson to Mallory, 24 Sept. 1861, Letterbook, Tredegar Company Records, VSA/RV. In this letter Anderson suggested that the Tredegar do only the casting, leaving banding and rifling to the Norfolk Navy Yard ("to the Government," says the letter).

72. Anderson to Mallory, 30 Oct. 1861, ibid. Herein Anderson specified that twelve Brooke rifles were ordered.

73. Mallory to C. ap R. Jones, 11 Nov. 1861, *ORN*, Ser. 1, 6:742.

74. *ORN*, Ser. 2, 1:786. Yet, apparently, Brooke had designed an armor-piercing projectile by the end of September 1861 (Brooke Diary, cited in Brooke, "John Mercer Brooke," vol. 2).

75. The most recent biography of Gideon Welles is John Niven, *Gideon Welles: Lincoln's Secretary of the Navy* (New York, 1973); yet one must not overlook the still valuable one by Richard S. West, Jr., *Gideon Welles: Lincoln's Navy Department* (Indianapolis, 1943). On Fox, see John D. Hayes, "Captain Fox: *He* Is the Navy Department," *U.S. Naval Institute Proceedings* 95 (1965): 64ff. One must also keep in mind the extremely important *Diary of Gideon Welles*, 3 vols., ed. H. K. Beale and A. W. Brownsword (New York, 1960), and *Confidential Correspondence of Gustavus Vasa Fox, Assistant Secretary of the Navy*, 2 vols., ed. Robert M. Thompson and Richard Wainwright (New York, 1918–19). Yet it is indispensable to peruse the mass of Fox's unpublished correspondence in the Archives of the New York Historical Society.

76. Nickname of the most rabid secessionists of the South.

77. See, for instance, McKay to Welles, 8, 21 Mar., 20 Apr. 1861, Department of the Navy, Miscellaneous Letters Received, 1801–64, NARG 45.

78. Baxter, *Introduction of the Ironclad Warship*, p. 245; Robert W. Bruce, *Lincoln and the Tools of War* (Indianapolis, 1956), pp. 171ff.

79. *Report of the Secretary of the Navy in Relation to Armored Vessels* (Washington, D.C., 1864); Gideon Welles, "The First Ironclad *Monitor*," in *AW*, pp. 17ff. The members of the board were Commodore Joseph Smith, chief of the Bureau of Yards and Docks, president; Commodore Hiram Paulding; and Commander Charles H. Davis.

80. Raimondo Luraghi, *Storia della Guerra Civile Americana*, 5th ed., rev. (Milan, 1986), p. 283.

81. Admiral Adolphe Auguste Marie Lepotier correctly underscores that it is "a mistake

to consider only the maritime fronts and not the river ones" of the Civil War (*Les Leçons de l'histoire, 1861–1865: Mer contre terre* [Paris, 1945]), p. 83.

82. H. K. Beale, ed., "The Diary of Edward Bates, 1859–1866," *Annual Report of the American Historical Association* (Washington, D.C., 1933), 4:182; Charles B. Boynton, *History of the Navy during the Rebellion,* 2 vols. (New York, 1867), 1:498ff.; Eads to Welles, 8 May 1861, Gideon Welles Papers, LC; Welles to Secretary of War Cameron, 14 May 1861, *ORN,* Ser. 1, 2:277; Eads to Welles, 27 Apr. 1861, ibid. (enclosure to the preceding letter).

83. McClellan to Scott, 26 Apr. 1861, with an endnote by Scott dated 2 May 1861, *OR,* Ser. 1, 51, pt. 1:338–39.

84. Scott to McClellan, 3 May 1861, ibid., pp. 369–70; Scott to McClellan, 21 May 1861, ibid., pp. 386–87.

85. Meigs to Cameron, 25 June 1861, War Department, Quartermaster's General Office, Miscellaneous Letters Sent, NARG 92.

86. Welles to Rodgers, 16 May 1861, *ORN,* Ser. 1, 22:280; Rodgers to Welles, 7, 8 June 1861, ibid., pp. 282–83; Welles to Rodgers, 12 June 1861, ibid., p. 284; Rodgers to Welles (telegram), 12 June 1861, ibid., p. 286.

87. Rodgers to General Meigs, 11 July 1861, War Department, Quartermaster General's Office, Miscellaneous Letters Received, NARG 92; U.S. Postmaster General M. Blair to Meigs, 3 Aug. 1861, ibid.; Eads to Meigs, 23 Sept. 1861, ibid.

88. Eads to Meigs, 1 Aug. 1861, ibid.; Annual Report of Quartermaster General Meigs, 18 Nov. 1861, *OR,* Ser. 3, 2:786ff.; Contract with Eads, 7 Aug. 1861, printed as an enclosure to aforesaid report, ibid., pp. 816–17. The most complete study on the writing of the contract for the building of seven ironclad gunboats is in Edwin C. Bearss, *Hardluck Ironclad: The Sinking and Salvaging of the* Cairo (Baton Rouge, 1966), pp. 10ff.

89. James B. Eads, "Recollections of Foote and the Gunboats," *BL,* 1:338ff.; James M. Merrill, *Battle Flags South: The Story of the Civil War Navies on Western Waters* (Rutherford, N.J., 1970), pp. 37–38; John D. Milligan, *Gunboats Down the Mississippi* (Annapolis, 1965), p. 15.

90. See the news in the *St. Louis* (Missouri) *Daily Democrat,* 14 Oct. 1861.

91. Testimony of Henry W. Smith, Treasury Department, Office of the Third Auditor, War Claims, NARG 217; Testimony of Louis W. Bogy, ibid.; Foote to Rodgers, 28 Sept. 1861, *ORN,* Ser. 1, 22:352; Foote to Eads, 29 Oct. 1861, ibid., p. 387; Meigs to Foote, 15 Nov. 1861, ibid., p. 431.

92. Foote to G. V. Fox, 11 Jan. 1862, *ORN,* Ser. 1, 22:491ff.; Enclosure B, ibid., p. 495.

93. Welles to Foote, 30 Aug. 1861, ibid., p. 307; Foote to Welles, 28 Nov. 1861, ibid., p. 444.

94. H. A. Wise to Hon. F. P. Blair, 1 Aug. 1861, ibid., pp. 295ff.; Foote to Frémont, 16, 28 Oct. 1861, ibid., p. 395; George D. Wise to Foote, 11 Dec. 1861, ibid., pp. 471–72; G. V. Fox to Foote, 29 Dec. 1861, ibid., p. 512; S. L. Phelps to Foote, 21 Jan. 1862, ibid., p. 512; G. V. Fox to Foote, 27 Jan. 1862, ibid., p. 522.

95. Eppa Hunton to Benjamin, 8 May 1861, War Department Collection of Confederate Records, Letters Received by the Confederate Secretary of War, NARG 109; Governor of Tennessee, Isham Harris, to President Davis, 13 June 1861, ibid.; Walker to General Twiggs, 17 July 1861, War Department Collection of Confederate Records, Letters Sent by the Confederate Secretary of War, NARG 109; M. C. Galloway to Walker, 18 Apr. 1861

(telegram), *ORN,* Ser. 1, 22:786; Governor Harris to Walker, 22 Apr. 1861, ibid., pp. 786–87.

96. *ORN,* Ser. 2, 1:259; *Dictionary of American Naval Fighting Ships,* 8 vols. (Washington, D.C., 1959–81), 6:269.

97. Mallory to Huger, 15 May 1861, with post scriptum, Navy Department Collection, Confederate Area File 5, NARG 45.

98. L. Gwathmey to Paymaster J. W. Nixon, 17 June 1861, ibid.

99. Statement by Lt. Joseph Fry, commanding the gunboat *Ivy,* 18 Aug. 1861, ibid.

100. Mallory to Hollins, 31 July 1861, ibid; see the original letter, which includes the log of the trip, in Hollins Papers, ZB File, NHD/W.

101. M. C. Galloway to Secretary of War Walker, *ORN,* Ser. 1, 22:786; Governor Harris to Walker, 22 Apr., 8 May 1861, ibid., pp. 786–87, 788; General Josiah Gorgas to Walker, 29 Apr. 1861, ibid., p. 788. Evidently, people got worried even before the real danger appeared and thus risked obtaining results contrary to those desired.

102. Pillow to Walker, 20 June 1861, *ORN,* Ser. 1, 22:789–90.

103. Brooke Diary, 30 July 1863, in "John Mercer Brooke."

104. "Autobiography of Commodore George Nicholas Hollins," *Maryland Historical Magazine* 34 (1939): 228ff.; Charles L. Dufour, *The Night the War Was Lost* (Garden City, N.Y., 1960), pp. 61–62.

105. *ORN,* Ser. 2, 1:472; Merrill, *Battle Flags South,* pp. 68–69.

106. Mallory to Hollins, 22 Nov. 1862 (this is a misprint: it should read 1861), *ORN,* Ser. 2, 1:514ff. In Comptroller's Contracts, Treasury Department Collection of Confederate Records, NARG 365, there are several contracts signed by Hollins or Kennon.

107. Mallory to R. D. Minor, 19 Nov. 1861, Navy Department Collection, Confederate Area File 5, NARG 45.

108. Diary of R. D. Minor, 22 Nov. 1861, Minor Family Papers, VHS/RV.

109. Mallory to Memminger, 3 Dec. 1861, Treasury Department Collection of Confederate Records, Letters Received by the Confederate Secretary of the Treasury, NARG 365. In this letter Mallory requests the intercession of the congressional Finance Committee in order that the funds be sent to New Orleans. Mallory to Memminger, 22 Feb. 1862, ibid., in which the writer stated that the Navy Department was in a difficult position because the Treasury was slow in sending funds to New Orleans.

110. Report by Mallory to President Davis, 27 Feb. 1862, *ORN,* Ser. 2, 2:149ff.

111. Mallory to Bolling Baker, 17 Mar. 1864, Navy Department Collection, Confederate Subject File A: Naval Ships, NARG 45.

112. William M. Robinson, Jr., *The Confederate Privateers* (1928; reprint, Columbia, S.C., 1991), pp. 514–15.

113. James Morris Morgan, *Recollections of a Rebel Reefer* (New York, 1917), pp. 54ff.

114. *ORN,* Ser. 1, 16:725ff., includes many clippings from newspapers about the action. See also Hollins to Mallory, 12 Oct. 1861, ibid., pp. 727–28; General Duncan to General Twiggs, 14 Oct. 1861, ibid., p. 728; Mallory to Hollins, 28 Oct. 1861, ibid., p. 730; Warley, commanding the *Manassas,* to Mallory, no date, ibid., p. 730/a; Hollins to Warley, 20 Jan. 1862, which quotes a letter from Mallory. Federal reports are in ibid., pp. 703ff.

115. Rodgers to Welles (telegram), 4 Sept. 1861, and letter of same date, *ORN,* Ser. 1, 22:309.

116. *OR,* Ser. 1, 4:179ff. Also Davis to Polk, 4 Sept. 1861, ibid., p. 181; Polk to Kentucky Governor Beriah Magoffin, 8 Sept. 1861, *OR,* Ser. 1, 52, 2:141ff. Kentucky had declared

itself neutral soon after the bombardment of Fort Sumter, yet preponderant power in the state lay with Union men; see Luraghi, *Storia della Guerra Civile Americana,* pp. 325ff. Of the Confederate gunboats that went upriver, one, the *Tuscarora,* was accidentally set on fire during the trip and was lost.

117. Polk to Mallory, 15 Oct. 1861, *ORN,* Ser. 1, 22:794; Polk to Price, 29 Nov. 1861, ibid., p. 805; Scharf, *Confederate States Navy,* pp. 243ff.

118. Scharf, *Confederate States Navy,* pp. 243ff. Charles William Read, "Reminiscences of the Confederate States Navy," *SHSP,* 1:331ff., purports the theory of Hollins's excessive "prudence." This writer, however, calculates that it was almost impossible for the Confederate gunboats to have arrived at Memphis before December, at best. By this date, several Union ironclad gunboats did arrive and were ready for action and capable of inflicting on the Confederates a rough treat. See also *ORN,* Ser. 2, 1452ff.

119. *ORN,* Ser. 2, 1:454ff.

120. Walter Chandler, "The Memphis Navy Yard: An Adventure in Internal Improvement," *West Tennessee Historical Society Papers* 1 (1947): 68ff. The attempt to build a navy yard there was abandoned before the Civil War began. Oddly, naval ships were built there by private enterprise during World War II.

121. The contract with J. T. Shirley, 24 Aug. 1861, provided for a penalty for late delivery. See Treasury Department Collection of Confederate Records, Comptroller's Contracts, NARG 365.

122. The data are in Shirley's contract. Other information was supplied by the late William E. Geoghegan, of the Smithsonian Institution, who conducted painstaking research into Confederate ironclads, tracing their plans. See also U.S. Navy Department, Bureau of Construction, Equipment and Repair, which includes several drafts of Confederate warships, NARG 19.

123. Mallory to Memminger, Aug. 1861, estimate note 8, Treasury Department Collection of Confederate Records, Letters Received by the Confederate Secretary of the Treasury, NARG 365.

124. *ORN,* Ser. 2, 1:549. Ample information about the Tifts is to be found in Felix Senac, *Saga of Felix Senac; Being the Legend and Biography of a Confederate Agent in Europe,* ed. Regina Rapier (Atlanta, Ga., 1972). Senac, a relative of Mallory, born in Pensacola, Florida, was a paymaster in the C.S. Navy. Stationed at Key West, he was very friendly with the Tifts. The editor of the book is a direct descendant of Senac. See also Joseph T. Durkin, S.J., *Stephen R. Mallory: Confederate Navy Chief* (Chapel Hill, 1954), pp. 235ff.; in which it appears that the Tifts, although loyal to the South, tried to salvage interests in the North that the war, obviously, disrupted.

125. *ORN,* Ser. 2, 1:546–47.

126. Ibid., p. 546.

127. Asa and Nelson Tift to Mallory, 26 Aug. 1861, ibid., p. 571.

128. Mallory to the brothers Tift, 28 Aug., 5 Sept. 1861, ibid., pp. 601, 602.

129. Undated letter, C.S. Navy Papers, CM/RV, which confirms that the plans for the future ironclad *Mississippi* were given to the Tifts by the naval secretary, who had them from Porter and who also sent a naval constructor (Joseph Pierce, here and elsewhere always spelled Pearce), and the chief engineer E. M. Ivens (who was a civilian staff member of the Tredegar but who enjoyed the trust of the navy). See also Naval History Division, *Civil War Naval Chronology, 1861–1865,* 6 vols. (Washington, D.C., 1961–66), 6:271–72.

130. To calculate with some accuracy the displacement of a ship of the time is not easy. Sometimes specifications are missing; when they are supplied, they are at best approximate. One does not know if the matter at hand is tonnage (meaning that the ship still lacks her armor and guns as well as ammunition supply, water, coal, and foodstuffs) or displacement, used today for warships. For the ironclad being built by the Tift brothers, figures in *Dictionary of American Fighting Ships,* reprinted in Naval History Division, *Civil War Naval Chronology,* 6:271, indicate a tonnage of 1,400 tons that involves an approximate calculation including only the wooden hull and nothing else (or "light weight" or "light displacement"; see ibid., p. 183). Because armor would have added another 1,000 tons, Rear Admiral W. M. Parks, "Building a Warship in the Southern Confederacy," *U.S. Naval Institute Proceedings* 69 (1923): 1299ff., calculated (according to my opinion, with acceptable approximation) what today is meant by standard displacement of the ship at 4,000 tons.

131. The brothers Tift to Mallory, 9 Oct. 1861, *ORN,* Ser. 2, 1:575–76.

132. The brothers Tift to Mallory, 13 Oct. 1861, ibid., p. 576; specifications, ibid., p. 575.

133. The brothers Tift to Mallory, 26 Aug. 1862, ibid., pp. 598ff.

134. The brothers Tift to Mallory, 4, 12 Nov. 1861, ibid., p. 579.

135. The brothers Tift to Mallory, 26 Aug. 1862, ibid., pp. 598ff.; Mallory to N. and A. Tift, same day, ibid.; Naval History Division, *Civil War Naval Chronology,* 2:185.

136. Mallory to the brothers Tift, 5 Sept. 1861, *ORN,* Ser. 2, 1:603; for the cost of the ironclad, see ibid., p. 468.

137. Stephen R. Mallory Diary, SHC/CHNC.

138. *ORN,* Ser. 2, 1:757, where Murray, too, among other things, says that it was he who conceived the idea of converting the *Merrimack.*

139. Murray Contract, 18 Sept. 1861, in Comptroller's Contracts, Treasury Department Collection of Confederate Records, NARG 365.

140. *ORN,* Ser. 2, 2:152.

CHAPTER SEVEN

1. Gideon Welles, "The First Ironclad *Monitor,*" *AW,* pp. 17ff.

2. *ORN,* Ser. 2, 1:90, 159; William C. Davis, *Duel between the First Ironclads* (Garden City, N.Y., 1975), pp. 14ff.

3. Neither would be ready in time to face the former *Merrimack.* Their draft varied from ten feet for the *Galena* to thirteen feet for the *New Ironsides.*

4. C. S. Bushnell to Welles, 9 Mar. 1877, *BL,* 1:748–49. See the lively narrative in Davis, *Duel between the First Ironclads,* pp. 15ff.

5. Ruth White, *Yankee from Sweden: The Dream and the Reality in the Days of John Ericsson* (New York, 1960), p. 82. This biography is not the best that might be expected, yet it is among the richest in information. A truly satisfactory biography of the great engineer and inventor is still lacking.

6. Ibid., p. 114.

7. Ibid., pp. 118, 130.

8. Bushnell to Welles, 9 Mar. 1877, *BL,* 1:748.

9. John Ericsson, "The Building of the *Monitor,*" *BL,* 1:730ff.

10. This placement was because a ram would have to penetrate at least three feet of

iron armor before reaching the vital parts of the hull unless the blow were dealt (as in the case of the former *Merrimack*) by a submerged ram.

11. Ericsson, "Building of the *Monitor*," *BL,* 1:730–31.

12. *The Diary of Gideon Wells,* 3 vols., ed. H. K. Beale and A. W. Brownsword (New York, 1960), 1:214–15; Welles, "The First Ironclad *Monitor*," *AW,* p. 749.

13. Welles to Bushnell, 19 Mar. 1877, *BL,* 1:749.

14. Robert S. McCordock, *The Yankee Cheesebox* (Philadelphia, 1938), p. 34. A complete description which shows that at least eleven firms were simultaneously put to work on the ironclad is found in William N. Still, Jr., Monitor *Building: A Historical Study of the Principal Firms and Individuals Involved in the Construction of U.S.* Monitor (Washington, D.C., 1988). This basic study makes short work of any theory that the Southern industrial plant might compete with the Northern one.

15. Bushnell to Welles, 19 Mar. 1877, *BL,* 1:748–49.

16. Davis, *Duel between the First Ironclads,* pp. 42ff.

17. Letter from J. L. Porter, published in *Charleston Mercury,* 19 Mar. 1862, also in *SHSP,* 19:8–9.

18. G. Ashton Ramsay, "The Most Famous Sea Duel: The *Merrimac* and the *Monitor*," *Harper's Weekly* 56 (1912): 11ff.

19. C. ap R. Jones to R. D. Minor, 29(?) Sept. 1861, Robert D. Minor Papers, VHS/RV.

20. John Taylor Wood, "The First Fight of Ironclads," *BL,* 1:692ff.

21. Mallory to Brooke, 8 Oct. 1861, John M. Brooke Papers, ZB File, NHD/W.

22. Brooke to Porter, 3 Apr. 1862, *SHSP,* 19:14–15.

23. John W. H. Porter, *A Record of Events in Norfolk County, from April 19th, 1861, to May 10th, 1862, with a History of the Soldiers and Sailors of Norfolk County, Norfolk City, and Portsmouth Who Served in the Confederate Army or Navy* (Portsmouth, Va., 1892), p. 341, J. L. Porter to the *Richmond Examiner,* 29 Mar. 1862.

24. General Huger, Commanding Army Forces in Norfolk, to Adjutant General Cooper, 14 Oct. 1861, *OR,* Ser. 1, 51, 2:345.

25. F. Forrest to S. S. Lee, 8 Nov. 1861, where he gives accurate guard dispositions, in French Forrest Letterbook, C.S. Navy Yard, Gosport, Va., VSA/RV.

26. F. Forrest to V. R. Morgan, 6 Dec. 1861, F. Forrest to General Huger, 9 Dec. 1861, F. Forrest to Reuben Thom and Lt. Gwynn, commanding marines, same day, ibid.

27. J. T. Mason to his mother, 21 Dec. 1862, John Thompson Mason Letters, M615, CM/RV.

28. Capt. Buchanan, Chief of the Bureau of Orders and Details, to R. D. Minor, 5 Feb. 1862, R. D. Minor Papers, ZB File, NHD/W; *BL,* 1:694; Royce G. Shingleton, *John Taylor Wood: Sea Ghost of the Confederacy* (Athens, Ga., 1979), pp. 21ff.

29. William N. Still, Jr., "The Common Sailor, Part 2: Confederate Tars," *Civil War Times Illustrated,* Mar. 1985, pp. 12ff.

30. Wood to Buchanan, 22 Jan. 1862, *ORN,* Ser. 2, 2:137; Mallory to Benjamin, 25 Jan. 1862, ibid.

31. Buchanan to Tucker, 10 Feb. 1862, *ORN,* Ser. 1, 6:766.

32. *BL,* 1:695.

33. Catesby ap R. Jones, "Services of the *Virginia* (*Merrimac*)," *SHSP,* 11:65ff., says that there were 330 men in the crew and praises their professional quality. For the order from the secretary of war, see F. Forrest to Hunter Davidson (a lieutenant serving on the iron-

clad), 10 Feb. 1862, Forrest Letterbook, C.S. Navy Yard, Gosport, Va., VSA/RV. For the testing of the guns see F. Forrest to Jones, 23 Nov. 1861, *ORN*, Ser. 1, 6:743; Jones to Brooke, 24 Jan. 1862, in George M. Brooke, Jr., "John Mercer Brooke, Naval Scientist," 2 vols. (Ph.D. dissertation, University of North Carolina, 1955), 2:809; on Wood's proficiency as an artillerist, see Wood to his wife, 9 Aug. 1858, John Taylor Wood Papers, SHC/ CHNC.

34. H. W. King (by order) to S. S. Lee, 18 Jan. 1862, Forrest Letterbook, C.S. Navy Yard, Gosport, Va., VSA/RV; Porter, *Record of Events*, pp. 337–38 (concerning eighty skilled workmen, listed by name); J. Thomas Scharf, *History of the Confederate States Navy from Its Organization to the Surrender of Its Last Vessel* (New York, 1887), pp. 153–54.

35. *BL*, 1:696.

36. F. Forrest to Engineer Quinn, 7 Feb. 1862, Forrest Letterbook, C.S. Navy Yard, Gosport, Va., VSA/RV.

37. General Wool to G. V. Fox, 21 Feb. 1862 (telegram), in *Confidential Correspondence of Gustavus Vasa Fox, Assistant Secretary of the Navy, 1861–1865*, 2 vols., ed. Robert M. Thompson and Richard Wainwright (New York, 1918–19), 1:428; Commodore Smith to Lt. Worden, 1 Jan. 1862, in which he announced that the latter would command the *Monitor*, *ORN*, Ser. 1, 6:515; Worden to Smith, 13 Jan. 1862, ibid., p. 516; Welles to Worden, 13 Jan. 1862 (commission to command the *Monitor*), ibid., p. 517; Worden to Welles, 17 Jan. 1862 (in which he states that he had assumed command), ibid., p. 522; G. V. Fox to Ericsson (telegram), 30 Jan. 1862, ibid., p. 538. Fox said: "Hurry her [the *Monitor*] for sea, as the *Merrimack* is nearly ready at Norfolk." This shows how tense was the race and how deep anxiety also moved the North. The name *Monitor*, chosen by Ericsson, was intended as a warning not only for the Confederates (who at the time were thought to have the advantage) but also for the European maritime powers because of their presumed sympathy for the South. See Ericsson to G. V. Fox, 20 Jan. 1862, *BL*, 1:731n. Worden had recently been exchanged as a prisoner of war by the Confederates. See J. P. Benjamin to Major Calhoun, 12 Nov. 1861, *OR*, Ser. 2, 3:739; Major Calhoun to Benjamin, 13 Nov. 1861, ibid., p. 740.

38. Report from General Henry A. Wise, n.d., cited by the Congressional Board of Inquiry into the loss of Roanoke Island, *OR*, Ser. 1, 9:188.

39. J. T. Mason to his mother, 11 Feb. 1862, Mason Letters, M615, CM/RV.

40. William R. Cline, "The Ironclad Ram *Virginia*, Confederate States Navy: Story of Her Launching and Accomplishments," *SHSP*, 32:243ff. Cline was a crew member of the *Virginia*.

41. F. Forrest to the commanding officer of the receiving ship *Confederate States*, V. R. Morgan, 17 Feb. 1862, Forrest Letterbook, C.S. Navy Yard, Gosport, Va., VSA/RV.

42. Catesby ap R. Jones to Brooke, 20 Feb. 1862, in Brooke, "John Mercer Brooke," 2:814.

43. John Sergeant Wise, *The End of an Era*, ed. C. C. Davis (New York, 1965), pp. 194– 95.

44. C. ap R. Jones to Brooke, 5 Mar. 1862, *SHSP*, 19:31; R. D. Minor to Brooke, 7 Mar. 1862, ibid., p. 32.

45. A difference exists in the indications given by the two main sources: Catesby ap R. Jones, "Services of the *Virginia*," and Porter, *Record of Events*, pp. 335ff. Here are the most remarkable differences: length, Jones: 275 feet; Porter: 262; Casemate, Jones: "about 160 feet"; Porter: 178.3; inclination of the walls, Jones: 36 degrees; Porter: 35 degrees.

46. Ferruccio Botti, "La 'nave invulnerabile' e le teorie del Generale Cavalli: Dal vascello in legno alla nave corazzata," *Rivista Marittima*, July 1988, pp. 107ff.; James P. Baxter III, *The Introduction of the Ironclad Warship* (1933; reprint, Hamden, Conn., 1968), pp. 90–91. Contrary to what Baxter said, not the French but Mallory, Brooke, and Porter truly followed Cavalli. No one can say if the three leading Confederates knew of Cavalli's writings, yet, given Brooke's encyclopedic knowledge as well as Mallory's inquisitiveness, we may wonder. Indeed, this appears highly possible for Brooke and without taking any merit away from the designer of the *Virginia*. Yet it must be underscored that according to the leaders of the C.S. Navy, as well as to Cavalli, the ultimate weapon was the rifled gun, something the U.S. Navy had not yet understood. Even the talented John Dahlgren declared his disbelief in rifled guns. See Dahlgren to Fox, 14 Feb. 1862, in *Confidential Correspondence of Gustavus Vasa Fox*, 1:423–24.

47. Scharf, *Confederate Sates Navy*, pp. 154ff.

48. Jones to Johnston, 10 Mar. 1864, Naval Collection, Confederate Area File 7, NARG 45; Wood to his wife, 26 Mar. 1862, John Taylor Wood Papers, SHC/CHNC; R. D. Minor to Jones, 20 Sept. 1861, *ORN*, Ser. 1, 6:731ff. ("Buchanan will probably be her captain," speaking of the ironclad).

49. See Charles L. Lewis, *Admiral Franklin Buchanan: Fearless Man of Action* (Baltimore, 1925). A satisfactory biography of Buchanan does not yet exist.

50. Davis, *Duel between the First Ironclads*, p. 41.

51. Mallory to Buchanan, 24 Feb. 1862, U.S. Department of State, General Records, Letters Sent by the Confederate Secretary of the Navy, NARG 59, also in *ORN*, Ser. 1, 6:776–77.

52. Welles to Worden, 20 Feb. 1862, *ORN*, Ser. 1, 6:659; N. Paulding, commanding the New York Navy Yard, to Worden, 4 Mar. 1862, ibid., p. 679; Worden (at sea) to Welles, 6 Mar. 1862, ibid., p. 684. About Worden (and his successors who would command the ironclad) see William N. Still, Jr., *Ironclad Captains: The Commanding Officers of the U.S.S. Monitor* (Washington, D.C., 1988).

53. George W. Gift, "The Story of the *Arkansas*," *SHSP*, 12:48ff.

54. *ORN*, Ser. 2, 1:780.

55. Mallory to Polk, 24 Dec. 1861, *ORN*, Ser. 1, 22:811. See also *ORN*, Ser. 2, 1:781. Mallory evidently alluded to the Battle of Belmont, fought during the early days of November along the Mississippi's right bank, when Federal gunboats had efficiently protected General Ulysses Grant's expeditionary corps.

56. *ORN*, Ser. 2, 1:549ff., 763, 782. Also William N. Still, Jr., *Iron Afloat: The Story of the Confederate Armorclad* (1971; reprint, Columbia, S.C., 1985), p. 82; F. P. Rose, "The Confederate Ram *Arkansas*," *Alabama Historical Quarterly* 12 (1953): 333ff.

57. Polk to Mallory, 25 Sept. 1861, *ORN*, Ser. 1, 22:792–93; Polk to Secretary of War Walker (telegram), 3 Aug. 1861, ibid., p. 792, where the scare of the enemy gunboats becomes truly distressing.

58. Scharf, *Confederate States Navy*, p. 306, n. 1, gives a biography of Brown, saying that he had entered the navy in 1834. Because there was as yet no Naval Academy, he served as a naval cadet beginning at a very early age. Brown must then have been born in 1820 or shortly before; he was therefore well past forty.

59. I. Brown to Polk, 30 July 1861, *ORN*, Ser. 1, 22:790–91.

60. I. Brown to Polk, 2 Aug. 1861, ibid., p. 791.

61. I. Brown to Polk, 24 Sept. 1861, Isaac Brown Papers, War Department Collection

of Confederate Records, Records Relating to Confederate Naval and Marine Personnel, NARG 109.

62. I. Brown to Polk, 27 Sept. 1861, ibid.

63. I. Brown to Polk, 5 Nov., 4 Dec. 1861, ibid.

64. James M. Merrill, "Confederate Shipbuilding at New Orleans," *Journal of Southern History* 28 (1962): 87ff.

65. The first of such contracts, entered into by Murray while he was still in Richmond, went wrong because in the meantime the coasts of Florida (where the timber had to come from) were blockaded by the Union fleet. After reaching New Orleans, Murray had to write a new contract with local producers. See *ORN,* Ser. 2, 1:754.

66. Merrill, "Confederate Shipbuilding at New Orleans," pp. 87ff.

67. *ORN,* Ser. 2, 1:760ff.

68. Ibid., p. 754.

69. Manuscript Memo by Engineer James Hamilton Tombs, W. V. and J. H. Tombs Papers, SHC/CHNC.

70. *ORN,* Ser. 2, 1:532–33.

71. Ibid., p. 532.

72. Mallory to Pierce, 17 Sept. 1861, Navy Department Collection, Confederate Area File 5, NARG 45.

73. *ORN,* Ser. 2, 1:541ff.

74. Ibid., pp. 553–54.

75. Jackson to Mallory, 25 Sept. 1861, ibid., p. 572.

76. The Tifts to Mallory, 8 Oct. 1861, ibid., p. 575.

77. Mallory to Warner, 19 Nov. 1861, Navy Department Collection, Confederate Area File 5, NARG 45.

78. The Tifts to Mallory, 9 Oct. 1861, *ORN,* Ser. 2, 1:575–76.

79. *ORN,* Ser. 2, 1:533.

80. F. Forrest to Master Armorer John Gregg, 14 Nov. 1861, French Forrest Letterbook, C.S. Navy Yard, Gosport, Va., VSA/RV; the Tifts to Mallory, 20, 23 Oct. 1861, *ORN,* Ser. 2, 1:577.

81. *ORN,* Ser. 2, 1:534. It was on this occasion that the Atlanta Rolling Mill (see Chapter 3) modified its machinery so as to be able to produce plate more than two inches thick.

82. *OR,* Ser. 1, 6:626.

83. The Tifts to Mallory, 10 Feb. 1862, *ORN,* Ser. 2, 1:589–90.

84. *ORN,* Ser. 2, 1:638. That a shaft of such size could be produced only in the North is clearly stated by a member of the Tredegar, John F. Tanner. See ibid., p. 775.

85. Salesbook, Tredegar Company Records, VSA/RV.

86. The Tifts to Mallory, 10 Feb. 1862, *ORN,* Ser. 2, 1:589ff.

87. The Tifts to Mallory (telegram), 15 Feb. 1862, ibid., p. 590.

88. R. D. Minor Diary, 15 Feb. 1862, Minor Family Papers, VHS/RV.

89. Mallory to the Tift brothers, 5 Sept. 1861, *ORN,* Ser. 2, 1:602.

90. *ORN,* Ser. 2, 1:481.

91. Memminger to Mallory, 7 July 1861, General Records of the Department of the Treasury, Treasury Department Collection of Confederate Records, Letters Sent by the Confederate Secretary of the Treasury, NARG 56.

92. Mallory to Memminger, 3 Dec. 1861, 22 Feb., 28 Mar., 7 Apr. 1862, Treasury De-

partment Collection of Confederate Records, Letters Received by the Confederate Secretary of the Treasury, NARG 365.

93. *ORN*, Ser. 2, 1:489.

94. S. L. Phelps to Foote, 9 Nov. 1861, *ORN*, Ser. 1, 22:394.

95. Mallory to Polk, 25 Dec. 1861, Navy Department Collection, Confederate Area File 5, NARG 45; Mallory to Brown, 25 Dec. 1861, *ORN*, Ser. 1, 22:812–13.

96. Edwin C. Bearss, "A Federal Raid up the Tennessee River," *Alabama Review* 17 (Oct. 1964): 261ff.

97. Raimondo Luraghi, *Storia della Guerra Civile Americana*, 5th ed., rev. (Milan, 1986), pp. 421ff.

98. General A. S. Johnston to Secretary of War Benjamin, 25 Feb. 1862, *OR*, Ser. 1, 7:426–27; Polk to Benjamin, 2 Mar. 1862, ibid., p. 427; Polk to Col. Jordan, 18 Mar. 1862, ibid., p. 437.

99. Joseph T. Durkin, S.J., *Stephen Russell Mallory: Confederate Navy Chief* (Chapel Hill, 1954), p. 203.

100. Welles to David Dixon Porter, 2 Dec. 1861, *ORN*, Ser. 1, 18:3; Welles to Farragut, 15, 23 Dec. 1861, 9, 20 Jan. 1862, ibid., pp. 5–7.

101. Welles to Farragut, 24 Feb. 1862, *ORN*, Ser. 1, 18:37.

102. Farragut to Welles, 14 Mar. 1862, ibid., pp. 64–65.

103. Charles L. Dufour, *The Night the War Was Lost* (Garden City, N.Y., 1960), p. 175.

104. Lovell to Benjamin, 27 Feb. 1862, *OR*, Ser. 1, 6:832.

105. Mallory to Mitchell, 13 Nov. 1861, *ORN*, Ser. 2, 1:466–67.

106. Mallory to Mitchell, 13 Nov. 1861, Navy Department Collection, Confederate Area File 5, NARG 45. The letter bears a note in Mitchell's handwriting which says that when he arrived in New Orleans on 22 November, he learned that Commodore Hollins had gone upriver with the flotilla. Therefore, Mitchell went to Columbus and there reported to Hollins.

107. *ORN*, Ser. 2, 1:452ff.

108. Lieutenant Commanding W. Dunnington to Paymaster J. W. Nixon, 31 Jan. 1862, ibid.; Lt. Comm. J. Fry to J. W. Nixon, 26 Feb. 1862, ibid.; Scharf, *Confederate States Navy*, pp. 243ff. The list of gunboats in Hollins's flotilla still remains approximate.

109. General Twiggs to Secretary of War Walker, 9 Aug. 1861, *OR*, Ser. 1, 53:722; General Polk to Walker, 13 Aug. 1861, ibid.; Walker to Twiggs, 24 Aug. 1861, ibid., p. 731. The initiative to build the floating batteries came from the army, and the navy acquired them even though it had not asked for them. One might wonder if Mallory was really happy that so many invaluable resources and labor had been squandered by such enterprises, for they could have been used more suitably to hasten the building of the ironclads. This was one of many examples of army interference with naval policy (usually with negative effects).

110. Hollins to Guthrie, 23 Nov. 1861, Navy Department Collection, Confederate Area File 5, NARG 45; Whittle to Gwathmey, 10 Dec. 1861, ibid.; Dufour, *The Night the War Was Lost*, pp. 105–6.

111. *ORN*, Ser. 2, 1:464; R. D. Minor to Renshaw, 2 Dec. 1861, ibid., p. 777.

112. President Davis to Lovell, 17 Oct. 1861, *OR*, Ser. 1, 6:645; Benjamin to Lovell, 19 Jan. 1862, ibid., p. 646.

113. Benjamin to Lovell, 14 Jan. 1862, *OR*, Ser. 1, 53:770.

114. Benjamin to Lovell, n.d., but probably 18 Jan. 1862, in Scharf, *Confederate States Navy,* p. 249.

115. Scharf, *Confederate States Navy,* pp. 250–51.

116. John D. Milligan, *Gunboats Down the Mississippi* (Annapolis, 1965), pp. 68ff. Ellet's battering rams would cooperate well with the U.S. Navy, whereas in the South the almost private character of Montgomery's flotilla (and of other ones) would lead to incessant wrangles with the naval forces.

117. R. D. Minor to Mallory, 31 Jan. 1862, Minor Family Papers, VHS/RV.

118. Dufour, *The Night the War Was Lost,* p. 176.

119. Mallory to McIntosh, 2 Mar. 1862, Navy Department Collection, Confederate Area File 5, NARG 45.

120. R. D. Minor Diary, 30 Jan. 1862, Minor Family Papers, VHS/RV.

121. A. Tift to N. Tift, 17 Feb. 1862, *ORN,* Ser. 2, 1:557.

122. Mallory to Mitchell, 24 Feb. 1862, ibid., p. 466.

123. Mallory to the Tift brothers, 7 Oct. 1861, ibid., p. 602.

124. The Tifts to Mallory, 14 Oct. 1861, ibid., pp. 576ff.

125. Mallory to the Tift brothers, 22 Jan. 1862, ibid., p. 604.

126. Shirley to Polk, 15 Jan. 1862, ibid., p. 795.

127. T. Jordan to John J. Guthrie, 18 Mar. 1862, *ORN,* Ser. 1, 22:838.

128. Still, *Iron Afloat,* p. 63.

129. I was able to peruse Henry Kennedy Stevens's private papers through the courtesy of Cynthia Elizabeth Moseley of Spartanburg, South Carolina, a descendant of relatives of the Confederate officer, who wrote a master's thesis at the University of North Carolina, Chapel Hill, in 1951 titled "The Naval Career of Henry Kennedy Stevens as Revealed in His Letters, 1839–1863." The episode is mentioned on page 24. I wish to thank Moseley for allowing me to quote from her thesis as well as from several letters in her possession, both of which are very important for the story of the *Arkansas.*

130. Grace T. Stevens to Sara Stevens, 11 Apr. 1862, H. K. Stevens Papers, Cynthia Moseley's private collection.

131. H. K. Stevens to his mother, 19 Apr. 1862, ibid.

132. Mallory to Mitchell, 15 Mar. 1863, *ORN,* Ser. 2, 1:466–67.

133. Mallory to the Tift brothers, 15 Mar. 1862, ibid., p. 605.

134. Mallory to the Tift brothers (telegram), 17 Mar. 1862, ibid., p. 606.

135. Mallory to the Tift brothers (telegram), 20 Mar. 1862, ibid., p. 592.

136. *OR,* Ser. 1, 6:626–27; *ORN,* Ser. 2, 1:637.

137. Mallory to the Tift brothers, 22 Mar. 1862, *ORN,* Ser. 2, 1:606.

138. The Tifts to Mallory, 21 Mar. 1862, ibid., p. 592.

139. Mallory to A. Sinclair, 21 Mar. 1862, ibid., p. 512.

140. Mallory to the Tift brothers, 5 Apr. 1862, ibid., p. 607.

141. *ORN,* Ser. 2, 1:435.

142. G. Minor to C. A. Newton, 13 Mar. 1862, to W. J. Cullen, 19 Mar. 1862, to J. W. Jett, 15 Apr. 1862, to T. B. P. Ingram [*sic*], 21 Apr. 1862, Navy Department Collection, Confederate Area File 5, NARG 45.

143. Mallory to W. C. Whittle, 5 Apr. 1862, *ORN,* Ser. 2, 1:449.

144. Mallory to Hollins, 10 Apr. 1862, to C. H. McBlair, same day, ibid., p. 798.

145. The Tifts to Mallory, 17 Apr. 1862, ibid., p. 597.

146. Ibid., pp. 538, 615.

147. Governor Moore to the Tift brothers, 15 Apr. 1862, ibid., p. 610.

148. Ibid., p. 479.

149. The Tifts to Mallory, 26 Aug. 1862, ibid., pp. 598ff.

150. Ibid., p. 489.

151. Naval History Division, *Civil War Naval Chronology, 1861–1865*, 6 vols. (Washington, D.C., 1961–66), 2:40.

152. David D. Porter, *Incidents and Anecdotes of the Civil War* (New York, 1885), p. 66; Porter to Grimes, 6 May 1861 (but actually 1862), in Scharf, *Confederate States Navy*, p. 267.

153. James Morris Morgan, *Recollections of a Rebel Reefer* (Boston, 1917), p. 71.

154. Farragut to Welles, 6 May 1862, *ORN*, Ser. 1, 18:155ff.

CHAPTER EIGHT

1. Robert W. Daly, *How the* Merrimac *Won: The Strategic Story of the C.S.S.* Virginia (New York, 1957), p. 82, remarks that during his stay in Richmond, Buchanan must have discussed with Mallory the possibilities and perspectives for the *Virginia*.

2. J. T. Mason to his mother, 10 Jan. 1862, James T. Mason Papers, M615, CM/RV, in which the plan looks complete in every detail, the objectives (to "open" the James River for reinstating water communications with Richmond) clearly defined, and the perspective of "breaking the blockade" on the ocean excluded. One wonders how a young cadet could have known all this (and written to his mother about it), yet it proves what little attention was paid to secrecy and security by both opponents in the Civil War, at least during its early days.

3. Butler to Scott, 27 May 1861, *OR*, Ser. 1, 2:52–53.

4. Butler to Scott, 29 May 1861, ibid., p. 54.

5. Raimondo Luraghi, *Storia della Guerra Civile Americana*, 5th ed., rev. (Milan, 1986), pp. 271ff.

6. For the extremely important activities of this board, much overlooked by historians, see Welles to Barnard, 26 July 1861, *ORN*, Ser. 1, 12:195. The board is carefully analyzed in *Samuel Francis Du Pont: A Selection from His Civil War Letters*, 3 vols., ed. John D. Hayes (Ithaca, N.Y., 1969), 1:xviiiff.

7. "First Report of Conference for the Consideration of Measures for Effectively Blockading the South Atlantic Coast," 5 July 1861, *ORN*, Ser. 1, 12:195ff.; "Second Report . . . ," 16 July 1861, ibid., pp. 198ff.; "Third Report . . . ," 26 July 1861, ibid., pp. 618ff. Then (of the greatest importance), "First Report of Conference for the Consideration of Measures for Effectively Blockading the Coast Bordering the Gulf of Mexico," ibid., 16:618ff. These are basic documents to study regarding the paternity of amphibious warfare.

8. Theodore Ropp, "Anaconda Anyone?", *Military Affairs* 27 (Summer 1963): 71ff.

9. John D. Hayes, "Sea Power in the Civil War," *U.S. Naval Institute Proceedings* 88 (Nov. 1961): 60ff.

10. Rowena Reed, *Combined Operations in the Civil War* (Annapolis, 1978). The aim of this book (certainly a good one), which seeks to credit McClellan with the idea of amphibious warfare, is not convincing. The amphibious strategy the Union adopted is quite different from the simple use of maritime transports to land troops on a coast *already in*

the hands of its own army. On McClellan see Edward Hagerman, "The Professionalization of George B. McClellan and Early Civil War Field Command," *Civil War History,* June 1975, pp. 113ff.

11. For this criticism see Luraghi, *Storia della Guerra Civile Americana,* pp. 377ff.

12. *OR,* Ser. 1, 5:41ff.; McClellan to Wool, 21 Feb. 1861, *OR,* Ser. 1, 91:15–16; George B. McClellan, *McClellan's Own Story* (New York, 1887), pp. 202–3, wherein the general expounds upon his plan and its dependence upon control of the James River as the specific line of operations.

13. Magruder to Davis, 10 Jan. 1861, *OR,* Ser. 1, 9:32.

14. Daly, *How the* Merrimac *Won,* pp. 82ff.

15. *ORN,* Ser. 2, 1:65ff. Curiously, the usually accurate historian William C. Davis, *Duel between the First Ironclads* (Garden City, N.Y., 1975), pp. 68ff., said that both the *Cumberland* and the *Congress* were screw ships.

16. Goldsborough to Welles, 16 Nov. 1861, *ORN,* Ser. 1, 6:437; Goldsborough to W. Smith, 18 Nov. 1861, ibid., p. 439; W. Smith to Welles, 21 Jan. 1862, ibid., p. 525.

17. Hayes, "Sea Power in the Civil War," p. 63.

18. Adolphe Auguste Marie Lepotier, *Les Leçons de l'histoire, 1861–1865: Mer contre terre* (Paris, 1945), p. 338.

19. Buchanan to Magruder, 2 Mar. 1862, in Admiral Buchanan's Letterbook, Franklin Buchanan Books, SHC/CHNC.

20. Magruder to General Cooper, 24 Feb. 1861, *OR,* Ser. 1, 9:44. ("No one ship can produce such an impression. . . . No important advantage can be obtained by the *Merrimac* than to demonstrate her power.") He ended by suggesting that the ironclad be left to protect Norfolk.

21. Hill Carter to Henry Bryan, with endorsement by Magruder, 19 Jan. 1862, *OR,* Ser. 1, 51:445; Magruder to General Cooper, 25 Feb. 1862, ibid., p. 480; Magruder to General Cooper, 1 Jan. 1862, ibid., 9:38ff.; Magruder to President Davis, 10 Jan. 1862, ibid., pp. 32ff.; Magruder to Buchanan, 3 Mar. 1862, ibid., p. 50.

22. Keeler to his wife, 6, 7 Mar. 1862, in William F. Keeler, *Aboard the U.S.S.* Monitor, *1862: The Letters of Acting Paymaster William Frederick Keeler to His Wife Anna,* ed. Robert W. Daly (Annapolis, 1964), pp. 27ff.

23. Buchanan to Tucker, 3 Mar. 1862, Admiral Buchanan's Letterbook, Buchanan Books, SHC/CHNC.

24. Buchanan to Mallory, 4 Mar. 1862, ibid.

25. Catesby ap R. Jones, "Services of the *Virginia (Merrimac),*" *SHSP,* 11:65ff.

26. J. Taylor Wood, "The First Fight of the Ironclads," *BL,* 1:696.

27. Davis, *Duel between the First Ironclads,* p. 78.

28. Daly, *How the* Merrimac *Won,* p. 105; H. Ashton Ramsay, "The Wonderful Career of the *Merrimac,*" *Confederate Veteran* 25 (July 1907): 313ff. Ramsay was the chief engineer of the *Virginia.*

29. John S. Wise, *The End of an Era* (1902; reprint, New York, 1965), pp. 196–97; J. T. Wood, "The First Fight of Ironclads," *BL,* 1:92ff.

30. William H. Parker, *Recollections of a Naval Officer, 1841–1865* (New York, 1883), pp. 252ff. Parker was in command of the gunboat *Beaufort.*

31. W. R. Cline, "The Ironclad Ram *Virginia,*" *SHSP,* 32:243ff.

32. Parker, *Recollections,* p. 52. Buchanan had sent in writing the same order to Com-

mander Tucker: Buchanan to Tucker, 3 Mar. 1862, Admiral Buchanan's Letterbook, Buchanan Books, SHC/CHNC.

33. Virginius Newton, "The Ram *Merrimac*," *SHSP,* 20:1ff.

34. Parker, *Recollections,* pp. 253–54.

35. Report by Captain Van Brunt to Secretary Welles, 10 Mar. 1862, *ORN,* Ser. 1, 7:10ff.

36. Charles O'Neil, "The Engagement between the *Cumberland* and the *Merrimac*," *U.S. Naval Institute Proceedings* 48 (1922): 863ff.

37. "Captain Eggleston's Narrative of the Battle of the *Merrimac*," *SHSP,* 41:170.

38. *ORN,* Ser. 2, 1:27ff.

39. Report of Captain Marston (officer in command) to Secretary Welles, 9 Mar. 1862, *ORN,* Ser. 1, 7:8ff.; *Memoirs of Thomas O. Selfridge, Jr., Rear Admiral U.S.N.* (New York, 1924), pp. 46ff.; T. O. Selfridge, Jr., "The Story of the *Cumberland*," *PMHSM,* 12:101ff.

40. Geo. Weber to brother Louis, 10 Mar. 1862, George Weber Letters, CM/RV.

41. Parker, *Recollections,* p. 253; Selfridge, "Story of the *Cumberland*," pp. 120ff.

42. Henry Reaney, "How the *Zouave* Aided the *Congress*," *BL,* 1:714ff.

43. Jones, "Services of the *Virginia*," p. 68 and notes, *SHSP,* 11:65ff.

44. "Captain Eggleston's Narrative," *SHSP,* 41:171ff.

45. F. S. Alger, "The *Congress* and the *Merrimac*," *New England Magazine,* May 18, 1899, pp. 687ff.

46. Davis, *Duel between the First Ironclads,* p. 89.

47. George U. Morris, second in command of the *Cumberland,* to Commodore William Radford, *ORN,* Ser. 1, 6:21; Selfridge, "Story of the *Cumberland*," p. 121.

48. "Captain Eggleston's Narrative," *SHSP,* 41:171.

49. Report by Buchanan to Mallory, 27 Sept. 1862, *ORN,* Ser. 1, 7:44ff.; Jones, "Services of the *Virginia*," p. 68.

50. J. T. Wood, "The First Fight of the Ironclads," *BL,* 1:692; William Morris, "The Story of the Confederate Ship *Virginia* (once *Merrimac*)," *SHSP,* 42:204ff.

51. Geo. Weber to brother Louis, 10 Mar. 1862, George Weber Letters, CM/RV; B. E. Colston, "Watching the *Merrimac*," *BL,* 1:712ff.

52. Buchanan's Report, *ORN,* Ser. 1, 7:44ff.; Wood, "First Fight of the Ironclads," pp. 692ff.

53. Jones, "Services of the *Virginia*," pp. 65ff.

54. Buchanan's Report, 27 Sept. 1862, *ORN,* Ser. 1, 7:44ff.; Geo. Weber to brother Louis, 10 Mar. 1862, Weber Letters, CM/RV; Personal manuscript narrative by Leonard Lorenzo Billings (a Union soldier, serving in the coast batteries), Raimondo Luraghi's private collection.

55. Reaney, "How the Gunboat *Zouave* Aided the *Congress*," *BL,* 1:714ff.

56. Report of Lt. Austin Pendergast to Secretary Welles, *ORN,* Ser. 1, 7:23–24.

57. Buchanan's Report, ibid., pp. 44ff.; Robert D. Minor to John M. Brooke, 11 Mar. 1862, *SHSP,* 19:5–6; Virginius Newton, "The Ram *Merrimac*," ibid., 41:201; "Captain Eggleston's Narrative," ibid., 41:66; Daly, *How the* Merrimac *Won,* p. 116; Parker, *Recollections,* p. 257.

58. W. Norris, "The Story of the Confederate States Ship *Virginia*," *SHSP,* 42:204ff.

59. B. R. Colston, "Watching the *Merrimac*," *BL,* 1:712.

60. Jones to Hunter Davidson, 20 Aug. 1862, *ORN,* Ser. 1, 7:58ff.; Jones, "Services of the *Virginia*," p. 70; Wood, "The First Fight of the Ironclads," p. 700.

61. There were 121 men killed in the *Cumberland*, 120 in the *Congress*, and an unknown number in other ships and on land. See *ORN*, Ser. 1, 7:22, 24. The *Virginia* had only 2 killed and 8 wounded (Buchanan to Mallory, 27 Mar. 1862, ibid., pp. 44ff.). Those killed on all Confederate ships numbered 27.

62. Robert D. Minor to J. M. Brooke, 8 Mar. 1862, *SHSP*, 19:5ff.

63. Foxhall A. Parker, "The *Monitor* and the *Merrimac*," *U.S. Naval Institute Proceedings* 1 (1874): 155ff.

64. Worden to Welles, 9 Mar. 1862, *ORN*, Ser. 1, 7:5.

65. Jones, "Services of the *Virginia*," p. 70; Arthur Sinclair, Jr., "How the *Merrimac* Fought the *Monitor*," *Hearst's Magazine*, Dec. 1913. Young Sinclair (son of Commander Sinclair, later detailed to command the *Mississippi*) had served on the *Virginia* as a non-commissioned officer and witnessed a pilot's identification of the *Monitor* upon her arrival during the night of 8 and 9 March.

66. Robert D. Minor to Mrs. Kell, 8 (? most possibly 18) Mar. 1862, in John McIntosh Kell, *Recollections of a Naval Life, Including the Cruises of the Confederate States Steamers* Sumter *and* Alabama (Washington, D.C., 1900), pp. 281ff. The mistake in the date of the letter must be ascribed to a misprint because in it Minor told about events that had not yet occurred on the eighth. See Colston, "Watching the *Merrimac*," *BL*, 1:712ff.

67. Sinclair, "How the *Merrimac* Fought the *Monitor*," p. 884.

68. Norris, "The Story of the C.S.S. *Virginia*," *SHSP*, 42:217.

69. "Captain Eggleston's Narrative"; James K. Rochelle to John R. Tucker, 30 Jan. 1865, *ORN*, Ser. 1, 7:49ff.; Parker, *Recollections*, p. 264.

70. George M. Brooke, Jr., "John Mercer Brooke, Naval Scientist" (Ph.D. dissertation, 2 vols., University of North Carolina, 1956), pp. 826ff.

71. James P. Baxter III, *The Introduction of the Ironclad Warship* (1933; reprint, Hamden, Conn., 1968), p. 293.

72. J. M. Brooke to Warley, 4 Jan. 1863, Naval Collection, Confederate Subject File AB, NARG 45.

73. Keeler, *Aboard the U.S.S.* Monitor, ed. Daly, pp. 36ff.

74. J. T. Wood to his wife, 20 Mar. 1862, John Taylor Wood Papers, SHC/CHNC, in which he expresses the disbelief of the *Virginia*'s crew when they learned that the *Monitor* had not been knocked out. S. Dana Greene, "In the *Monitor* Turret," *BL*, 1:719ff.

75. Jones, "Services of the *Virginia*," p. 72.

76. Daly, *How the* Merrimac *Won*, pp. 127ff.

77. Davis, *Duel between the First Ironclads*, p. 143.

78. McClellan's Report, 4 Aug. 1863, *OR*, Ser. 1, 5:5ff.

79. Barnard's Report, *OR*, Ser. 1, 11, pt. 1:106ff.

80. McClellan to Goldsborough, 5 Apr. 1862, *ORN*, Ser. 1, 7:205; Goldsborough to McClellan, 6 Apr. 1862, ibid., p. 206; McClellan's Report, 4 Aug. 1863, *OR*, Ser. 1, 11, 1:5ff. The failure of his plan because the *Virginia* fully controlled the waters is well explained on page 8.

81. Mallory to President Davis, 19 Aug. 1862, *ORN*, Ser. 1, 7:62; Mallory to Jones, 6 May 1863, ibid.

82. Mallory to Jones, 13 Mar. 1862, Jones Rogers Family Papers, vol. 33, 1806–66, LC.

83. *ORN*, Ser. 1, 7:56.

84. R. C. Foute, "Echoes from Hampton Roads," *SHSP*, 19:24ff.; Wise, *End of an Era*, p. 205.

85. Norris, "The Story of the Confederate Ship *Virginia*," *SHSP,* 42:221.

86. *Spectator,* "Thanksgiving Service on the *Virginia*," *SHSP,* 19:248ff.; Wood to his wife, Lola, 20 Mar. 1862, John Taylor Wood Papers, SHC/CHNC.

87. Wood to his wife, Lola, 4, 6, 7 May 1862, Wood Papers, SHC/CHNC; Wood, "The First Fight between Ironclads," *BL,* 1:703ff.

88. Mallory to Buchanan, 7 Mar. 1862 (confidential), General Records of the Department of State, Confederate States Navy Department, NARG 59. The letter is published in *ORN,* Ser. 1, 6:780ff. This letter need some consideration. It seems strange that it could have been sent on 7 March because Buchanan's answer, dated 19 March, states that Mallory's letter had reached him *the evening before* (18 March) and that it had been written *on 17 March.* The secretary's words about "an event" that "would eclipse all the glories of the combat at sea" sounds very odd if written when the ironclad had not yet given any measure of her capabilities. Yet everything becomes logical if Mallory did write the letter on the seventeenth, *after* the battle at Hampton Roads. Therefore the date of 7 March must be a lapse, either by Mallory or by the clerk who copied it. To this writer, the latter hypothesis seems probable. Buchanan in his answer paid no attention to the date of the seventh, which must have appeared to him clearly erroneous.

89. Buchanan to Mallory, 19 Mar. 1862, Admiral Buchanan's Letterbook, Buchanan Books, SHC/CHNC. This extremely important letter, not included in *ORN,* explains why the *Virginia* was unable to operate on the high seas: she, as well as her enemy, the *Monitor,* was totally unseaworthy.

90. J. T. Mason to his mother, 10 Jan. 1862, John Thompson Mason Letters, M615, CM/RV.

91. See the long and detailed description by Robert S. McCordock, *The Yankee Cheesebox* (Philadelphia, 1938), pp. 140ff.

92. *The Diary of Gideon Welles,* 3 vols., ed. H. K. Beale and A. W. Brownsword (New York, 1960), 1:62ff; Gideon Welles, "The First Ironclad *Monitor*," *AW,* pp. 17ff. Here comments on Secretary of War Stanton's dismay are particularly abrasive.

93. Welles to Fox, 10 Mar. 1862 (telegram), *ORN,* Ser. 1, 7:83; Fox to Montgomery Blair, 10 Mar. 1862 (telegram), ibid., p. 85; Fox to Sen. James W. Grimes, 13 Mar. 1862 (telegram), ibid., p. 98; Goldsborough to Fox, 16 Mar. 1862, in *Confidential Correspondence of Gustavus Vasa Fox,* 1:248.

94. See several of them in U.S. Navy Department, Miscellaneous Letters Received, 3:1862, NARG 45. For example, it was suggested to run into the ironclad with a high-freeboard ship fitted with many guns on her bow and capsize them on the deck of the enemy ship, thus sinking her (Letter of 6 Apr. 1862, by C. L. Pascal from Philadelphia). Or to fling against her an enormous iron ball attached by a chain to a barrel of powder that would be exploded electrically (Letter of 24 Mar. 1862 from Ramsey).

95. Davis, *Duel between the First Ironclads,* p. 146.

96. The specifications and projects for these ships are in Bureau of Construction and Repair, Bureau of Ships, NARG 19.

97. Fox to Ericsson, 18 Mar. 1862, Gustavus Vasa Fox Papers, NHSL/NY.

98. Ericsson to Fox, 19 Mar. 1862, John Ericsson Papers, ibid.

99. Ericsson to Fox, 12 Apr., 9 May 1862, ibid.

100. Fox to Ericsson, 20 Mar. 1862, Fox Papers, ibid.

101. Maury to Captain de la Marche, Depôt de la Marine, Paris, dated Richmond, 15

Mar. 1862, Matthew Fontaine Maury Papers, LC. See also Davis, *Duel between the First Ironclads,* p. 140.

102. Edward, Duke of Somerset, "The *Merrimac* and the *Monitor,*" *SHSP,* 16:218ff.

103. The secretary gave this order "within the hour" from the moment he learned that the *Virginia* had gone into battle. See Mallory to R.M.T. Hunter, 9 Apr. 1862, *ORN,* Ser. 1, 7:762ff.

104. William N. Still, Jr., *Iron Afloat: The Story of the Confederate Armorclad* (1971; reprint, Columbia, S.C., 1985), p. 94; John W. H. Porter, *A Record of Events in Norfolk County, Virginia, from April 19th, 1861, to May 10th, 1862, with a History of the Soldiers and Sailors of Norfolk County, Norfolk City, and Portsmouth Who Served in the Confederate States Army or Navy* (Portsmouth, Va., 1892), p. 330; Naval History Division, *Civil War Naval Chronology, 1861–1865,* 6 vols. (Washington, D.C., 1961–66), 6:293.

105. French Forrest to Lt. Comdr. Van R. Morgan, 10 Mar. 1862, inviting him to take aboard the receiving ship (which he commanded) the officers and men of the *Virginia, ORN,* Ser. 1, 7:741; F. Forrest to C. ap R. Jones, same date, ibid.

106. General Robert E. Lee to Magruder, 13 Mar. 1862, *ORN,* Ser. 1, 7:744–45.

107. Mallory to French Forrest, 19 Mar. 1862, General Records of the Department of State, C.S. Navy Department, NARG 59, also in *ORN,* Ser. 1, 7:747.

108. Mallory to French Forrest, 20 Mar. 1862, General Records of the Department of State, Records of the C.S. Navy Department, NARG 59, also in *ORN,* Ser. 1, 7:748.

109. Mallory to French Forrest, 23 Mar. 1862 (telegram), General Records of the Department of State, C.S. Navy Department, NARG 59, also in *ORN,* Ser. 1, 7:749.

110. Mallory to S. S. Lee, 24 Mar. 1862, General Records of the Department of State, C.S. Navy Department, NARG 59, also in *ORN,* Ser. 1, 7:748. Yet the expertise of the aged Forrest was not wasted because he was appointed head of the Bureau of Orders and Details.

111. Mallory to S. S. Lee, 24 Mar. 1862, General Records of the Department of State, C.S. Navy Department, NARG 59, also in *ORN,* Ser. 1, 7:750.

112. Buchanan to Mallory, 13 May, 3 June 1862, Admiral Buchanan's Letterbook, Buchanan Books, SHC/CHNC.

113. Mallory to Tattnall, 21 Mar. 1862 (telegram), 25 Mar. 1862, General Records of the Department of State, C.S. Navy Department, NARG 59, also in *ORN,* Ser. 1, 7:748–50.

114. James D. Bulloch, *The Secret Service of the Confederate States in Europe, or, How the Confederate Cruisers Were Equipped,* 2 vols. (1884; reprint, New York, 1959), 1:143ff.; Parker, *Recollections,* pp. 271ff.; Alexander A. Lawrence, *A Present for Mr. Lincoln: The Story of Savannah from Secession to Sherman* (Macon, Ga., 1961). The only full biography of Tattnall is Charles C. Jones, *The Life and Services of Commodore Josiah Tattnall* (Savannah, Ga., 1878). Even if in the main a eulogy, this book is nevertheless a treasure trove of information.

115. Mallory to Tattnall, 25 Mar. 1862, General Records of the Department of State, C.S. Navy Department, NARG 59.

116. J. T. Mason to his mother, 30 Mar. 1862, John Thompson Mason Letters, CM/ RV.

117. Buchanan to Mallory, 26 Mar. 1862, Admiral Buchanan's Letterbook, Buchanan Books, SHC/CHNC.

118. Tattnall to Mallory, 4 Apr. 1862, at 1 P.M., *ORN,* Ser. 1, 7:756–57. Also Daly, *How the* Merrimac *Won,* pp. 145–46.

119. James A. Semple (on board the *Virginia*) to R. D. Minor, 3 Apr. 1862, Minor Family Papers, VHS/RV. For changes made, Porter to Mallory, 7 Apr. 1862, *ORN*, Ser. 1, 7:764 (quoted by Mallory in his letter to R.M.T. Hunter, 9 Apr. 1862).

120. J. A. Semple to R. D. Minor, 3 Apr. 1862, Minor Family Papers, VHS/RV.

121. Chief Engineer H. Ashton Ramsay to Tattnall, 5 Apr. 1862, Ramsay to C. ap R. Jones, Apr. 1862, *ORN*, Ser. 1, 7:758ff. (The day of the last letter may be the same as the first one.)

122. Still, *Iron Afloat,* p. 37; Daly, *How the* Merrimac *Won,* pp. 145ff.

123. Mallory to S. S. Lee, 4 Apr. 1862 (letter), *ORN*, Ser. 1, 7:757ff.

124. Mallory to S. S. Lee, 4 Apr. 1862 (telegram), ibid., p. 758.

125. *OR,* Ser. 1, 11, pt. 1:10ff.

126. R. E. Lee to Mallory, 8 Apr. 1862, *ORN*, Ser. 1, 7:761.

127. Mallory to Tattnall, 8 Apr. 1862, ibid., p. 760.

128. Tattnall to Mallory, 10 Apr. 1862, ibid., pp. 764ff.

129. Charles C. Fulton to Union Secretary of War, 12 Apr. 1862, ibid., pp. 220ff.

130. Goldsborough to Welles, 12 Apr. 1862, ibid., p. 219.

131. Report of Comdr. W.N.W. Hewitt, Royal Navy, ibid., pp. 224–25.

132. Tattnall to Mallory, 12 Apr. 1862, ibid., p. 223.

133. Keeler, *Aboard the U.S.S.* Monitor, ed. Daly, p. 74. In Richmond Mallory had had built a replica of the *Monitor*'s turret and stated that armor-piercing projectiles designed by Brooke would pierce it as long as they were fired from no farther than fifty to one hundred yards (Daly, *How the* Merrimac *Won,* p. 140).

134. Mallory to Tattnall, 12 Apr. 1862, *ORN*, Ser. 1, 7:224. Mallory, turning to private entrepreneurs, had also ordered laid down a number of small ironclad gunboats for North Carolina's coastal waters.

135. McClellan, *McClellan's Own Story,* pp. 281ff., McClellan to Stanton (n.d., but according to McClellan, ibid., written "about 20 April 1862"), in which the general wrote: "Circumstances, among which I will now only mention uncertainty as to the power of the *Merrimac,* have compelled me to adopt the present line *(of operations)* as probably safer, though far less brilliant, than that of Urbana." To put McClellan's memoirs in proper critical perspective, see Stephen W. Sears, "The Curious Case of General McClellan's Memoirs," *Civil War History* 2 (1988): 101ff.

136. Tattnall to Mallory, 19 Apr. 1862, *ORN*, Ser. 1, 7:756–57; Tattnall to Barney, 18 Apr. 1862, ibid., p. 767.

137. Tattnall to Tucker, 20 Apr. 1862, ibid., p. 768.

138. General Joseph E. Johnston to Tattnall, 28 Apr. 1862, *ORN*, Ser. 2, 1:633.

139. Tattnall to Mallory, 21 Apr. 1862, *ORN*, Ser. 1, 7:769–70.

140. Mallory to S. S. Lee, 22 Apr. 1862 (telegram), ibid., p. 772.

141. Mallory to S. S. Lee, 24 Apr. 1862, ibid., p. 773.

142. Mallory to S. S. Lee (confidential), 30 Apr. 1862, ibid., pp. 778ff.; Mallory to the Secretary of War, 16 Apr. 1862, *OR,* Ser. 1, 11, pt. 3:538; Notes of R. E. Lee, 17 Apr. 1862, ibid., p. 539.

143. Tattnall to Gen. J. E. Johnston, 30 Apr. 1862, *ORN*, Ser. 1, 7:777.

144. Mallory to S. S. Lee, 22, 23, 24 Apr. 1862, ibid., p. 772.

145. Mallory to S. S. Lee, 1 May 1862, ibid., p. 779.

146. J. E. Johnston to R. E. Lee, 27 Apr. 1862, *OR,* Ser. 1, 11, pt. 3:469; J. E. Johnston to Huger, same date, ibid., pp. 469–70; J. E. Johnston to R. E. Lee, 29 Apr. 1862, ibid.,

p. 473; General Order, 2 May 1862, ibid., p. 489; J. E. Johnston to Tucker, 2 May 1862, *ORN,* Ser. 1, 7:782. Two reasons pushed Johnston to order the retreat: the need to concentrate all the Confederate forces available for the defense of Richmond and the supposed impossibility of holding the Yorktown line when faced with the heavy and very heavy guns McClellan was gathering. See Report by Gen. J. E. Johnston, 19 May 1862, *OR,* Ser. 1, 11, pt. 1:725–26. See also Joseph E. Johnston, *Narrative of Military Operations during the Late War between the States,* ed. Frank Vandiver (1874; reprint, Bloomington, Ind., 1959), pp. 117ff. Both these motives are debatable. For example, one might stress the resistance that entrenchments would turn out to be able to oppose against heavy artillery fire. It is true, however, that Johnston could correctly hold that he had no alternatives.

147. Mallory to S. S. Lee (confidential), 30 Apr., 1 May 1862, *ORN,* Ser. 1, 7:778–79.

148. J. E. Johnston to Tucker, 2 May 1862, ibid., p. 782; Mallory to S. S. Lee, 3 May 1862, ibid., p. 783.

149. Mallory to Tattnall, 5 May 1862 (telegram), and 6 May 1862, ibid., p. 785.

CHAPTER NINE

1. Report of General Johnson K. Duncan, commanding the Confederate forts, 30 Apr. 1862, *OR,* Ser. 1, 6:521; William B. Robertson, "The Water-battery at Fort Jackson," *BL,* 2:99ff. Captain Robertson commanded this battery, which turned out to be most efficient.

2. Lovell to Secretary of War Judah Benjamin, 6 Feb. 1862, *OR,* Ser. 1, 6:822–23; Benjamin to Lovell, 8 Feb. 1862, ibid., p. 823; Lovell to Benjamin, 12 Feb. 1862, ibid., pp. 825–26; George G. Garner to General Samuel Jones, 28 Mar. 1862, ibid., pp. 866–67.

3. Report of Mallory to Davis, 27 Feb. 1862, *ORN,* Ser. 1, 18:830–31; President Davis to Louisiana Governor Thomas O. Moore, 17 Apr. 1862, *OR,* Ser. 1, 6:878.

4. Hollins to Mallory, 9 Apr. 1862 (telegram), *ORN,* Ser. 2, 1:519; Hollins to Mallory, 11 Apr. 1862, ibid., p. 520; Hollins to Mallory, 11 Apr. 1862 (telegram), *ORN,* Ser. 1, 18:844.

5. Mallory to Hollins, 10, 11 Apr. 1862, *ORN,* Ser. 2, 1:519.

6. Hollins himself acknowledged this before the congressional Committee of Inquiry on the fall of New Orleans, *ORN,* Ser. 2, 1:520.

7. James Morris Morgan, *Recollections of a Rebel Reefer* (Boston, 1917), pp. 69–70; Charles W. Read, "Reminiscences of the Confederate States Navy," *SHSP,* 1:331ff.; see also in *ORN,* Ser. 2, 1:517–18, the places from which the several telegrams were sent as well as the addressees.

8. Later Hollins held that he had an amazing plan to attack and destroy Farragut's powerful fleet with his small gunboats. Such a plan, when studied carefully, appears to be a product of fantasy rather than of tactical thought. Indeed, should he have been right and the secretary wrong, his duty as an officer was to carry out his orders as best he could without causing needless complications and behaving in a way that impaired discipline. His plan appears to have been as follows. Because his ships had pivot guns and some iron protection forward, while the enemy had most of his guns in broadside, he hoped, by descending the river with the help of the current, to attack with the bow on so as to inflict serious damage to the Federal ships before they could succeed in making a quarter turn. That these ships had their sides well protected by heavy chains coiled about them he did not seriously consider. How he might suppose that Farragut would be so careless as to be surprised is not made clear. Charles W. Read (unanimously acknowledged as a most competent and daring officer in the C.S. Navy) gave a poor appraisal of Hollins, whom he rated as very brave in talking yet very reticent to act. See Read, "Reminiscences," pp. 335,

338ff., wherein he charges Hollins with shunning the action in front of him and going elsewhere to seek "amazing" enterprises. For Hollins's plan against Farragut's fleet, see *ORN,* Ser. 2, 1:474ff.

9. *ORN,* Ser. 2, 1:476; James M. Merrill, *Battle Flags South: The Story of the Civil War Navies on the Western Waters* (Rutherford, N.J., 1970), p. 141.

10. *ORN,* Ser. 2, 1:441.

11. Governor Moore to President Davis, 17 Apr. 1862, *OR,* Ser. 1, 6:878; Davis to Moore, same date, ibid.; Captain Whittle to General Lovell, 11 Apr. 1862, ibid., p. 650; Randolph to General Lovell, 11 Apr. 1862 (telegram), *ORN,* Ser. 1, 18:844.

12. *ORN,* Ser. 2, 1:441. This message, quoted by Whittle in his deposition before the Joint Special Committee of Inquiry about the fall of New Orleans, must have been dated 18 April 1862.

13. Whittle to Mitchell, 18 Apr. 1862, *ORN,* Ser. 1, 18:323–24.

14. John Wilkinson, *The Narrative of a Blockade Runner* (New York, 1877), pp. 32ff. Captain Wilkinson was the executive officer of the ironclad, who assumed command after McIntosh was mortally wounded; therefore, he was an excellent witness. Wilkinson says the ironclad carried twelve guns still unmounted, whereas Commodore Mitchell said sixteen, adding that they were poorly mounted (Mitchell to Mallory, 19 Aug. 1862, *ORN,* Ser. 1, 18:289). Another officer of the *Louisiana,* Lieutenant William C. Whittle, Jr., son of the commodore, says that four days were needed to mount the cannons and that two of them never were mounted (W. C. Whittle, Jr., to Editors, n.d., *BL,* 2:48). J. Thomas Scharf, *History of the Confederate States Navy from Its Organization to the Surrender of Its Last Vessel* (New York, 1887), p. 200, reports testimony from young Whittle.

15. Wilkinson, *Narrative,* pp. 32ff.; Scharf, *Confederate States Navy,* pp. 278ff.; Mitchell to Mallory, 19 Aug. 1862, *ORN,* Ser. 1, 18:289–90; *ORN,* Ser. 2, 1:452ff.

16. Mitchell to Mallory, 19 Aug. 1862, *ORN,* Ser. 1, 18:289ff. One must keep in mind that because the *Louisiana* was moored, she could use not more than a maximum of eight cannons, that is, those forward and to starboard. The strength of the Confederates' naval guns thus fell to twenty-two, and its ratio to the enemy's was 12.25:1.

17. Stevenson to Mitchell, 21 Apr. 1862, *ORN,* Ser. 1, 18:328; Mitchell to Duncan, 23 Apr. 1862, ibid.

18. "The Opposite Forces in the Operations at New Orleans, La.," *BL,* 2:73ff.; Scharf, *Confederate States Navy,* p. 278, n. 1. Seven of the Federal warships were detailed to protect Porter's mortar boats, but these were nevertheless at Farragut's disposal.

19. Report of General Lovell, 22 May 1862, *OR,* Ser. 1, 6:512ff., states that the forts had "65–70" cannons. The complete summary is to be found in *BL,* 2:75.

20. Morgan, *Recollections,* p. 71.

21. *ORN,* Ser. 2, 1:538, 604.

22. Duncan to Mitchell, 22 Apr. 1862, *ORN,* Ser. 1, 18:370; Mitchell to Duncan, 22 Apr. 1862, ibid., p. 324. See also General Duncan's Report in *OR,* Ser. 1, 6:521ff.

23. Whittle to Mitchell, 23 Apr. 1862, *ORN,* Ser. 1, 18:329; Mitchell to Whittle, 23 Apr. 1862, ibid.; Mitchell to Duncan, 23 Apr. 1862, ibid., p. 325.

24. Robertson, "The Water-battery," *BL,* 2:99–100; see also Report of General Duncan, *OR,* Ser. 1, 6:521ff.

25. Duncan to Mitchell, 24 Apr. 1862, at hours 3:30, *ORN,* Ser. 1, 18:330.

26. See the description in Raimondo Luraghi, *Storia della Guerra Civile Americana,* 5th ed., rev. (Milan, 1986), pp. 516ff.

27. Mitchell to Mallory, 19 Aug. 1862, *ORN,* Ser. 1, 18:289ff.

28. Warley to Mallory, 13 Aug. 1862, ibid., pp. 338ff.; Documents and statements from Warley, ibid.

29. Read to Whittle, two letters, 1 May 1862, ibid., pp. 332ff.; Read, "Reminiscences," pp. 72–73. The *McRae,* reduced to a floating wreck, was used, with the authorization by the Federals, to carry the wounded to New Orleans, where she soon sank.

30. Beverly Kennon, "Fighting Farragut below New Orleans," *BL,* 2:76ff.; A. F. Warley, "The Ram *Manassas* at the Passage of the New Orleans Forts," ibid., pp. 89ff.

31. The upper deck of the ironclad was protected by an iron wall, only a few inches thick, designed only against rifle fire of sharpshooters and utterly useless against artillery shells. McIntosh was wounded by splinters from this wall and from the upper deck itself. See Scharf, *Confederate States Navy,* p. 283, n. 1.

32. *ORN,* Ser. 2, 1:552ff.

33. The Tift brothers to Mallory, 26 Aug. 1862, ibid., pp. 598ff.

34. ORN, Ser. 2, 1:438, 487ff.

35. Private Diary of Farragut, in *Life and Letters of Admiral David Glasgow Farragut, First Admiral of the United States Navy, Embodying His Journal and Letters,* ed. Loyall Farragut (New York, 1879), pp. 261ff.; General Order by Flag Officer Farragut, 20 Apr. 1862, *ORN,* Ser. 1, 18:162.

36. J. T. Mason to his mother, 6 June 1862, John Thompson Mason Letters, M615, CM/RV.

37. J. M. Baker, "Reminiscences," in J. Thomas Scharf Papers, C.S. Navy Records, MdHS/BM; Wilkinson, *Narrative,* pp. 52ff.

38. Mitchell to Mallory, 19 Aug. 1862, *ORN,* Ser. 1, 18:299ff.

39. Wilkinson, *Narrative,* pp. 56–57.

40. The true reason why the ironclad did not try a desperate sallying seems to be that she had not even on board men enough to man the guns.

41. Mallory to S. S. Lee, 3 May 1862, *ORN,* Ser. 1, 7:783; Tucker to Mallory, 8 May 1862, ibid., pp. 786–87.

42. Tucker's Report, *ORN,* Ser. 1, 7:786–87.

43. On Lincoln's strategic mind, see Colin R. Ballard, *The Military Genius of Abraham Lincoln* (Cleveland, Ohio, 1952). Ballard was a brigadier general in the British army.

44. Lincoln to Goldsborough, 7 May 1862, *ORN,* Ser. 1, 7:326; Welles to Goldsborough, 8 May 1862, ibid., p. 330. This action had been suggested by McClellan a couple of days earlier: see McClellan to Fox, 4 May 1862, *ORN,* Ser. 1, 7:309; Col. J. J. Astor to Goldsborough, 4 May 1862, ibid. It did not seem that the commodore had any intention of doing so, yet the president immediately grasped the importance and far-reaching implications of such an initiative and ordered its immediate execution. He fitted it into a larger and more intelligent plan.

45. Goldsborough to Rodgers, 7 May 1862, *ORN,* Ser. 1, 7:327, in which the commodore stated, "It is the desire of the President of the United States that the expedition should start at once to night."

46. Rodgers to Goldsborough, 9, 11 May 1862, ibid., pp. 328–29; Tucker to Mallory, 8 May 1862, ibid., pp. 786–87.

47. See Mallory's telegram of 5 May, ibid., p. 785.

48. J. E. Johnston to B. Huger, 27 Apr. 1862, *OR,* Ser. 1, 11, pt. 3:111; J. E. Johnston to R. E. Lee, 29 Apr. 1862, ibid., p. 473; B. Huger to R. E. Lee, 29 Apr. 1862, ibid., p. 474;

Huger to J. E. Johnston, 29 Apr. 1862, ibid.; R. E. Lee to Huger, 30 Apr. 1862, ibid., pp. 476–77; Secretary of War G. W. Randolph to Huger, 3 May 1862, ibid., p. 490; R. E. Lee to Huger, 7 May 1862, ibid., p. 497.

49. Goldsborough to Lincoln, 9 May 1862, *ORN*, Ser. 1, 7:330ff.; Goldsborough to Welles, 9 May 1862, ibid., pp. 331–32.

50. J. T. Wood to his wife, Lola, 8 May 1862, John Taylor Wood Papers, SHC/CHNC; J. T. Wood, "The First Fight," *BL*, 1:709. Flag Officer Tattnall once again ordered a shot fired into the wind to show his disdain for the fleeing enemy. Yet, wisely, he did not follow them. Goldsborough to G. V. Fox, 2 May 1862, in *Confidential Correspondence of Gustavus Vasa Fox, Assistant Secretary of the Navy*, 2 vols., ed. Robert M. Thompson and Richard Wainwright (New York, 1918–19), 1:265–66.

51. Goldsborough to Fox, 8 May 1862, in *Confidential Correspondence of Fox*, 1:267–68.

52. Abstract Log of U.S.S. *Dacotah*, *ORN*, Ser. 1, 7:333–34.

53. Wood, "The First Fight," p. 709.

54. Tattnall's Report, 14 May 1862, *ORN*, Ser. 1, 7:335ff.

55. Wood, "The First Fight," p. 710; C. ap R. Jones, "Services of the *Virginia*," *SHSP*, 11:74; Tattnall's Report, *ORN*, Ser. 1, 7:355ff.

56. J. T. Mason to his mother, 6 June 1862, Mason Papers, M615, CM/RV. Tattnall offered a less dramatic explanation: according to him, the pilots' patriotism was unquestionable. It was a case of cowardice (*ORN*, Ser. 1, 7:335ff.).

57. Jones, "Services of the *Virginia*," p. 74; Wood, "The First Fight," p. 710.

58. R. E. Lee to his wife, 13 May 1862, Robert E. Lee Papers, VHS/RV.

59. Keeler to his wife, 12 May 1862, in William F. Keeler, *Aboard U.S.S.* Monitor, *1862: The Letters of Acting Paymaster William Frederick Keeler to His Wife Anna*, ed. Robert W. Daly (Annapolis, 1964), pp. 119ff.

60. Goldsborough to Welles, 12 May 1862, *ORN*, Ser. 1, 7:342–43.

61. R. D. Minor to his brother, 30 Apr. 1862, Minor Family Papers, VHS/RV; R. D. Minor to Secretary of War Randolph, 1 May 1862, ibid.

62. John B. Jones, *A Rebel War Clerk's Diary at the Confederate States Capital*, 2 vols., 1866. New ed. by Howard Swiggett (New York, 1935), 1:125; Thomas C. De Leon, *Four Years in Rebel Capitals* (1890; reprint, New York, 1962), pp. 217ff. The latter gives the best picture of events.

63. Scharf, *Confederate States Navy*, p. 711. Instead, John Taylor Wood ("The First Fight," p. 711) speaks of three 32-pounders and two 64-pounders. It is extremely difficult to reconcile the numbers, but it seems reasonable to assume that the guns mentioned by Wood were those served by the *Virginia*'s sailors. In his (usually excellent) comment about the letters by Keeler (*Aboard the U.S.S.* Monitor, p. 127) Daly holds that the fort at Drewry's Bluff originally had only three cannons and that the *Virginia*'s crew, commanded by Catesby ap R. Jones, served one. How this can be reconciled with the detailed narrative of Wood is hard to understand.

64. William C. Davis, *Duel between the First Ironclads* (Garden City, N.Y., 1975), p. 153.

65. Rodgers to Goldsborough, 16 May 1862, *ORN*, Ser. 1, 7:357–58. Confederate losses were seven dead and eight wounded (Farrand to Mallory, 15 May 1862, *ORN*, Ser. 1, 18:7–8).

66. David D. Porter, "The Opening of the Lower Mississippi," *BL*, 2:22ff. (the Lincoln quotation is on p. 243).

67. Welles to Farragut, 20 Jan. 1862, *ORN,* Ser. 1, 18:7–8.

68. John D. Milligan, *Gunboats Down the Mississippi* (Annapolis, 1965), p. 79; Robert C. Black III, *The Railroads of the Confederacy* (Chapel Hill, 1952), pp. 200ff.

69. S. H. Lockett, "The Defense of Vicksburg," *BL,* 3:482ff.; Luraghi, *Storia della Guerra Civile Americana,* pp. 586ff.

70. Beauregard to Captain of Engineers D. E. Harris, 21 Apr. 1862, *ORN,* Ser. 1, 23:696ff.; Adjutant General T. Jordan to E. K. Marshall, 20 Apr. 1862, in Alfred Roman, *The Military Operations of General Beauregard in the War between the States,* 2 vols. (New York, 1884), 1:564–65; Beauregard to Captain D. B. Harris, 21 Apr. 1862, ibid., pp. 366ff. (see also *ORN,* above); Beauregard to Harris, same date, ibid.

71. *ORN,* Ser. 2, 1:552; Lovell to General Cooper, 22 May 1862, *ORN,* Ser. 1, 18:263ff.

72. Lockett, "Defense of Vicksburg," pp. 482ff.; Lovell to Beauregard, 14 May 1862, *OR,* Ser. 1, 15:735; Lovell to Beauregard, 26 May 1862, *OR,* Ser. 1, 52, 2:318.

73. W. Faxon to Farragut, 13 Mar. 1863, *ORN,* Ser. 1, 19:661; the promotion was made retroactive to 16 July 1862.

74. Captain Craven to his wife, 3 June 1862, *ORN,* Ser. 1, 18:528; Commander J. S. Palmer to Farragut, 13 May 1862, ibid., pp. 489ff.

75. An ample picture of these events, which do not concern the C.S. Navy except indirectly, is in Luraghi, *Storia della Guerra Civile Americana,* pp. 585ff.; Edwin C. Bearss, *Rebel Victory at Vicksburg* (Vicksburg, 1963), pp. 51ff.; Milligan, *Gunboats Down the Mississippi,* pp. 79ff.

76. Private Diary of Commander H. H. Bell, 1862, n. 3, *ORN,* Ser. 1, 18:697ff.

77. *OR,* Ser. 1, 17, pt. 2:661, says the forces of General Van Dorn in Vicksburg in July 1862 numbered 9,916 men.

78. Van Dorn's Report, 9 Sept. 1862, *OR,* Ser. 1, 15:15ff.; Beauregard to Lovell, 10 June 1862, ibid., p. 752; Van Dorn to President Davis, 24 June 1862 (telegram), Jefferson Davis Papers, MUL/OO.

79. *ORN,* Ser. 2, 1:782–83.

80. This is the opinion of William N. Still, Jr., *Iron Afloat: The Story of the Confederate Armorclad* (1971; reprint, Columbia, S.C., 1985), pp. 62ff., and one must certainly agree with him.

81. McBlair to Tidball, 25 Apr. 1862 (telegram), *ORN,* Ser. 2, 1:798; ibid., p. 782.

82. *ORN,* Ser. 2, 1:781.

83. Henry Kennedy Stevens to his mother, 10 May 1862, H. K. Stevens Papers, Cynthia E. Moseley private collection.

84. Read, "Reminiscences," pp. 331ff.; M. L. Smith to Mallory, 21 May 1862, in Roman, *General Beauregard,* 1:370.

85. Mallory to McBlair, 24 May 1862, ZB File, NHD/W; H. K. Stevens to his mother, 29 May 1862, Stevens Papers, Moseley private collection.

86. Scharf, *Confederate States Navy,* p. 306, n. 1; George W. Gift, "The Story of the *Arkansas,*" *SHSP,* 12:115ff.; J. Grimball to his father, Grimball Family Papers, SHC/CHNC. Both Gift and Grimball were among the best officers aboard the ironclad.

87. Isaac N. Brown, "The Confederate Gunboat *Arkansas,*" *BL,* 3:572ff.; Mallory to Brown, 28 May 1862, ibid., p. 572.

88. Brown to General Ruggles, 4 June 1862, *OR,* Ser. 1, 15:749–50.

89. Brown, "Confederate Gunboat *Arkansas,*" pp. 572ff.; Read, "Reminiscences," pp. 331ff.; Gift, "Story of the *Arkansas,*" pp. 115ff., 163ff., and 215ff.; Harriet Gift Castlen, *Hope*

Bids Me Onward (Savannah, Ga., 1945), pp. 64ff. This book by Gift's daughter is a potpourri of writings and memoirs of her father, mixed together without much sense; later (yet starting on 19 December 1862, after the *Arkansas* story) it includes letters by Gift to his wife, the originals of which are in the George Washington Gift Letters, 1862–70, SHC/CHNC.

90. Brown to Ruggles, 29 May 1862, *OR*, Ser. 1, 15:746–47.

91. Brown to Ruggles, 4 June 1862, *ORN*, Ser. 1, 18:647–48; Brown, "Confederate Gunboat *Arkansas*," pp. 572ff.; Castlen, *Hope Bids Me Onward*, p. 64.

92. H. K. Stevens to his mother, 20 June 1862, Stevens Papers, Moseley private collection.

93. Brown, "Confederate Gunboat *Arkansas*," pp. 572ff.; Brown to Ruggles, 22 June 1862, Naval Collection, C.S. Navy, Confederate Area File 5, NARG 45, also in *OR*, Ser. 1, 15:762–63. In this letter Brown speaks of recovering three cannons from aboard the gunboats; Still, *Iron Afloat*, p. 65, speaks of four and six.

94. There is some discrepancy about carriages. Brown ("Confederate Gunboat *Arkansas*," p. 572) holds that these were manufactured in Jackson and that one of the two builders made five of them. Gift ("Story of the *Arkansas*," pp. 211–12) says that four had arrived from Memphis and were made of railroad iron; the other six were manufactured in Canton under the direction of H. K. Stevens. Yet all agree that they arrived in oxdrawn wagons conducted by Stevens.

95. Gift, in Castlen, *Hope Bids Me Onward*, p. 63; Meta (Morris) Grimball Diary, 1860–66, passim, SHC/CHNC; W. N. Still, Jr., "Confederate Shipbuilding in Mississippi," *Journal of Mississippi History* 30 (1968): 291ff.

96. H. K. Stevens to his mother, 25 Apr. 1862, Stevens Papers, Moseley private collection; *SHSP*, 1:349; Brown to Ruggles, 9 June 1862, *OR*, 1, 15:751–52.

97. Appointment of Read to Memphis, 20 May 1862, Naval Collection, C.S. Navy, Area File 5, NARG 45.

98. Read, "Reminiscences," pp. 331ff.

99. Lynch to Mallory, n.d., *SHSP*, 1:360; Brown, "Confederate Gunboat *Arkansas*," pp. 572ff.

100. Brown, "Confederate Gunboat *Arkansas*," p. 572; Read, "Reminiscences," pp. 331ff.; Gift, "Story of the *Arkansas*," pp. 205ff. About the broadside guns of the *Arkansas*, there is some disagreement among the three sources cited. On this matter, see the discussion in Luraghi, *Storia della Guerra Civile Americana*, p. 609, n. 48.

101. Farragut to Porter, 26 June 1862, *ORN*, Ser. 1, 18:588; Alfred W. Ellet to Stanton, 28 June 1862, ibid., p. 590; Luraghi, *Storia della Guerra Civile Americana*, pp. 598ff.

102. Brown to Ruggles, 22 June 1862, *OR*, Ser. 1, 15:762ff.

103. Brown, "Confederate Gunboat *Arkansas*," pp. 572ff.

104. President Davis to M. L. Smith, 14 June 1862, *OR*, Ser. 1, 15:754.

105. Van Dorn to President Davis (telegram), 24 June 1862, Jefferson Davis Papers, MUL/OO; Davis to Van Dorn, 26 June 1862, *OR*, Ser. 1, 15:767.

106. Brown to Ruggles, 20 June 1862, *ORN*, Ser. 1, 23:700; *SHSP*, 1:351.

107. Van Dorn to Ruggles, 24 June 1862, *ORN*, Ser. 1, 18:650.

108. Brown to Ruggles, 25 June 1862, *OR*, Ser. 1, 15:765–66.

109. Abstract from the Papers of Acting Master's Mate Wilson, C.S. Navy, *ORN*, Ser. 1, 19:132ff.

110. Bearss, *Rebel Victory at Vicksburg*, pp. 240ff.

111. Almost the whole day of 14 July was lost because the powder had become damp and had to be dried out in the sun. See Brown, "Confederate Gunboat *Arkansas*," pp. 573ff.

112. Isaac N. Brown to Alfred T. Mahan, 9 May 1883, Naval Collection, C.S. Navy Papers, Confederate Area File 5, NARG 45; J. Grimball to his mother, 31 July 1862, Grimball Family Papers, SHC/CHNC; C. Graves to his wife, 14 July 1862, Charles I. Graves Papers, SHC/CHNC.

113. Reports by commanding officers Gwyn *(Tyler)* and Walke *(Carondelet), ORN,* Ser. 1, 18:37ff.

114. Castlen, *Hope Bids Me Onward,* pp. 67ff.; *SHSP,* 12:50ff.

115. Log of the U.S. steam sloop *Richmond, ORN,* Ser. 1, 19:747ff.; Log of the U.S. steam sloop *Hartford,* ibid., pp. 705ff.

116. Stevens to his mother, 15 July 1862, Stevens Papers, Moseley private collection.

117. Boyce House, "Confederate Navy Hero Puts the Flag Back in Place," *Tennessee Historical Quarterly* 19 (1960): 172ff.

118. L. S. Flatau, "A Great Naval Battle," *Confederate Veteran* 25 (1917): 458–59.

119. J. E. Fiske to John M. Comstock, 24 July 1862, John Henry Comstock Papers, SHC/CHNC; Brown to Mallory (telegram), 15 July 1862, *ORN,* Ser. 1, 19:64–65.

120. Van Dorn to Davis (telegram), 15 July 1862, *ORN,* Ser. 1, 19:65.

121. J. E. Fiske to J. M. Comstock, 24 July 1862, Comstock Papers, SHC/CHNC; Van Dorn to Davis, 15 July 1862, *ORN,* Ser. 1, 19:65–66.

122. The *Winona* began to sink and was saved with much distress and almost totally disabled (E. T. Nichols to Farragut, 16 [?] July 1862, *ORN,* Ser. 1, 19:24–25).

123. J. E. Fiske to J. M. Comstock, 24 July 1862, Comstock Papers, SHC/CHNC.

124. *Oneida* ship diary, 15 July 1862, SHC/CHNC, where one feels the awful distress created by the ironclad *Arkansas* in the minds of U.S. crews. The ironclad is here called "iron monster," and the diary goes on at great lengths to specify that the broadsides from the *Richmond* did her no damage. See also July 17, 1862, ibid., where it is said that the Union ships were compelled to keep their fires stoked, to be ready for action at any moment. See also Private Diary of Captain H. H. Bell, U.S. Navy, *ORN,* Ser. 1, 19:711–12; Still, *Iron Afloat,* p. 75.

125. Bearss, *Rebel Victory at Vicksburg,* pp. 281–82.

126. Stevens to his mother, 2 Aug. 1862, Stevens Papers, Moseley private collection.

127. Gift, "Story of the *Arkansas,*" pp. 205ff.

128. Ibid.

129. Stevens to his mother, 9 Aug. 1862, Stevens Papers, Moseley private collection.

130. Read, "Reminiscences," p. 331. The crew of the *Arkansas,* like that of the *Virginia,* fought in the river batteries at Port Hudson, protecting from the southern side that part of the Mississippi remaining in Confederate hands, thanks mainly to the heroic action of the ironclad.

CHAPTER TEN

1. Rembert W. Patrick, *Jefferson Davis and His Cabinet* (Baton Rouge, 1961), p. 255.

2. *JC,* 5:303.

3. *ORN,* Ser. 2, 1:431.

4. Mallory to President Davis, 27 Aug. 1862, Jefferson Davis Papers, DUL/DNC, in

which the secretary stressed that he wanted the inquiry made at once, and in depth, so as to warrant to the navy a full acknowledgment of its deeds.

5. Stephen R. Mallory Diary, 24 June 1862, SHC/CHNC.

6. Mallory to President Davis, 27 Aug. 1862, Davis Papers, DUL/DNC.

7. Mallory to his wife, 31 Aug. 1862, Stephen Russell Mallory Papers, UFL/GF.

8. The *Report of Evidence Taken before a Joint Special Committee* of *Both Houses of the Confederate Congress to Investigate the Affairs of the Navy Department* (Richmond, [1863]) is reprinted in *ORN,* Ser. 2, 1:431ff., albeit without the contracts, which, however, can be found in the originals in Comptroller's Contracts, NARG 365.

9. Report of a Conference in reference to the occupation of points on the Atlantic coast, 5 July 1861, *OR,* Ser. 1, 53:64ff.; Second report, 13 July 1861, ibid., pp. 67ff.; Welles to Major Barnard, U.S. Corps of Engineers, 26 June 1861, *ORN,* Ser. 2, 12:195; Third report, ibid., pp. 201ff.; Welles to Du Pont, 3 Aug. 1861, ibid., p. 207; First report of conference for the consideration of measures for effectively blockading the coast bordering on the Gulf of Mexico, 9 Aug. 1861, *ORN,* Ser. 1, 16:618ff.

10. Du Pont to his wife, 28 June 1861, in *Samuel Francis Du Pont: A Selection of His Civil War Letters,* 3 vols., ed. John D. Hayes (Ithaca, N.Y., 1969), 1:85–86; Du Pont to his wife, 26 July 1861, ibid., pp. 112–15; Welles to Du Pont, 5 Aug. 1861, ibid., p. 126 (also in *ORN,* Ser. 1, 12:207); Percival Drayton to Du Pont, 2 July 1862, ibid., 2:150, n. 2; Du Pont to Welles, 3 June 1863, ibid., 3:152ff. (also in *ORN,* Ser. 1, 14:68ff.); Du Pont to G. V. Fox, 6, 16 Dec. 1861, in *Confidential Correspondence of Gustavus Vasa Fox, Assistant Secretary of the Navy, 1861–1865,* 2 vols., ed. Robert M. Thompson and Richard Wainwright (New York, 1918–19), 1:76ff.

11. Commander Paul E. Speicher, in a letter of 6 Feb. 1933, in "AWC Lectures" about "Union Joint Operations in the Civil War," USMHI/CP, underscores that in the operational plan from the Blockade Board, amphibious operations were clearly indicated and their strategic objective was the conquest of "forts and seaports"; Speicher adds that the operational plan against New Orleans was made personally by Gustavus Vasa Fox. See also John D. Hayes, "Sea Power in the Civil War," *U.S. Naval Institute Proceedings* 77 (Nov. 1961): 60ff.

12. Barron to Mallory, 31 Aug. 1861, *ORN,* Ser. 1, 6:138ff.; John G. Barrett, *The Civil War in North Carolina* (Chapel Hill, 1963), pp. 37ff.

13. Rush C. Hawkins, "Early Coastal Operations in North Carolina," *BL,* 1:632ff.

14. Daniel Ammen, "Du Pont and the Port Royal Expedition," *BL,* 1:671–72; E. Milby Burton, *The Siege of Charleston, 1861–1865* (Columbia, S.C., 1970), pp. 66ff.

15. Ambrose Burnside, "The Burnside Expedition," *BL,* 1:660ff. Even though General McClellan (who showed a fine understanding of the potential of sea power) had approved the organization of the division and accepted its objectives, the initial idea seems to have originated with Burnside himself and the navy. See Robert W. Daly, "Burnside's Amphibious Division," *Marine Corps Gazette* 35 (Dec. 1951): 30ff. The contention by the late Rowena Reed, *Combined Operations in the Civil War* (Annapolis, 1978), pp. 36ff., that McClellan intended to push the expedition forward into Confederate territory does not seem to be wholly acceptable. In the general's memoirs, the order he gave Burnside, instead, recommended great caution: McClellan to Burnside, 7 Jan. 1862, in George B. McClellan, *McClellan's Own Story* (New York, 1887), pp. 206ff.

16. William H. Parker, *Recollections of a Naval Officer, 1841–1865* (New York, 1883), p.

224. Because of shallow water and their large size, no Union warship was able to follow the two Confederate gunboats.

17. G. V. Fox to Goldsborough, 24 Feb. 1862: the taking of New Bern "gives us a fine base to push any number of troops into the interior" (*ORN,* Ser. 1, 6:664ff.).

18. Charles C. Jones to his parents, 18 Mar. 1862, Charles Colcock Jones, Jr., Collection, UGL/AG; Alexander A. Lawrence, *A Present for Mr. Lincoln: The Story of Savannah from Secession to Sherman* (Macon, Ga., 1961), pp. 41ff.

19. Emanuel R. Lewis, *Seacoast Fortifications of the United States* (Washington, D.C., 1970), pp. 50–51; Ralston B. Lattimore, *Fort Pulaski National Monument* (Washington, D.C., 1954).

20. Lawrence, *A Present for Mr. Lincoln,* pp. 51–52.

21. Report of General Gillmore, 20 Oct. 1865, *OR,* Ser. 1, 6:148ff.

22. John E. Johns, *Florida during the Civil War* (Gainesville, Fla., 1963), pp. 62ff.

23. James M. Merrill, *The Rebel Shore: The Story of Union Sea Power in the Civil War* (Boston, 1957), p. vi.

24. Catherine Ann Devereux Edmondston, *Journal of a Secesh Lady: The Diary of Catherine Ann Devereux Edmondston, 1860–1865,* ed. Beth Gilbert Crabtree and James W. Patton (Raleigh, N.C., 1979), pp. 117ff.

25. *Brockenburn: The Journal of Kate Stone, 1861–1868,* ed. John Q. Anderson (Baton Rouge, 1955), p. 181.

26. Elizabeth Allston Pringle, *Chronicles of Chicora Woods* (Atlanta, Ga., 1976), p. 189.

27. Rev. Charles C. Jones to Lt. Charles C. Jones, Jr., 26 Apr. 1862, in Robert Mason Myers, ed., *The Children of Pride: A True Story of Georgia and the Civil War* (New Haven, 1972), pp. 884ff.

28. Special Order No. 206 from the Adjutant General, 5 Nov. 1861, *OR,* Ser. 1, 6:309.

29. A. L. Long, *Memoirs of Robert E. Lee* (New York, 1886), pp. 138ff.

30. Mallory to Conrad, 10 May 1861, *ORN,* Ser. 2, 2:67ff.; William N. Still, Jr., "Confederate Naval Strategy: The Ironclad," *Journal of Southern History* 27 (1961): 330ff.

31. Adolphe Auguste Marie Lepotier, *Les Leçons de l'histoire, 1861–1865: Mer contre terre* (Paris, 1945), p. 139; Robert W. Daly, *How the* Merrimac *Won: The Strategic Story of the CSS* Virginia (New York, 1957), p. 185.

32. Edwin C. Bearss, *Rebel Victory at Vicksburg* (Vicksburg, 1975), p. 281.

33. Mallory to William Porcher Miles, 9 Dec. 1863, *ORN,* Ser. 1, 15:699ff.; Buchanan to Mallory, 18 Mar. 1862, Admiral Buchanan's Letterbook, Franklin Buchanan Books, SHC/CHNC; J. M. Brooke to Warley, 4 Jan. 1863, Naval Collection, C.S. Navy, Subject File AD, NARG 45.

34. Mallory to A. G. Brown, 18 Feb. 1865, Naval Collection, Subject File, NARG 45.

35. G. W. Gift to the newspaper *Sun,* 3 Feb. 1863, George W. Gift Letters, SHC/CHNC.

36. William N. Still, Jr., *Confederate Shipbuilding* (Athens, Ga., 1969), pp. 50ff. See also Chapter 3 above.

37. T. M. Jones to General J. H. Forney, 14 May 1862, *OR,* Ser. 1, 6:660.

38. R. D. Minor to his wife, 11 Feb. 1864, Minor Family Papers, VHS/RV.

39. Still, *Confederate Shipbuilding,* pp. 33ff.

40. W. Bevershaw Thompson, commanding the Engineers of North Carolina coast defense, to Col. Warren Winslow, 25 July 1861, *ORN,* Ser. 1, 16:713; Thompson to Col. Thomas Allen, 26 July 1861, ibid.; Barrett, *Civil War in North Carolina,* pp. 33ff.

41. Sidney C. Kerksis and Thomas S. Dickey, *Heavy Artillery Projectiles of the Civil War, 1861–1865* (Kennesaw, Ga., 1972), p. 236.

42. Beauregard to Cooper, 30 July 1863, *OR,* Ser. 1, 28, 2:244; Beauregard to Brooke, 31 July 1863, ibid., p. 248.

43. Brooke to R. Anderson, 28 Mar. 1862, Letterbook, Tredegar Company Papers, VSA/RV. The data given by the authoritative Warren C. Ripley, *Artillery and Ammunition of the Civil War* (New York, 1970), p. 129, do not agree in part with those given by Brooke himself, at least for the 7-inch cannon. See Diary of J. M. Brooke, in George M. Brooke, Jr., "John Mercer Brooke, Naval Scientist" (Ph.D. dissertation, 2 vols., University of North Carolina, 1955), p. 828.

44. Brooke to Catesby ap R. Jones, 28 Jan. 1864, Letters Received, Selma Foundry Papers, NARG 45. In this letter Brooke said also that smoothbore heavy guns were cast because the South lacked industry, which made it difficult to obtain proper projectiles for rifled guns and because of the bad use of them by inexperienced officers. The South, in other words, was beginning to feel the lack of skilled officers, not only of technical means. See also Edward Porter Alexander, "Confederate Artillery Service," *SHSP,* 9:98ff.

45. E. A. Archer to Brooke, 29 Oct. 1887, in Brooke, "John Mercer Brooke," p. 850.

46. Unsigned letter from the Office of Ordnance and Hydrography, 27 Jan. 1862, Colin J. McRae Papers, ASDAH/MA.

47. Ethel Armes, *The Story of Coal and Iron in Alabama* (1910; reprint, New York, 1973), pp. 157–58.

48. J. W. Lapsley to McRae, 8 Feb. 1862, McRae Papers, ASDAH/MA.

49. William N. Still, Jr., "Selma and the Confederate States Navy," *Alabama Review* 14 (Jan. 1962): 20ff. See also Chapter 3 above.

50. McRae to Mallory, 1 Aug. 1862, Letterbook, vol. 1, Selma Foundry Papers, NARG 45.

51. Special Order No. 1, "Quartermaster General Gvt. Foundry," Letterbook, vol. 2, ibid., announcing, on 20 Feb. 1863, the acquisition of the plant.

52. Special Order signed by Gen. Rains and Chambliss to Rains, 17 Apr. 1863 (telegram), Letterbook, vol. 2, ibid.

53. Jones to Brooke, 1 June 1863, Letterbook, vol. 3, ibid.

54. Armes, *Story of Coal and Iron in Alabama,* pp. 142ff.; Jones to Brooke, 5 June 1863, Letterbook, vol. 3, Selma Foundry Papers, NARG 45.

55. Jones to Brooke, 1 June 1863, Letterbook, vol. 3, Selma Foundry Papers, NARG 45.

56. Jones to Brooke, 18 June 1863, and Jones to Mallory, 20 June 1863, ibid.

57. Jones to Brooke, 13, 24 June 1863, ibid.

58. Jones to Brooke, 29 June, 6 July 1863, ibid.

59. Jones to Brooke, 22 July 1863, ibid.

60. Jones to Brooke, 1, 6, 14 Aug. 1863, ibid.

61. Armes, *Story of Coal and Iron in Alabama,* p. 144. It appears that the owners of the Brierfield Furnace did not understand that they should send to the Selma Foundry only the best pig iron. See Jones to Brooke, 1 Aug. 1863, Letterbook, vol. 3, Selma Foundry Papers, NARG 45, in which the proposal was made to offer a bonus to the owners of Brierfield (rejected) of $10 a ton if they would send only the best iron. Evidently, it was a problem of fitness of the furnace (later overcome) and not of ill-will.

62. Walter W. Stephen, "The Brooke Guns from Selma," *Alabama Historical Quarterly* 20 (1958): 462ff.

63. Armes, *Story of Coal and Iron in Alabama,* p. 144.

64. Record of Operations, 2 vols., Selma Foundry Papers, NARG 45.

65. J. M. Brooke to Warley, 4 Jan. 1863, Naval Collection, C.S. Navy, Subject File AD, NARG 45; also Brooke, "John Mercer Brooke," pp. 827ff.

66. R. D. Minor to R. Anderson, 1 Aug. 1862, Letterbook, Tredegar Company Records, VSA/RV; Thomas B. *[sic]* Dickey, "The Armor Puncher," *Civil War Times Illustrated* 18 (Aug. 1979): 24ff.; Kerksis and Dickey, *Heavy Artillery Projectiles of the Civil War,* passim, with photographs of armor-piercing projectiles still in existence.

67. Welles to Du Pont, 6 Jan. 1863, in *Samuel Francis Du Pont,* ed. Hayes, 2:352–53.

68. Du Pont to Welles, 7, 15, 27 Mar. 1863, *ORN,* Ser. 1, 13:740, 755, 787.

69. T. A. Honour to his wife, Beekie, 7 Sept. 1863, Theodore A. Honour Papers, SCL/CSC, who gives particulars about the April battle; D. E. Howe to T. Jordan, 23 Apr. 1863, *ORN,* Ser. 1, 4:84. The records of the battle are in ibid., pp. 3ff. for the Federals and pp. 74ff. for the Confederates.

70. T. A. Honour to his wife, Beekie, 18 Apr. 1863, Honour Papers, SCL/CSC, where he, writing from James Island, said that a projectile from a Brooke rifle had pierced the armor of the "most formidable" Union ironclad, the *Passaic.* Also Lepotier, *Les Leçons de l'histoire: Mer contre terre,* p. 237.

71. Lepotier, *Les Leçons de l'histoire: Mer contre terre,* p. 270.

72. The C.S. Navy by law had granted this rank to any officer coming from the U.S. Navy. See *A Digest of the Military and Naval Laws of the Confederate States from the Commencement of the Provisional Congress to the End of the First Congress under the Permanent Constitution,* ed. W. W. Lester and W. J. Bromwell (Columbia, S.C., 1864), p. 209. The C.S. Navy soon had thirty-eight captains and commanders. See *Register of Officers of the Confederate Navy, 1862* (N.p., n.d. [Richmond, 1862]), pp. 20ff.

73. See the observations by Tom H. Wells, *The Confederate Navy: A Study in Organization* (University, Ala., 1971), pp. 73–74.

74. Mallory to Davis, 6 Jan. 1862, *ORN,* Ser. 2, 2:124–25.

75. *Register of the Commissioned and Warrant Officers of the Navy of the Confederate States to January 1, 1864* (Richmond, 1864), pp. 75ff.

76. Ibid., pp. 73–74.

77. J. Taylor Wood to Catesby ap R. Jones, 30 Aug. 1862, *ORN,* Ser. 2, 2:256–57.; M. Mason to the Chairman of the Senate Committee on Naval Affairs, 2 May 1864, ibid., pp. 648ff.

78. *Register, 1864,* pp. 76–77.

79. Ibid., pp. 78–79; General Order, 2 June 1864, Savannah Squadron Papers, EUL/AG (also in *ORN,* Ser. 2, 2:658).

80. S. S. Lee to Mallory, 31 Oct. 1864, *ORN,* Ser. 2, 2:753ff.

81. Lepotier, *Les Leçons de l'histoire: Mer contre terre,* p. 336.

CHAPTER ELEVEN

1. Mallory to Bulloch, 11 Jan. 1862, *ORN,* Ser. 2, 2:129.

2. James D. Bulloch, *The Secret Service of the Confederate States in Europe, or, How the Confederate Cruisers Were Equipped,* 2 vols. (1884; reprint, New York, 1959), 1:109.

3. *Confederate Foreign Agent: The European Diary of Major Edward C. Anderson,* ed. William S. Hoole (University, Ala., 1976), p. 22.

4. Walker to Anderson, 18 May 1861, *OR,* Ser. 4, 1:332–33; Anderson, *Confederate Foreign Agent,* pp. 31ff.

5. Anderson, *Confederate Foreign Agent,* pp. 35–36; Bulloch, *Secret Service,* 1:110.

6. Bulloch to A. Dudley Mann, 3 Oct. 1861, *ORN,* Ser. 2, 2:96–97.

7. Bulloch, *Secret Service,* 1:111ff.; Anderson, *Confederate Foreign Agent,* p. 55. The editor of Anderson's book gives the tonnage of the *Fingal* as 463 (p. 141, n. 50). Evidently, he refers (or should have referred) to effective loading room, while the number 800, given in English tons of 2,240 pounds (1,016.047 kilograms), likely refers to gross tonnage.

8. Bulloch, *Secret Service,* 1:112. On the account of the army and the states of Georgia and Louisiana, the *Fingal* carried no less than fourteen thousand Enfield rifles and one million cartridges.

9. On Low, see William S. Hoole, *Four Years in the Confederate Navy: The Career of Captain John Low of the CSS Fingal, Florida, Alabama, and Ajax* (Athens, Ga., 1964).

10. While the *Fingal* was approaching Holyhead during a pitch-dark night, she rammed and sank a small collier, the *Siccardi,* probably Italian rather than Austrian, as Bulloch states. He instructed Fraser, Trenholm and Company to pay damage claims. See Bulloch, *Secret Service,* 1:115ff.

11. James H. North Diary, 8, 9 Oct. 1861, James H. North Papers, SHC/CHNC; North to Mallory, 9 Oct. 1861, *ORN,* Ser. 2, 2:97–98; Mallory to North, 9 Oct. 1861, ibid., pp. 98–99.

12. Bulloch, *Secret Service,* 1:116ff.

13. Tattnall to J. S. Kennard, 5, 12 Dec. 1861, C.S.A. Navy Collection, UGL/AG. (The Joel S. Kennard Papers are the property of Mary E. Woods, of Athens, Georgia. Her courtesy in allowing their use is highly appreciated.)

14. Bulloch, *Secret Service,* 1:116ff.

15. Mallory to Bulloch, 30 Nov. 1861, *ORN,* Ser. 2, 2:113–14; Mallory to Davis, 5 Jan. 1862, ibid., pp. 124–25. On the *Trent* Affair, see Chapter 5 above, n. 106.

16. Mallory to Bulloch, 11 Jan. 1862, *ORN,* Ser. 2, 2:129. During the meeting at Richmond Mallory had at length stressed with Bulloch his ideas about the need to build seagoing ironclads in Europe. See Bulloch, *Secret Service,* 1:380.

17. Mallory to Bulloch, 14 Jan. 1862, *ORN,* Ser. 2, 2:131; Bulloch, *Secret Service,* 1:139. Mallory suggested (but did not insist) that Bulloch cooperate with North.

18. Bulloch to Mallory, 22 Jan. 1862, *ORN,* Ser. 2, 2:134–35.

19. Bulloch, *Secret Service,* 1:151.

20. *ORN,* Ser. 2, 2:182–83.

21. Mallory to Memminger, 14 Apr. 1862, Treasury Department Collection of Confederate Records, Letters Received by the Confederate Secretary of the Treasury, NARG 365.

22. Mallory to Memminger, 19 Apr. 1862, ibid.

23. North to Mallory, 25 July 1862, *ORN,* Ser. 2, 2:228–29.

24. James M. Mason to Secretary of State Judah P. Benjamin, 18 Sept. 1862, *ORN,* Ser. 2, 3:528–29.

25. Ephraim D. Adams, *Great Britain and the American Civil War,* 2 vols. (New York, 1925), 1:289; Lynn M. Case and Warren F. Spencer, *The United States and France: Civil War Diplomacy* (Philadelphia, 1970), passim. On Stringer, who remains a shadowy figure, see Warren F. Spencer, *The Confederate Navy in Europe* (University, Ala., 1983), p. 72.

26. North to Thomson, 11 Apr. 1862, *ORN,* Ser. 2, 2:182.

27. North to Mallory, 14 Apr. 1862, ibid., p. 185.

28. Mallory to North, 5 May 1862, ibid., p. 191; North to Mallory, 29 Mar. 1862, ibid., pp. 176–77.

29. Specifications of hull, masts, etc., of an ironclad iron steamship, etc., ibid., pp. 193ff. For the contract, ibid., p. 189.

30. North to Mallory, 7 June 1862, ibid., p. 206.

31. Plans for the ironclad *Glasgow* or *Santa Maria,* drawn by constructors James and George Thomson, Clyde Bank Iron Shipyard, Glasgow, Scotland, Naval Collection, C.S. Navy, Subject File: Construction of Ships, NARG 45. The composition of the battery for the ironclad is not clear. See *ORN,* Ser. 2, 2:220ff., Alterations and extra fittings, frigate No. 61; which states that the guns in broadsides would be six per side, leaving four to be mounted (on pivots?) over the deck bow and stern. For the installation of rifled Whitworths, see North to Mallory, 11 Nov. 1862, ibid., pp. 295ff.

32. Frank J. Merli, *Great Britain and the Confederate Navy, 1861–1865* (Bloomington, Ind., 1970), p. 142. Merli reproduces on pages 139ff. the plans of the ironclad as made by the late Patrick Geoghegan, of the Smithsonian Institution, who showed them in the original to this writer.

33. Bulloch to North, 18 May 1862, *ORN,* Ser. 2, 2:192–93.

34. Bulloch to Mallory, 11 Apr. 1862, ibid., pp. 183ff.

35. Bulloch, *Secret Service,* 1:383.

36. Mallory to Bulloch, 30 Apr. 1862, *ORN,* Ser. 2, 2:186–87.

37. Bulloch to Mallory, 4 July 1862, ibid., p. 212. In this message Bulloch says that he had contracted for three ironclads. This three, most possibly, is an error in decoding. At any rate, the letter indicates clearly that two ships are involved.

38. Several papers relating to ships 294 and 295, Principal dimensions, Miscellaneous Papers, CLCA/LGB. These unpublished (and overlooked) records provide the correct figures regarding the dimensions and characteristics of the two ironclads. Those given by several authors (including the authoritative Merli, *Great Britain and the Confederate Navy,* p. 182, and Spencer, *Confederate Navy in Europe,* pp. 81–82) are based on *ORN,* Ser. 2, 2:222ff., which contains Bulloch's requests but not the definitive plans and therefore are less precise.

39. Description of armor plating, etc., Miscellaneous Papers, CLCA/LGB. Bulloch (*ORN,* Ser. 2, 2:224) gives the thickness of the internal bulwark as twelve inches, while the specifications herein cited set it at nine inches.

40. Specification of a pair of marine steam engines, with screw propellers, of 350 hp nominal, by English Admiralty Rule, Miscellaneous Papers, CLCA/LGB.

41. Bulloch to Mallory, 4, 21 July 1862, *ORN,* Ser. 2, 2:212, 222ff.

42. On Coles, see Sir Leslie Stephen and Sir Sidney Lee, *The Dictionary of National Biography* (London, 1960), 4:774–75; G. A. Ballard, "British Battleships of 1870: The *Monarch,*" *Mariner's Mirror* 17 (1931): 113ff.; but above all the ideas Coles himself expressed in "Shoot-proof Gun-shields as Adapted to Iron-cased Shields," *Journal of the Royal United Service Institution* 4 (June 1860): 280ff., and "The Turret versus the Broadside System," ibid. 11 (1868): 434ff.

43. *ORN,* Ser. 2, 2:226.

44. William Laird to Bulloch, 15 Oct., 4, 5 Dec. 1862, Old Letterbook, CLCA/LGB. On the last date, the final meeting as well as the signing of the contract took place.

45. Contract dated 5 Dec. 1862 between C. P. Coles and the Laird brothers, Contract Book, CLCA/LGB.

46. Mallory to Bulloch, 30 Apr. 1862, *ORN,* Ser. 2, 2:186–87.

47. Coles, "Shoot-proof Gun-shields."

48. Merli, *Great Britain and the Confederate Navy,* p. 318.

49. G. V. Fox to J. M. Forbes, 1 Apr. 1863, Gustavus Vasa Fox Papers, Naval Historical Society Collection, NHSL/NY.

50. Bulloch, *Secret Service,* 1:382ff.

51. Mallory to Bulloch, 8 Aug., 20 Sept. 1862, *ORN,* Ser. 2, 2:234–35, 270–71.

52. Mallory to Memminger, 21 Aug., 22 Sept. 1862, Treasury Department Collection of Confederate Records, Letters Received by the Confederate Secretary of the Treasury, NARG 365; Douglas B. Ball, "Confederate Finance, 1861–1865: Economic Policy Making in the South during the Civil War" (Ph.D. dissertation, University of London, 1974), p. 157.

53. Mallory to Memminger, 2 Jan. 1863, Treasury Department Collection of Confederate Records, Letters Received by the Confederate Secretary of the Treasury, NARG 365.

54. J. M. Mason to Benjamin, 18 Sept. 1862, *ORN,* Ser. 2, 3:529ff.; Mason to Mallory, 18 Sept. 1862, ibid., p. 531. The most careful analysis of how cotton certificates arrived in England is in Spencer, *Confederate Navy in Europe,* pp. 89ff.

55. Mallory to Memminger, 12 Jan. 1863, Treasury Department Collection of Confederate Records, Letters Received by the Confederate Secretary of the Treasury, NARG 365.

56. Bulloch to Mallory, 24 Sept. 1862, *ORN,* Ser. 2, 2:274ff.

57. Mallory to Bulloch, 7 May 1862, ibid., p. 191. On this subject see Douglas H. Maynard, "The Confederacy's Super *Alabama,*" *Civil War History* 5 (Mar. 1959): 8off.

58. See Spencer, *Confederate Navy in Europe,* which deals with the question at some length. In the meantime there was in England a private speculator, George N. Sanders, who had proposed to the Confederate government the organization of a line between Europe and the South by means of special armed ships. It was Sanders who first got cotton certificates in Richmond. His idea failed (and one cannot see how it might have succeeded); yet, from this Mason and Sinclair got the idea of financing shipbuilding by such certificates.

59. Maynard, "The Confederacy's Super *Alabama.*"

60. Bulloch to Mallory, 10 Sept., 7 Nov. 1862, *ORN,* Ser. 2, 2:263ff., 291ff.

61. Bulloch to Mallory, 18 Dec. 1862, ibid., pp. 309ff.; Bulloch to North, 3 Nov. 1862, ibid., pp. 289ff.; Bulloch, *Secret Service,* 1:386.

62. Mallory to Bulloch, 1 Dec. 1862, *ORN,* Ser. 2, 2:307.

63. J. Taylor Wood to Catesby ap R. Jones, 30 Aug. 1862, ibid., pp. 256–57.

64. R. D. Minor to R. Anderson, 19 Sept. 1862, Letterbook, June 1869–January 1877, Tredegar Company Records, VSA/RV.

65. Sales Book, 1 Oct. 1862, ibid.

66. George M. Brooke, Jr., "John Mercer Brooke, Naval Scientist" (Ph.D. dissertation, 2 vols., University of North Carolina, 1955), 2:867. The ship had a total of six guns. Yet J. Thomas Scharf, *History of the Confederate States Navy from Its Organization to the Surrender of Its Last Vessel* (New York, 1887), p. 727, says that the ironclad was armed with four cannons, which looks incorrect, in light of what is reported by the Tredegar Company Records, VSA/RV.

67. E. Milby Burton, *The Siege of Charleston, 1861–1865* (Columbia, S.C., 1970), pp. 124ff.; William N. Still, Jr., *Iron Afloat: The Story of the Confederate Armorclad* (1971; reprint, Columbia, S.C., 1985), pp. 8off.

68. *Charleston Daily Courier,* 11, 13 Mar., 12 May 1862.

69. Journal of the South Carolina Executive Council, passim, SCDAH/CSC.

70. Burton, *Siege of Charleston,* p. 123.

71. A. F. Warley to R. D. Minor, 27 Sept. 1862, Minor Family Papers, VHS/RV.

72. The present state of the records does not allow one to say whether the *Palmetto State* was launched or commissioned in October. Still, *Iron Afloat,* p. 82, seems inclined toward the first hypothesis; Burton, *Siege of Charleston,* pp. 125ff., toward the second. The delay in launching her was owing to the need to remove about two thousand tons of mud from the bottom of the harbor so that the ship would not ground at the moment she descended into water. See Voucher dated 23 Aug. 1862 from Charleston, Naval Collection, C.S. Navy Subject File, NARG 45.

73. J. L. Porter to J. M. Eason, 20 June 1862, in Scharf, *Confederate States Navy,* p. 671, where also are found more consistent data about the two ironclads.

74. William H. Parker, *Recollections of a Naval Officer, 1841–1865* (New York, 1883), p. 288.

75. Alfred Roman, *The Military Operations of General Beauregard in the War between the States* (New York, 1884), 2:56ff.

76. Parker, *Recollections,* pp. 293ff., gives a lively narrative of the battle. As for the official papers, see Ingraham to Mallory, 1 Feb. 1863, *ORN,* Ser. 1, 13:617ff., and Tucker to Ingraham, 31 Jan. 1863, ibid., p. 619.

77. The commanding officer of the *Mercedita,* Stellwagen, to Rear Admiral Du Pont, 31 Jan. 1863, *ORN,* Ser. 1, 13:579–80.

78. Paroling consisted of a pledge by the prisoners not to take up arms again until duly exchanged, under threat of retaliation. Paroling was frequently used by both sides throughout the Civil War, and, in general, was respected.

79. Commander Le Roy, of the *Keystone State,* to Rear Admiral Du Pont, 31 Jan. 1863, *ORN,* Ser. 1, 13:581–82; Report of losses on the said ship, ibid., p. 852.

80. Parker, *Recollections,* pp. 124ff.

81. Still, *Iron Afloat,* pp. 124ff.

82. Jacob Schirmer Diary, 31 Jan. 1863, SCHS/CSC.

83. J. Tattnall to Mallory, n.d., in Scharf, *Confederate States Navy,* p. 542.

84. Petition from forty-seven Savannah citizens to the president, 19 July 1862, and Memo from Mallory, n.d. (but July 1862), Jefferson Davis Papers, MUL/OO.

85. Dabney Minor Scales Diary, 9, 10 Dec. 1862, DUL/DNC; W. R. Taylor, C.R.P. Rodgers, R. Danby, and A. S. Mackenzie to Du Pont, 20 June 1863, *ORN,* Ser. 1, 14:273ff.

86. Ingraham to Warner, 5 Apr. 1862, James H. Warner Papers, ZB File, NHD/W; Voucher 104, 5 Apr. 1862, with the costs for executing the order, ibid.

87. Scales Diary, 11 Dec. 1862, DUL/DNC. A cadet aboard the *Atlanta* observed that the officers' quarters were so dark that they always needed candlelight (H. B. Littlepage to C. ap R. Jones, 16 Feb. 1863, *ORN,* Ser. 1, 13:819–20).

88. Scales Diary, 12 Jan., 3, 5 Feb., 20 Mar. 1863, DUL/DNC. Scales notes that the draft of water of the ship, already exorbitant, increased by two feet when sixty tons of coal were taken aboard. Sinclair to R. L. Page, 19 Apr. 1863, *ORN,* Ser. 1, 14:692.

89. Du Pont to Henry A. Wise, 16 Jan. 1863, *Samuel Francis Du Pont: A Selection from His Civil War Letters,* 3 vols., ed. John D. Hayes (Ithaca, N.Y., 1969), 3:358–59.

90. Beauregard to R. L. Page (telegram), 5 Apr. 1863, and Mallory to Page (telegram),

5 Apr. 1863, Savannah Squadron Papers, EUL/AG. Tattnall (like the other elderly man, Ingraham at Charleston) had been transferred to a land command in accordance with Mallory's policy of putting aside by instituting in a provisional navy the strict standard of seniority, opening the way to younger officers held to be more energetic. Tattnall, a strict disciplinarian, had bowed to the order, yet he had been very disappointed. See E. F. Neufville to J. I. Kolloch, 9 Feb. 1863, in "The Kolloch Letters," *Georgia Historical Quarterly* 34 (Sept. 1950); 241–43, 36–62.

91. Tattnall to Mallory, 23 Apr. 1863, in Charles C. Jones, Jr., *The Life and Services of Commodore Josiah Tattnall* (Savannah, Ga., 1878), p. 224.

92. Brooke to Page, 15 Apr. 1863, Savannah Squadron Papers, EUL/AG; List of cannons of the *Atlanta*, 2 Apr. 1863, ibid. These documents are only partially reproduced in *ORN*, Ser. 1, 14:695–96; the originals have been used here.

93. Brooke to Page, 16 Apr. 1863, Savannah Squadron Papers, EUL/AG; Brooke to Page, 9 May 1863, ibid., where Brooke announces the sending of the new gun.

94. Du Pont to Welles, 17 June 1863, *ORN*, Ser. 1, 14:263.

95. Page to Webb, 13 May 1863, Savannah Squadron Papers, EUL/AG.

96. Webb to Mallory, 15 June 1863, *ORN*, Ser. 1, 14:287. A fine expounding of the matter is in Still, *Iron Afloat*, pp. 128ff. See also Alexander Lawrence, *A Present for Mr. Lincoln: The Story of Savannah from Secession to Sherman* (Macon, Ga., 1961), pp. 121ff.

97. G. A. Mercer to I. M. Crady, 28 June 1863, Savannah Squadron Papers, EUL/AG; W. W. Gordon to General Taliaferro, 28 June 1863, ibid.

98. Webb to Mallory, 10 June 1863, *ORN*, Ser. 1, 14:710–11.

99. Webb to Mallory, 1 June 1863, ibid., p. 705; Webb to E. J. Johnston, 1 June 1863, ibid.

100. Documents on the battle are in ibid., pp. 263ff., 287ff., and 697ff.

101. Buchanan to Mitchell, 6 June 1863, John K. Mitchell Papers, VHS/RV.

102. Bulloch, *Secret Service*, 1:114ff., Clement A. Evans, ed., *Confederate Military History: A Library of Confederate States History Written by Distinguished Men of the South*, 13 vols. (1899; reprint without vol. 13, New York, 1962), 12:73.

103. John B. Jones, *A Rebel War Clerk's Diary at the Confederate States Capital*, 2 vols., 1866, New ed. by Howard Swiggett (New York, 1935), 1:353–54.

104. George Anderson Mercy Diary, 15 Mar. 1862ff., SHC/CHNC; C.F.M. Spotswood to Mitchell, 14 Apr. 1863, John K. Mitchell Papers, VHS/RV; Lawrence, *A Present for Mr. Lincoln*, p. 77.

105. Memo from Mallory, July 1862, Jefferson Davis Papers, MUL/OO.

106. R. E. Lee to G. W. Smith, 7 Sept. 1862, *OR*, Ser. 1, 19, pt. 2:599; J. F. Gilmer to Secretary of War G. W. Randolph, 10 Sept. 1862, *OR*, Ser. 1, 51, 2:616–17. Following the suggestions from such letters, which were transmitted to him, President Davis decided against the opening of the obstructions until the motive capabilities of the ironclad would be tested. For a second attempt, see Longstreet to Secretary of War Seddon, 6 Mar. 1863, *OR*, Ser. 1, 18:910; Longstreet to R. E. Lee, 27, 30 Mar., 3, 4 Apr. 1863, ibid., pp. 944, 950, 958; Seddon to Longstreet, 7 Apr. 1863, ibid., p. 967, which shows that Mallory (albeit with some prudence) was not against participating in the operation because, according to General Longstreet, there was only one enemy ironclad in Hampton Roads.

CHAPTER TWELVE

1. Dudley to Seward, 11 Dec. 1861, Records of the Department of State (Union), Consular Correspondence (Liverpool), NARG 59. The Confederates, too, kept a sharp eye on enemy activities and succeeded in unmasking several dangerous U.S. secret agents operating in Great Britain. Among these were a surgeon, a lawyer, and a preacher. See Mallory to Bulloch, 23 May 1863, C.S.A. Papers, Folder 9-A, CM/RV.

2. James D. Bulloch, *The Secret Service of the Confederate States in Europe, or, How the Confederate Cruisers Were Equipped,* 2 vols. (1884; reprint, New York, 1959), 1:152–53.

3. Bulloch to Mallory, 21 Mar. 1862, ibid., pp. 161–62. Frank Lawrence Owsley, Jr., *The C.S.S. Florida: Her Building and Operations* (Philadelphia, 1965), pp. 17ff., gives the best account of the affair. See also Warren F. Spencer, *The Confederate Navy in Europe* (University, Ala., 1983), and Frank J. Merli, *Great Britain and the Confederate Navy, 1861–1865* (Bloomington, Ind., 1970).

4. Among other works, see Spencer, *Confederate Navy in Europe,* pp. 38ff.

5. North to Mallory, 22 Feb. 1862, *ORN,* Ser. 2, 2:147; Merli, *Great Britain and the Confederate Navy,* p. 67.

6. Bulloch, *Secret Service,* 1:156ff.

7. Emma Maffitt, *The Life and Service of John Newland Maffitt* (New York, 1906), pp. 30ff. This basic book, published by the Neale Publishing Company, which specialized in Confederate writings, includes many documents not available elsewhere, particularly a portion of Maffitt's diary; therefore, together with the Maffitt Papers in SHC/CHNC, it remains the major source of information about Maffitt.

8. Bulloch to Low, 21 Mar. 1862, in Bulloch, *Secret Service,* 1:157ff.; also in *ORN,* Ser. 1, 1:756–57.

9. Bulloch to Maffitt, 21 Mar. 1862, in Bulloch, *Secret Service,* 1:159; also in *ORN,* Ser. 1, 1:757–58.

10. Low to Bulloch, 1 May 1862, in Bulloch, *Secret Service,* 1:163, also in *ORN,* Ser. 1, 1:757–58.

11. Owsley, *C.S.S. Florida,* pp. 24ff.

12. Maffitt to Mallory, 1 Aug. 1862, in Maffitt, *Maffitt,* pp. 242–43; Maffitt Diary, 7 Aug. 1862, ibid., p. 245.

13. This is the name given by Maffitt (Diary, pp. 246ff., in Maffitt, *Maffitt*) and by Bulloch, *Secret Service,* 1:167. The name *Prince Albert,* used by Owsley, *C.S.S. Florida,* is an oversight.

14. Maffitt Diary, John N. Maffitt Papers, SHC/CHNC.

15. Extracts from the journal of Lt. J. N. Maffitt (which excerpt parts of Maffitt's diary), *ORN,* Ser. 1, 1:764. Adding these extracts to what is printed in Maffitt, *Maffitt,* and to other unpublished parts in Maffitt Papers, SCH/CHNC, it is possible, as Owsley, *C.S.S. Florida,* correctly states, to reconstruct almost the whole diary.

16. Log of the *Florida,* vol. 1, Claims Commission and Court Records, Department of State (Union), NARG 76; Smooth Log of the *Florida,* written by Midshipman John A. Wilson, Naval Collection, C.S. Navy Records, NARG 45; Abstract Log of the *Florida,* partially reproduced in *ORN,* Ser. 1, 1:769ff.; Maffitt Diary, Maffitt, *Maffitt,* p. 246.

17. Maffitt Diary, Maffitt, *Maffitt,* p. 246.

18. Maffitt to Bulloch, 20 Aug. 1862, *ORN,* Ser. 1, 1:760; Maffitt, *Maffitt,* p. 246.

19. Maffitt Diary, Maffitt, *Maffitt,* pp. 246ff.

20. Extracts from the Journal of Lt. J. N. Maffitt, *ORN,* Ser. 1, 1:765.

21. Log of the *Florida,* Claims Commission, NARG 76; Maffitt Diary, Maffitt, *Maffitt,* pp. 250ff.; Extracts from the Journal of Lt. J. N. Maffitt, *ORN,* Ser. 1, 1:765ff.

22. *ORN,* Ser. 1, 1:766.

23. C. H. Hein, Confederate Agent in Havana, to Secretary of State Judah P. Benjamin, 3 Sept. 1862, ibid., pp. 760ff.; Extracts from the Journal of Lt. J. N. Maffitt, ibid., pp. 766–67; Maffitt Diary, Maffitt, *Maffitt,* pp. 250–51.

24. Log of the *Florida,* Claims Commission, NARG 76.

25. Maffitt Diary, Maffitt, *Maffitt,* pp. 253–54.

26. Ibid., p. 253.

27. Preble to Farragut, 4 Sept. 1862, *ORN,* Ser. 1, 1:432; Owsley, *C.S.S.* Florida, pp. 40ff.

28. Chief Engineer F. C. Dade to Preble, 9 Oct. 1862, *ORN,* Ser. 1, 1:444–45.

29. The best description of the short yet severe ordeal is in Maffitt Diary, Maffitt, *Maffitt,* pp. 253ff.

30. Abstract of the Log of U.S.S. *Oneida, ORN,* Ser. 1, 1:432–33. Preble was relieved following the engagement. He was then readmitted, yet full clearance for him came only after the war, thanks also to highly favorable testimony by Maffitt. The two later became warm friends.

31. Buchanan to French Forrest, 12 Sept. 1862, Admiral Buchanan's Letterbook, Franklin Buchanan Books, SHC/CHNC; Abstract of the Log of the *Florida,* Naval Collection, NARG 45.

32. Maffitt to his daughter Florie, 8 Sept. 1862, Maffitt, *Maffitt,* pp. 260–61.

33. Buchanan to Maffitt, 7 Sept. 1862, Maffitt, *Maffitt,* p. 256; Buchanan to Mallory, 8 Sept. 1862, Buchanan to Maffitt, 24 Sept. 1862, Buchanan to Mallory, 26 Sept. 1862, Admiral Buchanan's Letterbook, Buchanan Books, SHC/CHNC; Mallory to Maffitt, 8 Oct. 1862, *ORN,* Ser. 1, 1:761.

34. Maffitt Diary, Maffitt, *Maffitt,* pp. 257ff.

35. Maffitt's Journal, J. N. Maffitt Papers, SHC/CHNC.

36. Mallory to Maffitt, 25 Oct. 1862, *ORN,* Ser. 1, 1:762–63.

37. Buchanan to Farrand, 20 Nov. 1862, Admiral Buchanan's Letterbook, Buchanan Books, SHC/CHNC.

38. Maffitt Diary, Maffitt, *Maffitt,* p. 265.

39. Buchanan to Mallory, 1 Jan. 1863, Admiral Buchanan's Letterbook, Buchanan Books, SHC/CHNC.

40. Buchanan to Maffitt, 16 Jan. 1863, ibid.

41. Maffitt Diary, Maffitt, *Maffitt,* p. 266.

42. Buchanan to Maffitt, 6 Jan. 1863, Admiral Buchanan's Letterbook, Buchanan Books, SHC/CHNC.

43. Maffitt Diary, Maffitt, *Maffitt,* pp. 267–68.

44. Buchanan to Mallory, 19 Jan. 1863, Admiral Buchanan's Letterbook, Buchanan Books, SHC/CHNC.

45. C. W. Quinn, Chief Engineer of the *Florida,* Diary, CM/RV.

46. Maffitt Diary, Maffitt, *Maffitt,* pp. 267ff.

47. Bulloch, *Secret Service,* 1:225.

48. Ibid., pp. 228ff.

49. Mallory to Bulloch, 30 Apr., 3 May 1862, *ORN,* Ser. 2, 2:186–87, 190.

50. Mallory to North, 2 May 1862, ibid., p. 188.

51. Bulloch to Mallory, 19 Apr. 1862, ibid., pp. 185–86.

52. Mallory to Semmes, 29 May 1862, Correspondence, Admiral Semmes Papers, ASDAH/MA.

53. Semmes to Mallory, 20 June 1862, ibid.; Semmes to North, *ORN,* Ser. 1, 1:771.

54. Merli, *Great Britain and the Confederate Navy,* p. 89.

55. Semmes to Kell, Galt, and Howell, 9, 12 July 1862, Correspondence, Admiral Semmes Papers, ASDAH/MA.

56. Spencer, *Confederate Navy in Europe,* p. 55.

57. Wilbur D. Jones, *The Confederate Rams at Birkenhead: A Chapter in Angelo-American Relations* (Tuscaloosa, Ala., 1961), pp. 27ff.

58. According to George W. Dalzell, *The Flight from the Flag: The Continuing Effect of the Civil War upon the American Carrying Trade* (Chapel Hill, 1940), p. 131n., Bulloch's man was Victor Buckley, a clerk in the Foreign Office. Yet Dalzell does not indicate the source of his information. See also Douglas H. Maynard, "Plotting the Escape of the *Alabama,*" *Journal of Southern History* 20 (1954): 197ff.

59. The best analysis of the problem is in Merli, *Great Britain and the Confederate Navy,* passim.

60. Bulloch, *Secret Service,* 1:237ff.

61. Bulloch to Butcher, 30 July 1862, *ORN,* Ser. 1, 1:773–74.

62. Bulloch, *Secret Service,* 1:243–44. The preceding narrative is based substantially on Bulloch's recollections.

63. Bulloch to McQueen, 28 July 1862, *ORN,* Ser. 1, 1:771–72 (even though this letter was written by Bulloch, it was pro forma signed by his agent in London).

64. Bulloch to Mallory, 3 Aug. 1862, ibid., p. 775.

65. Raphael Semmes, *Memoirs of Service Afloat during the War between the States* (New York, 1869), p. 360.

66. Bulloch, *Secret Service,* 1:253.

67. Bulloch to Mallory, 11 Aug. 1862, *ORN,* Ser. 2, 2:235–36.

68. C.S.S. *Alabama* Journal, vol. 1, 20–27 Aug. 1862, Admiral Semmes Papers, ASDAH/MA; Bulloch to Mason, 1 Sept. 1862, *ORN,* Ser. 1, 1:775ff.; Bulloch to Mallory, 10 Sept. 1862, ibid., pp. 776–77.

69. Bulloch to Mallory, 10 Sept. 1862, *ORN,* Ser. 1, 1:776–77. There is a difference between Bulloch's letter to the secretary, which dates the event as 23 August, and Semmes's manuscript diary, in ASDAH/MA, which places it on the twenty-fourth. As Bulloch wrote his letter later, whereas Semmes wrote his diary daily, I have accepted the second date. See also Semmes, *Memoirs,* pp. 409ff.

70. C.S.S. *Alabama* Journal, vol. 1, Admiral Semmes Papers, ASDAH/MA, also partially reproduced in *ORN,* Ser. 1, 1:783ff.

71. Semmes to Mallory, 4 Jan. 1863, *ORN,* Ser. 1, 1:778ff. The bond was the pledge from the ship's owner to pay the Confederacy an amount of money equal to the assumed value of the ship at the end of the war. The bond system was frequently used by the Confederate raiders in cases of enemy traders carrying neutral goods or for ships left afloat to transfer to them the crews of those previously destroyed.

72. E. C. Anderson to his mother, from on board the *Alabama,* 22 Dec. 1862, Edward Clifford Anderson, Jr., Letters, G. W. and E. C. Anderson Papers, SHC/CHNC; Bulloch, *Secret Service,* 1:264ff.

73. John McIntosh Kell, *Recollections of a Naval Life, Including the Cruises of the Confederate States Steamers* Sumter *and* Alabama (Washington, D.C., 1900), p. 194.

74. C.S.S. *Alabama* Journal, vol. 1, Admiral Semmes Papers, ASDAH/MA; Semmes, *Memoirs*, pp. 472ff.

75. Semmes, *Memoirs*, p. 547.

76. Report of Commander M. C. Blake, of the *Hatteras*, 21 Jan. 1863, *ORN*, Ser. 1, 2:18ff.

77. C.S.S. *Alabama* Journal, vol. 1, Admiral Semmes Papers, ASDAH/MA.

78. Semmes to Mallory, 12 May 1863, *ORN*, Ser. 1, 2:683ff.

79. Owsley, *C.S.S.* Florida, pp. 187ff., Appendix A.

80. C. W. Read to Maffitt, 6 May 1863, *ORN*, Ser. 1, 2:644.

81. Maffitt to Read, 6 May 1863, ibid., p. 645.

82. Read to Mallory, 30 July 1863, ibid., p. 654.

83. Jim D. Hill, *Sea Dogs of the Sixties* (New York, 1961), pp. 178ff.

84. Read to Mallory, 19 Oct. 1864, *ORN*, Ser. 1, 2:655ff.

85. *ORN*, Ser. 1, 2:273ff., esp. Welles to R. Adm. S. P. Lee (telegram), 13 June 1863; Welles to Commo. C. K. Stribling (telegram), 13 June 1863; Welles to R. Adm. Paulding (telegram), 13 June 1863, as well as the answers by the addressees; "Cruise of the *Clarence, Tacony, Archer*," *SHSP*, 23:274ff.; Owsley, *C.S.S.* Florida, pp. 86ff.; Charles L. Dufour, *Nine Men in Gray* (Garden City, N.Y., 1963), pp. 142ff.

86. Maj. Andrews to U.S. Secretary of War Stanton, 27 June 1863, *ORN*, Ser. 1, 2:329; Welles to Alpheus Hardy & Co., 3 July 1863, ibid., pp. 379–80.

87. Read to Mallory, 19 Oct. 1864, ibid., pp. 655ff.

88. John Low to Barron, Mar. 1864, ibid., pp. 718–19.

89. Maffitt to Mallory, 11 May, 27 July, Sept. 1863, ibid., pp. 618ff., 652ff., 659ff.

90. Semmes to Mallory, 5 Aug. 1863, ibid., pp. 689–90.

91. The best study of the South African adventure of the *Alabama* is Edna Bradlow and Frank Bradlow, *Here Comes the* Alabama: *The Career of a Confederate Raider* (Cape Town, 1958).

92. C.S.S. *Alabama* Journal, vol. 2, Admiral Semmes Papers, ASDAH/MA.

93. Semmes to Mallory, 22 Dec. 1863, *ORN*, Ser. 1, 2:706ff.

94. C.S.S. *Alabama* Journal, vol. 2, Admiral Semmes Papers, ASDAH/MA.

95. C.S.S. *Alabama* Journal, vol. 1, ibid.

96. M. F. Maury to R. D. Minor, 21 Apr. 1863, R. D. Minor Papers, VHS/RV; Mallory to Maury, 7 Nov. 1862, *ORN*, Ser. 2, 2:295.

97. Bulloch, *Secret Service*, 2:261ff.

98. M. F. Maury to R. D. Minor, 21 Apr. 1863, Minor Papers, VHS/RV.

99. W. L. Maury to Robert Maury, 4 Jan. 1863, and to Anne Maury, 4 Jan. 1863, Maury Family Papers, UVL/CV.

100. Log of the *Georgia*, Apr. 9, 1863, to Jan. 18, 1864, C.S.A. Navy Department, CM/RV; Monthly Return, List of Prizes Captured by the C.S.S. *Georgia*, Maury Family Papers, UVL/CV; Bulloch, *Secret Service*, 2:262–63; James Morris Morgan, *Recollections of a Rebel Reefer* (Boston, 1917), passim (he served on the *Georgia*).

101. Log of the *Georgia*, C.S.A., Navy Department, CM/RV; W. L. Maury to Anne Maury, 20 May 1863, Letters, Box 147, Maury Family Papers, UVL/CV; Governor of Bahia to W. L. Maury, 13, 19 May 1863, ibid.

102. Log of the *Georgia*, C.S.A., Navy Department, CM/RV; Morgan, *Recollections of*

a Rebel Reefer, p. 163; R. Adm. G. Roze to W. L. Maury, 9 Nov., 7 Dec. 1863, Letters, Box 147, Maury Family Papers, UVL/CV; W. L. Maury to Barron, *ORN*, Ser. 1, 2:807–8.

103. W. L. Maury to Barron, 27 Dec. 1863, *ORN*, Ser. 1, 2:809.

104. C. F. Adams to Count Sclopis, 17 June 1872, Carte varie (miscellaneous papers), Fondi Aggregati, Fondo Sclopis: affare dell'*Alabama*, AS/T.

105. Dalzell, *Flight from the Flag*, pp. 237ff.

106. Adolphe Auguste Marie Lepotier, *Les Leçons de l'histoire: Les corsairs du sud et le pavillon etoilé: De l'*Alabama *à l'*Emden (Paris, 1936), on which is based much of the discussion that has preceded and that will follow.

CHAPTER THIRTEEN

1. Adolphe Auguste Marie Lepotier, *Les Leçons de l'histoire, 1861–1865: Mer contre terre* (Paris, 1945), p. 237.

2. Giambelli also built another infernal machine, of huge dimensions. By means of a small ship, he carried it against a large pontoon bridge built by the Spaniards and blew it up, almost killing their general, the Duke Alessandro Farnese, also an Italian. See Raimondo Luraghi, introductory essay to *Le Opere di Raimondo Montecuccoli*, 2 vols. (Rome, 1988), 1:66.

3. J. S. Barnes, *Submarine Warfare, Offensive and Defensive* (New York, 1869), pp. 18ff. Herein is reproduced the report by Bushnell to the American Philosophical Society, 8 June 1798.

4. Admiral Lord St. Vincent observed that a power which had command of the sea should never encourage any device that would undermine such command. See Barnes, *Submarine Warfare*, pp. 30ff.; E. Taylor Parks, "Robert Fulton and Submarine Warfare," *Military Affairs*, 24 (Winter 1961–62): 177ff.; also, for more detail, the next chapter of this book.

5. Bernard Brodie, *Sea-Power in the Machine Age* (Princeton, 1943), pp. 269–70.

6. See a long paper on torpedo warfare, n.p., n.d., in Minor Family Papers, VHS/RV., also [Victor E.K.R.] von Scheliha, *A Treatise on Coast Defense Based on the Experience Gained by the Officers of the Corps of Engineers of the Army of the Confederate States* (1868; reprint, Westport, Conn., 1971), pp. 221ff. On von Scheliha, a lieutenant colonel in the Confederate service, commanding the engineers in the Department of the Gulf of Mexico, see Ella Lonn, *Foreigners in the Confederacy* (Chapel Hill, 1940), pp. 143ff.; and Fitzgerald Ross, *Cities and Camps of the Confederate States*, ed. R. B. Harwell (Urbana, Ill., 1958).

7. The letter in which Volta notified Francesco Castelli of the experiment is in the *Epistolario di Alessandro Volta*, ed. Francesco Massardi et al., 3 vols. (Bologna, 1949–52), 1:162ff.

8. Philip K. Lundeberg, *Samuel Colt's Submarine Battery: The Secret and the Enigma* (Washington, D.C., 1974), pp. 7ff.

9. Brodie, *Sea-Power in the Machine Age*, pp. 259ff.

10. See Meriwether Stuart, "Dr. Lugo, an Austro-Venetian Adventurer in Union Espionage," *Virginia Magazine of History and Biography* 90 (July 1982): 339ff.

11. H. Davidson to Jefferson Davis, 2 Aug. 1874, with enclosure, dated May 1874, C.S.A. Navy Department, CM/RV, reproduced in *Jefferson Davis, Constitutionalist: His Letters, Papers and Speeches*, 10 vols., ed. Dunbar Rowland (Jackson, Miss., 1923), 7:387ff.

12. H. Davidson, "Electrical Torpedoes as a System of Defense," *SHSP*, 5:1ff.

13. R. O. Crowley, "The Confederate Torpedo Service," *Century Illustrated Monthly Magazine,* June 1898, pp. 290ff.

14. H. Davidson to Davis, 28 May 1867, Davis to Davidson, 3 July 1867, in *Jefferson Davis, Constitutionalist,* ed. Rowland, 7:107, 109; Lee to Davidson, 10 June 1867, Letterbook, Robert E. Lee Papers, VHS/RV.

15. Jefferson Davis, *The Rise and Fall of the Confederate Government,* 2 vols. (New York, 1881), 2:207ff.

16. J. Thomas Scharf, *History of the Confederate States Navy from Its Organization to the Surrender of Its Last Vessel* (New York, 1887), pp. 750ff.

17. Frances Leigh Williams, *Matthew Fontaine Maury: Scientist of the Sea* (New Brunswick, N.J., 1963), pp. 372ff., and p. 620, n. 4. The other biography, frequently cited, by Maury's daughter (Diana Fontaine Maury Corbin, *A Life of Matthew Fontaine Maury, U.S.N. and C.S.N.* [London, 1888]), although containing some information unavailable elsewhere, must be used with much caution because of its extreme bias in favor of Maury and because of many—and sometimes major—mistakes, as, for example, putting events of 1861 in 1862 (ibid., p. 200).

18. Even the Academy of Sciences of Turin, capital of the Kingdom of Sardinia, conferred upon him a Medal of Honor.

19. Williams, *Maury,* pp. 237ff.

20. All this comes out clearly both from the wrangle about the Naval Retiring Board and from the one with Bache and the great physicist Joseph Henry. See on this point Williams, *Maury,* passim, whose pages, even if openly and uncritically favorable to Maury, clearly show his bias and scarce propensity to understand other people's viewpoints and reasons in both cases.

21. M. F. Maury to B. Franklin Minor, 11 June 1861, Letters, Box 14, Maury Papers, LC.

22. Williams, *Maury,* pp. 572–73.

23. The first marine torpedoes "were designed in Richmond, and were first successfully used in the waters of the James river," wrote the son of M. F. Maury, Richard L. Maury, who at the time was his close collaborator (*SHSP,* 31:326ff.).

24. *Jefferson Davis, Constitutionalist,* ed. Rowland, 7:391, with a note by Isabel Maury, a daughter of M. F. Maury, dated 17 Jan. 1902, in margin to the pamphlet by Davidson.

25. An Account by Maury about Confederate Torpedoes, dated 18 Nov. 1865, Maury Papers, LC; Electrical Equipment Book, ibid.

26. See, for example, M. F. Maury to B. F. Minor, 11 Aug. 1861, as well as several others in Letters, Maury Papers, LC, which give samples of the tone used by the oceanographer regarding the secretary of the navy. See also Williams, *Maury,* pp. 380–81. The articles appeared in the *Richmond Examiner* in September and October 1861.

27. S. R. Mallory to his son "Buddy," 27 Sept. 1865, Stephen R. Mallory Diary, SHC/CHNC; Joseph T. Durkin, S.J., *Stephen R. Mallory: Confederate Navy Chief* (Chapel Hill, 1954), pp. 43–44, 85–86.

28. M. F. Maury to B. F. Minor, 2 Aug. 1861, Letters, Box 14, Maury Papers, LC; R. L. Maury, "The First Marine Torpedoes," *SHSP,* 31:326ff.

29. Maury to B. F. Minor, 8 July 1861, Letters, Box 14, Maury Papers, LC; Maury, "The First Marine Torpedoes." Two days later, on 9 July 1861, the Federals discovered the first Confederate torpedo in the Potomac (*ORN,* Ser. 1, 4:566).

30. Lundeberg, *Samuel Colt,* pp. 31ff.

31. Buchanan to R. D. Minor, 5 Oct. 1861, *ORN,* Ser. 1, 6:304a.

32. R. D. Minor to J. M. Brooke, 16 Oct. 1861, Minor Family Papers, VHS/RV; R. D. Minor to M. F. Maury, 11 Oct. 1861, *ORN,* Ser. 1, 6:304a. Another attack, also directed by Minor, was organized a little later, yet also with no results. See R. D. Minor to M. F. Maury, 21 Oct. 1861, Minor Family Papers, VHS/RV.

33. I. Brown to General Polk, from Norfolk, Virginia, 2 Aug. 1861, *ORN,* Ser. 1, 22:791; Polk to Benjamin, 10 Oct. 1861, ibid., p. 793.

34. Samuel Tate to General A. S. Johnston, 4 Nov. 1861, *OR,* Ser. 1, 4:512–13.

35. Brown to Polk, from Memphis, 4 Dec. 1861, War Department Collection of Confederate Records, Records Relative to Confederate Naval and Marine Personnel, NARG 109.

36. M. F. Maury to R. H. Maury, 11 Jan. 1862, Naval Collection, Confederate Area File 5, NARG 45.

37. Mallory to Polk, 25 Dec. 1861, and Commodore Whittle to Gwathmey, 10 Dec. 1861, ibid.

38. A. L. Saunders to Polk, 5 Dec. 1861, *ORN,* Ser. 1, 22:807.

39. Milton F. Perry, *Infernal Machines: The Story of Confederate Submarine and Mine Warfare* (Baton Rouge, 1965), p. 11.

40. Comdr. S. L. Phelps, U. S. Navy, to Flag Officer A. H. Foote, 10 Feb. 1862, *ORN,* Ser. 1, 22:571ff.

41. A. H. Foote to Welles (telegram), 4 Mar. 1862, *ORN,* Ser. 1, 22:551–52.

42. Betty Maury Diary, 8 July 1861, Maury Papers, LC.

43. Organization of the Army of Northern Virginia, 30 Apr. 1862, *OR,* Ser. 1, 11, pt. 3:479ff.

44. G. J. Rains to D. H. Hill, 14 May 1862, *OR,* Ser. 1, 11, pt. 3:516; Scharf, *Confederate States Navy,* p. 752.

45. A. P. Mason to D. H. Hill, including an extract of McClellan's report, *OR,* Ser. 1, 11, pt. 3:511.

46. Note by D. H. Hill in an exchange of letters with Rains, ibid., p. 510.

47. Aide de Camp G. Moxley Sorrel to Gen. Rains, 11 May 1862, ibid., pp. 509ff.; A. D. Mason to D. H. Hill, 12 May 1862, ibid., p. 511.

48. Note by G. W. Randolph to the correspondence re. to General Rains, ibid., p. 510.

49. Special Order 140, 18 June 1862, ibid., p. 608.

50. Opposition came from his wife. See Betty Maury Diary, 5 June 1861, Maury Papers, LC.

51. Maury to Governor Letcher of Virginia, 8 Oct. 1861, Letters, Maury Papers, LC.

52. Testimony of J. M. Brooke, *ORN,* Ser. 2, 1:785.

53. Conrad to Mallory, 9 Dec. 1861, ibid., pp. 750–51; *JC,* 1:606ff.; Naval Station, Fluvanna, Payroll, Naval Collection, C.S. Navy, Subject File X, NARG 45.

54. *ORN,* Ser. 2, 1:731–32.

55. *ORN,* Ser. 1, 7:544ff.

56. Maury to Randolph, 1 May 1862, *OR,* Ser. 1, 11, pt. 3:487. It is thus very doubtful that Maury ever used it, as held by Perry, *Infernal Machines,* pp. 14ff. Perhaps he gave it to the army, hoping that it would be used by Rains's Torpedo Bureau.

57. Mallory to Davidson, 30 June 1862, *ORN,* Ser. 1, 7:546.

58. M. F. Maury to R. D. Minor, 21 Apr. 1863, Letters, Maury Papers, LC; Mallory to Bulloch, 20 Sept. 1862, *ORN,* Ser. 2, 2:269ff.

59. Warren F. Spencer, *The Confederate Navy in Europe* (University, Ala., 1983), pp. 128ff.

60. Enlisting Articles, C.S. Naval Submarine Battery Service, *ORN*, Ser. 1, 10:11; Scharf, *Confederate States Navy,* p. 753.

61. Perry, *Infernal Machines,* p. 31.

62. G. W. Rains to W. J. Walthall, 21 June 1879, Jefferson Davis Papers, TUL/NOL.

63. See Dean Snyder, "Torpedoes for the Confederacy," *Civil War Times Illustrated* 24 (Mar. 1985): 40ff.

64. Lt. Col. Alfred L. Rives, commanding Engineers, to Generals E. Kirby Smith and J. Johnston (endorsed by the Secretary of War), 20 Aug. 1863, *OR,* Ser. 1, 27, pt. 2:173–74; Special Order, 18 Aug. 1863, by commander of the Arkansas District, *ORN,* Ser. 1, 26:190–91.

65. T. E. Courtenay to Col. Clark, 19 Jan. 1864, *ORN,* Ser. 1, 26:186–87.

66. Snyder, "Torpedoes for the Confederacy," p. 45.

67. Secretary of War Seddon to Courtenay, 9 Mar. 1864, *OR,* Ser. 4, 3:202–3; William M. Robinson, Jr., *The Confederate Privateers* (1928; reprint, Columbia, S.C., 1991), pp. 325–26.

68. This was used as a floating headquarters by General Butler. At the moment of the explosion he was aboard, together with General Schenck and Rear Admiral Porter. All aboard were rescued. See David D. Porter, *Incidents and Anecdotes of the Civil War* (New York, 1885), pp. 263ff.

69. G. V. Fox to Gen. Halleck, 5 May 1865 (telegram), *ORN,* Ser. 1, 12:135.

70. Uriel Wright to President Davis, 11 Aug. 1864, *OR,* Ser. 4, 3:580; Mallory to Secretary of War, 11 Aug. 1864, ibid., p. 581; C. Williams to President Davis, Aug. 1864, ibid., pp. 581ff.; Perry, *Infernal Machines,* pp. 130ff.

71. Maxwell to Z. McDaniel, 16 Dec. 1864, *OR,* Ser. 1, 42, pt. 1:954–55; McDaniel to General Gabriel Rains, 17 Dec. 1864, ibid., p. 956; Rains to Secretary of War, 17 Dec. 1864, ibid.; General Grant to Halleck, 9, 11 Aug. 1864, ibid., p. 17; Horace Porter, *Campaigning with Grant* (Bloomington, Ind., 1961), pp. 273–74.

72. T. H. Stevens to John Rodgers, 4 July 1862, *ORN,* Ser. 1, 7:543.

73. Payroll of C.S.S. *Torpedo,* General Records of the Department of the Treasury, NARG 56.

74. R. Anderson to T. S. Rhett, 29 Dec. 1862, Letterbook, June 1860–5 January 1877, Tredegar Company Records, VSA/RV; R. Anderson to Beauregard, 12 Jan. 1863, ibid.

75. Barnes, *Submarine Warfare,* pp. 6ff.

76. This was the Boynton-Crowley battery system; see H. Davidson to Mallory, 18 Nov. 1862, *ORN,* Ser. 1, 8:848–49.

77. H. Davidson to C. ap R. Jones, 25 Oct. 1862, *ORN,* Ser. 1, 7:60–61.

78. W. T. Jeans, *Lives of the Electricians* (London, 1887), pp. 185ff.; Barnes, *Submarine Warfare,* pp. 151ff.

79. Diaries, 17 Dec. 1864, and the French Admiral Chabannes to Maury, 10 Apr. 1865, Letters M 620A, Maury Papers, LC.

80. Pamphlet compiled by the scientist's son, ibid.

81. Davidson, "Electrical Torpedoes," pp. 1ff.

82. G. J. Rains, "Torpedoes," *SHSP,* 3:255ff.

83. G. Rains to D. H. Hill, 30 May 1863, *OR,* Ser. 1, 18:1082–83.

84. General Gabriel Rains Papers, CM/RV. For telling me about this bulky folder, in part evidently increased and reworked after the war, and for locating it, I am greatly indebted to my warm friend, Lee A. Wallace, Jr., chief historian in the National Military Park Service and a fine scholar on Confederate military history, as well as to the late Eleanor C. Brockenbrough, at the time chief librarian at the Confederate Museum, Richmond, Virginia, and another warm friend of mine. The document, found buried under a heap of newspaper clippings, is most likely in whole or in part the "book" or "manuscript" compiled by Rains and shown by him to President Davis. It is, it seems, the one that, according to Perry, *Infernal Machines,* p. 42, was supposedly lost.

85. "Torpedoes—Defensive," Rains Papers, CM/RV. The Austrians, during the siege of Venice in 1849, had made use of such an aerial fire device, albeit far less sophisticated than Rains's.

86. "Experiments," ibid.

87. "Galvano Electrical Torpedo; Magneto Electrical Torpedo; three kinds of Torpedoes," ibid.

88. "Sensitive Fuse; Several Types of Fuses," ibid.; von Scheliha, *A Treatise on Coast Defense,* pp. 231ff.

89. John B. Jones, *A Rebel War Clerk's Diary at the Confederate States Capital,* 2 vols., 1866, New ed. by Howard Swiggett (New York, 1935), 1:245. The editor confused General Gabriel J. Rains with his brother, General James E. Rains, both on page 233 of volume 1 and in the Index. Yet the diarist had clearly indicated "G. J. Rains."

90. "Notes," Rains Papers, CM/RV. It is interesting to find here the evidence that Fretwell served under Rains. See also Mallory to Ware, 20 Oct. 1863, Naval Collection, Paymaster Ware's Correspondence, NARG 45, a letter that bears witness, among other things, to the dire financial straits the torpedo service had to work under.

91. "Submarine Torpedo Mortar Battery," Rains Papers, CM/RV; Rains to the Bureau of Engineers, 8 Sept. 1863, War Department Collection of Confederate Records, NARG 109.

92. T. Jordan to Maj. Harris, 8 Dec. 1862, *OR,* Ser. 1, 14:700–701; Circular letter from Gen. R. S. Ripley, 26 Dec. 1862, ibid., pp. 732ff.

93. Isaac N. Brown, "Confederate Torpedoes in the Yazoo," *BL,* 3:580; Scharf, *Confederate States Navy,* pp. 752–53.

94. The best account of the Union operation is in Edwin C. Bearss, *Hardluck Ironclad: The Sinking and Salvaging of the* Cairo (Baton Rouge, 1966), pp. 88ff.

95. Porter to Welles, 17 Dec. 1862, *ORN,* Ser. 1, 23:544. For other records relating to the case, see ibid., pp. 544ff. See also the testimony of the captain of the *Cairo: Memoirs of Thomas O. Selfridge, Jr., Rear Admiral U.S.N.* (New York, 1924), p. 75.

96. Mallory to Ware, Naval Collection, Paymaster Ware's Correspondence, NARG 45.

97. Barnes, *Submarine Warfare,* pp. 70ff.

98. Captain Bradbury to Colonel Duff, 9 Jan. 1864, *OR,* Ser. 1, 34, pt. 2:854ff.

99. Rains to N. L. Rives, from Augusta, 1, 4 May 1863, War Department Collection of Confederate Records, Register of Letters Received, vol. 7, chap. 3, Engineer Department, NARG 109; Rains to Rives, from Charleston, 8 Sept., 5, 26 Nov. 1863, ibid.; Rains to Rives, from Mobile, 11 Mar. 1864, ibid.

100. N. L. Rives to Rains, 7 Jan. 1863, War Department Collection of Confederate Records, Engineer Department, Letters Sent, vol. 7, chap. 3, NARG 109.

101. Special Order No. 1241 of General Beauregard, 3 Dec. 1862, War Department

Collection of Confederate Records, Records Relating to Confederate Naval and Marine Personnel, Capt. Gray Papers, NARG 109. Toward the end of the war, Gray became disaffected and was put under arrest because he was suspected of trying to desert, which he himself later proved true, for he placed himself at Federal disposition after the city fell. See M. M. Gray to Rear Admiral Dahlgren, 22 Mar. 1865, *ORN,* Ser. 1, 16:378.

102. Alfred Roman, *The Military Operations of General Beauregard in the War between the States, 1861 to 1865,* 2 vols. (New York, 1884), 2:13–14.

103. G. C. De Lisle to Beauregard, 25 May 1863, *OR,* Ser. 1, 14:948ff.

104. N. L. Rives to Rains, 25 Feb. 1864, War Department Collection of Confederate Records, Letters Sent, vol. 2, chap. 3, Engineer Department, NARG 109; Chief of Staff T. Jordan to Maj. Harris, 8 Dec. 1862, *OR,* Ser. 1, 14:700–701; Roman, *Military Operations of General Beauregard,* 2:48.

105. G. J. Rains, "Torpedoes," *SHSP,* 3:255ff.

106. Report of Second Engineer Stephens, U.S. Navy, *ORN,* Ser. 1, 13:700ff.

107. Admiral Porter to Welles, 14 July 1863, *ORN,* Ser. 1, 25:282–83.

108. Contract with J. R. Fretwell to procure fifty Singer model torpedoes with forty pounds of powder each, 16 Apr. 1863, Naval Collection, Paymaster Ware's Correspondence, NARG 45; I. Brown to Fretwell, from Yazoo City (telegram), 19 June 1863, ibid.; I. Brown to Fretwell, 29 June 1863, ibid., with a request that the torpedoes be modified so as to contain thirty rather than forty pounds of powder.

109. Report of damage sustained by USS *Commodore Barney, ORN,* Ser. 1, 9:147–48.

110. F. T. Wade to G. Welles, 13 May 1864, *ORN,* Ser. 1, 10:143; H. Davidson to President Davis, 5 Dec. 1881, *SHSP,* 24:285ff.; Barnes, *Submarine Warfare,* pp. 99ff.

111. J. S. Barnes to Rear Adm. S. P. Lee, 10 May 1864, *ORN,* Ser. 1, 10:10–11.

112. Barnes, *Submarine Warfare,* pp. 231ff.

113. "The Circumventor of the Devil," Rains Papers, CM/RV.

114. Mallory's opinion reported by H. Davidson, *SHSP,* 24:286.

115. G. J. Rains, "Torpedoes," *SHSP,* 257ff.; Davis, *Rise and Fall,* 2:220; Scharf, *Confederate States Navy,* p. 768; Perry, *Infernal Machines,* pp. 199ff.

CHAPTER FOURTEEN

1. W. H. Dickinson, *Robert Fulton, Engineer and Artist: His Life and Works* (London, 1913).

2. E. Taylor Parks, "Robert Fulton and Submarine Warfare," *Military Affairs* 24 (Winter 1961–62): 117ff.

3. J. S. Barnes, *Submarine Warfare, Offensive and Defensive* (New York, 1869) pp. 30–31.

4. It is impossible to determine whether Fulton's boat was a true *submarine* or a *submersible.* The first is an underwater boat that can also sail on the surface, whereas the second is a surface boat that can submerge. Therefore, the submarine can easily sail while submerged but is unseaworthy when on the surface, whereas the contrary is true for the submersible. From a hydrostatic viewpoint, a submarine is a vessel whose ratio between displacement in immersion and displacement in emersion is minor or equal to 1.1. A submersible is one in which the ratio oscillates between 1.3 and 1.5. A truly satisfactory submarine (in the scientific sense of the word) was built only after World War II, when propulsive power went nuclear, following experiments made by the Germans toward the end of the conflict. World Wars I and II were fought exclusively with fleet submarines

that sailed (and attacked) mainly on the surface, using diving primarily to escape the enemy. At the beginning the distinction was not clear and inventors initially focused mainly on submarines, which consequently, like the Confederate *Hunley,* when on the surface, were unseaworthy. For Fulton's test see Parks, "Robert Fulton," p. 178.

5. Cyril Field, *The Story of the Submarine* (London, 1908), pp. 62ff.

6. Parks, "Robert Fulton," pp. 179, 181–82.

7. "La Navigation sous-marine," *Cahiers de Salorges,* no. 15 (n.d.): 31ff. Herein is reproduced an article that appeared in the *Annales de la Société Royale Académique de Nantes et de la Loire Inférieure* 13 (1832): 338.

8. Naval History Division, *The Submarine in the United States Navy* (Washington, D.C., 1969), p. 6.

9. L. M. Goldsborough to Comdr. William Smith, 27 Oct. 1861, *ORN,* Ser. 1, 6:353.

10. Allan Pinkerton, *The Spy of the Rebellion: Being a True History of the Spy System of the United States during the Late Rebellion* (New York, 1883), pp. 395–96.

11. Milton F. Perry, *Infernal Machines: The Story of Confederate Submarine and Mine Warfare* (Baton Rouge, 1965), p. 93.

12. W. R. Anderson to W. G. Cheeney, 26 Nov. 1862, Sales Book, 1836–1900, pp. viii–4, Tredegar Company Records, VSA/RV; see also the authoritative witness [Victor E.K.R.] von Scheliha, *A Treatise on Coast Defense Based on the Experience Gained by Officers of the Corps of Engineers of the Army of the Confederate States* (1868; reprint, Westport, Conn., 1971), p. 300n.

13. W. R. Anderson to W. G. Cheeney, 13 May 1862, Sales Book, 1836–1900, pp. viii–4, Tredegar Company Records, VSA/RV.

14. General E.R.S. Canby to U.S. Secretary of the Navy, G. Welles, 18 Jan. 1864, *ORN,* Ser. 1, 6:411ff., with enclosures from which it is learned that the seizure of the Southern mail occurred on 22 November 1863. The submarine designs are also herein: Major Jackson, U.S. Army, to Lt. Col. C. R. Christensen, 13 Mar. 1865, *ORN,* Ser. 1, 22:103ff.

15. Biographical data on Hunley and McClintock in Eustace Williams Collection, Miscellaneous Papers, SHC/CHNC.

16. William M. Robinson, Jr., *The Confederate Privateers* (1928; reprint, Columbia, S.C., 1991), p. 167.

17. The commander of the *Pioneer,* John K. Scott, to the Confederate Secretary of State, n.d. (but 29 Mar. 1862), *ORN,* Ser. 2, 1:399–400.

18. Perry, *Infernal Machines,* p. 95.

19. F. H. Hatch to J. P. Benjamin, 1 Apr. 1862, with enclosures, *ORN,* Ser. 2, 1:399–400.

20. W. A. Alexander, "Thrilling Chapter in the History of the Confederate States Navy: Work on Submarine Boats," *SHSP,* 30:164ff.

21. J. R. McClintock to M. F. Maury, n.d., Letters, Box 46, Maury Papers, LC. This letter was written several years after the war, probably in 1870–71, according to Robinson, *Confederate Privateers,* p. 171.

22. Buchanan to Mallory, 14 Feb. 1863, Admiral Buchanan's Letterbook, Franklin Buchanan Books, SHC/CHNC.

23. Buchanan to Mallory, 3 Mar. 1863, ibid.

24. Alexander, "Thrilling Chapter," pp. 164–65.

25. Buchanan to Mallory, 14 Feb. 1863, Admiral Buchanan's Letterbook, Buchanan

Books, SHC/CHNC; Description of submarines, Miscellaneous Papers, Williams Collection, ibid.

26. Information obtained from questioning deserters from the enemy, *ORN*, Ser. 1, 15:227–28; Alexander, "Thrilling Chapter," p. 164.

27. Alexander, "Thrilling Chapter," pp. 165ff.

28. Harry von Kolnitz, "The Confederate Submarine," *U.S. Naval Institute Proceedings* 43 (Oct. 1937): 1453ff.

29. Characteristics of submarines, Miscellaneous Papers, Williams Collection, SHC/CHNC.

30. Buchanan to Mallory, 3 Mar. 1863, Admiral Buchanan's Letterbook, Buchanan Books, SHC/CHNC.

31. P.G.T. Beauregard, "Torpedo Service in Charleston Harbor," *AW,* pp. 513ff.

32. Beauregard to "Quartermasters and Railroad Agents on Lines from Charleston, S.Ca., to Mobile, Ala.," 7 Aug. 1863, *OR*, Ser. 1, 29, pt. 2:265.

33. H. S. Hunley to J. R. McClintock, 15 Aug. 1863, Horace S. Hunley Papers, Williams Collection, SHC/CHNC.

34. Chief of Staff T. Jordan to B. A. Whitney, 15 Aug. 1863, *OR*, Ser. 1, 27, pt. 2:285.

35. Alexander, "Thrilling Chapters"; Comment, Miscellaneous Papers, Williams Collection, SHC/CHNC.

36. Alexander, "Thrilling Chapter," pp. 164ff.

37. Narration, Williams Collection, SHC/CHNC.

38. Alexander, "Thrilling Chapter," passim.

39. Beauregard to Flag Officer Tucker, 17 Oct. 1863, including a request for help to refloat the *Hunley,* James H. Rochelle Papers, DUL/DNC; Extract from Journal of Operations, kept at Confederate Headquarters, Charleston, S.C., 15 Oct. 1863, *ORN*, Ser. 1, 15:692; Beauregard, "Torpedo Service," pp. 513ff.

40. Perry, *Infernal Machines,* p. 102.

41. C. L. Stanton, "Submarines and Torpedo Boats," *Confederate Veteran* 3, No. 9 (1914): 398.

42. Alexander, "Thrilling Chapter," pp. 171–72.

43. Special Order 271, 14 Dec. 1863, *OR*, Ser. 1, 28, 2:553.

44. Alexander, "Thrilling Chapter," p. 172.

45. George E. Dixon to Capt. John F. Cothran, 5 Feb. 1864, Letters, Williams Collection, SHC/CHNC.

46. Lt. F. J. Higginson to R. Adm. Dahlgren, 18 Feb. 1864, *ORN*, Ser. 1, 15:328; Report of the Commission of Inquiry on the sinking of the *Housatonic,* 7 Mar. 1864, ibid., pp. 332–33.

47. Report by Lt. Col. G. M. Dantzler, Commanding battery on Sullivan's Island, 19 Feb. 1864, ibid., p. 335.

48. Footnote by Gen. Beauregard, 20 Feb. 1864, ibid., p. 336.

49. Beauregard to Adj. Gen. Cooper, 21, 27 Feb. 1864 (telegrams), ibid.

50. H. W. Felden to H. J. Leary, 10 Mar. 1864, ibid., p. 337; Capt. M. M. Gray of the Torpedo Bureau to Gen. Dabney H. Maury, 29 Apr. 1864, ibid., pp. 337–38.

51. Comment, Williams Collection, SHC/CHNC.

52. R. Adm. Dahlgren to Capt. S. C. Rowan, 19 Feb. 1864, *ORN*, Ser. 1, 15:338.

53. Beauregard, "Torpedo Service," p. 516.

54. Capt. Francis D. Lee to Aide de Camp Thomas Jordan, 22 Oct. 1862, *OR*, Ser. 1, 14:648. For the slow beginning, see a statement by F. D. Lee in Beauregard, "Torpedo Service," p. 517.

55. Beauregard to Mallory, 31 Oct. 1862, *OR*, Ser. 1, 14:661.

56. F. D. Lee to T. Jordan, 8 Nov. 1862, ibid., pp. 670–71.

57. F. D. Lee to Commodore Ingraham, two letters, 8 Nov. 1862, ibid., pp. 671–72; Ingraham to F. D. Lee, 8 Nov. 1862, ibid.

58. F. D. Lee to T. Jordan, 16 Dec. 1862, 6, 28 Jan. 1863, ibid., pp. 1018–19.

59. F. D. Lee to T. Jordan, 25 Mar. 1863, ibid., pp. 843–44.

60. Beauregard to the Secretary of War, 26 Mar. 1863, ibid., p. 844.

61. F. D. Lee to T. Jordan, 11 July 1863, *OR*, Ser. 1, 28, pt. 2:191.

62. Statement of Capt. F. D. Lee in Beauregard, "Torpedo Service," pp. 513ff.

63. Carlin to Beauregard, 22 Aug. 1863, *ORN*, Ser. 1, 14:498–99; Beauregard to Carlin, 23 Aug. 1863, ibid., p. 500.

64. Capt. S. C. Rowan, commanding the *New Ironsides,* to R. Adm. Dahlgren, 28 Aug. 1863, ibid., p. 497; Ens. B. H. Porter to Capt. Rowan, 28 Aug. 1863, ibid., p. 498; Extract from log book of the *New Ironsides,* ibid.

65. Beauregard, "Torpedo Service," p. 217; Herbert Ravenal Sass, "The Story of the Little *David,*" *Harper's Magazine* 186 (1943): 620ff.

66. See the letter from F. D. Lee to A.N.T. Beauregard, aide-de-camp to the general, 25 July 1863, cited in E. Milby Burton, *The Siege of Charleston, 1861–1865* (Columbia, S.C., 1970), p. 213; also David C. Ebaugh, "David C. Ebaugh on the Building of the *David,*" *South Carolina Historical Magazine* 54 (Jan. 1964): 322ff. Ebaugh claims, in a letter dated 4 Oct. 1862 and there enclosed, to have made the original draft of the torpedo boat.

67. A very accurate design of the torpedo boat found in von Scheliha, *Treatise on Coast Defense,* following p. 300.

68. On the assault boats of the Royal Italian Navy, suffice it to cite Virgilio Spigai, *100 Uomini contro due flotte* (Livorno, 1954); Ufficio Storico della Marina Militare, *La Marina Italiana nella Seconda Guerra Mondiale,* vol. 14, *I Mezzi d'assalto* (Rome, 1972; a new revised and enriched edition is forthcoming).

69. William T. Glassel, "Reminiscences of Torpedo Service in Charleston Harbor," *SHSP,* 14:225–26; John Johnson, *The Defense of Charleston Harbor Including Fort Sumter and the Adjacent Islands* (Charleston, 1890), pp. xxxi ff.; Beauregard, "Torpedo Service," pp. 517–18; Burton, *Siege of Charleston,* pp. 219ff.

70. W. T. Muse to Glassel, 6 Sept. 1863, *ORN,* Ser. 1, 15:11; J. W. Otey to Glassel, 18 Sept. 1863, ibid. When he was deck officer on the ironclad *Chicora,* Glassel had seen the assault boat *Torch* and became very interested in her. He had also participated in a failed attempt to attack enemy ships with torpedoes carried by oared boats. Transferred to the ironclad *North Carolina* at Wilmington, he applied to be sent back to Charleston to assume voluntary command of the *David* (Burton, *Siege of Charleston,* pp. 219ff.).

71. James H. Tombs, "Memoirs," Naval Collection, C.S.N. Subject File A, NARG 45; Flag Officer J. R. Tucker to Glassel, 22 Sept. 1863, *ORN,* Ser. 1, 15:12.

72. Glassel, "Reminiscences of Torpedo Service," p. 230.

73. Beauregard, "Torpedo Service," p. 518.

74. Glassel, "Reminiscences of Torpedo Service," pp. 230–31.

75. Glassel, "Reminiscences of Torpedo Service," pp. 231ff.; Captain Rowan, commanding the *New Ironsides,* to R. Adm. Dahlgren, 6 Oct. 1863, *ORN,* Ser. 1, 15:13.

76. I have mainly followed here Glassel's clear account, "Reminiscences of Torpedo Service." See also Report of Secretary Mallory, 30 Nov. 1863, *ORN*, Ser. 1, 15:19; Beauregard to Adj. Gen. Cooper, 6 Oct. 1863, Flag Officer J. F. Tucker to Gen. Beauregard, 6 Oct. 1863, and Chief Engineer Tombs to Flag Officer Tucker, 6 Oct. 1863, ibid.

77. Charles C. Jones, Jr., to Eva Eve, Charles C. Jones Papers, UGL/AG; Beauregard, "Torpedo Service," p. 518.

78. U.S.N. Carpenter T. H. Bishop to Captain Rowan, 24 Nov. 1863, *ORN*, Ser. 1, 15:17–18.

79. R. Adm. Dahlgren to Welles, 30 Nov. 1863, ibid., p. 17; Rowan to Dahlgren, 28 Nov. 1863, ibid.; Extract from the Diary of R. Adm. Dahlgren, 18 Nov. 1863, ibid., pp. 18–19.

80. The powerful British battleships were, in effect, sunk; yet the shallow water enabled their decks to remain clear; later it was possible to raise and repair them. See (among other sources) Marco A. Bragadin, *Che ha fatto la marina?* (Milan, 1955), pp. 191ff.

81. Beauregard, "Torpedo Service," p. 519; Augustine T. Smythe, "Torpedo and Submarine Attacks on the Federal Blockading Fleet off Charleston during the War of the Secession," *1907 Year Book* (Charleston, S.C., 1907), pp. 53ff.

82. Extract of notebook of J. H. Tombs, *ORN*, Ser. 1, 15:358–59; also J. H. Tombs, Memoirs, Naval Collection, C.S. Navy Subject File A, NARG 45.

83. F. D. Lee to Gen. T. Jordan, 8 Mar. 1864, *ORN*, Ser. 1, 15:358.

84. Burton, *Siege of Charleston,* p. 227.

85. The two were of Italian origin; the former captain of the Austro-Hungarian navy Luigi Contri (or Conti?) and Dr. Orazio Lugo de Antonzini (Antongini?), born near Venice and also serving in the imperial Habsburg armed forces. See Meriwether Stuart, "Dr. Lugo: An Austro-Venetian Adventurer in Union Espionage," *Virginia Magazine of History and Biography* 90 (July 1982): 339ff. Also the letter by Stuart to this writer, now in my private archive.

86. Francis D. Lee to Capt. A.N.T. Beauregard, 15 Oct. 1863, *OR*, Ser. 1, 28, pt. 2:420; General Beauregard to T. Stoney, 25 Nov. 1863, ibid., p. 525.

87. T. Stoney to Gen. T. Jordan, 26 Jan. 1864, *OR*, Ser. 1, 35, pt. 1:546.

88. Lt. Col. A. L. Rives to Capt. F. D. Lee, 27 Jan. 1864, *OR*, Ser. 1, 35, pt. 1:548–49.

89. E. Gotheil, Superintendent of the Iron Works of the Corps of Engineers at Savannah, to Flag Officer W. W. Hunter, 31 Aug. 1864, Savannah Squadron Papers, EUL/AG; Flag Officer J. R. Tucker to W. W. Hunter, 18 Mar. 1864, *ORN*, Ser. 1, 15:718.

90. Memo by John A. Curtis, n.d., C.S. Navy Papers, VSA/RV; Mallory to Chief Engineer Henry A. Wright, 10 June 1864, Marsden Bellamy Papers, SHC/CHNC; H. Davidson to Mallory, 11, 15 Apr. 1864, *ORN*, Ser. 1, 9:603; U.S. Captain Gansevoort to R. Adm. S. P. Lee, 12 Apr. 1864, ibid., pp. 599–600.

91. Mallory to Bulloch, 16 Apr., 18 July 1864, *ORN*, Ser. 2, 2:627–28, 688–89.

92. Bulloch to Mallory, 26 Jan. 1865, ibid., pp. 790–91.

93. R. Adm. Dahlgren to Commodore G. S. Blake, 27 May 1865, *ORN*, Ser. 1, 16:339.

94. *ORN*, Ser. 1, 15:passim.

95. Dahlgren to Welles, 12 Oct. 1863, ibid., p. 16.

96. Dahlgren to G. V. Fox, 7 Oct. 1863, *ORN*, Ser. 1, 16:13ff. The message was labeled "confidential," and in it the rear admiral made several schematic drafts of the torpedo boat, going so far as to submit a first summary plan for building such boats.

CHAPTER FIFTEEN

1. Bulloch to Mallory, 23 Jan. 1863, *ORN,* Ser. 2, 2:344ff.

2. Slidell to Secretary of State Benjamin, 23 Jan. 1863, with memorandum of colloquy, *ORN,* Ser. 2, 3:572ff.

3. James D. Bulloch, *The Secret Service of the Confederate States in Europe, or, How the Confederate Cruisers Were Equipped,* 2 vols. (1884; reprint, New York, 1959), 2:22.

4. Slidell to Benjamin, 11 Jan. 1863, *ORN,* Ser. 2, 3:638–39.

5. Memminger to Mallory, 5 Jan. 1863, Treasury Department press copies, War Department Collection of Confederate Records, NARG 109.

6. Slidell to Benjamin, 28 Oct. 1862, *ORN,* Ser. 2, 3:569ff.

7. Benjamin to Slidell, 15 Jan. 1863, ibid., pp. 564ff.

8. L.Q.C. Lamar to Benjamin, 20 Mar. 1863, ibid., pp. 716ff.

9. Douglas B. Ball, "Confederate War Finance, 1861–1865: Economic Policy Making in the South during the Civil War" (Ph.D. dissertation, University of London, 1974), p. 172. John Schwab, *The Confederate States of America, 1861–1865: A Financial and Industrial History of the South during the Civil War* (New York, 1901), p. 35, calculates that the Confederacy did not bank more than £500,000. Ball's figure appears to be more accurate.

10. Memminger to Mallory, 11 Apr. 1863, *ORN,* Ser. 2, 2:400.

11. Mallory to Memminger, 3 Apr. 1863, Treasury Department Collection, Letters Received by the Confederate Secretary of the Treasury, NARG 365.

12. Mallory to Memminger, 23 Apr., 22 May 1863, with enclosure of the secret bill and its amendments, ibid.

13. Comptroller's Contracts, order dated 16 May 1863, with "Erlanger" annotated in the margin, ibid.

14. Bulloch, *Secret Service,* 2:25ff.

15. Chasseloup-Laubat to Arman, 6 June 1863, BB4 1345 I, "Voruz et Arman concernant les navires construits à Nantes et Bordeaux," AMV.

16. H. Hotze to Benjamin, 14 May 1863, *ORN,* Ser. 2, 3:767ff.; Bulloch to McRae, 10 Aug. 1863, Treasury Department Collection, Comptroller's Contracts, NARG 365; Charles S. Davis, *Colin J. McRae; Confederate Financial Agent* (Tuscaloosa, Ala., 1961), p. 35; Bulloch, *Secret Service,* 2:28.

17. Arman to J. Voruz, 10 June 1863, BB4 1345 I, "Voruz et Arman," AMV.

18. Mallory to Memminger, 5 June 1863, Treasury Department Collection, Letters Received by the Confederate Secretary of the Treasury, NARG 365.

19. Mallory to Bulloch, 7 May, 6 June 1863, *ORN,* Ser. 2, 2:416ff., 417ff.

20. Mallory to Memminger, 5 June 1863, Treasury Department Collection, Letters Received by the Confederate Secretary of the Treasury, NARG 365.

21. Bulloch to Mallory, 8 July 1863, *ORN,* Ser. 2, 2:452ff.

22. Bulloch to Mallory, 9 July 1863, ibid., pp. 455ff.

23. J. Voruz to his son, 14 July 1863, ibid., pp. 462–63; Bulloch, *Secret Service,* 2:32ff. The first man who tried to have ironclads for the Confederacy built in France had been M. F. Maury, who for that purpose had many and complicated contacts with Arman, Slidell, and others. On the tangled story (from which, in the end, nothing came) see Warren F. Spencer, *The Confederate Navy in Europe* (University, Ala., 1983), pp. 155ff.

24. Arman-Bulloch Contract, 16 July 1863, BB4 1345 I, AMV.

25. Mallory to Memminger, 30 July, 13 Aug. 1863, Treasury Department Collection, Letters Received by the Confederate Secretary of the Treasury, NARG 365.

26. Spencer, *Confederate Navy in Europe*, pp. 153ff.

27. Mallory to Barron, 30 Aug. 1863, Samuel Barron Papers, WM/W, also in *ORN*, Ser. 2, 2:485ff.

28. The matter is clearly discussed by Wilbur D. Jones, *The Confederate Rams at Birkenhead: A Chapter in Anglo-American Relations* (Tuscaloosa, Ala., 1961).

29. Frank J. Merli, *Great Britain and the Confederate Navy, 1861–1865* (Bloomington, Ind., 1970), pp. 101ff.

30. Bulloch, *Secret Service,* 1:330–31. At Richmond it was obvious that she was a warship: the navy had even detailed her commanding officer, Lieutenant John R. Hamilton. See Mallory to Bulloch, 8 Oct. 1862, *ORN,* Ser. 2, 2:280; Bulloch to Fraser, Trenholm & Co., 24 Nov. 1862, ibid., p. 302.

31. Bulloch to Mallory, 16 May 1863, *ORN,* Ser. 2, 2:423ff.

32. The *Alexandra* was never returned to the Confederates because the British government, by a series of claims, still held her up to April 1864. Thereafter used as a blockade runner, she was seized in the Bahamas, again by British authorities. See Spencer, *Confederate Navy in Europe,* p. 103.

33. Bulloch to Mallory, 30 June 1863, *ORN,* Ser. 2, 2:444ff.

34. Lord Cowley to Lord Russell, 24 Aug. 1863, Foreign Office 5, France, PRO/L.

35. Secretary of Foreign Affairs to Home Office, 1 Sept. 1863, ibid.

36. C. F. Adams to Lord Russell, 5 Sept. 1863, Foreign Office 5/1000, PRO/L.

37. Jones, *Confederate Rams,* pp. 67ff.

38. Bulloch to Mallory, 20 Oct. 1863, *ORN,* Ser. 2, 2:507ff.

39. Bulloch to Mallory, 13 May 1864, ibid., pp. 653ff. The two ironclads were commissioned in the Royal Navy with the names *Scorpion* and *Wivern* and served for many years. One ended her career in Bermuda, the other in Hong Kong.

40. North to Mallory, 14 Dec. 1863, 18 Feb. 1864, ibid., pp. 566, 587; Merli, *Great Britain and the Confederate Navy,* pp. 154ff. The ironclad, christened *Denmark,* was launched with difficulty because of her bulk and proved to be speedy, logging twelve knots. The Royal Danish Navy altered her several times. She was scrapped in 1907. See Merli, *Great Britain and the Confederate Navy,* pp. 315–16, nn. 44, 46, and 49. As for the *Canton* (also known by her cover name of *Pampero*), see Douglas H. Maynard, "The Confederacy's Super *Alabama,*" *Civil War History* 5 (Mar. 1959): 80ff.

41. General Order, 1 Nov. 1863, by which Barron assumed command of a squadron on the Atlantic Ocean, General Records of the Department of State, C.S. Navy, NARG 59; Diary of Commodore Barron, *ORN,* Ser. 2, 2:813ff.

42. McRae to Mallory, 1 Aug. 1862, Naval Collection, Letterbook 1, Selma Foundry Papers, NARG 45.

43. Emil Newman to his sister, 11 Jan. 1863, Newman Family Papers, Special Collections, RUL/HT; Howard C. Westwood, "The Battle of Galveston," *U.S. Naval Institute Proceedings* 109 (Jan. 1983): 49ff.

44. Mallory to J.D.B. De Bow, 19 Aug. 1862, James D. B. De Bow Papers, DUL/DNC; Mallory to Secretary of War G. W. Randolph, 24 Sept. 1862, *ORN,* Ser. 1, 19:78–79.

45. Mallory to I. N. Brown, 23 Sept. 1862, Naval Collection, C.S. Navy, Confederate Area File 5, NARG 45; J. E. Fiske to J. Comstock, 24 July 1862, John H. Comstock Papers, SHC/CHNC.

46. Mallory to naval agents Weldon and McFarland, 16 Sept. 1862, Naval Collection, C.S. Navy, Confederate Area File 5, NARG 45; Paymaster Taylor to Mallory, 13 Nov. 1862, 23 Jan. 1863, ibid., Confederate Subject File A.

47. Mallory to J. H. Carter, Naval Collection, C.S. Navy, Confederate Area File 5, NARG 45.

48. Contract with Constructors R. Moore and J. Smoker, 1 Nov. 1862, Treasury Department Collection, Comptroller's Contracts, NARG 365.

49. Mallory to Barron, 20 Oct. 1862; French Forrest to Barron, 6 Oct. 1862, Samuel Barron Papers, WM/W. Both letters are also in *ORN,* Ser. 1, 23:703ff.

50. Barron to E. C. Minor, 20 Oct. 1862, Naval Collection, Confederate Area File 5, NARG 45; Barron to Mallory, 30 Oct. 1862, *ORN,* Ser. 1, 23:705.

51. H. K. Stevens to Lt. McCarrick, 4 Nov. 1862; Carter to John Roy, 17 Apr. 1863, Naval Collection, C.S. Navy, Confederate Area File 5, NARG 45.

52. Major Brent to General Stevenson, 24 Feb. 1863, ibid.

53. W. F. Brand, "The Capture of the *Indianola,*" *Maryland Historical Magazine* 4 (1909): 353ff.

54. Edwin C. Bearss, *The Campaign for Vicksburg,* 3 vols. (Dayton, Ohio, 1985–86), 1:625ff.

55. Albert T. Jones to Lynch, 4 Sept. 1862; G. Minor to A. T. Jones, 27 Sept. 1862, Shelby Iron Company Papers, UAL/TA.

56. William R. Hunt to J. A. Wall, 14 Mar. 1863, ibid.

57. I. Brown to General Pemberton, 9 Dec. 1862, *OR,* Ser. 1, 17, pt. 2:788. The matter is thoroughly discussed in William N. Still, Jr., *Iron Afloat: The Story of the Confederate Armorclad* (1971; reprint, Columbia, S.C., 1985), pp. 143ff., and, with more detail, in "The Confederate Ironclad *Missouri,*" *Louisiana Studies* 4 (Summer 1965): 107ff.

58. J. H. Carter to Gen. M. L. Smith, 28 Jan. 1863, War Department Collection of Confederate Records, Records Relating to Confederate Naval and Marine Personnel, NARG 109; Carter to Mallory, 1 Feb. 1863, Naval Collection, Jonathan H. Carter Correspondence, NARG 45.

59. Carter to Paymaster Nixon, 6 Feb. 1863, and Carter to J. M. Waskam, 11 Feb. 1863, Naval Collection, Carter Correspondence, NARG 45.

60. Carter to Mallory, 1 Apr. 1863, ibid.

61. Ironclad Plans, Bureau of Ships, NARG 19; A. M. Jackson to Gen. Hurlbut, 14 Apr. 1865, *ORN,* Ser. 1, 27:142. The Federals who captured her stated that she carried one 11-inch and two 6-inch guns. J. Thomas Scharf, *History of the Confederate States Navy from Its Organization to the Surrender of Its Last Vessel* (New York, 1887), p. 530, says four guns because in addition to the 11- and 9-inch the ironclad had "two heavy 36 pounders." I have followed the date given by Still, *Iron Afloat,* p. 148, which is usually authoritative, even though no documentation is provided.

62. J. R. Anderson to Mallory, 25, 31 Mar. 1863, Letterbook, Tredegar Company Records, VSA/RV.

63. Commo. Lynch to Secretary of War Seddon, 26 Jan. 1863, *ORN,* Ser. 1, 8:856–57.

64. Mallory to Lynch, 2 Oct. 1862, ZB File, William F. Lynch Papers, NHD/W.

65. G. Elliott to Vance, 27 Jan. 1864, Governor Vance Papers, NCDAH/RNC. The matter is well analyzed in Still, *Iron Afloat,* pp. 150ff.

66. John G. Barrett, *The Civil War in North Carolina* (Chapel Hill, 1963), pp. 182ff. A

good biography of Vance is Glenn Tucker, *Zeb Vance: Champion of Personal Freedom* (Indianapolis, Ind., 1965).

67. Lynch to Vance, 14 May 1863, Governor Vance Letterbook 2, NCDAH/RNC.

68. Mallory to Davis, 30 Nov. 1863, *ORN*, Ser. 2, 2:588ff.

69. Barrett, *Civil War in North Carolina*, pp. 129–30; James M. Merrill, *The Rebel Shore: The Story of Union Sea Power in the Civil War* (Boston, 1957), p. 102.

70. William N. Still, Jr., "The Career of the Confederate Ironclad *Neuse*," *North Carolina Historical Review* 43 (June 1966): 1ff.

71. Contract with Martin and Elliott, 17 Sept. 1862, Treasury Department Collection, Comptroller's Contracts, NARG 365.

72. Martin and Elliott to Mallory, 10 Oct. 1862, William Francis Martin Papers, SHC/CHNC.

73. Contract, 1 Dec. 1862, with Martin and Elliott of Elizabeth City, N.C., for the construction within a year of an ironclad, Treasury Department Collection, Comptroller's Contracts, NARG 365. Mallory anticipated the launching for 31 March 1863.

74. J. G. Porter to General Halleck, 27 Dec. 1862, *OR*, Ser. 1, 18:68ff.; Major Garrard to Col. J. Mix, 17 Dec. 1862, ibid., p. 69.

75. Barrett, *Civil War in North Carolina*, pp. 144ff.; Still, *Iron Afloat*, p. 156.

76. Gen. J. G. Foster to Halleck, 24 July 1863, *OR*, Ser. 1, 27, pt. 2:963–64; Gen. E. E. Potter to Col. S. Hoffman, 28 July 1863, ibid., pp. 964ff. The distress and panic caused by the raiders is well depicted by Catherine Ann Devereux Edmondston, *Journal of a Secesh Lady: The Diary of Catherine Ann Devereux Edmondston*, ed. Beth Gilbert Crabtree and James W. Patton (Raleigh, N.C., 1979), pp. 436ff. She adds that the enemy at Tarboro destroyed not only the hull of the gunboat but also the timber collected there.

77. Lee to President Davis, 20 Jan. 1864, *OR*, Ser. 1, 33:1101–2.

78. Mallory to Randolph, 28 Oct. 1862, *ORN*, Ser. 1, 8:843.

79. Randolph to Mallory, 29 Oct. 1862, ibid., p. 814.

80. J. W. Cooke to Martin and Elliott, Martin Papers, SHC/CHNC; Mallory to Vance, 4 Nov. 1862, *ORN*, Ser. 1, 8:814.

81. *The Papers of Zebulon Baird Vance*, ed. Frontis W. Johnson (Raleigh, N.C., 1963–), 1:306n; Gilbert Elliott, "The Confederate Ram *Albemarle*: Her Construction and Service," in Walter Clark, ed., *Histories of the Several Regiments and Battalions from North Carolina in the Great War, 1861–1865*, 5 vols. (Goldsboro, N.C., 1901), 5:315ff. On Cooke, see Edmondston, *Journal of a Secesh Lady*, pp. 421ff.

82. Vance to Mallory, 21 Nov. 1862, *ORN*, Ser. 1, 8:845–46.

83. J. T. Wood to Mallory, 14 Feb. 1863, ibid., pp. 859–60.

84. Mallory to Vance, 23 June 1863, with copy of letter from Cooke to Mallory, Governor Vance Letterbook 2, NCDAH/RNC.

85. Lynch to Vance, 14 May 1863; the governor's aide-de-camp to W. Gwynn, 18 May 1863, ibid.

86. Elliott, "Confederate Ram *Albemarle*," p. 315; Scharf, *Confederate States Navy*, pp. 402ff.; Edmondston, *Journal of a Secesh Lady*, p. 446.

87. Mallory to J. L. Porter, 14 Oct. 1863, ZB File, John Luke Porter Papers, NHD/W; Elliott, "Confederate Ram *Albemarle*," p. 316. The date of launching can be deduced from Edmondston, *Journal of a Secesh Lady*, pp. 473–74, which describes the complicated launching.

88. Mallory's Report to President Davis, 30 Nov. 1863, *ORN,* Ser. 1, 9:797ff.

89. Contract dated 16 Oct. 1862 with F. M. Jones for the construction of an ironclad's hull and the application of the armor, at a cost of $120,000, Treasury Department Collection, Comptroller's Contracts, NARG 365. Scharf, *Confederate States Navy,* p. 671, says that the contract was signed with J. M. Eason, who evidently should provide engines, fitting out, and the like.

90. Scharf, *Confederate States Navy,* p. 671. Much of the money needed to build the ironclad was once again contributed by Charleston's women.

91. Alexander Lawrence, *A Present for Mr. Lincoln: The Story of Savannah from Secession to Sherman* (Macon, Ga., 1961), pp. 128–29.

92. Biographical Data, Henry F. Willinck Papers, EUL/AG.

93. Contract dated 2 Nov. 1862 for two gunboats, to cost $36,000; Mallory to Willinck, 14 Jan. 1862, ibid.

94. Mallory to Willinck, 11 Aug. 1862, ibid.

95. Contract dated 13 Sept. 1862, with H. F. Willinck, Treasury Department Collection, Comptroller's Contracts, NARG 365.

96. Because of the industrial inadequacy of the South, the *Milledgeville* could not be launched until 21 December 1864 and, still unfinished, would be scuttled, so as not to fall into enemy hands when the Federals took Savannah.

97. J. L. Porter to Willinck, 11 Aug. 1862, Willinck Papers, EUL/AG.

98. Warner to Tattnall, 6 Nov. 1862, J. H. Warner Letterbook, CNM/CG. On 3 March 1863 Warner mailed Tattnall the invoice for the engines (ibid.).

99. J. M. Brent to Willinck, 22 July 1862; Willinck to Brent, 23 July 1862, Willinck Papers, EUL/AG.

100. William N. Still, Jr., *Savannah Squadron* (Savannah, Ga., 1989), p. 8.

101. Tattnall (commanding the Naval Station) to W. W. Hunter, 30 June 1863, Savannah Squadron Papers, EUL/AG.

102. Hunter to Tattnall, 30 June 1863, Hunter to Mallory, 30 June 1863, *ORN,* Ser. 1, 14:713–14.

103. Tattnall to Conrad, 3 Feb. 1864, *ORN,* Ser. 1, 15:708–9.

104. Commander of the ironclad, J. R. Pinkney, to Hunter, 3 Aug. 1863; Hunter's letter, dated 4 Aug., to appoint a commission of inquiry, and report from such commission on the same date, Savannah Squadron Papers, EUL/AG.

105. Warner to Hunter, 7, 22 Aug. (telegram) 1863, ibid.

106. John E. Johns, *Florida during the Civil War* (Gainesville, Fla., 1963), p. 72.

107. Comdr. G. U. Morris to R. Adm. T. Bailey, commanding the West Gulf Blockading Squadron, 24 Apr. 1863, *ORN,* Ser. 1, 17:421.

108. G. W. Gift to his wife, 18 Apr. 1863, George W. Gift Letters, SHC/CHNC; McLaughlin to Mallory, 26 Jan. 1864, A. McLaughlin Letterbook, CNM/CG.

109. A. McLaughlin to C. ap R. Jones, 16 June, 26 Dec. 1863, *ORN,* Ser. 1, 17:869–70.

110. Governor Shorter to Mallory, 1 May 1862, Governor Shorter Papers, ASDAH/MA.

111. Charles C. Simms to C. ap R. Jones, 20 Mar. 1864, *ORN,* Ser. 1, 21:885–86.

112. McRae to Mallory, 8 Apr. 1862, Colin J. McRae Papers, ASDAH/MA.

113. McRae to Mallory, 15 Apr. 1862, ibid.

114. Contract with H. D. Bassett, 1 May 1862, Treasury Department Collection, Comptroller's Contracts, NARG 365.

115. Still, *Iron Afloat,* p. 194.

116. Buchanan to R. D. Minor, 4 Jan. 1862, Minor Family Papers, VHS/RV; Buchanan to Mallory, 13 May 1862, Buchanan to French Forrest, 26 May, 3 June 1862, Admiral Buchanan's Letterbook, Franklin Buchanan Books, SHC/CHNC.

117. Buchanan to French Forrest, 12 Sept. 1862, Admiral Buchanan's Letterbook, Buchanan Books, SHC/CHNC.

118. Mallory to Acting Naval Constructor W. Waggner, 26 June 1862, with the order to report to Selma and hasten the construction to the utmost, Naval Collection, C.S. Navy, Confederate Area File 6, NARG 45.

119. Mallory to Farrand, 1 Aug. 1862, ZB File, NHD/W; Mallory to Warner, 2 Aug. 1862, Warner Papers, CNM/CG. Until that time Farrand had commanded the seacoast batteries at Drewry's Bluff, Virginia, where he had in 1862 repulsed the attempted attack by Northern ironclads against Richmond.

120. Mallory to Farrand, 2 Sept. 1862, Naval Collection, C.S. Navy, Confederate Area File 6, NARG 45.

121. Contract dated 16 Sept. 1862 with P. E. Montgomery and A. Anderson (for the *Nashville*). Completion was anticipated by 30 May 1863, at a cost of $660,872, with an advance of $50,000. The deadline could not be met. The contract for the *Tennessee* (and for a twin that could never be commissioned because the launching was bad) was made with Bassett. Several other contracts were also closed with S. D. Porter and J. M. Watson for two large ironclads 160 feet long and a third 180 feet long, to be built at Owens Bluff, on the Tombigbee River. None was completed (Treasury Department Collection, Comptroller's Contracts, NARG 365).

122. The name really should be the *Tennessee II,* the first one being the twin to the *Arkansas,* laid down at Memphis and never completed. Yet because the Memphis one never was commissioned, it is usual to designate as the *Tennessee* the vessel built at Selma.

123. Buchanan to Mallory, 26 Sept., 6 Oct. 1862, Admiral Buchanan's Letterbook, Buchanan Books, SHC/CHNC.

124. Buchanan to G. Minor, 9 Oct. 1862; Buchanan to Farrand, 11 Oct. 1862, ibid.

125. Buchanan to Mallory, 15 Oct. 1862, with attached letter from Farrand, ibid.

126. Buchanan to E. H. Edwards, 27 Oct. 1862, Buchanan to Farrand, 15 Nov. 1862, ibid.

127. Buchanan to Mitchell, 20 Nov. 1862, Buchanan to Farrand, 20 Nov. 1862, ibid.

128. Buchanan to Farrand, 26 Nov. 1862, ibid.

129. Buchanan to I. Brown, 9 Feb. 1863, ibid.

130. Buchanan to Mallory, 6 Apr., 13 May 1863, ibid.

131. Buchanan to Mallory, 26 Nov. 1862, 19 Jan., 25 May 1863, Buchanan to Farrand, 19 Dec. 1862, Buchanan to Mitchell, 8 Apr., 3 July 1863, Buchanan to Surgeon General Spotswood, 8 Sept. 1863, ibid.

132. William N. Still, Jr., "Selma and the Confederate States Navy," *Alabama Review* 15 (Jan. 1962): 19–20; Still, *Iron Afloat*, pp. 192–93.

133. Buchanan to Farrand, 23 May 1863, Admiral Buchanan's Letterbook, Buchanan Books, SHC/CHNC; Farrand to Fisher, 6 May, 13 Apr., 1 June 1863, Naval Collection, C.S. Navy, Confederate Subject File A, NARG 45.

134. Buchanan to Mallory, 27 July 1863, Admiral Buchanan's Letterbook, Buchanan Books, SHC/CHNC; Ethel Armes, *The Story of Coal and Iron in Alabama* (1910; reprint, New York, 1973), p. 145. Captain Johnston, who commanded the *Tennessee,* credits the providing of the armor to the Atlanta Rolling Mill. See J. D. Johnston, "The Ram *Tennes-*

see at Mobile Bay," *BL,* 4:40ff. The truth lies somewhere in between because most of the iron came from Alabama and was then rolled in Atlanta. See McRae to Harris, 11 Oct. 1862, Colin J. McRae Papers, ASDAH/MA.

135. Buchanan to Mallory, 21 Oct. 1863, Admiral Buchanan's Letterbook, Buchanan Books, SHC/CHNC.

136. Buchanan to Mitchell, 11 Dec. 1863, John K. Mitchell Papers, VHS/RV.

137. C. ap R. Jones to Buchanan, 17 Dec. 1863, Naval Collection, Selma Foundry Papers, Letterbook vol. 3, NARG 45.

CHAPTER SIXTEEN

1. Richard I. Lester, *Confederate Finance and Purchasing in Great Britain* (Charlottesville, Va., 1975), p. 49.

2. Louise B. Hill, *State Socialism in the Confederate States of America* (Charlottesville, Va., 1936), p. 9; Samuel Bernard Thompson, *Confederate Purchasing Operations Abroad* (Chapel Hill, 1935), passim.

3. Frank L. Owsley, *King Cotton Diplomacy: Foreign Relations of the Confederate States of America,* 2d ed., rev. by Harriet Chappel Owsley (Chicago, 1959), p. 369. The text comes from the Confederate newspaper in London, the *Index.* About its able editor, Henry Hotze, see Charles P. Cullop, *Confederate Propaganda in Europe, 1861–1865* (Coral Gables, Fla., 1969).

4. Thomas E. Taylor, *Running the Blockade: A Personal Narrative of Adventures, Risks and Escapes during the American Civil War,* new ed. (London, 1912), pp. 10ff.; E. Merton Coulter, *The Confederate States of America, 1861–1865* (Baton Rouge, 1950), pp. 250ff.

5. James D. Bulloch, *The Secret Service of the Confederate States in Europe, or, How the Confederate Cruisers Were Equipped,* 2 vols. (1884; reprint, New York, 1959), 2:234; Raimondo Luraghi, *The Rise and Fall of the Plantation South* (New York, 1978), pp. 134–35.

6. Bulloch, *Secret Service,* 2:224ff.

7. Luraghi, *Rise and Fall of the Plantation South,* p. 134. The name *Ad-Vance* meant either an honor to the governor's wife (Adelaide Vance) or the audacity of the enterprise.

8. Hill, *State Socialism,* p. 12.

9. Benjamin to Mallory, Memminger, and Seddon, 15 Sept. 1863 (with signatures of approval by the three addressees), C.S.A. Archives, Department of State, LC.

10. *OR,* Ser. 4, 3:78ff., 80ff.

11. Luraghi, *Rise and Fall of the Plantation South,* pp. 135ff.

12. Lester, *Confederate Finance,* p. 49.

13. Bulloch to Mallory, 16 Sept. 1864, *ORN,* Ser. 2, 2:723ff.

14. Accounts of cotton shipped to various ports, Papers of George A. Trenholm, Box 1, LC. In his report to the president, dated 10 Dec. 1864, Secretary of War Seddon gave a slightly higher figure: 27,299 bales (13,649,500 pounds) valued at $5,296,006. See *OR,* Ser. 4, 3:928ff.

15. Secretary of the Treasury Trenholm to President Davis, 12 Dec. 1864, *OR,* Ser. 4, 3:953ff.

16. Seddon to Davis, 10 Dec. 1864, ibid., pp. 928ff. Unfortunately, I could not make use of the excellent book by Stephen R. Wise, *Lifeline of the Confederacy: Blockade Running*

during the Civil War (Columbia, S.C., 1988), because this chapter had already been written when I received the book. It seems, however, that Wise's work confirms with more and complete data my conclusions here.

17. E.T.S. Nepveux, *George Alfred Trenholm* (Charleston, S.C., 1973), pp. 85ff.

18. Richard D. Goff, *Confederate Supply* (Durham, N.C., 1969), p. 247.

19. *The Diary of Gideon Welles,* 3 vols., ed. H. K. Beale and A. W. Brownsword (New York, 1960), 2:127.

20. Charles W. Quinn, *Florida's* Chief Engineer, Diary, CM/RV.

21. Frank L. Owsley, Jr., *The C.S.S.* Florida: *Her Building and Operations* (Philadelphia, 1965), p. 103.

22. See Lynn M. Case and Warren F. Spencer, *The United States and France: Civil War Diplomacy* (Philadelphia, 1970), pp. 436ff. About Trémont (who, it seems, was called Pesterman), see ibid., p. 669, n. 32. It seems hard to believe that he was a "patriot" (as the U.S. diplomats said), mainly because of the large monetary reward he asked for "to cover his expenses" (ibid., p. 439).

23. John Bigelow, *France and the Confederate Navy, 1862–1868: An International Episode* (New York, 1888), pp. 1ff, which prints many of the documents consigned by the informer.

24. Drouyn de Lhuys to Chasseloup-Laubat, 25 Sept., 12 Oct. 1863, Voruz to Chasseloup-Laubat, 16 Oct. 1863, Arman to Chasseloup-Laubat, 16 Oct. 1863, BB 4 1345 I, AMV, in which he claimed that the documents produced by Dayton were false and asked authorization to proceed with the work on the sloops (yet not to put weapons on board).

25. Drouyn de Lhuys to Chasseloup-Laubat, 16 Oct. 1863, ibid., in which he asks that weapons not be put on the sloops.

26. Bulloch to Mallory, 18 Feb. 1864, *ORN,* Ser. 2, 2:588ff.

27. Mallory to Col. W. H. Stevens, 10 Mar. 1864, *ORN,* Ser. 1, 9:802; Commo. French Forrest to Lt. Comdr. M. T. Clark, 22 Mar. 1864, ibid.; Ordnance Report of C.S.S. *Virginia,* James River Squadron, 26 May 1864, Minor Family Papers, VHS/RV.

28. Unfortunately, the *Texas* was never put into commission. Launched in January 1865, she was still being fitted out when Richmond fell into enemy hands. Her hull was considered to be among the best ever built in the Confederacy. See Naval History Division, *Civil War Naval Chronology, 1861–1865,* 6 vols. (Washington, D.C., 1961–65), 6:314.

29. *Memoirs of Thomas O. Selfridge, Jr., Rear Admiral U.S.N.* (New York, 1924), pp. 68–69.

30. For the military events on the Virginia front in 1864 see Raimondo Luraghi, *Storia della Guerra Civile Americana,* 5th ed., rev. (Milan, 1986), pp. 965ff.

31. Acting Rear Adm. S. P. Lee to Welles, 7 June 1864, *ORN,* Ser. 1, 10:129; William H. Parker, *Recollections of a Naval Officer, 1841–1865* (New York, 1883), pp. 334ff.

32. Mallory to Mitchell, 6 May 1864, *ORN,* Ser. 1, 10:625; Mallory to Secretary of War Seddon, 7 May 1864, ibid., p. 628; Mitchell to Mallory, 11, 16 May 1864, ibid., p. 639.

33. Maj. G. Williams to Mason, 1 Mar., 18 May 1864; Stevens to General Bragg, 17 May 1864, Charles T. Mason Papers, VHS/RV. All these papers highlight the problems the Corps of Engineers faced in clearing the obstructions. See Mallory to Seddon, 19 May 1864, *OR,* Ser. 1, 51, pt. 2:946–47.

34. Mitchell to Mallory, 24 May, 20 June 1864, *ORN,* Ser. 1, 10:653, 704–5.

35. T. R. Rootes, interim commander of the C.S. Squadron, to J. C. Minor, 21 Nov. 1864, Minor Family Papers, VHS/RV; Mitchell to Mallory, 22 Nov. 1864, *ORN*, Ser. 1, 10:588–89.

36. Flag Officer Tucker to Rochelle, 16 Dec. 1863, James H. Rochelle Papers, DUL/DNC; Report of the Secretary of the Navy, 16 Dec. 1863, *ORN*, Ser. 1, 15:697; Tucker to W. G. Dozier, 27 Jan. 1864, ibid., p. 705.

37. Report of the Secretary of the Navy, 30 Apr. 1864, *ORN*, Ser. 1, 15:732–33.

38. Buchanan to Mallory, 20 Sept. 1863, Admiral Buchanan's Letterbook, Franklin Buchanan Books, SHC/CHNC.

39. G. W. Gift to his wife, 19 June 1863, George W. Gift Letters, SHC/CHNC.

40. Buchanan to C. ap R. Jones, 15 Dec. 1863, *ORN*, Ser. 1, 20:856–57. Buchanan was prepared for this. See Buchanan to Mallory, 31 Aug. 1863, Admiral Buchanan's Letterbook, Buchanan Books, SHC/CHNC.

41. Mallory's Report to the President, *ORN*, Ser. 2, 2:630ff.

42. Buchanan to Mallory, 18 Nov. 1863, Admiral Buchanan's Letterbook, Buchanan Books, SHC/CHNC.

43. William N. Still, Jr., in his authoritative *Iron Afloat: The Story of the Confederate Armorclad* (1971; reprint, Columbia, S.C., 1985), questions whether all the *Tennessee*'s guns came from Selma. But see C. ap R. Jones to Brooke, 6, 11, 31 Jan. 1864, Naval Collection, Selma Foundry Papers, NARG 45 (the last letter mentions the delivery of the fourth gun). The Foundry Book, ibid., also noted the delivery of other guns: two on 17 February, one on 27 February, one on 6 March, and one on 7 March. In addition, the foundry sent fifty-three shells and ninety-two 7-inch shots. Last see Lt. Eggleston to C. ap R. Jones, 26 Jan. 1864, and Buchanan to C. ap R. Jones, 30 Jan. 1864, *ORN*, Ser. 1, 21:870–71. Buchanan stated that on 26 January all the guns had been mounted on the *Tennessee;* see Buchanan to Mitchell, 26 Jan. 1864, J. K. Mitchell Papers, VHS/RV. Evidently, however (as Still also surmises) as soon as the Selma guns came in, they were mounted in place of others, perhaps put on provisionally. See also the testimony of the commanding officer of the *Tennessee,* James D. Johnston, in *BL,* 4:401ff. Today the *Tennessee* guns are in the Washington Navy Yard Museum, where I inspected them and noted that they are marked with an "S," the mark of the Selma Naval Foundry.

44. Buchanan to Mitchell, 26 Jan. 1864, J. K. Mitchell Papers, VHS/RV.

45. Buchanan to C. ap R. Jones, 30 Jan. 1864, *ORN*, Ser. 1, 21:871–72.

46. Secretary of War Seddon to Gen. D. H. Maury (telegram), 23 Feb. 1864, ibid., p. 879; Buchanan to Gen. Polk, 1 Apr. 1864, with a letter from Commodore Mitchell, ibid., pp. 889–90.

47. Buchanan to Mitchell, 11 Mar. 1864, Mitchell Papers, VHS/RV.

48. Buchanan to Mitchell, 13 Mar. 1864, ibid.

49. Buchanan to C. ap R. Jones, 29 Apr. 1864, *ORN*, Ser. 1, 21:895; Diary of John C. O'Connell, Assistant Engineer of the *Tennessee,* printed in C. Carter Smith, Jr., ed., *Two Naval Journals, 1864, at the Battle of Mobile Bay* (Chicago, 1964), p. 1.

50. O'Connell's Diary in Smith, ed., *Two Naval Journals;* J. D. Johnston, "The Ram *Tennessee,*" *BL,* 4:401ff.

51. Farragut to his family, 8 Aug. 1864, in *The Life of David Glasgow Farragut First Admiral of the United States Navy, Embodying His Journal and Letters,* ed. Loyall Farragut (New York, 1879), p. 429; Alfred Thayer Mahan, *The Gulf and Inland Waters* (New York, 1883), p. 221.

52. Mahan, *The Gulf and Inland Waters,* pp. 221ff.; Ethel Armes, *The Story of Coal and Iron in Alabama* (1910; reprint, New York, 1973), pp. 145ff.

53. J. R. Eggleston to C. ap R. Jones, 26 Jan. 1864, *ORN,* Ser. 1, 21:870–71.

54. Buchanan to J. D. Johnston, 30 July 1864, *ORN,* Ser. 1, 21:909.

55. J. Thomas Scharf, *History of the Confederate States Navy from Its Organization to the Surrender of Its Last Vessel* (New York, 1887), pp. 389ff.

56. General R. E. Lee to President Davis, 2 Jan. 1864, *OR,* Ser. 1, 33:1061.

57. Mallory to Cooke, 15 Jan. 1864, *ORN,* Ser. 1, 9:799–800.

58. J. T. Wood to C. ap R. Jones, 26 Feb. 1864, ibid., p. 800.

59. R. D. Minor to Mallory, 16 Feb. 1864, R. D. Minor Papers, VHS/RV.

60. B. P. Loyall to R. D. Minor, 7 Apr. 1864, ibid.

61. R. D. Bacot to his sister, 19 Mar. 1864, Richard D. Bacot Papers, NCDAH/RNC.

62. General Pickett, commanding the North Carolina Department, to Adjutant General Samuel Cooper, 15 Feb. 1864, *OR,* Ser. 1, 33:92ff.

63. R. D. Bacot to his sister, 19 Mar. 1864, Bacot Papers, NCDAH/RNC.

64. Bragg to Hoke, 12 Apr. 1864, *OR,* Ser. 1, 51, pt. 2:320.

65. No report from the Confederates has been found. Apart from the number and names of the brigades, their effective strength is hard to calculate. Yet the average for a Confederate brigade was about fifteen hundred men who would have to be increased by a regiment of cavalry and one of artillery. The number of seven thousand men and thirty to forty guns is probably an underestimate. The best accounts of the Confederate military campaign against Plymouth are D. H. Hill, Jr., "North Carolina," in *Confederate Military History,* 4:222ff., and John W. Graham, "The Capture of Plymouth," in Walter Clark, ed., *Histories of the Several Regiments and Battalions from North Carolina in the Great War, 1861–1865,* 5 vols. (Goldsboro, N.C., 1901), 5:175ff.

66. The exact number is 2,834. See *OR,* Ser. 1, 33:301.

67. Graham, "Capture of Plymouth," pp. 176ff.

68. Gilbert Elliott, "The Confederate Ram *Albemarle:* Her Construction and Service," in Clark, ed., *Histories of the Several Regiments,* 5:315ff.

69. Hill, "North Carolina," pp. 223ff.

70. Memorial on the Construction of the *Albemarle,* Peter Evans Smith Papers, SHC/CHNC.

71. Catherine Ann Devereux Edmondston, *Journal of a Secesh Lady: The Diary of Catherine Ann Devereux Edmondston,* ed. Beth Gilbert Crabtree and James W. Patton (Raleigh, N.C., 1979), p. 446; Elliott, "Confederate Ram *Albemarle,*" pp. 315ff.

72. Hill, "North Carolina," pp. 222ff.

73. John W. Graham to his father, 24 Apr. 1864, William Alexander Graham Papers, SHC/CHNC; J. W. Graham, "Capture of Plymouth," in Clark, ed., *Histories of the Several Regiments,* 5:177.

74. J. W. Graham to his father, 29 Apr. 1864, Graham Papers, SHC/CHNC.

75. Graham, "Capture of Plymouth," p. 180.

76. Comm. Flusser to Davenport, 17 Apr. 1864, *ORN,* Ser. 1, 9:634–35.

77. Cooke to Mallory, 23 Apr. 1864, ibid., pp. 656–57. This is the most reliable account of the battle because it was written on the spot. Gilbert Elliott, in his essay "Confederate Ram *Albemarle,*" says that the ironclad got under way on the morning of the eighteenth. The disagreement is perhaps trifling because the whole night of 17–18 April was lost because of the need to repair damage.

78. Cooke to Mallory, 23 Apr. 1864, *ORN,* Ser. 1, 9:636–37.

79. Scharf, *Confederate States Navy,* p. 405.

80. Elliott, "Confederate Ram *Albemarle,*" p. 319; Gilbert Elliott, "The First Battle of the Confederate Ram *Albemarle,*" *BL,* 4:625ff.; Cooke to Mallory, 23 Apr. 1864, *ORN,* Ser. 1, 9:626ff.

81. Elliott, "Confederate Ram *Albemarle,*" pp. 319–20.

82. The account of the battle and of the following action of the *Albemarle* is best given by Cooke's report, *ORN,* Ser. 1, 9:656ff.; by Elliott, "Confederate Ram *Albemarle*"; by Graham, "Capture of Plymouth"; and in Graham's letter to his father of 24 Apr. 1864, Graham Papers, SHC/CHNC.

83. General Wessels to General Peck, 18 Aug. 1864, *OR,* Ser. 1, 33:296ff.

84. J. T. Wood to President Davis, 21 Apr. 1864, *ORN,* Ser. 1, 9:658; Extract from Mallory's report, 30 Apr. 1864, ibid.; List of Union losses, *OR,* Ser. 1, 33:301.

85. Gen. John T. Peck to see Gen. Butler, 25 Apr. 1864, *OR,* Ser. 1, 33:287ff.

86. Resolution of thanks by the Confederate Congress, *ORN,* Ser. 1, 9:658. See Edmondston, *Journal of a Secesh Lady,* pp. 550ff., for the exultation of Confederate people, not only in Richmond.

87. Abstract of events in the Pamlico subdistrict, Apr. 1864, *OR,* Ser. 1, 33:312.

88. Bragg to Beauregard, 22 Apr. 1864, in Alfred Roman, *The Military Operations of General Beauregard in the War between the States, 1861 to 1865,* 2 vols. (New York, 1884), 2:539; R. D. Bacot, Notebook with sketches of the *Neuse,* Bacot Papers, SHC/CHNC.

89. Personal note by President Davis at the end of a letter by Bragg to Beauregard, 28 Apr. 1864, in Roman, *Military Operations of General Beauregard,* 2:197.

90. Beauregard to Bragg, 23, 24 Apr. 1864, *ORN,* Ser. 1, 9:807–8. Still, in *Iron Afloat,* p. 162, says that the *Neuse* weighed anchors on 27 April, a date which appears logical but does not agree with the records cited. See also William N. Still, Jr., "The Career of the Confederate Ironclad *Neuse,*" *North Carolina Historical Review* 43 (Jan. 1966): 1ff., n. 43.

91. Adjutant General Samuel Cooper to Beauregard, 15 Apr. 1864 (telegram), Bragg to Beauregard, 23 Apr. 1864, in Roman, *Military Operations of General Beauregard,* 2:539ff.; also Edmondston, *Journal of a Secesh Lady,* p. 551.

92. Beauregard to Hoke, 1 May 1864, *OR,* Ser. 1, 51, pt. 2:882ff.

93. James C. Long to Sarah McKay, 30 May 1864, McKay and Stiles Family Papers, SHC/CHNC; Report by a deserter from the *Albemarle, ORN,* Ser. 1, 9:768ff.

94. G. V. Fox to Ericsson, 22 Apr. 1864, *ORN,* Ser. 1, 9:683.

95. G. V. Fox to R. Adm. S. P. Lee, 23 Apr. 1864 (telegram), ibid.

96. Scharf, *Confederate States Navy,* pp. 411ff.; *ORN,* Ser. 2, 1:54ff.

97. Captain Smith operation's order, *ORN,* Ser. 1, 9:735–36.

98. The distance can be calculated from the battle plan in *BL,* 4:630.

99. Narrative of the fight between the *Sassacus* and the *Albemarle,* in which the commanding officer of the first ship states that before the battle he had ordered that a wall be constructed to separate the two boilers so the explosion of one did not involve the other or the ship would have sunk (F. A. Roe Collection, Box 144m, NHF/W).

100. Edmondston, *Journal of a Secesh Lady,* pp. 556, 560.

101. Davis to Beauregard, 4 May 1864 (telegram), in Roman, *Military Operations of General Beauregard,* 2:547.

102. F. D. Graham, "Fifty-sixth Regiment," in Clark, ed., *Histories of the General Regiments,* 3:349ff.

103. Beauregard to Davis, 4 May 1864 (telegram), in Roman, *Military Operations of General Beauregard*, 2:547; Beauregard to Hoke, 5 May 1864, 12 noon (telegram), ibid., pp. 547–48. General Bragg's order was to leave half a regiment at Washington, North Carolina, and at Plymouth, or practically nothing. See Bragg to Beauregard, 5 May 1864, ibid., p. 547.

104. John G. Barrett, *The Civil War in North Carolina* (Chapel Hill, 1963), p. 227.

105. Report of the Court of Inquiry on the loss of C.S.S. *Raleigh*, *ORN*, Ser. 1, 10:24–25.

106. J. R. Randall to his fiancée, 3 June 1864, James Ryder Randall Papers, SHC/CHNC.

107. There are no official Confederate records on this episode except the report of the court of inquiry, which concludes by ascribing the accident to the flimsy structure of the vessel. The very interesting Union records, on which this narrative is based, are in *ORN*, Ser. 1, 10:18ff.

108. Lt. J. B. Cushing to Welles, 21 May 1864, *ORN*, Ser. 1, 10:77.

109. R. Adm. S. P. Lee to Welles, 21 June 1864, ibid., pp. 176ff.

CHAPTER SEVENTEEN

1. J. Thomas Scharf, *History of the Confederate States Navy from Its Organization to the Surrender of Its Last Vessel* (New York, 1887), p. 718.

2. J. T. Wood to C. ap R. Jones, 30 Aug. 1862, *ORN*, Ser. 2, 2:256–57.

3. Royce G. Shingleton, *John Taylor Wood: Sea Ghost of the Confederacy* (Athens, Ga., 1979), p. 62.

4. Adolphe Auguste Marie Lepotier, *Les Leçons de l'histoire: Les corsaires du Sud et le Pavillon Etoilé, 1861–1865, de l'*Alabama *à l'*Emden (Paris, 1936), p. 190.

5. Scharf, *Confederate States Navy*, p. 122, n. 2.

6. Wood to his wife, Lola, 3, 5, 6 Oct. 1862, John Taylor Wood Papers, SHC/CHNC; U.S. Commodore Harwood to Secretary Welles, 10 Oct. 1862, with the report from Acting Master T. P. Ives of 8 Oct. 1862, *ORN*, Ser. 1, 5:118; Commo. Harwood to Comdr. Magaw, 25 Oct. 1862, ibid., p. 119.

7. Scharf, *Confederate States Navy*, p. 719, who, by mistake, gives the date as 28 November; Acting Master N. Provost to Commo. Harwood, 29 Oct. 1862, *ORN*, Ser. 1, 5:137–38.

8. Commo. Harwood to Secretary Welles, 5 Nov. 1862, *ORN*, Ser. 1, 5:138–39; Welles to Harwood, 17 Nov. 1862, ibid., pp. 140–41.

9. Shingleton, *John Taylor Wood*, p. 69.

10. Wood to Hoge, 7 July 1863, *ORN*, Ser. 1, 9:80.

11. President Davis to General Lee, 16 Sept. 1863, *OR*, Ser. 1, 29, pt. 2:725–26; Scharf, *Confederate States Navy*, p. 122.

12. Shingleton, *John Taylor Wood*, pp. 74–75.

13. Welles to Commo. Harwood, 25 July 1863, with enclosure, *ORN*, Ser. 1, 5:310; Harwood to Welles, 25 July 1863, with his plan for countering the attack, ibid.

14. Wood initially had a skirmish with enemy naval explorers at the mouth of the Piankatank River, then, throughout the night, he sailed uselessly up and down Chesapeake Bay seeking enemy ships. He finally moved to a new base along the Rappahannock River. See Shingleton, *John Taylor Wood*, pp. 75–76.

15. Rosser to H. C. Lee, 5 Sept. 1863, *OR*, Ser. 1, 29, 1:76ff.

16. *ORN,* Ser. 2, 1:190, 202; Scharf, *Confederate States Navy,* p. 122; Shingleton, *John Taylor Wood,* pp. 79ff.

17. Sommers to Welles, 8 Sept. 1863, *ORN,* Ser. 1, 5:332. The surrender was speeded up by the cowardice of Captain Robinson, who shut himself in his stateroom. For the proceedings of the court-martial held on the officers of the two ships, see ibid., pp. 335ff.

18. Wood to Mallory, 25 Aug. 1863, with detailed report enclosed, *ORN,* Ser. 1, 5:344–45.

19. J. McCabe to Welles, 25 Sept. 1863, *ORN,* Ser. 1, 5:344; President Davis to Mrs. Wood, 25 Aug. 1863, Wood Papers, SHC/CHNC; Scharf, *Confederate States Navy,* pp. 124ff.

20. Wood to his wife (telegram), 27 Aug. 1863, Wood Papers, SHC/CHNC; Scharf, *Confederate States Navy,* pp. 126–27.

21. Mallory to Hoge, 21 Sept. 1863, *ORN,* Ser. 1, 9:180.

22. J. H. Crawford, "John Yates Beall, Gallant Soldier," *SHSP,* 33:71; John W. Headley, *Confederate Operations in Canada and New York* (New York, 1906), pp. 241ff. This book is possibly the best source about Beall.

23. Scharf, *Confederate States Navy,* p. 719.

24. U.S. Commander Gansevoort to General Foster, 28 Sept. 1863, *OR,* Ser. 1, 29:138–39; Scharf, *Confederate States Navy,* p. 720; Headley, *Confederate Operations,* pp. 245ff.

25. General Lockwood to General Schenck, 15 Nov. 1863 (telegram), and Gen. Lockwood's report, 16 Nov. 1863, *OR,* Ser. 1, 29:639–40.

26. Scharf, *Confederate States Navy,* p. 721. Some members of the commando, among them Beall's brother, were not exchanged until five months later.

27. Lee to President Davis, 20 Jan. 1864, *OR,* Ser. 1, 33:1101; Lee to Gen. G. E. Pickett, 20 Jan. 1864, ibid., p. 1102; Lee to Commander Wood, 20 Jan. 1864, Wood Papers, SHC/CHNC; President Davis to Wood, 6 Jan. 1864, Scrapbook, ibid.

28. Mallory to Hoge, 17 Oct. 1863, Papers of Francis L. Hoge, Lt. C.S.N., H-490, CM/RV.

29. On all this, see Chapters 15 and 16.

30. Mallory to Hoge, 16 Jan. 1864, Papers of Hoge, CM/RV.

31. Col. J. C. Ives to Hoge, 3 Oct. 1863, with orders to lay torpedoes at Wilmington, Papers of Hoge, CM/RV; Ives to Secretary of War Seddon, 5 Oct. 1863, ibid., Mallory to Hoge, 9 Dec. 1863, with orders to lay torpedoes in Petersburg's waters, etc., ibid.

32. Wood to Gift, 20 Jan. 1864, *ORN,* Ser. 1, 9:449; J. K. Mitchell to Gift, 21 Jan. 1864, ibid., p. 450; Gift to his wife, 21 Jan. 1864, George W. Gift Letters, SHC/CHNC.

33. J. K. Mitchell to French Forrest, 27 Jan. 1864, Papers of Hoge, CM/RV.

34. B. P. Loyall, "Capture of the *Underwriter,*" *SHSP,* 27:136ff.

35. Extract of report of Secretary Mallory, *ORN,* Ser. 1, 9:454; Wood to the commander of Marine Corps, Colonel L. Y. Beall, 15 Feb. 1864, ibid., pp. 453–54.

36. Gift to his wife, 27 Jan. 1864, Gift Letters, SHC/CHNC.

37. Daniel B. Conrad, "Capture and Burning of the Federal Gunboat *Underwriter* in the Neuse, off New Bern, N.C., in February 1864," *SHSP,* 19:93ff., which mentions only one of Gift's launches. Yet see Gift to C. ap R. Jones, 13 Feb. 1864, *ORN,* Ser. 1, 9:493.

38. Wood to Mallory, 11 Feb. 1864, *ORN,* Ser. 1, 9:451–52.

39. Scharf, *Confederate States Navy,* p. 396. As a midshipman, Scharf participated in the expedition in one of Gift's launches. His eyewitness report is extremely valuable.

40. Loyall, "Capture of the *Underwriter,*" pp. 138–39.

41. Gift to his wife, 7 Feb. 1864, Gift Letters, SHC/CHNC.

42. Graves to Commander Davenport (commanding all U.S. naval forces in the sounds), 2 Feb. 1864, *ORN,* Ser. 1, 9:441–42.

43. Loyall, "Capture of the *Underwriter,*" p. 139.

44. *ORN,* Ser. 2, 1:228. The young cadet who expressed that thought was Palmer Saunders, of the James River Squadron, who fell in the battle; see Loyall, "Capture of the *Underwriter,*" p. 139.

45. Scharf, *Confederate States Navy,* p. 397.

46. Wood to Davis and to Mallory, 4 Feb. 1864, *ORN,* Ser. 1, 9:451; Wood's Report, 11 Feb. 1864, ibid.; Scharf, *Confederate States Navy,* pp. 397ff.; Conrad, "Capture and Burning of the Federal Gunboat *Underwriter,*" pp. 95–96; Loyall, "Capture of the *Underwriter,*" pp. 140–41.

47. Gift to his wife, 7 Feb. 1864, Gift Letters, SHC/CHNC.

48. Loyall, "Capture of the *Underwriter,*" p. 142; *ORN,* Ser. 1, 9:443ff.

49. Pickett to R. E. Lee, 16 Feb. 1864, with report enclosed, 15 Feb. 1864, *OR,* Ser. 1, 33:92ff.

50. *JC,* 3:747.

51. David D. Porter, *The Naval History of the Civil War* (New York, 1886), p. 472.

52. G. V. Fox to Adm. S. P. Lee, 8 Apr. 1864, *ORN,* Ser. 1, 9:589.

53. Scharf, *Confederate States Navy,* pp. 643ff.; Naval History Division, *Civil War Naval Chronology, 1861–1865,* 6 vols. (Washington, D.C., 1961–66), 6:323.

54. This seems the most probable series of events, even though a detailed study of them (William Harden, "The Capture of U.S.S. *Water Witch* in Ossabaw Sound, Ga., June 2–3 1864," *Georgia Historical Quarterly* 3 [Mar. 1919]: 111ff.) says that the conception of the plan is of uncertain origin and that Pelot "was designated" to execute it.

55. Hunter to Pelot, 31 May 1864, Savannah Squadron Papers, EUL/AG, also in *ORN,* Ser. 1, 15:491.

56. Pelot to Hunter, 1 June 1864 and telegram, same date; Pelot to Hunter, 2 June 1864 (two telegrams); Hunter to Pelot, 2 June 1864 (telegram), Savannah Squadron Papers, EUL/AG, also in *ORN,* Ser. 1, 15:492ff.

57. H. Golder to Hunter, 3 June 1864 (telegram); Price to Hunter, 5 June 1864, Savannah Squadron Papers, EUL/AG; Hunter to S. S. Lee, 9 June 1864, *ORN,* Ser. 1, 15:500.

58. Hunter to Mallory, 4 June 1864 (telegram), Savannah Squadron Papers, EUL/AG, also in *ORN,* Ser. 1, 15:498.

59. S. S. Lee to Hunter, 15 June 1864 (telegram) and letter of 16 June 1864, W. H. Hunter Papers, DUL/DNC; Scharf, *Confederate States Navy,* pp. 649–50.

60. Mallory to Hunter, 24 June 1864, *ORN,* Ser. 1, 15:504; Hunter to Price, 21 July 1864, ibid., p. 505.

61. Hunter to Mallory, 8 June 1864, *ORN,* Ser. 1, 15:499–500; Mallory to Hunter, 15 June 1864, Hunter Papers, DUL/DNC.

62. Shingleton, *John Taylor Wood,* pp. 116ff.

63. Mallory to Bulloch, 22 Feb. 1863, *ORN,* Ser. 2, 2:368.

64. Journal of Midshipman Clarence Cary, with sketch of the ship, Records of Boundary and Claims Commissions and Arbitrations, Navy Department, Cruisers, NARG 76; Naval History Division, *Civil War Naval Chronology,* 4:309–10; Scharf, *Confederate States Navy,* p. 806; *ORN,* Ser. 2, 1:268.

65. U.S. Navy Commander Clary to Welles, 9 Sept. 1864, *ORN,* Ser. 1, 3:183–84.

66. Mallory to Maffitt, 24 Feb. 1865, *ORN*, Ser. 2, 2:804ff.

67. This plan is clearly demonstrated by the use of ships of greatest speed and shortest range (Mallory to Bulloch, 19 Aug. 1864, *ORN*, Ser. 2, 2:707–8), even if the orders Mallory gave Wood allowed the latter ample discretion, as was Mallory's style; Mallory to Wood, 23 July 1864, Scrapbook, Wood Papers, SHC/CHNC. But see also Scharf, *Confederate States Navy*, pp. 808ff.

68. Lepotier, *Les Leçons de l'histoire: Les corsaires du Sud et le Pavillon Etoilé*, p. 190.

69. President Davis to Bragg, 24 Oct. 1864, *OR*, Ser. 1, 51, pt. 2:1048; President Davis to Hon. S. J. Person, 15 Dec. 1864, ibid., 42, pt. 3:1273.

70. At least, this is what is said in Shingleton, *John Taylor Wood*, p. 122, who, however, gives only vague references to his sources; the normally reliable Scharf, *Confederate States Navy*, p. 806, instead says one rifled 32-pounder, a lighter rifled one, and a bronze howitzer; *ORN*, Ser. 2, 1:268 says five guns: one 84-pounder, two 24-pounders, and two 32-pounders, adding that this was the armament as of 28 September 1864 and that the ship later would have "3 guns." Naval History Division, *Civil War Naval Chronology*, 6:309, avoids the matter by saying "3 guns," without further defining them.

71. The diary of Captain Crenshaw is published in its essential parts in *Alabama Historical Quarterly* 1 and 2 (1939–40).

72. Wood to Paymaster C. L. Jones, 11 July 1864, 3G Pkg. 18, GHS/SG.

73. Mallory to Bulloch, 25 July 1864, *ORN*, Ser. 2, 2:689.

74. John T. Wood, "The *Tallahassee's* Dash into New York Waters," *Century Magazine* 56 (1898): 408–17.

75. Wood to Mallory, 31 Aug. 1864, *ORN*, Ser. 1, 3:701ff.; Wood, "The *Tallahassee's* Dash," passim.

76. Admiral Paulding to Naval Commander in Hampton Roads, 12 Aug. 1864 (telegram), *ORN*, Ser. 1, 3:140; Commander W. R. Taylor to Welles, 13 Aug. 1864 (telegram), ibid.; Commander J. Downes to Welles, 13 Aug. 1864 (telegram), ibid.; Welles to Downes, 13 Aug. 1864 (telegram), ibid., p. 141; Welles to President of Maritime Underwriters Co. of New York, 13 Aug. 1864 (telegram), ibid., in which he stated that a fleet had been unleashed against the "pirate."

77. Wood to Mallory, 31 Aug. 1864, *ORN*, Ser. 1, 3:701ff.; Wood to Mallory, 6 Sept. 1864, ibid., pp. 705–6; Governor McDonnel to Wood, 19 Aug. 1864, ibid., pp. 706ff.; and several letters by Governor McDonnel to British authorities. For a full analysis of the problem see Mary Elizabeth Thomas, "The C.S.S. *Tallahassee:* A Factor in Anglo-American Relations, 1864–1865," *Civil War History* 21 (June 1975): 148ff.

78. U.S. Consul at Halifax, M. M. Jackson, to Secretary of State Seward, 19 Aug. 1864 (telegram), *ORN*, Ser. 1, 3:156; Jackson to Seward, 20 Aug. 1864 (telegram), ibid.; Welles to Rear Adm. Paulding, 20 Aug. 1864 (telegram), ibid.

79. List of vessels captured . . . etc., *ORN*, Ser. 1, 3:703ff.

80. Gift to his wife, 28 Sept. 1864, Gift Letters, SHC/CHNC; Note on the cruise of the *Olustee, ORN*, Ser. 1, 3:836; Scharf, *Confederate States Navy*, pp. 807–8.

81. Extracts from Journal of C.S.S. *Chickamauga, ORN*, Ser. 1, 3:710ff.; Scharf, *Confederate States Navy*, pp. 808–9; John Wilkinson, *The Narrative of a Blockade Runner* (New York, 1877), pp. 209ff., which indicates that Wilkinson, even though he was an able blockade runner, did not fully understand the spirit of raids by naval commandos.

82. "Memoirs of J. Y. Beall," in Headley, *Confederate Operations*, pp. 242ff.; Crawford, "John Yates Beall," pp. 73ff.

83. Gift to his wife, 4 Oct. 1863, Gift Letters, SHC/CHNC.

84. W. H. Murdaugh to Mallory, 7 Feb. 1863, *ORN,* Ser. 1, 2:828ff.

85. Gift to his wife, 6, 16 Nov. 1863, 13 Jan. 1864, Gift Letters, SHC/CHNC; R. D. Minor to Buchanan, 2 Feb. 1864, *ORN,* Ser. 1, 2:822ff.; Wilkinson, *Narrative,* pp. 172ff.

86. Headley, *Confederate Operations,* pp. 248ff. Headley's book (he participated in Confederate operations on Lake Erie) includes substantial parts of Beall's diary.

87. Crawford, "John Yates Beall," p. 74. Beall would have proceeded, but his men told him that it would be suicidal to do so. See ibid., pp. 250–51.

88. Crawford, "John Yates Beall," p. 255.

89. Mallory to Thompson, 19 Dec. 1864, in Headley, *Confederate Operations,* p. 310.

90. For an almost complete record of Beall's trial see ibid., pp. 340ff.

91. "Records of Trial and Execution of the Sentence of John Yates Beall," Records of the Judge Advocate General (U.S.), NARG 153; Crawford, "John Yates Beall," pp. 75ff. Beall's tombstone carries the simple inscription: "Died in Defense of my Country."

CHAPTER EIGHTEEN

1. "Extracts from Journal of Captain Semmes, C.S.N. . . ," *ORN,* Ser. 1, 3:569ff.

2. Vessels bonded by the C.S.S. *Alabama,* 1862 to 1864, *ORN,* Ser. 1, 3:677ff.; Vessels overhauled by C.S.S. *Alabama,* 1862 to 1864, ibid.; J. Thomas Scharf, *History of the Confederate States Navy from Its Organization to the Surrender of Its Last Vessel* (New York, 1887), pp. 796ff.

3. John McIntosh Kell, "Cruise and Combats of the *Alabama,*" *BL,* 4:600ff.

4. Raphael Semmes, *Memoirs of Service Afloat during the War between the States* (New York, 1869), pp. 749–50; John McIntosh Kell, *Recollections of a Naval Life, Including the Cruises of the Confederate States Steamers* Sumter *and* Alabama (Washington, D.C., 1900), pp. 242–43.

5. Extracts from Journal of Captain Semmes, *ORN,* Ser. 1, 3:676.

6. Slidell to Semmes, 12 June 1864 (two letters), *ORN,* Ser. 2, 3:647; Semmes, *Memoirs,* p. 751.

7. Scharf, *Confederate States Navy,* p. 802.

8. Mallory to Barron, 3 Dec. 1863, 5 Apr. 1864; W. P. Campbell to Barron, 8 Mar. 1864, William C. Whittle Papers, NPL/NV.

9. The *Kearsarge* had already called at Flushing several times for repairs (Captain John A. Winslow to Welles, 16 May 1864, *ORN,* Ser. 1, 3:37; Winslow to Ambassador Dayton, 17 May 1864, ibid.).

10. John M. Browne (surgeon on board the *Kearsarge*), "The Duel between the *Alabama* and the *Kearsarge,*" *BL,* 4:615ff.

11. The French Minister of Marine, Chasseloup-Laubat, to Dayton, 15 June 1864, *ORN,* Ser. 1, 3:58; Kell, "Cruise and Combats of the *Alabama.*"

12. Semmes always denied having known that the enemy ship had been "ironclad" (Semmes to Barron, Official Report, 21 June 1864, *ORN,* Ser. 1, 3:649ff.; Semmes, *Memoirs,* pp. 753ff.). His executive officer, John M. Kell, was in complete agreement with Semmes in denying that his captain had ever been informed of the armor (see Kell's article, "Cruise and Combats of the *Alabama,*" written in 1866 for the *Century Magazine* and reprinted in 1888 in *BL,* 4, 600ff., as well as his *Recollections,* pp. 245ff.) The opposite thesis was expounded by Lieutenant Arthur Sinclair in his reminiscences (*Two Years on the* Alabama [Boston, 1896], p. 261). Sinclair, an officer on board the *Alabama,* gave a narrative of the

battle which is considered "subjective, yet amazingly honest," by Warren F. Spencer, *The Confederate Navy in Europe* (University, Ala., 1983), p. 247, n. 14.

13. The experienced seaman Bulloch underscores the superiority of the *Kearsarge*'s ordnance because the two heavy 11-inch Dahlgrens could cause terrible damage to a wooden hull (James D. Bulloch, *The Secret Service of the Confederate States in Europe, or, How the Confederate Cruisers Were Equipped*, 2 vols. [1884; reprint, New York, 1959], 1:278–79).

14. Semmes to Barron, 5 July 1864, *ORN*, Ser. 1, 3:664.

15. Kell, *Recollections*, p. 245.

16. Semmes to Confederate agent Bonfils, 14 June 1864, *ORN*, Ser. 1, 3:648; Semmes to Barron, 14 June 1864, ibid.

17. G. T. Sinclair to Barron, 20 June 1864, Whittle Papers, NPL/NV.

18. Semmes, *Memoirs*, pp. 751–52.

19. Browne, "Duel," p. 615; Bulloch, *Secret Service*, 1:278.

20. Dayton to Winslow, 16 June 1864, *ORN*, Ser. 1, 3:57–58. The *Niagara* then carried twelve 15-pounder Parrotts, twenty 11-inch Dahlgrens, a 24-pounder howitzer, and two other rifled 12-pounders. See *ORN*, Ser. 2, 1:160.

21. Semmes to Barron, 27 June 1864, *ORN*, Ser. 1, 3:649–50; Semmes, *Memoirs*, pp. 753ff.; Kell, "Cruise and Combats of the *Alabama*," and *Recollections*, pp. 245ff.

22. Sinclair, *Two Years*, pp. 259ff.

23. See Norman C. Delaney, *John McIntosh Kell of the Raider* Alabama (University, Ala., 1973), pp. 216ff.

24. Sinclair, *Two Years*, pp. 265ff. In addition to Sinclair's account, the reconstruction of the battle is based on the memoirs of Semmes and Kell; in *BL*, 4:600ff., which includes the account by Kell and (on the Union side) by Surgeon J. M. Browne. See also Winslow to Welles, 20, 21 June 1864, *ORN*, Ser. 1, 3:59ff.; Semmes to Barron, 21 June 1864, ibid., pp. 649ff.

25. The piece of the sternpost of the *Kearsarge* with the unloaded shell still stuck in it is on display at the Museum of American History of the Smithsonian Institution in Washington, D.C.

26. The duration of the exchange of projectiles is given by the chief gunner of the *Kearsarge*, F. A. Graham, to the Executive Officer, 20 June 1864, *ORN*, Ser. 1, 3:64.

27. The Federals later lamented the British "unfair" behavior because the yacht left without giving the Confederates to them. Yet it seems that Captain Winslow, formerly a good friend of Semmes's, was happy to see him escape imprisonment. See Winslow to Welles, 21 June 1864, *ORN*, Ser. 1, 3:60–61; Kell, *Recollections*, p. 248. From the viewpoint of the law of war, the question is cleared by a historian (of Union inclination), James Russell Soley, in *BL*, 4:621–22n, in which he states that the intervention of the *Deerhound* was perfectly lawful because requested (albeit very generously) by Winslow himself. Consequently, once aboard a neutral ship the prisoners were legally free.

28. Browne, "Duel," p. 261.

29. George T. Sinclair to Barron, 21 June 1864, Whittle Papers, NPL/NV; Muster Roll of the *Alabama*, ibid.; Surgeon Browne to Winslow, 19 June 1864, *ORN*, Ser. 1, 3:60.

30. Frank L. Owsley, Jr., *The C.S.S.* Florida: *Her Building and Operations* (Philadelphia, 1965), pp. 103ff.

31. C. A. Dana to Secretary Stanton, 29 Nov. 1863, *OR*, Ser. 1, 31, pt. 2:71ff.

32. Grant to Meade, 9 Apr. 1864, *OR*, Ser. 1, 33:827ff.; Grant to Stanton, 22 July 1864, ibid., 34, pt. 1:8ff.; Ulysses S. Grant, "Preparing the Campaign of 1864," *BL*, 4:97ff.

33. *The Life of David Glasgow Farragut, First Admiral of the United States Navy, Embodying His Journal and Letters,* ed. Loyall Farragut (New York, 1879), pp. 265–66; Alfred Thayer Mahan, *The Gulf and Inland Waters* (New York, 1895), p. 185.

34. The effective force of General Banks is given as thirty-one thousand men in "The Opposing Forces in the Red River Campaign," *BL,* 4:367.

35. We need not concern ourselves about the motives (mainly political) that stimulated the Union leaders to undertake the strategically erroneous Red River campaign. They are exhaustively and masterfully probed by Ludwell H. Johnson, *The Red River Campaign: Politics and Cotton in the Civil War* (Baltimore, 1958).

36. Farragut to his family, 3 Sept. 1862, *Life of Farragut,* p. 294.

37. Farragut to Welles, 22 Jan. 1864, *ORN,* Ser. 1, 21:52ff.; Alfred Thayer Mahan, *Admiral Farragut* (New York, 1892), pp. 243ff.; Farragut to his son Loyall, 2 Mar. 1864, *Life of Farragut,* pp. 362–63.

38. Farragut to General Asboth, 30 May 1864, Miscellaneous Manuscripts Collections, USNA/AM.

39. Buchanan to Mitchell, 13 Mar. 1864, J. K. Mitchell Papers, VHS/RV.

40. Gift to his wife, 18, 19 June 1864, George W. Gift Letters, SHC/CHNC.

41. Buchanan to C. ap R. Jones, 29 Apr. 1864, *ORN,* Ser. 1, 21:895–97.

42. Buchanan to C. ap R. Jones, 7 May 1864, ibid., 896.

43. Brooke to Jones, 15 Jan. 1864, Jones to McCorkle, 28 Jan. 1864, Jones to Buchanan, 22 Jan. 1864, McCorkle to Brooke, 25 Jan. 1864, Naval Collection, Selma Foundry Papers, NARG 45; Jones to Buchanan, 28 Jan. 1864, *ORN,* Ser. 1, 21:871; Buchanan to Jones, 30 Jan. 1864, ibid.

44. Jones to Buchanan, 2 May 1864, Naval Collection, Selma Foundry Papers, NARG 45.

45. William N. Still, Jr., *Iron Afloat: The Story of the Confederate Armorclad* (1971; reprint, Columbia, S.C., 1985), p. 204.

46. Farragut to Welles, 25 May 1864, *ORN,* Ser. 1, 21:298; Welles to the Commanding Officer of the *Manhattan,* 7 June 1864, ibid., p. 323.

47. Commander T. Craven to Welles, 3 July 1864 (telegram), ibid., p. 359.

48. Welles to Farragut, 25 June 1864, ibid., p. 344; Porter to General Canby, 1 July 1864, ibid., p. 368; Maj. Christensen to Farragut, 9 July 1864, ibid.

49. Naval History Division, *Monitors of the U.S. Navy* (Washington, D.C., 1969).

50. "The Journal of Private Charles Brother, USMC, on the U.S.S. *Hartford,*" in C. Carter Smith, Jr., ed., *Two Naval Journals, 1864, at the Battle of Mobile Bay* (Chicago, 1964), pp. 18ff.

51. Canby to Granger, 31 July 1864, *OR,* Ser. 1, 39, pt. 2:216; Canby to Farragut, 29 July 1864, *ORN,* Ser. 1, 21:390.

52. Gen. D. Maury to Gen. Cooper, 3 June 1864, *ORN,* Ser. 1, 21:901; Buchanan to C. ap R. Jones, 14 June 1864, ibid., p. 902.

53. "The Opposing Forces at Mobile," *BL,* 4:400.

54. Emanuel R. Lewis, *Seacoast Fortifications of the United States: An Introductory History* (Washington, D.C., 1970), pp. 42ff.

55. Gen. Canby to Halleck, 9 Aug. 1864, *ORN,* Ser. 1, 21:524; Scharf, *Confederate States Navy,* pp. 552–53, says instead twenty-seven guns: three 10-inch Columbiads, four rifled 32-pounders, and some twenty smoothbores.

56. This is the number of guns given by Scharf, *Confederate States Navy,* p. 533. Yet

ORN, Ser. 1, 21:524, gives eighteen. Probably some were fieldpieces or small ones, useless for naval defense.

57. [Victor E.K.R.] von Scheliha, *A Treatise on Coast Defense Based on the Experience Gained by Officers of the Corps of Engineers of the Army of the Confederate States* (1868; reprint, Westport, Conn., 1971), pp. 104ff. The Prussian von Scheliha commanded the Confederate Corps of Engineers in the Gulf of Mexico. See Chief Engineer (and Scheliha's second in command) L. J. Freneaux to Gen. D. H. Maury, 2 June 1864, *ORN*, Ser. 1, 21:899ff.

58. Mahan, *Farragut*, pp. 259–60.

59. Ibid., p. 260.

60. General Order No. 10, 12 July 1864, *ORN*, Ser. 1, 21:397ff.; Scharf, *Confederate States Navy*, p. 559.

61. C. ap R. Jones to the commanding officer of the *Tennessee*, J. D. Johnston, 10 May 1864, Naval Collection, Selma Foundry Papers, NARG 45, only partially reproduced in *ORN*, Ser. 1, 21:898.

62. Farragut to Welles, 22 Jan. 1864, *ORN*, Ser. 1, 21:52–53; Farragut to Bailey, 26 Mar. 1864, ibid., p. 268.

63. Abstract Log of C.S.S. *Tennessee*, *ORN*, Ser. 1, 21:984ff.; Daniel B. Conrad, "Capture of the C.S. Ram *Tennessee* in Mobile Bay, August 1864," *SHSP*, 19:72ff.

64. Granger to Christensen, 3, 5 Aug. 1864, *OR*, Ser. 1, 39, pt. 2:225–26.

65. This narrative of the battle of Mobile Bay is based essentially on *ORN*, Ser. 1, 21:405ff.; *BL*, 4:379ff.; *SHSP*, 19:72ff.; *Life of Farragut*, pp. 407ff.; Mahan, *Farragut*, pp. 269ff.; "Journal of C. O'Connell, C.S.N.," and "Journal of Private Charles Brother, USMC," in Smith ed., *Two Naval Journals*; Commodore Foxhall A. Parker, U.S.N., "The Battle of Mobile Bay," in "Naval Actions and History," in *PMHDM*, pp. 109ff. Also very helpful are Bern Anderson, *By Sea and by River; The Naval History of the Civil War* (New York, 1962); E. B. Potter and Chester W. Nimitz, eds., *Sea Power: A Naval History* (Englewood Cliffs, N.J., 1960); and Still, *Iron Afloat*.

66. C. ap R. Jones to Gen. Page, 25 July 1864, *ORN*, Ser. 1, 21:908.

67. For many years (and, indeed, today) the catastrophe that overwhelmed the *Tecumseh* was ascribed either to an error by Commander Craven, who would have "disobeyed" Farragut's orders and changed course on his own initiative (see Scharf, *Confederate States Navy*, p. 561) or to Craven's impatience to strike the *Tennessee*, which could be glimpsed beyond the channel, by shortening the course (Mahan, *Farragut*, p. 274). Since starting my study of the battle of Mobile Bay, both through a long and painstaking analysis of the records available and through visits to the scene of the battle, I have been considering that the thesis of a voluntary change of tack by the *Tecumseh* could not possibly be upheld. I then began to hypothesize that the Federal ironclad had undergone the same mishap as the French battleship *Bouvet* on 18 March 1915 during the attempt to force the passage of the Dardanelles, when, hit (and disabled) by Turkish artillery, she went off her course and ended in the minefield. The *Bouvet* sank in a few minutes, dragging with her almost her whole crew. My hypothesis would have remained intact except that in 1967, during research organized by the Smithsonian Institution with the support of the U.S. Army Corps of Engineers, the wreck of the *Tecumseh* was located by divers and found to have in her hull two cannon shot holes, each about a dozen inches across (9 inches by 14, to be exact). See the article by Herman Schaden, "Divers Write *Tecumseh's* Last Chapter," *Washington Evening Star*, 4 Aug. 1967. Still, the newspaperman's observation, according to which the

ironclad had *first* hit a torpedo, *then* was hit by Confederate artillery fire, does not seem tenable. The projectiles that pierced her low in her hull quite probably did so because Southern gunners, following the advice of the able artillerist Catesby ap R. Jones, fired low against ironclads so as to strike them (as they did the *Tecumseh*) just below their waterline.

68. That Farragut had cried: "Damn the torpedoes, full speed ahead!" is probably a legend, made up much later, yet this in no way detracts from his gallantry and daring.

69. "The Journal of Private Charles Brother, USMC," in Smith, ed., *Two Naval Journals,* p. 45.

70. Still, *Iron Afloat,* pp. 209–10.

71. Mahan, *Farragut,* pp. 281ff.

72. The draft of the *Tennessee* was 11.5 feet, whereas that of the *Manhattan,* the largest of the enemy ironclads, was the same and that of the *Winnebago* and *Chickasaw* only 6 feet.

73. See Adm. Angelo Jachino, *La Campagna navale di Lissa, 1866* (Milan, 1966), pp. 440ff.

74. This was something that even Buchanan came to realize later. See Buchanan to Mallory, 29 Aug. 1864, *ORN,* Ser. 1, 21:576ff.

75. F. A. Parker, "The Battle of Mobile Bay," *PMHSM,* p. 236.

76. "The Journal of John C. O'Connell," in Smith, ed., *Two Naval Journals,* p. 6.

77. *ORN,* Ser. 1, 21:405ff.; Scharf, *Confederate States Navy,* pp. 573ff.

78. Robert D. Minor to his wife, 19 Aug. 1864, Minor Family Papers, VHS/RV; the captain of the ironclad *Fredericksburg,* T. Rootes, to J. M. Brooke, 4 Oct. 1864, Mitchell Papers, ibid.; Rootes to Mitchell, 19 Aug., 4, 5 Oct. 1864, ibid.; Mitchell to General Field, 12 Aug. 1864, *ORN,* Ser. 1, 10:351; Mitchell to Mallory, 14 Aug. 1864, ibid., p. 352; O. P. Johnston to Comdr. T. Rootes, 19 Aug. 1864, ibid., pp. 367–68; Mitchell to Mallory, 22 Oct. 1864, ibid. p. 586; Scharf, *Confederate States Navy,* pp. 734ff.

79. Pinkney to Elliott, 2 June 1864, Governor Vance Papers, NCDAH/RNC; R. D. Minor to his wife, 14 May 1864, Minor Family Papers, VHS/RV; Mallory to Cooke, 26 May 1864, *ORN,* Ser. 1, 10:659.

80. Morris to Barron, 18 Feb. 1864, C. M. Morris Letterbook, Claims and Arbitrations, NARG 76.

81. Welles to Commo. Stribling, 10 July 1864, *ORN,* Ser. 1, 3:101; Welles to Adm. Paulding, 10 July 1864 (telegram), ibid. p. 102; Welles to Adm. Stringham, 12 July 1864 (telegram), ibid. p. 103.

82. Morris to Mallory, 12, 16 May 1864, Morris Letterbook, Claims and Arbitrations, NARG 76; Mallory to Morris, 2 June 1864, *ORN,* Ser. 1, 3:612–13.

83. Morris to Mallory, 21 June, 2, 13 July 1864, *ORN,* Ser. 1, 3:617–18, 621, 623ff.; Scharf, *Confederate States Navy,* p. 815.

84. Morris to Barron, Report with many enclosures, 16 Oct. 1864, ibid., pp. 631ff.; T. K. Porter to Morris, 20 Feb. 1865, ibid., p. 637; Collins to Welles, 31 Oct. 1864, ibid., p. 255.

85. Owsley, *C.S.S.* Florida, pp. 144–45. The rest of the *Florida's* story was prosaic. Supported by the world's diplomatic opinion, Brazil asked that the cruiser be returned, the prisoners freed, and those responsible for the violation chastised. With many circumlocutions, Secretary Seward admitted that he was in the wrong. The prisoners were freed, yet the *Florida* could not be returned because, while in Union hands, she, "in an accidental

way," sank while at anchor. Captain Collins was court-martialed and discharged from the navy. Yet a few months later, Secretary Welles declared the sentence null and void, restored him to the service, and later made him an admiral. By this time, the Confederacy and its navy had ceased to exist.

86. Elliott to Governor Vance, 11 May 1864, Governor Vance Letterbook, NCDAH/RNC; Pinkney to Elliott, 2 July 1864, ibid.

87. W. B. Cushing, "The Destruction of the *Albemarle*," *BL,* 4:634ff.

88. Alexander F. Warley, "Notes on the Destruction of the *Albemarle*," *BL,* 4:641–42.

89. Cushing to Adm. D. D. Porter, 30 Oct. 1864, *ORN,* Ser. 1, 10:611ff.; Warley to Mallory, 28 Oct. 1864, ibid., p. 624. If the Confederacy had had an industrial plant worth its name, refloating the ship would have presented no problems, as proved when the British raised the battleships *Queen Elizabeth* and *Valiant,* sunk by Italian assault boats in the harbor of Alexandria, Egypt, in 1941.

90. See Raimondo Luraghi, *Storia della Guerra Civile Americana,* 5th ed., rev. (Milan, 1986), passim.

91. Hardee to Hunter, 27 Nov. 1864, *ORN,* Ser. 1, 16:465.

92. Hunter to Comdr. Kennard, of the *Macon,* 27 Nov. 1864 (two letters), ibid.

93. Hunter to Comdr. Carnes of the *Sampson,* 29 Nov. 1864 (two letters), Savannah Squadron Papers, EUL/AG; Comdr. Dalton of the *Isondiga* to Hunter, 1 Dec. 1864, ibid.

94. Hardee to Hunter, 2, 8 Dec. 1864, ibid.

95. Hunter to Comdr. Brent, 29, 30 Nov. 1864, *ORN,* Ser. 1, 16:468–69; Brent to Hunter, 1 Dec. 1864, ibid., p. 470; Hunter to Hardee, 2 Dec. 1864, ibid.; Hunter to Comdr. W. Gwathmey of the *Georgia,* 8 Dec. 1864, ibid., p. 473; Hunter to Hardee, 9 Dec. 1864, ibid., p. 475; Gwathmey to Hunter, 9 Dec. 1864, ibid.; Hunter to Brent, 6 Dec. 1864, Savannah Squadron Papers, EUL/AG.

96. Hardee to Hunter, 10 Dec. 1864, at 10:00 P.M., Savannah Squadron Papers, EUL/AG.

97. Scharf, *Confederate States Navy,* pp. 651ff. Scharf, a midshipman on board the *Sampson,* says that Hunter personally went to the bridge with the gunboat (which was his flagship) by Hardee's order. Hardee's letter, cited in note 96, does not say so. Perhaps Hunter went because, given the importance of the task, he wanted it carried out under his own supervision.

98. Gen. Hazen (U.S. Army) to Adj. Gen. of the XV Corps, 9 Jan. 1865, *OR,* Ser. 1, 44:109ff.

99. Maj. Hitchcock to Gen. Slocum, 15 Dec. 1864, ibid., pp. 718ff.

100. Jefferson Davis, *The Rise and Fall of the Confederate Government,* 2 vols. (New York, 1881), 2:571ff.

101. Alexander Lawrence, *A Present for Mr. Lincoln: The Story of Savannah from Secession to Sherman* (Macon, Ga., 1961), p. 192.

102. William N. Still, Jr., *The Savannah Squadron* (Savannah, Ga., 1989), p. 18; Lawrence, *A Present for Mr. Lincoln,* pp. 194ff.; Henry Lee Graves to Mrs. Sarah D. Graves, 28 Dec. 1864, in Richard B. Harwell, ed., *A Confederate Marine* (Tuscaloosa, Ala., 1963), pp. 124ff.

103. Sherman to Gen. Webster, 23 Dec. 1864, *OR,* Ser. 1, 44:787ff.

104. Mallory to Tattnall, 10 Dec. 1864, *ORN,* Ser. 1, 16:476.

105. Orders to Captain Brent, 18 Dec. 1864, ibid., p. 482.

106. Brent to Hunter, 24 Dec. 1864, ibid., p. 483.

107. Mallory to Hunter, 14 Dec. 1864, Savannah Squadron Papers, EUL/AG; S. S. Lee to Hunter, 17 Dec. 1864, ibid.

108. Dahlgren to Welles, 23 Dec. 1864, *ORN*, Ser. 1, 16:140ff.

109. Scharf, *Confederate States Navy*, p. 653.

110. Still, *Savannah Squadron*, p. 20.

CHAPTER NINETEEN

1. John G. Barrett, *The Civil War in North Carolina* (Chapel Hill, 1963), pp. 262ff.

2. Porter to Welles, 17 Jan. 1865, *ORN*, Ser. 1, 11:436ff.

3. William N. Still, Jr., *Iron Afloat: The Story of the Confederate Armorclad* (1971; reprint, Columbia, S.C., 1985), p. 254.

4. Mallory to Mitchell, 16 Jan. 1865, *ORN*, Ser. 1, 11:797–98.

5. Mallory to Mitchell, 21 Jan. 1865, ibid., p. 803.

6. Mallory to Mitchell, 21 Jan. 1865, at 9:00 P.M., ibid., p. 804; J. Thomas Scharf, *History of the Confederate States Navy from Its Organization to the Surrender of Its Last Vessel* (New York, 1887), p. 740.

7. Scharf, *Confederate States Navy*, pp. 740ff.; Still, *Iron Afloat*, p. 185.

8. Raphael Semmes, *Memoirs of Service Afloat during the War between the States* (New York, 1869), pp. 803ff.; John McIntosh Kell, *Recollections of a Naval Life, Including the Cruises of the Confederate States Steamers* Sumter *and* Alabama (Washington D.C., 1900), pp. 266ff.

9. Dahlgren to Welles, 16 Jan. 1865, *ORN*, Ser. 1, 16:171; List of losses, ibid., p. 179.

10. R. Milby Burton, *The Siege of Charleston, 1861–1865* (Columbia, S.C., 1970), pp. 317ff.

11. *Charleston Daily Courier*, 20 Feb. 1865; Burton, *Siege of Charleston*, pp. 300ff.; Still, *Iron Afloat*, pp. 200ff.

12. F. S. Parker (by order from General Bragg), Special Order 59, 10 Mar. 1865, *ORN*, Ser. 1, 12:190–91; William N. Still, Jr., "The Career of the Confederate Ironclad *Neuse*," *North Carolina Historical Review* 43 (Jan. 1966): 1ff.

13. Mallory to Semmes, 2 Apr. 1865, *ORN*, Ser. 1, 12:191, with the order to scuttle the fleet; A. O. Wright, "The Destruction of the Fleet," in *Record of the Confederate Sailor Devoted to the History of the Confederate Navy and Those Who Served in It* 1 (1925): 8ff.; Semmes, *Memoirs*, pp. 811ff.

14. Scharf, *Confederate States Navy*, p. 746.

15. Ibid., pp. 747ff.; Semmes, *Memoirs*, pp. 817ff.

16. C. ap R. Jones, to General Taylor, 15 Mar. 1864, *ORN*, Ser. 1, 22:271.

17. George Gift to his wife, 30 Apr. 1865, George W. Gift Letters, SHC/CHNC; Gift to Milton, 4 May 1863, Governor Milton Letterbook, FHSC/TF; Wilson to Canby, 17 Apr. 1865, 10:00 A.M., *OR*, Ser. 1, 46, pt. 2:383; Townsend to Wilson, 5 June 1865, ibid., p. 960; "Wilson's Raid through Alabama and Georgia," *BL*, 4:759ff.

18. Canby's Report to the Chief of Staff, 1 June 1865, *OR*, Ser. 1, 49, pt. 1:91ff.

19. Thatcher to Welles, 12 Mar. 1865, *ORN*, Ser. 1, 22:64; Canby to Thatcher, 16 Mar. 1865, ibid., p. 65. Canby may have chosen the eastern shore of the bay because his troops came in the main from Pensacola, Florida, so as not to isolate them from their base. The Confederate commander, General Dabney H. Maury, was greatly relieved, for, if the en-

emy had come from the western shore, he would have invested the city directly and the Confederates would probably have been hopelessly trapped. See D. H. Maury, "The Defense of Mobile in 1865," *SHSP*, 3:1ff.

20. D. H. Maury to Jefferson Davis, 25 Dec. 1871, *SHSP*, 3:5ff.; Maury, "The Defense of Mobile in 1865," in which the former Confederate leader variously states that his forces numbered eight thousand (p. 2) or nine thousand (p. 4). See also Dabney H. Maury, *Recollections of a Virginian* (New York, 1894).

21. D. H. Maury to Davis, 25 Dec. 1871, "Remarks," *SHSP*, 3:10ff.

22. General Steele (U.S.) to the Adj. Gen., 17 Apr. 1865, *OR*, Ser. 1, 49, pt. 1:282ff.; Commander of the *Nashville* Bennett to Farrand, 15 Apr. 1865, *ORN*, Ser. 1, 22:99ff.

23. Canby to Thatcher, 16 Mar. 1865, *ORN*, Ser. 1, 22:65; Thatcher to Welles, 21 Mar. 1865, ibid., pp. 66–67; Canby to Thatcher, 24 Mar. 1865, ibid., p. 67.

24. Thatcher to Canby, 27 Mar. 1865, *ORN*, Ser. 1, 22:67–68; Comdr. Gillis to Thatcher, 30 Mar. 1865, ibid., p. 71; Scharf, *Confederate States Navy*, p. 594.

25. Thatcher to Chief Engineer Smock, n.d., but probably 28 Mar. 1865, *ORN*, Ser. 1, 22:68; Canby to Thatcher, 28 Mar. 1865, ibid.

26. Canby to Thatcher, 30 Mar. 1865, ibid., p. 69.

27. Thatcher to Welles, 3 Apr. 1865, ibid., p. 70; Commo. Gamble to Thatcher, 29 Mar. 1865, ibid., p. 72.

28. Comdr. Dyer to Thatcher, 2 Apr. 1865, ibid., pp. 72–73; Scharf, *Confederate States Navy*, p. 594, mistakenly classified the *Rodolph* as an ironclad.

29. Scharf, *Confederate States Navy*, pp. 594ff.

30. The Mayor of Mobile, R. H. Slough, to General Granger, 12 Apr. 1865, *ORN*, Ser. 1, 22:94; Maury, "The Defense of Mobile in 1865," pp. 8ff.

31. The original plan to sail up the Alabama River as far as Selma had to be given up because that city had fallen into enemy hands.

32. Carter to Gen. Buckner, 30 Mar. 1865, Naval Collection, Carter Letterbook, NARG 45.

33. Mallory to Bulloch, 27 Feb. 1865, *ORN*, Ser. 2, 2:798.

34. Read to Mallory, 22 Apr. 1865, *ORN*, Ser. 1, 22:168ff.

35. Carter to Mallory, 28 Apr. 1865, ibid., p. 170.

36. Col. C. Everett to Adj. Gen., 24 Apr. 1865 (telegram), ibid., p. 145; W. Hoffman to commanding officers of the forts, 24 Apr. 1865, and other messages from Union authorities, ibid., 146ff.

37. Mallory to Davis, 2 May 1865, Davis to Mallory, 3 May 1865, in *Jefferson Davis, Constitutionalist: His Letters, Papers and Speeches*, 10 vols., ed. Dunbar Rowland (Jackson, Miss.), 1923), 6:586ff.

38. Thatcher to Welles, 15 May 1865, *ORN*, Ser. 1, 22:177ff.

39. Mallory to Bulloch, 18 July 1864, *ORN*, Ser. 2, 2:687ff.

40. Campbell to Barron, 7 Mar. 1864, William C. Whittle Papers, NPL/NV; Notes, mainly from 1 Nov. 1863, to 16 May 1864, Douglas French Forrest Diary, VSA/RV.

41. James D. Bulloch, *The Secret Service of the Confederate States in Europe, or, How the Confederate Cruisers Were Equipped*, 2 vols. (1884; reprint, New York, 1959), 2:131ff.

42. Bulloch to Mallory, 16 Sept. 1864, *ORN*, Ser. 2, 2:723ff.; Bulloch to Mallory, 20 Oct. 1864, ibid., p. 736.

43. Memoirs, James Iredell Waddell Papers, NCDAH/RNC; published as *C.S.S. Shenandoah: The Memoirs of Lieutenant Commanding James I. Waddell*, ed. James D. Horan

(New York, 1960). A cue to help us in judging Waddell "the man" is a copy of the *History,* by Herodotus, in ancient Greek, printed at Leipzig, Germany, in 1839, with pencil notes in Waddell's hand, to be found among the Waddell Papers, NCDAH/RNC. This shows that the man, sometimes called "a kind of a Captain Bligh," was not a stranger to the classic Southern education. See also William C. Whittle, Jr., "The Cruise of the *Shenandoah,*" *SHSP,* 35:235ff.

44. Dabney Minor Scales Diary, CM/RV; Bulloch to Waddell, 5 Oct. 1864, *ORN,* Ser. 1, 3:749ff.; Barron to Waddell, 5 Oct. 1864, ibid., pp. 655ff.; George W. Groh, "Last of the Rebel Raiders," *American Heritage* 10 (Dec. 1958): 48ff.

45. Waddell to Mallory, 25 Jan. 1865, *ORN,* Ser. 1, 3:759ff. CM/RV has a collection of clippings under the heading "Australian Newspapers"; remarkable among them is the *Melbourne Argus,* 26 Jan. 1865, with news of the arrival of the *Shenandoah* with Confederate flag flying. It also voices admiration for the flawless Confederate uniforms, which (the paper writes) in gold and gray were similar to the old ones of the French navy. The *Illustrated Australian News,* giving the list of the officers, underscores their martial presence.

46. Midshipman James T. Mason Diary, vol 1, CM/RV; Dabney Minor Scales Diary, ibid.; Abstract Log of C.S.S. *Shenandoah, ORN,* Ser. 1, 3:785ff.; *Memoirs of Waddell,* passim.

47. Drouyn de Lhuys to Chasseloup-Laubat, 30 Oct. 1864, AMV, BB 4 1346/II; Arman to the Commissaire général, 30 Oct. 1864, ibid.; Bulloch, *Secret Service,* 2:73ff. The other ironclad, the *Cheops,* was commissioned in the Prussian navy with the name of *Prinz Adalbert* and served until 1878 (information kindly supplied by the late William Geoghegan of the Smithsonian Institution). The Danes had named their ironclad the *Starkodder,* from a mythological hero (Diary of Bennett Wood Green, Surgeon aboard C.S.S. *Stonewall,* UVL/CV).

48. Bulloch to Mallory, 10 Jan. 1865, including the contract with Arnous de la Rivière, *ORN,* Ser. 1, 3:720ff.

49. "Captain Thomas Jefferson Page," with contributions from several Confederate officers, including Virginius Newton, of the *Stonewall,* and torpedo expert Hunter Davidson, at the time commanding the blockade runner *City of Richmond, SHSP,* 17:219ff.; Lee Kennett, "The Strange Career of the *Stonewall,*" *U.S. Naval Institute Proceedings* 94 (Feb. 1968): 74ff.; Edwin Strong, Thomas Buckley, and Annetta St. Clair, "The Odyssey of C.S.S. *Stonewall,*" *Civil War History* 30 (4 Dec. 1984): 306ff.

50. Bulloch to Barron, 19, 21 Dec. 1864, Whittle Papers, NPL/NV; Bulloch to H. Davidson (commanding the *City of Richmond*), 10 Jan. 1865, *ORN,* Ser. 1, 3:726ff.

51. Drouyn de Lhuys to Chasseloup-Laubat, 4 Feb. 1865, AMV, BB 4 1346/II. Drouyn de Lhuys pretended to be astonished and ordered information from the French ambassador at Copenhagen (Bulloch to Page, 10, 16 Jan. 1865, *ORN,* Ser. 1, 3:730–31).

52. The French Consul in Galicia to Chasseloup-Laubat, 3 Feb. 1865, AMV, BB 4 1346/II; Drouyn de Lhuys to Chasseloup-Laubat, 5 Feb. 1865, informing him that the *Stonewall* was at El Ferrol (perhaps she was still in navigation, near La Coruña, because she moored at El Ferrol some days later), ibid.; Bulloch to Mallory, 11 Feb. 1865, *ORN,* Ser. 1, 3:736; Page to Bulloch, 12 Feb. 1865, ibid., p. 737; Bulloch to Page, 14, 21 Feb. 1865, ibid.

53. Diary of Surgeon B. W. Green of the *Stonewall,* UVL/CV; Slidell to Benjamin, 9 Feb. 1865, *ORN,* Ser. 1, 3:735.

54. Page to Bulloch, 19 Mar. 1865, ibid., p. 741.

55. Page to Bulloch, 25, 27 Mar. 1865, ibid., 741, 745; Kennett, "Strange Career of the *Stonewall.*"

56. Steam Log of C.S.S. *Stonewall,* kept by Chief Engineer W. P. Brooks, CM/RV, where it is said that the final discharge of the crew took place on 19 May 1865. This steam log shows in the frontispiece, "Fragata H. *Nuestra Salud del Carmen,*" yet it is written in English. This was the fifth name of the ship. Her career was not yet over. Spain gave her up to the United States, which on 2 November 1865 commissioned her with the Confederate name *Stonewall.* Captain Thomas Craven was court-martialed because he had not accepted battle at El Ferrol. Finally, the ironclad was sold to the shogun of Japan and, with the new name of *Japan,* made a long trip around the Americas and arrived at Yokohama on 24 April 1866. Meanwhile the shogun, who had commissioned the ironclad with the name of *Kotetsu-kan,* was defeated and the new imperial Japanese government commissioned the vessel into the imperial navy with the name of *Azuma,* her eighth and last name. As such, she, at last, saw battle against some rebellious Daimios. Thanks to an exceedingly calm sea, she could steer with ease and made short work of the wooden ships of the Daimios. She was decommissioned and sold for scrap in 1888.

57. Dabney Minor Scales Diary, CM/RV, lists thirty-seven merchantmen captured by the raider (eight in 1864), for a total value of $1,294,081.30. See Waddell to Lord Russell, 6 Nov. 1865, *ORN,* Ser. 1, 3:783ff.

Bibliography
Primary Sources

Manuscripts

INTRODUCTORY NOTE

When the Confederate authorities, after their defeat, evacuated Richmond on 2 April 1865, they tried to carry the government archives away from the capital. The records of the Navy Department were partially but amply destroyed when the building of the military departments went up in flames (see Dallas D. Irvine, "The Fate of Confederate Archives," *American Historical Review* 44(1939)823ff.; Naval History Division, *Civil War Naval Chronology, 1861–1865* [Washington, D.C., 1961–66], 5:76ff.). Yet Commander William H. Parker personally saw many of the Navy Department's records being packed up to be sent elsewhere (see Parker, *Recollections of a Naval Officer, 1841–1865* [New York, 1883], p. 350).

These records got as far as Charlotte, North Carolina. There, near the local navy yard, the navy's archives were almost totally destroyed. This was done basically because the North had threatened in a more or less veiled way to prosecute Southern naval men both for "piracy" and for using "unlawful" weapons (such as torpedoes), tools of war that, however, the Federals had hurried to adopt. The fact remains that the naval archives suffered destruction first at Richmond and then in Charlotte. On such matters we have the testimony of Mallory himself, who on 25 May 1877 wrote to Lieutenant James H. Rochelle that the greatest part of the records was destroyed *"upon and soon after the evacuation of Richmond"* (see the James H. Rochelle Papers, DUL/DNC).

Thus was created the legend that writing the history of the Confederate States Navy was almost impossible because of the lack of records. Yet some important parts of the Confederate naval archives survived. To these must be added the private collections held by officers and personnel of the vanished Southern navy and also foreign archives as well as the Confederate correspondence intercepted by the Federals.

All these papers, however, are spread about in more than fifty disparate archives, libraries, and repositories, thus making the work of the researcher particularly tiring.

Here, nevertheless, is a summary landscape of the documentation that has been found, with the warning that, because of space limits, I have not quoted all the several collections consulted and that, moreover, there may be others still waiting to be brought to light.

UNITED STATES

Guides to Archives and Lists of Sources

The basic guide for Confederate records held in the National Archives still is Henry Putney Beers, *Guide to the Archives of the Government of the Confederate States of America* (Washington, D.C.: Government Printing Office, 1968). It is generally a reliable guide, compiled by an able and experienced archivist who spent years working in the National Archives. It has a few mistakes, as on page 380, where it says that the Huntington Library, San Marino, California, has the papers of Confederate lieutenant Beverly Kennon. This is wrong; the papers are those of another one of the same name, of another historical period. Of primary importance is a twin volume: Kenneth W. Munden and Henry P. Beers, *Guide to Federal Archives Relating to the Civil War* (Washington, D.C.: Government Printing Office, 1962).

Obviously, as anyone who has engaged in archival research knows, collections are subject from time to time to being rearranged and, normally, when this is done, the National Archives prints many readers' guides that are of the utmost importance to the scholar. See, for example, Carmelita S. Ryan, *Preliminary Inventories, No. 169, Treasury Department Collection of Confederate Records* (Washington, D.C.: National Archives, 1969). Extremely useful also are the small readers' guides that accompany collections that are in whole or in part microfilmed.

All American archives generally publish guides to their collections, updating them from time to time. See, for example, for the extremely important Southern Historical Collection, Chapel Hill, North Carolina, Susan S. Blosser and Clyde N. Wilson, Jr., *The Southern Historical Collection: A Guide to Manuscripts* (Chapel Hill, 1970), with several supplements, the first of which appeared in 1975.

Other useful guides are published by other archives. Among the most important is the Robert W. Woodruff Library, Emory University, *Manuscript Sources for Civil War History* (Atlanta, Ga., 1990).

Alabama State Department of Archives and History, Montgomery, Alabama

Superior to any other collection here housed are Admiral Semmes Papers, which, considered lost, reemerged recently and have sometimes been overlooked; Colin J. McRae Papers, notable especially for the acquisition of the Selma Cannon Foundry; W. Phineas Browne Papers, very important for the problem of the coal supply for the C.S. Navy; Governor Shorter Papers; Baltic Construction Papers.

Charleston Library Society, Charleston, South Carolina

William G. Hinson Collection (important for the submarine *Hunley*); Wilmot G. De Saussure Letters; as well as a copy of the book by John Johnson, *The Defense of Charleston Harbor* (Charleston, 1890), with annotations in the author's handwriting.

Confederate Museum, Eleanor C. Brockenbrough Library, Richmond, Virginia

This collection is one of the most rewarding, even if it appears that historians have not given it the attention it deserves. Yet it contains many records of the utmost importance. Some examples are the original of the Provisional Constitution of the Confederate States of America; Log of the cruiser *Georgia*, 9 April 1863–18 January 1864; Log of the cruiser *Shenandoah*, 29 October 1864–21 July 1865; a descriptive list of the crew of the *Tennessee;* Diary of G. W. Quinn, chief engineer of the *Florida;* Diary of James T. Mason, on board the *Shenandoah;* Diary of Dabney Minor Scales, very important for the *Shenandoah;* Diary of W. P. Brooks, chief engineer of the *Stonewall;* Francis L. Hoge Papers, of the utmost importance for torpedo warfare and the Confederate commandos; many letters (not yet inventoried) by Mallory, by President Davis, by Governor Vance of North Carolina, by Commodore Barron and other naval officers, as well as by the secretaries of the treasury, Memminger and Trenholm, and by General R. E. Lee; the Papers of Chief Constructor John Luke Porter, among which is the draft by his own hand and autographed by himself of the first plan of the *Virginia,* entitled *Merrimac* Gun Deck, 1861, as well as the other original plans for the *Virginia.* Also included are the James D. Bulloch Papers; Raphael Semmes Papers; Matthew F. Maury Papers; the extremely important John Thompson Mason Papers; and the General Gabriel J. Rains Papers, where, hidden beneath a bunch of newspaper clippings, is the renowned manuscript written by Rains for President Davis, with outstanding data and drafts about torpedo warfare.

Confederate Naval Museum, Columbus, Georgia

In this museum, now named for James W. Woodruff, Jr., is the basic Letterbook of James H. Warner, chief engineer, Columbia Naval Iron Works, as well as the Letterbook of Augustus McLaughlin and the C.S. Navy Yard Logbook and Account Book.

Duke University Library, Durham, North Carolina

This is among the most conspicuous collections, second only to the NA and the SHC/CHNC. Some of the most important collections are the Clement Claiborne Clay Papers, which has important letters by Mallory, as also do the Jefferson Davis Papers, William W. Hunter Papers, and James D. B. De Bow Papers. Of great interest are also the James H. Rochelle Papers, Joseph N. Barney

Papers, Francis W. Dawson Papers, Beauregard Papers, and Francis W. Pickens Papers. Then there are the Diary of Raphael Semmes (information on the James River Squadron) and that of Dabney Minor Scales (copy), basic on many points, especially for the ironclad *Atlanta* (the original is in CM/RV).

East Carolina University Library, Greenville, North Carolina

Elizabeth Gordon Griffin Papers, interesting correspondence on the construction of the ironclad *Albemarle*.

Emory University Library, Atlanta, Georgia

Willink Brothers Papers, very important for naval construction at Savannah; Savannah Squadron Papers, narrative of the squadron operating on the Savannah River; William W. Hunter Papers, one of the several collections (others are in DUL/DNC and in TUL/NOL) in which are separated the papers of this officer who had a notable part in the life of the Confederate navy. A fairly large part of his correspondence is not published in the *ORN*.

Florida Historical Society Collection, Tampa, Florida

Located near the library of the University of South Florida, this collection includes the important Governor John Milton Papers, with much correspondence of the governor and Mallory.

Georgia Historical Society, Savannah, Georgia

William P. Brooks Papers; C. Lucian Jones Papers, information about the ironclad *North Carolina,* with some letters from Mallory, as well as on the projected expedition of J. T. Wood against Point Lookout.

Georgia State Archives, Atlanta, Georgia

Adjutant General Office; Naval Matters, various information about the Georgia navy. Extremely important—because they contain the continued controversy between the governor and the Confederate authorities—are the Governor Brown Papers, with many of Mallory's letters.

Library of Congress, Washington, D.C.

The Confederate States of America Archives contains several collections essential for the history of the Southern navy. First and foremost are the so-called Pickett Papers, which include the whole Confederate diplomatic correspondence and which I perused because they include a goodly part of records not printed in *ORN,* Ser. 2, vol. 3.

There follow the Navy Department Papers, mainly Box 119, with many records relating to the cruiser *Sumter,* as well as important information about the volunteer navy.

Then come the Matthew Fontaine Maury Papers, a monumental collection with important data about torpedo warfare, as well as the diaries (Box 59) and correspondence of Maury with his children; the Jones Roger Family Papers, containing letters of the highest interest, exchanged between Mallory and Catesby ap R. Jones; and the James H. Hammond Papers.

Last but not least, dwarfing in importance any other collection, are the Papers of George A. Trenholm. These contain invaluable information on the financial activities of the firm that had such a large part in supporting the war effort (especially on the naval side) of the Confederacy; on blockade running; and personal correspondence of Trenholm when he became secretary of the treasury.

Basic also are several collections of Federal records. The Low Mill Family Papers, with letters from U.S. merchant sailors, offer much information about the activities of Confederate raiders; Gideon Welles Papers; David Dixon Porter Papers; Louis Goldsborough Papers; Andrew Hull Foote Papers; and John A. Dahlgren Papers.

Louisiana State University, Department of Archives, Baton Rouge, Louisiana

Edward J. Means Letterbook, with several letters addressed to Mallory, John L. Porter, and other Confederate naval personnel.

Mariners Museum, Newport News, Virginia

Contains many plans and drafts of C.S. naval shipbuilding.

Maryland Historical Society, Baltimore, Maryland

When J. Thomas Scharf began to write his *Confederate States Navy,* in addition to his personal recollections he put together a sizable correspondence with former members of the Southern navy, as well as clippings and papers. All these are in the J. Thomas Scharf Papers. There is very little information that he has not used or cited in his book.

Miami University Library, Oxford, Ohio

Jefferson Davis Papers, with outstanding materials on the first phase of the defense of Vicksburg and the ironclad *Arkansas* as well as the defense of Mobile.

Mississippi Department of Archives and History, Jackson, Mississippi

Governor's Correspondence, with material on riverine operations.

National Archives, Washington, D.C.

This is still the most important repository for Confederate naval records. Many of these have been printed in the *Official Records,* both military and naval. Yet it is necessary to bear in mind that not all of the papers held by the National Archives and stamped "copied" have been published and that not all of those published carry that mark. It is therefore always useful, if one can, to check the printed papers against the original manuscripts. In this way, I was able to discern some mistakes of great importance in the papers printed in both *ORN* and *OR.*

Following is a list of the major collections in the National Archives, in order of importance and size.

Record Group 45, Naval Records Collection of the Office of Naval Records and Library, includes the major collection of Confederate naval papers, put together by order of the U.S. secretary of the navy immediately after the end of the war. These are in two sections: first, Subject File, where the subjects are earmarked by a letter and which is by far the larger collection. Outstanding here are the seven volumes of the Selma Naval Gun Foundry Papers, of the highest importance and to date used very little. Correspondence of officers such as John J. Guthrie, George W. Gift, James H. Tombs (or Tomb; the spelling varies), and the report (unpublished) by J. Taylor Wood about the action on the Piankatank and the narrative (unpublished) by H. Ashton Ramsay in the *Virginia-Monitor* fight are also to be found here, under the caption "Battles and Casualties to Ships, etc." Second is the Area File, which contains records from varied sources, but always concerning naval operations and problems and distributed according to eight areas: Area 4, Atlantic Ocean from the Arctic to the Antarctic, excluding the American coast to the north of the equator; Area 5, Mississippi River and its branches and tributaries; Area 6, Gulf of Mexico; Area 7, American waters north of North Carolina, inclusive of the Great Lakes; Area 8, American waters from North Carolina, south to the Amazon Delta; Area 9, Pacific Ocean from the Arctic to the Antarctic; Area 10, waters of Asia, Oceania, and Indian Ocean; Area 11, records relating to Washington, D.C.

Record Group 109, War Department Collection of Confederate Records. Many important papers of the C.S. Navy ended up in this collection, which in the main keeps records relating to the C.S. Army. Among such naval papers, there are many that can offer important information on the activities of the Office of Ordnance and Hydrography, torpedo warfare, the evolution of naval ordnance, shipyards, and naval construction, as well as the outstanding collection of the Records Relating to Confederate Naval and Marine Personnel and the volumes of Letters Sent by the Confederate Secretary of the Treasury (press copies), many of which are excellent for the history of the navy. Other papers useful for the C.S. Navy are to be found in the Letterbook of the Department of South Carolina and Georgia.

Record Group 365, Treasury Department Collection of Confederate Records. Outstanding herein are the Letters Received by the Confederate Secretary of the Treasury, whose importance for naval history cannot be overrated. Here are to be found at least 260 letters by Secretary Mallory, almost all unpublished, many of which are of the greatest importance and relate not only to the navy's financial problems but also to naval operations, designs and plans of construction, plus other records among which are the Comptroller's Contracts, the original contracts for Confederate shipbuilding.

Record Group 56, General Records of the Department of the Treasury, contains two volumes of Letters Sent by the Confederate Secretary of the Treasury (March–October 1861 and October 1864–March 1865), many of them sent to Mallory. The collection is completed by the press copies of RG 109 and other letters to be found in the Library of Congress.

Record Group 59, General Records of the Department of State, contains several letters by Secretary Mallory, generally published; correspondence (intercepted) relating to cruiser warfare; and other papers on the Norfolk Navy Yard. The diplomatic correspondence of the Confederacy is of outstanding importance for naval history, yet most has been printed in *ORN*. Basic in this record group is the diplomatic and consular correspondence of the Union government, with a wealth of information relating to Confederate cruisers, Confederate shipbuilding overseas, and the activity of Southern agents in foreign countries.

Record Group 84, Foreign Service Posts of the Department of State, contains much Confederate correspondence intercepted by Federals.

Record Group 19, Records of the Bureau of Ships, contains many construction plans for Confederate warships.

Record Group 76, Boundary and Claims Commissions and Arbitrations, has many records relating to Confederate raiders, used after the war by the U.S. government for the contention with Great Britain about the responsibility of the British in building Southern commerce destroyers.

In addition to these record groups, many interesting records may be found in the following: Record Group 37, Hydrographic Office; Record Group 74, Bureau of Ordnance; as well as in all the collections of Federal papers relating to the naval war. These have been carefully perused by this writer, especially the logs of U.S. warships.

Naval Historical Foundation, Washington, D.C.

Not a part of the Library of Congress, this is located in the same building as the Naval Historical Center. It has several collections of papers of Southern naval officers and personalities, such as the Daniel B. Conrad Diaries; yet, above all, it contains papers of U.S. naval officers, very important for the history of the C.S. Navy, including the David Glasgow Farragut Papers, Porter Family Papers, John A. Dahlgren Papers, Samuel P. Lee Papers, and Rodgers Family Papers.

Naval History Division, Washington, D.C.

This repository, located in the building of the National Archives, yet not belonging to it, contains papers that at one time were held by the U.S. secretary of the navy. Particularly, the ZB File includes substantial correspondence of Confederate naval officers, among them Matthew F. Maury, John L. Porter, Jonathan Carter, James H. Warner, Isaac N. Brown, Ebenezer Farrand, Charles H. McBlair, and James H. Tombs; the last one has a particularly important narrative about the attack by the C.S. torpedo boat *David* against the U.S. ironclad *New Ironsides*.

New York Historical Society Library, New York, New York

Here, in the Naval Historical Society Collection, are two outstanding groups of papers, from two of the most prominent and brilliant foes of the C.S. Navy: the Gustavus Vasa Fox Papers, of which only a small part was published, and the John Ericsson Papers; both are basic to understanding the thought and strategy of the two men and the menace that the Southern navy had to face. There are also two important letters by Confederate officer James H. Rochelle.

New York Public Library, New York, New York

Here are some letters of Commodore Hollins for the year 1862 and also a few Confederate papers. There is also a major portion of the John A. Dahlgren Papers. In the records of the U.S. rear admiral one may gather invaluable information about operations against the Confederates on the Atlantic coast. Last, there are the John Bigelow Papers, with copies, made by Union spies, of correspondence between French shipbuilders, Bulloch, and Slidell.

Norfolk Public Library, Norfolk, Virginia

To be found here are the William C. Whittle Papers, of importance for some aspects of the activity of the C.S. Navy in Europe. See also UVL/CV.

North Carolina Department of Archives and History, Raleigh, North Carolina

Basic are Governor Vance's Letterbooks, with the letters sent by the governor, and the Governor's Papers, containing letters received and other papers. The Adjutant General Letterbooks, as well as the Richard H. Cabot Papers, are very useful for the history of the ironclad *Neuse;* James Iredell Waddell Papers, with the letter of 5 November 1865 to Lord Russell; and the Charles A. Anderton Papers are very useful also.

Rice University Library, Houston, Texas

Newmann Family Papers, as well as a narrative *de visu* of fighting in Galveston's waters.

South Carolina Department of Archives and History, Columbia, South Carolina

Military Affairs, 1860–1865: Confederate Navy Papers. A very valuable collection of records on the South Carolina navy and the first days of naval war in the Palmetto State; Journal of the South Carolina Executive Council, also very useful for the early period; Letters Received by the Governor, many to Francis H. Pickens, Milledge L. Bonham, and Andrew G. Magrath.

South Carolina Historical Society Library, Charleston, South Carolina

John R. Cheeves Collection; Jacob D. Schirmer Diary; *Year Book of the City of Charleston,* several annuals, all with valuable information.

South Caroliniana Library, Columbia, South Carolina

Richard H. Bacot Papers (letters and a pocket notebook); he served on board the ironclads *Charleston* and *Neuse.* The papers of Bacot should be filled out with Ada Bacot Papers (Richard's sister); Mary Amarinthia Snowden Papers; Edward W. Barnwell Letters; George E. Dixon Letter (fitting out of submarines, on the

Hunley); Engineers Department Papers; Edward H. Edwards Papers; Theodore A. Honour Letters (on the *Hunley*).

Southern Historical Collection, Chapel Hill, North Carolina

Here is, with the exception of the National Archives, the most important collection of records for the history not only of the C.S. Navy but of the Confederacy itself and of the whole South.

So many papers have been checked, examined, and studied there while I was writing this book that only a limited number of them can be mentioned here. For reasons of space, I will mention the most important ones which would be useful for anyone studying the C.S. Navy.

First, perhaps, in importance are the Franklin Buchanan Books, where is to be found the Letterbook of Admiral Buchanan, which escaped publication in *ORN* and is of outstanding importance, mainly for the operations of the *Virginia* and for Mobile Bay. Then are the Edward Clifford Anderson Papers, with much on the *Alabama;* Arnold and Appleton Family Papers; Marsden Bellamy Papers; John Mercer Brooke Papers, a few letters; Francis Thornton Chew Papers, including the important diary on secret missions abroad: Bermuda, Nova Scotia, France, Great Britain, as well as navigation aboard the *Shenandoah;* John Henry Comstock Papers, important for the ironclad *Arkansas;* Forrest Family Papers, some letters of the two Forrests of the C.S. Navy; George Washington Gift Letters; Charles Iverson Graves Papers; John Berkeley Grimball Papers and Meta Grimball Diary (they had a son in the Confederate marines); Bartlett Shipp Johnston Papers, some letters received from C.S. Navy veterans; Eli Spinks Hamilton Papers, some letters about the ironclads of the James River Squadron; William Alexander Hoke Papers and William Calder Papers, on the coast defense of North Carolina; Evander McIvor Law Papers, in which are enclosed the papers of Milledge L. Bonham, very useful for disclosing Mallory's naval strategy about the ironclads; Edward M. L'Engle Papers; John Newland Maffitt Papers, with unpublished parts of his diary; Stephen Russell Mallory Papers, a few documents plus the irreplaceable diary; William Francis Martin Papers and Peter E. Smith Papers, with much on naval construction in North Carolina, mainly about the *Albemarle;* George A. Mercer Diary; James Morris Morgan Papers, a few letters on his Confederate service; James Heyward North Papers, some letters and an important pocket diary: other letters sent from Europe by North are to be found in the Chisolm Family Papers; Richard Lucien Page Logs, important on the defense of Fort Morgan at Mobile Bay; Ruffin Thomson Papers and James Ryder Randall Papers, important for the naval base at Wilmington, North Carolina; James H. Tombs Papers, included in the collection of his sons who were both officers in the U.S. Navy: much on the Confederate commandos; Lewis Neale Whittle Papers, a few letters; Eustace Williams Collection, important for submarine operations; Wirt Family Papers, some letters by J. M. Baker, a Confederate naval officer; John Taylor Wood Papers, indispensable for many subjects, mainly the ironclad *Virginia* and the commandos.

Tulane University Library, New Orleans, Louisiana

Louisiana Historical Association Collection; Alfred C. Van Benthuysen Papers, very important for the history of Confederate marines; William W. Hunter Papers, one of the several groups into which Hunter's correspondence is subdivided, of which thirty-four letters remain unpublished, among them three of Mallory's; Jefferson Davis Papers, with important letters of General Gabriel J. Rains, basic for torpedo warfare; the Diary of John Roy, agent of the secretary of the navy.

U.S. Army History Institute Archives, Carlisle Barracks, Pennsylvania

In the *Civil War Times Illustrated* Collection housed here there are, under the heading of Blockade Running, the Dr. Wendell Pierce Papers and the William Robert Dalton Papers, which contain information on the Confederate cruiser *Nashville.*

U.S. Naval Academy, Chester W. Nimitz Library, Annapolis, Maryland

Of great importance for all operations in the Mississippi Delta, in the Gulf of Mexico, and especially at Mobile Bay are the David Glasgow Farragut Papers.

University of Alabama Library, Tuscaloosa, Alabama

Shelby Iron Company Papers, outstanding for the relations of this firm with the Confederate navy.

University of Florida Library, Gainesville, Florida

Here is the basic collection of the private letters of Secretary Mallory in the Stephen Russell Mallory Papers.

University of Georgia Library, Athens, Georgia

Charles C. Jones, Jr., Papers, important for all the operations about Savannah and Georgia's waters; C.S. Navy Collection (copies: originals are owned by Mary E. Woods, Athens, Georgia), many letters by Tattnall; Nelson Tift Diary (copy; original in Dougherty County Courthouse, Albany, Georgia); some letters of W. W. Hunter while he was in command at Savannah.

University of Virginia Library, Charlottesville, Virginia

The most remarkable collections for Confederate naval history are the Maury Family Papers, mainly Box 147, with the letters of William L. Maury, very important for the operations of the CSS *Georgia;* the Autobiographical Notes and Diary, 24 January–20 May 1865, of Bennett W. Green, surgeon on board the ironclad *Stonewall;* and the William C. Whittle Papers, which complete the collection held at NPL/NV.

Valentine Museum, Richmond, Virginia

Confederate Papers—Miscellaneous contain a letter by Mallory that is important for the activity of the Atlanta Rolling Mill.

Virginia Historical Society Library, Richmond, Virginia

Contains correspondence of major importance (and sometimes overlooked) for the history of the C.S. Navy: John K. Mitchell Papers, with much unpublished material on the activities of the Bureau of Orders and Details which he directed for a long time; the outstanding Robert D. Minor Papers and Minor Family Papers (two different collections, which creates some problems of individuation for the researcher), absolutely indispensable, also for the number of letters by other naval officers to be found there, as well as the diary of R. D. Minor; Charles T. Mason Papers, with information about submarine warfare along the James River; Schockoe Foundry Records; Robert E. Lee Papers, which offer much material on naval history because of the intermingling between land and sea operations.

Virginia State Archives, Richmond, Virginia

This is one of the most important archives for the history of the C.S. Navy. Bulkiest among its holdings are the Tredegar Company Records, 1836–1900. Preserved intact are the whole, massive correspondence, the Account Books, the Foundry Books, and all the papers of the firm that built the armor of the *Virginia,* cast many Brooke cannons, and built torpedoes and submarines.

Then there are the Confederate Navy Records (several records gathered by H. R. McIlwain); General P.G.T. Beauregard Papers, 1862–1865; Day Books of Commodore French Forrest; Order Book and Letterbook of the C.S. Navy Yard at Gosport; Diaries of Douglas French Forrest, naval officer, son of the commodore; and a series of papers about the cruiser *Florida,* ironclad *Richmond,* the duel between the *Virginia* and the *Monitor,* the torpedo boat *Squib* and its operations, and the cruiser *Rappahannock.*

William and Mary College, Earl Gregg Swem Library, Williamsburg, Virginia

The most important collection is the Samuel Barron Papers, most of which, however, have been printed in *ORN.*

Many records remain in the hands of private parties. The most important among these collections, which I consulted thanks to the kindness of the owner, remains that of Cynthia Moseley, of Spartanburg, South Carolina. Included are copies of the personal letters of Commander Henry Kennedy Stevens which, in addition to shedding light on the personality of this officer, provided irreplaceable information on the construction and operations of the ironclad *Arkansas.*

GREAT BRITAIN

Useful information about the British and Irish archives is found in *A Guide to Manuscripts Relating to America in Great Britain and Ireland,* new rev. ed., ed. by John W. Raimo (London: Mansell Publishing, 1979).

Cammel Laird Company Archives, Liverpool

These archives, usually ignored, contain records of the highest interest, indispensable for understanding the contracting problems Bulloch had to solve (especially to acquire the patent on the armored turret designed by Captain Cowper P. Coles), as well as the technical features of the ships built in the Laird shipyards at Liverpool for the C.S. Navy. Pertinent are Miscellaneous Papers, Contract Book, and Old Letterbook.

Public Record Office, London

The basic collection for the subject matter is Foreign Office 5/755-2625; General Correspondence: America, United States of, 1861–1905, divided into several series. This collection contains far more than it pledges because there are also records that should belong to other collections (France, for example), yet that somehow relate to the United States, for example, "Confederate Ships Sold to British Subjects, 1863–64" (Vol. 1008); "Case of the Ironclads Built at Birkenhead" (Vols. 1001–1004); "Case of the *Alexandra*" (Vols. 1048–49); "Case of the Rappahannuck" (Vol. 1052); "Case of the *Oretos [sic]* or *Florida* (Vol. 1313); and "Case of the *Alabama*" (Vols. 1318–1832). The collection PRO 30/32, Lord John Russell Papers, contains the correspondence of the secretary, which has largely been published; and FO 519, Cowley Papers, semiofficial correspondence of the British ambassador in Paris.

FRANCE

A very useful guide is *Guide des sources de l'histoire des Etats-Unis dans les archives françaises* (Paris: France Expansion, 1976).

Archives de la Marine, Chateau de Vincennes, Paris

All the records held here are of outstanding importance, even if some of them do not deal directly with the C.S. Navy. Yet some are indispensable for the evolution of naval shipbuilding and ordnance in the second half of the nineteenth century. Above all, see 7 DD 1 65, Devis d'armement of several ships, among them the renowned floating batteries of the Crimean War; BB 8 1106ff, Conseil des Travaux, with the basic interventions and relations by Paixhans. More specifically on Confederate naval activity is the huge collection BB 4 1345/i, Campagnes, of capital importance both for the cruise of the *Sumter* and her movements in French overseas waters and for Confederate naval shipbuilding in France. Of course, on this problem paramount is the correspondence of the French naval minister (BB 4 1346/ii).

ITALY

Accademia delle Scienze, Torino

Here are the papers of Count Federico Sclopis di Salerano, who after the Civil War chaired the Arbitration Commission that handled the contest between the

United States and Great Britain regarding the Confederate raiders built in England. The papers are in Fondi Aggregati—Fondo Sclopis, and are divided largely into two groups: Letters received by Count Sclopis regarding the *Alabama* (1872) and Miscellaneous Papers used by him to draft the decision. The records and Sclopis's considerations are much more unbiased and believable than those presented by both the United States and Great Britain.

Printed Sources

NEWSPAPERS

Throughout the Civil War, the South had a great variety of newspapers, often of small size and published on very poor paper because of the restrictions imposed by the blockade and wartime occurrences. Their information was often inexact, sensational, almost always biased, and should be handled with much care. At the same time, however, they offer a lively picture of the opinions and impressions formed by the public about wartime operations (and not only about naval ones). One of the richest collections is found in LC, another, very rich, in SCL/CSC. Newspaper collections are scattered throughout the archives and libraries of the United States.

MAJOR COLLECTIONS OF SOURCES

The Annals of the War, Written by Leading Participants North and South. Philadelphia: The Times Publishing Co., 1879.

When the U.S. government decided to start the imposing publication of the *OR,* it was decided, as the basic standard, to print only papers synchronous with the war events; nothing, that is, written *post factum* would be included. Yet it was soon understood that gathering the statements of participants while still alive would be of the highest interest to future historians. Several steps were therefore taken, among the first of which was probably that of the *Philadelphia Weekly Times.* The narratives printed in that magazine were later gathered in this volume, fifty-six in all, among which are many of great usefulness for naval history.

Battles and Leaders of the Civil War. Ed. Robert U. Johnson and Clarence C. Buel. New York: Century, 1887–88. 4 vols.

This is the major collection of narratives from participants on both sides. The papers are arranged chronologically, with frequent appendixes of comments or debate. It is basic and indispensable. Yet, because this collection derives from an antecedent serial publication in the *Century Magazine,* one should also check that magazine because several important papers have been omitted from the published volumes.

A Compilation of the Messages and Papers of the Confederacy, Including the Diplomatic Correspondence. Ed. J. D. Richardson. Nashville, Tenn.: U.S. Publishing Co., 1906. 2 vols.

Some useful papers and records.

The Confederate Records of the State of Georgia. Ed. Allen D. Candler. Atlanta, Ga., 1909–14. 6 vols.

Many important letters, both on the Georgia navy and the Confederate navy. Five volumes were published irregularly up to 1914; the sixth volume remains in manuscript and is in the Georgia State Archives.

Confederate Veteran. "Published Monthly in the Interest of Confederate Veterans and Kindred Topics." Nashville, Tenn., 1893–1932. 40 vols.

Together with much material of little historical relevance there are, especially in the first issues, many important papers by witnesses and participants in the events. Should not be overlooked.

Great Britain: Case of Great Britain as Laid before the Tribunal of Arbitration. London: HMSO, 1872. 3 vols.

The British answer on the subject of the *Alabama* claims.

Histories of the Several Regiments and Battalions from North Carolina in the Great War, 1861–1865, Written by Members of the Respective Commands. Ed. Walter Clark. Goldsboro, N.C., 1901. 5 vols.

Volume 4 is of special importance for the naval war, yet useful information is to be found in the whole work.

Jefferson Davis, Constitutionalist: His Letters, Papers and Speeches. Ed. Dunbar Rowland. Jackson, Miss.: Little & Ives Co., 1923. 10 vols.

Many important letters on the naval war.

Journal of the Congress of the Confederate States of America, 1861–1865 *(JC)*. Washington, D.C., 1904–5. 7 vols.

Of greatest importance for all the laws and acts relating to the navy passed by the House and Senate of the Confederacy.

Official Records of the Union and Confederate Navies in the War of the Rebellion *(ORN)*. Washington, D.C., 1894–1914. 30 volumes divided into two series, plus an index volume.

This collection is the compulsory starting point for any study of the Civil War at sea. The publication is most accurate even if it contains some fairly serious errors. For example, as noted by this writer, the important letter by Mallory to Buchanan in *ORN*, Ser. 1, 6:780–81, dated 7 March 1862, should be moved to volume 7 and be dated ten days later. In *ORN*, Ser. 2, 2:631–39, the narrative of 30 April 1864 should be moved to 5 November of the same year, and pages 743–49 should be moved back to the former place; the organizations of the Savannah and the Mobile squadrons, pages 630 and 745–46, should be inverted; the narrative on page 598 attributed to Mallory is clearly a forgery by Union propaganda. These errors notwithstanding, the *ORN* is a collection of sources of outstanding importance and usefulness. Whenever possible, one should check the printed papers against the originals held in archives.

Papers of the Military Historical Society of Massachusetts (*PMHSM*). Boston: Houghton Mifflin, 1894–1918. 14 vols.

Similar to the *SHSP* from the Northern viewpoint, albeit far more limited. Volume 12 is fully devoted to the naval war; yet important information is scattered throughout the collection.

Southern Historical Society Papers (*SHSP*). Richmond, Va., 1876–1959. 52 vols.

An outstanding, indispensable collection of wartime reminiscences, papers, and records from Confederate military and political men. It is of the greatest importance, following the *OR,* for gathering evidence about the South's wartime activities. Volumes 44–52 contain the Proceedings of the Confederate Congress.

A great help for orienting oneself in this massive publication is *An Index-Guide to the Southern Historical Society Papers, 1876–1959,* James I. Robertson, Jr., Editor in Chief (Millwood, N.Y., 1980), 2 vols. Robertson and his collaborators have produced a superb research tool. I have only to remember the difference of working on the *SHSP* before and after 1980 to be grateful to the editors.

U.S. Bureau of the Census. Eighth Census of the United States.

Washington, D.C.: Government Printing Office, 1862–66, several volumes and appendixes. The Preliminary Report was reprinted in Washington in 1963 under the title *The United States on the Eve of the Civil War.*

U.S. Department of State: Correspondence Concerning Claims Against Great Britain. Washington, D.C.: Government Printing Office, 1869–71. 7 vols.

Contains the correspondence submitted by the United States to the International Court of Arbitration about the controversy with Great Britain upon the so-called *Alabama* Claims, that is, the building in Great Britain of commerce destroyers and other warships for the Confederacy. Enclosed in the volumes is *The Case of the United States to Be Laid before the Tribunal of Arbitration to Be Convened at Geneva* (Washington, D.C.: Government Printing Office, 1872). Very important and interesting material, even if put together according to methods that have nothing to do with objective research for historical truth.

The War of the Rebellion: A Compilation of the Official Records of the Union and Confederate Armies (*OR*). Washington, D.C., 1880–1901. 79 volumes in 129 parts, divided into 4 series, plus a volume of index and an atlas.

An incredible number of records useful for the naval history of the Civil War are included in this monumental collection, and not only papers dealing directly with the activities of the C.S. and U.S. navies, later reprinted in the *ORN.* Most of the nonreprinted ones are by non-naval authorities, yet from them, given also the peculiar character of the maritime war amply stressed in this book, one may gather a vast amount of basic information about the Civil War at sea and the struggle between sea and land.

To orient oneself in the veritable jungle of the *OR*, one might use the following: *Military Operations of the Civil War: A Guide-Index to the Official Records of the Union and Confederate Armies, 1861–1865*, comp. Dallas D. Irvine et al. (Washington, D.C.: National Archives and Records Service, 1977–80), 5 vols. in 9 parts.

CONFEDERATE IMPRINTS

During its limited life, the Confederacy printed a great number of books and pamphlets of basic importance for the history of the navy. In addition to others quoted in the notes, I will mention here only those books that are indispensable to any serious study of the Confederate navy.

The City Intelligencer; or, Stranger's Guide. Richmond: MacFarlane & Fergusson, 1862; reprint, Richmond, 1960. Very useful because it has all the names and addresses of the various naval and military institutions in the city.

A Digest of the Military and Naval Laws of the Confederate States from the Commencement of the Provisional Congress to the End of the First Congress under the Permanent Constitution. Analytically arranged by W. W. Lester and Wm. J. Bromwell. Columbia, S.C., 1864.

Elements of Seamanship. Prepared as a textbook for the midshipmen of the Confederate States Navy by Wm. H. Parker, commanding C.S. school-ship *Patrick Henry.* Richmond, 1864.

Laws for the Army and Navy of the Confederate States. Richmond, 1861.

Minority Report of the Special Committee to Investigate the Affairs of the Navy Department. Richmond, 1863. The opinions of the minority, hostile to Mallory.

Ordnance Instructions for the Confederate States Navy Relating to the Preparation of Vessels of War for Battle, to the Duties of Officers and Others When at Quarters, to Ordnance and Ordnance Stores and to Gunnery. Prepared by Order of the Navy Department. London: Saunders, Otley and Co., 1864.

Register of the Commissioned and Warrant Officers of the Navy of the Confederate States to January 1, 1863. Richmond: MacFarlane & Fergusson, 1862.

Register of the Commissioned and Warrant Officers of the Navy of the Confederate States to January 1, 1864. Richmond: MacFarlane & Fergusson, 1864.

Register of the Officers of the Confederate Navy, 1862. N.p., n.d. [Richmond, 1862].

Regulations for the Interior Police of the Confederate States School-Ship Patrick Henry. N.p., n.d. [Richmond, 1863].

Report from the Joint Select Committee to Investigate the Management of the Navy Department. N.p., n.d. [Richmond, 1864]. The final majority report.

Report of Evidence Taken before a Joint Special Committee of Both Houses of the Confederate Congress to Investigate the Affairs of the Navy Department. N.d. [1863]. Includes thirty-two contracts for building warships. Published (without the contracts, for which, anyway, it is better to check the original) in *ORN,* Ser. 2, 1:431ff.

The Statutes at Large of the Provisional Government of the Confederate States of America, from the Institution of the Government, February 7, 1861, to Its Termination, February 18, 1862, Inclusive, Arranged in Chronological Order. . . . Richmond, E. Smith, Printer to Congress, 1864.

Many other documents published by the Confederacy useful for naval history that were consulted are listed in the following:

Crandall, Marjorie. *Confederate Imprints.* 2 vols. Boston: Athenaeum, 1955.
Harwell, Richard Barksdale. *More Confederate Imprints.* Richmond: State Library, 1957; and *Confederate Imprints in the University of Georgia Library.* Athens, Ga.: University Press of Georgia, 1964.

LETTERS, CORRESPONDENCE, AND DIARIES

Anderson, Edward C. *Confederate Foreign Agent: The European Diary of Major Edward C. Anderson.* Ed. William S. Hoole, University, Ala.: University of Alabama Press, 1976.
Andrews, Eliza Frances. *The Wartime Journal of a Georgia Girl.* Ed. Spencer Bidwell King, Jr. Atlanta: Cherokee Publishing Co., 1976.
Browne, Henry R., and Symmes E. Browne. *From the Fresh-Water Navy, 1861–1864: The Letters of Acting Master's Mate Henry R. Browne and Acting Ensign Symmes E. Browne.* Ed. J. D. Milligan. Annapolis, Md.: Naval Institute Press, 1970. Very important letters by two Union sailors.
Castlen, Harriet Gift. *Hope Bids Me Onward.* Savannah, Ga.: Chatham Printing Co., 1945. Contains many letters by George W. Gift to his fiancée, later his wife. Yet some are incomplete and with mistakes or misprints; it is therefore necessary to check the originals in SHC/CHNC.
Chesnut, Mary Boykin. *The Private Mary Chesnut: The Unpublished Civil War Diaries.* Ed. C. Vann Woodward and Elisabeth Muhlenfold. New York: Oxford University Press, 1984. This is the heretofore unpublished diary of Mary Boykin Chesnut. What had appeared before was instead a later compilation that the writer put together in 1875 which, although based on memories and perhaps notes written at the time, better belongs to memorialist literature than to diaries. See *Mary Chesnut's Civil War,* ed. C. Vann Woodward (New Haven: Yale University Press, 1981).
Crenshaw, Edward. "Diary." *Alabama Historical Quarterly* 1 and 2 (Fall and Winter 1930, Spring, Summer, Fall, and Winter 1940): 261ff., 438ff., 52ff., 221ff., 365ff., and 465ff.
Dawson, Sarah Morgan. *A Confederate Girl's Diary.* Ed. James J. Robertson, Jr. Bloomington: Indiana University Press, 1960. A new and more complete edition has been published recently, yet too late to be used for this book.
Du Pont, Samuel Francis. *A Selection from His Civil War Letters.* 3 vols. Ed. John D. Hayes. Ithaca, N.Y.: Cornell University Press, 1969.
Ebaugh, David C. "David C. Ebaugh on the Building of the *David.*" *South Caro-*

lina Historical Magazine 44 (Jan. 1953): 32ff. Important letters by one of the builders of the torpedo boat.

Edmondston, Catherine Ann Devereux. *Journal of a Secesh Lady: The Diary of Catherine Ann Devereux Edmondston, 1860–1865.* Ed. Beth Gilbert Crabtree and James W. Patton. Raleigh, N.C.: Department of Archives and History, 1979. Important for amphibious Union operations in North Carolina and the ironclad *Albemarle.*

Farragut, David Glasgow. *The Life of David Glasgow Farragut, First Admiral of the United States Navy, Embodying His Journal and Letters.* Ed. Loyall Farragut. New York: D. Appleton and Co., 1879.

Fleming, Robert H. "The Confederate Naval Cadets and the Confederate Treasury: The Diary of Midshipman Robert H. Fleming." Ed. G. Melvin Herndon. *Georgia Historical Quarterly* 50 (1966): 207ff.

Forrest, French Douglas. *Odyssey in Gray: A Diary of Confederate Service, 1863–1865.* Ed. William N. Still, Jr. Richmond: Virginia State Library, 1979. This is the diary that in this book is quoted directly from the manuscript in VSA/RV.

Fox, Gustavus V. *Confidential Correspondence of Gustavus Vasa Fox, Assistant Secretary of the Navy, 1861–1865.* 2 vols. Ed. Robert M. Thompson and Richard Wainwright. New York: Naval History Society, 1918–19. A collection of great importance, which, however, contains only a minor part of the correspondence of Fox, whose letters are in NHSL/NY.

Fullam, George Townley. *The Journal of George Townley Fullam, Boarding Officer of the Confederate Sea Raider* Alabama. Ed. Charles G. Summersell. University, Ala.: University of Alabama Press, 1973.

Gayle, Richard H. "Extracts from the Diary of Richard H. Gayle, CSN." Ed. Frank E. Vandiver. *Tyler's Quarterly Historical and General Magazine,* No. 30 (Oct. 1948): 86ff.

Gorgas, Josiah. *The Civil War Diary of General Josiah Gorgas.* Ed. Frank E. Vandiver. University, Ala.: University of Alabama Press, 1947.

Graves, Henry Lea. *A Confederate Marine: A Sketch of Henry Lea Graves with Excerpts from the Graves Family Correspondence, 1861–1865.* Ed. Richard B. Harwell. Tuscaloosa, Ala.: Confederate Publishing Co., 1963.

Hoole, W. S., ed. "Letters from a Georgia Midshipman on the CSS *Alabama.*" *Georgia Historical Quarterly* 59 (1970): 416ff.

Jones, John B. *A Rebel War Clerk's Diary at the Confederate States Capital,* 2 vols. 1866. New ed. by Howard Swiggett. New York: Old Hickory, 1935.

Kean, Robert Garlick. *Inside the Confederate Government: The Diary of Robert Garlick Kean, Head of the Bureau of the War.* Ed. Edward Younger. New York: Oxford University Press, 1957. Has some information of the relations between the army and the navy, as does the diary of Gorgas cited above.

Keeler, Frederick. *Aboard the USS* Monitor, *1862: The Letters of Acting Paymaster William Frederick Keeler to His Wife Anna.* Ed. Robert W. Daly. Annapolis, Md.: U.S. Naval Institute, 1964.

Low, John. *The Logs of CSS* Alabama *and the CSS* Tuscaloosa, *1862–1863, Kept by Lieut. John Low.* Ed. W. S. Hoole. University, Ala.: Confederate Publishing Co., 1972.

Maffitt, Emma. *The Life and Services of John Newland Maffitt.* New York: Neale Publishing Co., 1906. Publishes many diary entries and letters of John N. Maffitt.

McClellan, George B. *McClellan's Own Story.* New York: Charles L. Webster and Co., 1887. Even if this book was put together late (see Stephen W. Sears, "The Curious Case of General McClellan's Memoirs," *Civil War History* 2 [1988]: 101ff.), it nevertheless contains many important letters that vividly recall the great strategic impact of the Confederate ironclad *Virginia.*

"The Middleton Correspondence." *South Carolina History Magazine* 53 (1962): 33ff., 61ff., 164ff., and 204ff.; 54 (1964): 28ff., 95ff., 158ff., 212ff.; and 55 (1965): 33ff., 98ff.

Minor, H. T., Jr. "I Am Getting a Good Education." *Civil War Times Illustrated,* 13 and 14 (Nov. and Dec. 1974): pp. 25ff. and 24ff. The unpublished diary by a cadet of the Confederate Naval Academy.

Myers, Robert Mason, ed. *The Children of Pride: A True Story of Georgia and the Civil War.* New Haven: Yale University Press, 1972. A splendid collection of the letters of the Jones family. Because many are missing, however, it is indispensable to check the Charles C. Jones, Jr., Papers in UGL/AG.

"La Navigation Sous-marine." *Cahiers des Salorges,* No. 15 (n.d.): 31ff. Letter and document relative to Brutus de Villeroy.

Newton, James K. "The Siege of Mobile." Ed. Stephen E. Ambrose. *Alabama Historical Quarterly* 20 (Winter 1958): 595ff.

Nichols, S. O. "Fighting in North Carolina Waters." Ed. Roy F. Nichols. *North Carolina Historical Review* 40 (1963): 75ff. Letters of a young Union sailor important for the actions of the Confederate ironclad *Albemarle.*

Ruffin, Edmund. *The Diary of Edmund Ruffin.* 3 vols. Ed. William K. Scarborough. Baton Rouge: Louisiana State University Press, 1972–80. Provides a clear idea of the impact of the Northern threat from the sea.

Smith, C. Carter, ed. *Two Naval Journals, 1864, at the Battle of Mobile Bay.* Chicago: Wyvern Press of S.F.E. Inc., and Mobile, Ala.: Graphics, Inc., 1964.

Stone, Kate. *Brockenburn: The Journal of Kate Stone, 1861–1868.* Ed. John Q. Anderson. Baton Rouge: Louisiana State University Press, 1955.

Vance, Zebulon Baird. *The Papers of Zebulon Baird Vance.* Ed. Frontis W. Johnson. Raleigh, N.C.: State Department of Archives and History, 1963–. A multivolume work still being published.

Vandiver, Frank E., ed. *Confederate Blockade Running through Bermuda, 1861–1865: Letters and Cargo Manifests.* Houston: University of Texas Press, 1946.

Waring, Mary. *Miss Waring's Journal: 1863 and 1865, Being the Diary of Miss Mary Waring during the Final Days of the War between the States.* Chicago: Wyvern Press of S.F.E., Inc., and Mobile, Ala.: Graphics, Inc., 1964.

Watson, Robert. "The Yankees Were Landing Below Us: The Journal of Robert Watson, CSN." Ed. William N. Still, Jr. *Civil War Times Illustrated* 15 (Apr. 1976): 12ff.

Welles, Gideon. *The Diary of Gideon Welles.* 3 vols. Critical ed. by H. K. Beale and A. W. Brownsword. New York: Norton, 1960.

Whitman, G. W. "Civil War Letters of G. W. Whitman from North Carolina."

Ed. J. M. Loring. *North Carolina Historical Review* 1 (Winter 1973): 73ff. Important for New Bern.

MEMOIRS AND REMINISCENCES

Given the high standard of education and the spread of literacy that in the last century characterized the United States of America, memoirs and reminiscences by former participants in the naval war are abundant. All, Confederates and Federals, provide information of the highest interest for reconstructing the operations and events of the Civil War at sea, and particularly of the C.S. Navy. Memoirs must be handled with care by researchers, both because people's memories are likely, with the passing of time, to fade and also because of the bias evident in many of them. Here is a summary list of those that this writer found helpful.

A fairly good help for tracking down titles of books about the Civil War at sea is Myron J. Smith, Jr., *American Civil War Navies: A Bibliography* (Methuen, N.J.: Scarecrow Press, 1972).

Alexander, W. A. "The Confederate Submarine Torpedo Boat *Hunley.*" *Gulf States Historical Magazine* 1 (Sept. 1902): 82ff. He was a member of the crew.

Ammen, Daniel. *The Old Navy and the New.* Philadelphia: Lippincott, 1891.

Baker, W. W. *Memoirs of Service with John Yates Beall, CSN.* Introduction by Douglas Southall Freeman. Richmond: Richmond Press, 1910.

Beauregard, Pierre G. T. "Defense of Charleston, South Carolina." *North American Review* 144 (May 1886): 30ff.

Bigelow, John. *Retrospections of an Active Life.* 2 vols. New York: Baker and Taylor, 1909.

Brooke, St. George T. "The *Merrimac-Monitor* Battle." *Trans-Alleghany Historical Magazine* 7 (Oct. 1902): 30ff. He was a midshipman in the *Nansemond.*

Bulloch, James Dunwoody. *The Secret Service of the Confederate States in Europe, or, How the Confederate Cruisers Were Equipped.* 2 vols. New York: Putnam, 1884; reprint, New York, 1959, with an introduction by Philip Van Doren Stern. The information it contains (together with letters, or parts of them, some of which are extremely difficult to find elsewhere) is absolutely indispensable.

Conrad, Daniel B. "What the Fleet Surgeon Saw of the Fight in Mobile Bay, August 1864, Whilst on the Confederate Ironclad *Tennessee.*" *United Service Magazine* 7 (Sept. 1892): 261ff.

Corbin, Diana Fontaine. *A Life of Matthew Fontaine Maury . . . Compiled by His Daughter, Diana Fontaine Maury Corbin.* London: S. Low, Marston, Searle, & Rivington, 1888. Badly written, biased, and unreliable, but contains much correspondence not printed elsewhere.

Crowley, R. O. "The Confederate Torpedo Service." *Century Illustrated Monthly Magazine,* June 1898, pp. 200ff. He was an electrician in the torpedo service.

Dahlgren, Madeleine V. *Memoirs of John A. Dahlgren, Rear Admiral, U.S. Navy.* Boston: J. R. Osgood, 1882.

Davidson, Hunter. "The Electrical Submarine Mine, 1861–1865." *Confederate Veteran,* No. 16 (1909): 456ff.

————. "Mines and Torpedoes during the Rebellion." *Magazine of History,* No. 8 (Nov. 1908): 255ff.

Davis, Jefferson. *The Rise and Fall of the Confederate Government.* 2 vols. New York: D. Appleton, 1881 (several reprints; the last one, New York, 1958, with an introduction by Bell I. Wiley). Even if President Davis wanted to give this book a historical tone, it still remains his version of events based both on his recollections and on information supplied by former Confederate soldiers and politicians.

Dawson, Francis W. *Reminiscences of Confederate Service, 1861–1865.* Charleston: News and Courier Book Presses, 1882. He served on board the *Nashville* and other ships.

De Leon, Thomas C. *Four Years in Rebel Capitals.* 1890. Reprint. New York: Collins, 1962.

Harrison, Mrs. Burton. *Recollections Grave and Gory.* New York: Scribner's, 1911. She was the sister of Midshipman Clarence Cary, who served on board the *Nashville* and the *Chickamauga.*

Headley, John W. *Confederate Operations in Canada and New York.* New York: Neale Publishing Co., 1906.

Hobart, Pasha. (Augustus C. Hobart-Hampton.) *Sketches from My Life.* London: Longmans, Green, 1886.

Hollins, G. N. "Autobiography of Commodore G. N. Hollins." *Maryland Historical Magazine* 34 (Sept. 1939): 228ff.

Huse, Caleb. *The Supplies for the Confederate Army: How They Were Obtained in Europe and How Paid For.* Boston: Marvin, 1904. Reprint. Dayton, Ohio: Morningside Bookshop, 1976. Huse was in charge of supplying the army, but his thin reminiscences are also useful for the navy.

Jones, Catesby ap. R. "The Ironclad *Virginia.*" *Virginia Magazine of History and Biography* 49 (Oct. 1941): 297ff.

Kell, John McIntosh. *Recollections of a Naval Life, Including the Cruises of the Confederate States Steamers* Sumter *and* Alabama. Washington, D.C.: Neale Publishing Co., 1900.

Mahan, Alfred Thayer. *From Sail to Steam: Recollections of a Naval Life.* New York: Harper and Brothers, 1907.

Maury, Dabney H. *Recollections of a Virginian.* New York: Scribner's, 1894.

Morgan, James M. *Recollections of a Rebel Reefer.* Boston: Houghton Mifflin, 1917.

Parker, William H. *Recollections of a Naval Officer, 1841–1865.* New York: Scribner's, 1883. One of the best Confederate naval reminiscences.

Porter, David D. *Incidents and Anecdotes of the Civil War.* New York: Appleton, 1885.

Porter, John W. H. *A Record of Events in Norfolk County, Virginia, from April 19th, 1861, to May 10th, 1862, with a History of the Soldiers and Sailors of Norfolk County, Norfolk City, and Portsmouth Who Served in the Confederate States Army or Navy.* Portsmouth, Va.: W. A. Fisher, 1892.

Pringle, Elizabeth Allston. *Chronicles of "Chicora Wood."* Atlanta: Cherokee Publishing Co., 1976.

Record of the Confederate Sailor Devoted to the History of the Confederate Navy and Those Who Served in It. Richmond: United Confederate Veterans, 1925. Intended to be published periodically but never got beyond the first issue. Yet it contains many important written memoirs.

Roman, Alfred. *The Military Operations of General Beauregard in the War between the States, 1861 to 1865.* 2 vols. New York: Harper and Brothers, 1884.

Selfridge, Thomas O. *Memoirs of Thomas O. Selfridge, Jr., Rear Admiral U.S.N.* New York: Putnam's, 1924.

Semmes, Raphael. *Memoirs of Service Afloat during the War between the States.* New York: J. P. Kennedy and Sons, 1869. This is the first version of Semmes's recollections, more bitter and polemical but closer to the events, hence more spontaneous and believable.

Sinclair, Arthur. "How the 'Merrimac' Won." *Hearst's Magazine* 24 (Dec. 1913): 884ff.

———. *Two Years on the* Alabama. Boston: Lee and Shepard, 1896.

Taylor, Richard. *Destruction and Reconstruction.* New York: Longmans Green, 1879. Reprint with an Introduction by R. B. Harwell, 1955.

Taylor, Thomas E. *Running the Blockade: A Personal Narrative of Adventures, Risks and Escapes during the American Civil War.* New ed. London: Murray, 1912.

Tindall, William. "The True Story of the *Virginia* and the *Monitor*." Introduction by Milledge L. Bonham. *Virginia Magazine of History and Biography* 32 (Jan. 1923): 1ff; (Apr. 1923): 89ff.

Waddell, James I. *CSS* Shenandoah: *The Memoirs of Lieutenant-Commanding James I. Waddell.* Ed. James D. Horan. New York: Crown, 1960.

Watson, William. *The Adventures of a Blockade Runner, or, Trade in Time of War.* London: T. Fisher, 1898. Only incidentally refers to the Confederate navy.

Wilkinson, John. *The Narrative of a Blockade Runner.* New York: Sheldon and Co., 1877. Includes many other naval memories in addition to those of trade by a naval blockade runner.

Wise, John S. *The End of an Era.* Boston: Houghton Mifflin, 1902. Reprint with an Introduction by Curtis Carrol Davis, New York: Yoseloff, 1965.

SECONDARY WORKS CONTAINING WORTHWHILE SOURCES

Many books written after the war with the declared intent of telling about operations are authentic sources (some, like Scharf, are indispensable) because the authors themselves participated in the events they describe. If on the one hand they lack objectivity, on the other hand, they gathered true treasure troves of information, often not to be found elsewhere. They gathered the reminiscences of those still living who had participated in the naval conflict yet wrote rarely, if ever.

Barnes, James S. *Submarine Warfare Offensive and Defensive.* New York: D. Van Nostrand, 1869. Produced by a Union naval officer who frequently had to confront the terrible submarine weapon, this book contains particulars of the highest importance.

Bigelow, John. *France and the Confederate Navy, 1862–1865*. 1888. Reprint. New York: Bergman Publishers, 1968. Written to uphold the North's contentions but rich with information on Southern naval construction in France and the failure of these plans.

Boynton, Charles B. *The History of the Navy during the Rebellion*. 2 vols. New York: D. Appleton and Co., 1867–68. This may be considered the Union's "companion" to Scharf's book. The author is really the spokesman for the Union naval secretary and, even if he is very biased, furnishes data that cannot be found elsewhere.

Campaigns of the Civil War. 16 vols. New York: Scribner's, 1883. The last three volumes are titled *The Navy in the Civil War*. Written some time after the Civil War, it has a pro-Union bias but contains much information. The first part, *The Blockade and the Cruisers*, written by Professor James R. Soley, even if written in a competent and well-balanced way, is more indirect. The second part, however, *The Atlantic Coast*, written by Rear Admiral Daniel Ammen, and especially the third part, *The Gulf and Inland Waters*, written by Alfred Thayer Mahan, contain much direct information (the last two fought in the U.S. Navy), and that of Mahan has acute insights.

Clayton, William F. *A Narrative of the Confederate States Navy*. Weldon, N.C.: Harrel's Printing Co., 1910.

Johnson, John. *The Defense of Charleston Harbor Including Fort Sumter and the Adjacent Islands*. Charleston: Walter, Evans and Cogswell Co., 1890. Written by a distiguished Confederate engineer who took part in the first plan for defending that port city. Also furnishes details of the highest importance on naval and submarine operations.

Jones, Charles C., Jr. *The Life and Services of Commodore Josiah Tattnall*. Savannah, Ga.: Morning News Printing House, 1878.

Parker, William H. "The Confederate States Navy." In *Confederate Military History*, vol. 12. Ed. Clement A. Evans. Atlanta, Ga.: Confederate Publishing Co., 1899. Written in a cursory way by an officer of the C.S. Navy who had been in command of the C.S. Naval Academy. Provides much firsthand information.

Porter, David D. *The Naval History of the Civil War*. New York: Sherman Publishing Co., 1886. The author, one of the most important enemies of the C.S. Navy who operated against it both on the Mississippi and in the Atlantic, offers, in a chaotic way and full of bias, some very valuable information.

Rochelle, James H. *Life of Rear Admiral John Randolph Tucker*. Washington, D.C.: Neale Publishing Co., 1903.

Scharf, J. Thomas. *History of the Confederate States Navy from Its Organization to the Surrender of Its Last Vessel*. New York: Rogers and Sherwood, 1887. This book is an indispensable source for the history of the Southern navy. The author, one of its officers, mixes personal recollections with a vast amount of information assembled through a protracted exchange of correspondence with former Confederate naval, military, and political men. Muddled and chaotic, it lacks even the appearance of a historical narrative, yet it is still authoritative. An invaluable treasure trove of information.

Sprunt, James. *Chronicles of Cape Fear River, 1660–1916.* Raleigh, N.C.: Edwards and Broughton, 1916. Some information on the ironclad *Raleigh* and blockade runners.

————. *Tales and Traditions of the Lower Cape Fear.* 1896. Reprint. Spartanburg, N.C., 1973.

von Scheliha, [Victor E.K.R.]. *A Treatise on Coast Defense Based on the Experience Gained by Officers of the Corps of Engineers of the Army of the Confederate States.* 1868. Reprint. Westport, Conn., 1971. The author was in command of the C.S. Corps of Engineers in the Confederate Department of the Gulf of Mexico, very important for torpedo warfare and maritime obstructions.

Wright, A. O. "The Destruction of the Fleet." In *Record of the Confederate Sailor Devoted to the History of the Confederate Navy and Those Who Served in It* 1 (1925): 8ff. Intended to be a periodical publication but only one issue was published.

CHRONOLOGIES

Long, E. B., with Barbara Long. *The Civil War Day by Day: An Almanac, 1861–1865.* Garden City, N.Y.: Doubleday, 1971. Contains most of the important events of the Civil War; very useful for placing naval actions in the general picture.

Naval History Division. *Civil War Naval Chronology, 1861–1865.* 6 vols. Washington, D.C.: Naval History Division, Office of the Chief of Naval Operations, 1961–66. An utterly indispensable work, compiled with extreme care and detail and without noticeable error. The book contains essays and records as well as an accurate picture of Confederate naval units.

Secondary Sources

INTRODUCTORY NOTE

The reader of this section is requested never to forget that the research for the present book was closed in 1988. Even if later more books on the subject were published (several of them of primary importance), I decided not to rewrite any part of this volume. Twenty-seven years of research (and toiling) were deemed enough: no writer can go on for a lifetime writing and rewriting the same book. This is why many books were not taken into account. Still, I checked them carefully and was able to ascertain (with some gratification) that none of them modifies or changes in any substantial way the conclusions reached in the present work. I included some of them in the following bibliography, which still remains far from complete.

This section contains only secondary works because other books that have any importance as printed sources are listed above. What follows is designed, in part, as a critical appraisal; therefore it has no pretension of being complete. Many works have been omitted, even though consulted, because they were not considered indispensable or for lack of space. If one adds books inevitably overlooked, it will be easily understood that this is only a partial list.

This is intended to be a topical and critical biography, mainly to indicate just some of the important works on the different topics relating to the Confederate States Navy. Therefore, the titles are distributed according to topic and not merged into an alphabetical list. Inside each topic the titles are divided between books and articles and given in alphabetical order. I hope that this will help the researcher (who normally looks at a specific problem and confronts the almost impossible task of locating all the books relative to it if merged in a general alphabetical listing) find it easier to locate the writings on specific topics.

BIBLIOGRAPHIES

Albion, Robert G. *Naval and Maritime History: An Annotated Bibliography.* Mystic, Conn.: Marine Historical Association, 1963 (with supplements, 1966 and 1968).

Coletta, Paolo E. *An Annotated Bibliography of U.S. Marine Corps History.* Lanham, Md.: University Press of America, 1985.

——. *A Bibliography of American Naval History.* Annapolis, Md.: Naval Institute Press, 1981.

——. *A Selected and Annotated Bibliography of American Naval History.* Lanham, Md.: University Press of America, 1987.

Smith, David R. *The* Monitor *and the* Merrimac, *A Bibliography.* Los Angeles: University of California, Los Angeles, Library, 1968.

Smith, Myron J., Jr. *American Civil War Navies: A Bibliography.* Metuchen, N.J.: Scarecrow Press, 1972.

GENERAL STUDIES: NAVAL STRATEGY

There is no general history of the American Civil War at sea that can be considered wholly satisfactory, and for the Confederate navy, the lacuna is total. Scharf's work, despite its title, is a chaotic heap of information (albeit quite valuable) and not a critical narrative. On the problems of naval strategy, however, these are some excellent works that are sometimes overlooked by historians.

Books

Anderson, Bern. *By Sea and by River: The Naval History of the Civil War.* New York: Knopf, 1962. The author, a former rear admiral in the U.S. Navy, in this book reveals a good general strategic outlook on the problem. Unfortunately, he does not understand Confederate naval strategy and remains anchored in the old legend that the Southern navy was designed to break the blockade and therefore should be considered a failure.

Beringer, Richard E., Herman Hattaway, Archer Jones, and William N. Still, Jr. *Why the South Lost the Civil War.* Athens: University of Georgia Press, 1986.

Of primary importance; absolutely indispensable. The two chapters "The Impact of the Blockade" and "The Union Navy and Combined Operations," written by Still, are outstanding, and clarify the related problems in a definitive way.

Coulter, E. Merton. *The Confederate States of America, 1861–1865.* Baton Rouge: Louisiana State University Press, 1950. A study rich in details and reflections on the naval war on the Confederacy's domestic front.

Genovese, Eugene D. *The Political Economy of Slavery.* New York: Pantheon, 1965.

———. *The World the Slaveholders Made.* New York: Pantheon, 1969. Like the first book, this one gives a clear analysis of the structural weaknesses of Southern industry.

Jones, Virgil C. *The Civil War at Sea.* 3 vols. New York: Holt, Rinehart and Winston, 1961–62. Contains hundreds of small facts but lacks a general vision. Poorly understands Confederate naval strategy. Lists many sources, but it seems that he did not use them in his text. In sum, he left things as they were. An authentic history of the Civil War at sea still has to be written.

Lepotier, Adolphe Auguste Marie. *Les Leçons de l'histoire, 1861–1865: Mer contre terre.* Paris: Mirambeau, 1945. The most important work with respect to the naval strategy of the American Civil War. The author, a distinguished writer on naval subjects, a former captain and then admiral in the French navy, considers with extraordinary insight the strategic parameters generated by the amphibious offensive of the Federals and the Confederate response.

———. *Les Leçons de l'histoire, 1861–1865: Les Corsaires du Sud et le pavillou étoilé. De l'*Alabama *à l'*Emden. Paris: Societé d'Éditions Géographiques, Maritimes et Coloniales, 1936. This extremely important work by then Lieutenant Lepotier, although dealing with commerce destroying, provides the first critical and total picture of the naval strategy of the Civil War that he would complete after World War II in *Mer contre terre,* cited above.

Luraghi, Raimondo. *Gli Stati Uniti.* Turin: UTET, 1972.

———, ed. *La Guerra Civile Americana.* Bologna: Il Mulino, 1978.

———. *The Rise and Fall of the Plantation South.* New York: New Viewpoints, 1978.

———. *Storia della Guerra Civile Americana.* 1st ed. 1966; 5th ed, rev., Milan: Rizzoli, 1986.

Merrill, James M. *The Rebel Shore: The Story of Union Sea Power in the Civil War.* Boston: Little, Brown, 1957. This is the seminal work that, in American historiography, opened an era. In it, the naval historians of the United States could for the first time find a clear analysis of the Union's amphibious threat against the Confederacy's coasts.

Musicant, Ivan. *Divided Waters: The Naval History of the Civil War.* New York: HarperCollins, 1995.

Potter, E. B., and Chester W. Nimitz, eds. *Sea Power: A Naval History.* Englewood Cliffs, N.J.: Prentice-Hall, 1960. A good collective work that provides a good understanding of naval strategy, but with respect to Confederate strategy, again, presents the trite legend of "failed to break the blockade."

Reed, Rowena. *Combined Operations in the Civil War.* Annapolis, Md.: Naval Institute Press, 1978. Regrettably, the late author dedicated her pages essentially to support a thesis according to which the credit for Union amphibious operations belongs to General McClellan, a rash conclusion. There is discontinuity in the use of sources.

Roland, Charles P. *The Confederacy.* Chicago: University of Chicago Press, 1960. A good general picture of the Confederacy at war.

Stern, Philip van Doren. *The Confederate Navy: A Pictorial History.* New York: Doubleday, 1962. Much useful illustrative material.

Thomas, Emory M. *The Confederacy as a Revolutionary Experience.* Englewood Cliffs, N.J.: Prentice-Hall, 1971.

————. *The Confederate Nation.* New York: Harper & Row, 1979.

Vandiver, Frank E. *Their Tattered Flags: The Epics of the Confederacy.* New York: Harper's Magazine Press, 1970. With Thomas's *Confederate Nation,* it is among the best general histories of the Confederacy.

Wells, Tom H. *The Confederate Navy: A Study in Organization.* University, Ala.: University of Alabama Press, 1971. A doctoral dissertation published with scant revision. The author, a former naval officer, reveals a notable competence and furnishes interesting conclusions. Yet he never tries to understand Confederate naval strategy or the technological problems of the South. The result is a failure to understand the philosophy on which Southern naval organizational problems were based. It offers some information, but the conclusions are unacceptable.

West, Richard S. *Mister Lincoln's Navy.* New York: Longmans, 1957. Although the author is a notable naval historian, in this book he merely offers a list of facts and does not attempt to define and study Northern naval strategy.

Articles

Folk, W. "The Confederate States Naval Academy." *U.S. Naval Institute Proceedings* 40 (Sept. 1934): 1235ff.

Fornell, E. M. "Confederate Seaport Strategy." *Civil War History* 2 (Dec. 1956): 61ff.

Hayes, John D. "Sea Power in the Civil War." *U.S. Naval Institute Proceedings* 88 (Nov. 1961): 60ff.

Luraghi, Raimondo. "The Civil War and the Modernization of the American Society: Social Structure and Industrial Revolution in the Old South before and during the Civil War." *Civil War History* 18 (Sept. 1972): 230ff.

————. "La grande strategia della Guerra Civile Americana e l'avvento della guerra totale." *Revue Internationale d'Histoire Militaire* 39 (1978): 290ff.

————. "Le Guerre del risorgimento e la guerra tra gli Stati Americani; la rivoluzione tecnologica, logistica, tattica e stragegica." In *Italia e Stati Uniti nell'Età del Risorgimento e della Guerra Civile.* Florence: La Nuova Italia, 1966, pp. 213ff.

————. "L'ideologia della guerra industriale, 1861–1945." *Memorie Storiche Militari,* 1980, pp. 169ff.

———. "Il Sud degli Stati Uniti fino alla Guerra Civile." In *Annali della Facoltà di Scienze Politiche* 11–13 (1983–86). Genoa: Ed. Culturali Internazionali, 1986, 2:141ff.

Ropp, Theodore. "Anaconda Anyone?" *Military Affairs* 27 (Summer 1963): 71ff. A perceptive analysis of Northern naval strategy, and of the Civil War in general.

Thomas, Emory M. "The South and the Sea." *Georgia Historical Quarterly* 4 (Summer 1983): 159ff.

BIOGRAPHIES

Books

Davis, Charles S. *Colin J. McRae: Confederate Financial Agent.* Tuscaloosa, Ala.: Confederate Publishing Co., 1961. Confederate financial operations in Europe (of great interest to the navy) and the many reports by McRae about the latter appear to be well analyzed.

Delaney, Norman C. *John McIntosh Kell of the Raider* Alabama. University, Ala.: University of Alabama Press, 1973.

Donnelly, Ralph W. *Biographical Sketches of the Commissioned Officers of the Confederate States Marine Corps.* Alexandria, Va.: By the Author, 1973.

Dufour, Charles L. *Nine Men in Gray.* Garden City, N.Y.: Doubleday, 1963. An excellent portrait of Lieutenant Charles Read.

Durkin, Joseph T., S. J. *Stephen R. Mallory: Confederate Navy Chief.* Chapel Hill: University of North Carolina Press, 1954. This is the only extensive biography of Mallory, and it has many good points, but the author appears to have little interest in naval strategy and naval operations.

Hendrick, Burton J. *Statesmen of the Lost Cause: Jefferson Davis and His Cabinet.* New York: Literary Guild of America, 1939. A useful book even if dated and in part superseded by that of Rembert W. Patrick cited below.

Hill, Jim Dan. *Sea Dogs of the Sixties.* 1935. Reprint. New York: Barnes and Co., 1961. Excellent biographical sketches of Bulloch, Wilkinson, Read, and Waddell, together with other important naval men.

Hoole, William S. *Four Years in the Confederate Navy: The Career of Captain John Low of the CSS* Fingal, Florida, Alabama, *and* Ajax. Athens: University of Georgia Press, 1964.

Lewis, Charles L. *Admiral Franklin Buchanan: Fearless Man of Action.* Baltimore, Md.: Norman Remington, 1929. A truly satisfactory biography of Buchanan is still lacking.

———. *David Glasgow Farragut.* 2 vols. Annapolis, Md.: U.S. Naval Institute, 1914–43. Much better than the biography of Buchanan cited above.

Lonn, Ella. *Foreigners in the Confederate Army and Navy.* Chapel Hill: University of North Carolina Press, 1940.

Mahan, Alfred Thayer. *Admiral Farragut.* New York: D. Appleton, 1892. Essential for understanding Farragut's tactical and strategic thought.

Niven, John. *Gideon Welles: Lincoln's Secretary of the Navy.* New York: Oxford University Press, 1973. The best biography of the head of the Northern navy.

Patrick, Rembert W. *Jefferson Davis and His Cabinet.* Baton Rouge: Louisiana State University Press, 1961.

Roberts, Walter. *Semmes of the* Alabama. Indianapolis: Bobbs-Merrill, 1930. Dated. It is hoped that a critical biography of Semmes will finally be written.

Senac, Felix. *Saga of Felix Senac: Being the Legend and Biography of a Confederate Agent in Europe.* Ed. Regina Rapier. Atlanta, Ga.: Privately printed, 1972.

Shingleton, Royce G. *John Taylor Wood: Sea Ghost of the Confederacy.* Athens: University of Georgia Press, 1979. As a, biography, it is quite weak, but there is nothing better.

Taylor, John M. *Confederate Raider: Raphael Semmes of the* Alabama. New York: Brassey's, 1994.

Tucker, Glenn. *Zeb Vance: Champion of Personal Freedom.* Indianapolis: Bobbs-Merrill, 1965. A good biography of the governor of North Carolina; also discusses his many relations with naval operations.

Wakelyn, Jon L. *Biographical Dictionary of the Confederacy.* Westport, Conn.: Greenwood Press, 1977. This is less a dictionary than a collection of the biographies of leading Confederates.

Weatherford, W. D. *James Dunwoody Bronson De Bow.* Charlottesville, Va.: Historic Publishing Co., 1935 (Southern Sketches, No. 2).

West, Richard S., Jr. *Gideon Welles: Lincoln's Navy Department.* Indianapolis: Bobbs-Merrill, 1943.

———. *The Second Admiral: A Life of David Dixon Porter.* New York: Coward-McCann, 1937.

Williams, Frances Leigh. *Matthew Fontaine Maury: Scientist of the Sea.* New Brunswick, N.J.: Rutgers University Press, 1963.

Williams, T. Harry. *Beauregard: Napoleon in Gray.* Baton Rouge: Louisiana State University Press, 1955. An excellent biography of the general and also his relations with maritime operations.

Articles

Bradford, Gamaliel. "Raphael Semmes: A Last Confederate Portrait." *Atlantic Monthly* 112 (Oct. 1913): 469ff. An excellent portrait of Admiral Semmes.

Grant, Richard S. "Captain William Sharp of Norfolk, Virginia, USN-CSN." *Virginia Magazine of History and Biography* 57 (Jan. 1949): 44ff.

Hayes, John D. "Captain Fox: *He* Is the Navy Department." *U.S. Naval Institute Proceedings* 95 (Sept. 1965): 64ff.

Holt, T. "The Organization of the Confederate Navy." *American Historical Quarterly* 7 (Winter 1945): 537ff.

Knapp, V. "William Phineas Browne, Business Man and Pioneer Mine Operator in Alabama." *Alabama Review* 2, No. 2 (1949): 108ff.

Melvin, Philip. "Stephen Russell Mallory, Southern Naval Statesman." *Journal of Southern History* 10 (May 1944): 137ff.

Robbins, P. "Caleb Huse: Confederate Agent." *Civil War Times Illustrated* 17 (Aug. 1978): 30ff.

Roberts, William B. "James D. Bulloch and the Confederate Navy." *North Carolina Historical Review* 24 (July 1947): 315ff.

Willis, V. B. "James D. Bulloch." *Sewanee Review* 34 (Oct.–Dec. 1926): 386ff.

NAVAL CONSTRUCTION AND TECHNOLOGICAL PROBLEMS AND ORDNANCE

Books

Armes, Ethel. *The Story of Coal and Iron in Alabama.* 1910. Reprint. New York: Arno Press, 1973.

Black, Robert C., III. *The Railroads of the Confederacy.* Chapel Hill: University of North Carolina Press, 1952.

Brewer, James H. *The Confederate Negro: Virginia's Craftsmen Military Laborers, 1861–1865.* Durham, N.C.: Duke University Press, 1969.

Bruce, Kathleen. *Virginia Iron Manufacture in the Slave Era.* New York: Century Co., 1931; reprint, New York: A. M. Kelley, 1968.

Bruce, Robert W. *Lincoln and the Tools of War.* Indianapolis: Bobbs-Merrill, 1956. Extremely useful for understanding the technological and industrial strength of the North and how high technology influenced the war.

Canfield, Eugene B. *Notes on Naval Ordnance of the American Civil War, 1861–1865.* Washington, D.C.: American Ordnance Association, 1960.

Daniel, Larry J., and Riley W. Gunter. *Confederate Cannon Foundries.* Union City, Tenn.: Pioneer Press, 1977. Absolutely fundamental.

Dew, Charles B. *Ironmaker to the Confederacy: Joseph R. Anderson and the Tredegar Iron Works.* New Haven: Yale University Press, 1966.

Johnson, Angus J. *Virginia Railroads in the Civil War.* Chapel Hill: University of North Carolina Press, 1961.

Kerksis, Sidney G., and Thomas S. Dickey. *Heavy Artillery Projectiles of the Civil War, 1861–1865.* Kennesaw, Ga.: Phoenix Press, 1972.

Ripley, Warren. *Artillery and Ammunition of the Civil War.* New York: Van Nostrand Reinhold, 1970.

Still, William N., Jr. *Confederate Shipbuilding.* Athens: University of Georgia Press, 1969. A work of enormous importance, absolutely indispensable.

———. *Monitor Builders: A Historical Study of the Principal Firms and Individuals Involved in the Construction of USS* Monitor. Washington, D.C.: National Park Service, 1988. Gives a clear idea of the power and modernity of Northern industry.

Vandiver, Frank E. *Ploughshares into Swords: Josiah Gorgas and Confederate Ordnance.* Austin: University of Texas Press, 1952. Indispensable for the relations between the Confederate Army Ordnance Bureau and the navy.

Articles

Allard, Dean C. "Naval Technology during the American Civil War." *American Neptune* 49 (Spring 1984): 114ff.

Chandler, Walter. "The Memphis Navy Yard: An Adventure in Internal Improvement." *West Tennessee Historical Society Papers* 1 (1947): 68ff.

Dickey, Thomas S. "The Armor Punchers." *Civil War Times Illustrated* 18 (Aug. 1979): 24ff.

Donnelly, Ralph W. "The Charlotte, North Carolina, Navy Yard." *Civil War History* 5 (May 1959): 12ff.

———. "Confederate Copper." *Civil War History* 1 (Dec. 1955): 355ff.

Eisterhold, J. A. "Savannah, Lumber Center of the South Atlantic." *Georgia Historical Quarterly* 57 (Winter 1973): 526ff.

Lander, Ernest M., Jr. "Charleston: Manufacturing Center of the Old South." *Journal of Southern History* 26 (1960): 330ff.

Layton, E. Colin. "Colin McRae and the Selma Arsenal." *Alabama Review* 19 (Apr. 1966): 125ff.

Melton, Maurice. "The Selma Naval Ordnance Works." *Civil War Times Illustrated* 14 (Dec. 1975): 18ff.

Merrill, James M. "Confederate Shipbuilding at New Orleans." *Journal of Southern History* 27 (1962): 87ff.

Parks, W. M. "Building a Warship in the Southern Confederacy." *U.S. Naval Institute Proceedings* 69 (Aug. 1923): 1299ff.

Stavinsky, Leonard P. "Industrialism in Ante-Bellum Charleston." *Journal of Negro History* 36 (1951): 302ff.

Stephen, Walter W. "The Brooke Guns from Selma." *Alabama Historical Quarterly* 20 (Aug. 1958): 462ff. A study of first importance on the Selma foundry and the exceptional quality of the cannons produced.

———. "The Sunken Guns of the Chattahoochee River." *Alabama Historical Quarterly* 20 (Winter 1958): 619ff.

Still, William N., Jr. "Confederate Shipbuilding in Mississippi." *Journal of Mississippi History* 30 (Nov. 1968): 291ff.

———. "Facilities for the Construction of War Vessels in the Confederacy." *Journal of Southern History* 31 (Aug. 1965): 285ff.

———. "Selma and the Confederate States Navy." *Alabama Review* 14 (Jan. 1962): 19ff.

———. "Technology Afloat." *Civil War Times Illustrated* 14 (Nov. 1975): 4ff.

Vandiver, Frank E. "The Shelby Iron Works in the Civil War: A Study of Confederate Industry." *Alabama Review* 1 (Jan. 1948): 12ff.; (Apr. 1948): 111ff; and (July 1948): 203ff.

———. "The South Carolina Ordnance Board." *Proceedings of the South Carolina Historical Association,* 1945, pp. 14ff.

Weller, Jac. "The Confederate Use of British Cannons." *Civil War History* 3 (June 1957): 135ff.

ECONOMIC, ADMINISTRATIVE, AND PERSONNEL PROBLEMS

Books

Andreano, Ralph, ed. *The Economic Impact of the American Civil War.* Cambridge, Mass.: Schenkman, 1962.

Hill, Louise B. *State Socialism in the Confederate States of America.* Charlottesville, Va.: Historic Publishing Co., 1936 (Southern Sketches, Ser. 1, No. 9). A fundamental study on the nationalization of foreign trade by the Confederacy and its consequences for more than naval matters.

Ramsdell, Charles W. *Behind the Lines in the Southern Confederacy.* Baton Rouge: Louisiana State University Press, 1944.

Schwab, John C. *The Confederate States of America, 1861–1865: A Financial and Industrial History of the South during the Civil War.* New York: Scribner's, 1901. Still remains indispensable.

Todd, Richard C. *Confederate Finance.* Athens: University Press of Georgia, 1954.

Articles

Andreano, Ralph L. "A Theory of Confederate Finance." *Civil War History* 2 (June 1956): 21ff.

Eckenrode, H. D. "Negroes in Richmond in 1864." *Virginia Magazine of History and Biography* 46 (July 1938): 193ff.

Ginsberg, Eli. "The Economics of British Neutrality during the American Civil War." *Agricultural History* 10 (1936): 147ff.

Herndon, Melvin G. "The Confederate States Naval Academy." *Virginia Magazine of History and Biography* 69 (July 1961): 300ff.

Lerner, Eugene M. "Inflation in the Confederacy." In *Studies in the Quantitative Theory of Money,* edited by Milton Friedman. Chicago: University of Chicago Press, 1955, 163ff.

———. "The Monetary and Fiscal Program of the Confederate Government, 1861–1865." *Journal of Political Economy* 52 (Feb.–Dec. 1954): 506ff.

———. "Money, Prices and Wages in the Confederacy, 1861–1865." *Journal of Political Economy* 53 (Feb.–Dec. 1955): 20ff.

Roberts, A. Sellew. "High Prices and the Blockade in the Confederacy." *South Atlantic Quarterly* 24 (Apr. 1925): 154ff.

Still, William N., Jr. "The Common Sailor, Part 2: Confederate Tars." *Civil War Times Illustrated* 24 (Mar. 1985): 12ff.

THE WAR OF THE IRONCLADS IN AMERICA

Books

Bathe, Greville. *Ship of Destiny: A Record of the US Frigate* Merrimac, *1854–1862.* St. Augustine, Fla.: n.p., 1951.

Baxter, James P., III. *The Introduction of the Ironclad Warship.* 1933. Reprint. Hamden, Conn.: Archon Books, 1968. Fundamental even if it does not examine closely Confederate ironclad strategy.

Bright, Leslie, W. H. Rowland, and J. C. Bardon. *C.S.S. Neuse: A Question of Iron and Time.* Raleigh, N.C.: Division of Archives and History, 1981.

Daly, Robert W. *How the* Merrimac *Won: The Strategic Story of the CSS* Virginia. New York: Thomas Y. Crowell Co., 1957. A fundamental work that opened truly a new era in interpretation.

Davis, William C. *Duel between the First Ironclads.* Garden City, N.Y.: Doubleday, 1975.

Elliott, Robert G. *Ironclad in the Roanoke: Gilbert Elliott's* Albemarle. Shippensburg, Pa.: White Mane, 1994.

McCordock, Robert S. *The Yankee Cheese Box.* Philadelphia: Dorrance, 1938.

Melton, Maurice. *The Confederate Ironclads.* New York: Thomas Yoseloff, 1968.

Still, William N., Jr. *Iron Afloat: The Story of the Confederate Armorclad.* 1971. Reprint. Columbia: University of South Carolina Press, 1985. A fundamental and indispensable work for every serious scholar.

————. *Ironclad Captains: The Commanding Officers of the* U.S.S. Monitor. Washington, D.C.: U.S. Department of Commerce, 1988.

Trexler, Harrison. *The Confederate Ironclad Virginia* ("Merrimac"). Chicago: University of Chicago Press, 1933.

U.S. Corps of Engineers, Savannah District. *CSS* Georgia. Savannah, Ga., n.d.

Articles

A. "Archeologists Excavate USS *Monitor.*" *Carolina Comments* 27 (Nov. 1979): 1ff.

Botti, Ferruccio. "La 'Nave Invulnerabile' e le teorie del generale Cavalli." *Rivista Marittima,* July 1988, pp. 107ff.

Davis, Charles H. "History of the U.S. Steamer *Merrimack.*" *New England Historical and Genealogical Register* 27 (July 1874): 245ff.

Demaree, Albert L. "Our Navy's Worst Headache: The *Merrimack.*" *U.S. Naval Institute Proceedings* 88 (Mar. 1962): 67ff.

Dorset, P. S. "James B. Eads: Navy Shipbuilder, 1861." *U.S. Naval Institute Proceedings* 101 (Aug. 1975): 76ff.

Hess, Earl J. "Northern Response to the Ironclad: A Prospect for the Study of Military Technology." *Civil War History* 31 (June 1985): 126ff.

Holcombe, Robert. "The *Richmond* Class Confederate Ironclads." *Confederate Historical Association of Belgium News* 15 (Sept. 1978): 26.

House, Boyce. "Confederate Hero Puts the Flag Back in Place!" *Tennessee Historical Quarterly* 19 (June 1960): 172ff.

Luraghi, Raimondo. "La corazzata 'Americana' *Re d'Italia.*" *Rassegna Storica del Risorgimento* 65 (Jan.–Mar. 1978): 11ff.

MacLean, Malcolm. "The Short Cruise of the CSS *Atlanta.*" *Georgia Historical Quarterly* 40 (1956): 130ff.

McClinton, Oliver W. "The Career of the Confederate Ram *Arkansas.*" *Arkansas Historical Magazine* 7 (Winter 1948): 329ff.

Melton, Maurice. "The First and Last Cruise of the CSS *Atlanta.*" *Civil War Times Illustrated* 10 (Nov. 1971): 4ff.

Milligan, John D. "Charles Ellet and His Naval Steam Ram." *Civil War History* 9 (June 1963): 121ff.

————. "Charles Ellet, Naval Architect: A Study in Nineteenth Century Professionalism." *American Neptune* 31 (Jan. 1971): 52ff.

Millis, Walter. "The Iron Sea Elephants." *American Neptune* 10 (Jan. 1950): 15ff.

Moore, Michael. "The Other *Mississippi.*" *U.S. Naval Institute Proceedings* 106 (Feb. 1980): 54ff.

Morgan, J. M. "The Pioneer 'Ironclad,' CSS *Manassas*." *U.S. Naval Institute Proceedings* 43 (Oct. 1917): 2275ff.

Newton, J. G. "How We Found the *Monitor*." *National Geographic* 147 (Jan. 1975): 48ff. The wreck was found off Cape Hatteras.

Oliver, Frederick. "The Officers of the *Monitor* and *Merrimac*." *Shipmate* 23 (Aug. 1963): 6ff.

O'Neil, Charles. "The Engagement between the *Cumberland* and the *Merrimac*." *U.S. Naval Institute Proceedings* 48 (June 1922): 863ff.

Smith, Alan C. "The *Monitor-Merrimac* Legend." *U.S. Naval Institute Proceedings* 66 (Mar. 1940): 385ff.

Snow, Elliot. "The Metamorphosis of the '*Merrimac*.'" *U.S. Naval Institute Proceedings* 52 (Nov. 1931): 1518ff.

Still, William N., Jr. "The Career of the Confederate Ironclad *Neuse*." *North Carolina Historical Review* 43 (Jan. 1966): 1ff.

———. "Confederate Behemoth: The CSS *Louisiana*." *Civil War Times Illustrated* 16 (Nov. 1977): 20ff.

———. "The Confederate Gunboat *Arkansas*." *Collegere: Mississippi State College for Women* 3d issue, 1967, pp. 28ff.

———. "The Confederate Ironclad *Missouri*." *Louisiana Studies* 4 (Summer 1965): 101ff.

———. "Confederate Naval Policy and the Ironclad." *Civil War History* 9 (June 1963): 145ff.

———. "Confederate Naval Strategy: The Ironclad." *Journal of Southern History* 27 (Aug. 1961): 330ff. This short essay opened a new era in the historiography of the Confederate ironclad navy.

———. "The Confederate States Navy at Mobile, 1861 to August 1864." *Alabama Historical Quarterly* 30 (Fall and Winter 1968): 127ff.

———. *The Savannah Squadron*. Savannah, Ga.: Coastal Heritage Press, 1989.

NAVAL CONSTRUCTION AND SUPPLY IN EUROPE, THE WAR ON
TRADE, AND INTERNATIONAL PROBLEMS

Books

Adams, Ephraim Douglass. *Great Britain and the American Civil War*. 2 vols. in 1. New York: Russell & Russell, 1925.

Bernath, Stuart L. *Squall Across the Atlantic: American Civil War Prize Cases and Diplomacy*. Berkeley: University of California Press, 1970.

Bradlow, Edna, and Frank Bradlow. *Here Comes the* Alabama: *The Career of a Confederate Raider*. Cape Town, South Africa: A. A. Balkema, 1958.

Browning, Robert M., Jr. *From Cape Charles to Cape Fear: The North Atlantic Blockading Squadron during the Civil War*. Tuscaloosa: University of Alabama Press, 1993.

Case, Lynn M., and Warren F. Spencer. *The United States and France: Civil War Diplomacy*. Philadelphia: University of Pennsylvania Press, 1970.

Clara, Giovanni. *Appunti di diritto bellico marittimo.* Livorno: Istituto di Guerra Marittima, 1983.

Cullop, Charles P. *Confederate Propaganda in Europe, 1861–1865.* Coral Gables, Fla.: University of Miami Press, 1969.

Dalzell, George W. *The Flight from the Flag: The Continuing Effect of the Civil War upon the American Carrying Trade.* Chapel Hill: University of North Carolina Press, 1940.

Ellison, Mary. *Support for Secession: Lancashire and the American Civil War.* Chicago: University of Chicago Press, 1972. Explodes the legend according to which English workers would have massively supported the North, showing that the attempt of the Confederates to build warships in Great Britain and run the blockade had considerable popular support.

Goff, Richard D. *Confederate Supply.* Durham, N.C.: Duke University Press, 1969.

Jenkins, Brian. *Britain and the War for the Union.* 2 vols. Montreal: McGill–Queen's University Press, 1964.

Jones, Wilbur D. *The Confederate Rams at Birkenhead: A Chapter in Anglo-American Relations.* Tuscaloosa, Ala.: Confederate Publishing Co., 1961.

Lester, Richard I. *Confederate Finance and Purchasing in Great Britain.* Charlottesville: University Press of Virginia, 1975.

Merli, Frank J. *Great Britain and the Confederate Navy, 1861–1865.* Bloomington: Indiana University Press, 1970.

Owsley, Frank Lawrence. *King Cotton Diplomacy: Foreign Relations of the Confederate States of America.* 2d ed., rev. by Harriet Chappel Owsley. Chicago: University of Chicago Press, 1959.

Owsley, Frank Lawrence, Jr. *The C.S.S.* Florida: *Her Building and Operations.* Philadelphia: University of Pennsylvania Press, 1965.

Poolman, Kenneth. *The* Alabama *Incident.* London: W. Kimber, 1958.

Robinson, Charles M. *Shark of the Confederacy: The Story of the C.S.S.* Alabama. Annapolis, Md.: Naval Institute Press, 1994.

Robinson, William M., Jr. *The Confederate Privateers.* 1928. Reprint. Columbia: University of South Carolina Press, 1991. Still of utility.

Spencer, Warren F. *The Confederate Navy in Europe.* University, Ala.: University of Alabama Press, 1983.

Thompson, Samuel B. *Confederate Purchasing Operations Abroad.* Chapel Hill: University of North Carolina Press, 1935.

Wise, Stephen R. *Lifeline of the Confederacy: Blockade Running during the Civil War.* Columbia: University of South Carolina Press, 1988. Excellent. Published too late to be used for this book.

Articles

Anderson, S. "Blockade versus Closing Confederate Ports." *Military Affairs* 41 (Dec. 1973): 190ff.

Baxter, James P., III. "The British Government and Neutral Rights, 1861–1865." *American Historical Review* 34 (Oct. 1928): 9ff.

————. "Some British Opinion as to Neutral Rights, 1861–1865." *American Journal of International Law* 23 (1919): 517ff.

Delaney, N. C. "At Semmes' Hands." *Civil War History Illustrated* 18 (June 1979): 22ff. Important on the sinking of the *Hatteras*.

————. "Matamoros: Port for Texas during the Civil War." *Southwestern Historical Quarterly* 58 (1955): 473.

Dyer, Brainerd. "Confederate Naval and Privateering Activity in the Pacific." *Pacific Historical Review* 3 (1934): 433ff.

Eiseman, B. "Darr Kom die *Alabama*." *U.S. Naval Institute Proceedings* 101 (Apr. 1975): 72ff.

Elliott, Charles B. "The Doctrine of Continuous Voyage." *American Journal of International Law* 1 (Jan. 1907): 62ff.

Geoghegan, William W. "The South's Scottish Sea Monster." *American Neptune* 29 (Jan. 1969): 5ff.

Groh, George W. "Last of the Rebel Raiders." *American Heritage* 10 (Dec. 1958): 48ff.

Hanna, Kathryn A. "Incidents of the Confederate Blockade." *Journal of Southern History* 5 (May 1945): 214ff.

Harrison, Royden. "British Labor and the Southern Confederacy." *International Review of Social History* 7 (1957): 78ff.

Higginbotham, Don. "A Raider Refuels: Diplomatic Repercussions." *Civil War History* 4 (1958): 129ff.

Kennett, Lee. "The Strange Career of the *Stonewall*." *U.S. Naval Institute Proceedings* 94 (Feb. 1968): 77ff.

Khasigian, Amos. "Economic Factors and British Neutrality." *Historian* 25 (1963): 451ff.

Kinnaman, Stephen. "Inside the *Alabama*." *Naval History* 4 (Summer 1990): 54ff.

Krein, David F. "Russell's Decision to Retain the Lairds' Rams." *Civil War History* 22 (June 1976): 158ff.

Lester, Richard I. "Confederate Fiscal Procurement Activity in Great Britain during the Civil War." *Military Collector and Historian* 27 (Winter 1975): 163ff.

————. "Construction of Confederate Ironclad Rams in Great Britain." *Military Collector and Historian* 26 (Summer 1974): 73ff.

Logan, Frenise A. "Activities of the *Alabama* in Asian Waters." *Pacific Historical Review* 31 (May 1962): 143ff.

Luraghi, Raimondo. "Guerre Civile Americaine et alliances etrangeres: Les 'Quasi-alliances' Europeenes pendant la Guerre de sécession (1861–1865)." In *Forces Armées et Systèmes d'Alliance*. Montpellier: Fondation pour les études de defense nationale, 1981, pp. 369ff.

Mallison, W. Thomas, Jr. "A Survey of International Law of Naval Blockade." *U.S. Naval Institute Proceedings* 102 (Feb. 1976): 44ff.

Maynard, Douglas H. "The Confederacy's Super *Alabama*." *Civil War History* 5 (Mar. 1959): 80ff.

————. "The Escape of the *Florida*." *Virginia Magazine of History and Biography* 47 (Apr. 1953): 171ff.

————. "Plotting the Escape of the *Alabama*." *Journal of Southern History* 20 (May 1954): 197ff.

————. "Union Efforts to Prevent the Escape of the *Alabama*." *Mississippi Valley Historical Review* 41 (June 1964): 41ff.

Owsley, Frank Lawrence, Jr. "The Capture of the CSS *Florida*." *American Neptune* 22 (Jan. 1962): 45ff.

————. "The CSS *Florida's* Tour de Force at Mobile Bay." *Alabama Review* 15 (Oct. 1962): 110ff.

Price, Marcus W. "Masters and Pilots Who Tested the Blockade of the Confederate Ports, 1861–1865." *American Neptune* 21 (Apr. 1961): 81ff.

————. "Ships That Tested the Blockade of the Carolina Forts." *American Neptune* 8 (Apr. 1948): 196ff.

————. "Ships That Tested the Blockade of the Georgia and East Florida Ports." *American Neptune* 25 (Apr. 1955): 97ff.

————. "Ships That Tested the Blockade of the Gulf Ports, 1861–1865." *American Neptune* 11 (Oct. 1951): 262ff., and 12 (Jan.–July 1952): 52ff., 154ff., and 229ff.

Rentz, W.O.K. "The Confederate States Ship *Georgia*." *Georgia Historical Quarterly* 56 (Fall 1972): 307ff.

Schmidt, Louis B. "The Influence of Wheat and Cotton on Anglo-American Relations during the Civil War." *Iowa Journal of History and Politics* 16 (1918): 400ff.

Smith, John David. "Yankee Ironclads at Birkenhead? A Note on Gideon Welles, John Laird and Gustavus Vasa Fox." *Mariner's Mirror* (Great Britain) 1 (1881): 77ff.

Spencer, Warren F. "Drouyn de Lhuys et les navires confederés en France." *Revue d'histoire diplomatique* 70 (Oct.–Dec. 1963): 324ff.

Strong, Edwin, Thomas Buckley, and Annetta St. Clair. "The Odyssey of C.S.S. *Stonewall*, 1864–1865." *Civil War History* 30 (Dec. 1894): 306ff.

Thomas, Mary Elizabeth. "The C.S.S. *Tallahassee*: A Factor in Anglo-American Relations." *Civil War History* 21 (June 1975): 148ff.

Trexler, Harrison. "Coaling the Confederate Commerce Raiders." *Georgia Historical Quarterly* 17 (Mar. 1933): 13ff.

Wallace, Lee A., Jr. "The CSS *Stonewall* and Her Captain." *Museum of the Confederacy Newsletter* 10 (May 1973).

Woodworth, Celia. "The Confederate Raider *Shenandoah*." *U.S. Naval Institute Proceedings* 99 (June 1973): 66ff.

THE SUBMARINE WAR, TORPEDO BOATS, AND THE COMMANDOS

Books

Barnes, Robert H. *United States Submarines*. New Haven: H. F. Morse Association, 1944.

Bearss, Edwin C. *Hardluck Ironclad: The Sinking and Salvaging of the* Cairo. Baton Rouge: Louisiana State University Press, 1966. The complete operation of the first, illustrous victim of Confederate torpedoes.

Kinchen, O. A. *Confederate Operations in Canada and the North: A Little Known Phase of the American Civil War.* North Quincy, Mass.: Christopher Publishing House, 1970.

Lundeberg, Philip K. *Samuel Colt's Submarine Battery: The Secret and the Enigma.* Washington, D.C.: Smithsonian Institution Press, 1974.

Perry, Milton F. *Infernal Machines: The Story of Confederate Submarine and Mine Warfare.* Baton Rouge: Louisiana State University Press, 1965. A basic work but has some serious gaps.

Articles

Blair, C. H. "Submarines of the Confederate States Navy." *U.S. Naval Institute Proceedings* 78 (Sept. 1952): 1115ff.

Bolander, Louis H. "The *Alligator:* First Federal Submarine of the Civil War." *U.S. Naval Institute Proceedings* 44 (June 1938): 845ff.

Donnelly, Ralph W. "A Confederate Navy Forlorn Hope." *Military Affairs* 27 (Summer 1964): 73ff.

Hagerman, G. "Confederate Submarines." *U.S. Naval Institute Proceedings* 103 (Sept. 1977): 74ff.

Kelly, Albert N. "Confederate Submarines." *Virginia Magazine of History and Biography* 61 (July 1953): 293ff.

Mazet, H. "Tragedy and the Confederate Submarines." *U.S. Naval Institute Proceedings* 68 (1942): 669ff.

Naval History Division. *The Submarine in the U.S. Navy.* Washington, D.C.: N.d. [1970].

Parks, E. Taylor. "Robert Fulton and Submarine Warfare." *Military Affairs* 25 (Winter 1961): 177ff.

Pelzer, John, and Linda Pelzer. "Hijack! Confederates on Lake Erie." *Civil War Times Illustrated* 22 (Sept. 1983): 10ff.

Sass, Herbert R. "The Story of the Little *David.*" *Harper's Magazine* 186 (1943): 620ff.

Shingleton, R. G. "Cruise of CSS *Tallahassee.*" *Civil War Times Illustrated* 15 (May 1976): 30ff.

Smythe, Augustine T. "Torpedo and Submarine Attacks on the Federal Blockading Fleet off Charleston during the War of Secession." *Charleston Yearbook,* 1907, 53ff.

Snyder, Dean. "Torpedoes for the Confederacy." *Civil War Times Illustrated* 24 (Mar. 1985): 40ff.

Stuart, Meriwether. "Dr. Lugo: An Austro-Venetian Adventurer in Union Espionage." *Virginia Magazine of History and Biography* 90 (July 1982): 339ff. An important essay because it states how Union spies were nested right in the Torpedo Bureau of the Confederate navy.

Thomason, D. W. "Three Confederate Submarines: Operations at New Orleans, Mobile and Charleston, 1862–1864." *U.S. Naval Institute Proceedings* 69 (Jan. 1941): 39ff.

von Kolnitz, Harry. "The Confederate Submarine." *U.S. Naval Institute Proceedings* 43 (Oct. 1937): 1453ff.

Winer, Frank H. "Transplanted Torpedoman." *U.S. Naval Institute Proceedings* 100 (July 1974): 80ff.

Woolson, Allen M. "Confederates on Lake Erie." *U.S. Naval Institute Proceedings* 99 (Apr. 1973): 69ff.

NAVAL OPERATIONS AND ACTIVITIES IN GENERAL

Books

Bearss, Edwin C. *The Campaign for Vicksburg.* 3 vols. Dayton, Ohio: Morningside, 1985–87.

———. *Decision in Mississippi.* Jackson, Miss.: Committee on the War between the States, 1962.

———. *Rebel Victory at Vicksburg.* Vicksburg, Miss.: Centennial Commission, 1963.

Cooling, B. Franklin. *Forts Henry and Donelson: The Key to the Confederate Heartland.* Knoxville: University of Tennessee Press, 1987.

Dufour, Charles E. *The Night the War Was Lost.* Garden City, N.Y.: Doubleday, 1960.

Gosnell, H. Allen. *Guns on the Western Waters.* Baton Rouge: Louisiana State University Press, 1949.

Gragg, Rod. *Confederate Goliath: The Battle of Fort Fisher.* New York: Harper Collins, 1991.

Hearn, Chester G. *The Capture of New Orleans, 1862.* Baton Rouge: Louisiana State University Press, 1995.

Lewis, Emanuel R. *Seacoast Fortifications of the United States: An Introductory History.* Washington, D.C.: Smithsonian Institution Press, 1970.

Merrill, James M. *Battle Flags South: The Story of the Civil War Navies on the Western Waters.* Rutherford, N.J.: Fairleigh Dickinson University Press, 1970.

Milligan, John D. *Gunboats down the Mississippi.* Annapolis, Md.: Naval Institute Press, 1965. Milligan's book and Merrill's above have practically outclassed all earlier studies on the war on the western waters (with the exception, still, of that of A. T. Mahan).

Articles

Bearss, Edwin C. "Civil War Operations in and around Pensacola." *Florida Historical Quarterly* 36 (Oct. 1957): 125ff.; 39 (Jan.–Apr. 1962): 330ff.

———. "A Federal Raid up the Tennessee River." *Alabama Review* 17 (Oct. 1964): 261ff.

———. "The Fiasco at Head of the Passes." *Louisiana History* 4 (Fall 1963): 301ff.

———. "The Union Raid down the Mississippi and up the Yazoo." *Military Affairs* 27 (Fall 1962): 108ff.

———, with W. P. Nash. "Fort Henry." *Civil War Times Illustrated* 4 (Nov. 1965): 9ff.

King, Joseph E. "The Fort Fisher Campaigns, 1864–1865." *U.S. Naval Institute Proceedings* 87 (Aug. 1951): 842ff., and 88 (Feb. 1952): 197ff.

Robbins, P. "When the Rebels Lost Ship Island." *Civil War Times Illustrated* 17 (Jan. 1979): 4ff.

Trexler, Harrison A. "The Confederate Navy Department and the Fall of New Orleans." *Southwest Review* 19 (Fall 1933): 88ff.

Turner, Maxine. "Naval Operations on the Apalachicola and Chattahoochee Rivers, 1861–1865." *Alabama Historical Quarterly* 26 (Fall–Winter 1974): 60ff.

Werner, H. O. "The Fall of New Orleans, 1862." *U.S. Naval Institute Proceedings* 88 (Apr. 1962): 78ff.

OPERATIONS IN VARIOUS STATES AND CITIES

Books

Barrett, John G. *The Civil War in North Carolina.* Chapel Hill: University of North Carolina Press, 1963.

Bergeron, Arthur W., Jr. *Confederate Mobile.* Jackson: University Press of Mississippi, 1991.

Bryan, T. Conn. *Confederate Georgia.* Athens: University of Georgia Press, 1961.

Burton, E. Milby. *The Siege of Charleston, 1861–1865.* Columbia: University of South Carolina Press, 1970.

Carse, Robert. *Department of the South: Hilton Head Island in the Civil War.* Columbia, S.C.: State Printing Co., 1961.

Cauthen, Charles C. *South Carolina Goes to War, 1860–1865.* Chapel Hill: University of North Carolina Press, 1960.

Coleman, K. *Confederate Athens.* Athens: University Press of Georgia, 1969.

Corley, Flory C. *Confederate City: Augusta, Georgia, in the Confederacy.* Columbia: University of South Carolina Press, 1965.

Johns, John E. *Florida during the Civil War.* Gainesville: University of Florida Press, 1963.

Lawrence, Alexander. *A Present for Mr. Lincoln: The Story of Savannah from Secession to Sherman.* Macon, Ga.: Ardivan Press, 1961.

Russell, James M. *Atlanta, 1847–1890.* Baton Rouge: Louisiana State University Press, 1988.

Standard, Diffie W. *Columbus, Georgia, in the Confederacy: The Social and Industrial Life of the Chattahoochee River Port.* New York: William Frederick Press, 1954.

Turner, Maxine. *Navy Gray: A Story of the Confederate Navy on the Chattahoochee and Apalachicola Rivers.* Tuscaloosa: University of Alabama Press, 1988.

Winters, John D. *The Civil War in Louisiana.* Baton Rouge: Louisiana State University Press, 1963.

Wise, Stephen R. *Gate of Hell: The Campaign for Charleston Harbor.* Columbia: University of South Carolina Press, 1994.

Articles

Fornell, Earl W. "The Civil War Comes to Savannah." *Georgia Historical Quarterly* 43 (Sept. 1959): 120ff.

———. "Mobile during the Blockade." *Alabama Historical Quarterly* 23 (Spring 1961): 29ff.

Jones, J. P. "Wilson's Raiders Reach Georgia: The Fall of Columbus." *Georgia Historical Quarterly* 59 (Fall 1975): 313ff.

Mobley, Joe A. "The Siege of Mobile, August 1864–April 1865." *Alabama Historical Quarterly* 38 (Winter 1976): 250ff.

Yonge, Julien C. "Pensacola in the War for Southern Independence." *Florida Historical Quarterly* 38 (Apr. 1959): 120ff.

CONFEDERATE STATES MARINES

Books

Donnelly, Ralph W. *The History of the Confederate States Marine Corps.* Washington, N.C.: By the Author, 1976. Thus far it is the only whole book on the Confederate marines: sound, complete, and reliable.

———. *Service Records of Confederate Enlisted Marines.* Washington: N.C.: By the Author, 1979. Completes the work above as well as the other by the same author cited under the heading of "Biographies."

Articles

Donnelly, Ralph W. "Battle Honors and Services of Confederate Marines." *Military Affairs* 23 (Spring 1959): 37ff.

———. "Confederate Navy and Marine Corps Commissions." *Military Collector and Historian* 30 (Fall 1978): 137ff.

Laughlin, P. "Rebel Marine." *Marine Corps Gazette* 37 (Nov. 1953): 53ff.

Marion, A. P. "Marines for the Confederacy." *Civil War Times Illustrated* 17 (Nov. 1978): 28ff.

McClellan, Edwin N. "The Capture of Fort Fisher." *Marine Corps Gazette* 5 (Mar. 1920): 59ff. Devotes much attention to Confederate marines.

McGlone, J. E. "The Lost Corps: The Confederate States Marines." *U.S. Naval Institute Proceedings* 98 (Nov. 1972): 68ff.

THESES AND DISSERTATIONS

Ball, Douglas B. "Confederate Finance, 1861–1865: Economic Policy Making in the South during the American Civil War." Ph.D. diss., University of London, London School of Economics, 1974 (later printed in briefer format under the title *Financial Failure and Confederate Defeat* [Urbana: University of Illinois Press, 1991]).

Bright, Samuel R. "Confederate Coast Defense." Ph.D. diss., Duke University, 1961.

Brooke, George M., Jr. "John Mercer Brooke, Naval Scientist." Ph.D. diss. 2 vols. University of North Carolina, 1956 (later published but, it seems, with some condensation).

Lenti, Roberto. "Per una storia della cantieristica genovese del xvii secolo: La construzione della *San Giovanni Battista*." M.A. thesis, University of Genoa, 1970.

Macino, Giorgio. "Il Concetto di neutralità nella sua strutturazione giuridica e nella sua evoluzione storico-politica. Connessioni e sviluppi della preda marittima." M.A. thesis, University of Genoa, Italy, 1973.

Maynard, Douglas H. "Thomas H. Dudley and Union Efforts to Thwart Confederate Activities in Great Britain." Ph.D. diss., University of California, Los Angeles, 1951.

Melton, Maurice. "The Savannah Squadron: A Study in Failure." M.A. thesis, University of Georgia, 1971.

Moseley, Cynthia E. "The Naval Career of Henry Kennedy Stevens as Revealed in His Letters, 1839–1863." M.A. thesis, University of North Carolina, 1951.

Perry, Percival. "Naval Stores Industry in the Antebellum South, 1789–1861." Ph.D. diss., Duke University, 1947.

Rodiman, William. "The Confederate Cruiser *Florida*." M.A. thesis, University of Alabama, 1939.

Still, William N., Jr. "The History of the CSS *Arkansas*." Ph.D. diss., University of Alabama, 1958.

Todd, Herbert H. "The Building of the Confederate States Navy in Europe." Ph.D. diss., Vanderbilt University, 1940.

Index

About the Author

Raimondo Luraghi was born in Milan, Italy, in 1921. He is a professor of American history and director of graduate studies in the history of the Americas at the University of Genoa. He has also served as a visiting professor at several colleges and universities in the United States over the past thirty-five years.

He is the author of several books of military and naval history concerning the American Civil War. His Italian-language history of the conflict was a best-seller in Italy. He is a member of both the International Bureau of Military History and the U.S. Association for Military History.